FILM STUDY
A Resource Guide

FILM STUDY
A Resource Guide

Frank Manchel

Rutherford • *Madison* • *Teaneck*
Fairleigh Dickinson University Press

Associated University Presses, Inc.
Cranbury, New Jersey 08512

Library of Congress Cataloging in Publication Data

Manchel, Frank.
  Film study: a resource guide.

  Includes bibliographies.
  1. Moving-pictures—Bibliography. 2. Moving-pictures—Study and teaching.
I. Title.
Z5784.M9M34   791.43'07   72-3262
ISBN 0-8386-1225-3

Printed in the United States of America

For Sheila,
to Whom This Book
and Author
Are Dedicated

Contents

Acknowledgments

I wish to thank the following publishers for having given me permission to quote from published works:

American Federation of Film Societies, for permission to quote from Daniel Rosenblatt, "Dreams in the Dream Factory," *Film Society Review*, 1963.

The British Film Institute, for permission to quote from Peter John Dyer, "Youth and the Cinema," *Sight and Sound*, Winter 1959–1960.

Doubleday & Company, Inc., for permission to quote from *From Movielot to Beachhead*, copyright 1945 by Cowles Magazine, Inc. Reprinted by permission of Doubleday & Company, Inc.

Indiana University Press, for permission to quote from Robert Richardson, *Literature and Film*, 1971.

The Macmillan Company, for permission to quote from Joseph T. Klapper, *The Effects of Mass Communication*, 1960, and for permission to quote from Walter Lippmann, *Public Opinion* (copyright 1922 by Walter Lippmann, renewed 1950 by Walter Lippmann). Also for permission to quote from Eric Larrabee and David Reisman, "Company Town Pastoral: The Role of Big Business in *Executive Suite*," *Mass Culture: The Popular Arts in America*, 1957.

Random House, Inc., for permission to quote from Ralph Ellison, *Shadow and Act*, 1964.

Simon and Schuster, Inc., for permission to quote from Erwin Panofsky, "Style and Medium in the Motion Pictures," *Film: An Anthology*, Daniel Talbot, ed., 1959.

University of California Press, for permission to quote from Dorothy B. Jones, "Hollywood War Films: 1942–1944," *Hollywood Quarterly*, 1945, and to quote from Ernest Callenbach, "Editor's Notebook," *Film Quarterly*, 1962–1963.

Variety, for permission to reprint its graph, "U.S. Theatrical Boxoffice: 1946–1971," *Variety*, May 10, 1972.

I wish to thank as well the following people who graciously allowed me to quote from their published works: Edgar Dale, Raymond Durgnat, Anthony W. Hodgkinson, Lewis Jacobs, Arthur Knight, John Howard Lawson, Robert Richardson, and Richard Schickel.

This book on film study makes no claim to be the product of original research into unpublished materials. It is based simply on years of viewing films that others have made and reading books that others have written. Their work has made mine easier. My debts are too vast to list in so short a space. My only claim to originality, and a small one at that, is in the area of organization, arrangement, and interpretation. I trust that the afore-mentioned acknowledgments outline the beginnings of my obligations to others. In addition, I wish to give my special thanks to Professor Louis Forsdale for his initial support in this study as well as Professor Milton A. Kaplan for his patient advice. The Motion Picture Association of America was very helpful in getting me information about the Movie Code, and I was further helped in obtaining necessary material by such wonderful aides as Miss Judy Blanchard, Miss Cindy Cannon, Mrs. Winifred Gadue, Mrs. Claire Buckley, and Mr. Phil Lyman. Typing this manuscript was a hor-rendous job and a great deal of thanks go to Mrs. Evelyn Kyle, Miss Jo Ann Cook, Miss Jody Jarvis, Mrs. Marie Schwenn, and Mrs. Lynn Lanctot. I am also indebted to my colleagues, Dr. Virginia Clark and Dr. Littleton Long, whose editorial comments were invaluable. I want also to express a debt owed my editor, Mr. Leslie Bialler, for giving me the extra incentive to finish. Finally, I wish to express my love and gratitude to my wife, Sheila, and to my sons, Steven and Gary, whose consideration, patience, and encour-agement made everything else possible.

Introduction

The question of educating the public to a better more critical appreciation of the films is a question of the mental health of nations.

Béla Balázs, Theory of Film

This is not a methods book on how to teach about film, though it does offer in each of its eight chapters observations on current practices. Nor is this book an attempt to list definitively the various sources or materials connected with film study, though such a work would be welcome. It is a survey designed to describe six popular approaches to the study of the cinema, along with a practical analysis of selected books, materials and information about motion picture rentals.

It comes at a time when film study programs are rapidly increasing in the schools. In spite of this activity, most institutions still continue to relegate movies to the status of a textbook, an audio-visual aid to stimulate students to learn more about other academic subjects. No doubt A-V films, like textbooks, serve a variety of useful purposes. But there are many films, like books, which are works of art and deserve special consideration. Long ago educators realized such books existed. Now they have grasped that the same is true for the cinema.

While there is considerable interest—particularly among young people—in learning more about movies, few instructors are able to present useful film programs. Not only do lean budgets and poor facilities limit their efforts, but the instructors themselves often have only limited knowledge about movies. They have not considered the principles of film art, or how these principles stem from the nature of the medium. Therefore, it comes as no surprise that film study in many schools is unsatisfactory, and that teachers need and want help in remedying the situation.

There are a number of groups and individuals trying to provide that help: workshops at national conventions and regional meetings, special summer courses, the efforts of the American Film Institute and sectional organizations, state-subsidized programs and aggressive academic departments. But the average teacher is often bewildered by offers of help. He needs assistance in choosing between the quality and suitability of the programs, the procedures for joining and participating in the activities, and

in following up the suggestions made at these meetings. This book tries to help film students find useful sources of information about such film study aids.

There are other problems confronting confused teachers. We live in a cavalier age where irresponsible suggestions are not only available but popular. Articles and books continue to appear suggesting that anyone can teach about film. No training is necessary; all you need to do is walk into a classroom and get students "involved" with the "relevance" of film and they will have a "meaningful experience." Behind these over-used and ill-defined concepts lie the false assumptions that we have nothing to learn from the past and anything new must be better than what has come before. I do not accept these assumptions. Certainly we can enjoy a film just by seeing it. Yet a knowledge of history leads to a deeper appreciation of movies, and an understanding of film aesthetics increases our sense of enjoyment. This book reaffirms what competent teachers have always maintained: that good teaching provides bridges between the past and the present which are meaningful and enjoyable. Where mediocrity and dullness are, bad teaching is also. Here methods and materials need revision. But we should not confuse change with progress. How to improve our teaching is a complex problem. And the best that can be said about a simple solution to a complex problem was phrased by H. L. Mencken, "It is simple, direct and it is wrong."

In considering change, it is useful to examine where we are. This book is organized so that the six most common approaches to film appreciation can be examined: a representative genre; stereotyping; thematic approach; comparative media; a representative period; and the history of film. None of the approaches has been exhaustively discussed. Appropriate materials (films, books, articles) have been suggested to help film students explore the subject further.

Each film entry, depending upon its context, is listed alphabetically and contains, in addition to its titles, the releasing company (country of origin), the film gauge (16mm, 35mm or 8mm), the year of its initial release, running time in minutes, special information (black and white or color, cinemascope prints, subtitles, etc.), and a special code abbreviation of the American distributor who has the film for rental, lease or sale. These special codes are listed alphabetically in Appendix II.[1]

The following is a typical entry:

The Prime of Miss Jean Brodie (Fox—16mm: 1969, 116 min., b/w, sound, R-FNC)

Ronald Neame directed this memorable film about the Edinburgh

---

1. Extremely helpful in cross-checking my list was a very useful book edited by James L. Limbacher, *Feature Films on 8mm and 16mm, Third Edition. A Directory of Feature Films Available for Rental, Sale or Lease in the United States* (New York: R. R. Bowker Company, 1971).

spinster, Jean Brodie, who shocks her colleagues at a staid school for girls by snubbing the prescribed curriculum and developing her own coterie of "Brodie girls." Maggie Smith is superb as the dogmatic school teacher who preaches the virtues of Mussolini and Franco, warps young minds, and ends up alone. Unfortunately, Jay Presson Allen based the screenplay on the stage play which, in turn, had been adapted from Muriel Spark's novel. The book should have been the original source since it is much stronger.

After the title comes the country of origin (or studio name when dealing with American films), that it is a 16mm print, first released in 1969, with a running time of 116 minutes, in black and white, with sound, and that it can be (R) rented from Films Incorporated. (S) would indicate that it is for sale; and (L) for lease. Also included is a brief description plus key personalities connected with the film. More often than not useful articles dealing with the movie or its cast will be footnoted on the page. Space and emphasis, however, sometimes require additional footnoting elsewhere and readers should check the index for more possible information.

In preparing the material and selecting the films, I have also used the following criteria:

1. The films had to be available to schools and students.

2. The range of the films had to represent the history of motion pictures, significant genres, and important artists.

3. The films, for the most part, had to demonstrate aesthetic excellence. I have drawn upon the judgment of recognized and respected film critics and film historians as well as my own preferences.

4. The major emphasis is on fiction films: as a result, the majority of movies chosen are well-known theatrical films from different countries.

Books, monographs and screenplays have been, for the most part, annotated in the text proper. These annotations, chiefly critical and descriptive, suggest, in my opinion, the best of the existing materials now available in libraries and book stores. Each has been read by me, and in most cases my opinions have been checked against book reviews by major scholars in many of the reputable film periodicals. The dates given suggest the best editions to study; the publishers listed are American, whenever possible; and asterisks are used to indicate paperback editions available at the time of this writing. To keep abreast of the new editions, readers should consult *Paperbound Books in Print*. Those who wish to study these works or purchase them should consult Appendix V, which lists major archives, libraries and rare book dealers.

Over the years, I have found it useful to consider the art of film as a systematic ordering of images which might be said to have its own language, composition and literature. Such metaphorical extensions of traditional terms provide us with the means of approaching a new medium in familiar terms. What I mean by *language,* therefore, is the audio-visual mode of

expression which is characteristic of film, and yet shares with other "languages" the traditional properties of being systematic, symbolic, learned,
socially employed and consistently evolving under the pressure of cultural
change. By *composition*, I refer mainly to the arrangement of filmic properties, such as images and sounds, which create the total film. And *literature*
suggests the films which represent the outstanding achievements of the
cinema.

Finally, this book is not meant as a substitute for an individual's need
to devise and develop an approach to film teaching which is right for his
students and himself. Only he knows what is best for him. But for too long
movies have been ignored as a significant art form and as a valuable mode
of expression. My hope is that you will find in the following pages materials
and suggestions that will help change this situation. It is intended as a
survey which offers practical advice to students of film.

FILM STUDY
A Resource Guide

1
Film Literature

The highest function of motion picture art is to express the people to themselves. The voice of the screen is the voice of common humanity trying to put into living words its thoughts and emotions, its ideals and its dreams.
William C. DeMille, Hollywood Saga

BACKGROUND

Important to any film teacher is a perspective that allows him to unify what appear to be disparate elements. In developing this perspective, it is helpful to ask the following questions: Why teach about films at all? What do we mean by film study? My assumption—and the basic premise of this book— is that first we need to consider what we want to do and why before we attempt to make a sensible decision concerning teaching materials, approaches and assignments.[1]

In answering these questions for myself, I find it helps to remember what movies have done for me. Since my purpose in teaching is to affect my students, I assume that what film does for me it can do for them. Thinking back over my life, I realize that movies have brought me to places I'd never been and provided experiences I'd never thought possible. They have changed my outlook on life, helped shape my career and influenced my opinions, values and actions. They have caused me to investigate not only myself but also my relationship to other people and the world in which we live. They have broadened my mode of expression and aided me in communicating with people all over the globe, regardless of distance, age, or background. And they have given me an incredible amount of pleasure.

I believe that movies have this and much more to offer. That is why I teach about film and argue for film study in the schools.

But none of us expects to find a way of accomplishing all these aims within the narrow range of our influence. Nor should anyone expect it of us!

---

1. The strategy for this opening argument is suggested by James Knapton and Bertrand Evans, *Teaching a Literature-Centered English Program* (New York: Random House, 1967), pp. 1–31.

After all, we teach in a variety of schools, made up of widely different faculties which are committed to an assortment of purposes. Our budgets, training, and interests are equally varied. What's more, students are different not only from building to building and year to year, but from seat to seat. Every time you walk into a classroom, you relate to dynamic individuals and not static robots. Given such divergence, how could anyone profess to know one method that would work for everyone?

We should begin by accepting the fact that there is no one answer to what "film study" means or what it should include. And yet the impossibility of the answer suggests a starting point. Diversity, not uniformity, seems to be the key to film study. It follows from that position that people should be creative, experimental, and ambitious. Learning situations should provide a safe cushion for failure. Teachers should avoid using inflexible critical conclusions. And as students become more interested in history, criticism, appreciation, and production, they should have the opportunity to pursue these and other concerns. By study and practice, they should learn that asking the right questions is often more useful than having the right answer. Film study, no matter what the variables are, should stimulate students' imaginations about the world of film and then help them to explore fruitfully the many interesting possibilities.

Although film study first appeared in the schools, mainly in English departments, in the early 1900s, teachers still fluctuated between an analytical and a humanistic approach. One of the earliest reports implies that educators considered the first motion pictures a moral and social threat.[2] To insure that children's minds would not be polluted, only audio-visual moving pictures were allowed in the classrooms. Straining to avoid the menace of a commercial product in the pure realms of Academia, teachers used the instructional movie, with its major concern for transmitting information, as a substitute for the fiction film. Thus, they attempted to reduce the stigma of entertaining students with a theatrical movie during the school day, and motion pictures as teachers' aids gained a strong hold in institutions.[3] In the thirties, the Payne Fund Studies pointed out that it was the

---

2. Robert W. Neal, "Making the Devil Useful," *The English Journal* 2, no. 4 (December 1913) : 658–60.

3. The most exhaustive study to date on the film in the secondary school, and the one which this section rests most heavily on, is Stuart Selby, "The Study of Film as an Art Form in American Secondary Schools" (Doctor of Education Report, Teachers College, Columbia University, 1963). In addition, the following are also useful sources: Ronald Polito, "The History of Film Teaching in the American School System," *Screen Education* 31 (September–October 1965) : 10–18; Edouard L. de Laurot, "Audio-Visualism versus Education," *Film Culture* 1 (Winter 1955) : 6–13; David C. Stewart, "Toward Film Study," *Film Study in Higher Education*, David Stewart, ed. (Washington: American Council on the Arts, 1966), pp. 1–15; Colin Young, "Films are Contemporary: Notes on Film Education," *Arts in Society* (Winter 1966–67), pp. 23–33; Frank Manchel, "Film Education in Our Time," *Screen Education* 40 (July–August 1967) : 6–12; Anthony W. Hodgkinson, "Education Comes First," *Screen Education* 43 (March–April 1968) : 6–13; Helen W. Concon, "Screen Education in American High Schools," *Screen Education* 45 (July–August 1968) : 6–12; Robert Geller and Sam Kula, "Toward Filmic Literacy: The Role of the American Film Institute," *The Journal of Aesthetic Education* 3, no. 3 (July

responsibility of educational institutions to teach about the harmful effects of the commercial film. Since then secondary schools have tacitly designated that responsibility to the English departments. The rationale is that this department develops human ideals and suitable attitudes. The English teacher in the past had done this through teaching the rudiments of language while claiming that an analysis of a literary work would lead to moral and spiritual upheaval.[4] The film was viewed as a form of nonverbal communication that could transmit these values more rapidly than words, and thus was a valuable adjunct to the curriculum.

Following World War II and prior to the 1960s, teachers' attitudes reverted to the idea of film as an instructional medium rather than a humanistic experience. As late as 1965, one observer commented, "Today, film study in the public school still exists in scattered groups throughout the country, but only vestiges remain of the once vital film study movement of the 30's."[5]

But much has happened since. Significant groups of educators meeting at Lincoln Center, Dartmouth, Waltham, and Aspen—to name just a few places—have helped define the problems and needs of film teachers.[6] Organizations like the American Film Institute and Eastman Kodak have started to work on projects to reduce waste and duplication in workshops, conferences, and newsletters. Best of all, teachers everywhere have initiated and developed film programs at a staggering rate, and movies are beginning to enjoy their long-overdue status in academic circles. All this testifies to the fact that film study is more important now than ever before. And with all this ferment, there is equal fervor about which is the best way to study film.

Each teacher makes a number of important assumptions in choosing an approach to film study, but underlying every consideration is his concern for the best possible learning experience for the students. The most important factor in selecting films is not the age or subject of the movie, but the quality of the film. If it is a well-done picture, it will provide a worthwhile experience.

The catch, of course, is what constitutes a worthwhile film. Each of us has his own answer. But in teaching, we need a set of standards by which our choices are explainable to others. If we are helping students to develop standards, taste, and discrimination about movies, we should be able to show how a film has integrity, order, and coherence. In this instance, the

---

1969) : 91–112; Paddy Whannel, "Film Education and Film Culture," *Screen* 10, no. 3 (May–June 1969) : 49–59; and "Approaches to Film Teaching: A Seminar Discussion," *Screen* 11, no. 1 (January–February 1970) : 14–26.

4. For the most delightful disclaimer to this theory, read Pauline Kael, "It's Only a Movie," *Film Study in Higher Education*, pp. 127–44.

5. Polito, "History of Film Teaching," p. 16.

6. Accounts of these meetings are referred to in the following: *Film Study in Higher Education;* Jane Anne Hannigan and David J. Powell, eds. *The Waltham Conference: Screen Education in the United States* 1975–K–12 (New York: Films Incorporated, 1968) ; *The Journal of Aesthetic Education* 3, no. 3 (July 1969) .

neophyte can get considerable help in film aesthetics by examining the work of reputable movie critics and historians.[7] At the same time, it helps to study the principles of film art and to develop a personal perspective. For over thirty years teachers introduced students to film study through a discussion of the language of film. It is an approach worth considering now.

FILM AS LANGUAGE[8]

Since all technological media are referred to as "new languages," the assumption is that this metaphor indicates a naive comparison between a very complex print-oriented system and loose, simple, visual communications. There is nothing simple about film language. Students examining it should remember that using any language effectively requires skill.

Just as print-oriented literacy requires a recognition of words and patterns, so film literacy requires recognition of pictures. The form and function of those images with relation to sound and movement require analysis if an idea or emotion is to be meaningfully communicated. Furthermore modern teachers of communication show that the print-oriented society of the past 500 years is being replaced by a multi-media culture. The point is that schools need to think seriously about visual literacy programs.

Anthony Hodgkinson has cogently stated the basic assumptions about teaching film language:

1. Human beings express themselves and communicate with each other in a variety of modes (speech, writing, pictures, actions, etc.). Each of these modes may be called "a language."
2. Films and television, taken as essentially similar (in that they both present moving pictures on a screen accompanied by sounds), constitute a particularly rich and complex "language" (mode of expression and communication), embracing elements of most other languages—notably mime and gesture, speech, pictures, music, sounds.
3. Communication is only possible when agreement is reached between communicator(s) and receiver(s) on the meaning to be attached to the symbols used and the manner in which they are used. . . . We call these conventions of a language *vocabulary* and *grammar*.
4. These agreed conventions derive from human usage of the language and are subject to variation from time to time, place to place, person to person, except where language is dead (e.g., Latin) or is artificially and arbitrarily constructed (e.g., Volapuk).
5. Although the *basic* conventions of the mother-tongue and non-verbal "universal" languages (e.g., facial expressions, pictures) are learned outside the formal education system by exposure (this also applies, of course, to the screen language, to which children are informally exposed almost from birth), it is generally accepted that the schools have the

7. Appendix I lists the names of leading film critics.
8. Particularly helpful in studying film as a language is *Ralph Stephenson and J. R. Debrix, *The Cinema as Art*, rev. ed. (Baltimore: Penguin Books, 1969).

responsibility to formalize and develop knowledge of vocabulary and grammar, and the recognition and practice of individual styles of use of language.

6. Because of the strongly print-oriented nature of Western society since Gutenberg, our schools tend to limit their responsibilities largely to one mode of communication—printed or written words. Other modes—speech, mime, picture, etc.—are relegated to minor positions in the curriculum, if indeed they are taught at all.[9]

With these assumptions in mind, we now turn to the grammar and vocabulary of film language.

THE GRAMMAR OF THE FILM

The "grammar" of the film refers to theories that describe visual forms and sound combinations and their functions as they appear and are heard in a significant relationship during the projection of a film. Thus, film grammar includes the elements of motion, sound, picture, color, and film punctuation. It avoids editing and montage, which concern film composition. Obviously, this metaphor helps to assess more effectively the relationship among the various mass-media languages. It has disadvantages as well as advantages. Simplifications are always distortions and the disadvantages need to be noted so that we may be reminded of the dangers of overgeneralizing.

First, each medium limits the effectiveness of its communication by the nature of the medium's structure. Print can do things that film cannot. But the reverse is also true. What we need to understand is what each can do best. Far too often we refuse to consider the limitations of either and exploit them for selfish reasons. In making an analogy between languages and their grammars, the teacher helps to describe a significant code of a particular language and to compare it with other codes used by the older media. In this fashion, students increase their perception and help develop the newer languages.

Second, what are the characteristics of film language that many people take for granted? Since the cinema was born in the current industrial age, it presents us with the only language of known origin. That language has now advanced to the point where it holds a prominent place in society. However, we still know very little about film language and grammar, and they are nowhere as defined as the more established languages.

Third, film grammar mainly describes what has taken place, it does not present a formula for making films. This may be because we try to verbalize about a medium which is basically nonverbal. Primarily, the film is concerned with conveying gestures, thoughts, and feelings rather than words.

9. Anthony Hodgkinson, "Teaching the Screen Language: A Basic Method," *Screen Education Yearbook* (London, 1965) : 57–58.

The problems involved with this form of communication have been described by Béla Balázs in his discussion of the silent film.[10] He maintains that expressions and gestures are part of a world language which for economic reasons must be understood by everyone.

Fourth, the classification that follows is not meant to be definitive. Its main value is in enabling us to generalize about the alternatives that have been open to filmmakers so that when we come to evaluating the finished product we can indicate the ingenuity, creativeness, and craftsmanship in outstanding films.

Fifth, grammatical technique indicates the possible forms and sound combinations and is an aid to understanding film literature. The total film is divided into elements of sight and sound.[11] The visual aspect centers around the *shot,* which in turn is subdivided into *fixed shots* and *motion shots.* Fixed shots are determined by the distance from the subject and by the angle of the camera. Included in this category are *long, medium* and *close* shots. Motion shots are those that suggest movement to the spectator. Typical are shots that *pan, zoom, tilt, dolly, travel,* and *boom.* All of these shots can be shown in *slow, normal* and *fast* motion.[12]

The concept of *size* is related to shots. Since it is the camera that directs the viewer's eyes, the filmmaker manipulates the dimensions and proportions of people, places, and things for creative purposes. Thus, small-scale models, properly constructed and photographed, can substitute for actual people or objects. In science-fiction films, for example, individuals can appear in contrast as giants or minute insects.

Both shots and sizes are influenced by *framing.* The restriction of a predetermined screen limits the director in what he can and cannot show. It helps him to select only those images that are important to the artistic presentation of the subject. It allows him to organize and arrange the various elements of lights, shadows, and objects (people included) in each shot. And by limiting what can be seen by the audience, framing controls our attention and provides a unity to the film. Different kinds of framing—*dramatic, split,* and *oblique*—are used to increase the action and suspense in films. In simplified terms, the filmmaker composes much in the style of the painter or the photographer, only his arrangements are basically mobile. The motion both in and from shots provides the dynamic aspects uncommon in the static arts.

Framing also allows for the advantages of *filmic space.* Because of the camera's mobility and speed, film can multiply, divide, add, and fragment space. It can create new objects from old ones, reshape present perspectives

---

10. Béla Balázs, *Theory of Film: Character and Growth of a New Art,* Edith Bone, trans. (New York: Roy, 1953), pp. 44–45.

11. For a more complete review of film grammar and composition, see the section at the end of this chapter, "Aesthetics."

12. For definitions of these terms and others, see the Glossary.

and control almost every appearance that we see on the screen.

What film can do to space it can also do to *time*. Flexibility is always the key word. Movies are able to involve us in a continuous present tense,[13] while at the same moment and without any observable visual contrast, show past, current, and future time. A useful way of labeling *filmic time* is suggested by the terms "physical," "psychological," and "dramatic." *Physical time* involves the duration of the actual scene along with its projection time; *psychological time* is our personal, subjective impression of time while we watch the movie; *dramatic time* is the manipulation of the natural time necessary for the scenes presented. Like filmic space, filmic time tends to mix a variety of its many possibilities within a single motion picture. As a result, filmmakers use slow, fast, and stopped motion along with flashbacks to repeat, extend, shorten or change the action in a movie.

Another way of manipulating reality is by optical distortions. Through the use of *soft-focus*, the filmmaker idealizes his romantic and epic heroes, provides symbolic representations and creates an impression of fantasy. Soft-focus may also be used to suggest dizziness, dream-like states of consciousness, flashbacks, and depth perception within a particular shot. Similarly *double-exposures* help the artistic quality of a film. They are useful for suggesting the supernatural, the internal states of mind, screen metaphors and a method of joining the present and the past. A third optical distortion is the *negative image,* which is useful for evoking the mysterious, the fantastic and the unnatural. Like other elements of film grammar, their success depends upon their context within the film itself and not as separate entities.

In addition, the filmmaker has learned how to create a unique effect with settings. Not only can he manipulate dimensions, but technical experts have developed rare methods of artificially creating a specific atmosphere through the use of such techniques as *glass shots, mirror shots, matte shots, optical printing, rear and front projection,* and *miniatures.*[14] Naturally, the creative use of costumes and make-up also contribute to the artistic effect of the scene.

Lighting is another consideration. More important to the artist than illuminating the scene suitably, is what kind and how much light he should use. With the help of lens openings, filters, reflectors and set ups, the film presents a mood or tone, suggests significant details, provides objects and performers with specific characteristics, and also creates an emotional state. Often there are many subtleties and nuances that the spectator views but rarely perceives. One of the most frequent types of lighting is *high key,*

---

13. Stephenson and Debrix, *Cinema as Art,* p. 90.
14. Lengthier discussions of these terms are available in Raymond Fielding, *The Technique of Special-Effects Cinematography* (New York: Hastings House, 1965) and Raymond Spottiswoode *et al., The Focal Encyclopedia of Film and Television Techniques* (New York: Hastings House, 1969).

generally employed with supernatural and suspense films where the intent is to suggest a terrifying and depressing effect. *Color* provides an added dimension to lighting. In the hands of experts, it can increase the symbolic and dramatic effects of a shot, scene, or film. It can help establish emotion, feeling, and thought. As is the case with any aspect of film grammar, lighting is ineffective if it calls attention to itself and does not blend with the other aspects in the movie.

Film punctuation is yet another factor. Like artists in the traditional narrative arts, the filmmaker manipulates time by starting a new episode, a new scene, and a new point of view. Here camera techniques other than *straight cuts* can be used to suggest transitions: *fades, dissolves, wipes, mixes, iris-out* and *iris-in, turn-overs,* and *titles.* By such means, an artist can suggest sadness, the passing of time, or a change in mood. He can also eliminate unnecessary material and space, move the story in any direction he chooses, make comparisons and contrasts, create suspense and establish important relationships.

Sound also has a number of important subdivisions, the most common being *music, speech, natural sounds* and *sound effects.* Sound provides an added dimension to the film experience because it brings another sense into play. Music, since it is married to the sound film itself, needs to be carefully constructed, arranged, and controlled. Used effectively, it can heighten visual effects, stress moods, recall prior events and foreshadow dramatic situations. Every type of music has proven successful in the cinema at some time or other. Suitability is in every instance the determining factor. Not only can traditional scores be used, but the filmmaker, by virtue of his control over sound recording, can create new musical sounds electronically, most commonly through amplification or by making marks on the sound track directly.[15]

As with visual distortions, so with sound manipulations: by creatively reproducing desired sound effects, the artist can increase the film's emotional impact. He can select, multiply, intensify, and invent the sounds we hear. And depending upon his skill, he can orchestrate them into the precise mood of the movie. Various sounds, like visual images, can act as transitional devices, generally in the form of a recurrent melody.

Speech is another asset. Not only does it liberate the image to work with visual ideas alone, but it allows the filmmaker to choose appropriate dialogue and sounds to create a more artistic effect. He therefore has one further device for controlling our emotions and attention. Interestingly, the absence of sound is also useful for the very same reasons.

A basic principle in filmmaking is that sound should not dominate the visual composition. In either sight or sound, the artist is judged by his ability to select, shape, and unify the various elements of film grammar.

---

15. See pages 47–48 for listing of source materials on film music.

THE VOCABULARY OF THE FILM

Like the vocabulary of spoken and written languages film vocabulary has denotations and connotations. The meanings are constantly changing in tune with changes in our culture and experiences. Consequently, anyone who has taught for a day knows the value of a mutual understanding of important terms. It is difficult to discuss whether a cut is good or bad unless we first agree that it is a cut. No doubt some students will need help in developing a basic film vocabulary. The most effective way to help them is by extensive screenings of good films and *not* by lists of specific terms. If you want to kill someone's love for movies, turn the projection of a film into a vocabulary drill. Although those who have grown up with television and film will already have an extensive knowledge of key terms, it might help, at the appropriate moment, to discuss the current meanings of such words as *distortion, reality, fantasy, genre, theme, structure, filmic time, filmic space, content, function, setting, character, illusion, irony,* and *symbol.* As is the case with all vocabulary, the word is not an end in itself, and it is always wise to anchor your definition to a particular film.

FILM COMPOSITION

The meaning of film composition derives from many complex elements. It is not just a handmaiden to film literature. And many viewers, realizing that movies are a collaborative art, sometimes ignore the contributions of individuals in composing the shots, scenes, sounds, and sequences of the cinema. A better understanding of what is involved in the making of a film should heighten a viewer's appreciation of a well-composed motion picture.

Basically, film composition is *editing* or *montage.* The differences in theoretical approaches range from ridiculing the advent of sound and color to claiming that film is the most significant form of communication in the world today. It is pointless to maintain that the theories of montage derived from Pudovkin, Eisenstein, Balázs or Arnheim are supreme, nor is it correct to ignore the aesthetic treatises of Kracauer, Lawson, or Montagu, or the documentary influences of Flaherty and Grierson. A more useful position is to study each of them and extract the most helpful ideas. In addition, a comparison between verbal composition and film composition should show that selection, organization and development are necessary for both. Each is concerned with a point of view, coherence, meaningful symbolic content, rhythm and forceful, unobtrusive grammar.

In most instances, a film is composed to convey an emotion, feeling, or concept to an audience. Grammar is used to select, arrange, and codify that meaning. Thus every shot and sound should be integrally arranged and timed to make as clear as possible the intention of the scene in its relative position to preceding and following shots. Essentially, the technique is called editing or *montage*. The latter is an older term originating from the efforts of the great Russian filmmakers of the twenties. They tried to distinguish between joining various elements of film together and the creative cutting of separate shots into an artistic whole. Today, their basic ideas have been expanded to include a variety of approaches. The original intention still persists—that of developing significant effects by joining two separate images together to create a new concept which is greater than the sum of its parts.[16]

Stephenson and Debrix refer to the newer theories of Marcel Martin: *narrative* and *expressive* montage. The former joins individual shots into a chronological scheme for the purpose of presenting a story. The latter joins disjunctive shots in order to create a specific, sudden effect when the two unrelated images clash.[17]

Another interesting approach to montage is presented in an involved but important discussion of synchronization by Kracauer. He divides his significant concepts into three major categories: (a) Synchronism—asynchronism; (b) parallelism—counterpoint; (c) actual and commentative sound. *Synchronism* represents the normal union of sight and sound we find in our natural lives (we hear and speak to an individual simultaneously).

Asynchronism represents a union of sight and sound not found in our natural lives, in which the source of a sound is not visual (we stare at a book and hear the words of someone not present who often spoke about the book).

Parallelism refers to a situation where sight and sound duplicate each other's actions, a form of tautology. This redundancy can be either synchronous or asynchronous. *Counterpoint* represents the creative union of two different aspects of sight and sound with both forming a single significant effect (a smiling, friendly salesman is shown as a hypocrite). This relationship can also be either synchronous or asynchronous.

The last contrast is between naturalistic sounds which fit into the screen story (*actual*) and those which talk over the visuals (*commentative*), most evident in documentaries. The sum total of Kracauer's argument is twofold: (1) the better films are those where sight, not sound, predominates; and (2) images that reinforce verbalizations tend to flaw a movie's pace and effect.[18]

Such theories of editing underscore that the movement in each shot needs

---

16. See Chapter 7 for a list of books by Pudovkin and Eisenstein dealing with montage.
17. Stephenson and Debrix, *Cinema as Art,* pp. 130–31.
18. For other points of view, see Richard Corliss, "The Limitations of Kracauer's Reality," *Cinema Journal* 10, no. 1 (Fall 1970) : 15–22; Brian Henderson, "Two Types of Film Theory," *Film Quarterly* 24, no. 3 (Spring 1971) : 33–42; and Brian Henderson, "The Long Take," *Film Comment* 7, no. 2 (Summer 1971) : 6–11.

to be arranged to control the effect. Consequently, not all motion that would occur in real life need or should appear in the filmed version. Only movement that relates specifically to the continuation of the desired impression is necessary. Obviously, the filmmaker needs to be selective. Movements are tied to motivations, and motivations should be shown by relating them to a theme as well as a plot. That relationship is set up to correspond to the filmmaker's point of view. Thus, the content of a shot should contain a careful, complex arrangement of sounds, movements, and subjects, which when scrutinized will reveal a significant contribution to the total effect of the film.

Relationships can also be established by *parallel editing* and *referential crosscutting*. In both cases, by alternating the shots between simultaneous actions, the editor allows the audience to witness both events. By showing the connection between the two events, parallel editing interprets the actions and heightens the emotional tension of the film. Referential crosscutting involves a psychological comment. Where the traditional narrative arts use words to reveal the innermost thoughts of an individual, the filmmaker can depict abstract thought graphically through shots showing the action and reaction of performers to a given situation—without verbalization. In somewhat similar fashion, a film depicts a naturalistic interpretation of an environment by *decomposition*. Whereas the novelist lists specific characteristics, the filmmaker presents specific images.[19]

Rhythm is present in one form or another in all works of art: in film composition we have *timing*. The shorter the shots, the quicker the time. By alternating the length of the film strip, the duration of the movie is modified, which in turn affects the vital time-space relationship. A shot, action, or emotion can be controlled for emphasis, depending upon the effect the artist wants to achieve. The right length depends on a relationship among the image's form, content, and duration.[20] This is similar to the choice of a word, the arrangement of a sentence, the length of a paragraph, and the development of an idea in prose.

An analogy can be drawn between precise diction in a literary work and correct typecasting in film. Typecasting approximates the physical characteristics suggested by the script, and the performers objectify these traits on the screen. For some, casting is a photographic art, requiring special talents. For others, casting is not photography but the creative use of individuals stereotyped by previous appearances or roles into visual symbols. Whether they are stars or supporting actors, they can be used frequently as visual icons in much the same way that certain symbols like a swan, rose, or mountain were used by Yeats, Dylan Thomas, or Joyce. Each player becomes not only an actor but also a way of life.

19. For more information on this aspect of film composition, see Joseph and Harry Feldman, *Dynamics of the Film* (New York: Hermitage House, 1952), pp. 74–102.
20. Ivor Montagu, *Film World* (Baltimore: Penguin Books, 1964), p. 130.

Analogies between movies and the oral and written languages are useful in suggesting the similarities between scenes and paragraphs, shots and sentences, actors and words, cuts and commas. But it is important to remember they are *only* analogies. Film has its own unique form of expression and we should not lose sight of that.

FILM LITERATURE

Film literature is the best movies have to offer. It is a representation on film of certain values, truths, attitudes, assumptions, and ethical judgments concerning mankind. It is the contribution of a creative group of individuals who have fashioned raw materials into a significant work of art. And it represents an invaluable opportunity for students intent on becoming educated. As John Steinbeck wrote when he met people who claimed that literature was only print-oriented:

> . . . I run into people who seem to feel that literature is all words and that words should preferably be a little stuffy. Who knows what literature is? The literature of the Cro-Magnon is painted on the walls of the caves of Altamira. Who knows but that the literature of the future will be projected on the clouds? Our present argument that literature is the written word in poetry, drama, and the novel has no very eternal basis in fact. Such literature has not been with us very long, and there is nothing to indicate that it will continue with us very long (at least at the way it is going). If people don't read it, it just isn't going to be literature.[21]

Dr. Lennox Grey puts it another way:

> . . . it is conceivably historical accident that printing came before any other kinds of art reproduction, and that literature became a matter of letters instead of pictures.[22]

The discussion of film literature that follows is predicated upon three assumptions. First, film is a new form of literature, one that represents the period in which it is created; it is uneven in quality, it has certain limitations, restrictions, and conventions, and it requires a certain selectivity when presented in the schools. The comparison between film and traditional literature is not meant to emphasize the dramatic and narrative qualities of film to the neglect of cinematic terms, but to show metaphorically the relationship of film to literature. The artist's situation with regard to film literature, for example, is similar to that of the artist who uses traditional

---

21. John Steinbeck, quoted by Neil Postman, *Television and the Teaching of English* (New York: Appleton-Century-Crofts, 1961), p. 40.
22. Lennox Grey, "Communication and the Arts," *The Communication of Ideas*, Lyman Bryson, ed. (New York: Harper and Brothers, 1948), p. 130.

literary language. The poet must write in terms of poetry; the dramatist in terms of drama; and the novelist in terms of narrative fiction. So, the filmmaker must work in terms of film. While filmmakers are creators of a new type of art form, it would be a mistake to disassociate the new form completely from traditional literature and its purposes.

Second, the value of film goes beyond the realm of entertainment. Motion pictures have an effect upon the values and mores of mankind. As Ervin Panofsky writes:

> Whether we like it or not, it is the movies that mold more than any other single force, the opinions, the taste, the language, the dress, the behavior, and even the physical appearance of a public comprising 60 per cent of the population of the earth. If all the serious lyrical poets, composers, painters and sculptors were forced by law to stop their activities, a rather small fraction of the general public would become aware of the fact and a still smaller fraction would seriously regret it. If the same thing were to happen with the movies, the social consequences would be catastrophic.[23]

Third, there is a need for teaching film in the colleges and public schools. It is a valuable and stimulating art form which communicates ideas and emotions of vital consequence to students and faculty alike. It influences our culture generally and our lives specifically. If there is any possibility that education and art combined can improve man's condition, we would be mad not to bring the art of the film into our classrooms.

FILMS[24]

The Art Director (Fox—16mm: n.d., 8 min., color, sound, R-TMC/L-TMC)
This short illustrates the job of the art director; it starts with his work on the script and shows his invaluable assistance on set designs.

The Cinematographer (Paramount—16mm: 1949, 10 min., b/w, sound, R-TMC/LTMC)
By showing how the filmmaker operates on a Hollywood lot during the shooting of a feature film, we get some practical ideas about equipment, lighting, and a variety of lenses and how they are used to effect moods.

Basic Film Terms: A Visual Dictionary (Adams-Renan—16mm: 1970, 15 min., color, sound, R-PYR/S-PYR)
Sheldon Renan directed this delightful and very useful movie about film syntax, which shows the uses and effects of various lenses, camera angles and editing.

---

23. Erwin Panofsky, "Style and Medium in the Motion Pictures," *Critique* 1, no. 3 (January–February 1947). Reprinted in *Film: An Anthology,* edited by Daniel Talbot (New York: Simon and Schuster, 1959), pp. 16–17.
24. A more extensive list of films useful for teaching purposes is compiled by *Robert W. Wagner and David L. Parker, *A Filmography of Films about Movies and Movie-Making* (Rochester: Eastman Kodak Company, 1969).

BOOKS

Introductory

* Amelio, Ralph J. *Film in the Classroom: Why to Use It, How to Use It.* Dayton: Geo. A. Pflaum, 1971.

In this short and simplistic guide to film study on the secondary school level, an Illinois high school teacher offers sample formats, lesson plans and other related material.

* Amelio, Ralph J. with Anita Owen and Susan Schaefer. *Willowbrook Cinema Study Project.* Dayton: Geo. A. Pflaum, 1969.

An imaginative outline of a two-semester course on the secondary school level designed to explore the intellectual and aesthetic aspects of the film medium. Some useful hints on writing, producing and discussing feature-length and short films are to be found.

* "The Film Issue," *Arts in Society* 4, no. 1 (Winter 1966–67).

A useful and critical collection of articles by such respected writers as Ernest Callenbach, Richard Dyer MacCann, Colin Young, Willard Van Dyke, George Amberg and Robert Steele. In addition, some wonderful material on Robert Rossen, the early years of movies, and a symposium on film by thirteen motion picture directors. Beautifully illustrated.

* Baker, Fred with Ross Firestone (editors). *Movie People At Work in the Business of Film.* New York: Douglas Book Corporation, 1972.

This is a fine and very readable introduction to the movie business as seen and commented upon by such key personalities as producer Roger Lewis, distributor David Picker, director Sidney Lumet, screenwriter Terry Southern, actor Rod Steiger, editor Aram Avakian, composer Quincy Jones, exhibitor Walter Reade, Jr., and film critic Andrew Sarris.

* Beckoff, Samuel. *Motion Pictures.* New York: Oxford Book Company, 1953.

This handy little textbook is one of the best of the early approaches to film study and has fifteen short, sensible chapters for use in the secondary school. Very similar in content to *Exploring the Film,* but not nearly so magnificently produced.

Bluem, A. William, with the collaboration of Jason E. Squire (editors). *The Movie Business, American Film Industry Practice.* New York: Hastings House, 1972.

In an attempt to present a realistic account of the many business practices and procedures that are often alluded to but never really revealed in film books and articles, the editors secured the cooperation of 43 top professional people who agreed to talk honestly and openly about their experiences. Among the contributors (producers, directors, screenwriters, agents, distributors and financial wizards) are Dennis Friedland, William Goldman, Charlton Heston, Stanley Kramer, David V. Picker, Sydney Pollack, Saul Rittenberg, Gordon Stulberg and Stirling Silliphant.

* Bobker, Lee R. *Elements of Film.* New York: Harcourt, Brace and World, Inc., 1969.

Bobker admirably succeeds in his attempt to combine the technical and aesthetic elements in film for the purposes of helping serious students of movies to learn more about the art of the cinema. The author, a knowledgeable film teacher, has organized the first six of his eight chapters on scripting, imagery, sound, editing, directing, and acting. The last two concern comments on the contemporary cinema and the nature of film criticism. Each chapter begins with a theoretical point of view, followed by a practical application, and then concludes with lists of suitable films for screening plus a supplementary bibliography.

* Butler, Ivan. *The Making of Feature Films: A Guide.* Baltimore: Penguin Books, 1971.
  This very readable and interesting book is compiled mainly from personal interviews with some of the most famous names in America and Britain. Each chapter deals with specific aspects of filmmaking: production, screenwriting, directing, acting, cinematography, art design, costuming, special effects, continuity, editing, composing, sound, distribution, and censorship.

* Callenbach, Ernest. *Our Modern Art: The Movies.* Chicago: Center for Liberal Education, 1955.
  Written by the editor of *Film Quarterly* and a long-time student of the cinema, this book is still a valuable model on how to discuss motion pictures. There are eleven different chapters on specific movies such as *The Ox-Bow Incident, Paisan, The Navigator, All the King's Men, The Informer,* and *The River.* The discussion begins with general background information on the history of a particular genre or technique and then moves into discussion questions about the film itself.

* Casty, Alan. *The Dramatic Art of the Film.* New York: Harper and Row, 1971.
  By studying the film from the point of view of technique and dramatic function, Casty offers his readers some valuable insights into the art of motion pictures. His early chapters stress how films are created through the use of the camera, through the arrangements of shots and through editing. Later chapters explore how technology and drama interact wtih sound, color and lighting. The concluding section treats the fusion of cinematic elements into various film styles.

* Casty, Alan (editor). *Mass Media and Mass Man.* New York: Holt, Rinehart and Winston, 1968.
  This is a good introduction for neophytes in film study dealing with the sight-and-sound media as originators, molders and communicators of ideas, opinions and values in society today. The anthology includes essays by Dwight Macdonald, Marshall McLuhan, Federico Fellini, Susan Sontag and Pauline Kael.

Elliott, Godfrey M. (editor). *Film and Education: A Symposium on the Role of the Film in the Field of Education.* New York: Philosophical Library, 1948.
  One of the best of the early attempts by a host of educators to discuss the useful limits and potential of the 16mm "educational film" in the public schools. The term refers to any and all movies whose uses are intended to "inform, orient, or motivate its audiences to some useful end."

Fensch, Thomas. *Films on the Campus.* South Brunswick, N.J., and New York: A. S. Barnes and Company, 1970.

For students interested in the depth and range of various film programs across American campuses—their rationales, requirements, staff and student body—Fensch offers a valuable and informative guide. He also includes his first-hand impressions of individuals, works-in-progress, and sample assignments.

* Fischer, Edward. *The Screen Arts: A Guide to Film and Television Appreciation*. New York: Sheed and Ward, 1960.

In his ten general and uneven chapters, this pioneer film educator discusses the essential points about writing, directing, acting and film grammar. Although oriented toward church groups, the book presents some useful information on forming a film study group in the public schools.

* Fulton, Albert R. *Motion Pictures: The Development of an Art from the Silent Films to the Age of Television*. Norman: University of Oklahoma Press, 1960.

Although the author is particularly interested in the relationship between the technical and historical aspects of film, he provides some good observations on the adaptation of literary and theatrical works to the screen. Furthermore his sixteen chapters—starting with the birth of the "machine" and continuing to the present marriage between it and art—are well-written, useful, and enjoyable. Also valuable are his apt illustrations, sensible glossary, and short list of film credits.

* Giannetti, Louis D. *Understanding Movies*. Englewood Cliffs, N.J.: Prentice-Hall, Inc., 1972.

Starting with the basic premise that movies consist mainly of images and sound, Giannetti builds from a narrow approach to pictures, movement, editing and sound to a stimulating discussion of the complex interaction between cinema and the traditional arts. He concludes with a useful section on various film theories. Neophytes will find the reading nontechnical but not patronizing.

* Gottesman, Ronald and Harry M. Geduld (editors). *Guidebook to Film: An Eleven-in-One Reference*. New York: Holt, Rinehart and Winston, Inc., 1972.

This useful but sketchy book contains brief descriptive comments about a number of areas in film study: Reference works, history books, reviewers, film techniques, theses, museums, film schools, equipment, and bookstores.

* Hall, Stuart *et al. Film Teaching: Studies in the Teaching of Film Without Formal Education—Four Courses Described*. London: British Film Institute, 1964.

Four authors describe their film teaching approaches, emphasizing the social effects of film as well as the use of the medium by directors for personal expression. Particularly helpful are Roy Knight's suggestions on teacher training and Albert Hunt's adult education program. Also valuable are four outlines of courses designed to teach the history of the cinema, film criticism, directing, and the qualities of motion pictures.

* Hodgkinson, A. W. *Screen Education: Teaching a Critical Approach to Cinema and Television*. New York: Unesco, 1964.

Based upon the international conference on Film and Television teaching held at Leangkollen, Oslo, Norway, in October 1962, this report by one of the pioneers of screen education provides a good introduction to the aims and methods of visual literacy. The monograph is short, readable, and has some informative appendices about recommended materials.

* Jones, G. Williams. *Sunday Night at the Movies.* Richmond: John Knox Press, 1967.

A simple but helpful book for church groups who need aid in initiating discussions about the interrelationship between films and religion. Jones suggests some basic steps in planning, executing and following-up film programs. He also provides a topical list of 248 approved feature films and short subjects.

Katz, John Stuart (editor) . *Perspectives on the Study of Film.* Boston: Little, Brown and Company, 1971.

Stressing that the basic problems of film study today involve the importance, impact, and viability of the medium, Katz offers a variety of opinions from filmmakers, film critics, and professional educators as to what to do. The book is divided into four uneven sections: "Film Study and Education"; "The Film as Art and Humanities"; "The Film as Communications, Environment, and Politics"; and "Curriculum Design and Evaluation in Film Study."

* Kitses, Jim, with Ann Mercer. *Talking About the Cinema: Film Studies for Young People.* London: British Film Institute, 1966.

Another effort by the British Film Education Department to publish reports by practicing cinema teachers about their materials and methods. Kitses presents a fine introductory course on the thematic study of teenagers' images, breaking it down into week-by-week suggestions, specific films, and discussion questions.

* Kuhns, William and Robert Stanley. *Exploring the Film.* Dayton: George A. Pflaum, Publisher, 1968.

Graphically, this is one of the most marvelous film study texts ever produced and is a wonderful, quick introduction to the cinema. Teachers and students need more help with the brief and very limited narrative; the authors, recognizing this, have provided a companion book, *Teaching Program: Exploring the Film,* which attempts to offer further information to the faculty about reading lists, supplementary materials, and names of distributors. Unfortunately, in an effort to avoid pretension, the texts oversimplify and mislead serious students.

Kuhns, William. *Themes: Short Films for Discussion.* Dayton: Geo. A. Pflaum, 1968.

For those interested in an informal, student-centered approach to the study of short films in the public schools, Kuhns offers two special sections of information. First, each description of the 70-odd shorts mentioned is followed by a variety of suggestions for using the film in the classroom. Second, he presents clues to the possible themes and suitable curriculum slots that the pictures might easily fit into, plus helpful comments about the discussion procedure.

* Lindgren, Ernest. *The Art of the Film.* New York: The Macmillan Company, 1963. (Revised Edition)

This invaluable introduction to film appreciation first appeared in 1948 and has since become a recommended book on every teacher's reading list. Lindgren divides his efforts into three main sections. Part One is on the mechanics of filmmaking, including the division of labor and a brief history of film equipment complete with related comments on its value to students. Part Two deals with technique, with an emphasis on editing, sound, and acting. Part Three is concerned with film criticism and some useful guidelines for teaching young people to enjoy movies. The volume also has a helpful bibliography and glossary.

* MacCann, Richard Dyer, (editor). *Film and Society.* New York: Charles Scribner's Sons, 1964.

One of the great values of this anthology is that only a few of the articles are found elsewhere. Another advantage is that it helps students in doing research papers. MacCann has divided the text into seven sections. He starts with the history of film, moves through audience values, the relationship between the screen and society, censorship, and finishes with the influence of television on motion pictures. Among the 39 articles are contributions by Terry Ramsaye, Richard Griffith, Arthur Mayer, Allardyce Nicoll, Mervyn LeRoy, Irving Thalberg, John Grierson, Bosley Crowther, and Jean Benoit-Levy.

* McKowen, Clark *et al. It's Only a Movie.* Englewood Cliffs, N.J.: Prentice-Hall, Inc., 1972.

This cleverly designed book which attempts to introduce reluctant movie students to the excitement of film in the classroom is high on graphics and low on written material. The authors put their faith in response-oriented teaching, but just in case you have doubts as to how it operates a teacher's manual is available.

* Mallery, David. *Film in the Life of the School: Programs, Practices and New Directions.* Boston: National Association of Independent Schools, 1968.

Teachers will find this concise, 50-page booklet a fast, informative, and pleasant guide to beginning film study work in the public schools. The author knows what he is talking about and has provided newcomers with some thoughtful and sensible ideas.

* Maltin, Leonard (editor). *TV Movies.* New York: Signet Books, 1969.

In the best and most complete of these capsule books on TV films, Maltin comments on more than 8,000 films. He provides his readers with brief comments, and includes titles, dates, running times, cast and rates each film by assigning it a number of stars.

Manchel, Frank. *Movies and How They Are Made.* Englewood Cliffs, N.J.: Prentice-Hall, Inc., 1968.

Strictly for children. This book follows a film from the first idea for a plot on through to the grand opening in a Hollywood theater. Youngsters get a chance very early in school to learn about the basic stages of production, screen writing, directing, casting, financing, shooting, editing, and acting.

* Manvell, Roger. *Film.* Revised Edition. Harmondsworth, England: Penguin Books, 1946.

This book offers one of the best introductions to film study, particularly in Manvell's opening chapters on the unique characteristics of film art. Almost as good is his final section on the relationship that existed between movies and the English in the years following World War II. While some of the material now seems outdated, the basic principles still are useful as is the chapter on starting a film society.

Manvell, Roger. *The Living Screen: Background to the Film and Television.* London: George G. Harrap and Company, Ltd., 1961.

One of the first to discuss the similarities and dissimilarities of the two screens, this book offers a nontechnical and useful introduction to media literacy. It now appears rather stodgy, but could serve as a useful model upon which to build a more modern foundation.

Manvell, Roger. *What is a Film?* London: Macdonald and Company, 1965.

In this informal and nontechnical exploration of the film as an art form, Manvell begins by discussing the birth of the medium and then goes quickly into the behind-the-scenes activities of directors, producers, actors, writers, technicians, distributors, and exhibitors. He concludes his overview with some general chapters on television, documentaries, and animated films.

Minus, Johnny and William Storm Hale. *The Movie Industry Book (How Others Made and Lost Money in the Movie Industry).* Hollywood: 7 Arts Press, 1970.

Designed primarily for businessmen in the film field, the book points out pitfalls in contractual matters. Among the topics covered are the steps in putting together a movie package, copyright, censorship, limited partnerships, uniform commercial codes, obscenity, working forms for producers and distributors, short contracts, and magazine reviews. Very interesting reading.

* Peters, J. M. L. *Teaching About the Film.* New York: International Documents Service, 1961.

This UNESCO publication, which emphasizes British methods, is one of the best books on screen education yet written. No one has come close to Peters's excellent chapter on "Understanding Film Language," in which he provides 33 stills from Lean's *The Fallen Idol,* a shooting script, and a well-balanced, informative narrative on how filmmakers express themselves. He also has chapters on appreciation and criticism as well as superb practical suggestions for classroom teaching. This one is a must.

* Rosenberg, Bernard and David Manning White (editors). *Mass Culture: The Popular Arts in America.* New York: The Free Press, 1957.

This useful introduction to the study of mass media contains a number of significant essays by Kracauer, Powdermaker, Wolfenstein and Leites, Elkin, Gans and Larrabee, and Reisman.

* Ross, T. J. *Film and the Liberal Arts.* New York: Holt, Rinehart and Winston, Inc., 1970.

The purpose of this anthology is to relate film study to the traditional college curriculum through sets of essays concerning individual themes and movies. For the most part, the organization works, particularly in the sections on "Film and Rhetoric," with contributions by André Malraux, André Bazin, Stephen Crane, and James Agee; "Film and the Visual Arts," including articles by Parker Tyler, Arnold Hauser, Rudolf Arnheim, and Josef von Sternberg; and "Film and Esthetics," which includes the observations of Jean-Luc Godard, Michelangelo Antonioni, Luis Buñuel, Jack Kerouac and J. B. Priestly. A good list of recommended films is also available.

* Samuels, Charles Thomas (editor). *A Casebook on Film.* New York: Van Nostrand Reinhold Company, 1970.

Recognizing the need for film students to write well, Samuels uses very effectively the casebook approach to research. He divides his text into two sections. First comes the material on the theory of film, including articles from such heavyweights as Panofsky, Hauser, Deren, Sarris, Pudovkin, Bluestone, Simon, Brustein, and Warshow. Then comes the theoretical application. Students are asked to see and write on three films: *The Graduate, Bonnie and Clyde,* and *Blow-up.* Each film assignment is preceded by four model essays. For example, Samuels presents students working on *The Graduate* with reviews by Kauffmann, Friedenberg, Farber and Changas, and Brackman. The book also has a selective glossary, a list of suggested projects, and a good bibliography.

* Sarris, Andrew (editor). *The Film.* New York: The Bobbs-Merrill Company, Inc., 1968.

This brief anthology is also concerned with student writing. It contains essays that center on directors from three countries. First are Americans (Stanley Kubrick, Elia Kazan, and Jerry Lewis), second are French (François Truffaut, Robert Bresson and the New Wave), finally there are the Italians (Michelangelo Antonioni and Federico Fellini). Sarris's format is to have critics—e.g., Kael, Archer, Alpert and Simon—comment on the filmmakers; then he adds a few stimulating questions for group discussion to be followed by writing assignments.

* Scheuer, Steven H. *Movies on TV.* New York: Bantam Books, 1969.

This is the most recent edition of a handbook that first appeared in 1958. It briefly describes and rates nearly 7000 feature films shown on American television. Included in the reviews are production dates and credits.

* Schillaci, Anthony and John M. Culkin (editors). *Films Deliver: Teaching Creatively with Film.* New York: Citation Press, 1970.

Several years ago Fordham University's National Film Study Project developed some useful and innovative materials for screen educators. The authors of this handy little book have collected the major results and presented them in four clearly defined sections: a rationale for film study ("What Films Can Do for Teachers and Students"), case studies of specific teaching units ("How It's Being Done Today"), practical tips for student filmmaking ("The Nitty-Gritty of Films in Education"), and extensive appendices that contain annotated filmographies and bibliographies.

* Schillaci, Anthony, OP. *Movies and Morals.* Notre Dame, Ind.: Fides Publishers, Inc., 1968.

Father Schillaci has written a good little book for religious institutions on the value of films for emotional maturity and moral development. In readable prose, he describes the place of film study in a spiritual education.

* Sheratsky, Rodney E. *Film: The Reality of Being.* New Jersey Association of Teachers of English I:1 (April 1969).

This 12-page monograph is a fine introduction to the study of film in the secondary school. Written by one of the best screen educators in the East, it presents sound advice based upon years of experience.

* Sheridan, Marion C. *et al. The Motion picture and the Teaching of English.* New York: Appleton-Century-Crofts, 1965.

Ever since its publication, this volume has been the "whipping boy" of film intellectuals because of its heavy-handed literary emphasis. Nevertheless, thousands of English teachers have found its opening chapters on film technique and language helpful bridges out of a staid literary program. This is one of those books to sample rather than study.

* Slade, Mark. *Language of Change: Moving Images of Man.* Toronto: Holt, Rinehart and Winston of Canada Ltd., 1970.

Written with wit and insight, this book offers a good discussion of the impact that moving images have on a global community. Slade, unlike most modern critics of the communications revolution, offers some positive suggestions to the problems of information processing and outmoded learning procedures.

* Sohn, David A. *Film Study and the English Teacher.* Bloomington: Indiana University Audio-Visual Center, 1968.

Written by a filmmaker and teacher, this extraordinary twelve-page document is wonderful for landscaping the problems and possible solutions to an initial cinema program. Read this before you try the other introductory materials.

* Sohn, David A. *Film: The Creative Eye.* Dayton: Geo. A. Pflaum, 1970.

This book is a good introduction to the students of visual literacy. Through the use of an excellent graphic text, cogent and brief interviews, and outstanding short films, Sohn presents an invaluable introduction to film aesthetics.

* Solomon, Stanley J. *The Film Idea.* New York: Harcourt, Brace and Jovanovich, Inc., 1972.

Working from the basic premise that the narrative film needs to be examined independently from the traditional arts, Solomon divides his book into three main sections. Part One offers a nontechnical discussion of the basic principles of film form; Part Two examines the chronological growth of that film form; and Part Three studies a host of theories and aesthetics about film form.

Sontag, Susan. *Against Interpretation and Other Essays.* New York: Farrar, Straus and Giroux, 1966.

Only six of 26 chapters are directly about motion pictures, but Sontag's first two chapters are quite good in cautioning us against the dangers of overanalyzing a work of art, to the point where it destroys our interest or love for the opus itself. Also useful for film students is her highly praised essay "Notes on 'Camp.' "

Starr, Cecile (editor). *Ideas on Film: A Handbook for the 16mm. Film User.* New York: Funk and Wagnalls Company, 1951.

Basically a collection of articles taken from the pages of *The Saturday Review of Literature* where Starr had a column, this book offers some stimulating observations on understanding the attempts in the 1940s to bring nontheatrical films into educational circles. Among the many scholarly and well-known contributors are Rudolf Arnheim, Willard Van Dyke, Arthur Knight, Pearl S. Buck, Raymond Spottiswoode, and Arthur Mayer.

* Stewart, David C. *Film Study in Higher Education.* Washington, D.C.: The American Council on Education, 1966.

This report summarizes the work of leading film teachers who from 1964 to 1965 met first at Lincoln Center and then at Dartmouth to discuss the possible approaches to improving film study. Among its many useful materials are Jack Ellis's communication program, Arthur Knight's outline of film history materials, Hugh Gray's film aesthetics, and George C. Stoney's arguments for the art of the film. Here too is Pauline Kael's highly publicized attack on screen education. Stewart also has some valuable appendices on professional associations and archives.

* Taylor, Theodore. *People Who Make Movies.* New York: Doubleday, 1967.
An easy-to-read overview of the work behind the scenes is presented in this book along with some good illustrations of actual feature film productions.

* Thompson, Howard (editor). *The New York Times Guide to Movies on TV.* Introduction by Bosley Crowther. Chicago: Quadrangle Books, 1970.
By far the best source for short, witty, and sometimes great film reviews. Thompson also provides complete credits, dates, and a still from each film.

Wall, James M. *Church and Cinema: A Way of Viewing Film.* Grand Rapids: Eerdmans Publishing, 1971.
Written by the enlightened editor of the *Christian Advocate,* this slim and lightweight book deals effectively with the religious school's need to analyze the place of sex and censorship in American films. Wall's emphasis is on relating content and style to the filmmaker's aesthetic and philosophical standards.

Weaver, John T. (editor). *Forty Years of Screen Credits 1929–1969.* Two Volumes. Metuchen, N.J.: The Scarecrow Press, Inc., 1970.
This sweeping coverage of performers' credits, arranged alphabetically, offers the most exhaustive listing to date. Scholars should be warned, however, that it is not always accurate.

* Whitaker, Rod. *The Language of Film.* Englewood Cliffs, N.J.: Prentice-Hall, Inc., 1970.
Designed as a brief introduction to the study of film as a form of communication which is shaped by purposes, audiences, the medium itself, and the nature of the message, this book emphasizes two main points of view: the creative and the perceptual.

White, David Manning and Richard Averson (editors). *Sight, Sound and Society: Motion Pictures and Television in America.* Boston: Beacon Press, 1968.
This excellent introductory textbook for media students is divided into five well-balanced sections. Part One, "The Screen and its Audience," consists of four sociological essays by Seldes, Silvey, Schramm, and Hayakawa. Part Two, "Media and Messages," has a wonderful critical piece on film aesthetics by Robert Steele. Part Three, "Sight and Sound Communicators," is about the pressures exerted by the now-defunct studio system. Part Four, "The Controversial Screen," deals with the familiar media problems of violence, censorship, and political pressures; particularly useful is Philip French's "Violence in the Cinema." Part Five, "The Expanding Image," has a superb essay by Walter J. Ong and John Culkin's fine survey of high school film teaching principles. The book also has a good bibliography.

* Williams, Clarence and John Debes (editors). *Visual Literacy.* New York: Pitman Publishing Corporation, 1970.

These uneven and provocative essays taken from the first National Conference on Visual Literacy discuss (1) the philosophy of the meeting, (2) related research, (3) various types of media literacy, (4) visual literacy in the schools, and (5) community projects. The 56 papers, concisely edited, suggest the problems and the directions for several years to come.

* Wlaschin, Ken. *Bluff Your Way in the Cinema.* London: Wolfe Publishing Ltd., 1969.

If you have trouble understanding all the faddish terms and cults, read this iconoclastic and delightful approach to the jargon of film. Some samples of Wiaschin's work: "Auteur—French bluffing term for O.K. director," "Cliff hanger—the unexplained disappearance of an Antonioni heroine in the middle of a film," and "Quickie—nothing to do with sex. A cheap, hurriedly-made and usually shoddy film." Every teacher should have a copy to take to class.

* Wollen, Peter. *Signs and Meaning in the Cinema.* Bloomington: Indiana University Press, 1969.

The best introduction yet to the relationship between film and the other arts, with a strong emphasis on the value of linguistics to screen language. For beginners who need and value a useful survey of Eisenstein, the Auteur theory, and a provocative discussion of major directors, Wollen's well-written, concise, and enjoyable text is first rate.

Aesthetics

* Arnheim, Rudolf. *Film As Art.* Berkeley: University of California Press, 1957.

Originally published in 1933, this book is the first full-length discussion of the relationship between film technique and audience reactions. Arnheim, writing during the early days of sound, considered both sound and color liabilities to the art of the cinema, and thus parts of the treatise are defensive statements about the value of the silent screen. Nevertheless, much of what the distinguished theorist observes about cinematic technique is invaluable for serious students.

* Balázs, Béla. *Theory of the Film: Character and Growth of a New Art.* Translated by Edith Bone. London: Dennis Dobson Ltd., 1952.

Written by a filmmaker and a pioneer motion picture theorist, this posthumous book presents an important aesthetic and psychological analysis of silent movies. Balázs, although overly critical of American films and favorably disposed toward Russian movies, provides one of the best studies ever written of the artistic qualities possible in the cinema.

* Bazin, André. *What is Cinema?* Volume I. Essays Selected and Translated by Hugh Gray. Berkeley: University of California Press, 1967.

Bazin's first essays, translated and published ten years after his untimely death at 40, represent the work of the most important postwar critic in France. We are given a good understanding of the thoughts and feelings of this influential editor of *Cahiers du Cinema* whose love for Hollywood so affected rising directors like Truffaut, Resnais, and Godard that a "New Wave" of filmmakers revitalized the French Cinema. Two impeccable selections, "The Myth of Total Cinema" and "The Evolution of the Language of the Cinema," are excellent examples of Bazin's ability to use films as springboards for his stimulating theories of movies in general.

* Bazin, André. *What is Cinema?* Volume II. Essays selected and translated by Hugh Gray. Foreword by François Truffaut. Berkeley: University of California Press, 1971.

    Taken from the last two volumes of Bazin's *Qu' est-ce le Cinéma?*, these valuable translations deal with the great French critic's views on the western, on Chaplin and on neorealism. There are also two charming and witty articles on pinup girls and *The Outlaw*.

* Bellone, Julius (editor). *Renaissance of the Film*. New York: The Macmillan Company, 1970.

    This anthology is a collection of some of the most interesting criticism about a number of the best films since 1940. Among the reviewers are Eric Rhode, Andrew Sarris, Robert Brustein, James Agee, Pauline Kael, Jonas Mekas, Stanley Kauffmann, Norman H. Holland and Vernon Young.

* Benoit-Levy, Jean. *The Art of the Motion Picture*. Translated by Theodore R. Jaeckel. New York: Coward-McCann, Inc., 1946.

    Divided into two main sections (Education and Entertainment), the book provides the general reader with a good idea of the general categories of film and the technique and art of bringing them into the classroom. It is more useful today as a model for discussing the problems of movies in educational circles.

* Boyum, Joy, and Adrienne Scott. *Film as Film: Critical Responses to Film Art*. Boston: Allyn and Bacon, Inc., 1971.

    Emphasizing that their book offers a chance to study and practice good film criticism, the authors divide their work into two parts. The first chapters explore the problems of treating film as an art form. The second part offers an excellent collection of critical articles by significant critics on 25 important films: e.g., *Blow-Up, Bonnie and Clyde, 8½, The Graduate, Jules and Jim, Open City, The Seventh Seal,* and *Viridiana*.

Cavell, Stanley. *The World Viewed: Reflections on the Ontology of Film*. New York: The Viking Press, 1971.

    Concerned with what makes movies so important in our lives and how to evaluate the film's artistic merit, Cavell philosophically explores Hollywood's star system, directors, and famous films while at the same time he provides some stimulating observations on major European artists.

* Dickinson, Thorold. *A Discovery of the Cinema*. New York: Oxford University Press, 1971.

    Although more than half the pages in this slim and attractive volume are devoted to the silent film, the author makes some provocative comments about what he considers to be the four basic factors of film development—political and social climate, creative capacity of the artist, flexibility of movie equipment, and the audience. The book also contains recommended film viewing lists, and a brief bibliography and indices.

Durgnat, Raymond. *Films and Feelings*. Cambridge: M.I.T. Press, 1967.

    Relying on his postgraduate research at the Slade School, Durgnat spends almost half the book developing a stimulating introduction to film styles, from *The Birth of a Nation* to experimental film production in the 1960s. Film buffs may find his highly personal prose tough going.

Feldman, Joseph and Harry. *Dynamics of the Film.* New York: Arno Press, 1971.
Originally written in 1952, this highly readable book discusses film study in everyday terms and is an excellent source guide to the general understanding of film characteristics.

* Huss, Roy, and Norman Silverstein. *The Film Experience: Elements of Motion Picture Art.* New York: Harper and Row, 1968.
The authors' intentions are to increase the filmgoer's perception through three critical methods: (1) a discussion of "auteur" directors such as Griffith, Godard, and Kurosawa and the development of their techniques; (2) an analysis of the social significance evident in specific movies; and (3) an evaluation of the effect that films create. In eight well-written chapters dealing with the important elements in film technique, Huss and Silverstein effectively use stills, diagrams, a graphic story-board presentation, and a host of fine filmic examples to illustrate many abstract concepts. Students should be more informed about the art of film after reading this book.

* Jacobs, Lewis (editor). *Introduction to the Art of the Movies: An Anthology of Ideas on the Nature of Movie Art.* New York: The Noonday Press, 1960.
Jacobs's purpose is to survey the nature of film art through 36 articles written from 1920 to 1960. He has arranged his worthwhile anthology into four main sections. Students should find invaluable a number of exceptional essays by Herman Weinberg, Dorothy B. Jones, Jay Leyda, Seymour Stern, Dwight Macdonald, Paul Goodman, Maya Deren, Dudley Nichols, Hans Richter, and Slavko Vorkapich.

* Jacobs, Lewis (editor). *The Emergence of Film Art: The Evolution and Development of the Motion Picture as an Art Form from 1900 to the Present.* New York: Hopkinson and Blake, 1969.
Don't be deceived by the title of this book, which suggests a heavy emphasis on historical matters. The author skips quickly from country to country with little chronological transition, and after the early 1930s the selections are almost all theoretical and not bound to a specific period. But it is a superb collection of essays on the art of the cinema as seen through the eyes of some outstanding film critics. Invaluable are articles by Jacobs, Stern, Eisenstein, Cavalcanti, Lawson, Flaherty, Anderson, Benson, Bergman, Sarris, Kael, Richie, Antonioni, Young, Mekas, and Kauffmann. This book should be on every beginning student's shelf.

* Jacobs, Lewis (editor). *The Movies as Medium.* New York: Farrar, Straus and Giroux, 1970.
The most recent attempt by Jacobs to collect important essays about the fundamentals of film art is a further example of his excellent skill as an editor. This time he divides the anthology into four main parts: aims and attitudes, the nature of film expression, the plastic elements, and the plastic structure. Not only is the reader able to learn about the interlocking relationship between a filmmaker's intentions and finished results, but also there are many stimulating suggestions about film criticism useful for classroom

discussion. Some of the contributors are Ezra Goodman, Stanley J. Solomon, Robert Gessner, Ivor Montagu, Carl Dreyer, Sergei Eisenstein, Béla Balázs, Kurt Weill, Arthur Lennig, and Jonas Mekas.

* Kracauer, Siegfried. *Theory of Film: The Redemption of Physical Reality.* New York: Oxford University Press, 1960.

This is one of the most significant studies of film art yet written. Kracauer, concerning himself primarily with black-and-white film, discusses the development of film aesthetics as an outgrowth of photography and argues that motion pictures achieve greatness only when they record and reveal the visible world around us. This book should be read by all serious students of film.

* Lawson, John Howard. *Film: The Creative Process. The Search For An Audio-Visual Language and Structure.* New York: Hill and Wang, 1964.

Written in Russia by a blacklisted American screenwriter, this book has more than its share of acrimony against Hollywood movies and an over-emphasis on Soviet achievements. But when it comes to a theoretical discussion of film as Art, Lawson is magnificent. He bases his critical position on the importance of movies in helping rational man know the truth about himself and the world so that humans can control their destiny. Although the book has five sections, readers might do better to skip I and II on history and begin with his important chapters on film language, theory, and structure.

Linden, George W. *Reflections on the Screen.* Belmont, Calif.: Wadsworth Publishing Company, Inc., 1970.

Central to understanding this book is Linden's premise that films have a dual nature which synthesizes a variety of life experiences, discussed in terms of contrasting relationships such as outer/inner worlds, objective/subjective experiences. If you can get by some of the verbosity, you'll find it very helpful in exploring film in relation to the more traditional arts.

* MacCann, Richard Dyer (editor). *Film: A Montage of Theories.* New York: E. P. Dutton and Company, Inc., 1966.

This well-organized anthology contains 39 stimulating articles written by important filmmakers and critics. The author, hoping to shed some light on the controversies surrounding the art of the film, has grouped conflicting and valuable points of view under five main titles: "The Plastic Material," "Film and the Other Arts," "The Cinematic Essence," "Dream and Reality," and "An Evolving Art." Readers should enjoy the observations of Parker Tyler, Hollis Alpert, Rudolf Arnheim, George Bluestone, V. I. Pudovkin, René Clair, Dudley Nichols, Mack Sennett, Pauline Kael, and François Truffaut.

* Montagu, Ivor. *Film World: A Guide to Cinema.* Baltimore: Penguin Books, 1964.

Although this is another politically biased treatise—avowedly pro-Soviet and anti-West—Montagu provides some excellent chapters on the art of the film and gives invaluable suggestions for beginning students on what to look for in film analysis. Of the four uneven chapters, the most practical and useful section is the third, on film as a commodity. The first two demonstrate Montagu's Aristotelian urge to list, and the last chapter on film as a vehicle can easily be avoided.

* Spottiswoode, Raymond. *A Grammar of the Film: An Analysis of Film Technique.* Berkeley: University of California Press, 1950.

This early work, somewhat dated today, is an invaluable introduction for establishing the basic language and grammar of film. It is particularly helpful in illustrating and describing specific movie devices and forms.

* Stephenson, Ralph, and J. R. Debrix. *The Cinema as Art.* Revised Edition. Baltimore: Penguin Books, 1969.

This book is the best organized and most lucid introduction to the art of the film now available for beginning students. Stephenson, a former employee of the British Film Institute, and Debrix, formerly from the Institut des Hautes Etudes Cinématographiques in France, have combined the scholarship of many European countries and produced a readable, valuable, and important text on motion picture aesthetics. The nine chapters, which begin with a discussion of the film as art and end with a summary on reality and artistic creation, include names of many films as good examples to illustrate abstract theories. The book also has more than 50 well-chosen stills.

* Talbot, Daniel (editor). *Film: An Anthology.* New York: Simon and Schuster, 1959.

Although there is an abridged paperback edition of this splendid anthology available from the University of California Press, it is worth paying the extra money to get this complete collection of invaluable articles. The first section—"Aesthetics, Social Commentary and Analysis"—has some of the most significant articles ever published on the film including Panofsky's "Style and Medium in the Moving Pictures," Nicoll's "Film Reality: The Cinema and the Theater," Langer's "A Note on the Film," Agee's "Comedy's Greatest Era," and Warshow's "The Westerner." In the other two sections, the reader will find equally important essays by Pudovkin, Balázs, Arnheim, Eisenstein, Clair, Cocteau, Rotha, Jacobs, Kracauer, and Sadoul.

* Thomson, David. *Movie Man.* New York: Stein and Day, 1967.

Here is a good discussion of the complexities of film expression by the use of literary analogies and sociological speculations. For those who are already into serious film study, Thomson provides some useful insights into the works of Hitchcock, Lang, Hawks, Renoir, Godard, Anthony Mann, and Losey.

* Tyler, Parker. *The Hollywood Hallucination.* Introduction by Richard Schickel. New York: Simon and Schuster, 1970.

First published in 1944, this original and controversial commentary about Hollywood in the 1930s offers the reader a chance to study the dream theory criticism that so often tries to explain the complex relationship between movies and their audiences.

* Tyler, Parker. *Magic and Myth of the Movies.* Introduction by Richard Schickel. New York: Simon and Schuster, 1970.

This book was originally published in 1947. In it Tyler continues his stimulating analysis of the movies as the folk art of the American people. More time is spent here in bringing the 1940s into focus as commercial myths.

Tyler, Parker. *The Three Faces of the Film: The Art, the Dream, the Cult.* New York: Thomas Yoseloff, 1960.

By now the eccentric but fascinating critic had synthesized his writings on film and dream to present a good discussion of the cultural and aesthetic relevance of movies in our lives.

* Warshow, Robert. *The Immediate Experience: Movies, Comics, Theater, and Other Aspects of Popular Culture.* New York: Doubleday, 1962.

Written by a former editor of *Commentary* magazine and a man who dearly loved the popular arts, this book is a remarkable collection of essays by a fine film critic. His main value is in pointing out a movie's flaws rather than in identifying outstanding characteristics of a well-done film. Included here are his memorable essays on Westerns, Gangsters, *M. Verdoux,* and *The Best Years of Our Lives.*

Young, Vernon. *Vernon Young on Film: Unpopular Essays on a Popular Art.* Chicago: Quadrangle Books, 1972.

In this first collection of film essays by a lucid, knowledgeable critic who has written for the *Hudson Review* during the past twenty years, we are treated to a broad and fascinating range of cultural comments about film and society. The author displays wit, good standards, and an impressive acquaintance with a wide variety of movies. Teachers should find his extensive comments on short films extremely rewarding.

* Youngblood, Gene. *Expanded Cinema.* Introduction by R. Buckminster Fuller. New York: E. P. Dutton and Company, Inc., 1970.

Arguing as a post-McLuhanite, Youngblood claims that new technological extensions of film have become mandatory. Consequently, he offers an unusual and perceptive account of such advanced breakthroughs as computers, films, television experiments, laser movies, and multiple-projection environments.

Techniques[25]

The Production Process

Baddeley, W. Hugh. *The Technique of Documentary Film Production.* New York: Hastings House, 1963.

Written by an experienced filmmaker, this is a practical introduction to the basic principles of movie-making, starting with an excellent chapter on script writing. The reader will find much useful information in subsequent chapters on equipment, location work, lighting, and sound recording.

Millerson, Gerald. *The Technique of Television Production.* New York: Hastings House, 1961.

Although the emphasis is clearly on TV production, Millerson suggests *many* useful ideas on techniques directly applicable to film, e.g., visual continuity, lighting, camera placement, composition, and sound recording.

Reynerston, A. J. *The Work of the Film Director.* New York: Hastings House, 1970.

In addition to providing an extremely worthwhile philosophy on film direction, Reynerston, in lucid and accurate prose, gives a valuable introduction to such production areas as methods, sound, composition and acting. The illustrations in this book are valuable and plentiful.

---

25. This list was influenced by Raymond Fielding's excellent article, "Motion Picture Technique: A Basic Library," *Film Quarterly* 16, no. 3 (Spring 1963) : 48–49.

Souto, H. Mario Raimondo. *The Technique of the Motion Picture Camera.* Edited by Raymond Spottiswoode. New York: Hastings House, 1967.

Written by a Uruguayan filmmaker, this useful and comprehensive text deals with motion-picture cameras, not techniques. But the information is invaluable for producing different types of movies effectively.

Spottiswoode, Raymond. *Film and Its Techniques.* Berkeley: University of California Press, 1968.

Originally published in 1951, this is one of the most compact, complete, and informative texts on making movies. More than 80 percent of the book is devoted to the needs of low-budget filmmakers.

Spottiswoode, Raymond (general editor). *The Focal Encyclopedia of Film and Television Techniques.* New York: Hastings House, 1969.

Without question, this is the major text available today on basic film techniques. More than 1600 entries, alphabetically arranged and in clear print, are concisely presented, along with many helpful charts, diagrams, and illustrations.

Cinematography[26]

Alton, John. *Painting With Light.* New York: The Macmilian Company, 1949.

Although the design leaves much to be desired, this first major attempt at discussing studio camera techniques—particularly the difficulties connected in lighting interior and exterior scenes—is worth reading.

* Campbell, Russell (editor). *Photographic Theory for the Motion Picture Cameraman.* New York: A. S. Barnes and Company, 1970.

Despite the author's claim that the book is designed for readers just beginning film production, you might start with easier texts and then come back to this technical but worthwhile, up-to-date discussion of film stock, processing, sensitometry, image formation and tone rendering, grain structure and definition, printing, color photography and color balance.

* Campbell, Russell (editor). *Practical Motion Picture Photography.* Introduction by Walter Lassally. New York: A. S. Barnes and Company, 1970.

Beginners will find this a useful text in which to read about light meters, exposure controls, filters, and color rendering. A special feature of the book is the section on aerial and underwater filming.

* Caunter, Julien. *How to Make Movie Magic in Amateur Films.* Philadelphia: Chilton Books, 1971.

This title was originally two books entitled *How to do Tricks* and *How to do the Simpler Tricks.* Caunter has combined and revised them into a

---

26. Some related articles are: Charles Higham and Joel Greenberg, "North Lights and Cigarette Bulb: Conversations with Cameramen," *Sight and Sound* 36, no. 4 (Autumn 1967) : 192–97; George Mitchell, "The Cameraman: Part I," *Films in Review* 7, no. 1 (January 1956) : 7–18; George J. Mitchell, "Part II: The Cameraman," *Films in Review* 7, no. 2 (February 1956) : 67–76; Jack Jacobs, "James Wong Howe," *Films in Review* 12, no. 4 (April 1961) : 215–32; George J. Mitchell, "The ASC," *Films in Review* 18, no. 7 (August–September 1967) : 385–97; and Ralph Gerstle, "Optical Effects," *Films in Review* 5, no. 4 (April 1954) : 171–74.

Also see the following articles on color: James L. Limbacher, "Color's An Old Device," *Films in Review* 10, no. 6 (June 1959) : 346–50; Rudy Behlmer, "Technicolor," *Films in Review* 15, no. 6 (June–July 1964) : 333–51; and William Johnson, "Coming to Terms with Color," *Film Quarterly* 20, no. 1 (Fall 1966) : 2–22.

useful introduction to special effects filmmaking. Among the many things discussed are simple effects—including exposure, focusing, lens, diffusion, distortion, filter and dissolves—and more sophisticated techniques, including camera speed, reverse action, stop motion, animation, editing and directing.

Evans, Ralph. *Eye, Film and Camera in Color Photography*. New York: John Wiley & Sons, 1959.

The author of this perceptive, well-written, provocative guide to the relationship between common-sense filmmaking and the audience's emotional response was the head of Kodak's Color Technology Division.

Fielding, Raymond. *The Technique of Special Effects Cinematography*. New York: Hastings House, 1965.

This invaluable book goes to great lengths to distinguish between special photographic effects (visual effects, optical effects, process cinema) and mechanical effects (special sound effects, explosions, matte shots of various types). Mr. Fielding supplies information that you won't find anywhere else.

* Lipton, Lenny. *Independent Filmmaking*. With an Introduction by Stan Brakhage. San Francisco: Straight Arrow Books, 1972.

This is a superb guide to 8mm, Super 8-Single 8, and 16mm filmmaking. It is divided into ten worthwhile and heavily detailed chapters on such things as formats, film, cameras, lens, shooting, splicing and editing, sound and magnetic recordings, preparing the sound tracks, and the laboratory's role. A valuable index is also included.

* Maltin, Leonard. *Behind the Camera: The Cinematographer's Art*. New York: Signet Books, 1971.

The editor of *Film Fan Monthly* offers a valuable introductory essay on the history of the famous Hollywood cameramen from the beginnings of film history to the present, plus invaluable interviews with Arthur C. Miller, Hal Mohr, Hal Rossen, Lucien Ballard, and Conrad Hall. Also included are an Academy Award listing for cinematography plus a useful index.

* Marner, Terence St. John (editor). *Directing Motion Pictures*. New York: A. S. Barnes and Company, 1972.

This is another useful and easily readable book in a new series on professional film techniques. Marner divides his text and contributors' comments into nine valuable chapters on such things as the director's role, his preparation, the script, setting up shots, graphic continuity, lens and composition, viewpoint and movement, the director and acting, and rehearsal and improvisation. Also included are two film excerpts (*Now that the Buffalo's Gone* and *This Sporting Life*) as well as a helpful index.

Mascelli, Joseph V. (editor). *The Five C's of Cinematography*. Hollywood: Cinne Graphic Publications, 1965.

A superb book on filmmaking, conceived from the cameraman's point of view. It deals with the basic Cs of the director: camera angles, continuity, cut-ups, close-ups, and composition. Mascelli not only supplies easy-to-understand definitions but also 500 clear photographs and 41 diagrams.

Mascelli, Joseph V. and Arthur C. Miller (editors). *American Cinematographer Manual,* 3rd edition. Hollywood: American Society of Cinematographers, 1966.

Designed primarily for cinematographers and film production people, this extraordinary reference book provides invaluable information on particulars and products. The book also has a very useful index, plus Walter Beyer's fine discussion of wide-screen systems. Very technical at times.

Mercer, John. *An Introduction to Cinematography.* Champaign, Illinois: Stripes Publishing Company, 1967.
This film-production handbook contains a wealth of useful and practical information. It seems to be aimed primarily at the low-budget filmmaker, and that makes it unique.

Millerson, Gerald. *The Technique of Lighting for Television and Motion Pictures.* New York: Hastings House, 1972.
This is the definitive work to date on the art of creative lighting techniques. Written by an engineer with twenty years of experience with the BBC, the text is divided into twelve excellent sections starting with the basic principles to the art of lighting and moving to more advanced levels of theory and methodology. In addition, Millerson offers the reader a wealth of useful and clear illustrations.

Editing[27]

Burder, John. *The Technique of Editing 16mm Film.* New York: Hastings House, 1968.
A short, forceful introduction to such elementary matters as film gauge, equipment and editing facilities, principles of editing, and the mechanics of sound editing. It should be a useful book for beginning filmmakers.

Reisz, Karel and Gavin Miller (editors). *The Technique of Film Editing.* New York: Hastings House, 1968.
An enlarged edition of the 1953 original and the fifteenth reprinting of this highly important text. It should continue for at least another decade to be the best introduction to editing for three good reasons: depth, breadth, and scholarship.

Walter, Ernest. *The Technique of the Film Cutting Room.* New York: Hastings House, 1969.
Written by a very knowledgeable and experienced film editor, this text discusses in detail the basic responsibilities of the editor and his assistants, and the various stages of editing. Clearly written and with many helpful diagrams and illustrations.

Film Music[28]

Eisler, Hans. *Composing for the Films.* New York: Oxford University Press, 1947.
Based upon his creative work in the forties, the famed composer's book is an informative and readable discussion of his personal approach to film music.

---

27. I recommend two articles by Jean R. Debrix, "Film Editing: I," *Films in Review* 4, no. 1 (January 1953) : 21–24; and "Film Editing: II," *Films in Review* 4, no. 2 (February 1953) : 24–27.
28. In my opinion, the best articles on film music to date are William Johnson, "Face the Music," *Film Quarterly* 22, no. 4 (Summer 1969) : 3–19; and Douglas W. Gallez, "Theories of Film Music," *Cinema Journal* 9, no. 2 (Spring 1970) : 40–47. Other useful articles are Jeffrey Embler, "The Structure of Film Music," *Films in Review* 4, no. 7 (August–September 1953) : 332–35; Jack Jacobs, "Alfred Newman," *Films in Review* 10,

Foort, Reginald. *The Cinema Organ: A Description in Non-Technical Language of a Fascinating Instrument and How It is Played.* Vestal, N.Y.: Vestal Press, 1971.

Originally published in 1932, this book was mainly a music text covering the history of the organ in movie houses, instructions on how to play it, and suggestions on musical scores. The new edition brings the story forward to the present day.

Hofmann, Charles. *Sounds for Silents.* New York: Drama Book Specialists Publications, 1970.

This beautifully designed book treats the silent era and its musical accompaniments. It is a carefully written and expert account, which also has a record to illustrate the author's major points.

Manvell, Roger and John Huntley. *The Technique of Film Music.* New York: Hastings House, 1957.

Except for two historical chapters on the development of film music, the authors concentrate on the scores of the 1950s. Although this is heavy reading, their comments on the function of music in talkies as well as the musicians' responsibilities are important considerations.

Animation[29]

Andersen, Yvonne. *Make Your Own Animated Movies: Yellow Ball Workshop Film Techniques.* Boston: Little, Brown and Company, 1970.

Strictly for children. This clever and well-illustrated book offers many valuable suggestions for elementary school children. It condenses much of Anderson's method by successfully taking novices step-by-step through the exciting experience of making original films.

Andersen, Yvonne. *Teaching Film Animation to Children.* New York: Van Nostrand Reinhold Company, 1970.

---

no. 7 (August–September 1959) : 403–14; Harry Haun and George Raborn, "Max Steiner," *Films in Review* 12, no. 6 (June–July 1961) : 338–51; Edward Jablonski and William R. Sweigart, "Harold Arlen," *Films in Review* 13, no. 10 (December 1962) : 605–14; Dennis Lee Galling, "Arthur Freed," *Films in Review* 15, no. 9 (November 1964) : 521–44; Anthony Thomas, "Hugo Friedhofer," *Films in Review* 16, no. 8 (October 1965) : 496–502; Ken Doeckel, "Milklos Rozsa," *Films in Review* 16, no. 9 (November 1965) : 536–48; Rudy Behlmer, "Erich Wolfgang Korngold," *Films in Review* 18, no. 2 (February 1967): 86–100; Page Cook, "Bernard Herrmann," *Films in Review* 18, no. 7 (August–September 1967) : 398–412; Page Cook, "Franz Waxman," *Films in Review* 19, no. 7 (August–September 1968) : 415–30; Page Cook, "Ken Darby," *Films in Review* 20, no. 6 (June–July 1969) : 335–56; Douglas W. Gallez, "Theories of Film Music," *Cinema Journal* 9, no. 2 (Spring 1970) : 40–47; Jean-François Hauduroy, "Writing for Musicals: Interview with Betty Comden and Adolph Green," *Cahiers du Cinema in English* 2, CdC no. 174 (January 1966) : 42–48; Patrick Brion, "Filmography," *ibid.*, 49–50; William Alwyn, "Composing for the Screen," *Films and Filming* 5, no. 6 (March 1959) : 9, 34; Richard Fothergill, "Putting Music in its Place," *ibid.*, 10–11, 33; and Lionel Godfrey, "The Music Makers: Elmer Bernstein and Jerry Goldsmith," *Films and Filming* 12, no. 12 (September 1966) : 36–40.

29. The following articles are helpful: Andre Martin, "Animated Cinema: The Way Forward," *Sight and Sound* 28, no. 2 (Spring 1959) : 80–85; Jules V. Schwerin, "Drawings that are Alive: The Story of the Animated Film Cartoon," *Films in Review* 1, no. 6 (September 1950) : 6–9; John Halas, "Tomorrow's Animation," *Films in Review* 20, no. 5 (May 1969) : 293–96; Harriet Polt, "The Death of Mickey Mouse," *Film Comment* 2, no. 3 (Summer 1964) : 34–39; and Elodie Osborn, "Animation in Zagreb," *Film Quarterly* 22, no. 1 (Fall 1968) : 46–51.

Teachers with next to no experience in filmmaking and animation should benefit greatly from this straightforward text for public schools. The stills are worthwhile, the explanations are clear, and the practical advice is invaluable.

Halas, John in collaboration with Roger Manvell. *Art in Movement: New Directions in Animation.* New York: Hastings House, 1970.

This updated version of the 1959 publication contains history and factors governing animation, its uses, and the production of cartoons together with speculations about the future of the animated film. Statements from people in the field add weight to the authors' comments and make it well-worth owning.

Kinsey, Anthony. *How to Make Animated Movies: A Studio Handbook.* New York: The Viking Press, 1970.

Written by an art educator, this beautifully designed text is a wonderful introduction to the basic mechanics of animation production. The reader will find many practical suggestions about equipment, techniques, and editing, along with a very readable narrative and good illustrations.

Levitan, Eli L. *Animation Techniques and Commercial Film Production.* New York: Reinhold 1962.

Although the in-depth coverage of animation work done in the television film area is interesting and worth knowing about, the reader should be warned about the poor production quality of the book itself and the unreasonable cost.

Madsen, Roy. *Animated Film: Concepts, Methods, Uses.* New York: Interland Publishing, Inc., 1969.

Here is the best book yet on animation—one conceived and executed in an appealing manner. In 15 informative and engaging chapters, Dr. Madsen traces the history of animation, suggests novel and useful ways of making your own animated films, and provides a valuable bibliography, filmography, and glossary.

Manvell, Roger. *The Animated Film.* New York: Hastings House, 1954.

This very slight but interesting book discusses animation in relation to Britain's first full-length animated film, George Orwell's *Animal Farm*. The text is filled with many fine illustrations created by John Halas and Joy Batchelor for producer Louis de Rochemont's important movie.

* Stephenson, Ralph. *Animation in the Cinema.* New York: A. S. Barnes and Company, 1967.

A useful contribution from Peter Cowie's International Film Guide Series. This brief but important survey of the history of animation and the present practices throughout the world is a useful guide and contains cogent, accurate information.

Thomas, Bob. *Walt Disney: The Art of Animation. The Story of the Disney Studio Contribution to a New Art.* New York: The Golden Press, 1958.

Strictly for children. A charming and worthwhile introduction to the history of animation, plus a pleasant and romantic behind-the-scenes account of the production of *Sleeping Beauty*. The illustrations are of Disney favorites like Mickey Mouse, Donald Duck, Bambi, Goofy, Pluto, and many more.

Make-Up

Kehoe, Vincent J. R. *The Technique of Film and Television Make-Up.*
New York: Hastings House, 1958.
  The most useful book yet available, one written by a practical and experienced artist in the field. The information is heavily oriented to British
practices.

Art Direction[30]

Carrick, Edward. *Designing for Films.* New York: Crowell-Studio Publications, 1950.
  This edition of a book first published in 1941 was revised and expanded
to deal with color, film effects, and perspective. Handsomely printed, it
offers some useful ideas about the functions of the set designer. It stresses
the function of lighting in creating mood and tension. The best things
about the book are its lovely illustrations.

Screenwriting[31]

Herman, Lewis. *Educational Films: Writing, Directing and Producing for
Classroom Television and Industry.* New York: Crown Publishers, 1965.
  For those who want an informal but knowledgeable guide to practical
filmmaking this book may be just the thing.

* Herman, Lewis. *A Practical Manual of Screen Playwriting for Theater and
Television Films.* New York: World Publishing Company, 1952.
  In spite of the date, this book is a valuable resource for most of the aspects
of writing screenplays, particularly when it comes to visual aids.

Lawson, John Howard. *The Theory and Technique of Playwriting and
Screenwriting.* New York: G. P. Putnam's Sons, 1949.
  Here is a persuasive and useful approach to the fundamentals of dramatic
writing for the screen. It comes as an outgrowth of Lawson's original study,
written in 1935 and regarded by many theater people as a basic text. Still
valuable today.

Yoakem, Lola Goelet (editor). *TV and Screen Writing.* Berkeley: University of California Press, 1958.
  This practical collection of 17 essays written by the members of the

  30. See Leo K. Kuter, "Art Direction," *Films in Review* 8, no. 6 (June 1957) : 248–58;
Roger Hudson, "Three Designers: Ken Adams, Edward Marshall, Richard MacDonald,"
Sight and Sound 34, no. 1 (Winter 1964–65) : 26–31.
  31. Some related articles are: Elia Kazan, "The Writer and Motion Pictures," *Sight and
Sound* 27, no. 1 (Summer 1957) : 20–24; Tom Milne, "The Difference of George Axelrod,"
Sight and Sound 37, no. 4 (Autumn 1968) : 164–69; John Springer, "Charles Brackett,"
Films in Review 11, no. 3 (March 1960) : 129–40; DeWitt Bodeen, "Francis Marion: Part
I," *Films in Review* 20, no. 2 (February 1969) : 71–91; DeWitt Bodeen, "Francis Marion:
Part II," *Films in Review* 20, no. 3 (March 1969) : 129–52; Stephen Farber, "The Writer in
American Films," *Film Quarterly* 21, no. 4 (Summer 1968) : 2–13; Stephen Farber, "The
Writer II: An Interview with Alexander Jacobs," *Film Quarterly* 22, no. 2 (Winter 1968–
69) : 2–14; Robin Bean, "Through the Looking Glass: Frank Pierson," *Films and Filming*
15, no. 12 (September 1969) : 29–31; Richard Corliss, "The Hollywood Screenwriter," *Film
Comment* 6, no. 4 (Winter 1970–71) : 4–7; Carl Foreman, "Confessions of a Frustrated
Screenwriter," *idem.,* 22–25; Sam Fuller, "Ben Hecht: A Sampler," *idem.,* 32–39; Gary
Carey, "Written on the Screen: Anita Loos," *idem.,* 50–55; Paul Jensen, "The Career of
Dudley Nichols," *idem.,* 56–63; Michael Dempsey, "They Shaft Writers Don't They:
James Poe Interviewed," *idem.,* 64–73; and "Screenwriters Symposium," *idem.,* 86–100.

Writers Guild of America is a delightful source of information about approaches to genres, screen adaptations and the marketing of scripts. Among the many useful contributors are Hugh Gray, Jesse L. Lasky, Jr., Frank Gruber, Ivan Tors, Erik Barnouw, and Lois Jacoby.

Sound Recording

Cameron, Ken. *Sound and the Documentary Film*. London: Pitman and Sons, 1947.
   Although out-of-date and difficult to obtain, this fascinating and lucid approach to mixing by a respected documentary filmmaker is a worthwhile overview of sound editing.

Frayne, John G. and Halley Wolfe. *Elements of Sound Recording*. New York: John Wiley and Sons, Inc., 1949.
   At one time or another, this important text on the use of sound and its various production principles should be consulted. For many years, it was the number one book in the field.

Nisbett, Alec. *The Technique of the Sound Studio*. New York: Hastings House, 1962.
   Another book which demonstrates the interrelationship between the mass media. Although the emphasis here is definitely on broadcasting, filmmakers should find many valuable suggestions for sound movies.

Oringel, Robert S. *Audio Control Handbook*. New York: Hastings House, 1963.
   One of the few books on the subject which is both accurate and readable.

Wysotsky, Michael Z. *Wide-Screen Cinema and Stereophonic Sound*. Translated and with annotations by Raymond Spottiswoode. New York: Hastings House, 1971.
   First issued in the Soviet Union in 1965, this definitive work discusses all aspects of wide-screen and sound usage from the professional's point of view. The test is helped considerably by the excellent illustrations and diagrams.

Student Filmmaking[32]

Bare, Richard L. *The Film Director*. New York: The Macmillan Company, 1971.
   This practical and easy to read book offers an excellent introductory text to film and television directing.

Bayer, William. *Breaking Through, Selling Out, Dropping Dead, and Other Notes on Film Making*. New York: The Macmillan Company, 1971.
   Instead of the usual structured approach to film production, Bayer uses a dictionary format. He arranges alphabetically 70 individual topics connected with film and television making. Most unusual is his attempt to impress upon the very young filmmaker the competitive nature of the film business.

Brodbeck, Emil E. *Handbook of Basic Motion Picture Techniques*. New

---

32. Students who want to know more about opportunities for specific programs should write to the American Film Institute for their very useful booklet, *Guide to College Film Courses.*

York: American Photographic Book Publishing Company, Inc., 1969.

Students should find this book a valuable guide to basic film equipment, together with useful suggestions about methods of panning, visual composition, editing, and lighting. Although not designed specifically for neophytes, this reference book offers more than 200 movie illustrations, drawings, and diagrams from which beginning filmmakers could learn.

Brodbeck, Emil E. *Movie and Videotape: Special Effects.* Philadelphia: Chilton, 1968.

Every beginning filmmaker should examine this book's useful information on masks, filters, special lenses, mirrors, titles, sound, double exposures, backgrounds, animation, fog, smoke, water, and heat. The helpful illustrations are well chosen and well reproduced.

Colman, Hila. *Making Movies: Student Films to Features.* New York: The World Publishing Company, 1969.

Strictly for children. This lightweight introduction into various careers in filmmaking and the reasons why some of the professionals have succeeded should help motivate youngsters to learn more about film opportunities. Colman has an interesting behind-the-scenes section on the making of *Alice's Restaurant,* plus some good appendices on sample training programs.

* Eastman Kodak. *Movies with a Purpose.* Rochester: Eastman Kodak, 1968.

This brief, informative booklet is one of the best bargains for beginning student filmmakers. In clear and precise terms, the Kodak people describe the basic elements of Super 8 film production, and offer practical guidelines.

Ferguson, Robert. *How to Make Movies: A Practical Guide to Group Film-Making.* New York: The Viking Press, 1969.

In this marvelous introduction to beginning filmmaking, the author surveys all aspects of production, from movie equipment and scripting to practical advice on sight and sound filming techniques. Extremely useful are the nicely conceived and creatively displayed illustrations.

* Gaskill, Arthur L. and David A. Englander. *How to Shoot a Movie Story: The Technique of Pictorial Continuity.* New York: Morgan & Morgan, Inc., Publishers, 1960.

In simple, straightforward language, this cogent study takes you from a basic sequence right through the important steps of build-up, script, shooting and editing. Despite the somewhat dated illustrations, this work still remains one of the best introductions to good filmmaking procedures.

* Gessner, Robert. *The Moving Image: A Guide to Cinematic Literacy.* New York: E. P. Dutton and Company, 1968.

Written by one of the most well-known film pioneers, this worthwhile text first discusses the principles, patterns, and structures of film art and then offers practical steps for student film production. In 13 sensible, informative, and progressively more useful chapters, Gessner leads students through important stages of film production. Five appendices, including one on various tests for "plastic sensitivity, visual memory, and visual intelligence."

Gordon, George N. and Irving A. Falk. *Your Career in Film Making.* New York: Julian Messner, 1969.

Strictly for children. This book, to be skimmed quickly, offers a hasty overview of the various careers open to young people in filmmaking. Its 12 uneven chapters are often disappointing discussions of important subjects. Considering the audience, the authors have done a particularly poor job with illustrations.

Helfman, Harry. *Making Pictures Move*. New York: William Morrow and Company, 1969.

One of the finest books ever designed and executed for elementary school students. Helfman, imaginatively and with excellent help from illustrator Willard Goodman, suggests nine animation projects, all very valuable for understanding the fundamentals of animation and for having a good time. Every youngster should have a copy.

Kemp, Jerrold E. *et al. Planning and Producing Audio-Visual Material*. San Francisco: Chandler Publishers, 1967.

Don't be alarmed by the title of the authors's A-V emphasis. A good portion of this valuable resource book deals with useful discussions on shooting, composition, and sound recording. The suggestions are practical, adaptable to various situations, and supplemented with important appendices.

* Kuhns, William and Thomas F. Giardino. *Behind the Camera*. Dayton: Geo. A. Pflaum, 1970.

This publication provides a fine introduction to 16mm film production in the secondary schools and useful information about equipment, techniques and time-saving methods. In addition, readers should enjoy reading the diary account of a student-made film entitled *Sparrow*.

Larson, Rodger, with Ellen Meade. *Young Filmmakers*. New York: E. P. Dutton, 1969.

Former painter Larson reports on his film teaching project with black and Puerto Rican slum children in New York City, and provides us with practical information on budgets, equipment, and techniques for making student films. This book offers something to adult and child alike on movies, how they are made, and people.

Lewis, Jerry. *The Total Film-maker*. New York: Random House, 1971.

Taken from more than 500,000 taped feet of his lectures at the University of Southern California, this book quickly covers the general problems confronting the beginning filmmaker: production and post-production. Lewis, unfortunately, gives little thought to editing his comments or providing his readers with a necessary index. He is at his best in discussing comedy and at offering hints on how to handle crews and actors.

Lidstone, John and Don McIntosh. *Children as Film Makers*. New York: Van Nostrand Reinhold Company, 1970.

Starting with the simple premise that children can enjoy making films and at the same time learn a great deal, the authors design a program for young people and then suggest, show, and comment on what occurs. This is one of the clearest, best illustrated, and most readable texts on the student-made film for children.

* Livingston, Don. *Film and the Director: A Handbook and Guide to Film Making*. New York: Capricorn Books, 1969.

In ten straightforward chapters, this 1953 reissue of a sensible guide through the basic techniques of cutting, motion, acting, sound, and editing techniques provides students with an inexpensive source of useful information.

Lowndes, Douglas. *Film Making in Schools.* New York: Watson, Guptill Publications, 1968.

Secondary school teachers should find this one of the most worthwhile books in their film library, primarily because Lowndes orients his materials to their questions, needs, and varied situations. Here are valuable, concise, and accurate answers to problems about methods, equipment, and materials. The illustrations are well-selected and well-printed.

Manoogian, Haig P. *The Film-Maker's Art.* New York: Basic Books, 1966.

In lucid prose, this experienced film teacher offers practical suggestions on filmmaking procedures. First he considers the principles of film art, and then he introduces intelligent and valuable steps to production practices, aided by several appendices of actual student work. Very helpful for novices in film teaching.

Monier, Pierre. *The Complete Technique of Making Films.* New York: Ballantine Books, 1968.

Beginners in film production may be put off by this book's amazing ignorance of Super 8 film. But in almost every other area, Monier provides useful, accurate information.

* Pincus, Edward, assisted by Jairus Lincoln. *Guide to Filmmaking.* New York: Signet, 1969.

This is the best handbook for beginning students in filmmaking, simply because it is up-to-date, comprehensive, and well designed. Furthermore, this inexpensive paperback has several valuable appendices that teachers should own and have close by.

Proviser, Henry. *8mm/16mm Movie Making.* New York: American Publishing Company, 1970.

Readers will find the illustrations in this beginner's handbook extremely useful.

Rilla, Wolf. *A-Z of Movie-Making.* New York: The Viking Press, 1970.

Teachers should delight in this fine book that deals with the specifics of filmmaking: terms, planning stages, technical matters, use of live performers, and post-shooting techniques.

Roberts, Kenneth H. and Win Sharples Jr. *A Primer for Film Making: A Complete Guide to 16mm and 35mm Film Production.* New York: Pegasus, 1972.

For those who want a sound, useful and accurate guide to 16mm and 35mm filmmaking, this book is one of the best around. Being professional filmmakers themselves, the authors provide important technical but sensible information about raw film stock, lighting, costs, scripts, editing, optical effects, sound and music. The book also offers many useful and accurate illustrations plus superb appendices. This is one volume for every library.

* Smallman, Kirk. *Creative Film-Making.* New York: Collier Books, 1969.

This text is a quick and uneven account of film equipment and techniques which should be used gingerly.

2
A Representative Genre
of the Film

. . . no attempt was ever made before the movies began to please young and old, men and women, rich and poor, learned and ignorant, well-bred and vulgar, urban and provincial, cleric and peasant, by the same means. Everything that is strong and everything that is weak in the moving pictures must have its source in this same attempt at being universal—its wealth in money, its poverty in taste, its splendid achievements, and its disastrous failures.

Gilbert Seldes, The Movies Come from America

At some point in film study it is important to distinguish among the wide variety of movie genres—say documentaries and fiction films—together with their numerous subdivisions. It is also valuable to know something about the history, conventions, and outstanding examples of a particular genre if one is to develop critical standards in viewing films. This tells a student about film precedents, what is unique about the current movies, and where the innovations seem to be heading. Most important, the study of film types helps us, better than any other approach, to categorize, compare and contrast motion pictures.

When to begin can be determined only by the instructor and his students, and depends upon the group's age, experience, and interest. As for the question of how, three general methods seem most popular. One approach is to compare different genres in order to discern respective characteristics; here the emphasis is primarily on those particular features of one genre which set it off from others. A second approach is the historical one, in which the students study the development of certain genres—westerns, musicals, and comedies, for example. A third approach is to study a single genre as a way to define a type of film. Any one of these methods will acquaint students with the reasons for the study of movie categories and the methods connected with it.

55

Many film teachers today, for better or worse, base their programs on the traditional approaches to classifying literary types. In this respect, I find the best source for reviewing these current practices is a doctoral study, done more than twenty-five years ago, which directed its attention to answering the problems of why and how to study genres.[1] The same arguments are basically true for film categories. Ivin Ehrenpreis found that one approach is to set up Platonic types toward which all authors [filmmakers] strive but rarely reach. A second approach is to use traditional types, a procedure which may discourage the recognition of new types. (This is the great weakness for film study in two ways: first, it prevents people from recognizing film as a new art form; second, it limits the creative and original movie, which is outside the traditional scope of the categories.) A third approach is to erect a hierarchy of types, thereby establishing a ranking system for major and minor genres. But no one, either in Ehrenpreis's examination or in current film study, thinks of these categories as permanent and immutable forms of communication, into which films are classified by means of rigid and inflexible criteria. Each film instructor should define the characteristics of a specific genre or approach in terms of a definite context. He should know full well that films are classified by a cultural-historical process, and that the method he uses relates only to a specific time, purpose, group, and place.

It comes as no surprise that the most frequent reasons given for studying genres in the schools are those of convenience and organization. By arranging blocks of time to to examine various types, students are able to (1) gain explicit recognition of literature [film] itself; (2) move easily from an individual work to a number of works of the same type; (3) surmount various kinds of reading difficulties, or, in the case of film, visual illiteracy; (4) appreciate how individual attitudes are reflected by the themes continually used in a culture; (5) compare works of art; (6) gain a basis for appreciating a work in relation to a particular category.

Ehrenpreis notes that there are three implicit factors connected with these reasons for teaching genres. First is the value of teaching literature as literature [film as film] and not as historical and biographical material. Second is the value in knowing that there are specific types of literature [film] and what these types are. And third is the value accruing from teaching the appreciation of literature [film] through the study of types.[2]

Turning now to film classifications, we find that there are several ways of categorizing motion pictures. The two most practical approaches are found in David Mallery's *The School and the Art of Motion Pictures* and the Beograd (Belgrade) Film Institute's *An Essay in Terminology and Determination of Film Genres.* Mallery classifies the movies according to

1. Ivin Ehrenpreis, "The Types Approach to Literature," (Doctor of Education Project Report. New York: Teachers College, Columbia University, 1943).
2. Ivin Ehrenpreis, "Types Approach," pp. 83–85.

themes, treatments, and types; his method is an example of an eclectic approach.[3] More helpful to the serious student of film is the Beograd Institute's system,[4] which has as its aim the fixing of a complete and inclusive series of terms for existing genres, of defining these types, and of suggesting a procedure for interlocking the various kinds. The following is their scheme:

Film Genres

—Scheme—

Division according to criteria of structure and technique	Division according to criteria of aim and theme
Documentary	Newsreel
Fiction film	Magazine
Cartoon	Report
Graphic film	Propaganda film
Puppet film	Advertising film
Silhouette film	Trailer
Collage	Scientific-research film
Film with models	Popular science film
	Educational film
	Cultural film
	Industrial film
	Film on economics
	Film on art
	Nature film
	Travelogue
	Ethnographical film
	Social film
	Psychological film
	Melodrama
	Biographical film
	Historical film
	War film
	Adventure film
	Criminal film
	Spy film
	Thriller
	Western
	Phantasy film
	Science fiction
	Horror film
	Fairy tale
	Fable
	Burlesque

3. David Mallery, *The School and the Art of Motion Pictures* (Boston: National Association of Independent Schools, 1964) .
4. Beograd Film Institute. *Film Genres: An Essay in Terminology and Determination of Film Genres.* Belgrade: Beograd Film Institute, 1964.

Comedy
Parody
Satire
Music film
Opera
Operetta
Musical
Ballet
Film poem
Film critic
Abstract film
Free theme film

One of the most useful ways to explain the Beograd scheme is to apply it to a genre that is now widely patronized by the American public: war films. Two points should be made clear at the outset. First, types are selected for a particular purpose, both by the artists who work with them and by the viewers who see them. What may be suitable for one group may not be so for another. Secondly, genres that are now popular with the public may become unpopular. Our attitudes change. It is not my intention to prescribe a particular genre to study in the classroom but simply to show a representative approach to the study of genres. With this in mind, let us turn to the war-film genre.

DEFINITION

The Beograd Institute states that a war film "treats war events either on the front or behind enemy lines, and can be produced in any technique."[5] Another definition has been given by Dorothy B. Jones, who believes that war films can be categorized according to six aspects: "the Issues of the War; the Nature of the Enemy; the United Nations and Peoples; Work and Production; the Home Front; and the Fighting Forces."[6] A third approach, developed by members of Fordham's National Film Study Project, is to group war movies under four general categories: (1) war: the immediate threat; (2) war: the historical perspective; (3) what causes war?; and (4) the effects of war.[7] For the purposes of this chapter, a war film will be defined according to its aim, treatment, structure or technique, and will deal with the issues and participants involved in war. Since it is not my intention to describe definitively the war-film genre, the major emphasis will be lim-

---

5. The Beograd Film Institute, *Film Genres*, p. 12.
6. Dorothy B. Jones, "Hollywood War Films: 1942–1944," *Hollywood Quarterly* 1, no. 1 (October 1945) : 2.
7. David Sohn, Henry F. Putsch, and Rev. A. Schillaci, O.P., "Perspectives on War: A Teaching Unit of Films," *Media and Methods* 4, no. 4 (December 1967) : 8–15, 28. Reprinted in Anthony Schillaci and John M. Culkin (editors), *Films Deliver: Teaching Creatively with Film* (New York: Citation Press, 1970), pp. 145–62.

ited to Hollywood movies and those mainly concerned with the First and Second World Wars.

Before discussing the Documentary and Fiction movies, two major categories of the war film, it would be useful, because of its relevance to the subject, to consider the concept of propaganda and war films.

PROPAGANDA[8]

Every film, intentionally or not, in one form or another, is propaganda in the sense that each of us is personally affected by what we see and hear. This is no accident. The moviemaker deliberately tries to influence our emotions and attitudes by the creative handling of images and sounds. The important thing, therefore, is that we learn to discriminate among the forms and purposes propaganda can take.

One suggestion is to examine the history of the word itself. Up to World War I, "propaganda" was usually identified with religious teachings and public declarations to encourage conversion and faith. By 1917, the word had shifted its meaning to suggest treachery, and most people used it as a term for something repulsive. Later, John Grierson referred to it as "the art of public persuasion," while Paul Rotha, in 1931, divided it into two categories: (1) For "incidental background" material; (2) For a "specifically designed" purpose.[9] There are enough examples of both in the cinema. In discussing the term, therefore, we should be clear about our usage. As Ruth A. Inglis explains:

> If by "propaganda" is meant something deceitful or misleading, then, of course, the movie must have none of it. If we mean by "propaganda" any content which might change the ideas, sentiments, or values of those exposed to it, the motion picture can not in any conceivable way avoid being propagandistic. Movies necessarily carry images of people and implications regarding ideas and ideals which have relevance to the community at large.[10]

For our purposes, a propaganda war film is one that is created specifically to persuade the audience on matters of social, political, and economic ends and accomplishments connected with war, whether the techniques are documentary, fiction, animation, or whatever. Like Inglis, I don't find the concept of a propaganda war film necessarily offensive if there are two

---

8. A particularly good book on the history and uses of propaganda films for war is Leif Furhammer and Folke Isaksson, *Politics and Film* (New York: Praeger Publishers, 1971).

9. Quoted in Robert Vas, "Sorcerers or Apprentices: Some Aspects of Propaganda Films," *Sight and Sound* 32, no. 4 (Autumn 1963): 200.

10. Ruth A. Inglis, *Freedom of the Movies: A Report on Self-Regulation from the Commission on Freedom of the Press* (Chicago: University of Chicago Press, 1947), p. 13.

basic ingredients present. First, the propaganda war film can serve a valuable function if its aim is to boost morale. Richard Schickel, for example, found that during the Second World War, the motion picture's "greatest contribution was to the morale of the fighting men. . . ."[11] Second, propaganda war films are not offensive if the public is aware that they are specifically designed as propaganda and not solely as entertainment films. Unfortunately, the public doesn't always make the distinction.

Often film classics heralded as anti-war films are not that in fact. And from the vantage point of the present they seem mild and romantic. Robert Hughes points out:

The two best-known anti-war films of the past, *All Quiet on the Western Front* and *La Grande Illusion*, are concerned with the basic, well-known contradictions of war: men fight other men who are like themselves. Effective as they still are, both pictures are romantic in their idealization of the so-called good side of war, the camaraderie. But in a world of "total war," where mass extermination is a fact, whether in concentration camps or obliterated cities, they seem strangely dated. War and killing today are much more efficient and outrageously absurd. But there is almost no reflection of this fact in present day movies.[12]

It seems to many intelligent viewers like Hughes that movies that try to portray the evils of war actually glorify them. Consider, for example, *The Bridge on the River Kwai*, which was supposedly intended as an anti-war film. Both Hughes and James Baldwin have commented on the same point, namely that the film shows individuals who are deranged placed in positions of authority, and the system itself, the military command in particular, is never seriously questioned nor is the extent of such madness ever explored. "And speaking of absurdity," Hughes exclaims, "what of an 'anti-war' film [*The Bridge on the River Kwai*] which inspired at least one of its big audiences to scream at one point: 'kill him! kill him!' "[13] I have seen the same reaction twice in the last two years in public schools where the film has been shown to large groups. Gordon Gow, taking note of the audience's misplaced and excessive sympathy, placed some of the blame on Alec Guinness's performance. He found it to be too "straight." The book's author, Pierre Boulle, described Colonel Nicholson (Guinness) as the prototype of the legendary Indian Army officer "who provokes in those around him alternating bouts of anger and affection." Guinness, in creating the screen role, won more loyalty for a soldier's allegiance to duty than for the destructive nature of such a blind obedience. As Gow points out, Sam Spiegel, the film's pro-

11. Richard Schickel, *Movies: The History of an Art and an Institution* (New York: Basic Books, Inc., 1964), p. 138.
12. Robert Hughes, "Murder: A Big Problem," *Film: Book 2: Films of Peace and War,* edited by Robert Hughes (New York: Grove Press, 1962), p. 8.
13. Robert Hughes and James Baldwin, "Mass Culture and the Creative Artist: Some Personal Notes," *Daedalus* 89 (Spring 1960): 375.

ducer, was well aware of the intellectual conflict, "Man came into this world to build, and not to destroy. Yet he's thrown into the necessity of destroying, and his one everlasting instinct is to try to save himself from having to destroy."[14]

Sometimes, however, the filmmaker achieves his intentions. Kauffmann, for instance, argues that *La Grande Illusion* is one of the most powerful anti-war films ever made:

> Couched in terms of individual confrontation—a man with a man, rather than bloc against bloc or two hemispheres competing for outer space— *Grand Illusion* remains a towering film. By now it has attained the state of all good art that has lived some time among men: it moves us more than ever because it no longer surprises us.[15]

John Clellon Holmes is another commentator who writes how he, and many like him, were affected by anti-war movies, in particular, *All Quiet on the Western Front:*

> It has always astonished me that almost no one has perceived that one reason why we went through the war [World War II] so laconically, with so little rhetoric, and with our eye out mainly for personal survival (not only against the enemy, but against the military system itself) was that we knew that all wars were basically frauds, even just wars. After all, hadn't we learned precisely that in our local theatre?[16]

The point is that while propaganda does enter into filmmaking, the intentions and the effects often depend not so much on the movie itself as on the mind of the viewer. It is because we are so troubled over war and its influence in our times that teachers and students should explore the films that have been and are being made to influence the values and judgments of today's generation.

THE WAR FILM FROM 1914–1970

War films obviously are directly related to the prevailing attitudes and the economic, political, and social conditions in the country in which they are made. Very often, by examining these films we can learn about the opinions of the nation and the direction in which it is heading. Lewis Jacobs, for example, in discussing World War I movies, noted that the films reflected the change in public opinion during the first World War from

14. Gordon Gow, *Hollywood in the Fifties* (New York: A. S. Barnes and Company, 1971) , pp. 79–81.

15. Stanley Kauffmann, *A World on Film: Criticism and Comment* (New York: Harper & Row, 1966) , p. 3.

16. John Clellon Holmes, "15 Cents Before 6:00: The Wonderful Movies of the 'Thirties,' " *Harper's Magazine* 231 (December 1965) : 53.

tolerance to intolerance, from progressivism to reaction, and from pacificism to militarism.[17] Jack Spears, another respected film historian, described how a pro-war feeling started in America after Germany's march into Belgium, but it did not reach any great heights until after Woodrow Wilson's 1916 reelection on the argument that "he kept us out of war." Then the movies became more militant as war became more "unavoidable," and films like *Civilization* declined in popularity.[18] Their observations are just as accurate for our time. There has not been one worthwhile film made about the Vietnam War; moreover, as we try to extricate ourselves from that bloody and immoral mess, war films like *M*A*S*H, Kelly's Heroes, Tora! Tora! Tora!* and *Catch -22* satirize the stupidity of war itself.

For commercial, social, and political reasons, war films become more liberal toward the enemy and more critical of the allies once the real war is over. First, the enemy nations become sizeable markets for movies and the industry tries to secure as much popularity there as at home. Second, returning veterans relate the horrors and atrocities committed at the front by both sides and are quite cynical about romanticized and idealized versions of war. Finally, as loyalties change, we need the friendship and cooperation of our former enemies in case of a new war with new antagonists. Unfortunately, there are notable exceptions to this, as evidenced by such films as *The Green Berets, Guns of Navarone, Battle of the Bulge, The Train, Von Ryan's Express,* and *The Blue Max,* all of which either point up a senseless kind of personal heroism or in other ways glorify war.

Sometimes the protests against the war and these chauvinistic films begin during the war itself, as in the example of an advertisement printed in *Motion Picture Magazine* in February 1916:

> Strangely enough, these pictures have not presented to our view the actual proof of the toll of war. They have not shown us the millions of widows and the millions of orphans that are the results of this conflict. They have not proven to us the hopelessness, the despair, the hunger and suffering that have been inevitable consequences of the War. And—having failed to present these consequences . . . —these pictures have not been logical arguments in favor of Peace. They have been military—they have been martial in the extreme. . . .[19]

Almost fifty years later, David Robinson reaffirmed the same unrealistic approach to the early war films, commenting that many of the photographers were former cameramen for popular magazines. Consequently, the

17. Lewis Jacobs, *The Rise of the American Film: A Critical History,* with an essay "Experimental Cinema in America 1921–1947" (New York: Teachers College Press, 1968), p. 261.

18. Jack Spears, "World War I on the Screen: Part I," *Films in Review* 17, no. 5 (May 1966) : 274; Part II, *idem.,* 17 no. 6 (June–July 1966) : 347–65.
Also see Timothy J. Lyons, "Hollywood and World War I, 1914–1918," *The Journal of Popular Film* 1, no. 1 (Winter 1972) : 15–30.

19. Quoted from Lewis Jacobs, *The Rise of the American Film,* p. 253.

pictures taken during World War I have a stilted effect, as if the soldiers were posing or inadvertently getting in the camera's eye.[20]

One of the most graphic examples of how films change in their treatment of war issues and enemies can be seen in Hollywood's treatment of the German people.[21] War films, prior to America's entry into World War II, began to educate the general public on what was to be the image of their future enemy. Arthur Knight, in describing this development, uses Hitchcock's *Foreign Correspondent* (1940) as an illustration of Hollywood's more menacing mood, especially the abrupt conclusion in which the film's hero, Joel McCrea, radios America from a blitzed London: "The lights are going out in Europe! Ring yourself around with steel, America!"[22] There are other examples as well. The previous year, Warner Brothers Studio had produced the archetypal German espionage story, *Confessions of a Nazi Spy*. The film, based upon a sensational German spy trial in New York City, charged that German-American Bunds were centers for espionage, destruction and anti-American activities; that German diplomatic missions were merely subterfuges for undermining our country. According to one source:

> The effect was electric. Actors and directors received murder threats. German Charge d'Affaires Thomsen screamed "Conspiracy!" The picture was banned by many countries anxious not to offend Germany. In the United States, however, it made a profound impression.

> . . . *What Confessions of a Nazi Spy* said was nothing new. But the picture dramatized the dangers of Nazism, brought them vividly home to the American people. Isolationists began to charge Hollywood with being one-sided about the war in Europe. The charges mounted as more screen dramas told their stories against the backdrop of Nazi terror—*The Mortal Storm, Escape, Four Sons.*[23]

During the war years, Hollywood set its patterns on how Germans should be treated. They were to be stereotyped on two levels; either as brutes, in the form of the Gestapo, SS troops, and hired henchmen, or as German intellectuals trapped by their inability to deviate from a preconceived idea. William K. Everson describes the stereotype best:

> The World War II German villain. . . . At the highest level was a man of supreme intellect and culture, placidly listening to Wagner while his storm-troopers tried to beat a confession out of the hero. He was resolutely

20. David Robinson, "The Old Lie," *Sight and Sound* 31, no. 4 (Autumn 1962) : 203–4.
21. Two good sources for information are: Larry N. Landrum and Christine Eynon, "World War II in the Movies: A Selected Bibliography of Sources," *Journal of Popular Films* 1, no. 1 (Spring 1972) : 147–52; and Arthur F. McClure, "Hollywood at War: The American Motion Picture and World War II, 1939–1945," *idem.*, pp. 122–35.
22. Arthur Knight, *The Liveliest Art: A Panoramic History of the Movies* (New York: The Macmillan Company, 1957) , p. 243.
23. Editors of *Look, Movie Lot to Beachhead: The Motion Pictures Goes to War and Prepares for the Future.* With a Preface by Robert St. John (New York: Doubleday, Doran and Company, Inc., 1945) , p. 5.

dedicated to his cause, given to fanatic speeches, and a mastermind at keeping several jumps ahead of the opposition. But like all Germans (according to Hollywood), he was a methodical and regimentalized man, and it was this discipline that finally tripped him up when, at the crucial moment, he was unable to outguess the less intellectual, more emotional representative of the democracies.[24]

It is interesting to note that the German stereotype in war films made during World War II did not deviate much from the patterns set in World War I. Then the image was of a hideous Hun, usually embodied by Erich von Stroheim, George Siegmann, or Walter Long. The stories involving these stereotypes are generally the same. We fight fairly, while the enemy almost always uses cowardly and despicable tactics, despite, as Everson points out, "overwhelmingly numerical superiority that makes such tactics rather superfluous anyway."[25]

After the second World War, Hollywood's treatment of Germans changed. We were suddenly told that the real enemy was only a limited group in the now-conquered German nation. In an excellent analysis of post World War II movies dealing with wartime Germany, Martin Dworkin points out how films have tried to show that the ordinary German soldier was really "not to blame" for what happened. "It is the politicians who are—and they happen to be the Nazis."[26] Forgotten are the fact that Hitler and his party in 1932 had a plurality of seats in the Reichstag; emphasized is the misunderstanding over what the war was all about; glorified are the Nazi generals who, having realized they were losing the war because a madman was leading them, tried to kill Hitler; and romanticized are the German youths who goose-stepped into the devastated countries of Africa and Europe. Dworkin emphasizes that these films show that the German youths, who were portrayed as no different from our American boys, were outside of politics as was the "good scientist of the present . . . outside responsibility. . . ."[27]

In line with the propagandist function of the war film is Hollywood's treatment of heroes. American war heroes are usually the prototypes of the cowboy or gangster type heroes. Herbert Jacobson described the war hero as an outsider who was defending the community, much the same way as the Western hero is usually portrayed as a scout, a guide or a soldier. The war hero fits into the scheme of the cowboy whose inventiveness, marksmanship, and perseverance always will win out, given enough time. No matter how many people are involved in the conflict, in the final showdown the decision will depend upon one man's courage and fortitude.[28]

---

24. William K. Everson, *The Bad Guys: A Pictorial History of the Movie Villain* (New York: The Citadel Press, 1964), p. 130.
25. William K. Everson, *The Bad Guys,* p. 125.
26. Martin Dworkin, "Clean Germans and Dirty Politics," *Film Comment* 3, no. 1 (Winter 1965): 37. Also see Leslie Halliwell's two-part article, "Over the Brink," *Films and Filming* 14, no. 12 (September 1968): 54–60, and 15, no. 1 (October 1968): 58–62, 64.
27. Martin Dworkin, "Clean Germans," p. 41.
28. Herbert L. Jacobson, "Cowboy, Pioneer and American Soldier," *Sight and Sound* 22, no. 4 (April–June 1953): 189–190.

The male leads' bravado is surpassed only by their indestructibility.[29] However, John Howard Lawson sees the American war heroes as gangsters who glorify, on the screen, sex and murder.[30] American officers, according to Lawson, portray fascist leaders. The men are seen accepting war and killing, reasoning that it is a game of kill or be killed. No one questions the orders of superiors; there are no discussions on morality or the purpose of war. Officers expect their men to be killed, and the men have as their aim "to accomplish the greatest possible destruction before they die."[31]

In studying how the propaganda war films familiarize their audience with the effects of oppression, Knight describes how Hollywood used these movies as a ruse for exploiting the public's fascination with terror, horror and sadism. He points out that the films often depicted the savage Nazis as mentally disturbed beasts who took great pleasure in inflicting their inhuman tortures. The typical American hero, on the other hand, never resorted to such brutality; he was just a clean-cut youth caught in a troubled world.[32] Quite a different picture is presented after the war, particularly in films like *The Dirty Dozen, The Victors,* and *The Naked and the Dead.* Parker Tyler has provided a useful analysis of war film myths in *Magic and Myth of the Movies.* In a chapter entitled "The Waxworks of War," Tyler reviews the formulas of war movies, and points out the tendency to portray an individual who, regardless of his rank or popularity with his comrades, will achieve success against the maniacal enemy. Tyler cites the film *A Walk in the Sun* as the archetype of the Hollywood war film. This movie presents soldiers as average Americans, "nearly all former clerks," who are transformed into fighting men in a "stinking" war. With no choice except to do their duty and finish the dirty business at hand, they are reduced to a corps of soldiers who recognize as their one purpose for being killing the enemy and capturing a farmhouse which they are to hold until relieved by a larger force.[33]

With this background in mind, we can turn to the major categories of the war film. By beginning with the form that a movie may take—that is, its basic structure—we can see that since 1914, war films fall into two groups: documentary or fiction. And the majority of these moving pictures, intentionally or not, are pro-war, as Richard Whitehall accurately notes.[34]

A documentary war film can be defined as a movie that relates and interprets "facts" of real life by trying to preserve authentic features, either by

29. The Editors of *Look, Movie Lot,* p. 58.

30. In view of Lawson's almost unanimous praise of Russian filmmaking, it would be interesting to learn his views of the Russian movie war hero, something which he does not discuss in his writings.

31. John Howard Lawson, *Film in the Battle of Ideas* (New York: Masses and Mainstream, 1953), pp. 23–25.

32. Arthur Knight, *Liveliest Art,* pp. 246–47.

33. Parker Tyler, *The Magic and Myth of the Movies,* Introduction by Richard Schickel, (New York: Simon & Schuster, 1970), pp. 132–174.

34. Richard Whitehall, "One . . . Two . . . Three . . .: A Study of the War Film," *Films and Filming* 10, no. 11 (August 1964) : 8.

showing them as they actually occur in real life or as they appear in published works such as newspapers and factual books. A fiction war film generally presents some contrived action performed by professional actors. For the most part, movies made during the war are not so good as those made afterwards, the main exception being documentary films, which we turn to now.

DOCUMENTARY WAR FILMS

The documentary war film can be classified under the following subgroups: magazine, propaganda, newsreel, training, and report.

The magazine war films deal mainly with news reports of general or specific interest, often held together by a common theme; they are released in a series, and imitate the style of popular publications. Two major series used during the war were *The March of Time* and *The Army-Navy Screen Magazine.* The former, which began in 1935 by Time-Life, Inc. under the direction of Louis De Rochemont, used a new means of screen journalism to inform the public on current events. *The Army-Navy Screen Magazine,* on the other hand, was a bi-monthly series prepared for the servicemen wherever they were stationed to show them what was happening at home and abroad.

The propaganda film was designed to let the people know what the war was about and why we were involved in it. One of the best examples of this type is the *Why We Fight* series, under the supervision of Frank Capra. As Dorothy B. Jones points out,

> These films were designed to make the men in our Armed Forces acutely aware of the dangers of totalitarianism and of the outstanding contributions and sacrifices of our allies in the global struggle. Composed primarily of newsreel clips and stock-library footage, these pictures were widely shown in the United States and overseas; and they were carefully studied and admired by Soviet filmmakers, ever conscious of the great propaganda powers of the motion picture.[35]

March of Time

The Ramparts We Watch (35mm: 1943, 60 min., b/w, sound, R-AUD, CCM/S-CCM)
Under Louis de Rochemont's direction and with authentic newsreels laced with fictionalized scenes, this film propagandizes for America's entry into the European conflict.

Music in America (16mm: 1943, 17 min., b/w, R-MMA)
An example of how entertainers boosted the morale of the servicemen

35. Dorothy B. Jones, "Hollywood War Films," p. 13. See also William Thomas Murphy, "The Method of *Why We Fight,*" *The Journal of Popular Film* 1, no. 3 (Summer 1972) : 185–96.

during the war. Some good shots of Glenn Miller, Perry Como, Marian Anderson, and Art Tatum.

The Army-Navy Screen Magazine

The War—Issue 10 (1945). *Burma Outpost—Issue 22* (1945). *Battle of the United States—Issue 42* (1945).
Each of these 20-minute films, available from the Museum of Modern Art, was heavily influenced by the attitudes and desires of the troops themselves. In particular, the emphasis was on authoritative, first-hand reporting, with a snappy, everyday commentary delivered in a matter-of-fact voice.

Why We Fight

The Nazis Strike (16mm: 1943, 42 min., b/w, sound, R-AUD, MMA, TWF)
Capra and Anatol Litvak directed this account of the German invasion and defeat of Austria and Poland.

Divide and Conquer (16mm: 1943, 58 min., b/w, sound, R-AUD, CON, MMA, TWF)
Capra and Litvak again on the German war machine, this time attacking Denmark, Norway, and France.

By way of contrast to American propaganda films are the more elaborate and less honest Nazi war propaganda movies. These should be studied by responsible groups. In 1933, Dr. Goebbels and his Ministry of Propaganda began their infamous attempt to enslave the minds of the German people. Starting at first with Eisenstein's *Potemkin* as his model and then abandoning its fictional emphasis, Goebbels saw the advantage of reediting actual documentary footage so that a specific point could be made; in a sense he was rewriting history.[36]

Nazi Films

Propaganda Films II (1933–1937). *Blutendes Deutschland* (excerpt) (1933). *Hans Westmar, Einer von Vielen* (excerpt) (1934). *Fur Uns* (1937). (16mm: 27 min., b/w, sound, R-MMA)
The concept of rebirth through life in the Nazi Party, a recurrent theme in the Nazi movies of the period, is graphically depicted in the two excerpts showing first a newsreel account of the Nazi funeral of Horst Wessel and next, a fictionalized version. *Fur Uns* is an homage to early members of the party killed in the 1923 "beer hall putsch."

The Triumph of the Will (16mm: 1936, 120 min., b/w, sound. No English subtitles. The Museum also has a 40 min. version, with English titles, R-MMA).

---

36. To explore this concept further, see Penelope Houston, "The Nature of Evidence," *Sight and Sound* 36, no. 2 (Spring 1967) : 88–92; and Robert Vas, "Sorcerers or Apprentices," *idem.*, pp. 199–204. To learn something about the Japanese approach, read Leona Protas Schecter, "World War II on Japanese Screens," *Films in Review* 8, no. 3 (March 1957) : 108–10.

Leni Riefenstahl's technically brilliant film was a deliberate attempt to influence public attitudes favorably toward the Nazi Party both in Germany and the rest of the world. The movie centers on the 1934 Nuremburg rally; the major emphasis is on showing Hitler as the savior of the German people.[37]

Newsreels of World War II are used in many of the documentary and fiction films seen today. Usually scenes from them are spliced into the story lines of war films to provide a sense of realism. One of the most important aspects of wartime newsreels was that they gave the people on the home front, for the first time, the chance to hear and see the war in action. As the editors of *Look* explain:

> Since Pearl Harbor four-fifths of newsreel footage has dealt with some aspect of the total war. Newsreel cameras have accompanied bombers and fighters on thousands of plane raids; roved the Pacific with our naval task forces; portrayed historic landings in Africa, Italy and Normandy; revealed events of immense significance—raids on Tokyo, war in China, battles in the malarial slime of Jap-infested islands.[38]

Out of these newsreel accounts filmmakers have created some of the best documentaries on war.

Books

Fielding, Raymond. *The American Newsreel: 1911–1967*. Norman: University of Oklahoma Press, 1972.

For those looking for a fascinating and instructive history of the birth of American newsreels starting in Europe and the United States to their demise in the late sixties when television news replaced them, Fielding's book offers a lucid and informative narrative. His text is filled with interesting anecdotes and facts about the problems, personalities, and events that made newsreels a key part of the local weekly movie program for over fifty years. The book itself is satisfactorily bound, attractively illustrated, and the best source yet available on the subject.

---

37. For useful information on the films of Leni Riefenstahl, see: *Film Comment* 3, no. 1 (Winter 1965) : 1–31; Arnold Berson, "The Truth About Leni," *Films and Filming* 11, no. 7 (April 1965) : 15–19; David Gunston, "Leni Riefenstahl," *Film Quarterly* 14, no. 1 (Fall 1960) : 4–19; *Siegfried Kracauer, *From Caligari to Hitler: A Psychological History of the German Film* (Princeton: Princeton University Press, 1947) ; David Stewart Hull, *Film in the Third Reich: A Study of the German Cinema 1933–1945* (Berkeley: University of California Press, 1969) ; and Michel Delahaye, "Leni and the Wolf: Interview with Leni Riefenstahl," *Cahiers du Cinema in English* 5, CdC no. 170 (September 1965) : 48–55.

In addition there are a number of articles on Nazi propaganda films: Helmut Blobner and Herbert Holben, "Jackboot Cinema: The Political Propaganda Film in the Third Reich," *Films and Filming* 9, no. 3 (December 1962) : 13–19; David Stewart Hull, "Forbidden Fruit: The Nazi Feature Film, 1933–1945," *Film Quarterly* 14, no. 4 (Summer 1961) : 16–30; Herbert G. Luft, "Shadow of the Swastika," *Films and Filming* 7, no. 2 (November 1960) : 10–11; and POM, "The Nazis Return," *Films and Filming* 12, no. 7 (April 1966) : 36–39; Peter John Dyer, "The Rebels in Jackboots," *Films and Filming* 5, no. 6 (March 1959) : 13–15, 32–33, 35.

38. *Look, Movie Lot*, p. 26.

Newsreel Anthologies

Memorandum (Canada—16 mm: 1966, 58 min., b/w, sound, R-CON/S-CON)
Donald Brittain produced and directed this National Film Board movie which contrasts the Bergen-Belsen concentration camp in the sixties and the forties. By focusing attention on Bernard Laufer, a survivor who returns to the modern tourist attraction, we get a sense of horror and frustration as film clips taken from German and British documentary footage are edited into the present-day scenes.

Night and Fog (France:16mm: 1955, 31 min., color, sound, R-CON)
Alain Resnais's classic also contrasts the past with the present in such extermination camps as Buchenwald, Treblinka, and Auschwitz. It may well be the most terrifying account of genocide ever made, and few young people are able to sit through the scenes which detail the life in those hell holes.

Over There, 1914–1918 (France—16mm: 1963, 90 min., b/w, English narration, sound, R-CAL, Con/S-CON)
Jean Aurel's production, based upon clips from various newsreels and official government documentaries, records World War I from the individual infantryman's perspective.

The Sorrow and the Pity (France—16mm: 1972, 245 min., b/w, English subtitles, sound, R-CIV)
Marc Ophuls, following in the superb tradition of his father Max, directed this fascinating documentary about Germany's World War II occupation of France and the rise of the French underground. One comes away realizing, if he did not know before, that determined men will stop at absolutely nothing to gain their ends and that time will make it all seem understandable, if not forgivable.

The Spanish Turmoil (BBC—16mm: 1967, 64 min., b/w, sound, R-TIM/S-TIM)
This excellent documentary traces the rise of Franco's power and the succession of political crises that led to the Spanish Civil War, and eventually to World War II.

To Die in Madrid (Spain—16mm: 1965, 90 min., b/w, English narration, sound, R-AUD)
One of the finest documentary films ever made, this depressing picture of the Spanish Civil War is brilliant in technique, delivery, and impact. Directed by Frederic Rossif.

A Trip Down Memory Lane (Canada—16mm: 1966, 12 min., b/w, sound, R-CON)
Arthur Lipsett's National Film Board collection of newsreel clips since the early days of moving pictures presents a brief, incisive, and memorable history of stupidity and inhumanity, particularly in the war scenes.

Vivre (France—16mm: 1959, 8 min., b/w, English subtitles, sound, R-CON)
Carlos Vilandebo's French film, using well-chosen newsreel scenes shot all over the globe during the last 40 years, poignantly visualizes the misery and horror that war spawns. No dialogue is used or needed.

Another subgenre of the documentary war film is the training movie, the purpose of which is to teach our servicemen the techniques of war. One example of such films is *Fog* (Walt Disney—16mm: 1943, 18 min., color, sound, R-MMA). This animated movie was designed to orient pilots to the problems of aerial navigation. It is also an example of Disney's educational cartoons made for the war effort.

The reportage documentary is a more elaborate documentary survey of a particular event presented from a first-person point of view. These films constitute the best war documentaries. Some outstanding examples of this type are director John Huston's *The Battle of San Pietro* (16mm: 1944, 30 min., b/w, sound, R-MMA), a film about the attack and capture of an isolated Italian village; *The Fighting Lady* (16mm: 1944, 61 min., color, sound, R-MMA, WRS), the biography of the aircraft carrier *Essex* during the war; and *Victory at Sea*[39] (16mm: 1954, 84 min., b/w, sound, R-FNC/S-FNC), the film record of naval operations during World War II, accompanied by Richard Rodgers's excellent musical score. In addition, there is one particular British film that should be mentioned for its importance in the history of war documentaries: *Desert Victory* (16mm: 1943, 62 min., b/w, sound, R-MMA, CAL, CON, ILL, RAD, TWF, WIL/S-CON), the record of Rommel's Afrika Korps retreating 1300 miles through Africa.

The patterns of wartime documentaries and their effects upon other types of film have been the source of an interesting analysis by Douglas Gallez. He did a study of some of the best American wartime documentaries, among them *Report from the Aleutians, The Battle of San Pietro, Let There Be Light, The Fighting Lady, The Memphis Belle* and the *Why We Fight* Series. He defines documentary movies as "those factual films that inform the public about the doings of men in wartime."[40]

Although not intended as an analysis of cliches in fiction war films, Gallez's study provides an excellent review of how the documentary film influenced fiction movies. He points this out through discussion of significant scenes that have been used again and again: soldiers waiting for the enemy's attack, the American flag still flying after the battle is over, and heroic fliers returning to their bases of operation after successful raids on the enemy. The sound tracks are punctuated with machine-gun fire, the sputtering of engines, the explosions of downed planes and of bombs. In addition, there are many scenes of bombing missions, beginning with the fueling and loading of the bombers, the briefing of the crews, the overloaded jeeps carrying the men to their planes, the last-minute instructions before takeoff, and then the planes, one by one, leaving their bases. During the flight to their destination, the crews are seen as human beings with personal problems. Once over the target, there are the sounds of antiaircraft guns,

39. An abridged version, based on the 26-part TV series.
40. Douglas W. Gallez, "Patterns in Wartime Documentaries," *The Quarterly of Films, Radio and TV* 10, no. 2 (Winter 1955) : 125.

the fights with enemy planes, and the dropping of bombs. When the mission is completed, the planes return home, and we have the scenes of anxious officers and ground crews tensely waiting for the crippled ships to return. Suddenly there is the sound of the first returning bombers, then the counting of the planes, the stationing of emergency landing vehicles for the damaged ships, the emergency landings, and the depiction of fatigue. Almost always there are close-ups of the tired and weary men who fight the dirty war. In addition, there are often scenes of the battles, with the weather and the terrain as enemies that plague the foot soldier as well as the pilots. These are usually exemplified by showing men building airstrips or fighting jungle warfare. And finally, there are often shots of the men themselves: lonely but somehow existing, finding joy where they can, particularly in mail from home.

Gallez, in summarizing the patterns emerging from this genre, makes three major points. First, the filmmakers emphasized the personal touch by trying to let the audience identify with the combat troops. Second, every effort was made to stress the importance of teamwork in winning the war; no one individual was more important than another. And third, the war documentaries propagandized the religious and moral right of our fight. We were the men of peace, forced into combat to preserve justice. Once the battle ended, we would return to our quiet and gentle lives.[41]

THE FICTION WAR FILM

The fiction war film tends, as can be expected, to glorify battles and struggles. But the issues themselves are rarely explored with any concern for a social or historical point of view. Men die, women weep, and children are orphaned. Millions are maimed, tortured, and raped, while nations are leveled. Yet most of the fiction war films have a happy ending.

It is particularly sad that no intelligent perspective is presented in motion pictures made during wartime, but the anxiety of the people often misleads filmmakers and discourages them from delving into the complex issues or the reasons for the conflict itself. A distraught country, mobilized both at home and abroad, searches in its leisure moments for some escape and distraction from the long working hours, the nerve-racking headlines and the overwhelming loneliness. The film industry, on one hand patriotic and willing to serve the nation's needs, produces a stream of movies designed to bolster the audience's morale. On the other hand, this same industry, commercially based and tending toward exploitation, greedily makes any kind of film that a maximum-wage working force will blindly pay to watch. Even when the war is over, the same type of film retains its popularity at the box office, or as Robin Bean puts it, ". . . like the Western, the war

---

41. Douglas Gallez, "Patterns in Wartime Documentaries," pp. 134–35.

setting is almost a reliable proposition for a producer, providing it is not too moralistic about its subject."[42]

Despite the fact that the subject matter is basically the same, war films fall into many diverse categories. In classifying Hollywood feature films, Dorothy B. Jones analyzed 1313 pictures produced from 1942 to 1944 and found that three out of every ten were related to some aspect of the war.

> . . . it may surprise some people that only one-fourth to one-third of Hollywood's output was concerned with the conflict. However, to those who are familiar with the nature of the industry's product, who know the proportion of formula westerns, murder mysteries, domestic comedies, and musicals which go to make up the bulk of pictures turned out each year, it would appear that Hollywood gave a remarkably large proportion of its output to war topics.[43]

First, Dorothy B. Jones, working on the assumption that there were relatively few people in America who understood what World War II was about, concentrated on motion pictures that explained the United States' role in the war. She found that 43 war films were made on this topic. These films explained our stake in the war, and at the same time justified our way of life. She concluded that these movies were generally superficially made and added little to our understanding of the issues.

Second, she explored the war films dealing with the enemy, a group that constituted the major number of films made: 107, or 28.16 percent of the total. Most of the films released in 1942 covered stories about sabotage or espionage; only 2 of 64 films did not. This proved, in her opinion, to be an unfortunate emphasis, particularly at the start of the war. Frightened and misguided citizens became suspicious of foreigners living in America (film spies spoke with foreign accents and innocent-looking people often turned out to be dangerous aliens).[44] No one knew how many actual spies were living in the country, and isolated events became accepted as widespread occurrences. Not only did this help the Axis cause but it also helped divide the nation itself. Screen exaggerations, therefore, presented a serious threat and a disservice at the outset. As Miss Jones notes, these films contained the greatest examples of distortions in war films made during this period.

Third, she turned her attention to films depicting our Allies. These movies, she found, provided Americans with a general understanding of our friends. Some of the countries depicted were Russia, China, France, and England. These films in many respects were Hollywood's best war movies. What is surprising is that the people who wrote, produced, starred in and directed these movies knew very little about the citizens and countries they

---

42. Robin Bean, "The War Makers," *Films and Filming* 12, no. 5 (February 1966) : 63.
43. Dorothy B. Jones, "Hollywood War Films," p. 2.
44. The film *Bad Day at Black Rock* treats an aspect of this problem. Robert Ryan and some of his cronies kill a Japanese-American tenant farmer to prove their patriotism.

were depicting. No amount of research could overcome their lack of first-hand knowledge. And authentic costumes were no substitute for a perceptive understanding of the customs and values of individuals in Allied nations. Nevertheless, the films served a useful purpose by linking Americans to friendly powers abroad.

Fourth, Jones investigated the films covering American war production, and found that relatively few films in this area were made—21 in all. Not only were they few in number, but they were also poorly made. There seems to be no doubt that Hollywood failed deplorably in presenting the contribution of management and labor in the winning of the war.

Fifth, she analyzed movies made about the home front; there were only 40 films made in this category. Some of the home-front problems portrayed on the screen were housing shortages, civilian defense activities, life in wartime Washington, and juvenile delinquency. Her conclusions were that the Hollywood feature film failed to dignify the efforts of the home-front war or to interpret its value to the total war effort. Just the reverse was the case. These movies ridiculed, exaggerated, or sensationalized the dilemma. And the group most adversely affected by these exploitive films was the domestic audience itself.

Finally, Miss Jones evaluated the war films showing our servicemen in action, a total of 95 films, or 25 percent of the total war film production. The themes of these movies centered on such areas as the fighting man, his development in boot camp, his adventures in battle, and his leaves. Although she found some good films made in this category, Miss Jones believes that most of the pictures were undesirable and unfortunate. Musicals and comedies of the period, often done in poor taste, minimized the seriousness of the war. Melodramas, complete with arrogant, swashbuckling American heroes who *alone* delivered the crucial blow that brought victory, were seriously criticized by our Allies for downplaying their role in the war to exaggerate the United States' contribution. The point missed was that teamwork won the war, not individual heroism.

Miss Jones concluded her research by finding that "most of the war films produced by Hollywood were inconsequential, misleading, or even detrimental to the war program."[45]

In addition to Miss Jones's approach, we can classify the fiction war film into a number of subcategories: biographical, those based on branches of the armed services, adventure, spy films, prisoner-of-war pictures, socially conscious films, those having to do with civilian life and with rehabilitation, films emphasizing comedy or history.

The biographical war film, for example, has a plot based upon the life of some important individual, and the treatment generally allows many liberties with the facts. The overall tendency is to show how great a man we had among us, to present his qualities as godlike traits, and to depict his

45. Jones, "Hollywood War Films," p. 13.

actions as the outgrowth of divine destiny. World War II produced few good biographical films about Americans involved in the war; instead, the best such movies centered around two personalities from World War I: President Woodrow Wilson and Sergeant Alvin York.

Biographical War Films

American

Patton: Lust for Glory (Fox—16mm: 1969, 171 min., color, sound, R-FNC)
    Franklin J. Schaffner directed what is probably the best war biography to date. Based upon a number of books, the screenplay starts in 1943 when General George S. Patton (George C. Scott) assumes command of a demoralized tank battalion and defeats Rommel's Afrika Corps. From then on we get to see Patton's ego take on General Bradley, Field Marshal Montgomery and General Eisenhower. Balanced against Patton's negative characteristics are his successful military victories. So ambivalent is the drama that one is torn between bitterness and admiration for what must have been a very disturbed man. Scott is brilliant.

Sergeant York (Warners—16 mm: 1941, 134 min., b/w, sound, R-CHA, CON, UAS)
    Gary Cooper gives a creditable but overrated performance as the ex-Tennessee pacifist who singlehandedly captured more than a hundred Germans. Howard Hawks does his best directing in the first 30 minutes, before he gets to moralizing about supermen.[46]

Wilson (Fox—16mm: 1944, 154 min., b/w, sound, R-AUD, FNC)
    Henry King's treatment of Wilson (Alexander Knox) begins with the Princeton professor's entry into politics and stays with him until the disastrous defeat of his plan to involve this country in the League of Nations. At the time the movie was made, it served to show a parallel between Wilson's failure and Roosevelt's attempts to help form the United Nations.[47]

German

The Desert Fox (Fox—16mm: 1951, 91 min., b/w, sound, R-FNC)
    Director Henry Hathaway's romanticized account of Field Marshal Rommel weaves various military scenes and episodes of his domestic life together in an attempt to create sympathy for individual German officers who considered themselves apart and aloof from the Nazi war machine. In spite of James Mason's strong performance, the film itself is stiff and distasteful.

I Aim at the Stars (Columbia—16mm: 1960, 107 min., b/w, sound, R-AUD, BUC, IDE, NAT, NEW, ROA, SWA, TWY/L-COL)
    Probably the most sympathetic treatment of Wernher von Braun's life

---

46. The most useful information is available in George Carpozi, Jr., *The Gary Cooper Story* (New Rochelle: Arlington House, 1970); Homer Dickens, *The Films of Gary Cooper* (New York: Citadel Press, 1970); and Robin Wood, *Howard Hawks* (New York: Doubleday, 1968).
47. For more useful information see James Agee, "Wilson," *Agee on Film:* Vol. 1— *Reviews and Comments* (New York: McDowell, Obolensky, Inc., 1958), pp. 110–13; the script of *Wilson* is available in *Best Film Plays 1943–44,* edited by John Gassner and Dudley Nichols (New York: Crown, 1944); and Alexander Knox, "On Playing Wilson," *Hollywood Quarterly* 1, no. 1 (October 1945): 110–11.

up to the Korean War, director J. Lee Thompson's pseudo-documentary film tries to pacify critics of the scientist's war work by suggesting that he had no other choice. There is even a vulgar attempt at praising Americans for having gotten better Nazi scientists than those who fled to Russia.

Fiction Films on the Military Branches

Army

From Here to Eternity (Columbia—16mm: 1953, 118 min., b/w, sound, R-AUD, CCC, CWF, IDE, NAT, ROA, SWA, TWF, TWY, WHO/L-COL)

Fred Zinnemann directs a well-made version of James Jones's cynical account of Army life at the Schofield Barracks, Honolulu, in the days just before the attack on Pearl Harbor. In addition to Daniel Taradash's forceful screenplay, there are commendable performances by Frank Sinatra, Montgomery Clift, Burt Lancaster and Donna Reed.[48]

The Victors (Columbia—16mm: 1963, 147 min., b/w, sound, R-AUD, CCC, CHA, CON, CWF, IDE, ROA, SWA, TWY/L-COL)

Carl Foreman produced, wrote and directed this uneven and sweeping picaresque journey of a squad of American infantrymen marching through Europe in World War II. Surprisingly good performances by George Peppard and George Hamilton.[49]

A Walk in the Sun (Fox—16mm: 1945, 117 min., b/w, sound, R-ROA, WHO)

Director Lewis Milestone, using Robert Rossen's well-written, well-conceived script, creates a semi-realistic film about a Texas platoon in an infantry division in Italy. One of Richard Conte's better roles.

The Young Lions (Fox—16mm: 1958, 167 min., b/w, cinemascope, sound, R-FNC)

Based upon Irwin Shaw's best selling novel about people in war, Director Edward Dmytryk presents on an epic scale the story of three men: an uncommitted socialite, an ill-fated Jew, and a misguided Nazi. Although the screenplay is flabby, Montgomery Clift gives a strong performance as a Jew caught in an anti-semitic platoon.[50]

Navy

Destination Tokyo (Warners—16mm: 1944, 135 min., b/w, sound, R-UAS)

Delmer Daves wrote and directed this restrained but propagandist adventure yarn about a submarine mission into Tokyo Harbor to blow up ships and cargo. Strong performances by Cary Grant and John Garfield.

Task Force (Warners—16mm: 1949, 116 min., b/w, sound, R-UAS)

Again Daves directs and writes, only this sea yarn about the birth of naval aircraft is too spread out and unevenly edited. There are, however, some

---

48. For some good background information read Bob Thomas, *King Cohn* (New York: G. P. Putnam's Sons, 1967). Also helpful is Daniel Taradash, "Into Another World," *Films and Filming* 5, no. 8 (May 1959) : 9, 33.

49. Carl Foreman, "The Road to *The Victors*," *Films and Filming* 9, no. 12 (September 1963) : 11–12.

50. Romano Tozzi, "Edward Dmytryk," *Films in Review* 13, no. 2 (February 1962) : 86–101.

good newsreel shots and fine examples of mixing actual footage with a fictional narrative, starring Gary Cooper and Jane Wyatt.

They Were Expendable (MGM—16mm: 1945, 136 min., b/w, sound, R-FNC)

Director John Ford fashioned this memorable film as a tribute to the PT boats in action in the Pacific. Lots of blood and thunder, typical of war films in general, but with respectable acting from John Wayne and Robert Montgomery.

Air Force[51]

Command Decision (MGM—16mm: 1948, 111 min., b/w, sound, R-FNC)

Director Sam Wood does a good job of adapting this hit Broadway play about the psychological pressures on the military chiefs who decide how many lives they are willing to sacrifice to achieve their objectives. The film has an all-star cast, headed by Clark Gable, Walter Pidgeon, Van Johnson, and Charles Bickford.

Thirty Seconds over Tokyo (MGM—16mm: 1944, 135 min., b/w, sound, R-FNC)

The combination of Dalton Trumbo's screenplay and Mervyn LeRoy's direction make this film, based upon Captain Ted Lawson's diary, a patriotic interpretation of the first bombing mission over Tokyo.[52]

Twelve O'Clock High (Fox—16mm: 1949, 133 min., b/w, sound, R-FNC)

Henry King directs what was to be the prototype of the popular 1960s television series in this drama of a general's torment as he sends his men on dangerous missions. Although Gregory Peck has the lead, Dean Jagger steals the film.

The Military in Foreign Countries

All Quiet on the Western Front (Universal—16mm: 1930, 103 min., b/w, sound, R-CCC, CON, SWA, UNI/L-UNI)

This Lewis Milestone masterpiece is based upon Erich Maria Remarque's great novel about young Germans who learn that dying for the Fatherland in 1918 is without glory or honor. Lew Ayres gives a moving portrayal of Paul Bauner, the disillusioned patriot, in this film, of which only poor prints are available.[53]

The Ballad of a Soldier (Russia—16mm: 1960, 89 min., b/w, English subtitles, sound, R-AUD)

Director Grigori Chukrai composes a series of impressive images of a soldier on leave who falls in love on the way home to see his mother. Particularly impressive is the photography of Vladimir Nikolayev and Era Savaleva.[54]

---

51. Rudy Behlmer, "World War I Aviation Film," *Films in Review* 18, no. 7 (August–September 1967) : 413–33.

52. The script is available in *Best Film Plays, 1943–44*, edited by John Gassner and Dudley Nichols (New York: Crown, 1945).

53. For a good analysis of this film see John Cutts, "Classics Revisited: *All Quiet on the Western Front*," *Films and Filming* 9, no. 7 (April 1963) : 55–58. Also useful is Jack Spears, "Louis Wolheim," *Films in Review* 23, no. 3 (March 1972) : 158–77.

54. There is a script extract from the film available in *Films and Filming* 7, no. 10 (July 1961) : 22–23; 38–39; 41.

The Burmese Harp (Japan—16mm: 1956, 116 min., b/w, subtitles, sound, R-AUD)

Director Kon Ichikawa presents a long, terrifying epic of a Japanese soldier in the Burmese campaign of 1943–44 and the responsibility this one man felt after the war to bury the dead as expiation for his sins. An outstanding performance by Shoji Yasui.

The Cruel Sea (Britain—16mm: 1953, 121 min., b/w, sound, R-TWY, UNI)

Director Charles Frend puts together this graphic adventure of the officers and men of the *Compass Rose,* whose job it was to hunt down Japanese submarines in World War II.

In Which We Serve (Britain—16mm: 1942, 113 min., b/w, sound, R-WRS)

Noel Coward produced, wrote, starred in, and directed this impressive account of people, adrift on a life raft, who recall their past experiences. David Lean co-directed.

King and Country (Britain—16mm: 1964, 86 min., b/w, sound, R-AUD)

Joseph Losey does a remarkable job of bringing John Wilson's stage play to the screen. Tom Courtenay plays the sensitive and simple soldier who decided to walk away from war and now faces a court-martial. Dirk Bogarde is the arrogant and pitiful officer who refuses to face the horror of his own military organization. A brutal visual picture of World War I in the Enlish trenches.[55]

Paths of Glory (United Artists—16mm: 1957, 87 min., b/w, sound, R-UAS)

One of Stanley Kubrick's most outstanding films. Using a brilliant script, written by Calder Willingham and Jim Thompson and adapted from Humphrey Cobb's novel, Kubrick presents the cynical account of a World War I French Army Division being exploited by its officers. Adolphe Menjou portrays the vicious general, while Kirk Douglas turns in a splendid performance as the outraged officer who sees the injustice of certain military procedures.

The Adventure War Film[56]

Casablanca (Warners—16mm: 1943, 102 min., b/w, sound, R-CHA, CON, UAS)

Director Michael Curtiz presents a good example of how Hollywood takes the usual adventure yarn, with its emphasis on dramatic scenes filled with the unexpected, and often set in exotic places, and adapts these conventions to Vichy-France-ruled North Africa. The all-star cast consists of Humphrey Bogart, Ingrid Bergman, Claude Rains, Sydney Greenstreet and Peter Lorre. This is the film where Dooley Wilson plays the memorable song, "As Time Goes By."[57]

55. See James Leahy, *The Cinema of Joseph Losey* (New York: A. S. Barnes and Co., 1967); and Tom Milne, *Losey on Losey* (New York: Doubleday, 1968). Also Gilles Jacob, "Joseph Losey or the Camera Calls," *Sight and Sound* 35, no. 2 (Spring 1966): 62–67.
56. Gordow Gow, "Thrill a Minute: Adventure Movies of the 60's," *Films and Filming* 13, no. 4 (January 1967): 4–11.
57. There is an excellent section of articles on *Casablanca* in *Joseph McBride, ed., *Persistence of Vision: A Collection of Film Criticism* (Madison: The Wisconsin Film Society Press, 1968), pp. 93–110. See also Jack Edmund Nolan, "Michael Curtiz," *Films in Review* 21, no. 9 (November 1970): 525–48; and Leonid Kinskey, "*Casablanca:* It Lingers Deliciously in Memory 'As Times Goes By,'" *Movie Digest* 1, no. 5 (September 1972): 118–33.

Spy War Films

Five Fingers (Fox—16mm: 1952, 108 min., b/w, sound, R-FNC)
Director Joseph L. Mankiewicz gives this conventional tale of espionage some superb moments of suspense, and James Mason is splendid as "Cicero," World War II's famous German spy who operated as a valet to the British emissary in Turkey.

House on 92nd Street (Fox—16mm: 1945, 89 min., b/w, sound, R-FNC)
Henry Hathaway gets the credit for this semi-documentary account of how the FBI broke up a Nazi spy ring operating in New York. Particularly interesting is some wartime footage made and used by the Federal Bureau of Investigation.

The Maltese Falcon (Warners—16mm: 1941, 100 min., b/w, sound, R-CON, UAS)
John Huston's classic "private eye" film about Dashiell Hammett's Sam Spade is an excellent illustration of how the gangster film slowly was transformed during the Second World War into a vehicle for spy stories.[58] This particular version has such stalwarts as Bogart, Greenstreet, Lorre, and a stunning performance by Mary Astor.

The Man Who Never Was (Fox—16mm: 1956, 104 min., cinemascope, b/w, sound, R-FNC)
This English spy film, directed by Ronald Neame, is an original and engrossing story about a cold-blooded attempt by British Intelligence to decoy the Germans from finding out about the Normandy Invasion. A fine performance by Clifton Webb.

The Thirty-Nine Steps (Britain—16mm: 1935, 80 min., b/w, sound, R-FCE, WHO, WIL)
Hitchcock's classic spy film, starring Robert Donat and Madeleine Carroll, melodramatically presents an innocent young man trying to catch German spies before they or the police put an end to him. Avoid the remake of 1960.

The Great Escape (United Artists—16mm: 1963, 170 min., color, sound, R-CHA, UAS)
Director John Sturges took charge of this epic-like adventure of a mass escape by hundreds of prisoners held inside Germany during World War II and what happened to them. Particularly good are James Garner and Steve McQueen.[59]

The Prisoner-of-War Film

The Bridge on the River Kwai (Columbia—16mm: 1957, 161 min., color, sound, R-AUD, BUC, CCC, CHA, CON, CWF, IDE, NAT, NEW, ROA, SWA, TWF, TWY, WHO/L-COL)
David Lean's highly acclaimed and controversial movie concerns a warped, resolute British Colonel (Alec Guinness) who defies the Japanese

---

58. For a helpful analysis read Allen Eyles, "Great Films of the Century: *The Maltese Falcon,*" *Films and Filming* 11, no. 2 (November 1964) : 45–50. Also Penelope Houston, "The Private Eye," *Sight and Sound* 26, no. 1 (Summer 1956) : 22–24, 55.
59. Michael Ratcliffe, "The Public Image and the Private Eye of Richard Attenborough," *Films and Filming* 9, no. 11 (August 1963) : 15–17.

prison commander (Sessue Hayakawa), and uses the construction of a bridge as a method of restoring his men's morale. William Holden plays an American officer who escapes, only to return with commandos to destroy the bridge.[60]

La Grande Illusion (France—16mm: 1937, 111 min., b/w, English subtitles, sound, R-JAN)

Jean Renoir directed this brilliant film about prisoners of war in Germany during World War I. Contributing to the overall excellence are Jean Gabin, Erich von Stroheim, and Pierre Fresnay.[61]

King Rat (Columbia—16mm: 1965, 133 min., b/w, sound, R-AUD, CCC, CHA, CON, CWF, IDE, ROA, SWA, TWF, WHO/L-COL)

Bryan Forbes directed this underrated version of James Clavell's novel about life in Changi, a notorious Japenese prisoner-of-war camp with over 10,000 soldiers. Strong performances by George Segal, Tom Courtenay, James Fox, and James Donald.

Stalag 17 (Paramount—16mm: 1953, 120 min., b/w, sound, R-FNC)

Billy Wilder wrote the screenplay and directed this bitter-comic film adapted from the Broadway hit of life in a POW camp. William Holden is outstanding as Sefton, the wheeler-dealer who most of the men suspect is a traitor. This movie set the pattern for the popular TV series *Hogan's Heroes.*

Socially Conscious War Film

Crossfire (RKO—16mm: 1947, 85 min., b/w, sound, R-MMA)

Director Edward Dmytryk developed this Richard Brooks novel *The Brick Foxhole* about an anti-Semitic soldier who becomes a killer into a strong, sensitive film filled with suspense. Robert Ryan gives one of his best performances as Montgomery, the intolerant murderer.

Home of the Brave (United Artists—16mm: 1949, 88 min., b/w, sound, R-AUD, CHA, CON, FCE, IDE, NAT, TWY, WHO, WIL/L-UEI)

Mark Robson and Stanley Kramer combined talents to adopt Arthur Laurent's successful Broadway play about anti-Semitism, and change it into the story of a white man suffering from his prejudices about his black comrade.[62]

Sahara (Warners—16mm: 1943, 97 min., b/w, sound, R-BUC, CWF, TWF, TWY/L-COL)

Zoltan Korda fashioned this adventure story of members of a racially troubled American tank crew who wander lost through the desert and eventually take on an entire German division . . . and win. Bogart and Rex Ingram give the movie some good moments.

---

60. For two good reviews of this film, see Stanley Kauffmann, *A World on Film* (New York: Harper and Row, 1966), pp. 3–5; and James Kearns, "Classics Revisited: La Grande Illusion," *Film Quarterly* 14, no. 2 (Winter 1960) : 10–17.

61. There is an interesting article by Sessue Hayakawa, who plays the Japanese Commandant, discussing his feelings about the film. Cf. Sessue Hayakawa, "Nazis and Japs," *Films and Filming* 8, no. 5 (February 1962) : 21, 45; and Gordon Gow, "Potential: The Mirisch Brothers," *Flims and Filming* 18, no. 6 (March 1972) : 41–44.

62. Herbert G. Luft, "Mark Robson," *Films in Review* 19, no. 5 (May 1968) : 288–97.

Rehabilitation[63]

The Best Years of Our Lives (Goldwyn—16mm: 1946, 170 min., b/w, sound, R-SGS)

Acting, directing, screenwriting, and photography all meshed effectively to make this the best example of the problems of returning veterans as they try to readjust to civilian life. William Wyler directed; Robert E. Sherwood did the script; Greg Toland handled the camera; and Fredric March, Myrna Loy, Dana Andrews, and Teresa Wright excelled.[64]

The Men (United Artists—16mm: 1950, 85 min., b/w, sound, R-CHA, FCE, ICS, TWY, WIL)

Stanley Kramer, Fred Zinnemann, and Carl Foreman combined talents to create this poignant and pervasive film about the adjustment of paralyzed war veterans to civilian life. This was Marlon Brando's first film, and he is well supported by Teresa Wright and Jack Webb.

The Search (MGM—16mm: 1948, 103 min., b/w, sound, R-FNK)

Another Zinnemann effort with Montgomery Clift as the soldier who helps in rehabilitating displaced European children rescued from Nazi concentration camps.

The Civilian War Film

The Diary of Anne Frank (Fox—16mm: 1959, 170 min., b/w, sound, R-FNC)

George Stevens produced and directed this tragic story of two Jewish families who are driven to hiding from the Nazis in a factory attic in Amsterdam for two harassing years. During that time we see the hopes, frustrations and humanity of men, women, and children facing imminent destruction. Particularly strong performances by Joseph Schildkraut and Shelley Winters.[65]

Forbidden Games (France—16mm: 1952, 90 min., b/w, English subtitles, sound, R-JAN)

René Clément's sensitive and disturbing film about an orphaned girl befriended by a poor family during World War II. She and the youngest boy explore the problems of growing up, and there are many poignant scenes of innocence. This French movie then injects one of the most devastating of all conclusions.

Hiroshima Mon Amour (France—16mm: 1959, 88 min., b/w, subtitles, sound, R-CON)

Director Alain Resnais unfolds an intriguing love story of a French screen

---

63. For a good discussion of the rehabilitation films, see the following: Frank Fearing, "Warriors Return: Normal or Neurotic?" *Hollywood Quarterly* 1, no. 1 (October 1945) : 97–109; Roy E. Grinker and John P. Spiegel, "The Returning Soldier: A Dissent," *Hollywood Quarterly* 1, no. 3 (April 1956) : 321–26; and Frank Fearing, "A Reply," *idem.*, pp. 326–28.

64. Abraham Polonsky, "The Best Years of Our Lives: A Review," *Hollywood Quarterly* 2, no. 3 (April 1947) : 257–60.

65. Herbert G. Luft, "George Stevens," *Films in Review* 9, no. 9 (November 1958) : 486–96; *Dialogue with the World* (New York: Encyclopaedia Britannica Films, Inc., 1964), pp. 28–30; Albert Johnson, "The Diary of Anne Frank," *Film Quarterly* 12, no. 4 (Summer 1959) : 41–44; and Peter John Dyer, "The Diary of Anne Frank," *Films and Filming* 5, no. 10 (July 1959) : 21–22.

actress and a Japanese architect whose brief affair in postwar Hiroshima brings back many shattering memories for the woman. Very fine performances by Emmanuelle Riva and Eiji Okada.[66]

Judgment at Nuremberg (United Artists—16mm: 1961, 186 min., b/w, sound, R-CHA, UAS)

Director Stanley Kramer takes Abby Mann's classic TV production of the same name and fashions it into a memorable tableau of the Nazi war crimes trials in Nuremberg. The cast—Spencer Tracy, Burt Lancaster, Richard Widmark, Montgomery Clift and particularly Maximilian Schell—helps create one of the most important fiction films about World War II and its implications for our time.

Rome, Open City (Italy—16mm: 1945, 103 min., b/w, English subtitles, sound, R-CON)

Roberto Rossellini's film about Italy's days under German occupation is one of the most artistic films ever made about the lives of civilians at war. This originator of neorealistic movies centers on a priest who works with the underground in the final days of Nazi rule in Rome.

Mrs. Miniver (MGM—16mm: 1942, 135 min., b/w, sound, R-FNC)

William Wyler directed this propagandistic yet entertaining movie about the English populace and their lives during the Second World War. Good performances by Greer Garson and Walter Pidgeon.[67]

The Shop on Main Street (Czechoslovakia—16mm: 1964, 128 min., b/w, subtitles, sound, R-AUD, MMM)

Jan Kadar and Elmar Slos directed this memorable film which starts off as a comedy about a simple man who is made the "Aryan manager" of a Jewish button shop. Brtko (Josef Kroner) runs up against the old Jewish lady (Ida Kaminska) who not only doesn't understand what his title means, but also doesn't concern herself with making money. The two develop an unusual relationship which is put to the severest test when it is announced that all Jews are being deported. An unforgettable film with amazing performances by its stars.

Two Women (Italy—16mm: 1961, 105 min., b/w, subtitles, sound, R-AUD)

Vittorio de Sica's story of a mother and daughter who try to stay alive in Italy toward the end of World War II. Sophia Loren in her best role.

Comedy War Film

Dr. Strangelove (Columbia—16mm: 1964, 93 min., b/w, sound, R-COL)

Stanley Kubrick co-wrote, produced, and directed this masterpiece of war satire concerning an insane general's triggering the eventual destruction of

---

66. Louis Marcorelles, "Alain Resnais and Hiroshima Mon Amour," *Sight and Sound* 29, no. 1 (Winter 1959–60) : 12–14; Henri Colpi, "Editing Hiroshima Mon Amour," *idem.*, pp. 14–16; Richard Roud, "Conversation with Marguerite Duras," *idem.*, pp. 16–17; *Roy Armes, *The Cinema of Alain Resnais* (New York: A. S. Barnes & Co., 1968) ; and *John Ward, *Alain Resnais or The Theme of Time* (New York: Doubleday & Co., 1968) .

67. The film script is available in *Twenty Best Film Plays* edited by John Gassner and Dudley Nichols (New York: Crown, 1943) , pp. 293–332.

the world. This film is the best at presenting the lunacy of war in comedy.[68]

Kelly's Heroes (MGM—16mm: 1970, 145 min., color, sound, R-FNC)

Brian Hutton directed this tongue-in-cheek war movie about a discouraged platoon led by the smooth-talking Kelly (Clint Eastwood), who in the course of interrogating a captured German colonel discovers that a French bank in occupied territory close by contains a fortune of money in gold bars. So the resourceful Kelly convinces the tough sergeant Crapgame (Telly Savalas) to help Kelly and a far-out renegade tank commander (Donald Sutherland) to pull a "bank robbery" in the name of war and personal profit. All in all, the film is good, fast, and clever entertainment.

M*A*S*H (Fox—16mm: 1970, 113 min., color, sound, R-FNC)

In one of the wildest, most irreverent and hysterically funny films about war, Hawkeye Pierce (Donald Sutherland), Duke Forrest (Tom Skerritt) and Trapper John McIntyre (Elliott Gould) [69] join up with the 4077th Mobile Army Surgical Hospital in Korea, and divide their time between operating in surgical crises and destroying any semblance of military discipline. The greatest scenes in the film, however, center around the virile males' attack on the moral and physical scruples of a new senior nurse (Sally Kellerman), soon known to all as "Hot Lips." While not completely an anti-war film, the movie goes a long way in showing the horrors of combat. Robert Altman directed.[70]

Historical War Film

An Occurrence at Owl Creek Bridge (16mm: 1961, 27 min., b/w, sound, R-CON)

Robert Enrico directed this impressive adaptation of Ambrose Bierce's short story about a Confederate spy's hanging by a Union platoon. The movie is beautifully created and provides a terrifying comment on war.[71]

A Time out of War (16mm: 1954, 22 min., b/w, sound, R-CON)

Denis Sanders directed this version of a Civil War film about a momentary truce between two Union soldiers and a Confederate who for one brief afternoon decide to lay down their arms and share their thoughts.

La Guerre Est Finie (France—16mm: 1966, 121 min., b/w, subtitles, sound, R-AUD)

Alan Resnais directed this outstanding and emotionally taut Spanish Civil War story of Diego (Yves Montand), a doomed Spanish patriot who plays out his last days in contemporary Spain and France in a series of events involving love and politics. Although it tends to be prosaic in comparison with the

---

68. Stanley Kauffmann, *A World on Film*, pp. 14–19; Stanley Kubrick, "How I learned to Stop Worrying," *Films and Filming* 9, no. 9 (June 1963): 12–13; Frank Manchel, "Dr. Strangelove," *Media and Methods* 4, no. 4 (December 1967): 29–32; and Tom Milne, "How I Learned to Stop Worrying and Love Stanley Kubrick," *Sight and Sound* 33, no. 2 (Spring 1964): 68–72.

69. Richard Warren Lewis, "Playboy Interview: Elliott Gould," *Playboy* 17, no. 11 (November 1970): 77–94, 262, 264.

70. John Cutts, M*A*S*H*, "McCloud and McCabe: An Interview with Robert Altman," *Films and Filming* 18, no. 2 (November 1971), 40–44; and Kenneth Geist, "The Films of Ring Lardner Jr.," *Film Comment* 6, no. 4 (Winter 1970–71): 44–49.

71. Paul A. Schreivogel, *A Visual Study Guide* (Dayton: George A. Pflaum, 1969); and David Sohn *et al.* "Perspectives on War," p. 12.

French director's other films, Montand is first-rate as the ruthless old soldier fighting a losing battle.[72]

As one examines the war films in all categories, one comes to the realization that the film in treatment and emphasis responds to the influences of a mass audience. That means, of course, that endings are often contrived, that characters are stereotypes, that prevailing attitudes of the public are reinforced. Rarely do we have a film that represents an unpopular viewpoint or situation. The war is scarcely examined for its significance and its importance. This chapter may help illustrate not only the various types of categories films may fall into, but also how movies are related to the times in which they are made.

OTHER STUDIES ON GENRES

The Gangster Film[73]

* Baxter, John. *The Gangster Film.* New York: A. S. Barnes and Company, 1970.
    In this general and useful index to movies dealing with organized crime, Baxter divides his entries into two categories: (1) personalities and themes, and (2) film titles. He also has some helpful illustrations.

Lee, Raymond and B. C. Van Hecke. *Gangster and Hoodlums: The Underworld in Cinema.* With a foreword by Edward G. Robinson. New York: A. S. Barnes and Company, 1971.
    A very badly prepared introduction goes along with a very good pictorial survey of crime movies.

The Musical Film

* McVay, Douglas. *The Musical Film.* New York: A. S. Barnes and Company, 1967.
    This thumbnail sketch is a chronological survey of musicals from 1927

---

72. Michael Caen, "The Times Change," *Cahiers du Cinema in English* 8, CdC no. 174 (January 1966) : 58–61; Andrew Sarris, "Ode to the Old Left," *idem.,* p. 62.
    73. For study of the gangster genre, see the following: Robert Warshow, "The Gangster as Tragic Hero," *The Immediate Experience* (New York: Doubleday and Company, 1964) , pp. 83–88; Robert Siodmak, "Hoodlums: The Myth," *Films and Filming* 5, no. 10 (June 1959) : 10, 35; Richard Whitehall, "Crime Inc.: Part I," *Films and Filming* 10, no. 4 (January 1964) : 7–12; Richard Whitehall, "Crime Inc.: Part II," *Films and Filming* 10, no. 5 (February 1964) : 17–22; and Richard Whitehall, "Crime Inc.: Part III," *Films and Filming* 10, no. 6 (March 1964) : 39–44; John Howard Reid, "The Best Second Fiddle," *Films and Filming* 9, no. 2 (November 1962) : 14–18; Alan Warner, "Yesterday's Hollywood: Gangster Heroes," *Films and Filming* 18, no. 2 (November 1971) : 16–25; Charles T. Gregory, "The Pod Society Versus the Rugged Individualists," *The Journal of Popular Film* 1, no. 1 (Winter 1972) : 3–14; Maria-Teresa Ravage, "The Mafia on Film: Part One," *Film Society Review* 7, no. 2 (October 1971) : 33–39; "Part Two," *Film Society Review* 7, no. 3 (November 1971) : 32–36; "Part Three," *Film Society Review* 7, no. 4 (December 1971) : 37–40; "Part Four," *Film Society Review* 7, no. 5 (January 1972) : 41–44; and Stuart M. Kaminsky, *"Little Caesar* and Its Role in The Gangster Film Genre," *The Journal of Popular Film* 1, no. 3 (Summer 1972) : 208–27.

to 1966. It has a good bibliography and a much-needed index to specific titles. The comments are useful, provocative, and often accurate. Read this along with the Springer book for the most helpful approach to musical film.

* Springer, John. *All Talking! All Singing! All Dancing! A Pictorial History of the Movie Musical.* New York: The Citadel Press, 1966.

To date, this is the best source on the outstanding songs, performers, and films of the screen. Springer, in a pleasant, quick, and sensitive narrative, provides a valuable reference guide, as well as 500 illustrations, a name and title index, and valuable annotations for the hundreds of stills.[74]

Taylor, John Russell and Arthur Jackson. *The Hollywood Musical.* New York: McGraw-Hill and Company, 1971.

Starting with the definition that a true musical film is one that is totally controlled by music—swallowing the drama and other jumps into fantasy through song or dance scenes, rather than lyrical dramas (*The Umbrellas of Cherbourg*), Russell, the *London Times* film critic, offers an exhaustive and extremely useful study of Hollywood's popular genre. The second part of the book belongs to music critic Jackson who also offers an exhaustive listing of more than 1400 musicals, plus a detailed filmography of the 275 most popular and a complete index of over 2750 songs. This is a very good book to have around.

* Vallance, Tom. *The American Musical.* New York: A. S. Barnes and Company, 1970.

This book offers a comprehensive and valuable guide to American artists connected with film musicals, including some critical comments, credits and biographical information.

The Horror Film[75]

* Butler, Ivan. *The Horror Film.* Revised and expanded edition. New York: A. S. Barnes and Company, 1970.

This updated version stresses specific films within the matrix of the period

---

74. For some more information on musicals, see the following: David Vaughan, "After the Ball," *Sight and Sound* 26, no. 2 (Autumn 1956) : 89–91, 111; Edward Jablonski, "Filmusicals," *Films in Review* 6, no. 2 (February 1955) : 56–69; John Cutts, "Bye Bye Musicals," *Films and Filming* 10, no. 2 (November 1963) : 42–45; Lionel Godfrey, "A Heretic's Look at Musicals," *Films and Filming* 13, no. 6 (March 1967) : 4–10; George Sidney, "The Three Ages of the Musical," *Films and Filming* 14, no. 7 (April 1968) : 4–7; and Alan Warner, "Yesterday's Hollywood: Musicals and Comedies," *Films and Filming* 8, no. 1 (November 1971) : 18–33.

75. Some good articles are Derek Hill, "The Face of Horror," *Sight and Sound* 28, no. 1 (Winter 1958–59) : 6–11; William K. Everson, "A Family Tree of Monsters," *Film Culture* 1, no. 1 (January 1955) : 24–30; William K. Everson, "Horror Films," *Films in Review* 5, no. 1 (January 1954) : 12–23; Edward Connor, "The Return of the Dead," *Films in Review* 15, no. 3 (March 1964) : 146–60; Robert C. Roman, "Boris Karloff," *Films in Review* 15, no. 7 (August–September 1964) : 389–412; Vincent Price, "Mean, Moody and Magnificent," *Films and Filming* 11, no. 6 (March 1965) : 5–8; Leslie Halliwell, "The Baron, The Count and Their Ghoul Friends: Part One," *Films and Filming* 15, no. 9 (June 1969) : 12–16: Leslie Halliwell, "Part Two," *Films and Filming* 15, no. 10 (July 1969) : 12–16; Michael Armstrong, "Some Like it Chilled: Part I," *Films and Filming* 17, no. 5 (February 1971) : 28–34; "Part II," *Films and Filming* 17, no. 6 (March 1971) : 32–37; "Part III," *Films and Filming* 17, no. 7 (April 1971) : 37–42; "Part IV," *Films and Filming* 17, no. 8 (May 1971) : 76–82; Brian Murphy, "Monster Movies: They Came from Beneath the Fifties," *The Journal of Popular Film* 1, no. 1 (Winter 1972) : 31–44; and Dennis L. White, "The Poetic of Horror: More than Meets the Eye," *Cinema Journal* 10, no. 2 (Spring 1972) : 1–18.

and the conventions of the genre. The author comments upon the effect of the audience at the time of release. Easy and fast reading.

* Clarens, Carlos. *An Illustrated History of the Horror Film.* New York: Capricorn Books, 1967.

The best of the books to date, it is a well-researched record of the major movies, plus an invaluable cast and credit directory at the end. Also worthwhile are the clever and entertaining illustrations, which are thematically grouped.

* Drake, Douglas. *Horror.* New York: The Macmillan Company, 1966.

This is a more reflective book than the others on the relationship between history and the fictional tales in literature and on the screen. It is useful for background material on legends and superstitions, but almost worthless for film criticism.

* Gifford, Denis. *Movie Monsters.* New York: E. P. Dutton and Company, 1969.

The only value of this book is its handsome selection of stills characterizing man-made creations, the living dead, and the host of horror transformations.

Manchel, Frank. *Terrors of the Screen.* Englewood Cliffs: Prentice-Hall, Inc., 1970.

Strictly for secondary school students. This approach to the horror film emphasizes the personalities and background material behind the important supernatural and suspense tales, starting with Méliès at the turn of the century.

The Science Fiction Film[76]

* Baxter, John. *Science Fiction in the Cinema.* New York: A. S. Barnes and Company, 1970.

Since it is the only comprehensive book available on this subject, the text offers a wealth of information about films, key personalities, and credits. Regrettably, the illustrations are few and of limited value.

* Johnson, William (editor). *Focus on Science-Fiction Film.* Englewood Cliffs: Prentice-Hall, Inc., 1972.

For those interested in a useful casebook on the history and theoretical aspects of science-fiction movies, this one is a must. Among the films covered are *The Time Machine, Woman in the Moon, Shape of Things to Come, Dr. Cyclops, Destination Moon, When Worlds Collide,* and *Invasion of the Body Snatchers.*

---

76. Some useful information on that subject can be found in the following: Douglas Menville, *A Historical and Critical Survey of the Science-Fiction Film* (Master's thesis, University of Southern California, 1959); Francis Arnold, "Out of This World," *Films and Filming* 9, no. 9 (June 1963): 14–18; Richard Hodgens, "A Brief, Tragical History of the Science-Fiction Film," *Film Quarterly* 13, no. 2 (Winter 1959): 30–39; Penelope Houston, "Glimpses of the Moon: Science Fiction," *Sight and Sound* 22, no. 4 (April–June 1953): 185–88; Margaret Tarratt, "Monsters from the Id—An Examination of the Science Fiction Film Genre, Part I," *Films and Filming* 17, no. 3 (December 1970): 38–42; "Part II," *Films and Filming* 17, no. 4 (January 1971): 40–42; Gordon Gow, "Cinema of Illusion: Part One," *Films and Filming* 18, no. 6 (March 1972): 18–22; "Part Two," *Films and Filming* 18, no. 7 (April 1972): 40–44; "Part III," *Films and Filming* 18, no. 8 (May 1972): 40–44; and Larry N. Landrum, "A Checklist of Materials about Science Fiction Films of the 1950s," *The Journal of Popular Film* 1, no. 1 (Winter 1972): 61–63.

* Lee, Walter. *Reference Guide to Fantastic Films: Science Fiction, Fantasy and Horror.* Volume 1, A-F. Los Angeles: Chelsea-Lee Books, 1972.

This worthwhile study is the beginning of a much-needed index on the material connected with the history of fantastic films. It provides information on such things as titles of films, articles, different versions of the same story, dates for the completed film, countries involved in the productions, and credits. Hopefully, Lee's important work will stimulate similar studies in other genres.

The Western Film[77]

Corneau, Ernest N. *The Hall of Fame of Western Film Stars.* North Quincy, Mass.: The Christopher Publishing House, 1969.

A helpful directory of stars and directors connected with cowboy films, but poorly organized for locating information quickly. Lots of good shots of famous personalities are sprinkled throughout the text.

Everson, William K. *A Pictorial History of the Western Film.* New York: Citadel Press, 1969.

This is a very much condensed version of Everson's original work with Fenin in 1962, but a delight to read and look at. It should be read after the longer book.

* Eyles, Allen. *The Western: An Illustrated Guide.* New York: A. S. Barnes & Co., 1967.

A less-expensive directory than Corneau's, and it is not so accurate or useful. In neither case, however, should students be deterred from supplanting them with a more carefully indexed and organized volume.

---

77. The following is a selected list of articles: Peter John Dyer, "A Man's World," *Films and Filming* 5, no. 8 (May 1959) : 13–15, 32–33; George N. Fenin, "The Western— Old and New," *Film Culture* 2 (1956) : 7–10; George N. Fenin and William K. Everson, "The European Western: A Chapter from the History of the Western Film," *Film Culture* 20 (1959) : 59–71; Sidney Field, "Outrage: A Print Documentary on Westerns," *Film Quarterly* 18, no. 3 (Spring 1965) : 13–39; "The Six-Gun Gallahad," *Time* (March 30, 1959) , pp. 52–54, 57–60; Robert Warshow, "Movie Chronicle: The Westerner," *The Immediate Experience* (New York: Doubleday, 1964) , pp. 89–106; Frederick Woods, "Hot Guns and Cold Women," *Films and Filming* 5, no. 6 (March 1959) : 11, 30; Frank Manchel, "The Archetypal American," *Media and Methods* 4, no. 8 (April 1968) : 36–38, 39, 48; William K. Everson, "Europe Produces Westerns Too," *Films in Review* 4, no. 2 (February 1953) : 74–79; William K. Everson, "Stunt Men," *Films in Review* 6, no. 7 (August–September 1955) : 394–402; George Mitchell and William K. Everson, "Tom Mix," *Films in Review* 8, no. 8 (October 1957) : 387–97; Anthony Thomas, "Tim McCoy," *Films in Review* 19, no. 4 (April 1968) : 218–30; John Ford and Burt Kennedy, "Ford and Kennedy on the Western," *Films in Review* 20, no. 1 (January 1969) : 29–33; Richard Whitehall, "The Heroes Are Tired," *Film Quarterly* 20, no. 2 (Winter 1966–67) : 12–24; Lionel Godfrey, "A Heretic's View of Westerns," *Films and Filming* 13, no. 8 (May 1967) : 14–20; David Austen, "Gunplay and Horses: Howard Hawks Talks About His Way With Westerns," *Films and Filming* 15, no. 1 (October 1968) : 25–27; Jim Kitses, "The Rise and Fall of the American West: Borden Chase Interviewed," *Film Comment* 6, no. 4 (Winter 1970–71) : 14–21; Alan Warner, "Yesterday's Hollywood: Western Heroes," *Films and Filming* 18, no. 5 (February 1972) : 34–40; Lewis Beale, "The American Way West," *Films and Filming* 18, no. 7 (April 1972) : 24–30; David Austen, "Continental Westerns," *Films and Filming* 17, no. 10 (July 1972) : 36–42; Ralph Willett, "The American Western: Myth and Anti-Myth," *Journal of Popular Culture* 4, no. 2 (Fall 1970) : 455– 62; and Ralph C. Croizier, "Beyond East and West: The American Western and Rise of the Chinese Swordplay Movie," *The Journal of Popular Film* 1, no. 3 (Summer 1972) : 229–43.

* Fenin, George N. and William K. Everson. *The Westerns: From Silents to Cinerama.* New York: Bonanza Books, 1962.

This is the standard work in English and should be the starting point for American students. It has some fine sections on themes, conventions and directors. Two major criticisms are the authors' failure to list the sources of their research and the over-emphasis on "B" westerns and their minor cowboy actors.

* Kitses, Jim. *Horizons West.* New York: Doubleday and Company, 1969.

This auteur approach to western films centers on three directors popular in the 1950s and the 1960s: Anthony Mann, Budd Boetticher, and Sam Peckinpah. Even if most of the narrative is provocative speculation, Kitses discusses the Western with more sensitivity than most other writers on the subject.

Lahue, Kalton C. *Winners of the West: The Sagebrush Heroes of the Silent Screen.* New York: A. S. Barnes and Company, 1970.

Devoted exclusively to the western star, this book presents a helpful guide to biographical information about 38 of the silent screen's most popular heroes.

Manchel, Frank. *Cameras West.* Englewood Cliffs: Prentice-Hall, Inc., 1971.

Strictly for secondary students. This chronological account of the history of the Western emphasizes the close connection between the health of the American film industry and cowboy films in particular. Useful for background on some of the major outlaws often depicted in moving pictures.

3
Stereotyping in Film

***

The cinema, in many ways the dominant art of our time, has become—because of its nature—a mirror of the community in which it is produced, and it would seem that the relation between the film and society may well become a central problem for critical analysis.

J. A. Wilson, The Cinema 1952

***

Like traditional literature the film is an art that uses mankind as its subject. The film is therefore also a social document, in which may be found such problems as prejudice, poverty, and war. The factors that dictate the shape and direction of the film also influence the social comment of the artist. We should know more about these influences. It is not, however, a justifiable substitute for critical film standards. My intention in this chapter is to survey some principal studies and suggest materials that should further film study in the area of visual literacy. In particular, I am concerned with the film's frequent use of stereotypes and its effect on the audience.

I would like to begin by drawing upon the work of M. H. Abrams for a simple and manageable yet flexible frame of reference for a study of the art of the film in relation to social issues.[1] While there are many differences between film and the traditional arts, there are also many noticeable similarities in critical approaches to discussing the complete situation connected with any work of art. Abrams, in synthesizing the dozens of historical-theoretical patterns, suggests four basic components. First, there is the work itself, in this case the film. And since it is fashioned by a human, the second component is the *filmmaker*. Third, the film has a subject, consciously presented or deviously implied, which like the traditional arts, "is derived from existing things—to be about, or signify, or reflect something which either is, or bears some relation to an objective state of affairs." This third component, whether intended as a visual picture of human beings and actions, thoughts and emotions, or divine essences, is aptly termed *The Universe*.

***

1. M. H. Abrams, *The Mirror and the Lamp: Romantic Theory and the Critical Tradition* (New York: W. W. Norton and Company, Inc., 1958), pp. 6–7.

Finally, there is the audience: the viewers for whom the work is intended or to whose attention it has come.

On this framework of filmmaker, movie, universe, and audience I wish to consider film stereotypes. There are two basic reasons for this.

First, stereotypes are symbols of the world in which we live. The film teacher realizes (as do other educated people) that man needs to symbolize his world, that he needs to put his disordered perception into some order. Symbols, as well as myths and archetypes, are attempts to help explain our society. But there is a difference in quality between a myth and a stereotype. The former serves as a vehicle for primordial images that embody truths about man that have recurred throughout the ages. By using such images, the filmmaker takes advantage of a common denominator in human experience to evoke profound emotional responses. Stereotypes, on the other hand, are stock conventions or types that are repeated so often as to become clichés. And far too often the unimaginative filmmaker resorts to stereotypes to give ready-made answers to complex situations. The result is an emphasis on prejudice as well as a reinforcement of a limited point of view.

To put it another way, a myth, appropriately used, becomes invaluable for the insights it brings to a given situation; a stereotype usually has just the opposite effect. This form of cognition, in part, is forced upon man because of his need to symbolize the world around him. Susanne K. Langer, for example, feels that the arts are based upon man's need and ability to symbolize. Hence, symbolization becomes a basis for all creative, conceptual thinking.[2] In addition, symbols are for many people, according to Robert Bone, a national iconography. Bone points out what he feels to be the responsibility of image makers.

> The artist, or image-maker, is guardian of the national iconography. And since the power of images for good or evil is immense, he bears an awesome responsibility. If his images are false, if there is no bridge between portrayal and event, no correspondence between the shadow and the act, then the emotional life of the nation is to that extent distorted, and its daily conduct is rendered ineffectual or even pathological.[3]

The stereotyped movie also becomes an example of folk art. "For better or worse," as Dr. Paul Weitz comments, "they [American films taken altogether] are a real reflection, as are foreign films presented in the United States, which tend to represent the best of a given society."[4] The "worse" undoubtedly refers to the stock situations. Nevertheless, by studying the various stereotypes, students see a remarkable picture of countries and cultures.

---

2. Susanne Langer, *Philosophy in a New Key: A Study in the Symbolism of Reason, Rite and Art* (Cambridge: Harvard University Press, 1942), Chapters I and 4.
3. Robert Bone, "Ralph Ellison and the Uses of the Imagination," *Anger and Beyond,* Herbert Hill, ed. (New York: Harper and Row, 1966), pp. 100–101.
4. Dr. Paul Weitz, *New York Film Festival,* September 8, 1965.

Second, knowing about stereotypes helps us to understand their film use. We are able, at the same time, to view a record of society's prejudices, to learn how distortions have prevented us from developing our imagination, and to discover how we have been led toward an undesirable state of affairs. Furthermore, a rational understanding of the norms of the images presented to the public will help students who are searching for their own identity and, hopefully, will become responsible citizens. Films cannot avoid suggesting norms. As Frederick Elkin points out:

> In any society, the norms—the ideas of what are proper and improper, right and wrong, good and bad—are in part implicitly suggested. Every film . . . expresses some norms intentionally or unintentionally. By virtue of the fact that a movie occurs in given settings, has characters and tells a story, it suggests that depending upon the occasion, one type of behavior and feeling is appropriate; that some goals are worthy and others unworthy; that certain types of men are heroic and others are villainous; that some actions merit praise and others merit censure; that certain ideas are serious and others are comic; that certain relationships are unpleasant.[5]

If the film, therefore, has created stereotypes, let us examine what they are, the extent and the range of the process. Perhaps one of the best ways to do that is to investigate the various content analyses of films.

CONTENT ANALYSIS

In the classic definition of communication by Harold Lasswell, *"Who* says *What,* to *Whom,* through *What Medium,* with *What Effect,"* content analysis refers to the "what." The pioneer book on this method is Bernard Berelson's *Content Analysis in Communications Research,* in which the author defines content analysis as "a research technique for the objective, systematic and quantitative description of the manifest content of communication."[6] The three major assumptions about the technique are (1) that inferences based on the relationship between intent and content, or between content and effect have validity; (2) that by studying manifest content, a reliable meaning can be found; and (3) that there is a valid meaning to the quantitative description of communication. Without doubt, teachers find it useful to examine selected films for which there are already completed content analyses. Fortunately, some general content studies already exist.

The first major studies of the social content of film and its effects upon

5. Frederick Elkin, "The Value Implications of Popular Films," *Sociology and Social Research* 38 (May-June 1954) : 320.
6. Bernard Berelson, *Content Analysis in Communications Research* (Chicago: University of Chicago Press, 1952) , p. 18.

the audience were those of the Payne Fund.[7] The major concerns were

> Do the pictures really influence children in any direction: Are their conduct, ideals and attitudes affected by the movies? Are the scenes which are objectionable to adults understood by children, or at least by very young children? Do children eventually become sophisticated and grow superior to pictures? Are the emotions of children harmfully excited?

An example of the social content found in films was provided by Edgar Dale's *The Content of Motion Pictures*. His study was divided into three areas. First he covered the complete film production (1500 films) of major Hollywood studios in the years 1920, 1925, and 1930. Dale then categorized the important ten themes of the motion pictures according to their frequency in the films. He found in order of importance: love, crime, comedy, sex, mystery, war, travel, history, children, social propaganda. After this he proceeded to analyze 115 films selected from the period 1929–1931. Here his emphasis was on the treatment given various aspects of our society. His five major categories were Nature of American Life and Culture; Motivation of Characters; Crime; Delinquency and Violence; Relations of the Sexes; Depiction of Underprivileged people. These were then divided into subheadings. For example, under the first category were (a) Home; (b) Education; (c) Religion; (d) Economics; (e) Agriculture; (f) Industry and Commerce; etc. There were sixteen subheadings in all. In addition, these were divided into additional subheadings. He then made an intensive study of selected films (40 of the previous 115), which involved obtaining film scripts as well as taking copious notes during screenings. Each analysis summarized the important material connected with setting, characterization, plot development, sex, marriage, romantic love, crime, recreation, drinking, smoking, vulgarity, and goals of major characters.

The interested teacher might take some films from 1929–1931—*All Quiet on the Western Front, Hallelujah, Shanghai Express, Scarface*—and use Dale's findings as a basis for discussing social content and stereotyping in films. In his summary, Dale gives a balance sheet for motion picture content, which teachers might reproduce for their classes.

---

7. The series, entitled "Motion Pictures and Youth," consists of Herbert Blumer, *Movies and Conduct* (New York: Macmillan, 1933); Herbert Blumer and Philip M. Hauser, *Movies, Delinquency and Crime, ibid.;* W. W. Charters, *Motion Pictures and Youth: A Summary*, combined with P. W. Holaday and George D. Stoddard, *Getting Ideas From the Movies, ibid.;* Paul G. Cressey and Frederick M. Thrasher, *Boys, Movies and City Streets, ibid.;* Edgar Dale, *The Content of Motion Pictures*, combined with Edgar Dale, *Children's Attendance at Motion Pictures, ibid.*, 1933; Edgar Dale, *How to Appreciate Motion Pictures, ibid.;* 1933; W. S. Dysinger and Christian A. Ruckmick, *The Emotional Responses of Children to the Motion Picture Situation*, combined with Charles C. Peters, *Motion Pictures and Standards of Morality, ibid.;* Ruth C. Peterson and L. I. Thurstone, *Motion Pictures and the Social Attitudes of Children*, combined with Frank K. Shuttleworth and Mark A. May, *The Social Conduct and Attitudes of Movie Fans, ibid.;* Samuel Renshaw, Vernon L. Miller, and Dorothy Marquis, *Children's Sleep, ibid.* These have all been reissued by Arno Press, under the general editorship of Professor Martin Dworkin.

BALANCE SHEET FOR MOTION-PICTURE CONTENT[8]

The following aspects or problems have received attention, sometimes excessive, in the motion pictures	The following aspects or problems have received scant attention in the motion pictures
Life of the upper economic strata Metropolitan localities Problems of the unmarried and the young	Life of the middle and lower economic strata Small town and rural areas
Problems of love, sex, and crime Motif of escape and entertainment Interest appeal to young adults	Problems of the married, middle aged and old Other problems of everyday life Motif of education and social enlightenment Interest appeal to children and older adults
Professional and commercial world Personal problems in a limited field Comedy foreigner such as the dumb Swede Diverse and passive recreations	Industrial and agricultural world Occupational and governmental problems Representative foreigners such as the worker, business man Active and inexpensive recreations Social goals Causes and cures of crime
Individual and personal goals Variety of crimes and crime techniques Emphasis on the romance and the unusual in friendships Physical beauty Emphasis on physical action Sports and trivial matters frequently shown in newsreels	Emphasis on the undramatic and enduring in friendship Beauty of character Increased skill in analysis of motives and portrayal of character World news of an intellectual and perhaps of an undramatic type, results of scientific findings, pictures of real conditions in the different parts of the world

Noting the lack of reality in the stories, Dale concluded that motion pictures tended to stereotype society by over-emphasizing sensational aspects of sex, violence, and romantic love.[9] We need only quote Bob Hope's satirical comment about movies to see how far we have come: "Our big pictures this year have had some intriguing themes—sex perversion, adultery, and cannibalism. We'll get those kids away from their TV sets yet."[10]

Some verification of Dale's conclusions can be found in the statistical

8. Edgar Dale, p. 229.
9. Edgar Dale, p. 229.
10. Bob Hope. Quoted by Ezra Goodman, *The Fifty-Year Decline of Hollywood* (New York: Simon and Schuster, 1961), p. 425.

summary reported by Marie L. Hamilton, "1950's Productions."[11] Hamilton found that films tended to avoid the serious in favor of escapist fare as exemplified by the number of feature films produced in the United States during 1950. He classified by genre and by frequency of production: Drama (53), Comedies (57), Musicals (27), Adventure (26), Melodrama (74), Westerns (88), Documentaries (7) and long Cartoons (2). Hamilton's division of film subjects into categories such as theme (e.g., medical, ethnic, minority problems), milieu (e.g., show business, horse racing), and treatment (e.g., farce, burlesque, fantasy) will indicate further the film's tendency toward stereotyping. One additional value of this study by Hamilton, as Ellis suggests, is that it can provide a model for students to follow in categorizing films shown at local theatres for a particular semester. Students may also categorize films by having access to plot summaries printed in such publications as *Motion Picture Herald, Film Daily,* and the like.[12]

Dorothy B. Jones is another critic who analyzes distortions created in films. Following Dale's work, she concerned herself with how well film reflected reality. Having examined 100 selected films, she found that there were 188 major characters. An analysis of these characters revealed that 66⅔ percent of them were men, half of whom were affluent, and of these only 20 percent were married. Only 20 percent of the male characters were not Americans. A further distortion was the frequency of happy endings. In relation to her findings, Ellis writes

> In terms of Dorothy Jones' hypothesis it is possible to say that film characters do not mirror the demographic features of American population, and we can speculate as to whether the type of wants and the degree of attainment reflect realty.[13]

These early analyses on social content in film and the various distortions presented to the public have been supplemented by various studies on the nature of heroes and heroines in motion pictures. Although they are another form of stereotype, the analysis of the hero and heroine in the film graphs the development of the process of stereotyping.

THE HEROINE[14]

The heroine has changed considerably from her early status in motion pictures. A. J. Alexander did an analysis of the heroine as "the nongenue."

11. Marie L. Hamilton, "1950's Production," *Films in Review* 2, no. 1 (January 1951), 8–9.
12. Jack C. Ellis, "Approaches to Film as an Art Form: Handbook for College Teachers," (Doctoral dissertation, Teachers College, Columbia University, 1955), p. 272, n26.
13. Jack C. Ellis, "Approaches to Film as an Art Form: A Handbook for College Teachers," Doctor of Education Project Report (New York: Teachers College, Columbia University, 1955), p. 273, n29.
14. A useful study to consult is a series of articles by Kevin Gough-Yates: "The

Her distinguishing characteristic is the aspiration to love. In this aspiration she is not only participant and partner, but protagonist. When she assumes tragic grandeur she is a heroine, not according to the restricted definition, "the principal female character in a story," but in the larger sense, "a woman of heroic character, a female hero." In these respects, she is different from all other film conceptions of woman; her distinctions might properly be fixed with the label, "nongenue." And she is different from all other screen conceptions of the hero in that she is thoroughly modern, a brave new woman.[15]

The films that Alexander uses as examples are *Room at the Top, The Fugitive Kind, Hiroshima Mon Amour, Private Property, The Savage Eye, The Lovers,* and *Look Back in Anger.* One of the many helpful techniques in his analysis of stereotypes is the comparison of the stock Hollywood heroines with the new "nongenue." He points out that the stereotyped heroine performs as if in a Victorian morality play. By forsaking the bad boyfriend, she often gains a respectable and loving husband. Doris Day is the prototype of this old-fashioned virgin. The new stock heroine is quite different. She is emancipated. She breaks with conventions, admits the importance of sex, and is concerned with shaping a new morality for herself. Her important function is, according to the films reviewed, "not procreative but creative, not matrix but cynosure-lover."[16]

Bosley Crowther offers another view of stereotyped female heroines. He talks of Hollywood being a "supermarket" where talent is replaced with sensuality. Actresses that have won distinction for their performances—Joanne Woodward, Hope Lange, Lee Remick, Maria Schell, and Geraldine Page—are being ignored because of the industry's desire to cater to its mass audience of teenagers. The new stars are

Shirley MacLaine? She's a calculated nitwit, doomed to eternal immaturity. Doris Day? The perennial childbride, still acting as though she's likely to suck her thumb. Julie Andrews? A delightful young woman who appears typed in wholesome school-marm roles. Natalie Wood? An aging teenager with all the presence of the girl next door.

Then there is the whole range of charm girls—Debbie Reynolds, Jane Fonda, Sandra Dee, Carroll Baker, Carol Lynley, Ann-Margaret, Suzanne Pleshette, Yvette Mimieux. Not one seems much more adult than the alarmingly precocious Hayley Mills.[17]

Heroine—Part One," *Films and Filming* 12, no. 8 (May 1966) : 23–7; "Part Two," *Films and Filming* 12, no. 9 (June 1966) : 27–32; "Part Three," *Films and Filming* 12, no. 10 (July 1966) : 38–43; "Part Four," *Films and Filming* 12, no. 11 (August 1966) : 45–50; see also, Estelle Changas, "Slut, Bitch, Virgin, Mother: The Role of Women in some Recent Films," *Cinema* 6, no. 3 (Spring 1971) : 43–47; and *Take One* 3, no. 2 (November–December 1970) , devoted to "Women in Film."

15. A. J. Alexander, "A Modern Hero: The Nongenue," *Film Culture* 22–23 (Summer 1961) : 81–82.

16. *Ibid.*, pp. 81–82.

17. Bosley Crowther, "Where are the Women?" *New York Times Section* 2 (Sunday, January 23, 1966) , p. 11.

Another analysis of the stereotyped image of woman discussed the role of females in society and its effect upon screen versions. John Howard Lawson, writing from a vitriolic point of view, attacks the political and economic factors for the subservient position of women in our society.

> Cultural attitudes toward women reflect the *mores* of capitalism. These *mores* are not shaped by sentiment, literary artifice, or the arrogance of the "male animal." The frustrations of the middle class woman do not originate within the walls of her home; the petty occupations which paralyze her personal development are her small part of the toll exacted from her working class sisters. The root of the woman question must be sought in the system of production, which holds women in reserve as a potential threat to the wages of men, or employs them at a lower rate in order to reduce the whole level of wages. . . . Hollywood treats "glamor" and sex appeal as the sum-total of woman's personality.[18]

Lawson goes on to say that portraits of woman in Hollywood films are of three kinds: the criminal type or the one who starts the trouble; the perennial loser in the battle of the sexes; and the sexual dream wish of lustful males.[19]

Admitting that the types are not mutually exclusive, Lawson cites films such as *Leave Her to Heaven, The Lady Gambles, Without Warning, Rachel, Westward the Women, All About Eve, Las Vegas Story, Lydia Bailey, Moulin Rouge,* and *A Streetcar Named Desire* as some examples of how women are stereotyped in motion pictures. He notes an increasing emphasis on sadism, tending to make criminal conduct attractive and justifiable; a continued use of sexual promiscuity and homosexuality as appeals to the audience's emotions; and a preference for having women assume the responsibility for the ill treatment they receive because of their having aroused the male's baser instincts.

Probably the most extensive analysis on the stereotyping of men and women in films was done by Martha Wolfenstein and Nathan Leites in *Movies: A Psychological Study.* The authors examined the content of 166 American "A" movies released in New York after September 1, 1945 and then compared them with French and British films that the authors decided were typical products of the country. Two major weaknesses in the method are, first, their failure to recognize the importance of the motion picture code in determining the stereotypes described; and second, the danger in confusing subject matter with its effect on the audience.

In their study the authors point out that "Day-dreams contain clues to deeper-lying, less articulate aspirations, fears and wishes."[20] They believe that the protagonist in fiction is the symbolization of a common daydream

---

18. John Howard Lawson, *Film in the Battle of Ideas* (New York: Masses and Mainstream, 1953), pp. 60–61.
19. *Ibid.,* p. 62.
20. Martha Wolfenstein and Nathan Leites, *Movies: A Psychological Study* (New York: Free Press, 1950), p. 11. Reissued in 1970 by Arno Press.

and it is an image that the audience can relate to.[21] When people share a common culture, it is not unlikely that they also share common daydreams. The authors present an analysis of films made in the 1940s to see how the industry treated the recurrent "day-dreams which enter into the consciousness of millions of movie-goers."[22] Some of their conclusions reached are (1) the problem in American films concerning love was how to make it interesting while at the same time get it past the censors;[23] (2) there was a tendency to depict protagonists in American films as free agents and not restricted by family ties;[24] (3) violence was shown as a threat from the outside, rather than from within one's emotions and stability;[25] (4) there was a preoccupation with showing a conflict between what appeared to be bad and what was "really" bad, between the reality and the illusion of a person's actions and appearance. In this last category, the reader will find available in *Mass Culture* an analysis of what Wolfenstein and Leites call the "Good-Bad Girl;"[26] that is, the device of having Hollywood's heroines appear "bad" at the beginning of the film, but showing them to be "good" by the end. One outstanding film, fortunately available, that illustrates this thesis is Howard Hawks's *The Big Sleep* (Warners—16mm: 1946, 114 min., b/w, sound, R-AUD, CON, IDE, UAS, WIL), a story about a good-bad girl's relationship with a gangster and a murderer.

THE HERO

In addition to the many types of stereotyped heroines, we can find a stock collection of film heroes.[27] The most extensive analysis on the stereotyping of the hero is Kevin Gough-Yates's "The Hero," a series of four articles in *Films and Filming* on the major and minor motion picture heroes. Gough-Yates in his initial article points out that every culture creates and perpetuates stereotypes. Appropriately, costumes or the selection of the actor will immediately identify for the audience the forces of good and evil. While there are many reasons for individuals' becoming heroic in films and thereby creating many types of outstanding characters, all heroes have one thing in common: "They are all developments of or reactions to the traditional concept of the Epic hero, although they may have other characteristics in addition." The stereotyped Epic hero always defends a way of life, as evi-

21. *Ibid.*, p. 11.
22. *Ibid.*, p. 12.
23. *Ibid.*, p. 19.
24. *Ibid.*, p. 134.
25. Martha Wolfenstein and Nathan Leites, *Movies*, p. 176.
26. Martha Wolfenstein and Nathan Leites, "The Good-Bad Girl," *Mass Culture: The Popular Arts in America*, pp. 294–307.
27. Also useful in this connection is Clifford Odets, "The Transient Olympian: The Psychology of the Male Movie Star," *Show* (April 1963): 106–7; 130–33. Reprinted in *Sight, Sound and Society: Motion Pictures and Television in America*, pp. 186–200.

denced in such film epics as *The Longest Day, El Cid, Shane, The Last Train From Gunhill* and *Battleship Potemkin.*[28]

In the second article the author begins by identifying the Epic hero as that character in a film who embodies those factors which suggest divine destiny. The standard characterizations of the Epic hero are these: he usually has a mysterious past, is in search of an ideal, and is driven by fate toward an inevitable end. Gough-Yates then goes on to compare the Epic hero with a second stereotype in film: the Romantic or Byronic hero. This type of figure, driven by his desires, does not have the assurance of success characteristic of the Epic hero. Three other differences are that the Byronic character often has misguided ambitions, the Epic one does not; the former exists in any movie setting, the latter populates mostly historical films; and usually the Byronic hero fails in the end, which is not the case with the Epic type. "Because the Epic hero and his variants symbolize the inevitable, the Byronic hero can not succeed. If he does, he must be shown to have only apparent victory."[29]

In the third article, Gough-Yates concerns himself with heroes who have no desire for glory. They are neither Epic nor Romantic, but usually want to be left alone to follow their humble pursuits. Always these people are confronted with a particular moral decision. "They can choose one line of behavior or another, but whatever they decide makes their moral decision clear." They will then be evaluated by the choice they make and the manner in which it is handled. This hero becomes what Gough-Yates calls the Beidermeier hero, an average person who is forced to assert himself. This hero cannot, usually, control the force of destiny and rarely sees himself as performing significant acts, unlike the Epic and Romantic hero. In the end, all he desires is to return to his former, domesticated life.[30]

In the final article, Gough-Yates summarizes his previous work and introduces two new types of heroes.

There are two kinds of hero, however, who cause their own downfall or earn their condemnation by inaction. The first is the Anti-hero who refuses to adopt any kind of heroic attitude. He is the person who is apathetic or a coward. By implication he associates himself with the tyrant or bully. The second is the hero who begins from a virtually identical position to that of the potential Epic hero. Because of his human failings, he vacillates or suffers the consequences of his weakness by falling from a position of some stature.[31]

These Tragic heroes generally die, and the viewer is always made aware of

28. Kevin Gough-Yates, "The Hero: Part I," *Films and Filming* 12, no. 3 (December 1965) : 11–16.
29. Kevin Gough-Yates, "The Hero Part II," *Films and Filming* 12, no. 4 (January 1966) : 11–16.
30. Kevin Gough-Yates, "The Hero," *Films and Filming* 12, no. 5 (February 1966) : 25–30.
31. Kevin Gough-Yates, "The Hero." *Films and Filming* 12, no. 6 (March 1966) : 25.

their tragic flaws. The author concludes by suggesting that the climax of films generally tells the viewer what type of hero has been depicted.

The stereotyped myths about the heroes and heroines of film have long been a source of concern to film critic Parker Tyler. In his *The Hollywood Hallucination,* Tyler observes that films have a mythological basis as the result of " (a) the existence of the unconscious mind as a dynamic factor in human action, and (b) the tendency of the screen stories to emphasize—unintentionally—neuroses and psychopathic traits discovered and formulated by psychoanalysis."[32] To put it another way, he believes that the movie theater acts as the psychoanalytic clinic for the average person's waking dreams. In a later book, *Magic and Myth of the Movies,* he gives a provocative analysis of several films that teachers might find useful for study in class: *The Grapes of Wrath* (Fox—16mm: 1940, 128 min., b/w, sound, R-CON, FNC, MMA) ; *Arsenic and Old Lace* (Warners—16mm: 1944, 110 min., b/w, sound, R-UAS) , and *A Walk in the Sun* (Fox—16mm: 1945, 117 min., b/w, sound, R-ROA, WHO) . Tyler makes no assertion that these are the most artistic films. His point is that they represent the types of stereotyped myths usually presented on the screen.

SOCIAL DISTORTIONS

Having considered stereotyped images of men and women, let's now turn our attention to the stock responses to social attitudes. Some of the most popular pictures presented to the public concern Big Business, class systems, teenage problems, social institutions, and social problems in general.[33] Often the film's stereotypes reflect the times in which they are made.

One example of distortions that reflect the period in which they are presented is the stereotyped image of Big Business. As Eric Larrabee and David Reisman hypothesize

The Temper of the Times toward business can be read on numerous barometers, but few of them are as legible as the fictional and dramatic arts—where popular images are projected twice life-size, and the public attitudes and assumptions are converted into "stories." Business is not always shown here at its best; thus the demands of Allan Nevins, Edward N. Saveth, John Chamberlain, and others for a more favorable treatment of business life in history and in novels. Yet of all the media the most massive and the most revealing are not books but the movies, and recently it is to them that observers who look for a rapprochement between the world of business and the world of the arts and intellect have turned. If the

32. Parker Tyler, *The Hollywood Hallucination,* Introduction by Richard Schickel (New York: Simon and Schuster, 1970) , p. xvi.
33. A good example is William Sloan's article, "Two Sides of the Civil Rights Coin: A Discussion of *Troublemakers* and *A Time for Burning," Film Comment* 4, nos. 2 and 3 (Fall–Winter 1967) : 54–56.

images of business have been changing, it is on the screen that their new shapes will soon appear.[34]

Using the movie *Executive Suite* (MGM—16mm: 1954, 104 min., b/w, sound, R-FNC) as an example of the most obvious and the most revealing use of a business background, the authors point out the distortions involved over executive warfare in a furniture corporation. The stereotyped hero becomes a neutral engineer, who was once shown in films as hard and insensitive but who has now been spoiled and adulterated by power. Innocence and uninvolvement are replaced in the hero's climb to the Executive Suite by shrewdness and aggressiveness. Big business is portrayed as an arena where the forces of good and evil are arrayed against each other in the common events of daily management.

There are also stereotyped myths that interfere with our understanding of various economic classes. Geoffrey Nowell-Smith analyzes the general tendency for us "to see things under a mythical aspect—using the word 'myth' fairly loosely to cover the generalized images or ideas one has of things, ideas which are mythical only insofar as they are a substitute for direct knowledge or experience."[35] He points out that we must either accept or reject myths on a logical and not a moral basis. For him, myths represent lies which are the enemies of reason and truth. He cites as an example the film *Saturday Night and Sunday Morning* (Britain—16mm: 1961, 90 min., b/w, sound, R-WRS), the story of a young factory worker who spends his free time in the local bar, where he gets drunk, fights, and plays practical jokes. Middle-class viewers saw this movie, so Nowell-Smith explains, as the realistic expression of the working-class, while the working-class identified in a more limited sense with the type of ideal they desired, but were unable or afraid to do so because of moral or material reasons.

Another type of stereotyping deals with teenage problems and is subtly presented to the public by means of "realistic" films, movies that supposedly present life as it really is. Some examples, as analyzed by Robert Brustein, are films like *On the Waterfront* (Columbia—16mm: 1954, 108 min., b/w, sound, R-AUD, CCC, CON, CWF, ICS, IDE, NAT, ROA, SWA, TWF, TWY, WHO/L-COL): *The Goddess* (Columbia—16mm: 1958, 105 min., b/w, sound, R-AUD, IDE), *A Hatful of Rain* (Fox—16mm: 1958, 115 min., b/w, sound, R-FNC)., and *Edge of the City* (MGM—16mm: 1957, 85 min., b/w, sound, R-FNC). Brustein points out that these films follow a formula: one that is centered around Zolaesque naturalism, method acting, and an

34. Eric Larrabee and David Reisman, "Company Town Pastoral: The Role of Big Business in *Executive Suite*." *Mass Culture: The Popular Arts in America*, edited by Bernard Rosenberg and David Manning White (New York: The Free Press, 1957), p. 425.

35. Geoffrey Nowell-Smith, "Movie and Myth," *Sight and Sound* 32, no. 2 (Spring 1963): 60.

anti-hero. The films have only changed the luxurious settings from the unrealistic pictures of the past to "shanty-town slums in rotting southern or northern towns, the costumes, apparently acquired no longer from Main-bocher but from the surplus stores of the Salvation Army, hang on the actors as dashing as skivvies on a scarecrow."[36] Brustein feels that this change occurred because Hollywood considers the majority of its audience to be teenagers and panders to the adolescent's interest in films depicting his problems and his generation.

The principle has not changed since then as evidenced by such recent films on student rebellion as *The Strawberry Statement, If . . ., The Prime of Miss Jean Brodie, RPM, Getting Straight* and *Move.* The stereotyped images used in these films are no more honestly presented than those previously discussed.

Further examples of stereotyping are the filmic treatments of various professions.[37] Many of us can cite pictures which have portrayed "mad scientists," "tranquil pipe-smoking, idealistic, shabbily-dressed professors," and "materialistic doctors." One useful analysis of such stereotyping is presented by Daniel Rosenblatt, in which he lists the five major film treatments of psychoanalysis and mental illness:

(1) Psychosis as gothic excitement: sex, violence, murder, suicide . . . . . . (2) The psychiatrist as hero-villain (Negative transference, fear) . . . (3) The analyst as comic-relief (Negative transference, belittling . . . (4) Psychoanalytic Romanticism (Positive Transference) and (5) Finally we reach the current period of *Maturity.* Psychoanalysis is a technique which can be utilized in the treatment of the emotionally disturbed. The analyst is a kindly, 'warm' human being who has solved almost all of his personal problems, although he has a few, lovable failings. He smokes a pipe, wears glasses, no longer has a beard and is either a Jew or a Negro. Rod Steiger in *The Mark,* Sidney Poitier in The Linder-Kornfield *Pressure Point.*[38]

Some films which can be used to illustrate Rosenblatt's viewpoint are *David and Lisa* (Continental—16mm: 1962, 94 min., b/w, sound, R-WRS) ; and *Freud* (Universal—16mm: 1962, 140 min., b/w, sound, R-CCC, ROA, TFC, UNI, WHO/L-UNI) .

In addition, there are stereotypes that involve social situations. Here the

36. Robert Brustein. "The New Hollywood: Myth and Anti-Myth," *Film Quarterly* 13, no. 3 (Spring 1959) : 23. See also Leslie Halliwell, "America: The Celluloid Myth— Part One," *Films and Filming* 14, no. 1 (October 1967) : 12–16; Leslie Halliwell, "America: The Celluloid Myth—Part Two," *Films and Filming* 14, no. 2 (November 1967) : 10–14.
37. Other examples are the following: Edward Connor, "Angels on the Screen," *Films in Review* 9, no. 9 (August–September 1958) : 375–79; Jack Spears, "Baseball on the Screen," *Films in Review* 14, no. 4 (April 1968) : 198–217; Edward Connor, "Demons on the Screen," *Films in Review* 10, no. 2 (February 1959) : 68–77; Jack Spears, "The Doctor on the Screen," *Films in Review* 6, no. 9 (November 1955) : 436–44; Dr. Paul Bradlow, "Two . . . But not of a Kind: A Comparison of Two Controversial Documentaries About Mental Illness—*Warrendale* and *Titicut Follies,*" *Film Comment* 5, no. 3 (Fall 1969) : 60–61.
38. Daniel Rosenblatt, "Dreams in the Dream Factory," *Film Society* 1 (1963) : 33–34.

distortions are usually created by socially conscious directors. Penelope Houston cites four examples of such stereotyping, which were directed against the established stock images of society's sacrosanct institutions. First there were the Courts. In a film like *Trial* (MGM—16mm: 1955, 105 min., b/w, sound, R-FNC) , a murder trial becomes the vehicle for showing the ineffectiveness of our legal system and the danger from corrupt policemen who would rather rig a jury than lose an important and highly publicized case. Second, the police come under attack in a number of movies, in particular *The Desperate Hours* (Paramount—16mm: 1955, 112 min., b/w, sound, R-FNC) . Here we see the possible danger in asking help from law enforcement officials who might willingly turn a dangerous situation into a shooting match so as to gain votes in the next election. Third, the schools are criticized. *The Blackboard Jungle* (MGM—16mm: 1955, 101 min., b/w, sound, R-FNC) is used to show how difficult teaching conditions are increased by the apathy and incompetence of the staff. *Rebel Without A Cause* (Warners—16mm: 1955, 111 min., b/w, sound, R-AUD, CCC, CHA, CWF, IDE, NAT, ROA, SWA, TWF, TWY, WHO/L-WSA) is another instance where apathy allows juvenile gangsterism to operate in an ordinary secondary school. Finally there is the family itself. Again, *Rebel Without A Cause* serves as a useful illustration of how an unhappy and sick marriage further helps to complicate the lives of young people and force them into juvenile delinquency.[39]

Stereotyping also is seen in the treatment of social problems in society. Donald Lloyd Fernow, in a content analysis of social problems treated in the film up to 1952, categorized four major topics: International Relations, Economic Problems, Political Issues,[40] and Sociological Problems.[41] In his introduction, Fernow explained that the increasing complexities of living in a technological age, the danger of nuclear war, and the communication crisis among people everywhere have only intensified the need for everyone to become free from prejudice and ignorance. Under each of the four topics, he has subheadings: for example, under Sociological Problems are the following: (a) Minority Problems, and (b) The Ostracized or Stigmatized Individual. He gives further subdivisions: for example, under Minority Problems are (1) Races and Nationalities—i) Negro, ii) Oriental, iii) Indian, iv) Mexican, v) Others—and (2) Religious—i) Jewish, ii) Protestant, iii) Catholic. He concluded, in connection with this area, by stating

---

39. Penelope Houston, "Rebels Without Causes," *Sight and Sound* 25, no. 4 (Spring 1956) : 179. Other useful articles are Lionel Godfrey, "Because They're Young—Part One," *Films and Filming* 14, no. 1 (October 1967) : 42–48; Lionel Godfrey, "Part Two," *Films and Filming* 14, no. 2 (November 1967) : 40–45; and Robin Bean and David Austen, "USA: Confidential," *Films and Filming* 15, no. 2 (November 1968) : 16–28.

40. Read Raymond Durgnat, "Vote for Britain: A Cinemagoer's Guide to the General Election—Part One," *Films and Filming* 10, no. 7 (April 1964) : 9–14; Raymond Durgnat, "Part Two," *Films and Filming* 10, no. 8 (May 1964) : 10–15; and Raymond Durgnat, "Part Three," *Films and Filming* 10, no. 9 (June 1964) : 38–43.

41. A useful essay is Peter John Dyer, "American Young in Uproar," *Films and Filming* 5, no. 12 (September 1959) : 10–12, 32–37.

One of the characteristics of prejudice has been the categorizing of individuals within a group as a well delineated stereotype. The perpetuation of such stereotypes, in some instances over centuries, has frequently served the purposes of nefarious parties and further enhanced bigotry with its concomitant intolerance.[42]

Nevertheless, he found that Hollywood's treatment of Jews prior to World War I was sympathetic and compassionate. Between the wars, little attention was given to religious intolerance because the film industry considered it too touchy an area. After the Second World War, filmmakers sensed the public's desire to see films dealing with religious themes. As a result, two of the best films on anti-Semitism appeared in 1947; *Crossfire* (RKO—16mm: 1947, 85 min., b/w, sound, R-MMA) depicted the murder of a Jewish ex-GI while at the same time hitting hard at religious prejudice. Probably one of the best films to date on religious prejudice is *Gentleman's Agreement* (Fox—16mm: 1947, 118 min., b/w, sound, R-FNC), a story of a Protestant journalist posing as a Jew for six months, which exposed the evils and viciousness of anti-Semitism.

In his conclusion, Fernow wrote:

Those entertainment films depicting a social problem which have exercized the greatest influence have been those which have been the most popular with the audiences. Good drama with a well-defined story line and genuine characters, presented with deftness and artistry usually carry a social message to the audience with compelling poignancy and credibility. A social problem implies a social need for reform to allay it. This can best be done by the motion picture, through engendering in the public an awareness of the problem's existence and instilling in them a sense of responsibility to take rational action to correct it. An entertaining story whose characters are real, genuine people, which is told with sincerity and honesty, and which clearly and definitely presents its case is the best vehicle for accomplishing this purpose.[43]

As an example of film stereotyping at its worst, let us look at the treatment of black people in American movies.[44]

THE AFRO-AMERICAN IN HOLLYWOOD FILMS

The movies help shape our attitudes and opinions about people and nowhere can America's prejudice against Afro-Americans be more clearly seen than in the commercial cinema's ugly history of grotesque stereotypes of black citizens. A summary of those distasteful images is presented in Arun

42. Donald Lloyd Fernow, "The Treatment of Social Problems in the Entertainment Film" (Master's thesis, University of Southern California, 1952), pp. 114–15.
43. Donald Lloyd Fernow, "Treatment of Social Problems," p. 180.
44. Although not concerned primarily with film, a book useful for the study of *all* stereotypes is Orrin E. Klapp, *Heroes, Villains, and Fools: The American Character.* Englewood Cliffs, N.J.: Prentice-Hall, Inc., 1962.

Kumar Chaudhuri's Master's Thesis, which was concerned with the treatment of Negroes in the film from 1902 to 1950:

> A chronological overview of the Negro in the motion picture reveals that from its inception it has used the Negro in a stereotyped derogatory manner or as a means of "poking fun" and giving the general public incorrect ideas on the life and character of the group. Picturization of the Negro, for the most part, has been represented by the following stereotyped personalities up to World War II: clown, clod-hopper, scarecrow, stupid individual, devoted slave who "knows his place," and an "Uncle Tom"—submissive, servile. White actors, at first, were "made up" to perform the role of these types of characterization. After World War I Negro actors were employed to portray roles which represented them as being afraid of the dark, ghosts, police, and animals; or either as lazy or greedy individuals. The Landmark in the film in its relation to the Negro came with the production of "Emperor Jones" in which a Negro was the star and white characters assumed the less important roles; some progress was also shown in the production of "Arrowsmith" which gave the Negro a fair representation.[45]

No one denies that such derogatory images have been used, but the reasons for their being and the effects they have had on a world population are not generally known or understood. For that alone, it would be useful to trace the "origins" of black screen images.[46]

Starting with the first primitive films in the 1890s, black people were used for comic relief. At first, any key parts, comedy or otherwise, were done by white actors in black-face. Slowly, blacks were assimilated into the movie business, but almost always in grotesque parodies of their race. Black production companies and black-owned theaters were nonexistent and a black audience found great difficulty in forming a strong, cohesive voice.

The major treatment accorded Afro-Americans in films is best reflected, until 1915, in *The Birth of a Nation*. Griffith's artistic masterpiece is the work of a white supremacist who tried to show how black people, unless they had paternal white leaders, were incapable of governing themselves or controlling their passions. Lewis Jacobs accurately lists the naive and ignorant images that Griffith projected in 1915:

> The film was a passionate and persuasive avowal of the inferiority of the Negro. In viewpoint it was, surely narrow and prejudiced. Griffith's Southern upbringing made him completely sympathetic toward Dixon's exaggerated ideas, and the fire of his convictions gave the film rude strength. At one point in the picture a title bluntly editorialized that the South must be made "safe" for the whites. The entire portrayal of the Reconstruction days showed the Negro, when freed from white domina-

---

45. Arun Kumar Chaudhuri, "A Study of the Negro Problem in Motion Pictures," (Master's thesis, University of Southern California, 1951), pp. 92–93.

46. A more detailed study is being prepared by the author and will be published in 1973, tentatively entitled *Black Projections: The History of the Black American Film* (Englewood Cliffs, N.J.: Prentice-Hall, Inc., 1973).

tion, as arrogant, lustful, villainous. Negro congressmen were pictured drinking heavily, coarsely reclining in Congress with bare feet upon their desks, lustfully ogling the white women in the balcony. Gus, the Negro servant, is depicted as a renegade when he joins the emancipated Negroes. His advances on Flora, and Lynch's proposal to Elsie Stoneman, are overdrawn to make the Negro appear obnoxious and audacious. The Negro servants who remain with the Camerons, on the other hand, are treated with patronizing regard for their faithfulness. The necessity for the separation of Negro from white, with the white as the ruler, is passionately maintained throughout the film.[47]

Not only are these stereotypes the outgrowth of isolated incidents in the Reconstruction Period, but they appear on the screen and in the minds of the audience as evidence of widespread facts about life in the South everywhere and any time slaves are given authority between 1865 and 1873.[48]

There can be little doubt of the influence that the film had on future portrayals of the Negro. Ralph Ellison, for example, writes:

In the struggle against Negro freedom, motion pictures have been one of the strongest instruments for justifying some white Americans' anti-Negro attitudes and practices. Thus the South, through D. W. Griffith's genius, captured the enormous myth-making potential of the film form almost from the beginning. While the Negro stereotypes by no means made all white men Klansmen the cinema did, to the extent that audiences accepted its image of Negroes, made them participants in the South's racial ritual of keeping the Negro "in his place."[49]

The effect of the film's characters was revealed in the black people stereotyped in movies during the twenties. These motion pictures, depicting all Afro-Americans as clods or brutes, helped impress the white audience, as Peter Noble puts it, with the general idea that Negroes belonged in African jungles "and certainly not in 'civilized' America, where they could count themselves lucky even to be tolerated by the whites."[50]

Walter Lippmann has also commented upon the film's negative effect:

Historically it may be the wrong shape, morally it may be a pernicious shape, but it is a shape, and I doubt whether anyone who has seen the

47. Lewis Jacobs, *The Rise of the American Film: A Critical History*. With an essay "Experimental Cinema in America 1921–1947" (New York: Teachers College, Columbia University, 1968), p. 177.

48. For a more liberal interpretation of the Reconstruction Period, the reader may consult Kenneth M. Stampp, *The Era of Reconstruction 1865–1877* (New York: Alfred A. Knopf, 1965). Also helpful is Charles L. Hutchins, "A Critical Evaluation of the Controversies Engendered by D. W. Griffith's *Birth of a Nation*" (Master's thesis, University of Iowa, 1961).

49. Ralph Ellison, "Shadow and Act," *Shadow and Act* (New York: Random House, 1964), p. 276. Another excellent analysis of the effect is Thomas R. Cripps, "The Reaction of the Negro to *The Birth of a Nation*," *The Historian* 25, no. 3 (May 1963): 344–62. Reprinted in the Bobbs-Merrill Reprint Series in Black Studies BC-57.

50. Peter Noble, *The Negro in Films* (London: Skelton Robinson, 1950), p. 44. Reissued by Arno Press, 1970.

film and does not know more about the Ku Klux Klan than Mr. Griffith, will hear the name again without seeing these white horsemen.[51]

Lippmann's point of view is reinforced by the findings of Ruth Peterson and L. I. Thurstone,[52] who reported that some children developed negative attitudes toward Afro-Americans as a result of seeing *Birth of a Nation.*

To counteract these attitudes and at the same time provide black performers with demanding roles as well as giving Afro-American audiences a meaningful film experience, a number of independent black production companies came into existence. The most famous were the Lincoln Motion Picture Company, which began in 1916, and the Micheaux Film Company, which started in 1924. The former was run and operated by George and Noble Johnson; the latter by Oscar Micheaux, often referred to as "the Father of the Black Cinema."

The black companies found a welcome audience in the late teens and early 1920s, until a series of economic and technical events forced many of the production heads out of business. With the coming of sound, movies about and with black performers became primarily the responsibility of white filmmakers.

The next major milestone was passed in 1929 with the production of the first all-black film, *Hallelujah* (MGM—16mm: 1929, 107 min., b/w, sound, R-FNC). Director King Vidor claimed that his primary concern was in presenting an objective treatment of the Negro. Just how much his aim missed is pointed out by Jacobs. "The film turned out . . . to be a melo-dramatic piece replete with all the conventionalities of the white man's conception of the spiritual-singing, crap-shooting Negro."[53] Rotha comments that "The Negro was portrayed in a vacuum. Because his position in white society was never referred to, his behavior appeared to arise from his own nature rather than from environmental pressures."[54] However, it can at least be said of Vidor that his intentions were honorable, if ineffectual.

Films like *Hallelujah* rarely questioned the accepted images of blacks. The few Afro-American production companies around decided to accept those images as box-office values and made movies that imitated white standards and interpretations. Interestingly, light-skinned blacks got the best parts. (The assumption was that whiteness was the standard for excellence and the closer you came the better you were.)

This was the period in which some of Hollywood's finest and most controversial black film characters appeared: e.g., Stepin Fetchit, Willie Best,

51. Walter Lippmann, "Stereotypes," *Thought and Statement,* Second Edition, edited by William G. Leary and James Steel Smith (New York: Harcourt, Brace and World, 1960) , p. 228.
52. Ruth Peterson and L. I. Thurstone, *Motion Pictures and Social Attitudes of Children* (New York: The Macmillan Company, 1933) , p. 166.
53. Lewis Jacobs, *The Rise of The American Film,* p. 458.
54. Paul Rotha and Richard Griffith, *The Film Till Now* (New York: Vision Press, 1960) , p. 471.

Eddie "Rochester" Anderson, Mantan Moreland and Clarence Muse. Another controversial aspect of the period was the arbitrary way in which regional censors banned entirely films that presented, in the local censoring bodies' point of view, an insulting image, theme, or story. One such movie was The Emperor Jones (Krimsky-Cochran—16mm: 1933, 80 min., b/w, sound, R-RAD/S-RAD), which starred Paul Robeson[55] and Fredi Washington.

Beginning in the early 1940s, new black film interests and personalities gained recognition and fame, including Lena Horne,[56] Ethel Waters,[57] and the American Negro Theater in Harlem.

Studies tracing the rise of these new and significant performers during World War II and into the present are sparse.[58] The best work to date is Peter Noble's The Negro in Film, which covers the history of the black man in film up to 1948. He is particularly good for his handling of the stereotypes created by Stepin Fetchit, "Snowball," and "Sleep n' Eat." These were the performers who created the image for the American public

> that the American Negro was a happy, laughing dancing imbecile with permanently rolling eyes and widespread, empty grin. In films too numerous to mention actors like Fetchit demeaned themselves, bringing Negro dignity to its lowest common denominator.[59]

Another interesting study is V. J. Jerome's The Negro in Hollywood Films[60] which is a left-winger's analysis of the first major group of films concerning the Afro-American problem in our society. Considerable written material can be found about the following films: Home of the Brave (United Artists—16mm: 1949, 88 min., b/w, sound, R-AUD, CHA, CON, FCE, IDE, NAT, TWY, WHO, WIL/L-UEI), a war story in the Pacific that revolves around soldiers' feelings about a Negro comrade; Lost Boundaries (de Rochemont—16mm: 1949, 97 min., b/w, sound, R-WSA), the story of a light-skinned Negro doctor who passes for white; Pinky (Fox—16mm: 1949, 102 min., b/w, sound, R-FNC), the story of a Negro girl who passes for

55. For the best available information on Paul Robeson, see Arnold Schlosser, "Paul Robeson: His Career in the Theatre, in Motion Pictures, and On the Concert Stage" (Ph.D. thesis, New York University, 1970).

56. *Lena Horne and Richard Schickel, Lena (New York: Signet Books, 1965).

57. *Ethel Waters with Charles Samuels, His Eye is on the Sparrow: An Autobiography (New York: Doubleday and Company, 1951).

58. A useful article on the growth of the black film industry is Thomas R. Cripps, "Black Films and Film Makers: Movies in the Ghetto, B. P. (Before Poitier)," Negro Digest 18, no. 4 (February 1969) : 21–48. Reprinted in the Bobbs-Merrill Reprint Series in Black Studies BC-55. Also helpful are Langston Hughes and Milton Meltzer, Black Magic: A Pictorial History of the Negro in American Entertainment (Englewood Cliffs, N.J.: Prentice-Hall, Inc., 1967); William Lee Burke, "The Presentation of the American Negro in Hollywood Films, 1946–1961: an Analysis of a Selected Sample of Feature Films," Ph.D. thesis, Northwestern University, 1965); and Singer Alfred Buchanan, "A Study of the Attitudes of Writers of the Negro Press Toward the Depiction of the Negro in Plays and Films: 1930–1965," (Ph.D. thesis, University of Michigan, 1968).

59. Peter Noble, The Negro in Films, p. 49.

60. V. J. Jerome, The Negro in Hollywood Films (New York: Masses and Mainstream, 1950).

white; and *Intruder in the Dust* (MGM—16mm: 1949, 87 min., b/w, sound, R-FNC), the story of a southern Negro accused of murdering a white man.

Jerome takes the filmmakers to task for what he considers to be the shoddy way in which these films treat their themes. He argues that the movies are a box-office concession to a socially conscious public, but really distort the problems involved. In connection with Jerome's pamphlet, the reader should study Ralph Ellison's excellent treatment of the same films in his essay "The Shadow and the Act." Ellison argues that the movies represent the white man's changing attitude toward the Negro, as evidenced by the fact that the motion pictures manifest basic and uncomfortable negative attitudes toward Negroes:

> Are Negroes cowardly soldiers? (*Home of the Brave*) ; are Negroes the real polluters of the South? (*Intruder in the Dust*) ; have mulatto Negroes the right to pass as white, at the risk of having black babies, or if they have white-skinned children of having to kill off their "white" identities by revealing to them that they are, alas, Negroes? (*Lost Boundaries*) ; and finally, should Negro girls marry white men or—wonderful non sequitur— should they help their race? (*Pinky*).[61]

As Ellison rightly points out, these films are about what white people think of Negroes, and not about Negroes themselves.

Two other useful analyses can be helpful in appraising recent movies on the Afro-American. Albert Johnson's "Beige, Brown, or Black,"[62] is an analysis of films such as *Island in the Sun* (Fox—16mm: 1957, 119 min., color, cinemascope, sound, R-FNC), a study of miscegenation; the remake of *Imitation of Life* (Universal—16mm: 1959, 124 min., color, sound, R-CCC, TFC, UNI, WHO), the story of an individual who is able to pass as white; and *The World, the Flesh and the Devil* (MGM—16mm: 1959, 95 min., b/w, sound, R-FNC), the story of the sole surviving Negro alive in New York City after an atomic attack who is soon joined by two white survivors. Johnson concludes that the theme of interracialism as exemplified in the films is "vague, inconclusive and undiscussed."[63]

A more recent study done by Johnson, "The Negro in American Films: Some Recent Works,"[64] discusses *One Potato, Two Potato* (Cinema V— 16mm: 1965, 92 min., b/w, sound, R-CAL, CCC, CHA, CON, CWF, ROA, SWA, TFC, TWF, TWY, WHO/L-TWF), a story of miscegenation, again; *Paris Blues* (United Artists—16mm: 1961, 98 min., b/w, sound, R-UAS), an account of American expatriate jazzmen; *Lilies of the Field* (United Artists—16mm: 1963, 97 min., b/w, sound, R-AIM, AUD, IDE), an over-

61. Ralph Ellison, "Shadow and Act," p. 277.
62. Albert Johnson, "Beige, Brown or Black," *Film Quarterly*, 13 (Fall 1959) : 38–43.
63. *Ibid.*, p. 43.
64. Albert Johnson, "The Negro in American Films: Some Recent Works," *Film Quarterly* 18, no. 4 (Summer 1965) : 14–30. By way of comparison, read Sidney Harmon, "How Hollywood is Smashing the Colour Bar," *Films and Filming* 5, no. 6 (March 1959) : 7, 30.

rated attempt to show the Negro as "he really is"; *Pressure Point* (United Artists—16mm: 1962, 89 min., b/w, sound, R-CHA, UAS), a story of a pseudo-intellectual struggle between a Negro psychiatrist in a Federal prison and a white prisoner; *Guns of the Trees* (Jonas Mekas—16mm: n.d., 75 min., b/w, sound, R-FMC), a portrayal of the Afro-American in urban society; and *The Cool World* (Shirley Clarke—16mm: 1964, 90 min., b/w, sound, R-OST/S-OST), an account of troubles among Harlem's young people. Johnson's essay ends with some valuable suggestions about the types of Negro films that should be made in order to create more positive impressions. He argues, for example, that the biographies of outstanding black intellectuals who were ahead of their time should be filmed; that documentaries should be made on the paradoxical relationships existing between blacks and whites; and that black film roles must become more sophisticated.

Ever since the strong human rights movement began in the early 1960s, black films have gotten a stronger hold on longevity. Today audiences are familiar with a host of key personalities such as Sidney Poitier, Harry Belafonte, Gordon Parks, Richard Roundtree, Godfrey Cambridge, Ossie Davis, Ruby Dee, Diana Sands, Ivan Dixon, Melvin Van Peebles, Sammy Davis, Jr., James Earl Jones, Roscoe Lee Browne, Woody Strode and many, many others. Outside the established system, independent filmmakers and those just starting out in ghetto film workshops across the nation offer us signs of a strong, healthy cinema.

Students will find that the most up-to-date bibliography is Edward Mapp's recent book, which focuses attention mainly on black production in the 1960s.[65]

In my opinion, the best film about blacks made up to 1970 is *Nothing But A Man* (Cinema V—16mm: 1963, 92 min., b/w, sound, R-ADF, AUD/L-CCM). Although Michael Roemer and Robert Young are both white men, they have been the only filmmakers operating in the commercial cinema to dare portray in sensitive and humane terms the struggle of a young black couple in a segregated society. The film is somewhat dated by the absence of any statement of the radical black position at the end of the sixties, but Ivan Dixon and Abbey Lincoln give two of the strongest Afro-American performances in the history of black screen images.[66]

The point to glean from these brief comments is that the public influences the kinds of film images that movies project. The Afro-American has been and continues to be distorted on the screen because an ignorant and prejudiced audience remains visually illiterate about the types presented and the effects such stereotypes have on our imagination.

---

65. Edward Mapp, *Blacks in American Films: Today and Yesterday* (Metuchen, N.J.: The Scarecrow Press, Inc., 1972).

66. Frank Manchel, "Film Study: *Nothing But a Man*," *Media and Methods* 4, no. 2 (October 1967): 10–13; Frank Manchel, "Movies and Man's Humanity," *Teaching The Humanities: Selected Readings* edited by Sheila Schwartz (New York: Macmillan Company, 1970), pp. 192–200; and Saul B. Cohen, "Michael Roemer and Robert Young: Film Makers of *Nothing But A Man*," *Film Comment* 3, no. 2 (Spring 1965): 8–13.

THE EFFECTS OF STEREOTYPING ON THE AUDIENCE

The stereotyping of American life in motion pictures obviously has had, and continues to have, a considerable impact on the audience. One commentator on film myths and symbols, John Clellon Holmes, puts it this way:

> It has been said that if you would understand the mind of my generation you must start with World War II, on the theory that a widespread attitude is shaped by a common experience. . . . It was the experience of moviegoing in the 1930s and early 1940s, and it gave us a fantasy life in common, from which we are still dragging up the images that obsess us.[67]

Siegfried Kracauer explains stereotyping in film somewhat differently by pointing out, "To be sure, American audiences receive what Hollywood wants them to want; but in the long run audience desires, acute or dormant, determine the character of Hollywood films."[68] This impact or interconnection between Hollywood stereotypes and the audience has too frequently been ignored by our educational system. This must change. The material of the movies is too great a part of our daily lives, thoughts, and actions. In a large sense, many of what we consider commonplace viewpoints may be reflections of film stereotypes. We could minimize the effect of stereotyping on impressional individuals if we could help the audience become more aware of movie clichés. Unfortunately this process is rarely examined in our schools. Somewhere, the study of film stereotypes should be included in the education of American children.

The easiest way, obviously, is to examine books and articles that have made an analysis of film stereotypes. This approach, which is analogous to translations and their imitations, is not so good as seeing the images in the context of the film. However, in dealing with movies, the films are not always available. In other cases, some distributors' rental prices are prohibitive.

In teaching about stereotypes, teachers should show how they diminish a work of art. There is also value in showing how they (1) prevent the viewer from thinking for himself; (2) present a distorted viewpoint which is artistically bad, and (3) become a vicious weapon for propaganda purposes by manipulating an audience. We should, however, be careful not to talk about films being considered "good" or "bad" according to sociological values. The same stipulation that Northrop Frye makes about literature is apropos for film: namely, the responsibility for art's correct images depend upon the audience:

---

67. John Clellon Holmes, "15 Cents Before 6:00 P.M.: The Wonderful Movies of the 'Thirties,'" *Harper's Magazine* 221 (December 1965) : 51.

68. Siegfried Kracauer, "National Types as Hollywood Presents Them," *Mass Culture: The Popular Arts in America*, p. 259. Other useful studies are Roger B. Dooley, "The Irish on the Screen: 1," *Films in Review* 8, no. 5 (May 1957) : 211–17; Roger B. Dooley, "The Irish on the Screen: II," *Films in Review* 8, no. 6 (June 1957) : 259–70; Jack Spears, "The Indian on the Screen," *Films in Review* 10, no. 1 (January 1959) : 18–35; and Robert Larkin, "Hollywood and the Indian," *Focus on Film* 2 (March–April 1970) : 44–53.

There's no such thing as a morally bad novel: its moral effect depends entirely on the moral quality of the reader, and nobody can predict what that will be. And if literature isn't morally bad, it isn't morally good either.[69]

But we need to remember that while morality is within the audience, who may need to be educated, there is a legitimate concern about the stereotyped images presented by the artists.

It is not enough to say that literature is art and therefore not morally good or bad. As Herbert Hill points out:

For the serious writer there must be a fundamental connection between artistic means, that is, technique and discipline, with social and moral conviction, and a recognition of the significant relationship between individual freedom and social necessity, between form and content.[70]

It is also a question of how people perceive the images on the screen. Walter Lippmann, who originated the term "stereotyping," feels that "for the most part we do not see first, and then define, we define first and then see."[71] If this is true, our viewing habits are based upon selective exposure.[72] That is, we generally choose what we wish to see. On the other hand, what we do not want to see, we consciously avoid; this is what is meant by cognitive dissonance.[73]

Relating this to film images presented to the public becomes easy once we recognize that the film industry is interested in selling a product. Therefore, it tries to anticipate what the audience will want to see and what it will avoid. When the industry discovers a successful stereotype it continues to use that cliché as long as the public accepts it. Besides reducing the number of artistic films that can be produced, this method encourages the audience to accept repeated stereotyped images as reality. Lippmann points out:

Photographs have the kind of authority over imagination today, which the printed word had yesterday, and the spoken word before that. They come, we imagine, directly to us without meddling, and they are the most effortless food for the mind conceivable. Any description in words, or even any inert picture, requires an effort of memory before a picture exists in the mind. But on the screen the whole process of observing, describing, reporting, and then imagining has been accomplished for you.

69. Northrop Frye, *The Educated Imagination* (Bloomington: Indiana University Press, 1964), p. 80.

70. Herbert Hill, "Introduction," *Anger and Beyond,* Herbert Hill, ed. (New York: Harper and Row, 1966), p. xiv.

71. Walter Lippmann, "Stereotypes," *Thought and Statement,* Second Edition, William G. Leary and James Steel Smith, eds. (New York: Harcourt, Brace and World, 1960), p. 221.

72. Charles R. Wright, *Mass Communications* (New York: Random House, 1959), pp. 73–74.

73. For a more detailed discussion, see Jack W. Brehm and Arthur Cohen, *Explorations in Cognitive Dissonance* (New York: John Wiley and Sons, 1962); and Leon Festinger, *A Theory of Cognitive Dissonance* (Evanston: Row, Peterson and Company, 1957).

Without more trouble than is needed to stay awake the result which your imagination is always aiming at is reeled off on the screen.[74]

Thus we can see that film stereotypes are effective because of the authority of the photograph.

Perhaps one of the best ways to begin studying the effects of stereotypes on the audience is to define what we mean by the "audience." The most useful book to date for helping us to do that is Leo A. Handel's study, *Hollywood Looks at Its Audience*. Handel points out that there is no distinction made among " (1) the potential audience; (2) the actual audience; (3) the average weekly motion picture attendance; (4) the maximum number of admissions or potential audience for a motion picture; and (5) the average number of admissions for a motion picture."[75] The significance of this is that when Hollywood attempts to present a stereotype for a particular audience, it has very little to go on. In addition, when critics and sociologists claim that an audience has rejected or accepted an image, it is difficult to determine what audience is being discussed.

The book itself is an examination of the statistical efforts made by Hollywood producers to pretest the stories and images that the public will most readily respond to. Handel points out that most audience research is carried out with great speed, that many respondents do not quite understand questions asked them in interviews and questionnaires, that very often it is difficult to isolate the effects of previous movies in discussing recent films, that it is difficult to assess the validity of these tests, and, in addition, that not all moviegoers are in a position to decide for themselves what films they see.[76] He declares that "the most primitive kind of communication research pertains to the extent and nature of the audience."[77] Particularly valuable are Handel's findings that audiences are fluid rather than rigid and change both in structure (age, sex, and socioeconomic groups) and with the seasons.

Since stereotyping affects the movie audience, it is important that we understand the makeup of that audience. Handel points out the types of people who go to the movies:

Male and female patrons attend at about equal rates.

Younger people attend more frequently than older people.

Persons in higher socio-economic brackets attend more frequently than those in lower levels.

The more years a person has spent in school, the more frequently he sees motion pictures.[78]

---

74. Walter Lippmann, "Stereotypes," p. 227.
75. Leo Handel, *Hollywood Looks at Its Audience: A Report of Film Audience Research* (Urbana: University of Illinois Press, 1950), p. 94. Reissued by Arno Press, 1970.
76. *Ibid.*, pp. 12, 13, 15.
77. *Ibid.*, p. 93.
78. *Ibid.*, p. 199.

What, then, are some of the effects upon these people?

No one who lived through the marriage of Grace Kelly to Prince Rainier doubts that such an influence exists. Bernard Rosenberg and David Manning White observed that more correspondents covered that event than reported the Normandy Invasion of June 6, 1944.[79] Rosenberg and White went on to say that "It is probably true that the 'average' American's knowledge about the lives, loves and neuroses of the demi-gods and goddesses who live in the Olympian heights of Beverly Hills far surpasses his knowledge of current affairs local, state and national combined."[80] It should be pointed out that while there is no reliable way to measure the movies' effect on adolescents, it does not mean that movies have no influence on the public and children in particular.[81]

For the past twenty years, educators have tried to measure the effect of stereotyping on the attitudes of people who attend the movies. Hoban and Van Ormer's work constitutes the most comprehensive film research up to 1950 and is a useful starting point. In regard to the general attitudes of the motion picture audience, they concluded:

> If the conclusions regarding the impact of films on the learning of infor-mation could be generalized to attitudes (and there is no evidence to sup-port such generalization), it might be postulated that the force of motion pictures on general attitudes may be greater than that of verbal media alone, when the influence is measured in long-term effects, and when con-ditions required in the development of general attitudes is satisfied. This postulate is somewhat feasible when reminiscent effect is taken into con-sideration, and when a relationship between specific and general attitude is assumed. However, research is needed on the long-term attitudinal effects of films to substantiate this postulate.[82]

Peterson and Thurstone, using an attitude scale of a paired comparison schedule, studied the effect of motion pictures on the social attitudes of children. One of their major concerns was with measuring the effect that a motion picture could have on attitudes relating to nationality, race, crime, war, capital punishment, and the punishment of criminals. They found that "motion pictures have definite lasting effects on the social attitudes of children and that a number of pictures pertaining to the same issue may have a cumulative effect on 'attitude.'"[83]

Shuttleworth and May, in working with two groups of school children in

---

79. Bernard Rosenberg and David Manning White, *Mass Culture: The Popular Arts in America* (New York: The Free Press, 1957), p. 254.

80. Bernard Rosenberg and David Manning White, *Mass Culture*, p. 254.

81. A useful essay is Nancy Ellen Dowd, "Popular Conventions," *Film Quarterly* 22, no. 3 (Spring 1969): 26–31.

82. Charles Hoban and Edward Van Ormer, *Instructional Film Research 1918–1950*, Technical Report SDC 269–7–19 (Long Island, New York: Special Devices Center, 1950), pp. 5, 18. Reissued by Arno Press, 1972.

83. Ruth Peterson and L. I. Thurstone, *Motion Pictures and Social Attitudes of Children*, p. 66.

Grades 5–9, attempted to measure the responses on examinations by children who went to the movies two or three times a week in contrast to those who went once a month. Recognizing the influence of interacting experiences on the child, they postulated the theory of "specific influence": in effect, this theory holds that when the movies continually present consistent patterns of conduct and personality, there is a carry-over to an individual child's behavior. They concluded that movies do exert an influence, but that the influence is specific for a given child and a given movie.[84] While it was shown that movie children (those who went to the movies more often) made a poorer showing on the educational tests, one wonders whether the tests themselves were valid.

Stereotypes can sometimes be helpful. It seems plausible that teachers can improve understanding among adolescents by instigating a study of various social problems treated in motion pictures. For example, if a teacher wanted to reinforce the view that prejudice was harmful to our society, he could show films like *Intruder in the Dust, Gentleman's Agreement,* and *Home of the Brave.* This view seems to be supported by Herbert Blumer, who in his writings presents several theories about the types of responses movies may elicit. His investigations found no proof that the public reacts uniformly to a stereotype. He did, however, find that there are people who imitate patterns of conduct presented in movies.[85]

Another concern, in the last decade, has centered on the effects of stereotyped patterns of violence, and the effect movies can have on stimulating aggressive behavior or acting as a cathartic release from fantasy drives. Feshback postulates that symbolic expressions of aggression or involvement in vicariously oriented aggressive activity could weaken a student's future aggressive behavior if the conditions were appropriate.[86] Berkowitz questions Feshback's catharsis hypothesis on the grounds that conditions that would be appropriate for such fantasy reduction are extremely slight for most of the population.[87] Dickens and Willams in summarizing the research conducted between 1960–1963 on aggression and violence in the mass media report that

> The greatest restriction in attempting to generalize any degree of the above findings to the possible deleterious effects of violence in the mass media lies in the fact that aggressive behavior in the experiments involved

84. Frank K. Shuttleworth and Mark A. May, *The Social Conduct and Attitude of Movie Fans* (New York: Macmillan, 1933.) Reissued by Arno Press, 1970.

85. For a more detailed study of the Payne Fund Work, read the propagandized account by Henry Forman, *Our Movie Made Children* (New York: Macmillan, 1933); a rebuttal by Mortimer Adler, *Art and Prudence* (New York: Longmans & Green, 1937); and a rebuttal to Adler by Paul Cressey, "The Motion Picture Experience as Modified by Social Background and Personality," *American Sociological Review* 3 (August 1938) : 516–25.

86. Seymour Feshback, "The Drive Reducing Function of Fantasy Behavior," Journal of *Abnormal Psychology* 50 (January 1955) : 3–11.

87. Leonard Berkowitz, *Aggression: A Social Psychological Analysis* (New York: McGraw-Hill, 1962) .

not other adults or children, but toys or dolls—themselves fantasy figures. . . . These studies, however, demonstrate two important points: (a) films or cartoons depicting violence can stimulate behavioral patterns which might be defined as aggressive, and (b) children do seem willing and able not only to learn but also to imitate particular patterns of behavior as presented by a mass medium.[88]

In the most impressive study on the effects of mass communication, Klapper examined and collated over 1000 writings dealing with the field, and concluded that there were some indicative findings that would serve as valid perspectives by which to view the disorganized and generally inconclusive research. Klapper listed five generalizations, but noted that he was in no way committed to them and speculated that future research would "modify and perhaps annihilate the schema."[89] Klapper's generalizations are these:

1. Mass communication *ordinarily* does not serve as a necessary and sufficient cause of audience effects, but rather functions among and through a nexus of mediating factors and influences.
2. These mediating factors are such that they typically render mass communication a contributory agent, but not the sole cause, in a process of reinforcing the existing conditions. (Regardless of the condition in question—be it the vote intentions of audience members, their tendency toward or away from delinquent behavior, or their general orientation toward life and its problems—and regardless whether the effects in question be social or individual, the media are more likely to reinforce than to change.)
3. On such occasions as mass communications does function in the service of change, one of two conditions is likely to exist. Either:
   a. the mediating factors will be found to be inoperative and the effect of the media will be found to be direct; *or*
   b. the mediating factors, which normally favor reinforcement, will be found to be themselves impelling toward change.
4. There are certain residual situations in which mass communication seems to produce direct effects, or directly and of itself to serve certain psycho-physical functions.
5. The efficacy of mass communication, either as a contributory agent or as an agent of direct effect, is affected by various aspects of the media and communications themselves or of the communication situation (including, for example, aspects of textual organization, the nature of the source and medium, the existing climate of public opinion, and the like).[90]

The most recent book and the least useful is *Violence and the Mass Media,* a collection of essays by social scientists who touch "only incidentally" on

88. Milton Dickens and Frederick Williams, "Mass Communications," *Review of Educational Research* 34 (April 1964) : 218.
89. Joseph T. Klapper, *The Effects of Mass Communication* (Glencoe: The Free Press, 1960) , p. 8.
90. *Ibid.,* p. 98.

such elements as "the breakdown of social institutions, or sexual frustration, or growing moral laxity, or economic deprivation, or population pressure."[91] Although Larsen begins by admitting that neither his authors nor anyone else can prove that our age is more violent than any previous period in history, the writers insist on making the mass media the whipping boy for society's troubles. In each of the anthology's eight sections, the "experts" deplore the violence in the world without treating its basic roots in life itself. Little concern is given to who runs these mass-media establishments, how they are operated, or the connection between the various branches of business and the social codes of our country. Just as interesting is the absence of any sensible comment about the children's attitudes to violence on the screen. For many youngsters, this emphasis on violence is an amusing and distracting pastime which can easily be dismissed in time for the next activity in the busy schedule. When this is not the case and some negative psychological reaction results, here is where we should have reliable information on what to do, how to help. No one gets this from *Violence and the Mass Media*.[92]

In connection with violence in movies, there are two interesting monographs that react against simplistic attitudes on condemning mass media. One of them, "Companion to Violence and Sadism in the Cinema," has the philosophy that the audience wants violence and that the suspense connected with physical violence in films is related to pity and terror. For those who object to certain screen representations the editors point out:

> If you wish to diminish the public demand for screen violence, first banish it from the history books (Cannae, Agincourt, The Thirty Years War, Waterloo, the Somme, Arnheim). Banish it from the headlines. Not a word please about megadeaths and overkill; we don't wish to know that. Eradicate crimes of violence and notions of punishment as retaliatory. Remove at their root children's temper tantrums, bowdlerize their dreams, eradicate egoism. Remove the masses' feeling of helplessness in the hands of the law, the state, the politicians. And then when you have done all that, do let us know.[93]

Some of the topics covered in the monograph are criminals, famous monsters, sadistic females, *élan vital* of the Japanese Cinema, and the psychology of aggression.

The second monograph, *Puritans Anonymous,* deals with the varied aspects of puritanism in films. The editors define and discuss puritanism as

First, the British version of orthodox Calvinism; second the Protestant-

---

*91. Otto N. Larsen, (editor), *Violence and the Mass Media* (New York: Harper and Row, 1968), p. 3.
92. Also useful in Michael Armstrong, "On Violence . . .," *Films and Filming* 15, no. 6 (March 1969) : 20–31.
93. Ian Johnson and Raymond Durgnat (eds.), "Companion to Violence and Sadism in the Cinema," *Motion* 6 (Autumn 1963) : 63.

bourgeois-capitalistic nexus established by Max Weber and R. H. Tawney; and third, that mixture of religion and rationalism which became Christian orthodoxy once theologians had married the thought of Plato to that of St. Paul, and which Matthew Arnold evolved into its agnostic form. Behind these looms a broader sense—applying to all those philosophies that aspire, not like Aristotle's to a judicious balance of selfishness and altruism, but, like Plato's to an actual *eradication* of "unworthy" impulses, however deeply they plunge into the soul. In that sense, every moral code has its own puritanism. Puritanism may be pessimistic ("we are all born corrupted, our wills must be broken for our own good"), or optimistic ("we are all born innocent and kind *really*"); there are puritanisms of reason (Aldous Huxley), of power, of success, of sensuality (D. H. Lawrence).

"High culture" is traditionally associated with Christian-rationalist "purification"—the academic world even thinks of itself as the "saving remnant," "the salt of the earth." But "low culture," from folk art to the best in the mass media, has a lower moral polarity, an Aristotelian, even a Rabelaisian, relaxation.[94]

The authors go on to explain how the new fields of sociology, anthropology and depth psychology have forced a reexamination of all cultural values, including artistic ones. And what Johnson and Durgnat conclude is that puritanism, in any moral code, may well be the consequence of the censor's deep-rooted anxiety, distrust and hatred. They ask,

Is "moral striving" itself a trap; the devil-a-monk-would-be quoting scripture for his own purposes, happy to hate sin so long as he is allowed to hate something? or are puritan *ideals* essential to every morality?[95]

Some films discussed in this monograph and available for classroom illustration are *Night of the Hunter* (United Artists—16mm: 1955, 91 min., b/w, sound, R-UAS), a textbook illustration of the man who identifies himself with God; *Wild Strawberries* (Sweden—16mm: 1957, 90 min., b/w, English subtitles, sound, R-JAN), a theme covering the male's humiliation; and Robert Bresson's *Le Journal d'Un Curé de Campagne* (France—16mm: 1951, 92 min., b/w, English subtitles, sound, R-AUD), a film that correlates the outside world with men's inner conflicts.

CENSORSHIP AND SELF-CONTROL

The threat of censorship is undoubtedly a factor in film stereotyping. Since the stereotyping of American life has been so widespread and has en-

---

94. Ian Johnson and Raymond Durgnat (editors), "Puritans Anonymous," *Motion* 6 (Autumn 1963) : 3.
95. *Ibid.*, pp. 10–18.

compassed so many social, political, and economic problems, filmmakers have frequently stepped on the sensitive toes of certain segments of society. It is small wonder then that there have been so many attempts to coerce the industry into producing only certain types of films, and those only in prescribed ways. Movies and their myths have long been a source of controversy, going as far back as 1908 when New York's mayor closed all the nickelodeons in town "because of the serious opposition by the rectors and pastors of practically all the Christian denominations in the city and because of the further objections of the Society for the Prevention of Crime."[96] The theaters reopened only after they had promised that no films which tended to degrade the morals of society would be shown.

Pressure groups were successful in helping to get passed laws to outlaw certain films as being indecent. Ordinances were enacted that gave the police the right to shut movie houses that showed "harmful films," and when the exhibitors appealed, the high courts, such as the Supreme Court of Illinois, ruled that the ordinances were necessary "to secure decency and morality in the moving-picture business, and that this purpose falls within the police power."[97]

The history of the movie industry's fight with the censors has been recorded in a number of books. The basic issue seems to be whether or not film as an art has the right to create whatever images, stereotyped or not, that it wants. The philosophical question can be seen in the contrasting positions on freedom and art taken by Susanne Langer and Mortimer Adler. Langer's two books—*Philosophy in a New Key: A Study in the Symbolism of Reason, Rite and Art*[98] and *Feeling and Form: A Theory of Art Developed from "Philosophy in a New Key"*[99]—show her pragmatic viewpoint and argue that society and the individual must be allowed to interact. The artist gives form to reality, and the communication between the artist and the audience is the basis of the creative experience. Therefore, the artist needs his freedom. The opposing point of view is taken by Mortimer Adler in *Art and Prudence: A Study in Practical Philosophy*,[100] in which he argues for an absolute value by which the work in art has to be measured. Things are either right or wrong in relation to the ideal. Thus, there must be some standards for artists outside the work of art, and hence the need for censorship. In spite of their differences, both of the authors recognize the importance of art as a channel for the individual's self-realization.

---

96. Mauritz Hallgren, *Landscape of Freedom* (New York: Howell Soskin and Company, 1941) , p. 339.
97. James Jackson Kilpatrick, *The Smut Peddlers* (Garden City, N.Y.: Doubleday and Company, 1960) , p. 171.
98. Susanne K. Langer, *Philosophy in a New Key: A Study in the Symbolism of Reason, Rite and Art* (Cambridge: Harvard University Press, 1942) .
99. Susanne K. Langer, *Feeling and Form: A Theory of Art Developed from "Philosophy in a New Key"* (New York: Charles Scribner's & Sons, 1953) .
100. Mortimer Adler, *Art and Prudence: A Study in Practical Philosophy* (New York: Longmans, Green, 1937) .

BOOKS OF FILM CENSORSHIP[101]

Beman, Lamar Taney (editor). *Selected Articles on Censorship of the Theater and Moving Pictures.* New York: Jerome S. Ozer, Publisher, Inc., 1971.

Originally published in 1931, this superb collection deals with many quotations and essays from the various pressure groups of the 1920s and 1930s who vigorously attacked the film industry. The book also contains an extremely useful bibliography covering the estimated effects that movies have on the American public.

Carmen, Ira H. *Movies, Censorship and the Law.* Ann Arbor: University of Michigan Press, 1966.

In this valuable study, Carmen covers the history of American motion picture censorship beginning in 1915 when the Supreme Court denied the freedom of the press to films and traces the various changes of thought which have occurred up to 1965. Most fascinating about the legal history is the arbitrary ways that state and local censors select to interpret the law.

* Cogley, John. *Report on Blacklisting. I: The Movies.* New York: The Fund for the Republic, Inc., 1956. Reissued by Arno Press in 1970.

Starting in January 1955, ten reporters and investigators headed by Cogley, then executive editor of *The Commonweal,* began an investigation of blacklisting in the mass media. This first-volume report is a valuable document on unseen political and economic pressures of studio life.

* Crowther, Bosley. *Movies and Censorship.* New York: Public Affairs Committee, 1962.

A very simplified and short pamphlet describing some basic ideas about censorship. It offers some sensible, practical, and useful ideas for public meetings where the discussion stays mainly on a superficial level.

Ernst, Morris, and Pare Lorentz. *Censored: The Private Life of the Movies.* New York: Jerome S. Ozer, Publishers, Inc., 1971.

Originally published in 1930, this work by the famed attorney and the great documentary filmmaker chronicled the legal decisions made by local and state censorship bodies and made a persuasive argument against any form of legislative control of movies.

Farber, Stephen. *The Movie Rating Game.* Washington, D. C.: Public Affairs Press, 1972.

Here is the most complete and useful discussion of the meaning and purpose of the controversial rating symbols. In nine informative chapters, the author provides historical background, inside information, and specific recommendations for improvement. Also included are a number of valuable appendices about studio contract stipulations, typical objections of the rating board, and types of censorship restrictions.

---

101. One of the best articles on censorship and the cinema is Richard Corliss, "The Legion of Decency," *Film Comment* 4, no. 4 (Summer 1968) : 24–61. Other useful material are John Wilcox *et al.* "The Small Knife: Studies in Censorship," *Sight and Sound* 25, no. 4 (Spring 1956) : 206–11, 220; Neville March Hunnings, ". . . And Loss of Paradise: The Origins of Censorship in England," *Sight and Sound* 27, no. 3 (Winter 1957–58) : 154–54; Neville March Hunnings, "The Silence of Fanny Hill," *Sight and Sound* 35, no. 3 (Summer 1966) : 134–38; and Herbert Levy, "The Case Against Film Censorship," *Film in Review* 1, no. 3 (April 1950) : 1-2, 38–42.

Houseman, John. *Run-Through: A Memoir.* New York: Simon and Schuster, 1972.
    Although not really concerned about film, this nostalgic and marvelous autobiography by one of the most respected names in the American theater presents some invaluable insights into censorship with his discussions on the WPA Federal theater and the production of *Citizen Kane.*

Hunnings, Neville March. *Film Censors and The Law.* London: George Allen & Unwin, 1967.
    In updating and expanding his articles on censorship for *Sight and Sound,* Hunnings has given a lengthy and remarkably good documentation of censorship in Britain since the Cinematograph Act of 1909. Although problems of other nations are dealt with, it is mainly in England that the story of ignorance, arrogance and apathy is best described.

Inglis, Ruth A. *Freedom of the Movies: A Report on the Self-Regulation from the Commission on Freedom of the Press.* Chicago: University of Chicago, 1947.
    One of the most detailed records about the rise of internal industry censorship and the pressures that filmmakers encountered during the past thirty years. Inglis is good on facts and provocative in presentation.

Kahn, Gordon. *Hollywood on Trial.* New York: Boni and Gaer, 1948. Reissued by Arno Press, 1970.
    In this valuable and fascinating account of the indictment against the famed Hollywood Ten, Kahn has a rib-tickling time with Ginger Rogers's mother.

Martin, Olga J. *Hollywood's Movie Commandments: A Handbook for Motion Picture Writers and Reviewers.* New York: Arno Press, 1970.
    Originally published in 1937, this invaluable commentary on the taboos of the American production code offers a stimulating background to the ingenious attempts by Hollywood producers and directors to present realism and humor in their films. There is also a useful section explaining the censorship of other countries in the early thirties.

Moley, Raymond. *The Hays Office.* New York: The Bobbs-Merrill Company, 1945. Reissued by Jerome S. Ozer, 1971.
    This interesting and for the most part accurate description of the organization that Will Hays began in 1922 is a readable introduction to the concept of self-censorship and the problems inherent in such an approach. Moley is good not only on background of the times, but also in providing invaluable information on particular personalities and significant events.

Nizer, Louis. *New Courts of Industry: Self Regulation Under the Motion Picture Code, Including an Analysis of the Code.* New York: Jerome S. Ozer, Publishers, Inc., 1971.
    Originally published in 1935, this carefully written and detailed account of the motion picture code attacks the problems inherent in the Hays Office and describes the methods used by the industry to resolve their difficulties.

* Randall, Richard S. *Censorship of the Movies: The Social and Political Control of a Mass Medium.* Madison: The University of Wisconsin Press, 1968.
    This now becomes the most valuable and up-to-date book on the changing

practices of film censorship. One comes away with the realization that yesterday's movies would all pass prohibitions today, and that the present crop of objectionable films would not have even been considered, let alone made, a handful of years back.

Schumach, Murray. *The Face on the Cutting Room Floor: The Story of Movie and Television Censorship.* New York: William Morrow and Company, 1964.

Although the author remains neutral, he presents a worthwhile lucid survey about personalities and events over the past forty years, including very good reports on the political pressures for censorship and the consequences resulting from such actions.

Trumbo, Dalton. *Additional Dialogue: Letters of Dalton Trumbo 1942–1962.* Edited by Helen Manfull. New York: M. Evans and Company, Inc., 1970.

Here is a sensitive and poignant account of an outstanding screenwriter who became one of the famous Hollywood Ten, blackballed by the industry for more than a decade. Through lucid and informative letters, we learn how Trumbo and others earned their bread, survived the social and political hatred of people within and outside the industry, and won.[102]

Vaughn, Robert. *Only Victims: A Study of Show Business Black Listing.* With a foreword by Senator George McGowan. New York: G. P. Putnam's Sons, 1972.

In this well-written and detailed account of the activities of the House Un-American Activities Committee, Vaughn presents the most important and valuable book on the subject to date.

* Vizzard, Jack. *See No Evil: Life Inside a Hollywood Censor.* New York: Simon and Schuster, 1970.

Written by the man who for many years was on the inside of the Hollywood Code Office, this book provides some interesting and sobering anecdotes about movie censorship.

The Code has been revised in light of current social, political, and economic conditions.[103] But the most dramatic shift has been the new labeling game begun on November 1, 1968. Films are now designated *G, PG* (formerly *M*, later *GP*), *R* and *X*. *G* means that it's safe to take anyone to the film. *PG* says pretty much the same thing, except the producers feel that it's best to have a parent give his permission before an adolescent hears a four-letter word or empathizes with a promiscuous line of thought. The catch is that no proof of parent permission is required at the box-office. *R* steps up the admission price because it theoretically requires the adolescent to be accompanied by an adult. And *X* means no one under 17 admitted.[104]

Contrary to public opinion, the biggest money-makers are not the *X* films. As Fletcher Knebel points out:

---

102. See also William Starr *et al.*, "Dalton Trumbo: An Interview," *Film Society Review* 7, no. 2 (October 1971) : 24–32.
103. See Appendix IV: The Motion Picture Code to date.
104. For a good, entertaining discussion read, Gene Shalit, "The Rating Game," *Look* 34, no. 22 (November 3, 1970) : 82, 86–89.

Variety's year-end survey shows that of the seven films that yielded $11 million or more in rental fees to distributors in 1969, only one, *Midnight Cowboy*, was an alienated-youth influx thing. The rest were "family" pictures, returning millions to the distributors last year—*The Love Bug*, $17; *Funny Girl*, $16.5; *Bullitt*, $16.4; *Butch Cassidy and The Sundance Kid*, $15; *Romeo and Juliet*, $14.5; and *True Grit*, $11.5. *Cowboy* ranked seventh at $11. (In movie parlance, a "family" film can include scores of instant corpses, done in murder, slaughter, war, perfidity, accident or more domestic annoyance, but positively no action by live human reproductive organs between the killing.) [105]

The most powerful form of censorship is the self-regulation created by the producers and distributors themselves. Started in 1922, under the direction of Will Hays, and with the intention of protecting the industry against outside interference, the Motion Picture Association of America has for more than forty-five years been the most formidable policeman in filmmaking. It operated, at least up to November 1, 1968, mainly through a motion picture code which prescribed what could and could not be shown in films.[106] Students, in considering stereotypes in movies, would do well to study the code for some insights into just what the filmmaker was allowed to present. Consider, for example, Rule 21 of the Code:

Resolved, that those things which are included in the following list shall not appear in pictures produced by the members of this association, irrespective of the manner in which they are treated;

1. Pointed Profanity—by either title or lip—this includes the words "God," "Lord," "Jesus," "Christ," (unless they be reverently in connection with proper religious ceremonies), "hell," "damn," "Gawd," and every other profane and vulgar expression however it is spelled;

2. Any licentious or suggestive nudity—in fact or in silhouette; and any lecherous or licentious notice thereof by other characters in the picture;

3. The illegal traffic of drugs;

4. Any reference of sex perversion;

5. White slavery;

6. Miscegenation (sex relationships between white and black races) ;

7. Sex hygiene and venereal diseases;

8. Scenes of actual childbirth—in fact or silhouette;

9. Children's sex organs;

10. Ridicule of the clergy;

11. Willful offense to any nation, race, or creed;

And be it further *resolved,* that special care be exercised in the manner in which the following subjects be treated, to the end that vulgarity and suggestiveness be eliminated and that good taste be emphasized:

1. The use of the flag;

2. International relations (avoiding picturizing in an unfavorable

---

105. Fletcher Knebel, "Hollywood: Broke—And Getting Rich," *Look* 34, no. 22 (November 3, 1970) : 52.
106. See Appendix III for the 1927 section of the Code, often listed as "The Don'ts and Be Carefuls."

light another country's religion, history, institutions, prominent people, and citizenry) ;

    3. Arson;

    4. The use of firearms;

    5. Theft, robbery, safe-cracking, and dynamiting of trains, mines, buildings, etc. (having in mind the effect which a too-detailed description of these may have upon the moron) ;

    6. Brutality and possible gruesomeness;

    7. Techniques of committing murder by whatever method;

    8. Methods of smuggling;

    9. Third degree methods;

    10. Actual hangings or electrocutions as legal punishment for crimes;

    11. Sympathy for criminals;

    12. Attitude toward public characters and institutions;

    13. Sedition;

    14. Apparent cruelty to children and animals;

    15. Branding of people or animals;

    16. The sale of women, or of a woman selling her virtue;

    17. Rape or attempted rape;

    18. First night scenes;

    19. Man and woman in bed together;

    20. Deliberate seduction of girls;

    21. Surgical operations;

    22. The institution of marriage;

    23. The use of drugs;

    24. Titles or scenes having to do with law enforcement or law-enforcing officers;

    25. Excessive or lustful kissing, particularly when one character or the other is a "heavy."

In sum, films create stereotypes which add, detract or reinforce existing points of view, thereby providing us with a reflection not only of the time in which they were made but also a perspective on the spiritual and social growth of a nation. By understanding these film conventions, we can learn about the need for more honest movies as well as appreciate the obstacles faced by commercial artists.

4
A Thematic Approach

His clothes are comfortable and sexually explicit. His manners, except to barmen, seem abominable. He is only secure,
communicative, really himself, in his hang-out at the back
of a candy store. His father is an ineffectual, out-of-touch
shadow, a bantering voice behind a newspaper or a cocktail-
shaker. His mother is foolish, puzzled but indulgent. He
has a battered car, a high-fi and a buddy. He is furiously
loyal and often demonstrates his affection with a right to
the jaw. He hates cops and cinema managers. He knows
and tacitly accepts prostitutes, homosexuals, drug addicts and
petty crooks. Sketched in from dozens of random descriptions, feature by feature like a wanted man's poster, he is
today's teenager.
                    Peter John Dyer, "Youth and the Cinema"

In spite of the advantages of the previously mentioned approaches, they all
tend to deal with movies from an external point of view; the thematic approach, on the other hand, stresses the inner unity of a film and the need
for us to become engaged with the motion picture itself. In seeing *Intruder
in the Dust,* for example, we become involved not only with Lucas Beauchamp's problems but also with the style and techniques that director Clarence Brown used in bringing Faulkner's famous novel to the screen. And we
examine as well our feelings and reactions to the artistic merit of the
production.

Students benefit from discussions centering on the complex relationship
between the content and style of a well-made film. They want to know more
about particular ideas, issues, and personalities. Our job, then, is to provide
available films which are related to these concerns. Sometimes the thematic
program best begins with social discussions rather than with film analyses.
This is because their interest is individual and personal, and the students
are exploring themselves. Gradually, by encouraging discussion about the
film itself, we help overcome superficial and false reactions to the problems
in movies and in life. The point to remember is that a student's feelings

are important, and what he wants to say and do needs to relate to what we want to achieve in the classroom. In this chapter, I'd like to offer a thematic grouping of films useful in developing a student's understanding, appreciation, and enjoyment of movies.[1]

If we intend to teach about critical awareness, there are at least two basic steps we should take. The first is to motivate our students *to think imaginatively* about films. That is, they should be encouraged to speculate, to question, to fantasize about the work they have seen. And second, we need to *discipline* their sensibilities, reinforcing the positive and creative responses, and showing, when errors in judgment occur, where they have been misled. Let me be quite clear on this point. I'm not suggesting that we teach students to accept our ideas or values. I *am* suggesting that they learn how we arrive at our criteria so that they can point out our mistakes or else use our experience as a building block to their own set of standards. When young people are able to develop their imagination and taste, they often appreciate and enjoy film more. As Louis and Joan Rosengren Forsdale have pointed out:

> The most profound reason for teaching about film is to enable the student to engage himself with the medium at the richest and deepest level possible *when he chooses to.* Pauline Kael's plea that teachers should not teach film, lest they ruin by their stultifying academic approaches this peculiarly "natural" medium of pleasure for millions, both overestimates the power which teachers have in shaping taste—either constructively or destructively—and underestimates the efficacy of any medium.[2]

One of the most helpful ways to motivate youngsters' imagination is through the identification process. The idea is to match the adolescent's strong feelings for a kindred soul within a work of art and thereby provide a sensitive and profound experience. Such an aesthetic sensation is an important part of a human being's growth and development. It helps shape his values and his life. Furthermore, the aesthetic experience offers a rare chance for perceiving and revealing mankind's worth and substance. Such being the case, teachers would do well to introduce thematic units into the film study curriculum.

The question arises as to which themes are best for which group. My favorite, at present, concerns the personal problems of young people as they appear on the screen. At a time when students are actively searching for answers, attempting revolutionary changes, and facing the challenge of

---

1. See Raymond Durgnat, "Style in Film-Making: I—This Damned Eternal Triangle," *Films and Filming* 11, no. 2 (December 1964): 14–18; "II—Truth is Stranger Than Fiction," *Films and Filming* 11, no. 3 (January 1965): 44–48; "III—Getting Cinema on the Right Wave Length," *Films and Filming* 11, no. 4 (February 1965): 46–50; "IV—Alexander and the Greats," *Films and Filming* 11, no. 5 (March 1965): 18–22; "V—Who Really Makes the Movies?", *Films and Filming* 11, no. 6 (April 1965): 44–48; "VI— Expressing Life in Celluloid," *Films and Filming* 11, no. 7 (May 1965): 44–48; and Susan Sontag, "On Style," *Partisan Review* 31 (Fall 1965): 545–60.
2. Louis and Joan Rosengren Forsdale, "Film Literacy," *Teachers College Record* 67 (May 1966): 616.

identity, what better way to show the art of the film than to examine movies that appeal to young people most? Not surprising is the fact that since the beginning of time, all men have asked the same questions about *God, Knowledge, Man, the State,* and *Love.* To illustrate how these broad categories may be used in the schools, I have chosen five general headings, suggested by Dwight Burton, for a thematic approach to the personal problems of students: (1) Coming to Terms with Self; (2) Problems of Relations with Peers; (3) Family Problems; (4) Preparing for the Future Adult Role; (5) Moral and Philosophical Problems and Issues.[3] While film cannot bear the burden of helping young people to solve their personal problems, it helps to provide an open forum for an intelligent discussion of these eternal questions.

I have selected a variety of movies, some older ones, some contemporary. Naturally, each filmmaker approaches the issues differently. And it is obvious from the aforementioned topics that film offers an overabundance of examples. Each of us, because of classroom time, suitability and money, chooses the movies he feels will be most effective. My list, therefore, is not intended as a definitive one.

Two warnings should be sounded before we start. First, the film, even though it gives insights into human experience and personal problems, is only a part of the total life experience necessary for a broader understanding of the issues themselves. Therefore, the movies act as a wedge toward opening new horizons and not as a solution to the problems themselves. Second, the discussion should emphasize the art of the film and not the social commentary alone. If the movie is well-made the social consequences will be forthcoming.

COMING TO TERMS WITH SELF

Young people are self-centered. They are also very impressionable, and as a result often want to compare themselves with their peers, teachers, parents, and heroes. It is not uncommon to find teenagers worried about their appearances and their abilities in matters of love, friendship, leadership, physical prowess, and social status. Hollywood, recognizing that a large percentage of its audience is made up of adolescents, has used the image of the teenager as a reliable and marketable character in film after film. Since 1949, as Peter John Dyer explains, the image of the teenager has appeared more and more in motion pictures:

> His role, at first, was simple: to portray, as far as possible truthfully and with sympathy, the immediate problems of his generation. And this for a

---

3. Dwight L. Burton, *Literature Study in the High Schools* (New York: Holt, Rinehart, 1960), pp. 50–51. Further topics and groupings are suggested in *Screen Experience: An Approach to Film,* Sharon Fayen, ed. (Dayton: George M. Pflaum, 1969).

while he did. But when a host of often spurious "adult" films began to play their part—an admittedly indeterminate part—in establishing stereotypes of adolescent behavior, a chain reaction was set up between film, film-teenager and real-life teenager.[4]

Very often the movies superficially portray teenagers as lonely, shy, and uncertain individuals.[5] By looking at some of the following films, teachers may find material that will demonstrate to the adolescent his relationship to the filmmaker while at the same time helping him understand his own behavior.

Billy Liar (Britain—16mm: 1963, 96 min., b/w, sound, R-WRS)
    Director John Schlesinger creates the fantasized world of Billy Fisher (Tom Courtenay), a young man working in a funeral parlor who dreams of becoming a great writer. Julie Christie provides some romance for the awkward clerk.[6]

Captains Courageous (MGM—16mm: 1937, 116 min., b/w, sound, R-FNC)
    Rudyard Kipling's tale of a fifteen-year-old boy was brought to the screen in director Fleming's artistic and moving film. This story of a spoiled youngster who develops his ability to endure hardship is still an effective motion picture for young people. There is also a superb performance by Spencer Tracy as Manuel, the Portuguese sailor who helps the youngster to mature.[7]

Closely Watched Trains (Czechoslovakia—16mm: 1966, 89 min., b/w, subtitles, sound, R-AUD)
    Milos Hrma (Vaclav Neckar), a modest young man, begins his job as an apprentice platform guard at an inconspicuous railway station in the Czechoslovakian countryside during World War II. Within a short time he witnesses the immorality, idleness and amorous adventures of his superiors and makes a conquest of his own as well. Milos soon becomes involved with the underground and an abortive attempt to sabotage a Nazi train, which costs him his life. In his first movie, Jiri Menzel not only wrote a sensitive screenplay of Bohumil Hrabal's novel, but also directed this humorous and tragic film with distinction.[8]

David and Lisa (Continental—16mm: 1962, 94 min., b/w, sound, R-WRS)
    Frank and Eleanor Perry's film of a psychologically disturbed boy who meets a schizophrenic fifteen-year-old girl while they are both in a mental

    4. Peter John Dyer, "Youth and the Cinema: Part I—The Teenage Rave, *Sight and Sound* 29 (Winter 1959–1960) : 27.
    5. See Peter John Dyer, "Patterns of Cinema: American Youth in Uproar," *Films and Filming* 5, no. 12 (September 1959) : 10–12, 32–33; and "Youth and the Cinema: Part II—Candid Camera," *Sight and Sound* 6, no. 3 (Spring 1960) : 61–65. In addition, the reader will find it useful to check the index for books and material on the films that are mentioned here.
    6. See Gene Phillips, "John Schlesinger: Social Realist," *Film Comment* 5, no. 4 (Winter 1969) : 58–63; and John Schlesinger, "Blessed Isle or Fool's Paradise," *Films and Filming* 9, no. 8 (May 1963) : 8–10.
    7. See Peter Cowie, "Gallery of Great Artists: Spencer Tracy," *Films and Filming* 7, no. 9 (June 1961) : 8–9, 38.
    8. Two reviews of the film by Joseph Morgenstern and John Simon are available in *Film 67–86*, edited by Richard Schickel and John Simon (New York: Simon and Schuster, 1968) , pp. 119–21.

home is a good picture that shows some of the problems of emotionally disturbed children.[9]

Island of the Blue Dolphins (Universal—16mm: 1964, 101 min., color, sound, R-COU, CWF, ROA, TFC, UNI, WHO/L-UNI)

Director Robert Radnitz, in one of the rare Hollywood films that depicts the American Indian with integrity, presents a young Indian girl's loneliness on an island where she has been deserted by her family and her tribe. It is one of the best movies for children ever made.[10]

Loneliness of the Long Distance Runner (Britain—16mm: 1962, 103 min., b/w, sound, R-WRS)

Tom Courtenay as the eighteen-year-old boy from the London slums gives one of the best performances of a troubled adolescent available today. The film centers around a juvenile delinquent who is the outstanding runner in a reform school. Directed by Tony Richardson.[11]

The Member of the Wedding (Columbia—16mm: 1952, 91 min., b/w, sound, R-AUD, IDE)

Adapted from Carson McCuller's Broadway play, director Fred Zinnemann's film depicts a twelve-year-old girl's desire to belong. Many members of the original play are in the film: Ethel Waters, Julie Harris, and Brandon de Wilde.[12]

PROBLEMS OF CONFLICT WITH SOCIETY

Another major concern of adolescents is their desire for independence. Often this desire brings them in direct conflict with adults. Hollywood thrives on such encounters. Since a majority of the film audience consists of the rebellious generation, it has always been good business to make movies that appeal to young people. Another reason is that conflict of any sort provides excellent material for moving pictures. Unfortunately, the negative aspects of rebellions win film attention, rather than the constructive solutions. Far too often, motion pictures dealing with juvenile delinquency depict events rather than causes, and solutions are found because the endings are contrived.

---

9. See William Bayer, "An Interview with Frank Perry," *Film Comment* 1, no. 5 (Summer 1963) : 15–22; "Frank and Eleanor Perry," *Time* 81 (January 25, 1963) : 59, 61; "David and Lisa," *Life* 55 (October 4, 1963) : 133–34; Elizabeth Sussex, "David and Lisa," *Film Quarterly* 16, no. 4 (Summer 1963) : 43–44; and Robin Bean, "Portrait of a Young Actor on His Way Up to the Top: Keir Dullea," *Films and Filming* 12, no. 3 (December 1965) : 5–9.

10. See David Rider, "The Island of the Blue Dolphins," *Films and Filming* 11, no. 11 (July 1965) : 31–32.

11. See Tom Courtenay, "Screen Extract from *The Loneliness of the Long Distance Runner,*" *Films and Filming* 8, no. 12 (September 1962) : 10–13; Peter Baker, "*The Loneliness of The Long Distance Runner,*" *Films and Filming* 9, no. 2 (November 1962) : 32; and Peter Harcourt, "I'd Rather be Like I am: Some Comments on *The Loneliness of the Long Distance Runner,*" *Sight and Sound* 32, no. 1 (Winter 1962–63) : 16–19.

12. See Karel Reisz, "The Member of the Wedding," *Sight and Sound* 22, no. 4 (April–June 1953) : 197; and Richard Roud, "The Empty Streets," *Sight and Sound* 26, no. 4 (Spring 1957) : 191–95.

Another area in adolescent relationships that has won film attention relates to sexual morality and the social mores of dating. Here again we need to recognize, as Michael Milner points out, certain premises.

Starting with the parties who conceive the idea of making a motion picture, many factors affect its developmental stages until it emerges on the screen before an audience that has paid to view it. The very goal of the film, to be presented before a paying audience, indicates that it must be a commercial success. If not the prime purpose, making a profit is certainly one of the main reasons for producing a particular movie. Though sex is a basic drive, it does not have to occur in every motion picture produced. The fact that it does appear as an existing theme in most motion pictures should not be surprising since sex either is recognized as such and purposely is included or it exists in the story itself.[13]

Teenagers who view these motion pictures generally think very seriously about love, social morality, premarital relations, abortion, and prostitution. Unfortunately, most of the films distort the relationships between lovers and project a sensational and sordid view of sex.

Bad Boys (Japan—16mm: 1960, 90 min., b/w, English subtitles, sound, R-AUD)
Director Susumu Hani's interpretation, in comparison with the typical Hollywood treatment of juvenile delinquency, centers on a seventeen-year-old Japanese youth who refuses to conform to the standards of his reform school peers.[14]

The Blackboard Jungle (MGM—16mm: 1955, 101 min., b/w, sound, R-FNC)
Director Richard Brooks's film about hostility, violence, and apathy in an American school is an example of how Hollywood treats juvenile delinquency. This much should be said for the film, if little else; there are scenes

---

13. Michael Milner, *Sex on Celluloid* (New York: Macfadden-Bartell Corporation, 1964), p. 38. See also Raymond Durgnat, "Eroticism in Cinema: Part One—Definitions and Points of Departure—The Dark Gods," *Films and Filming* 8, no. 1 (October 1961) : 14–16, 40–41; "Part Two: The Deviationists—Saturnalia in Cans," *Films and Filming* 8, no. 2 (November 1961) : 33–34, 46; "Part Three: The Mass Media and Their Public—Cupid Versus the Legions," *Films and Filming* 8, no. 3 (December 1961) : 16–18, 46; "Part Four: The Subconscious—From Pleasure Castle to Libido Motel," *Films and Filming* 8, no. 4 (January 1962) : 13–15, 41, 46; "Part Five: The Sacred and the Profane— Flames of Passion, All Next Week," *Films and Filming* 8, no. 5 (February 1962) : 16–18, 40–41; "Part Six: Mind and Matter, An Analysis of French and Italian Styles—Some Mad Love and the Sweet Life," *Films and Filming* 8, no. 6 (March 1962) : 16–18, 41; "Part Seven: Symbolism—Another Word For It," *Films and Filming* 8, no. 7 (April 1962) : 13–15, 38–41; "Final Part: Midnight Sun," *Films and Filming* 8, no. 8 (May 1962) : 21–23, 46–49; and Eric Rhode, "Sensuality in the Cinema," *Sight and Sound* 30, no. 3 (Spring 1961) : 93–95. There is also a fine pictorial history of sex in the cinema done by Arthur Knight and Hollis Alpert for *Playboy*. In addition, two magazines that frequently deal with topic of sensuality are the following: *Ms.* (370 Lexington Avenue, New York 10017) and *Sexual Behavior* (1255 Portland Place, Boulder, Colorado 80302) .
14. See Donald Richie, "Oriental Bad Boys," *Films and Filming* 8, no. 12 (September 1962) : 65; Peter John Dyer, "London Festival," *Sight and Sound* 30, no. 1 (Winter 1960– 61) : 17–19; and James Blue, "Susumu Hani: An Interview," *Film Comment* 5, no. 2 (Spring 1969) : 24–36.

that are truly representative of the one percenters. Strong performances by Glenn Ford, Vic Morrow, and Sidney Poitier.[15]

Blue Denim (Fox—16mm: 1959, 89 min., b/w, sound, R-FNC)
Director Philip Dunne created one of the rare Hollywood films that depict with sensitivity and good taste the problems of teenage love and pregnancy. Good acting by Brandon de Wilde and Carol Lynley.[16]

The Cranes Are Flying (Russia—16mm: 1957, 94 min., b/w, English subtitles, sound, R-AUD)
Mikail Kalatozov's exceptional Russian film is about two young lovers caught in World War II. The effects of the war on this couple are a moving example of how the film can become art once it breaks with formula patterns.[17]

If . . . (Paramount—16mm: 1969, 111 min., b/w, sound, R-FNC)
Lindsay Anderson is mostly responsible for this splendid film about life in an English public school. We see how a group of boys begin a new term by settling down to the traditional life of chapel, classes and hazing. Then some of the senior students start to rebel, and what is begun as an attack on outworn academic rules turns into an assault on society itself. Don't miss this one.[18]

Lord of the Flies (Britain—16mm: 1963, 90 min., b/w, sound, R-WRS)
Peter Brook's adaptation of William Golding's novel about well-mannered English school children who become the survivors of a plane crash on a deserted island is almost a horror film about the savagery of children.[19]

Los Olvidados or *The Young and the Damned* (Mexico—16mm: 1951, 81 min., b/w., English subtitles, sound, R-AUD)
Luis Buñuel's film about juvenile delinquency in Mexico exemplifies some of the problems of young people who are frightened, lonely and misguided.[20]

15. See Penelope Houston, "The Blackboard Jungle," *Sight and Sound* 25, no. 1 (Winter 1955–56) : 150; and *Dialogue with the World* (New York: Encyclopaedia Britannica Films, Inc., 1964) , p. 51.
16. See "Blue Denim," *Films in Review* 11, no. 3 (March 1960) : 140; and *Dialogue with the World*, pp. 51–52.
17. See Michael Lifton, "The Cranes are Flying," *Film Quarterly* 13, no. 3 (Spring 1960) : 42–44; Peter John Dyer, "The Cranes are Flying," *Films and Filming* 5, no. 2 (November 1958) : 22; and Nina Hibbin, "Ivan the Magnificent," *Films and Filming* 9, no. 5 (February 1963) : 56–61.
18. See David Robinson, "Anderson Shooting *If*," *Sight and Sound* 37, no. 3 (Summer 1968) : 130–31; and Pauline Kael, *Going Steady* (Boston: Atlantic-Little, Brown, 1970) , pp. 279–86. The script is available from Simon and Schuster.
19. See Dorothy Oshlag, "Lord of the Flies," *Sight and Sound* 30, no. 4 (Autumn 1961) : 185; Tom Milne, "Lord of the Flies," *Sight and Sound* 33, no. 4 (Autumn 1964) : 194–95; Jackson Burgess, "Lord of the Flies," *Film Quarterly* 17, no. 1 (Winter 1963–64) : 31–32; Roger Manvell, "Study Guide for Lord of the Flies," *Screen Education Yearbook* (1966), pp. 107–10; Michael Philips, "Film Critique No. 4: Lord of the Flies," *Screen Education* 29 (May–June 1965) : 41–47; Peter Brook, "The French Gave Me My Freedom," *Films and Filming* 6, no. 1 (October 1960) : 7–8, 43; Peter Cowie, "Lord of the Flies," *Films and Filming* 10, no. 11 (August 1964) : 21–22; and Penelope Houston and Tom Milne, "Interview with Peter Brook," *Sight and Sound* 32, no. 3 (Summer 1963) : 108–13.
20. See Roy Edwards, "The Fifth Columnists," *Sight and Sound* 23, no. 4 (July–September 1953) : 21–23, 54; Tony Richardson, "The Films of Luis Buñuel," *Sight and Sound* 23, no. 2 (January–March 1954) : 125–30; Jacques Doniol-Valcroze and André Bazin, "Conversation with Buñuel," *Sight and Sound* 24, no. 3 (Spring 1955) : 181–85;

Picnic (Columbia—16mm: 1956, 115 min., b/w, sound, R-AUD, CCC, CHA, CWF, IDE, ROA, TWF/L-COL)

Joshua Logan's screen adaptation of William Inge's drama about a drifter's romance with a small-town girl is an example of the conflicts of young people with adult society. Strong performances by William Holden, Arthur O'Connell, and Rosalind Russell.[21]

The Prime of Miss Jean Brodie (Fox—16mm: 1969, 116 min., b/w, sound, R-FNC)

Ronald Neame directed this memorable film about the Edinburgh spinster, Jean Brodie, who shocks her colleagues at a staid school for girls by snubbing the prescribed curriculum and developing her own coterie of "Brodie girls." Maggie Smith is super as the dogmatic school teacher who preaches the virtues of Mussolini and Franco, warps young minds, and ends up alone. Unfortunately, Jay Presson based the screenplay on the stage play which, in turn, had been adapted from Muriel Spark's novel. The book should have been the original source since it is much stronger.[22]

FAMILY PROBLEMS

A third major problem of adolescents is their relationship with parents. Teenagers desire independence, but also want the advice and counsel of their parents. This paradoxical situation often results in frustrating experiences for the entire family. The filmmakers' point of view toward delinquents undoubtedly affects the audience's attitude toward the American adolescent—so much so, perhaps, that the word "adolescent" has almost a pejorative quality. Many movies depict the parents as responsible for the delinquent behavior of children. Frequently we are shown fathers who have incestuous emotions about their buxom daughters, divorced parents who have little time for their youngsters, henpecked husbands with neurotic wives, and mothers who are boring, indifferent, adulterous, or vain.[23] Sometimes we see the economic and social status of the family as a problem the adolescent has to cope with. Therefore, it is not surprising to find in movies that family problems are a major cause of adolescents becoming lonely, confused, unhappy, and rebellious. The film selections that follow may contribute to a better understanding of adolescent behavior as well as of film art:

Derek Prouse, "Interviewing Buñuel," *Sight and Sound* (Summer 1960) : 118–19; Tom Milne, "The Mexican Buñuel," *Sight and Sound* 35, no. 1 (Winter 1965–66) : 36–39; Emilio G. Rierra, "The Eternal Rebellion of Luis Buñuel," *Film Culture* 29 (Summer 1960) : 42–59; J. F. Aranda, "Surrealist and Spanish Giant: First Part of an Analysis of Buñuel's Work for the Cinema," *Films and Filming* 7, no. 1 (October 1961) : 17–18, 39; "Second Part," *Films and Filming* 7, no. 2 (November 1961) : 29–30, 45; and *Interviews with Film Directors*, Andrew Sarris, ed. (New York: Bobbs-Merrill Company, 1967) , pp. 42–50.

21. See Andrew Sarris, "A Thin Slice of Americana," *Film Culture* 2 (August 1956) : 26–27; and Gene Ringgold, "Rosalind Russell," *Films in Review* 21, no. 10 (December 1970) : 585–610.

22. See Pauline Kael, *Going Steady*, pp. 286–88.

23. See Eugene Archer, "Generation Without a Cause," *Film Culture* 2 (June 1956) : 18–21; and Penelope Houston, "Rebels Without Causes," *Sight and Sound* 25, no. 3 (Spring 1956) : 178–81.

Aparajito (India—16mm: 1958, 108 min., b/w, English subtitles, sound, R-AUD)
This film is the second part of Ray's trilogy on Apu, a boy from a broken Brahmin family. It depicts Apu's schooling through his university days, and is told with poetic simplicity.[24]

The Bicycle Thief (Italy—16mm: 1949, 87 min., b/w, English subtitles, sound, R-AUD, BUR)
Vittorio de Sica's tragic film shows how a young man's inability to find work in an indifferent world profoundly affects his relationship with his son.[25]

East of Eden (Warners—16mm: 1955, 115 min., color, sound, R-AUD, CCC, CHA, CWF, ICS, IDE, NAT, ROA, SWA, TWF, TWY, WHO/L-WSA)
Writer Paul Osborne condensed a small part of Steinbeck's sweeping novel about a modern Cain and Abel, and Elia Kazan turned it into a marvelous movie. James Dean, as Cal, the lonely adolescent who feels slighted by his father (Raymond Massey), provides a stirring experience as do Julie Harris (Abra, his girlfriend) and Jo Van Fleet (Kate, his mother).[26]

Georgy Girl (Britain—16mm: 1966, 100 min., b/w, sound, R-COL)
Silvio Narizzano directed this fresh and delightful film about a plump girl (Lynn Redgrave) who sacrifices everything to mother someone else's child. Fine performances by Redgrave, James Mason and Alan Bates.[27]

The 400 Blows (France—16mm: 1959, 98 min., b/w, English subtitles, sound, R-JAN)
François Truffaut directed this film about the private world of twelve-year-old Antoine Doinel, which is filled with loneliness and fear. An unhappy home life leads this French boy into despair and then into trouble.[28]

24. See Albert Johnson, "Aparajito," *Film Quarterly* 12, no. 4 (Summer 1959) : 45–47; Marie Seton, "Journey Through India," *Sight and Sound* 26, no. 4 (Spring 1957) : 198–202; Satyajit Ray, "A Long Time on the Little Road," *ibid.*, 203–5; Eric Rhode, "Satyajit Ray, A Study," *Sight and Sound* 30, no. 3 (Summer 1961) : 132–36; Kobita Sarka, "Indian Family," *Films and Filming* 6, no. 7 (April 1960) : 29; Kobita Sarka, "The Great Three-In-One," *Films and Filming* 9 no. 3 (December 1964) : 57–58; Arlene Croce, "Pather Panchali and Aparajito," *Film Culture* 19 (August 1956) : 44–50; and Satyajit Ray, "From Film to Film," *Cahiers du Cinema in English* 3 (February 1966) : 12–19, 62–63.
25. See Douglas McVay, "Poet of Poverty: Part One—The Great Years," *Films and Filming* 10, no. 1 (October 1964) : 12–16; "Part Two: Umberto—And After," *Films and Filming* 10, no. 2 (November 1964) : 51–54; and Erich Rhode, "Why *Neo-Realism* Failed," *Sight and Sound* 20, no. 1 (Winter 1960–61) : 26–32.
26. See Michel Delahaye, "Preface to an Interview," *Cahiers du Cinema in English* 9 (CdC #183, October 1966) : 8–11; "A Natural Phenomenon: Interview with Elia Kazan," *Cahiers du Cinema in English* 9 (CdC #184, November 1966) : 12–35; and Patrick Brion, "Filmography," *Ibid.*, 36–39; and Robin Bean, "Dean—Ten Years After," *Films and Filming* 12, no. 1 (October 1965) : 12–15.
27. See Pauline Kael, *Kiss Kiss Bang Bang* (Boston: Little, Brown and Company, 1968), pp. 20, 22–3.
28. See "Special Truffaut Issue," *New York Film Bulletin* 3 (August 1962), 26 pp.; A. W. Richardson, "Les Quatre Cents Coups (The 400 Blows)," *Screen Education Yearbook* (1963) : 57–59; Eric Rhode, "Les Quatre Cents Coups," *Sight and Sound* 29, no. 2 (Spring 1960) : 89–90; Paul Rotha, "Les Quatre Cents Coups," *Films and Filming* 45, no. 7 (April 1960) : 21–22; Arlene Croce, "Les Quatre Cents Coups," *Film Quarterly* 13, no. 3 (Spring 1960) : 35–38; Judith Shatnoff, "François Truffaut—Anarchist Imagination," *Film Quarterly* 16, no. 3 (Spring 1963) : 3–11; Paul Ronder, "François Truffaut—An Interview," *Film Quarterly* 17, no. 1 (Fall 1963) : 3–13; Martin Perier, "Les Quatre Cents Coups," *Film Journal* 15 (March 1960) : 54–55; R. M. Franchi and Marshall Lewis, "Conversation with Truffaut," *Film Journal* 19 (April 1962) : 37–39; and Peter Davis, "Stilled Life," *ibid.*, pp. 34–36, 59–60.

The Graduate (Avco Embassy—16mm: 1967, 105 min., b/w, sound, R-AVC)
Mike Nichols directed this superb adaptation of Charles Webb's novel about Benjamin Braddock (Dustin Hoffman) who returns from a success-ful college career to the society of upper or middle-class America and runs smack into the screwed-up world of his wealthy parents and the Robinsons. Robert Surtees' photographic work is just right for moving us in and out of fantastic situations blended into naturalistic episodes of love, rebellion, and maturity. In addition to the remarkable music of Simon and Garfunkel, there are the widely acclaimed performances of Hoffman and Ann Bancroft.[29]

The Heiress (Paramount—16mm: 1949, 115 min., b/w, sound, R-CCC, UNI, WHO/L-UNI)
William Wyler's screen adaptation of Henry James's story about a rich, homely girl who wants to marry a fortune hunter is a good film for young people to see. The questions it poses about marriage and family relationships are worth discussing.[30]

How Green Was My Valley (Fox—16mm: 1941, 118 min., b/w, sound, R-FNC)
John Ford and Screenwriter Philip Dunne recreated Richard Llewellyn's poignant novel into a beautiful screen story about a coal mining family in Wales during the rise of labor unions. Choice performances are turned in by Walter Pidgeon, Maureen O'Hara, Donald Crisp and Roddy McDowall.[31]

Marty (United Artists—16mm: 1955, 91 min., b/w, sound, R-UAS)
In his first film, Delbert Mann, using Paddy Chayefsky's screenplay, trans-lated the original *Playhouse 90* TV show about two shy and lonely people into a major, low-budget masterpiece. In addition to Ernest Borgnine's out-standing performance, there are memorable moments provided by Betsy Blair and Esther Minciotti.

Nobody Waved Goodbye (Canada—16mm: 1964, 80 min., sound, R-AUD)
Don Owen directed the National Film Board's first full-length film, a moving and searching story about an adolescent boy trying to find a better way of life than the pathetic existence he sees his middle-class family going through.

A Raisin in the Sun (Columbia—16mm: 1961, 128 min., b/w, sound, R-AUD, CCC, CHA, CWF, IDE, NEW, ROA, SWA, TWF, TWY, WHO/L-COL)
Daniel Petrie directed Lorraine Hansberry's drama about the humor,

---

29. See Hollis Alpert, "The Graduate," *Film 68–69*, pp. 235–41; Pauline Kael, *Going Steady*, pp. 124–27; Robert L. Surtees, *"The Graduate's* Photography," *Films in Review* 19, no. 2 (February 1968) : 89–95; Anthony F. Macklin, ". . . Benjamin Will Survive: Interview with Charles Webb," *Film Heritage* 4, no. 1 (Fall 1968) : 1–6; Jacob Brack-man, "The Graduate," *The New Yorker* (July 27, 1968), pp. 34, 42, 46, 48, 50–52, 54–56, 58–66, and Barry Day, "It Depends How You Look at It," *Films and Filming* 15, no. 2 (November 1968) : 4–8.

30. See John Howard Reid, "A Little Larger Than Life: First Part of an Analysis of Wyler's Work for the Cinema," *Films and Filming* 6, no. 5 (February 1960) : 9–10, 32–33, "Second Part: A Comparison of Size," *Films and Filming* 45, no. 6 (March 1960) : 12, 31–32, 35; and Ken Doeckel, "William Wyler," *Films in Review* 22, no. 8 (October 1971) : 468–84.

31. See Donald Crisp, "We Lost So Much Dignity as We Came of Age," *Films and Filming* 6, no. 3 (December 1960) : 7, 41; Douglas McVay, "The Five Worlds of John Ford," *Films and Filming* 8, no. 9 (June 1962) : 14–17, 53. The script is available in *20 Best Film Plays*, John Gassner and Dudley Nichols, eds. (New York: Crown Publish-ers, 1943) .

pathos, and problems of a black family trying to overcome their own problems as well as taking a stand against an ignorant white community.[32]

Romeo and Juliet (Britain—16mm: 1954, 138 min., color, sound, R-WRS)
   Renato Castellani's film version of Shakespeare's immortal play about young people in love might profitably be compared with the more highly praised Franco Zeffirelli version of 1968.[33]

Shane (Paramount—16mm: 1953, 117 min., color, sound, R-FNC)
   George Stevens's often lauded film about the relationship between the archetypal gunfighter who desires peace and the young boy who worships him is, among other worthwhile things, a useful illustration of the problems involved with different generations.[34]

Sons and Lovers (Fox—16mm: 1960, 103 min., b/w, Cinemascope, sound, R-FNC)
   Jack Cardiff's screen adaptation of D. H. Lawrence's novel about a boy dominated by his mother is effectively presented. The film stars Dean Stockwell as the young man, Wendy Hiller as the domineering parent, and Trevor Howard as the ineffectual father.[35]

PREPARING FOR ADULT ROLES

   The fourth major area of adolescent problems centers around the roles these individuals will play as adults. Since every teenager is actively involved in thinking about his future, a well-selected series of films may help motivate him in his school work. Many adolescents believe that their adult success may well depend upon what they learn in school. In addition, some also believe that success is related to their own self-image. These factors, for better or worse, play an important role in a teenager's mental health. Unless he is adequately prepared for adult life, an adolescent clings to romantic notions that may prove injurious to his happiness. It is not uncommon to discover that many adolescents have unrealistic views of people such as

32. See "Raisin in the Sun," *Films in Review* 12, no. 5 (May 1961) : 298; John Cutts, "A Raisin in the Sun," *Films and Filming* 7, no. 10 (July 1961) : 27; and Sidney Poitier, "Thinking of Corruption," *Films and Filming* 7, no. 11 (August 1961) : 7.
33. See Ian Johnson, "Merely Players: The Impact of Shakespeare on International Cinema," *Films and Filming* 10, no. 7 (April 1964) : 41–48.
34. See Joanne Stang, "Hollywood Romantic: A Monograph on George Stevens," *Films and Filming* 5, no. 11 (July 1959) : 9–10, 33; Penelope Houston, "Shane and George Stevens," *Sight and Sound* 23, no. 2 (October–December 1953) : 71–77; Eugene Archer, "George Stevens and the American Dream," *Film Culture* (August 1957) : 2–4, 25–32; Herbert G. Luft, "George Stevens," *Films in Review* 11, no. 9 (April 1953) : 486; Alan Stanbrook, "The Return of *Shane*," *Films and Filming* 12, no. 8 (May 1966) : 37–41; "Viewing Report of *Shane*," *Screen Education* 26 (September–October 1964) : 76–77; Douglas McVay, "George Stevens: His Work, Part One," *Films and Filming* 22, no. 7 (April 1965) : 14; and "Part Two," *Films and Filming* 12, no. 8 (May 1965) : 16–19.
35. See Kenneth Cavander, "Sons and Lovers," *Sight and Sound* 29, no. 3 (Summer 1960) : 145; Pauline Kael, "Commitment and the Strait-Jacket," *Film Quarterly* 15, no. 4 (Fall 1961) : 4–13; John Gillett, "Sons and Lovers," *Film Quarterly* 14, no. 4 (Fall 1960) : 41–42; Charles Higham, "Jerry Wald and *Sons and Lovers*," *Film Journal* 30 (August 1962) : 63–77, 88–89; Gordon Gow, "Sons and Lovers," *Films and Filming* 6, no. 10 (July 1960) : 22; and Richard Whitehall, "Gallery of Great Artists: Trevor Howard," *Films and Filming* 7, no. 5 (February 1961) : 12–13, 36.

doctors, scientists, athletes, performers, lawyers, and teachers. And they often harbor unrealistic images of love and marriage. Very often the future is viewed not only as a time for achieving great heights in work, but, as David C. Beardslee and Donald D. O'Dowd have pointed out, as

> . . . an opportunity to find comfort, variety, interesting experiences, and pleasant acquaintances. For students, the occupation even specifies the personal qualities of its present and future members, providing a ready-made personality for those who cannot establish a secure identity from their own experience.
> By studying the connotations of occupational roles, it is possible to gain a picture of the values and symbols that characterize the thought and action of present-day students.[36]

Impressionable adolescents gain many of their attitudes and aspirations from motion pictures, and for that reason, it's worth examining the film-makers' treatment of the professions which have influenced young people's attitudes toward the adult world.

All About Eve (Fox—16mm: 1950, 130 min., b/w, sound, R-FNC)
Joseph Mankiewicz directed this ironic story of a young girl, Eve Harrington, who dreams about becoming a Broadway star. At first, Eve appears innocent to us, but as the story unfolds we come to recognize her as a repulsive personality. Splendid performances by Bette Davis, Anne Baxter, and George Sanders.[37]

All the King's Men (Paramount—16mm: 1949, 109 min., b/w, sound, R-AUD, CCC, CHA, CON, CWF, IDE, ROA, SWA, TWF, TWY)
Robert Rossen's expert direction of Robert Penn Warren's novel about the rise of a Louisiana demagogue is for many adolescents a major image of politicians. Particularly good are Broderick Crawford, John Ireland and Mercedes McCambridge.[38]

L'Avventura (Italy—16mm: 1960, 145 min., b/w, English subtitles, sound, R-JAN)
Antonioni's masterpiece ostensibly about the search for a lost woman is a compelling story about love and life. Many critics consider it one of the

---

36. David C. Beardslee and Donald D. O'Dowd, "Students and the Occupational World," *The American College: A Psychological and Social Interpretation of the Higher Learning*, Nevitt Sanford, ed. (New York: John Wiley and Sons, 1964) , p. 623.
37. See David Shipman, "Whatever Happened to Bette Davis," *Films and Filming* 9, no. 7 (April 1963) : 8–9; John Howard Reid, "Cleo's Joe: Part I—The Typewriter Years," *Films and Filming* 9, no. 11 (August 1963) : 44–48; "Part II—All About Eve and Others," *Films and Filming* 9, no. 12 (September 1963) : 13–16; Bette Davis, "What is a Star?" *Films and Filming* 11, no. 12 (September 1965) : 5–7; *Dialogue with the World, op. cit.,* pp. 49–50; Jacques Bontemp and Richard Overstreet, "Measure for Measure: Interview with Joseph L. Mankiewicz," *Cahiers du Cinema in English*, 8 (CdC #178, May 1966) : 28–42; and Lawrence J. Quirk, "Bette Davis," *Films in Review* 6, no. 10 (December 1965) : 481–99.
38. See Ernest Callenbach, *Our Modern Art the Movies* (Chicago: Center for Liberal Education, 1955) , pp. 58–66; and Alan Casty, *The Films of Robert Rossen* (New York: Museum of Modern Art, 1969) .

greatest films ever made. Memorable performances by Monica Vitti and Gabriele Ferzetti.[39]

Camille (MGM—16mm: 1936, 108 min., b/w, sound, R-FNC)
Students will find in George Cukor's film, adapted from Alexander Dumas's novel about love, the actress Greta Garbo, who for many of their parents symbolized the essence of femininity. Robert Taylor also gives a good, but often neglected, performance.[40]

City Lights (United Artists—8mm: 1931, 89 min., b/w, silent, R-MC)
One of Chaplin's masterpieces, this story about the love of a tramp and a blind girl is filled with humor and pathos.[41]

The Entertainer (Britain—16mm: 1960, 97 min., b/w, sound, R-WRS)
Lawrence Olivier portrays an egocentric song and dance man who alienates himself from his family as the result of his exploitation of them. Tony Richardson directs.[42]

The Goddess (Columbia—16mm: 1958, 105 min., b/w, sound, R-AUD, IDE)
Paddy Chayefsky's screenplay about a scheming girl who wants to become a movie star will not be forgotten by those who have seen it. It is typical of the treatment usually accorded Hollywood stars by socially conscious filmmakers, although not necessarily an accurate portrait. John Cromwell directs Kim Stanley in one of her best roles.[43]

---

39. See John Francis Lane, "Oh! Oh! Antonioni,' *Films and Filming* 8, no. 3 (December 1962) : 58–66; John Francis Lane, "The Face of '63—Italy," *Films and Filming* 9, no. 7 (April 1963) : 11–21; Michele Manceaux, "An Interview with Antonioni," *Sight and Sound* 30, no. 1 (Winter 1960–61) : 4–8; Richard Roud, "5 Films," *ibid.*, pp. 8–11; Penelope Houston, "L'Avventura," *ibid.*, pp. 11–13; Geoffrey Nowell-Smith, "The Event and the Image: Michelangelo Antonioni," *Sight and Sound* 33, no. 1 (Winter 1964–65) : 14–20; Roger Sandall, "L'Avventura," *Film Quarterly* 14, no. 4 (Summer 1961) : 51–54; John Bourgess, "L'Avventura," *Film Journal* 20 (August 1962) : 76–77, 89; and Jacques Doniol-Valcroze, "The R-H Factor and the New Cinema," *Cahiers du Cinema in English* 2 (January 1966) : 77–78.

40. See Carl Eric Nordberg, "Greta Garbo's Secret," *Film Comment* 6, no. 2 (Summer 1970) : 26–34; John Howard Reid, "So He Became a Lady's Man: First Part of Cukor's Work for the Cinema," *Films and Filming* 6, no. 11 (August 1960) : 9–10, 30, 34–35; "Women and Still More Women: Part II," *Films and Filming* 9, no. 2 (September 1960) : 10, 31–32; Richard Whitehall, "Garbo—How Good Was She?", *Films and Filming* 9, no. 12 (September 1963) : 42–48; Kenneth Tynan, "Garbo," *Sight and Sound* 23 (April-June 1954) : 187–90, 220; Derek Prouse, "Camille," *Sight and Sound* 25, no. 3 (Summer 1955) : 34–35; Louise Brooks, "Gish and Garbo: The Executive War on Stars," *Sight and Sound* 28, no. 1 (Winter 1958–59) : 12–17, 51; John Gillett and David Robinson, "Conversation with George Cukor," *Sight and Sound* 28, no. 4 (Autumn 1965) : 188–93; Joel Greenberg, "The Films of George Cukor," *Film Journal* 8 (July–August 1957) : 15–46; Romano Tozzi, "George Cukor," *Films in Review* 9, no. 2 (February 1958) : 53–64; and Gene Phillips, "George Cukor: An Interview," *Film Comment* 8, no. 1 (Spring 1972) : 52–55.

41. Theodore Huff, *Charlie Chaplin: A Biography* (New York: Pyramid Books, 1964), pp. 179–91.

42. See Douglas McVay, "Hamlet to Clown," *Films and Filming* 8, no. 12 (September 1962) : 16–19; Penelope Houston, "The Entertainer," *Sight and Sound* 30, no. 4 (Autumn 1960) : 194–95; Colin Young, "Tony Richardson: An Interview in Los Angeles," *Film Quarterly* 13, no. 4 (Summer 1960) : 10–15; Arlene Croce, "The Entertainer," *Film Quarterly* 14, no. 1 (Winter 1960) : 42; and James Merralls, "The Entertainer," *Film Journal* 18 (October 1961) : 15–17.

43. See Derek Prouse, "The Goddess," *Sight and Sound* 27, no. 4 (Autumn 1958) : 316–17; and Peter John Dyer, "The Face of the Goddess: Patterns of Cinema," *Films and Filming* 5, no. 9 (June 1959) : 13–15, 32–33.

Great Expectations (Britain—16mm: 1947, 115 min., b/w, sound, R-CON, UNI, WHO, WRS)

This film is a faithful adaptation by David Lean of Dickens's novel about a boy whose social pretensions cause him to become vain and arrogant.[44]

Hail the Conquering Hero (Paramount—16mm: 1944, 100 min., b/w, sound, R-UNI)

Preston Sturges's film story of a fabricated hero is one of the screen's most satiric comments about society. He centers attention on the wealthy Babbitts and their foibles. Eddie Bracken plays the phony-hero who returns to his small, rural community.[45]

The Hustler (Fox—16mm: 1961, 135 min., b/w, cinemascope, sound, R-FNC)

Robert Rossen's treatment of Walter Tevis's novel involves a pool shark's obsessive ambition to become the best. Particularly helpful for discussion is the character of the protagonist, "Fast Eddie," an individual many students have identified with. Superb performances by Paul Newman, George C. Scott, and Jackie Gleason.[46]

The Life of Emile Zola (Warners—16mm: 1937, 118 min., b/w, sound, R-CON, UAS)

Director William Dieterle's Academy Award winning film places its greatest emphasis on Zola's connection with the Dreyfus Case. Paul Muni, who portrays Zola, gives one of the screen's greatest performances, and demonstrates the need for integrity and perseverance. Also outstanding are Joseph Schildkraut and Donald Crisp.[47]

Lust for Life (MGM—16mm: 1956, 122 min., color, sound, R-FNC)

Director Vincente Minnelli's film, in brilliant color, depicts the despair and loneliness of Vincent Van Gogh as well as giving some excellent background to his greatest paintings. Anthony Quinn has one of his best roles as Paul Gauguin, Van Gogh's best friend and most caustic critic.[48]

---

44. See Chapter 5.

45. See Siegfried Kracauer, "Preston Sturges or Laughter Betrayed," *Films in Review* 11, no. 1 (February 1950) : 11–13, 43–47; Gordon Gow, "Conversation with Preston Sturges," *Sight and Sound* 25, no. 4 (Spring 1956) : 182–83; G. W. Stonier, "Preston Sturges," *Sight and Sound* 28, nos. 3–4 (Summer–Autumn 1959) : 185–86; Manny Farber and W. S. Poster, "Preston Sturges: Success in the Movies," *Film Culture* 26 (Winter 1962) : 9–16; and Eric Johnson, "Preston Sturges and the Theory of Decline," *ibid.*, pp. 17–20. The script is available in *Best Film Plays 1943–1944*, John Gassner and Dudley Nichols, eds. (New York: Crown Publishers, 1944).

46. *See Dialogue with the World*, pp. 39–42; Pauline Kael, "The Innocents and What Passes for Experience," *Film Quarterly* 15, no. 4 (Summer 1962) : 31; Peter Baker, "The Hustler," *Films and Filming* 8, no. 3 (December 1961) : 30; Robert Rossen, "The Face of Independence," *Films and Filming* 8, no. 11 (August 1962) : 7; Allen Eyles, "The Other Brando: The Surprising World of Paul Newman," *Films and Filming* 11, no. 4 (January 1965) : 7–11; Robin Bean, "Success Begins at Forty," *Films and Filming* 12, no. 4 (January 1966) : 5–8; Philip Oakes, "The Hustler," *Sight and Sound* 31, no. 1 (Winter 1961–62) : 40–41; Henry Hart, "Notes on Robert Rossen," *Films in Review* 13, no. 6 (June–July 1962) : 333–35; Henry Burton, "Notes on Rossen Films," *idem.*, pp. 335–41; John Springer, "A Rossen Index," *idem.*, pp. 341–42; Jean-Louis Noames, "Lessons Learned in Combat: Interview with Robert Rossen," *Cahiers du Cinema in English* 7, CDC no. 177 (April 1966) : 20–29; Patrick Brion, "Biofilmography," *idem.*, pp. 38–41; and Frank Manchel and Dan Ort, "Study Guide: *The Hustler*," *Screen Education* 42 (March–April 1968) : 54–62.

47. The script is available in *20 Best Film Plays*, edited by John Gassner and Dudley Nichols (New York: Crown Publishers, 1943).

48. See Penelope Houston, "Lust for Life," *Sight and Sound* 26, no. 4 (Spring 1957) : 207; and Alvin Marill, "Anthony Quinn," *Films in Review* 19, no. 8 (October 1968) : 465–81.

A Place in the Sun (Paramount—16mm: 1951, 120 min., b/w, sound, R-FNC)
Director George Stevens won an Oscar for his screen adaptation of Theodore Dreiser's novel about a confused, ambitious individual whose desire for money and glamor leads him to tragedy. Shelley Winters was given an Academy Award for her performance as the unattractive, poor working girl who becomes a victim of the young man's obsession with social success. Montgomery Clift and Elizabeth Taylor do outstanding jobs.[49]

Room at the Top (Britain—16mm: 1958, 116 min., b/w, sound, R-WRS)
Jack Clayton's screen adaptation of John Braine's novel of a poor man's climb up the social ladder at the expense of others as well as himself is a strong lesson for materialistic youths. Fine performances turned in by Laurence Harvey and Simone Signoret.[50]

MORAL AND PHILOSOPHICAL PROBLEMS AND ISSUES

Finally, we turn to the last major area of adolescent problems: the values of society. Everywhere we turn today, young people are openly and actively involved with the issues and problems that confront adults. They, too, are seeking a philosophy of life that allows them to understand our existence. They, too, are vitally concerned about civil liberties, war and its effects, modern society, and the relationships between people. Very often the arts provide all of us with the opportunity to examine society's values critically and rationally. Man's life is the very basis of the arts. Northrop Frye's explanation about literature, for example, is just as valuable for film:

> Literature does not reflect life, but it doesn't escape or withdraw from life either; it swallows it. And the imagination won't stop until it has swallowed everything. No matter what direction we start off in, the sign posts of literature always keep pointing the same way, to a world where nothing is outside the human imagination.[51]

It is, therefore, not unusual to find that some of the best films deal with the problems and issues of mankind.

Billy Budd (Allied Artists—16mm: 1962, 123 min., b/w, sound, R-CIN)
Herman Melville's story about a young sailor caught in the conflict between the demands of justice and the preservation of law and order is graphically depicted in Peter Ustinov's screen adaptation.[52]

49. See material on *Shane.*
50. See Pauline Kael, "Commitment and the Strait-Jacket," *Film Quarterly* 15, no. 1 (Fall 1961) : 4–13; Peter John Dyer, "Room at the Top," *Films and Filming* 5, no. 5 (February 1959) : 21; Laurence Harvey, "Following My Actor's Instinct," *Films and Filming* 7, no. 1 (October 1961) : 32; Simone Signoret, "On Being Under a Director's Spell," *Films and Filming* 8, no. 9 (June 1962) : 11–12; Peter Cowie, "The Face of '63: Britain," *Films and Filming* 9, no. 5 (February 1963) : 19–27; Alan Stanbrook, "Laurence Harvey," *Films and Filming* 10, no. 8 (May 1964) : 42–46; and Penelope Houston, "Room at the Top?", *Sight and Sound* 28, no. 3 (Spring 1959) : 56–59.
51. Northrop Frye, *The Educated Imagination* (Bloomington: University of Indiana Press, 1964) , 80.
52. See the following: *"Billy Budd* Script Extract," *Films and Filming* 8, no. 4 (January 1962) : 16–18, 42; John Cutts, "Film Review of *Billy Budd," Films and Filming*

Citizen Kane (RKO—16mm: 1941, 119 min., b/w, sound, R-AUD, CHA, FNC, IDE, JAN/L-FNC)
Widely regarded as one of the best films ever made, this movie traces the life of a prominent publisher and millionaire who became a major force in the period in which he lived. Even if students have never seen a film classic before, many of them would still be able to recognize the brilliance of Orson Welles's masterpiece.[53]

La Dolce Vita (Italy—16mm: 1961, 180 min., b/w, English subtitles, sound, R-AUD)
One of the most discussed films of all time, Fellini's motion picture is a cynical examination of contemporary upper-class Roman life. On a much larger scale, it is a discussion of modern life in general.[54]

Fury (MGM—16mm: 1936, 94 min., b/w, sound, R-ADF, FNC)
Fritz Lang's screen classic of the near lynching of an innocent man is an impressive commentary on mob violence. It became the model for many socially conscious films of later years. Strong performance by Spencer Tracy.[55]

Gentlemen's Agreement (Fox—16mm: 1947, 118 min., b/w, sound, R-FNC)
Elia Kazan's screen adaptation of Laura Z. Hobson's novel about anti-semitism in polite society provides a good basis for discussion of a vital problem in our culture. Good acting turned in by Gregory Peck, Dorothy McGuire, and Celeste Holm.[56]

The Grapes of Wrath (Fox—16mm: 1940, 128 min., b/w, sound, R-CON, FNC, MMA)
John Ford's screen adaptation of John Steinbeck's important novel about migrant workers vividly describes the plight and problems encountered by

---

9, no. 1 (October 1962) : 29–30; Peter John Dyer, "Film Review of *Billy Budd*," *Sight and Sound* 31, no. 4 (Autumn 1962) : 197; Pauline Kael, "Film Review of *Billy Budd*," *Film Quarterly* 16, no. 3 (Spring 1963) : 53–56; H. Turton, "Study Guide to *Billy Budd*," *Screen Education Yearbook* (1966) : 111–13; and Peter Ustinov, "Doing it all at Once," *Films and Filming* 6, no. 7 (April 1960) : 5, 32.

53. Almost every book in film history discusses this film. See *Dialogue with the World*, pp. 25–27; Marion Sheridan *et al.*, *Motion Pictures and the Teaching of English, op. cit.*, pp. 93–102; Boleslaw Sulik, "Film Critique No. 3: *Citizen Kane*," *Screen Education* 29 (May–June 1965) : 30–40; John Cutts, "Great Films of the Century: *Citizen Kane*," *Films and Filming* 10, no. 3 (December 1963) : 15–19; Andrew Sarris, "*Citizen Kane:* The American Baroque," *Film Culture* 2 (May 1962) : 14–16; Joseph McBride, "Welles Before Kane," *Film Quarterly* 23, no. 3 (Spring 1970) : 19–22; Joseph McBride, "Citizen Kane," *Film Heritage* 4, no. 1 (Fall 1968) : 7–18.

54. See "Script Extract of *La Dolce Vita*," *Films and Filming* 8, no. 5 (February 1962) : 14, 44; Raymond Durgnat, "La Dolce Vita," *ibid.*, pp. 31–32; John Francis Lane, "*La* (The) *Dolce* (Sweet) *Vita* (Life)," *Films and Filming* 7, no. 10 (June 1961) : 30, 34; Merando Morandini, "The Year of *La Dolce Vita*," *Sight and Sound* 29, no. 4 (Summer 1960) : 123–27; Eric Rhode, "La Dolce Vita," *Sight and Sound* 30, no. 1 (Winter 1960–61) : 34–35; and Gideon Bachmann, "An Interview with Fellini," *Sight and Sound* 33, no. 3 (Spring 1963) : 82–87. The script is available from Ballantine Books in New York.

55. See Gavin Lambert, "Fritz Lang's America: Part One," *Sight and Sound* 25, no. 1 (Summer 1955) : 15–21, 55; and "Part Two," *Sight and Sound* 25, no. 2 (Autumn 1955) : 92–97. The script is available in *20 Best Film Plays*, edited by John Gassner and Dudley Nichols (New York: Crown Publishers, 1943).

56. See Robin Bean, "Elia Kazan on 'The Young Agony,'" *Films and Filming* 8, no. 6 (March 1962) : 26–27, 34; Eugene Archer, "Elia Kazan—The Genius of a Style," *Film Culture* 2 (May 1956) : 5–7, 21–24; and *Dialogue with the World*, pp. 35–38.

many minorities in society. Fine acting by Henry Fonda, John Carradine, and Jane Darwell.[57]

Greed (MGM—16mm: 1923, 150 min., b/w, silent, R-FNC)
Erich von Stroheim's screen adaptation of Frank Norris's *McTeague* shows how human beings can become perverse as a result of an obsession for money. It is regarded by many film historians as one of the great motion pictures. Zasu Pitts gives one of the screen's immortal performances.[58]

High Noon (United Artists—16mm: 1952, 85 min., b/w, sound, R-AIM, CCC, CHA, CON, CWF, NAT, ROA, SPF, SWA, TWF, TWY, WHO, WIL)
Fred Zinnemann's classic Western is about a marshal whose integrity, courage, and conscience brings him into conflict with the philistine elements in society. Gary Cooper in one of his best roles.[59]

The Informer (RKO—16mm: 1935, 91 min., b/w, sound, R-AUD, FNC, IDE, JAN)
John Ford's great film about a slow-witted man, Gypo Nolan, who during the Irish rebellion turns traitor to the Irish cause is considered by many to be one of the ten best motion pictures ever made.[60]

Intruder in the Dust (MGM—16mm: 1949, 87 min., b/w, sound, R-FNC)
Clarence Brown's screen adaptation of William Faulkner's novel about the near lynching of a black man is considered by many to be one of the best films on race relations. Juano Hernandez is superb as Lucas Beauchamp.[61]

The Last Angry Man (Columbia—16mm: 1959, 100 min., b/w, sound, R-AUD, CCC, CON, CWF, IDE, ROA, SWA, TWF, TWY, WHO/L-COL)
Daniel Mann's film version of Gerald Green's novel about a Jewish doctor who dedicates his life to the help of underprivileged people is a strong plea

---

57. See Peter Cowie, "Fonda," *Films and Filming* 8, no. 8 (April 1962) : 22–23, 41; Henry Fonda, "Fonda on Fonda," *ibid.*, 9, no. 5 (February 1963) : 7–8; George Bluestone, *Novels Into Film* (Berkeley: University of California Press, 1961), pp. 147–69; and the script is available in *20 Best Film Plays*, edited by John Gassner and Dudley Nichols (New York: Crown Publishers, 1943).

58. See Dennis Marion, "Erich von Stroheim: The Legend and the Fact," *Sight and Sound* 31, no. 1 (Winter 1961–62) : 22–23, 51; Gavin Lambert, "Stroheim Revisited: The Missing Third in the American Cinema," *Sight and Sound* 22, no. 4 (April–June 1953) : 165–71, 204; Thomas Quinn Curtiss, "The Last Years of von Stroheim," *Film Culture* 4 (April 1958) : 3–5; Richard Watts, "A Few Reminiscences," *ibid.*, pp. 5–7; Lotte H. Eisner, "Homage to an Artist," *ibid.*, pp. 7–8; Lotte H. Eisner, "Notes on the Style of von Stroheim," *ibid.*, pp. 13–19; and Herman G. Weinberg, "Coffee, Brandy and Cigars 30," *ibid.*, pp. 21–22.

59. See George Fenin, "Son of Uncle Sam," *Films and Filming* 8, no. 1 (October 1962) : 49–52; and A. W. Hodgkinson, "High Noon," *The Film Teachers Handbook* (London: British Flm Institute, 1960) : 23–25. Also John A. Barsness, "A Question of Standard," *Film Quarterly* 21, no. 1 (Fall 1967) : 32–37; and Penelope Houston and Kenneth Cavander, "Interview with Carl Foreman," *Sight and Sound* 17, no. 5 (Summer 1958) : 220–23, 264.

60. See Alan Stanbrook, "Great Films of the Century: *The Informer*," *Films and Filming* 6, no. 11 (July 1960) : 10–12, 35; Michael Barkin, "Notes on the Art of John Ford," *Film Culture* 25 (Summer 1962) : 9–13; Ernest Callenbach, *Our Modern Art the Movies*, pp. 88–95; *Dialogue with the World*, pp. 58–59; George Bluestone, *Novels into Films*, pp. 65–90.

61. See *Dialogue with the World*, p. 59.

for humanitarian values. Another great performance by Paul Muni.[62]

A Man for All Seasons (Columbia—16mm: 1966, 120 min., color, sound, R-COL)
    Fred Zinnemann creates a film masterpiece out of Robert Bolt's screenplay based upon his successful stage play. Paul Scofield re-creates his original role of Sir Thomas More, the man whose courage and conscience led him to death and immortality.[63]

Modern Times (United Artists—8mm: 1936, 85 min., b/w, sound, S-Mc)
    Chaplin's great film parable, which he wrote, starred in, and directed, discusses the value of the individual in a mechanized world.[64]

Night and Fog (France—16mm: 1955, 31 min., color, sound, R-AUD)
    Probably the most powerful anti-war film available today, Resnais's motion picture is a documentary on the Nazi concentration camps, particularly Auschwitz.[65]

Odd Man Out (Britain—16mm: 1947, 117 min., b/w, sound, R-CON, JAN, WHO)
    Carol Reed's memorable film about an idealist who gives his life for his convictions is a powerful story not only about the man himself but also about those who come in contact with him. Superb performance by James Mason.[66]

The Ox-Bow Incident (Fox—16mm: 1943, 75 min., b/w, sound, R-FNC)
    William Wellman's excellent screen adaptation of Walter van Tilburg Clark's novel about mob violence in a small western town vividly presents the kind of people who form a lynching party.[67]

The Passion of Joan of Arc (France—16mm: 1928, 77 min., music and sound effects only, R-AUD, EMG, FCE/S-FCE)

---

62. See Peter Baker, "Last Angry Man," *Films and Filming* 6, no. 9 (May 1960) : 22; and John Howard Reid, "Portraying Life with Dignity: An Analysis of Daniel Mann's work for the Cinema," *Films and Filming* 8, no. 6 (March 1962) : 19–20.
    63. The script is available in paperback, Robert Bolt, *A Man for All Seasons: A Play in Two Acts* (New York: Vintage Books, 1962) .
    64. See Peter John Dyer, "Patterns of the Cinema: They Liked to Break the Rules," *Films and Filming* 5, no. 1 (October 1959) : 12–14, 28–29; Douglas McVay, "A Proper Charlie," *Films and Filming* 10, no. 2 (November 1964) : 10–15; Peter Cotes, "The Little Fellow's Self Portrait," *Films and Filming* 10, no. 2 (November 1964) : 11–13; Rene Micha, "Chaplin as Don Juan," *Sight and Sound* 23, no. 2 (January–March 1954) : 132–37; William Whitebait, "Modern Times," *Sight and Sound* 24, no. 3 (January–March 1955) : 140–41; and Margaret Hinxman, "An Interview with Chaplin," *Sight and Sound* 27, no. 4 (Autumn 1957) : 76–77.
    65. See Robert Hughes, editor, *Film: Book 2; Films of Peace and War* (New York: Grove Press, Inc., 1962) , and Roger Sandall, "Night and Fog," *Film Quarterly* 14, no. 3 (Spring 1961) : 43–44.
    66. See Andrew Sarris, "Carol Reed in the Context of His Time: Part One," *Film Culture* 2 (May 1956) : 14–17; and "Part Two," *Film Culture* 3 (August 1956) : 11–14, 28; James Agee, *Agee on Film, Volume One: Reviews and Comments* (New York: Grosset and Dunlap, 1967) , pp. 268–69, 289, 367–69; and Basil Wright, "A Study of Carol Reed," *The Year's Work in the Film—1949* (London: Longmans, Green and Company, 1950) , pp. 11–22.
    67. See George Bluestone, *Novels into Film*, pp. 170–196; *Dialogue with the World*, p. 61; Ernest Callenbach, *Our Modern Art, the Movies*, pp. 1–7; Marion Sheridan *et al.*, *The Motion Picture and the Teaching of English*, pp. 103–111; T. P. Turton, "Mary Beth Hughes," *Films in Review* 22, no. 8 (October 1971) : 485–97; and the script in *Best Film Plays 1943–44*, edited by John Gassner and Dudley Nichols (New York: Crown Publishers, 1944) .

Carl Dreyer's masterpiece of the trial of the young girl is one of the most visually moving experiences in film history. It is an excellent film technically, and Falconetti gives an immortal performance as the simple, doomed country girl.[68]

La Strada (Italy—16mm: 1954, 107 min., b/w, English subtitles, sound, R-AUD, MMM)
One of Fellini's great works, this story of a weak-minded girl, a repulsive strongman, and a philosophical "clown" is one of the memorable films depicting man's search for a way of life. Superb performances by Giulietta Masina, Anthony Quinn, and Richard Basehart.[69]

A Thousand Clowns (United Artists—16mm: 1965, 118 min., b/w, sound, R-UAS)
Fred Coe directed Jason Robards in the re-creation of his stage role as Murray, a nonconformist writer, who chooses to live his own life and avoid the dull world of commercial compromises. It is only when he realizes that society will take his nephew from him unless he conforms that Murray goes back to work for a grotesque TV comic. Good performances are turned in by Robards, Martin Balsam, Barbara Harris, and Barry Gordon.

Treasure of Sierra Madre (Warners—16mm: 1948, 126 min., b/w, sound, R-CHA, SWA, UAS)
John Huston's film classic about three individuals who search for gold is a sardonic and ironic story of what greed can do to some men. Outstanding performances by Humphrey Bogart, Walter Huston, and Tim Holt.[70]

The Trial (France—16mm: 1962, 118 min., b/w, sound, R-AUD)
Orson Welles's adaptation of Franz Kafka's novel about a young bank clerk, Joseph K, who is arrested for an unknown crime illustrates for many people the symbol of present day man in a mechanized society.[71]

---

68. See Alan Stanbrook, "Great Films of the Century: *The Passion of Joan of Arc,*" *Films and Filming* 7, no. 10 (June 1961) : 11–13, 40–41; Herbert G. Luft, "An Interview with Dreyer," *ibid.,* p. 4; Peter Cowie, "Dreyer at 65," *ibid.,* p. 10 (March 1964) : 45–46; Boerge Trolle, "The World of Carl Dreyer," *Sight and Sound* 25, no. 1 (Winter 1955–56) : 122–27; Carl Dreyer, "Thoughts of My Craft," *ibid.,* pp. 128–29; Tom Milne, "Darkness and Light: Carl Dreyer," *Sight and Sound* 34, no. 4 (Autumn 1965) : 167–72; and Kirk Bond, "The World of Carl Dreyer," *Film Quarterly,* 19, no. 1 (Fall 1965) : 26–38.
69. See Edouard de Laurot, "*La Strada*—A Poem on Saintly Folly," *Film Culture* 2 (May 1956) : 11–14; Anthony Quinn, "The Actor and His Mask," *Films and Filming* 6, no. 12 (September 1960) : 7–8; Federico Fellini, "The Bitter Life of Money," *Films and Filming* 7, no. 4 (January 1961) : 13, 38; Ian Johnson, "Gallery of Great Artists: Anthony Quinn," *Films and Filming* 8, no. 5 (February 1962) : 13–15, 42–43; and Peter Harcourt, "The Secret Life of Federico Fellini," *Film Quarterly* 20, no. 3 (Spring 1966) : 4–19.
70. See Fred Majdalany, "Viewing Report: *Treasure of Sierra Madre,*" *Screen Education* 28 (March–April 1965) : 50–51; and *Dialogue with the World,* pp. 64–65.
71. See Sergei Gerasimov, "All is not Welles," *Films and Filming* 5, no. 12 (September 1959) : 8; Peter Cowie, "Gallery of Great Artists: Orson Welles," *Films and Filming* 7, no. 7 (April 1961) : 10–13, 36–37, 39; John Cutts, "The Trial," *Films and Filming* 9, no. 3 (December 1963) : 25–26; Enrique Martinez and Richard Fleischer, "The Trial of Orson Welles," *Films and Filming* 8, no. 1 (October 1962) : 12–15; Robert Bean, "Pinning Down the Quicksilver," *Films and Filming* 6, no. 10 (July 1965) : 44–49; Orson Welles, "The Third Audience," *Sight and Sound* 33, no. 3 (January–March 1964) : 120–22; Michael Macliammoir, "Orson Welles," *Sight and Sound* 23, no. 3 (July–September 1954) : 36–38, 52; William S. Pechter, "Trials," *Sight and Sound* 33, no. 1 (Winter 1963–64) : 4–9; Ernest Callenbach, "The Trial," *Film Quarterly* 16, no. 3 (Summer 1963) : 40–43; and Parker Tyler, "Orson Welles and the Big Experimental Film Cult," *Film Culture* 29 (Summer 1963) : 30–35.

The Trial of Joan of Arc (France—16mm: 1962, 65 min., b/w, English subtitles, sound, R-CON)

Robert Bresson's impressive film about the French maid demonstrates how injustice is often committed in the name of justice as well as the ideological battle between empiricism and inspiration.[72]

The War Game (Britain—16mm: 1966, 50 min., b/w, sound, R-ADF, CON/S-CON)

This original BBC documentary was banned from the airways and released instead as a commercial film. Director Peter Watkins's exceptional pseudo-documentary is a fictional account of a nuclear war and the horrors that follow; fire storms that devastate villages; mass executions of helpless, injured people; and the psychological disaster to the survivors. An incredible motion picture.[73]

A thematic approach, we can thus see, enables us to study significant films while we are discussing important issues that bear directly on our students. The adolescent is able to see how the art of the film relates to the subject of the motion picture. Through such a study, it is hoped that young people will learn to understand, appreciate, and enjoy the cinema and learn something of value about themselves.

---

72. See Gordon Gow, "The Trial of Joan of Arc," *Films and Filming* 9, no. 4 (February 1963) : 36; Gordon Lambert, "Notes on Robert Bresson," *Sight and Sound* 22, no. 4 (July–September 1953) : 35–39; Robert Vas, "Trial of Joan of Arc," *Sight and Sound* 32, no. 1 (Winter 1962–63) : 37–38; and Marjorie Greene, "Robert Bresson," *Film Quarterly* 13, no. 3 (Spring 1960) : 4–10.
73. "Man's Right to Know Before He Dies: A Powerful New Anti-War Film From Britain, *The War Game*," *Film Comment* 3, no. 4 (Fall 1965) : 2–13; James Blue and Michael Gill, "Peter Watkins Discusses his Suppressed Nuclear Film *The War Game*," *idem.*, pp. 14–19.

5
Comparative Literature

Those people who deny that there can be any connection between the scenario and literature seem to me to have a wrong conception, not so much of film as of literature. Literature they seem to regard as something polite and academic, in other words, as something god-forsaken and superannuated, compounded of correct grammar and high-sounding ciceronian phrases. Such a conception reveals the feebleness of their sensibility. If you ask me to give you the most distinctive quality of good writing, I would give it to you in this one word: VISUAL. Reduce the art of writing to its fundamentals and you come to this single aim: to convey images by means of words. But to CONVEY IMAGES. To make the mind see. To project onto that inner screen of the brain a moving picture of objects and events, events and objects moving toward a balance and reconciliation of a more than usual state of emotion with more than usual order. That is a definition of good literature—of the achievement of every good poet—from Homer to Shakespeare to James Joyce or Ernest Hemingway. It is also a definition of the ideal film.

Sir Herbert Read, A Coat of Many Colours

Anyone who seriously intends to study the art of the film must, at some point, consider the strong ties between film and traditional literary forms.[1] The influence of the novel, poetry, and drama on motion pictures has been widely documented in almost every history of the cinema, and recently astute critics of the contemporary scene have started to explore the increasing influence of film on writers and dramatists. Then, too, there are many significant and striking similarities between the kinds of films and literary works that now exist. More often than not, the filmmaker and the poet, for example, use parallel techniques in terms of imagery and rhythm.[2] By

1. Part of the strategy for this section comes from Milton Allen Kaplan's work, *Radio and Poetry* (New York: Columbia University Press, 1949), pp. 171–92.
2. See Jean R. Debrix, "The Movies and Poetry," translated by Dorothy Milburn, *Films in Review* 4, no. 8 (October 1951) : 17–22.

examining critically the kinds of reciprocal influences these various forms exert, students gain a greater understanding of all literature.

Clearly, the strongest similarity between commercial films and the traditional literary forms is the great emphasis on narrative. And it is here that arguments about the relative merit of each medium generally begin. One school argues that although the narrative film in form and function is discursive, it is not like other narrative arts. Film differs from them and has its own conventions, restrictions, and techniques. A typical example is that the film—like the television story, the novel, and the radio play—has the freedom of movement that is denied the stage, although the contemporary stage, they acknowledge, has achieved amazing freedom. The filmmaker can shift time and place with amazing rapidity. By using visual and sound effects as well as print to introduce the setting and the characters, the filmmaker can move more rapidly than can the novelist. When he desires, the filmmaker like the novelist condenses or expands time and jumps over geographic limitations.

But there is another school of thought about these "unique" film techniques. In a well-written and thoughtful survey about movies and literature, Professor Robert Richardson has challenged a number of previously held theories.[3] For one thing, he attacks the idea that because film is basically a photographic medium it alone has the ability to handle the tangible, the actual world as it exists. He explains this is obviously not so, not only because the camera's eye is selective but also because the filmmaker is more concerned with creating a specific impression and not merely with recording reality. And it is precisely his emphasis on particular details to create his illusion of reality that relates him to centuries of literary men who have carefully selected specific examples in order to create a single and forceful image of an abstract idea.

Another controversy over film's unique techniques concerns the stream of images projected on the screen. Richardson argues persuasively that this technique is not related to film alone. He shows, through an apt examination of six lines from one of Keats's posthumous sonnets[4] published in 1848, that poets often change images without any formal prose logic. "The sense of process [in the Keats poem] motivates the sequence, and in

3. Robert Richardson, *Literature and Film* (Bloomington: Indiana University Press, 1969) .

4. The sonnet begins, "After dark vapors have oppress'd our plains/For a long . . ." Richardson cites the sestet to illustrate his point:

> The calmest thoughts come round us; as of leaves
>   Budding—fruit ripening in stillness—Autumn suns
> Smiling at eve upon the quiet sheaves—
> Sweet Sappho's cheek—a smiling infant's breath—
>   The gradual sand that through an hour-glass runs—
> A woodland rivulet—a Poet's death.

turn the slowly flowing sequence of images stirs in the reader a sense of organic process, and so one arrives by a logic of images and the rhythm of organic life at the only conceivable end, death. The quiet and powerful inevitability of such poetry is very much like the effect a good film sequence can provide."[5] Richardson discusses many other shared techniques, including the treatment of spectacle, mobility, point of view, speed, and sound. The overall point is that most literary forms share many common and important techniques.[6] And not merely on a superficial level which might be passed off as strained analogies. An artist, whatever his medium, needs to go beyond the simple act of reading and seeing, and appeal to the audience's far more important realms of perception, understanding, and imagination. He does this by creatively using all the existing techniques available in all the arts.

As you would expect, film critics differ among themselves about the significant relationship among the literary arts and its value for movies in particular. Kracauer, for example, doubts that the "mental world" is suitable for film content, arguing that it is the physical world that can best be present visually.[7] Kael, writing in reply to Kracauer, demonstrates her distaste for any distinctions among the arts:

> Who cares whether the objects on the screen are accessible to the stage, or, for that matter, to painting or the novel or poetry? Who started this divide and conquer game of aesthetics in which the different media are assigned their special domains . . . ?[8]

Andrew Sarris agrees in some measure with Kael. In his review of David Lean's *Dr. Zhivago* he writes: "the cherished belief of certain aestheticians that words are less 'cinematic' than images, and that every literary idea must be translated into a visual equivalent," is a fallacy.[9]

Differences among leading film theorists like Kracauer, Kael, and Sarris are valuable and significant for the stimulating thought they bring to a new art which is still seeking its own aesthetic. The search sometimes carries one group of film aestheticians too far; on the other hand, some critics may not be bold enough in freeing themselves from outworn positions. Students themselves, by examining the various relationships, help in advancing our understanding of the art of the film.

5. Richardson, *Literature and Film*, pp. 52–3.
6. Also useful to read is John Graham, "Damn Your A Priori Principles—Look!": W. R. Robinson Discusses the Movies as Narrative Art," *The Film Journal* vol. 1, no. 2 (Summer 1971) : 49–53; and John Graham, "Fiction and Film: An Interview with George Garrett," *idem.*, pp. 22–25.
7. Siegfried Kracauer, *Theory of Film: The Redemption of Physical Reality* (New York: Oxford University Press, 1960) , pp. 233–34.
8. Pauline Kael, "Is There a Cure for Film Criticism," *Sight and Sound* 31, no. 2 (Spring 1962) : 58. It has been reprinted in Miss Kael's book, *I Lost It at the Movies.*
9. Andrew Sarris, "Films," *The Village Voice* (December 30, 1965) , p. 15.

NOVELS AND FILMS

There are many similarities between the novel and the narrative film. Both have fluid boundaries which allow them to expand their actions through the experience of characters and feelings, although the novel frequently uses more real time than the film to describe situations. The physical appearance of a character or a setting can be communicated quickly to the discerning viewer. Both mediums can use dialogue and narration. Both can direct the audience's attention to particulars. In addition, both can condense or examine a moment at length. The two mediums develop specific situations, build plots, and examine character and environment created from the artist's imagination.

Richardson's *Literature and Film* has some excellent examples of how these similarities operate in practice. Citing novelists like Hawthorne, Twain, and Agee, Richardson demonstrates how the writer, like the filmmaker, uses sounds and dialects to make the book "ring with things actually heard."[10] I was particularly impressed with his chapter on "Verbal and Visual Languages," in which there is an invaluable comparison between verbs and movement in the film. Richardson bases his discussion on the fact that one of the most significant characteristics of forceful prose is a high percentage of verbs, and reminds us that:

> ". . . the film had, from the start, a built-in way to obtain the force and the movement which, in prose, comes from verbs. This was the simple fact that one could take pictures of things that were moving. When one photographed a man reaching for a gun on the wall, lifting it down, tucking it under his arm, opening the breach, inserting a shell, and swinging around to face the door, one had an image which requires six verbs to describe in words. Secondly, the camera itself could move, even if the subject stood still. In moving the camera three hundred and sixty degrees around an empty room, one adds the verbal force of turning, seeing, and following to a scene which in reality would be utterly motionless. Thirdly, when the peculiar power of editing had been discovered, film makers found that they had another verbal force at hand. One could join a series of static shots together in such a way as to produce a powerful tension, a sense of latent energy, and expectation of motion that would be hard to describe in prose (though perfectly possible) since one would need language that was at once static but compressed like a spring. . . . The fourth sort of verbal force available to the film is, of course, the actual verb on the sound track, where all the dramatic resources of the spoken word are just as available to the film as they have always been to the drama."[11]

Dialects and verbs are just two ways in which the languages of written and oral speech can be translated into the screen's visual language.

However, basic differences between the film and the novel do exist. While

---

10. Richardson, *Literature and Films,* pp. 57–63.
11. *Ibid.,* p. 67.

a novel is usually not read in one sitting, the film is seen all at once, and therefore does not rely so much on the viewer's memory. This may explain why Lawson feels that the book evolved as a "colloquy between writer and reader," the basic principle of which is that someone tells a story that requires a reader to remember material between sittings.[12] The film, on the other hand, by not relying heavily on the viewer's memory, is a shorter, more immediate, presentation. It may also explain why David Reisman feels there is an ironic difference between the novel and the film. Originally, Reisman conjectures, the novel had an important role in transforming society; it was used not so much as a vehicle for reforms but rather as a device where individuals could anticipate future roles that might emerge in their later lives. Now, he suspects, the film has replaced the *Bildungsroman* with its emphasis on protagonists, motives, and empathy.[13]

Since the filmmaker uses the camera, a remarkably fluid instrument which generally concentrates on significant content only, the motion picture is usually composed of a series of short episodes fused by the editor's and the viewer's imagination. In the novel and the stage play, there is often a need for the central plot to have greater development and greater continuation. In adapting the works of these mediums to the screen, the filmmaker picks up major episodes and cuts everything that is not significant, even transitions that are not vital to the main plot.

This emphasis on the significant naturally gives film an immediacy that may not be found in the novel. An example of this difference between the mediums is *Greed,* the film version of Frank Norris's *McTeague.* As Lawson points out:

> In the novel, the description of the wedding is contemplative, and gives an effect of lassitude and sadness. It mentions the guests, the sound of the melodion, the minister's low voice, and the noises of the street, heard in muffled monotone. The film-maker creates new value by showing a funeral procession through the window. The shocking contrast gives an urgency that is the opposite of the storyteller's diffuse observations.[14]

The difference is achieved mainly because the novel, in its attempt to be "contemplative," uses words. The film, with its emphasis on "urgency," uses visual images for a quicker reaction. The fact that *Greed* was a silent film helps explain that emphasis.

When a filmmaker attempts to translate concepts like "sacred" and "death" into visual terms, he readily sees the difficulty involved with handling abstractions. What must happen is that an image, a physical thing, has to take on metaphorical value, unless, of course, gesture alone is relied upon.

---

12. John Howard Lawson, *Film: The Creative Process* (New York: Hill and Wang, 1964), p. 213.
13. David Reisman, "The Oral Tradition, The Written Word and The Screen Image," *Film Culture* 2 (1956): 1–5.
14. John Howard Lawson, *Film: The Creative Process,* p. 213.

To illustrate how this is done, Joseph and Harry Feldman attempted to translate a sentence in Thackeray's *Vanity Fair* into visual terms. The sentence was "Unscared by the thunder of the artillery, which hurled death from the English line, the dark rolling column pressed on and up the hill." The shots in the shooting script were as follows:

1. A shot of two soldiers in contrasting attitudes, one crouching in the earth, his body shaking with fear, the other standing erect and calm, his face turned toward the enemy's fire.
2. A shot of very dark clouds breaking.
3. A shot of all sorts of cannon firing.
4. (a) a shot of one French soldier marching forward.
   (b) a shot of a line of French soldiers marching forward.
   (c) a shot of a column of French soldiers marching forward.
5. A shot of a hill.
6. A shot of an English line, entrenched on the top of a hill.
7. (a) Shots of dead soldiers.
   (b) Shots of dying soldiers.
   (c) Shots of guns and cannon.[15]

While by themselves the shots mean "nothing," when properly edited they convey the concepts of "unscared" and "death."

A study of novels that have been adapted to films seems to bear out the contention that the two mediums differ in the types of communication. The filmmaker who adapts a novel encounters a problem which is common in film, stage, television, and radio. The presentation moves inexorably by, and the audience is limited by time in understanding the meaning of the story; it does not have an opportunity to go back to an earlier portion of plot development for clarification.[16] This condition will be alleviated when films are made available to individual viewers for intensive study.

Another difference is that film-production costs constitute the most expensive overhead of all art media. A filmmaker must get viewers to pay admission to see his film. As a result this generally requires appealing to a relatively large segment of a population. It also requires a simplification of the involved story line with its several sub-plots. For more than sixty years, novels with strong narratives have been the most suited to screen adaptations. This tendency has resulted in almost every major western writer's having a portion of his work translated to the screen.[17] But no novelist has

15. Joseph and Harry Feldman, *Dynamics of the Film* (New York: Hermitage House, 1952) , p. 16. ·

16. Lester Eugene Asheim, "From Book to Film: Simplification," *Hollywood Quarterly* 5, no. 3 (Spring 1951) : 291–92. This is one of a series of four articles in *Hollywood Quarterly* which are extracts from Asheim's doctoral study.

17. The following is a selected list of articles on American, English, and World authors whose works have been brought to the screen. American Literature is represented by Kenneth W. Scott, "Hawkeye in Hollywood," *Films in Review* 9, no. 10 (December 1958) : 575–79; Richard B. Lillich, "Hemingway on the Screen," *Films in Review* 10, no. 4 (April 1959) : 208–18; Robert C. Roman, "Mark Twain on the Screen," *Films in Review* 12, no. 1 (January 1961) : 20–33; Robert C. Roman, "Poe on the Screen," *Films in Review*

been adapted more successfully or more often than Charles Dickens.

Since he is so popular and because criticism of a film adaptation of a novel invariably leads to a better understanding of the process involved in translation, students should find it useful to examine some examples of how a Dickens story is turned into a movie.

DICKENS IN THE FILM:
THE ADAPTION OF THREE BOOKS

No less an authority than Sergei Eisenstein, in his original and perceptive "Dickens, Griffith, and the Film Today," first established the influence and importance of the great English novelist to the early moving pictures. Throughout the essay, the famous Russian director emphasizes how Griffith, the father of film art, borrowed heavily from Dickens for visual techniques such as parallel editing, cross cutting, characterization, themes, and tone. So great was the novelist's effect in the first two decades of film that Sergei Eisenstein wrote, "all astonishment on this subject and the apparent unexpectedness [of the phenomenon] . . . can be ascribed only to our ignorance of Dickens."[18]

In 1947, director David Lean created one of the finest screen adaptations of a Dickens novel. *Great Expectations* (Britain—16mm: 115 min., b/w, sound, R-CON, UNI, WHO, WRS).[19] Two of the most difficult decisions Lean faced were the clarification of story line and the adaptation of dialogue. By comparing the opening pages of the novel with the opening scene

---

12, no. 8 (October 1961: 462–73; Stanley Fuller, "Melville on the Screen," *Films in Review* 19, no. 6 (June–July 1968) : 358–63; and Neil Leonard, "Theodore Dreiser and the Film," *Film Heritage* 2, no. 1 (Fall 1966) : 7–17.

English Literature is represented by Lucy Tupper, "Dickens on the Screen," *Films in Review* 10, no. 3 (March 1959) : 142–52; Robert C. Roman, "G. B. S. on the Screen," *Films in Review* 11, no. 7 (August–September 1970) : 406–18; Edward Connor, "Sherlock Holmes on the Screen," *Films in Review* 12, no. 7 (August–September 1961) : 409–18; Jack Edmund Nolan, "Graham Greene's Movies," *Films in Review* 15, no. 1 (January 1964) : 23–25; Rudy Behlmer, "Robin Hood on the Screen," *Films in Review* 16, no. 2 (February 1965), 91–110; Paul Jensen, "H. G. Wells on the Screen," *Films in Review* 18, no. 9 (November 1967) : 521–27; Margaret Tarratt, "An Obscene Undertaking," *Films and Filming* 17, no. 2 (November 1970) : 26–30; and William Thomaier, "Conrad on the Screen," *Films in Review* 21, no. 10 (December 1970) : 611–21.

World Literature includes John Ward, "Alain Robbe-Grillet: The Novelist as Director," *Sight and Sound* 37, no. 2 (Spring 1968) : 86–90; Richard Roud, "Two Cents on the Rouble," *Sight and Sound* 27, no. 5 (Summer 1958) : 245–47; and Richard Roud, "Novel Novel: Fable Fable?," *Sight and Sound* 31, no. 2 (Spring 1962) : 84–88.

Some general articles on film adaptations are Philip French, "All the Better Books," *Sight and Sound* 36, no. 1 (Winter 1966–67) : 38–41; Jerry Wald, "Screen Adaptation," *Films in Review* 5, no. 2 (February 1964) : 62–67; William Fadiman, "But Compared to the Original," *Films and Filming* 11, no. 5 (February 1965) : 21–23; Lionel Godfrey, "It Wasn't Like That in the Book," *Films and Filming* 13, no. 7 (April 1967) : 12–16; and John Schultheiss, "The 'Eastern' Writer in Hollywood," *Cinema Journal* 11, no. 1 (Fall 1971) : 13–47.

18. Sergei Eisenstein, *Film Form: Essays in Film Theory*. Edited and translated by Jay Leyda (New York: Meridan Books, Inc., 1957) , p. 201.

19. See Alvin H. Marill, "John Mills," *Films in Review* 22, no. 7 (August–September 1971) : 385–404.

of the film, we can learn something about the director's approach, which in turn helps illuminate several differences between screen and novel techniques. In the following passage from the novel, deletions in the film version are marked with brackets. All the underlined words indicate ideas that were translated visually.

[My father's family name being Pirrip, and my Christian name Philip, my infant tongue could make of both names nothing longer or more explicit than Pip. So I called myself Pip, and came to be called Pip.][20] [gave Pirrip as my father's family name], on the authority of his tombstone and my sister [Mrs. Joe Gargery, who married the blacksmith. As I never saw my father or my mother, and never saw any likeness of either of them (for their days were long before the days of photographs), my first fancies regarding what they were like, were unreasonably derived from their tombstones. The shape of the letters on my father's, gave me an odd idea that he was a square, stout, dark man, with curly black hair. From the character and turn of the inscription, "Also Georgiana Wife of the Above," I drew a childish conclusion that my mother was freckled and sickly. To five little stone lozenges,[21] each about a foot and a half long, which were arranged in a neat row beside their grave, and were sacred to the memory of five little brothers of mine—who gave up trying to get a living exceedingly early in that universal struggle—I am indebted for a belief I religiously entertained that they had all been born on their backs with their hands in their trousers-pockets, and had never taken them out in this state of existence.] Ours was the marsh country, down by the river, within, as the river wound, twenty miles of the sea. My first most vivid and broad impression of the identity of things, seems to me to have been gained on a memorable raw afternoon towards evening. At such a time I found out for certain, that this bleak place overgrown with nettles was the churchyard; [and that Philip Pirrip, late of this parish, and also Georgiana wife of the above] were dead and buried; [and that Alexander, Bartholomew, Abraham, Tobias, and Roger, infant] children [of the aforesaid, were][22] also dead and buried; and that the dark flat wilderness beyond the churchyard, intersected with dykes and mounds and gates, with scattered cattle feeding on it, was the marshes; and that the low leaden line beyond, was the river; and that the distant savage lair from which the wind was rushing, was the sea; and that the small bundle of shivers growing afraid of it all [and beginning to cry,] was Pip.

"Hold your noise!" cried a terrible voice, [as a man started up from among the graves at the side of the church porch.] "Keep still, you little devil, or I'll cut your throat!"

---

20. This was read on the soundtrack.
21. The infant tombstones were constructed on the set, and appear in shot-8 (four of them)!
22. This appears on the tombstone.

The shooting script for the film version follows:[23]

Shot   *Sound*

1. Exterior Thames Estuary Sunset. *Very Long Shot* of a small boy running from left to right along the bank of the Estuary. Camera pans and tracks with Pip . . . as he comes toward camera. A gibbet is built on the edge of the path, camera right, and Pip glances up at it as he passes. He continues running and moves out of the camera right.

    Dissolve to:

1. The wind is making a high-pitched, ghostly whistling noise. A marsh-bird calls.

2. Exterior Churchyard. *Medium Shot Pip.* He is carrying a bunch of Holly in his right hand. He climbs over a broken stone wall and camera pans right with him, as he walks past the tombstones and old graves in the churchyard. Camera continues panning as he makes his way toward one of the tombstones and kneels in front of it. Pip *Medium Long Shot.*

2. Wind continues. Creaking branches.

3. *Medium Shot* of Pip kneeling at the grave.

3. Wind continues crackling of branches. Continues to end.

4. *Medium Close Shot* Pip kneeling near the tombstone. Pip looks nervously toward the camera.

4. Wind gets louder. Owl calls.

5. *Long Shot* from Pip's eyeline of the leafless branches of a tree. The wind is blowing the branches, which look to Pip like bony hands clutching at him.

5. Wind and crackling of branches grows louder.

6. *Medium Close Shot* Pip looks round as in 4.

6. Wind continues.

7. *Medium Shot* of the trunk of an old tree from Pip's eyeline. The tree looks sinister to Pip.

7. Wind continues and sound of tree bending.

---

23. The following script is based on A. R. Fulton, but with some modification. See A. R. Fulton, *Motion Pictures* (Norman: University of Oklahoma, 1960), pp. 237–48.

8. *Medium Shot* Pip. He jumps up from the grave and runs away right to left toward the stone wall. Camera pans with him, then becomes static as he runs into the arms of a large, dirty uncouth and horrible-looking man, an escaped convict. Pip screams loudly.	8. Wind continues. Pip screams when convict grabs him.
9. Close up of Pip as hand covers his mouth.	9. Scream.
10. Close up on convict from waist up.	10. Convict: "Keep still, you little devil, or I'll cut your throat!"

Lean is concerned, in transferring Dickens's work to the screen, with maintaining the elements of suspense and shock. Any parts of the narrative that do not contribute to those effects are dropped from the screenplay.[24] Thus only the family association between Pip and the gravestones remains. His humorous opening comments, the verbal portrait of his father, and the boy's concern for his identity are cut. The director, in cinematic fashion, throws the audience off guard by suggesting danger near the tombstones and not behind the trees, from where Magwitch emerges. While the pace of the film is similar to the book—both give a lot of information very quickly[25]—the film moves with dramatic suddenness to catch and enthrall an audience.

A major change in adopting a novel to film is the reduction in time involved in telling the original story. Generally the reader spends more time with the novel than the filmgoer does with the motion picture. The writer and the filmmaker need to be conscious of this time difference. It affects the method of presentation and the content used. Some aestheticians feel that the time necessary for telling a story is itself a factor distinguishing the two mediums.[26] Clearly, the film, because of its physical time limitations, is more episodic in its communication; put another way, film makes a point and then moves quickly on to another incident. By comparison, the novelist needs more time for his exposition.

A fearful man, all in coarse gray, with a great iron on his leg. A man with no hat, and with broken shoes, and with an old rag tied around his head.

24. Useful in this connection is the Film-Critic Series *Extract of Great Expectations* (16mm.), produced by The British Film Institute, and distributed by Contemporary/McGraw-Hill. A. Jympson Harman, of *The London Evening News*, shows two ways of presenting the opening scene.

25. The author is indebted to Joan Rosengren's discussion in her class, "Film Education for Teachers," Summer 1965, for a comparison between the opening of the book and of the film.

26. Kracauer believes that the time element as used in the fiction film and in a novel is a difference in degree. Lawson, however, feels that time is crucial in fiction. "The novel is concerned with the memory of contemplations of past events," while the film weaves a pattern "in which all the parts are equally vivid, all having the same audio-visual impact on our consciousness." (Kracauer, *Theory of Film,* p. 262.)

A man who had been soaked in water, and smothered in mud and lamed by stones, and cut by flints, and stung by nettles, and torn by briars; who limped and shivered, and glared and growled; and whose teeth chattered in his head as he seized me by the chin.[27]

This descriptive paragraph is condensed by the filmmaker into one quick shot. Here the film moves more quickly than the novel. (Whether it communicates as much or more material is a matter for speculation.)

The episodic nature of the film obviously influences an adaptation of a novel. First the percentage of time devoted to telling the story is reduced. Asheim, in analyzing twelve novels that had been adapted for the screen,[28] wrote, "In every respect but one, the film reduces the proportion of the whole which is devoted to it [the story], or retains it in comparable relation to the whole."[29] The exception was *A Tale of Two Cities* (MGM—16mm: 1935, 128 min., b/w, sound, R-FNC).[30] There, the story of Sidney Carton occupies almost double the time in the film as compared to the book. (See Table I.) The film adaptation, moreover, focuses episodically on a major character, and all other characters and incidents are treated in their relationship to the protagonist. Table I indicates how the film changes the focus of the characters by magnifying the role of Carton, an attractive figure on the screen, and subordinating the rest of the characters.

TABLE I

Content Analysis of *A Tale of Two Cities*[31]

Content Aspects	Percentage	
	Book	Film
The story of Darnay and Lucie	28	19
The story of Dr. Manette	21	14
The story of Sidney Carton	18	36
The story of the Defarges	16	14
The story (stories) of Pross and Barsad	11	11

27. Charles Dickens, *Great Expectations* (New York: Hermitage Club, 1939), p. 12.
28. The twelve novels are *Pride and Prejudice, Jane Eyre, Wuthering Heights, The Good Earth, Victory, David Copperfield, A Tale of Two Cities, In This Our Life, The House of the Seven Gables, For Whom the Bell Tolls, Les Miserables, The Light That Failed, Main Street* (filmed as *I Married a Doctor*), *The Sea Wolf, Of Human Bondage, Kitty Foyle, The Grapes of Wrath, Dr. Jekyll and Mr. Hyde, Alice Adams, The Magnificent Ambersons, Anna Karenina, Huckleberry Finn, Tom Sawyer, The Virginian.*
29. Lester Eugene Asheim, "From Book to Film: A Comparative Analysis of the Content of Selected Novels and the Motion Pictures Based Upon them," (Doctoral study, University of Chicago, 1949), p. 69.
30. There are some useful articles on the film's star: Jack Jacobs, "Ronald Colman," *Films in Review* 9, no. 4 (April 1958) : 175–89; and Julian Fox, "Ronald Colman's Career: Part One," *Films and Filming* 18, no. 6 (March 1972) : 26–32; and "Part Two," *Films and Filming* 18, no. 7 (April 1972) : 34–39.
31. Lester Eugene Asheim, "From Book to Film," p. 69.

Historical treatment of the French Revolution	10	10
Commentary	9	5
Minor characters	8	8
The story of Jerry Cruncher	6	2

Since time must be contracted in adapting books to the screen, certain deletions occur no matter how faithful the screenplay is to the original narrative. In *Great Expectations* some of the characters who are omitted are Orlick, Trabb, Trabb's boy, The Avenger, and Miss Skiffins. In doing this, the screenwriter concentrates on the central story line and deletes any diverting or confusing interplay. Episodes are cut or condensed, in particular those involving Pip and Joe. These changes force the interplay between the two characters to be telescoped in one or two key scenes.[32]

As a result, the film adaptation changes the emphasis of the novel. The changes, however, do not deviate from the central theme of the book. In the film *David Copperfield* (MGM—16mm: 1935, 133 min., b/w, sound, R-FNC), the most important change occurred because director George Cukor wanted to emphasize Copperfield's youth (see Table II). To do this, Cukor stressed those characters which figured prominently in the boy's formative years.[33]

TABLE II

Content Aspects of *David Copperfield*[34]

	Percentage	
Content Aspects	Book	Film
David as a man	69	44
David as a boy	31	56
———————— Including sub-plots ————————		
Peggotty—Barkis, and Peggotty's family	20	26
The Wickfields, Uriah Heep, and David-Agnes	16	15
The Steerforth family	15	15
The Spendlows, and David-Dora	14	14
The Micawbers	11	10
Betsy Trotwood and Mr. Dick	10	20
Tommy Traddles	8	..

32. A. R. Fulton, *Motion Pictures*, p. 233.
33. Lester Eugene Asheim, "From Book to Film," p. 51.
34. *Ibid.*, p. 50.

In preparing a novel for film, the adapter stresses visual details. In the film, printed words become a succinct way of cinematically conveying information. In the film *David Copperfield,* Uriah Heep's successful conniving is shown by the polishing of a sign, "Heep and Wickfield." Here the single shot quickly conveys the change in situation and the status of the characters. Another technique is to photograph the actual page of the novel. The motion pictures of *David Copperfield* and *A Tale of Two Cities* begin with closeup shots of the scene described in the first page of the book itself: the former shows Dickens's preface; the latter, presents in abridged form, the key words in the paragraph: "It was the best of times, it was the worst of times. . . ."

Sound also helps to convey the story quickly. By combining sound with picture, the filmmaker can re-create realistically the rattling of a carriage or the attack on the Bastille much more succinctly than can the novel *A Tale of Two Cities.* In the film *Great Expectations,* sound is used effectively to emphasize startling effects in the graveyard scene and in Miss Haversham's room. Screaming sea gulls are heard in the rowboat chase, and a sound montage makes a cinematic metaphor of Mrs. Joe's words, which are drowned out by the wind.[35]

Film can use physical action to convey ideas that are described in the book. For example, in the novel *David Copperfield,* David's love for Dora is revealed in a letter to Agnes, while in the film he speaks his love to Dora in person. In *Great Expectations,* Dickens describes young Pip's fear of the convict, but in the film the sound track plays Magwitch's voice, and we see Pip reacting.

Another difference between the novel and the film is the ending, which often is changed in the movies. Unlike the book, the film is governed by censorship and popular taste. Before the 1950s most films ended happily. More recently, the story line has determined the ending. In the novels that Asheim talked about, there was a tendency to eliminate any content following the resolution once the audience was assured of a happy ending, whereas novelists tend to present later activities, such as marriages, births, and deaths, in order to resolve the sub-plots. For example, in *David Copperfield,* Dora dies after Micawber's denunciation of Heep. In the film, the situation is reversed in order to end the film with the emphasis on the main characters. However, such manipulations do not usually change the denouements in adaptations of Dickens.

---

35. A. R. Fulton, *Motion Pictures,* pp. 237–238.

Asheim reports that the films remained true to the resolutions in the books. In *David Copperfield* and *Great Expectations,* there is a happy ending emphasized either by showing the couples in an embrace or using a symbol to suggest the union of the two lovers. In *A Tale of Two Cities,* Carton is executed.

BOOKS

Introduction

* Althshuer, Thelma and Richard Paul Janaro. *Responses to Drama: An Introduction to Plays and Movies.* Boston: Houghton Mifflin Company, 1967.

In an attempt to increase visual literacy, the authors offer a basic but simplistic discussion about critical standards. The emphasis is on a historical perspective grounded in social comments.

* Bluestone, George. *Novels into Film.* Berkeley: University of California Press, 1961.

Originally published in 1957, this book is still one of the best studies now available on the essential relationships between books and movies. Bluestone divides his examination into two sections, "The Limits of the Novel and the Limits of the Film," followed by six chapters on *The Informer, Wuthering Heights, Pride and Prejudice, The Grapes of Wrath, The Ox-Bow Incident,* and *Madame Bovary.*

Enser, A. G. S. *Filmed Books and Plays: A List of Books and Plays from Which Films Have Been Made, 1928–1967. Revised and with a Supplementary List for 1968 and 1969.* New York: Seminar Press, 1971.

This book offers three indices: by film title, author, and change of original title. A typical film title entry has the name of the film, and underneath, the name of the filmmaker or the distributing company (usually in abbreviation) and the year the picture was registered. The book is intended primarily for librarians and film societies.

* Marcus, Fred H. (editor). *Film and Literature: Contrasts in Media.* Scranton: Chandler Publishing Company, 1971.

Starting from the position that film merits serious study in our schools, Marcus offers a good collection of familiar essays on the art of the film, including pieces by Balázs, Pudovkin, Durgnat, and Kauffmann. His second section of this worthwhile anthology treats specific translations from words to graphic images, such as *Catch-22, The Grapes of Wrath,* and *Tom Jones.*

Richardson, Robert. *Literature and Film.* Bloomington: Indiana University Press, 1969.

In nine well-written and highly profitable chapters, Richardson provides some excellent parallels and analogies between the various literary genres and film. Particularly useful are his observations on poetry and the perceptive and stimulating comparison between *La Dolce Vita* and *The Wasteland.*

* Robinson, W. R. (editor) with assistance from George Garrett. *Man and The Movies.* Baton Rouge: Louisiana State University Press, 1967.

Although this anthology is very uneven, the opening section on "The Art and Its Forms" has two very readable and helpful introductions to screen translations by Alan S. Downer and Martin C. Battestin. The former suggests a way of seeing films, and the latter is a good analysis of the film version of *Tom Jones*. Other valuable articles on film and book analogies are by O. B. Hardison, Richard Wilbur, Joseph Blotner, and Leslie Fiedler. If possible read Richard Jameson's stinging review of this book in "Manhandling the Movies," *Film Quarterly* 22, no. 3 (Spring 1969) : 4–11.

Screen Adaptations

* Agel, Jerome (editor). *The Making of Kubrick's 2001*. New York: Signet, 1970.
   This superb and delightful book contains some wonderful stories, insights, and illustrations about the origin, design, and impact of Stanley Kubrick's adaptation of his novel, written in collaboration with Arthur C. Clarke, *Journey Beyond the Stars*. After the film was completed, Clarke published its story in novel form: 2001: *A Space Odyssey* (New York: Signet, 1968).[36]

* Capote, Truman *et al. Trilogy: An Experiment in Multimedia. A Christmas Memory, Miriam, Among the Paths to Eden*. New York: The Macmillan Company, 1969.
   In this unique anthology, we have Capote's original stories, Eleanor Perry's wonderful screen adaptations, and some personal observations by director Frank Perry. The book, hopefully, will encourage publishers to produce more such invaluable materials in similar fashion.

Cocteau, Jean. *Diary of a Film*. New York: Roy, 1950.
   Although much of the book deals with incidentals about the making of *La Belle et La Bête* in France from August 1945 to June 1946, beginning students should find a discussion of the great filmmaker's basic techniques very useful. Unfortunately, the technical discussion presumes much background, and the neophyte would be wise to have a glossary nearby.

* Curry, George. *Copperfield '70: The Story of the Making of the Omnibus 20th Century-Fox Film David Copperfield*. New York: Ballantine Books, 1970.
   Here is another useful behind-the-scenes account of an all-star production of a Dickens classic—this time for an NBC-Television movie. The advantage, therefore, is in learning how TV adds to the adapter's problems. The book has 16 pages of photographs plus the Jack Pulman-Frederick Brogger screenplay.

* Mosley, Leonard. *The Battle of Britain: The Making of a Film*. New York: Ballantine Books, 1969.
   The author provides some insights into a spectacular failure and cites a number of problems that the producers faced in behind-the-scenes compromises with temperamental German and English World War II officers. In connection with this book, see Robin Bean, "Blazing the Trail: Harry Saltzman," *Films and Filming* 15, no. 12 (September 1969) : 4–7.

---

36. See also Don Daniels, "A Skeleton Key to *2001*," *Sight and Sound* 40, no. 1 (Winter 1970–71) : 28–33.

* Ross, Lillian. *Picture*. New York: Rinehart, 1952.

Originally printed as a *New Yorker* article, this book is a humorous yet invaluable record of John Huston's production of *The Red Badge of Courage*. No record of Hollywood's crass studio system has yet approached the intriguing reporting that Ross gives to the activities of studio production head Dore Schary, producer Gottfried Reinhardt, actor Audie Murphy, and director Huston himself. It should be on everyone's shelf. For a recent Huston translation, read Hans Koningsberger, "From Book to Film—Via John Huston," *Film Quarterly* 22, no. 3 (Spring 1969) : 2–4.

West, Jessamyn. *To See the Dream*. New York: Harcourt, Brace and Company 1956.

Written by the author of *The Friendly Persuasion,* this book describes how the film version of a novel is seen through the eyes of its original creator. Miss West presents an interesting account of her life as a screenwriter and technical advisor to director William Wyler, who made *The Friendly Persuasion* into an average movie, starring Gary Cooper, Anthony Perkins, and Dorothy McGuire.

FILMS

American Novels

For Whom the Bell Tolls (Paramount—16mm: 1943, 156 min., b/w, sound, R-SWA, TFC, WHO/L-UND)

Sam Wood directed Dudley Nichols's screen version of this Hemingway adventure of the Spanish Civil War and the American engineer who gave up his life in a hopeless cause. Strong performances by Gary Cooper, Ingrid Bergman, and Katina Paxinou.

The Good Earth (MGM—16mm: 1936, 138 min., b/w, sound, R-FNC)

Sidney Franklin directed this last production by Irving Thalberg. Based upon Pearl Buck's epic novel of hunger, plague, and the struggle for survival in China, the film remains a high point in screen adaptations. Outstanding performances by Paul Muni and Luise Rainer. The screenplay is available in Gassner and Nichols, *20 Best Film Plays* (New York: Crown Publishers, 1943).

The Haunting (MGM—16mm: 1963, 112 min., cinemascope, b/w, sound, R-AUD, FNC)

Director Robert Wise deserves the credit for this suspenseful translation of Shirley Jackson's novel about a strange young woman who gathers a group of people and takes them into a weird house. Good performances by Julie Harris, Claire Bloom, and Richard Johnson.

The Innocents (Fox—16mm: 1961, 99 min., cinemascope, b/w, sound, R-FNC)

Director Jack Clayton and screenwriter Truman Capote deserve the credit for this thrilling translation of Henry James's short novel *The Turn of the Screw,* a tale that pits two strange children against a bewildered governess and the haunting memories of her predecessors. Deborah Kerr gives a good performance as the frightened governess.[37]

Little Big Man (Fox—16mm: 1970, 139 min., color, sound, R-SWA)

Arthur Penn directed this uneven but still worthwhile screen adaptation of Thomas Berger's novel about the incredible Mr. Jack Crabb (Dustin Hoffman). In many respects this is a good spoof on the epic western films since we encounter a number of folk heroes plus famous incidents in the taming of the American frontier. Chief Dan George gives a memorable performance as Old Lodge Skins, the fatherly Indian chief who educates Crabb into manhood and wisdom.[38]

To Kill a Mockingbird (Universal—16mm: 1962, 129 min., b/w, sound, R-CCC, CWF, ROA, SWA, UNI, WHO/L-UNI)

Director Robert Mulligan and screenwriter Horton Foote combined talents to create a memorable film translated from Harper Lee's unusual story about Southern children escaping from a previous generation's prejudice. Gregory Peck gives an outstanding performance as their father.[39]

The Magnificent Ambersons (RKO—16mm: 1942, 88 min., sound, R-FNC, JAN)

Orson Welles wrote the screenplay and directed this remarkable screen version of Booth Tarkington's novel about the internal problems of a powerful midwestern family. Fine performances by Joseph Cotton, Tim Holt, and Agnes Moorehead.[40]

The Red Badge of Courage (MGM—16mm: 1951, 69 min., b/w, sound, R-FNC)

John Huston did a superb job in recreating many facets of Stephen Crane's classic story about the American Civil War where an innocent youth (Audie Murphy) learns to conquer fear. Some of the most memorable scenes of men at war are contained in this very significant film.[41]

---

37. Penelope Houston, "The Innocents," *Sight and Sound* 31, no. 1 (Winter 1961–62) : 39–40; Penelope Houston, "The Innocents," *Sight and Sound* 31, no. 2 (Summer 1961): 114–15; "Script Extract from *The Innocents*," *Films and Filming* 8, no. 3 (December 1961) : 14–15, 45; and Pauline Kael, "The *Innocents*, and What Passes for Experience," *Film Quarterly* 15, no. 4 (Summer 1962) : 21–27. The latter is available, in revised form, in Pauline Kael, *I Lost It at the Movies* (Boston: Little, Brown and Company, 1965) , pp. 147–55.

38. Gordon Gow, "Metaphor: An Interview with Arthur Penn," *Films and Filming* 17, no. 10 (July 1971) : 16–21; and Leo Braudy, "The Difficulties of Little Big Man," *Film Quarterly* 25, no. 1 (Fall 1971) : 30–33.

39. Lionel Godfrey, "Flawed Genius: The Works of Robert Mulligan," *Films and Filming* 13, no. 4 (January 1967) : 47–52.

40. Derek Prouse, "Notes on Film Acting," *Sight and Sound* 24, no. 4 (Spring 1955) : 174–180.

41. See N. Tucker, "The Red Badge of Courage," *Screen Education Yearbook* (1963) : 61–63; Eugene Archer, "Taking Life Seriously: A Monograph of John Huston, Part I—A Touch of Hemingway," *Films and Filming* 10, no. 12 (September 1959) : 13–14, 28, 35; "Small People in a Big World: Part II—A Touch of Melville," *Films and Filming* 6, no. 1 (October 1959) : 9–10, 25, 34; Gideon Bachmann, "How I Make Films: An Interview with John Huston," *Film Quarterly* 19, no. 1 (Fall 1965) : 3–13; Edouard Laurot, "An Encounter with John Huston," *Film Culture* 2 (May 1956) : 1–4; Eugene Archer, "John Huston—The Hemingway Tradition in American Film," *Film Culture* 19 (August 1956) : 66–101; and Garth Buckner, "A Director's Progress: John Huston in Perspective," *Film Journal* 4 (May 1955) : 1–15. Also, Lillian Ross, *Picture* (Baltimore: Pelican, 1962) . This was originally a series of articles on the making of the film, written by Ross for *The New Yorker* in 1950–51.

The Sun Also Rises (Fox—16mm: 1957, 129 min., color, sound, R-FNC)
Henry King directed Peter Viertel's exceptional screenplay taken from Hemingway's novel about the misfits of the lost generation who roamed Europe in the 1920s. Three superb performances by Tyrone Power, Ava Gardner, and Errol Flynn.

English Novels

Goodbye, Mr. Chips. (MGM—16mm: 1938, 114 min., b/w, sound, R-FNC)
Director Sam Wood was mainly responsible for this fine screen translation of James Hilton's nostalgic story of an English schoolmaster during the early years of the twentieth century. Outstanding performances by Robert Donat and Greer Garson.

Lost Horizon (Columbia—16mm: 1937, 120 min., b/w, sound, R-AUD, CCC, CHA, CON, CWF, IDE, TWF, TWY/L-COL)
Frank Capra deserves the credit for this memorable screen version of James Hilton's fantasy. According to Capra, the film was first shown to a preview audience that found it confusing and laughable. The director went home, considered the film print carefully, and decided to do away with the two opening reels, which is the version we have today. Jane Wyatt gives a fine performance as the ideal woman of Shangri-la.[42]

Mutiny on the Bounty (MGM—16mm: 1935, 132 min., b/w, sound, R-FNC)
Producer Irving Thalberg is responsible for this superb translation of Nordhoff and Hall's memorable sea saga about the villainous Captain Bligh and the idealistic Mr. Christian. Great performances by Charles Laughton and Clark Gable. Frank Lloyd directed.

Pride and Prejudice (MGM—16mm: 1940, 118 min., b/w, sound, R-FNC)
Aldous Huxley wrote the screenplay and Robert Z. Leonard directed Jane Austen's magnificent story about five daughters in pursuit of desirable mates. Delightful performances by Greer Garson, Laurence Olivier, Edmund Gwenn, and Edna May Oliver.

Tom Jones (United Artists—16mm: 1963, 115 min., color, sound, R-CHA, UAS)
Director Tony Richardson and playwright John Osborne created this masterly translation of Henry Fielding's novel about an eighteenth-century lovable rascal whose stimulating life in country manners explodes on the screen. Marvelous performance by Albert Finney. The Osborne script is available from Grove Press.

Wuthering Heights (Goldwyn—16mm: 1939, 104 min., b/w, sound, R-SGS)
Director William Wyler, using the screenwriting talents of Ben Hecht and Charles McArthur, created a sensitive, poignant film translation of Emily Bronte's masterpiece about the mysterious Heathcliff and the indomitable Catherine whose tortuous love affair destroyed two families. Outstanding performances by Merle Oberon, Laurence Olivier, and David Niven. The screenplay is available in Gassner and Nichols, *20 Best Film Plays*.

---

42. Roger Dooley, "Jane Wyatt," *Films in Review* 23, no. 1 (January 1972) : 28–40.

ADAPTATION OF THE STAGE PLAY

Theatrical works need to be rewritten if they are to succeed as films. The same factors that influence film–novel translations prevail in film–stage adaptations. The questions of how, when, where, and why are generally approached in three different ways.

First, the historical approach to the relationship between stage and screen is based on the thesis that the film play arose out of the nineteenth-century drama with its emphasis on panoramas, spectacles, fantasies, and melodramas. Nicholas Vardac places the motion picture in the larger development of drama.[43] He traces the stage's progress from the days of David Garrick to the works of D. W. Griffith, arguing that the early cinematic techniques were an outgrowth of the theater's need for innovation. It is precisely that close historical connection that prods many critics to judge film by its degree of independence from stage traditions. These same critics cite examples of the theater's negative influence on the early "photoplays," namely the immobile cameras, the exaggerated acting, and the awkward stage furnishings. Rarely do they mention such positive influences during those same years in terms of highly qualified performers, creative technicians, and brilliant theoreticians. People who quickly come to mind are Georges Méliès, D. W. Griffith, Max Reinhardt, and Sergei Eisenstein. The point, simply put, is that both mediums exert positive and negative influences on each other.

This brings us to the second approach: a comparison between films and the stage plays from which they are adapted. Allardyce Nicoll begins his invaluable study of such comparisons by examining the relationship between Shakespeare's age and the present world of the cinema and listing the usual arguments against the film as an art form.[44] Then, cleverly, he asks the reader to substitute *theater* for *cinema* and shows how the charges against the screen were almost the same as those leveled against Shakespeare's theater: it was designed to be popular, condemned by cultured men, dominated by clowns, controlled by ignorant financiers, appeared uneven in quality, often got revised by ghost writers, and disregarded the classical unities. Nicoll goes on to argue that the crucial difference between the two mediums is best seen in the treatment of characters. He suggests that the stage encourages stock figures while the screen cries out for individual characterizations. Erwin Panofsky, on the other hand, argues that just the reverse is true: film production, in contrast to the stage production, demands stock figures.[45]

---

43. A. Nicholas Vardac, *Stage to Screen* (Cambridge: Harvard University Press, 1949). Reissued by Benjamin Blom, 1968.

44. Allardyce Nicoll, *Film and Theatre* (New York: Thomas Y. Crowell Company, 1936), pp. 5–16. This chapter has been reprinted in Richard Dyer MacCann (ed.), *Film and Society* (New York: Scribners, 1964), pp. 29–31.

45. Erwin Panofsky, "Style and Medium in the Motion Pictures," *Film: An Anthology*, compiled and edited by Daniel Talbot (New York: Simon and Schuster, 1959), pp. 30–33.

Susan Sontag presents a third point of view:

> If an irreducible distinction between theatre and cinema does exist, it may be this. Theatre is confined to a logical or *continuous* use of space. Cinema (through editing, that is, through the change of shot—which is the basic unit of film construction) has access to an alogical or *discontinuous* use of space. In the theatre, people are either in the stage space or "off." When "on," they are always visible or visualizable in contiguity with each other. In the cinema, no such relation is necessarily visible or even visualizable.[46]

Sontag's main argument is that we need to approach the stage-screen controversy with new ideas.

A. R. Fulton emphasizes that the difference between the theater and the film is in the heavy reliance of the former on dialogue, while movies are more audio-visual oriented. The manner of presentation becomes the crucial point. In a film the attention of the audience can more easily be directed by camera angles and specific shots. The emphasis is achieved by editing. Fulton finds John Cromwell's film adaptation of *Abe Lincoln in Illinois* (RKO—16mm: 1940, 110 min., b/w, sound, R-CHA, FNC), to be a faithful translation of the main character, despite a considerable omission of dialogue which was compensated for by expanding the scope of the film version.[47]

Third, audience and financial pressures must be considered when discussing plays adapted to film. Because of the filmgoers' expectations and the capital investment in production, distribution, and exhibition, major changes occur in expository material and characterizations. Charles Gaupp finds that when a play is adapted to film, the outstanding technique is the exclusion of all material not directly related to the exposition of the main characters and their relation to the central plot.[48]

Through these three basic approaches to the comparative study of screen adaptations, students should sense the creative importance of judgment, selection, and execution. The artist, whatever his source, uses the raw materials to shape his ideas on how to imaginatively present his feelings and understandings to an unknown and varied audience.

BOOKS[49]

Introductory

Gaupp, Charles John Jr. "A Comparative Study of the Changes of Fifteen

46. Susan Sontag, "Film and Theatre," *Tulane Drama Review* 11, no. 1 (Fall 1966) : 29.
47. A. R. Fulton, *Motion Pictures*, pp. 201–14.
48. Charles Gaupp, Jr., "A Comparative Study of the Changes of Fifteen Film Plays Adapted from Stage Plays," (Doctoral study, University of Iowa, 1950).
49. Some useful articles on playwrights translated to the screen are: John Hans Winge, "Brecht and the Cinema," *Sight and Sound* 26, no. 3 (Winter 1956–57) : 144–47; Robert C. Roman, "O'Neill on the Screen," *Films in Review* 9, no. 6 (June–July 1958) : 296–305;

Film Plays Adapted from Stage Plays." Doctoral study, University of Iowa, 1950.

Although dated and difficult to obtain, this study on the various changes in certain aspects of exposition and characterization is worth reading because of its historical perspective on the various influences that studios exerted on screen writers. The plays discussed are *The Barretts of Wimpole Street, Brief Encounter, Dear Ruth, Gaslight, Here Comes Mr. Jordan, I Remember Mama, Lady in the Dark, Night Must Fall, Over Twenty-one, The Philadelphia Story, Pygmalion, Rope, Skylark, Watch on the Rhine,* and *The Women.*

Nicoll, Allardyce. *Film and Theatre.* New York: Thomas Y. Crowell Company, 1936. Reissued by Arno Press in 1972.

The best book available on the essential differences and similarities between the two dramatic arts. Don't let the publication date fool you.

Vardac, A. Nicholas. *Stage to Screen: Theatrical Method from Garrick to Griffith.* 1949. Reissued by Arno Press, 1970.

The author's main contention is that films surpass the stage in their ability to present reality. By tracing the growth of stage realism during the nineteenth century, Vardac points out that the course of events, so he believes, led inevitably to the birth of the motion picture. This scholarly and provocative book is well worth reading both for its stimulating discussion and its accurate footnotes to film history.

William Shakespeare[50]

Ball, Robert Hamilton. *Shakespeare on Silent Film: A Strange Eventful History.* New York: Theatre Arts Books, 1968.

In an informative and very readable narrative, Professor Ball provides a wealth of material, anecdotes, and insights concerning the creative and ingenious approaches to Shakespeare's plays during the first 27 years of film history. There are some fine stills, plus a useful bibliography, series of indices, and glossary of terms.

* Eckert, Charles W. *Focus on Shakespearian Films.* Englewood Cliffs: Prentice-Hall, Inc., 1972.

In this handy collection of useful and stimulating articles, Shakespearian students will find some good information on such films as *A Midsummer Night's Dream* (1935), *Henry V* (1944), *Hamlet* (1948), *Macbeth* (1948), *Romeo and Juliet* (1954), and *Othello* (1965). In addition, there are a valuable filmography and bibliography.

Kozintsev, Grigori. *Shakespeare: Time and Conscience.* Translated from the Russian by Joyce Vining. New York: Hill and Wang, 1966.

Although this book is not devoted entirely to film study, Kozintsev does

---

Richard Roud, "The Empty Streets," *Sight and Sound* 26, no. 4 (Spring 1957) : 191–95; Lionel Godfrey, "It Wasn't Like That in the Play," *Films and Filming* 13, no. 11 (August 1967) : 4–8; Donald Richie and Joseph L. Anderson, "Traditional Theater and Film in Japan," *Film Quarterly* 12, no. 1 (Fall 1958) : 2–9; and Frank Nulf, "Luigi Pirandello and the Cinema," *Film Quarterly* 24, no. 2 (Winter 1970–71) : 40–47.

50. Some useful articles are Geoffrey Reeves, "Shakespeare on Three Screens: Peter Brook Interviewed," *Sight and Sound* 34, no. 2 (Spring 1965) : 66–70; Meredith Lillich, "Shakespeare on the Screen," *Films in Review* 7, no. 6 (June–July 1956) : 247–60; Ian Johnson, "Merely Players," *Films and Filming* 10, no. 7 (April 1964) : 41–48.

discuss at length his prizewinning film *Hamlet*. What results are some invaluable production notes, behind-the-scenes observations on his technique, and a striking commentary on one artist and his world.

Manvell, Roger. *Shakespeare and the Film*. New York: Praeger Publishers, 1971.

Starting with the thesis that film offers unique advantages in presenting Shakespearian plays, Manvell, in a useful and detailed study, covers the history of Shakespeare on the screen from the first silent screen adaptations up to the present time. He is at his best once the Olivier years are covered and is particularly good at discussing the unique efforts of Kozintsev and Kurosawa. The book comes with a selected filmography and bibliography, plus a helpful index.

Morris, Peter. *Shakespeare on Film: An Index to William Shakespeare's Plays on Film*. Revised and Updated. Ottawa: Canadian Film Institute, 1972.

Originally published in 1964, this valuable and interesting critical survey covers screen adaptations of Shakespeare's plays from film beginnings up to 1971, and in addition offers an informative introductory essay about filming techniques, a detailed filmography, and a brief commentary on 50 films from the 1928 version of *Taming of the Shrew* to the 1971 *King Lear*.

* Whitehead, Peter and Robin Bean (editors). *Olivier-Shakespeare*. London: Lorrimer, 1966.

This brief but useful book on England's greatest actor provides a slight text, a filmography, and many superb stills.

George Bernard Shaw

Costello, Donald P. *The Serpent's Eye: Shaw and the Cinema*. Foreword by Cecil Lewis. Notre Dame: University of Notre Dame Press, 1965.

Although this text is mainly about Shaw and not about film aesthetics, Costello develops a valuable chronology of the great dramatist's work in motion pictures from 1914 to 1945 and his attitudes toward translations of his films. There is an invaluable discussion of *Pygmalion* on film plus some valuable appendices on his screen credits, the opening scenes for the film version of *The Devil's Disciple*, textual variations on a screen treatment of Act V of *Pygmalion*, and a complete scenario for a project film version of *Arms and the Man*. Unfortunately, at this time I do not find a *single* Shaw film available for 16mm rental.

SELECTED LIST OF
AMERICAN PLAYWRIGHTS ON FILM

Jack Gelber

The Connection (Films Around the World—16mm: 1962, 103 min., b/w, sound, R-AUD)

Shirley Clarke directed this fascinating screen adaptation of the story of eight drug addicts who are waiting in their Manhattan loft apartment for their "connection" to make a heroin delivery. To raise money to pay for the delivery, they have agreed to let a pseudo-documentary filmmaker make a movie of them playing jazz and relating anecdotes about themselves and their backgrounds.[51]

Lorraine Hansberry

A Raisin in the Sun (Columbia—16mm: 1961, 127 min., b/w, sound, R-AUD, CCI, CHA, CWF, IDE, NEW, ROA, SWA, TWF, TWY, WHO/L-COL)

Daniel Petrie directed and Hansberry wrote her own screen play in this story filled with humor, unrest, and pathos as the Younger family decides how to spend a $10,000 insurance check that the mother receives from her late husband's insurance policy.

William Inge

The Dark at the Top of the Stairs (Warners—16mm: 1960, 123 min., color, sound, R-AUD, CCC, CHA, ICS, NAT, ROA, SWA, TWF, TWY, WIL/L-WSA)

Delbert Mann directed this absorbing screen translation of a man, his wife, and their teenage daughter living in the mid-west and coming to terms with themselves and their problems. Good performances by Robert Preston, Dorothy McGuire, and Shirley Knight.[52]

LeRoi Jones

Dutchman (Britain—16mm: 1967, 55 min., b/w, sound, R-WRS/S-WRS)

Anthony Harvey directed this engrossing attack on racial prejudice when a mentally disturbed blonde (Shirley Knight) confronts a young black man (Al Freeman, Jr.) in a New York subway train.

Arthur Miller

A View from the Bridge (Continental—16mm: 1961, 114 min., b/w, sound, R-WRS)

Director Sidney Lumet and screenwriter Norman Roston combined talents to adapt this play of an Italian-American longshoreman whose sensuous desire for his niece destroys him as a man. Strong performances by Raf Vallone, Carol Lawrence, Morris Carnovsky, and Maureen Stapleton.

Eugene O'Neill

Long Day's Journey into Night (Embassy—16mm: 1962, 136 min., b/w, sound, R-AUD, CCC, ICS, IDE, ROA)

Sidney Lumet directed O'Neill's autobiographical play written in 1941 dealing with the four members of the Tyrone family whose lives reveal their frustrations, failures, and dreams. Strong performances by Katherine Hepburn, Jason Robards, and Ralph Richardson.[53]

51. See Basil Wright, *"The Connection-*Pro," *Film Quarterly* 15, no. 4 (Summer 1962) : 41–42; and Arlene Croce, ". . . Con," *ibid.*, pp. 42–45.

52. Lionel Godfrey, "The Private World of William Inge," *Films and Filming* 13, no. 1 (October 1966) : 19–24.

53. See Ernest Callenbach and Albert Johnson, "The Danger is Seduction: An Interview with Haskell Wexler," *Film Quarterly* 21, no. 3 (Spring 1968) : 3–14; and Dale Luciano, "Long Day's Journal into Night: An Interview with Sidney Lumet," *Film Quarterly* 25, no. 1 (Fall 1971) : 20–29.

Neil Simon

The Odd Couple (Paramount—16mm: 1968, 105 min., color, cinemascope, sound, R-FNC)
Gene Saks directs this hilarious story of two men: a virile, irresponsible slob and his finicky, fanatical housekeeping friend who decide to share an 8-room Manhattan apartment. Good performances by Walter Matthau and Jack Lemmon.

Tennessee Williams

Cat on a Hot Tin Roof (MGM—16mm: 1958, 108 min., color, sound, R-FNC)
Director Richard Brooks deserves the credit for this splendid version of Williams's plays about Maggie, the magnificent "cat" who wants a child but whose husband, the alcoholic ex-football player, can't forgive her for an event in the past. Superb performances by Elizabeth Taylor, Paul Newman, Burl Ives, and Jack Carson.

A Streetcar Named Desire (Warners—16mm: 1951, 122 min., b/w, sound, R-UAS)
Elia Kazan directed this remarkable adaptation dealing with the seedy southern belle Blanche du Bois (Vivien Leigh) who winds up her days as an alcoholic tramp in her brother-in-law's cheap apartment in New Orleans's slum district. At the time of the picture's release, it was considered not only to be one of the most powerful films ever made, but also boasted of having one of the finest casts ever to appear in one film: Brando, Leigh, Kim Hunter and Karl Malden. Everyone, except Brando, won Oscars and the New York critics chose the picture as the best of 1951.

Suddenly Last Summer (Columbia—16mm: 1960, 114 min., b/w, sound, R-AUD, CWF, IDE, NAT, SWA, TWF/L-COL)
Director Joseph L. Mankiewicz, using the screenplay by Williams and Gore Vidal, took a one-act Williams play from *Garden District* and made it into a thrilling film about a psychotic heroine, a practicing homosexual, a procuress-mother, a cannibalistic orgy, and a sadistic nun. Producer Sam Spiegel explained his movie as "a theme the masses could identify with."[54]

SELECTED LIST OF SHAKESPEARIAN FILMS

Hamlet (Britain—16mm: 1948, 152 min., b/w, sound, R-WRS)
Laurence Olivier directed and starred in this controversial Freudian interpretation. Other important roles were performed by Jean Simmons, Eileen Herlie, and Anthony Quayle. Brenda Cross has edited a book on the movie, *The Film Hamlet: A Record of Its Production* (London: Satwin Press, 1948).

Hamlet (Germany—16mm: 1964, 127 min., b/w, dubbed sound, R-AUD, ROA/S-CCM)
This German version in English was adapted and directed by Edward Dmytryk and Franz Peter Wirth and stars Maximilian Schell.

54. Peter Cowie, "Katherine Hepburn," *Films and Filming* 9, no. 9 (June 1963) : 21–23.

Henry V (Britain—16mm: 1945, 137 min., color, sound, R-WRS)
In one of the greatest screen translations ever made, Olivier directs and stars in what may be his finest work on the screen.[55]

Julius Caesar (MGM—16mm: 1953, 121 min., b/w, sound, R-FNC)
Joseph Mankiewicz directed this romantic and entertaining version, starring James Mason as Brutus, John Gielgud as Cassius, Marlon Brando as Antony, Edmund O'Brien as Casca, Louis Calhern as Caesar, Greer Garson as Calpurnia, and Deborah Kerr as Portia. John Culkin edited a handy paperback with useful material from the film together with the original play—William Shakespeare, *Julius Caesar: Complete Text, with scenes from the Screenplay* (New York: Scholastic Book Service, 1963).[56]

Macbeth (Britain—16mm: 1961, 107 min., color, sound, R-AUD, CCC, IDE)
George Schaeffer's original television production of this fine adaptation has an outstanding cast including Maurice Evans and Judith Anderson.

Macbeth (Republic—16mm: 1948, 95 min., b/w, sound, R-AUD, CHA, CON, FCE, IVY, TWY)
This controversial Orson Welles version is worth seeing for the original and imaginative editing that the director-star gives to Shakespeare's text.

The Merry Wives of Windsor (Austria—16mm: 1965, 97 min., color, sound dubbed, R-AUD)
Director George Tressler and producer-screenwriter Norman Foster teamed up to present this tuneful and beautifully photographed interpretation of the immortal Falstaff. The film is based more upon the opera by Otto Nicolai than on Shakespeare's play.[57]

A Midsummer Night's Dream (Czechoslovakia—16mm: 1961, 74 min., animation, color, sound, R-AUD)
This splendid puppet film is one of the best of its kind. Conceived and designed by the Czechoslovakian Jiri Vogta, the producer captures both a marvelous state of make-believe and the spirit of Shakespeare's play.

A Midsummer Night's Dream (Britain—16mm: 1969, 124 min., color, sound, R-AUD)
Peter Hall directed the Royal Shakespeare Company in this beautifully photographed version featuring David Warner, Diana Rigg, Bill Travers, Ian Richardson, and Barbara Jefford.[58]

Romeo and Juliet (Britain—16mm: 1966, 126 min., color, sound, R-AUD)
Paul Czinner produced and directed this intriguing and memorable ballet performance by Margot Fonteyn and Rudolph Nureyev. Also memorable

55. In this connection, it might be useful to look at Peter Whitehad and Robin Bean's little book, *Olivier-Shakespeare* (London: Lorrimer Films Ltd., 1966). Also helpful are Constance A. Brown, "Olivier's *Richard III:* A Reevaluation," *Film Quarterly* 20, no. 4 (Summer 1967) : 23–32; and Douglas McVay, "Hamlet to Clown," *Films and Filming* 8, no. 12 (September 1962) : 16–19.
56. Two useful articles are John Houseman, "Filming *Julius Caesar,*" *Films in Review* 4, no. 4 (April 1953) : 184–88; and John Houseman, "Filming Julius Caesar," *Sight and Sound* 23, no. 1 (July–September 1953) : 24–27.
57. Although the Welles film on Falstaff is not available, the reader will find the following article valuable: Joseph McBride, "Welles' *Chimes At Midnight,*" *Film Quarterly* 23, no. 1 (Fall 1969) : 11–20.
58. Gordon Gow, "In Search of a Revolution: Peter Hall," *Films and Filming* 15, no. 12 (September 1969) : 40–44.

is Kenneth MacMillan's superb choreography to the Royal Opera House's playing of Prokofiev's music.

The Taming of the Shrew (Columbia—16mm: 1966, 122 min., color, flat or cinemascope, sound, R-COL)

Franco Zeffirelli directed Burton and Taylor in this salty, free swinging romp through Shakespeare's tale of the violent-tempered Katharine and her lusty husband, Petruchio.[59]

Throne of Blood (Japan—16mm: 1957, 105 min., b/w, English subtitles, sound, R-AUD)

Director Akira Kurosawa created this masterly interpretation of *Macbeth*, and it well may be the greatest screen translation to date. Memorable performances by Toshiro Mifune and Isuzu Yamada.[60]

---

59. John Francis Lane, "The Taming of the Shrew," *Films and Filming* 13, no. 1 (October 1966) : 50–52.

60. J. Blumenthal, *"Macbeth* into *Throne of Blood,"* *Sight and Sound* 34, no. 4 (Autumn 1965) : 190–95.

6
A Representative Period of American Film (1913-1919)

> *If the historian tells you that the pictures you produced in 1910 were better than those you now lose money on, he is worthless to you. But if he fails to tell you the pictures of 1910 pointed the way to the right thing and that you have since departed from that way, discharge him as a fool.*
> *Gilbert Seldes,* The Seven Lively Arts

Movies are tied to the age in which they are made. It makes sense, then, to present certain courses in which the student can study film in a historical context. This gives interested people the opportunity to see a number of motion pictures in chronological order and to examine the social, economic, and artistic forces that helped to shape the form, technique, and content of the film.

The period in American films from 1913 to 1919 is a particularly profitable span of time to study. First, the year 1913 marked a major transition in movie making. The methods of production, distribution, and exhibition were going through significant changes, and the results set new patterns for decades to come. America was facing its first serious challenge from foreign competitors, the standard two-reelers were disappearing as the age of the feature film was being ushered in, and serious actors began to migrate to California in hopes of becoming part of an emerging new art form. Many of the old companies—Edison, Biograph, Selig, Essanay, Tanhouser, Lubin —began to die, and a new set of enterprising filmmakers began to take control.[1] This period has been labeled by some film historians as "the burgeon-

---

1. See Jeanne Thomas, "The Decay of the Motion Picture Patents Company," *Cinema Journal* 10, no. 2 (Spring 1972) : 34–40.

ing years,"[2] or the days of "lusty adolescence."[3] Whatever name we assign, the effect of those seven years upon the development of the film is undeniably great.

Second, the films made from 1913 to 1919 are striking evidence of the economic influence on motion pictures. In 1913, the United States housed more than 20,000 theaters. Every single evening, exhibitors projected over 96 million feet of film to an audience which totaled for the year more than 5 million. These addicted patrons paid collectively an estimated $3 million for their entertainment.[4] Such impressive figures spurred daring and opportunistic individuals into the motion picture business on the assumption that a fortune was to be made by anyone able to supply the audiences with a weekly change of program. By 1914, the United States produced over half of all the motion pictures in the world as the result of the virtual collapse of the film industries of France, Italy, Germany, Sweden, Norway, and England after the start of the first World War.[5] American producers, sensing an opportunity to make money quickly, released films designed to appeal to the public's wishes. As Arthur Knight explains,

> Laughter, love and make-believe—that was what the world wanted while war raged in Europe, and that was what the New Hollywood concentrated on. Romance, adventure, comedy, glamour—the studios took these basic elements and, in the years between 1915 and 1920, transformed them into a multi-million dollar business.[6]

This policy brought unexpected prosperity to the film industry. Owing to the revenue of those war years, the U.S. film industry acquired the financial vigor to survive the critical transition to sound in 1927 and the disastrous effects of the stock market crash in 1929.

From 1913 to 1919 the American movie developed a wide and permanent audience. People went to the cinema mainly to see moving pictures. This placed the emphasis on film production rather than on film art. Having an undiscriminating audience allowed producers, not artists, to gain control of the film world; as a result the pressures of regimentation, standardization, and economics became the major concerns, pressures that are still evident today.

Third, the period marks the development of a number of important

---

2. Kenneth MacGowan, *Behind the Screen: The History and Techniques of the Movies* (New York: Delacorte Press, 1965), p. 183.

3. Richard Schickel, *Movies: The History of an Art and an Institution* (New York: Basic Books, 1964), p. 60.

4. Henry Lanier in *The World's Work* (June 1914). Figures reprinted in Kalton C Lahue and Terry Brewer, *Kops and Custards: The Legend of Keystone Films,* with a foreword by Kent D. Eastin. (Norman: University of Oklahoma Press, 1968), p. 49.

5. Lewis Jacobs, *The Rise of the American Film: A Critical History with an Essay* "Experimental Cinema in America 1921–1947" (New York: Teachers College, 1968), p. 164.

6. Arthur Knight, *The Liveliest Art: A Panoramic History of the Movies* (New York: The Macmillan Company, 1957), p. 51.

trends: the rise of the large studios, the beginning of Hollywood's reign as the movie capital of the world, and the rising costs of films—the latter owing to legal entanglements, stars' exorbitant salaries, the attendant expenses of scripts, and producers involved in the process of film production. Some of the more important developments during these years included a star system, formula pictures, and the rise of advertising campaigns. This period also included three of the most significant men in the history of motion pictures: D. W. Griffith, Mack Sennett, and Charles Chaplin. By examining the motion pictures and theories developed by these seminal figures, students should see the importance of this period not only to the art of film but also to the contemporary screen.[7]

D. W. GRIFFITH

Almost every book written on the art of the film mentions the name of David Wark Griffith. He is generally recognized as the father of film narrative technique; as Alfred Hitchcock puts it, "Every time you see a movie, you see something that originated with D. W. Griffith."[8] Whether Griffith developed or originated all that is frequently attributed to him is a point of controversy, but his significance in the development of film is not.

By October 1, 1913, D. W. Griffith—actor, writer, director—had made 150 of the 400 films of his career, and he was preparing to go to California to seek more ambitious challenges. He had developed most of his ideas about technique, content, and form together with his brilliant cameraman, Billy Bitzer, at Biograph's 11 East 14th Street headquarters.[9] Over and over again his films depicted an American setting based upon tradition and sentiment where country folk were constantly menaced by the wiles of city slickers. Furthermore, Griffith had already assembled about him a cast of talented people who would help shape the style of film acting: e.g., Lillian and Dorothy Gish, Mae Marsh,[10] Henry B. Walthall, and Miriam Cooper.[11]

7. Major works will be discussed in the text; references of somewhat minor importance will be referred to in the footnotes.

8. Alfred Hitchcock. Quoted by William K. Everson, "David Wark Griffith," *Film Society* 1 (1963) : 26.

9. The most valuable sources of information about Griffith can be found at the Museum of Modern Art in New York. The best bibliographical information sources are Seymour Stern, *An Index to the Creative Work of David Wark Griffith*, Part II, Index Series 8, Special Supplement to *Sight and Sound* (September 1946) ; Robert M. Henderson, *D. W. Griffith: The Years at Biograph* (New York: Farrar, Straus and Giroux, 1970) ; and Robert M. Henderson, *D. W. Griffith: His Life and Work* (New York: Oxford University Press, 1972).

10. Harold Dunham, "Mae Marsh," *Films in Review* 9, no. 6 (June–July 1958) : 306–21.

11. The Museum of Modern Art has the best collection of Griffith films available for rental. Particularly good is the Griffith Biograph Program (16mm: 51 min., b/w) with *The Lonely Villa* (1909), *A Corner in Wheat* (1909), *The Lonedale Operator* (1911), *The Musketeers of Pig Alley* (1912), *The New York Hat* (1912). For articles related to these films see John Griggs, "Here Was an Actor: Henry B. Walthall's Magic Has Had a Life-long Effect," *Films in Review* 3, no. 3 (March 1952) : 118–24, 131; DeWitt Bodeen, "Dorothy Gish," *Films in Review* 19, no. 7 (August–September 1968) : 393–414; Theodore

By studying Griffith's films, we can see three major tendencies: attention to the development of narrative film techniques, sentimental treatment of the subject matter, and a strong literary emphasis. Griffith's technical revolutions in the making of film transitions, his innovative manipulation of time and space, his advancement of the editing process, and his great skill in directing actors were achievements that greatly influenced motion pictures.[12] Griffith's sentimentality—typical of the times—is evidenced, for example, in his concern with blonde, helpless heroines who enlist the sympathy of the audience and who finally, through many trials and tribulations, win their cause. The initial reaction is to dismiss Griffith's lovers as clumsy and silly. But after seeing his films time and again, one comes away feeling a sense of honesty in his treatment of young, inexperienced sweethearts whose awkwardness presents a genuine image of first love. Furthermore, Griffith's indebtedness to his literary background is evident; in particular, he was influenced by Browning, Tennyson, Dickens, Poe, and Whitman.[13]

Then came the great years from 1914 to 1916 when Griffith created *The Birth of a Nation* (Epoch—16mm: 1915, 195 min., b/w, silent, MMA)[14] and *Intolerance* (Griffith—16mm: 1916, 191 min., b/w, silent, R-AUD, EMG, MMA; 8mm: S-BLA, FCE).[15] The former is generally acknowledged as the first screen masterpiece because of its artistic, economic, and technical suc-

---

Huff, "40 Years of Feminine Glamour," *Films in Review* 4, no. 2 (February 1953) : 49–63; and Sheridan Morley, "Lillian Gish: Life and Living," *Films and Filming* 16, no. 3 (January 1970) : 12–15.

12. Some articles that will help to assess the importance of Griffith's influence on the growth of the film art are: Barret Braverman, "David Wark Griffith: Creator of Film Form," *Theatre Arts* 39 (April 1, 1945) : 240–50; William Everson, "David Wark Griffith," *Film Society* 1 (1963) : 26–32; Joseph and Harry Feldman, "The D. W. Griffith Influence," *Films in Review* 1, no. 5 (July–August 1950) : 11–14, 45; Seymour Stern, "11 East 14th Street," *Films in Review* 3, no. 8 (October 1952) : 399–406; Seymour Stern, "The Cold War Against David Wark Griffith," *ibid.* 7, no. 2 (February 1956) : 49–59; Seymour Stern, "The Soviet Director's Debt to Griffith," *idem.* 7, no. 5 (May 1956) : 202–9; G. Charles Niemeyer, "David Wark Griffith: In Retrospect, 1965," *Film Heritage* 1 (Fall 1965) : 13–24; Norman Silverstein, "D. W. Griffith and Anarchy in American Films," *Salmagundi* 1, no. 2 (Winter 1966) : 47–58; Paul Goodman, "Griffith and the Technical Innovations," *Moviegoer* 2 (Summer–Autumn 1964) : 51–54; and Julian Fox, "The Country Boys: An Aspect of Rural America in the Age of Innocence," *Films and Filming* 18, no. 8 (May 1972) : 28–36.

13. John Howard Lawson, *Film: The Creative Process: The Search for an Audio-Visual Language and Structure.* Preface by Jay Leyda (New York: Hill and Wang, 1964), 24–25; Seymour Stern, "Griffith and Poe," *Films in Review* 2, no. 9 (November 1951) : 23–28.

14. Helpful in studying this film are Seymour Stern's two monographs, *The Birth of a Nation,* Index Series No. 3, *Special Supplement* to *Sight and Sound* (July 1945) ; and "Griffith: 1—The Birth of a Nation," *Film Culture* 36 (Spring–Summer 1965) ; Charles L. Hutchins, "A Critical Evaluation of the Controversies Engendered by D. W. Griffith's Birth of a Nation" (Masters Thesis: University of Iowa, 1965) ; and D. W. Griffith, *The Rise and Fall of Free Speech in America* (1916) .

15. The most useful information is available in Stern's *Index to the Creative Work of David Wark Griffith,* and Theodore Huff, *Intolerance: The Film by David Wark Griffith, Shot-by-Shot Analysis* (New York: The Museum of Modern Art, 1966) . See also Harold Dunham, "Bessie Love," *Films in Review* 10, no. 2 (February 1959) : 86–99; Harold Dunham, "Bobby Harron," *Films in Review* 14, no. 10 (December 1963) : 607–18; and DeWitt Bodeen, "Blanche Sweet," *Films in Review* 16, no. 9 (November 1965) : 549–70.

cess.[16] The film presents a disillusioned southern artist's interpretation of the American Civil War and the Reconstruction Period that followed. *Intolerance* is the outcome of Griffith's astonishment and horror at the public reaction to *The Birth of a Nation*. It interweaves four stories of bigotry through the ages—Babylon, Christ, the French Revolution, and a modern tale of prejudice—held together by the scene of a mother rocking her baby. Although *Intolerance* was considered a financial disaster in 1916, it is without doubt one of the greatest films ever made.

Although biographies often divert readers from the work of art, they are sometimes useful in illuminating the achievements of certain authors or directors. By studying Griffith's life, the student should see the many financial, technical, and artistic problems that Griffith had to overcome in making important improvements in films.[17]

Books

Aitken, Roy E. as told to Al P. Nelson. *The Birth of a Nation Story*. Middleburg, Va.: William W. Denlinger, 1965.

Although Roy and Harry Aitken were close business partners with Griffith on the making of the *Birth*, Roy's memory on a number of key matters cannot always be trusted. The book, nevertheless, offers students many behind-the-scenes stories and figures about the crucial stages in the turbulent history of Griffith's classic.

* Barry, Iris, with an annotated list of films by Eileen Bowser. *D. W. Griffith: American Film-Maker*. New York: Museum of Modern Art, 1965.

This is a revised edition of Miss Barry's short and general monograph for a retrospective showing of Griffith films in 1940. It is particularly useful for Beaumont Newhall's interview with Bitzer and for a good annotated list of Griffith's films after 1914.

* Geduld, Harry M. (editor). *Focus on D. W. Griffith*. Englewood Cliffs, N.J.: Prentice-Hall, Inc., 1971.

Presented in this fine anthology are some of the best available articles on Griffith, written by Vardac, Arvidson, O'Dell, Jacobs, Gish, and von Stro-

---

16. The question of its social implications—justification of the Ku Klux Klan by distorting the role of the black community in the South—is treated in Chapter 3. The writer, nevertheless, wants to make clear that a teacher's showing of a film *does not imply* that he endorses the social content or philosophy of the film; it does mean, however, that he recognizes artistic achievement in the film. In connection, two interesting articles to read are Maxim Simcovitch, "The Impact of Griffith's *Birth of a Nation* on the Modern Ku Klux Klan," *The Journal of Popular Film* 1, no. 1 (Winter 1972) : 45–54; and Alan Casty, "The Films of D. W. Griffith: A Style for the Times," *The Journal of Popular Film* 1, no. 2 (Spring 1972) : 66–79.

17. A very good biographical 16mm film account of Griffith, *The Great Director* is available from Peter M. Robeck & Co., Inc., 4 West 16th Street, New York 10011. The reader might also enjoy reading Stern's two-part review of a very poor book on Griffith: Seymour Stern, "Biographical Hogwash: I," *Films in Review* 10, no. 5 (May 1959) : 336–41; Seymour Stern, "Biographical Hogwash: II," *Films in Review* 10, no. 6 (June 1959) : 336–41.

heim. Noticeably absent is any statement by Seymour Stern.[18] Best of all, however, are a host of personal statements by Griffith himself.

* Gish, Lillian with Ann Pinchot. *Lillian Gish: The Movies, Mr. Griffith and Me.* Englewood Cliffs: Prentice-Hall, Inc., 1969.

Although there are times when dates, movies, and incidents go contrary to established facts, Miss Gish offers one of the most moving and memorable accounts of the Griffith years. Just as valuable are her delightful insights into the early methods and dangers of film production.

* Griffith, Mrs. D. W. (Linda Arvidson). *When the Movies Were Young.* New York: E. P. Dutton, 1925. Reissued in 1968 by Benjamin Blom in New Work.

This is a second-best account of Griffith's early career at Biograph as recorded by his first wife. It is helpful in re-creating the atmosphere and conditions of the times, although there is almost nothing about technical developments.

Hart, James (editor). *The Man Who Invented Hollywood: The Autobiography of D. W. Griffith.* Louisville: Touchstone Publishing Company, 1972.

For the most part Griffith wrote this book between 1932 and 1940, with the help of the editor; he presents himself for today's readers as a naive genius who found it difficult to accept the limitations of a young toy in the early 1900s. Hart offers a valuable text of Griffith's contacts with the Gishs and Pickford as well as the director's version of the filming of the *Birth,* plus some superb photographs.

* Henderson, Robert M. *D. W. Griffith: His Life and His Work.* New York: Oxford University Press, 1972.

By far the best book on Griffith to date, covering his rise and fall in the movie industry, this important text offers a wealth of information in a clear and scholarly manner.

* Henderson, Robert M. *D. W. Griffith: The Years at Biograph.* New York: Farrar, Straus and Giroux, 1970.

An in-depth record of Griffith's beginnings in film with accurate, useful footnotes and information. It is more valuable as a resource book than as reading matter.

* O'Dell, Paul. *Griffith and the Rise of Hollywood.* With the assistance of Anthony Slide. New York: A. S. Barnes and Company, 1970.

A terse and factual overview of Griffith's work and influence in Hollywood starting with the *Birth,* this text offers a number of stimulating and useful observations on stars, producers and key Griffith films.

* Silva, Fred (editor). *Focus on the Birth of a Nation.* Englewood Cliffs: Prentice-Hall, Inc., 1971.

One of the best things about this useful collection are the editor's own introductory comments. In addition, the contributors include most of the important critics of the film: Sarris, Cripps, Noble, and Jacobs. Again, Stern's name is absent from the lists.

---

18. Seymour Stern has for more than forty years been the most resourceful and prolific writer on Griffith's life and achievements. Despite anyone's disagreements with his point of view, it is unthinkable that his voice would not be included in any significant anthology.

In addition, there are a number of history books and collections that offer further help to Griffith's students. Edward Wagenknecht's examination of the great director provides some rare material,[19] as do Lewis Jacobs's three chapters on Griffith in his excellent *The Rise of the American Film*.[20] Also, Kevin Brownlow's noteworthy book, *The Parade's Gone By*,[21] has an outstanding interview with Joseph Henabery, the actor who played Lincoln in *The Birth of a Nation*. And finally, there is Ezra Goodman's pathetic and controversial account of Griffith near the end of his life.[22]

MACK SENNETT

Biograph not only produced the father of film art but also the father of film comedy, Mack Sennett. He had come to the New York studio on January 17, 1908, after nine years of burlesque and music hall stints and within four years had learned Griffith's basic techniques for good, fast-paced films, a skill referred to in those early days as the style of "Biograph editing." In essence, this meant constantly changing camera angles, parallel editing, and close-up shots for psychological effects. On August 12, 1912, Sennett joined with two ex-bookmakers and set up the Keystone Film Company. The cocky actor-director-screenwriter then went into production, bringing with him from his former studio such talented people as Mabel Normand, Fred Mace, Ford Sterling, and Henry "Pathé" Lehrman. With this nucleus of creative individuals, Sennett began developing a unique brand of motion picture comedy.

Starting with the early efforts of French film fantasies and trick photography, the thirty-two-year-old Canadian introduced in 1913 a number of unusual touches, emphasizing the grotesque and the violent. In addition, Sennett developed a style of filmmaking that fitted in with the studios' need for quick, standardized pictures. And yet, as Wagenknecht puts it:

Sennett films were compounded of attractively diverse elements. There was a slight touch of madness about them—they defied both logic and gravity and hovered on the edge of fantasy—yet down to earth as they were, the girls who appeared in them glorified them with a touch of beauty. The result should have been a hodge-podge, but it was not, somehow; it was a world. How this was achieved was Sennett's secret, and this constitutes his final claim as an artist, for nobody else has ever been able to do it so well.[23]

19. Edward Wagenknecht, *Movies in the Age of Innocence* (Norman: University of Oklahoma Press, 1962).
20. Also available in Daniel Talbot (editor), *Film: An Anthology* (New York: Simon and Schuster, 1966).
21. Kevin Brownlow, *The Parade's Gone By* (New York: Alfred Knopf, 1968).
22. Ezra Goodman, *The Fifty-Year Decline and Fall of Hollywood* (New York: Simon and Schuster, 1961).
23. Wagenknecht, *Movies in Age of Innocence*, p. 40.

For Sennett, speed was crucial to comedy. He believed that all you needed was a situation in which one gag piled on another to result in a madcap hundred-foot film of incredible confusion. But Sennett's mark was not pace alone. He had the ability to see humor where others found suspense and horror. For example, where Griffith used the chase for excitement, Sennett used it for zaniness. His world of comedy centered on scoundrels, villains, phonies, and bums whose lives consisted of chasing pretty girls and outsmarting policemen.

Sennett was also the greatest developer of stars of the silent era. His cast credits read today like an honor roll; among the most famous were such performers as Charles Chaplin, Marie Dressler, Wallace Beery, Gloria Swanson, Roscoe "Fatty" Arbuckle, Mable Normand, Ford Sterling, Harry Langdon,[24] W. C. Fields, Ben Turpin, Mack Swain, Chester Conklin, Fred Mace, and Hal Roach.[25] He was truly "the king of comedy."[26]

Thankfully, a number of early Sennett films are available. The Museum of Modern Art has a "film anthology" of five of his comedies that runs for 95 minutes. The first selection, *Comrades,* was made in 1911, and the last film, *The Clever Dummy,* was finished in 1917.

The viewer thus has an opportunity not only to study Sennett's work but also to note the development of his art. In addition, there is a series of Sennett comedies available from the Audio Film Center, in which some of the many comedians developed by Sennett are starred: *Saturday Afternoon,* featuring Harry Langdon; *Leading Lizzie,* with Mabel Normand and Fatty Arbuckle; *Beach Flirt,* which introduces Sennett's famous Bathing Beauties; and *Fickleness of Sweedie,* an early appearance of the Keystone Kops. There are also a number of Sennett comedies that can be purchased from Blackhawk Films in 8mm size, including: *Because He Loved Her,* with Mae Busch; *The Desperate Scoundrel,* with the Keystone Kops; and *Teddy at the Throttle,* with Gloria Swanson.

---

24. Vernon L. Schonert, "Harry Langdon," *Films in Review* 18, no. 7 (October 1967) : 470–85.

25. Hal Roach, "Living with Laughter," *Films and Filming* 11, no. 1 (October 1964) : 23–25.

26. Related articles: Arthur Knight, "The 2-Reel Comedy—Its Rise and Fall," *Films in Review* 2, no. 8 (October 1951) , 29–35; Peter John Dyer, "They Liked to Break the Rules," *Films and Filming* 6, no. 6 (October 1959) : 12–14, 28–29; Raymond Durgnat, "World of Comedy: I," *Films and Filming* 11, no. 10 (July 1965) : 8–13; Raymond Durgnat, "World of Comedy: II," *Films and Filming* 11, no. 11 (August 1965) : 10–15; Raymond Durgnat, "World of Comedy: III," *Films and Filming* 11, no. 12 (September 1965) : 8–12; Raymond Durgnat, "World of Comedy: IV," *Films and Filming* 12, no. 1 (October 1965) : 16–20; Raymond Durgnat, "World of Comedy: V," *Films and Filming* 12, no. 2 (November 1965) : 14–19; Raymond Durgnat, "World of Comedy: VI," *Films and Filming* 12, no. 3 (December 1965) : 42–48; and Raymond Durgnat, "World of Comedy: VII," *Films and Filming* 12, no. 4 (January 1966) : 40–46. The Durgnat articles have been edited, updated and published in his book *The Crazy Mirror: Hollywood Comedy and the American Image* (New York: Horizon Press, 1969) .

Books[27]

Fowler, Gene. *Father Goose: The Story of Mack Sennett.* New York: Covici, Friede Publishers, 1934.

In a highly readable, but very unreliable narrative, Fowler traces Sennett's career from childhood to Mabel Normand's marriage to Lew Cody. The emphasis is on amusing, rather than on technical matters.

Lahue, Kalton C. *Dreams for Sale: The Rise and Fall of the Triangle Corporation.* New York: A. S. Barnes and Company, 1971.

For serious students, this informative and very significant book examines how Harry Aitken, the financial wizard who backed Griffith's *The Clansman,* formed the Triangle Film Corporation and started the era of great movie mergers. Together with Griffith, Sennett, and Ince, Aitken also helped develop at Triangle the budding careers of such famous silent film stars as W. S. Hart, Douglas Fairbanks and Norma Talmadge. Then, before anyone knew what had happened, the corporation folded. The story has never been adequately touched until now. More needs to be known, but from now on Lahue's narrative should be the starting point.

Lahue, Kalton C. *The World of Laughter: The Motion Picture Comedy Short, 1910–1930.* Norman: University of Oklahoma Press, 1966.

This book offers a good contrast between Sennett's work and his competitors in America's silent film era. Among the many useful insights provided by Lahue is his introductory chapter called "The American Comedy, 1910–1913." There is also a 39 page appendix listing filmographies of Billy Bevan, Chaplin, Keaton, Langdon, Laurel and Hardy, Lloyd, "Our Gang," Snub Pollard, Larry Semon, and Ben Turpin.

Lahue, Kalton C. and Terry Brewer. *Kops and Custards: The Legend of Keystone Films.* With a foreword by Kent D. Eastin. Norman: University of Oklahoma Press, 1968.

A clear and concise account of the famous "Fun Factory" which set the style and pace of American film comedy from 1912 until the early 1920's, this book offers a good study of how and why Sennett's comics were so important and successful. The book also provides an invaluable appendix of the Keystone films.

Lahue, Kalton C. *Mack Sennett's Keystone: The Man, the Myth, and the Comedies.* New York: A. S. Barnes and Company, 1971.

In this text, Lahue provides readers with some valuable new material on Sennett's techniques, plus a critical examination of the myths surrounding the father of film comedy. There is also a series of appendices, one of which includes a sample Keystone script. Although this is the best American book on Sennett, scholars should examine the Italian biography by Davide Turconi called *Il Fe delle Comiche* (Rome: Edizioni dell' Ateneneo, 1961).

Sennett, Mack, as told to Cameron Shipp. *King of Comedy.* New York: Doubleday and Company, 1954.

---

27. A very useful study has also been done by Robert Giroux, "Mack Sennett: Part I," *Films in Review* 19, no. 10 (December, 1968) : 593–612; and "Part II," *Films in Review* 20, no. 1 (January, 1969) : 1–28.

Another book designed more to entertain than to inform, this one spends more time in sentimentalizing over Sennett's love affair with Normand than in discussing his film style. Still, the author gives many fascinating anecdotes about his early career in films.

CHARLES SPENCER CHAPLIN

Just as Griffith influenced Sennett, so the first King of Comedy gave the movies its greatest comedian, Charles Spencer Chaplin. More people have seen his films than any others. More books and articles have been written about him than on any other individual in motion picture history. His favorite theme was that of the poor little fellow who finds dignity in a dream world, and just at the moment when he seems most successful, misfortune occurs. Yet Chaplin added little to movie technique or movie form.

The basic facts about his life prior to his Keystone days in 1914 are generally known. Born on April 16, 1889, the son of vaudevillians, he grew up for the first ten years mainly in the London slums. His father died an alcoholic and his mother suffered several mental breakdowns, leaving him alone most of those formative years from six to ten. Between the ages of eleven and twenty-four, he gained a favorable reputation as a comedian in music-hall stints, burlesque, and Fred Karno's Pantomime Company. Then on May 12, 1913, he accepted Kessel and Baumann's offer to work for Mack Sennett.

Chaplin did not fit in with the Keystone style of comedy. His insistence on subtlety and a slow build-up often had him at odds with Mabel Normand, Ford Sterling, and Pathé Lehrman. Fortunately for him, audiences and exhibitors immediately took to Chaplin, and Sennett decided against firing him. Between 1913 and 1919, Charles Chaplin developed his great art of pantomime, and he was generally hailed as the star of his era—the man with the pathetic expression, the foolish mustache, small derby, oversized shoes, pretentious cane, and ridiculous walk.

Many of his films between 1914 and 1919 are available on a rental basis from the Museum of Modern Art or Audio Film Center. There is even a greater number available for purchase in 8mm size from Blackhawk and Entertainment Films. Some fine shorts that will reveal his artistic style in 1915 are: *His New Job* (8mm: BLA), *A Night Out* (8mm: BLA), *The Champion* (8mm: BLA), *The Bank* (8mm: ENT), *Shanghaied* (8mm: ENT), *A Night at the Show* (8mm: ENT). Some outstanding films of 1916 are: *Carmen* (8mm: ENT), *Police* (8mm: BLA), *The Floorwalker* (8mm: ENT), *The Fireman* (8mm: ENT), *The Vagabond* (8mm: BLA), *One A. M.* (8mm: BLA), *The Count* (8mm: ENT), *The Pawnshop* (8mm: BLA), *Behind the Screen* (8mm: BLA), *The Rink* (8mm: BLA). In 1917, he created such masterpieces as: *Easy Street* (8mm: ENT), *The Immigrant*

(8mm: BLA), *The Cure* (8mm: BLA), *The Adventurer* (8mm: BLA).[28]

Chaplin's great contribution to films was his personality and his timing. Other producers used films simply as a frame for exhibiting their stars. The stories remained secondary to the players, mere vehicles for a contrived personality, and almost everything connected with production, distribution, and exhibition went into exploiting the players' mannerisms and physical qualities.

Books[29]

* Chaplin, Charles. *My Autobiography*. New York: Simon and Schuster, 1964.

Every student of Chaplin will find this must reading and will probably be disappointed by Chaplin's omissions and distortions of key events and films, particularly the absence of material on Laurel, Langdon, Campbell, and Linder. The one redeeming feature is the first 200 pages, which give some insight into the formative years in London and the United States.

* Chaplin, Charles Jr. *My Father, Charlie Chaplin*. With N. and M. Rau. New York: Popular Library, 1961.

Although the author makes no claim to a definitive biography, this account provides anecdotes and insights that only a son can supply. The narrative covers Chaplin's early life as well as first-hand accounts of the personal problems the star encountered in business, marriage, and criminal court proceedings.

Cotes, Peter and Thelma Niklaus. *The Little Fellow: The Life and Work of Charles Spencer Chaplin*. With a foreword by W. Somerset Maugham. New York: The Citadel Press, 1965.

This reissued and slightly altered account of a 1951 publication contains very little useful information, although almost a third of the slight volume consists of good illustrations from Chaplin's films. It suffers from undeveloped speculations and inaccurate research. Also, the authors see Chaplin as god-like and thus lack any objectivity in their evaluations.

* Huff, Theodore. *Charlie Chaplin: A Biography*. New York: Pyramid Books, 1964. (First published in 1951.) Reissued in 1972 by Arno Press.

By far, the single best source for Chaplin research to date. Not only does Huff help the reader with marvelous descriptions of individual films, but he

---

28. For a full description of these films, the reader may turn to *Theodore Huff, *Charlie Chaplin* (New York: Henry Schuman, 1951). The book is now available in paperback and is published by Pyramid Books in New York. In addition, see: Gerald D. McDonald, *et al.*, *The Films of Charlie Chaplin* (New York: Bonanza Books, 1965).

29. The two best bibliographical sources on Chaplin are Theodore Huff, "An Index to the Films of Charles Chaplin," *Special Supplement to Sight and Sound* Index Series No. 3 (March 1945), and Edward Wagenknecht, *The Movies in the Age of Innocence*. Some relevant articles are: "Charlie Chaplin's *Monsieur Verdoux* Press Conference," *Film Comment* 5, no. 4 (Winter 1969): 34–42; Terry Hickey, "Accusations Against Charles Chaplin for Political and Moral Offenses," *ibid.*, pp. 44–57; Jack Spears, "Chaplin's Collaborators," *Films in Review* 13, no. 1 (January 1962): 18–36; Jack Spears, "Max Linder," *Films in Review* 16, no. 5 (May 1965): 272–91; Peter Cotes, "The Little Fellow's Self Portrait," *Films and Filming* 11, no. 3 (December 1964): 11–13; David Madden, "Harlequin's Stick, Charlie's Cane," *Film Quarterly* 22, no. 1 (Fall 1968): 10–26; and Philip G. Rosen, "The Chaplin World-View," *Cinema Journal* 9, no. 1 (Fall 1969): 2–12.

provides us with a well-researched and lucidly written account of the ties between Chaplin's life and the themes of his pictures. This is the book to use in any study of Chaplin.

* McCaffrey, Donald W. (editor). *Focus on Chaplin.* Englewood Cliffs, N.Y.: Prentice-Hall, Inc., 1971.

Although this book contains a number of key critics, the editor should have taken time to point out the errors in some of the statements. John Montgomery's opening article, for example, states that Chaplin was 26 when he joined Sennett's company, when in fact he was 24. Despite these annoying editorial slips, the anthology is filled with good and useful information.

McDonald, Gerald D. *et al. The Films of Charlie Chaplin.* New York: Bonanza Books, 1965.

This is an excellent follow-up to the Huff book and contains valuable plot synopses, casts, and credits. Many of the stills in the book are to be found nowhere else. Although there are minor errors, the brief and effective textual comments provide a useful transition from page to page.

Payne, Robert. *The Great God Pan: A Biography of the Tramp.* New York: Hermitage House, 1952.

This book suggests much more than it gives. It seems to have been carelessly written, makes superficial gestures toward profundity and offers far too many unfounded generalizations. A good example of how some people get carried away with an interpretation of Chaplin's intellectual strength.

* Quigly, Isabel. *Charlie Chaplin: Early Comedies.* New York: E. P. Dutton and Company, Inc., 1968.

A brief but useful summary of the major research done on Chaplin's days at Sennett, Essanay, Mutual, and First National. In particular, students should find it an easy exercise to skim quickly through the excellent illustrations while still getting a good introduction to Chaplin's work.

* Sullivan, Ed. *Chaplin vs. Chaplin.* Los Angeles: Marvin Miller Enterprises, 1965.

Designed mostly for sensational purposes, this distasteful book provides the only readily available texts of the Lita Grey divorce papers and should be studied in terms of the snide comments made about Chaplin's morality. The shoddy evidence weighed heavily in his being barred from this country on September 19, 1952.

Tyler, Parker. *Chaplin: Last of the Clowns.* New York: The Vanguard Press, 1947.

A fascinating and original analysis of the relationship between Chaplin's youth and his art is offered in this often underrated extended essay.

THE STAR SYSTEM

The star system, which readily appealed to the mass audience, provided a valuable answer to the studio's concern with standardized products. Prior to 1910, filmgoers often referred to their favorite players as "the girl with the blonde curls" (Mary Pickford) or the "Biograph girl" (Florence Lawrence). But once the producers discovered that by publishing the names of their stars they would attract more customers, the star system began to dominate the industry. The movie fans soon had a score of favorites, including John Bunny, Charles Chaplin, Mary Pickford, Douglas Fairbanks, W. S. Hart, Theda Bara[30] and Rudolph Valentino. It was the popularity of stars like these that put the motion picture business on a firm financial basis.[31] As Richard Schickel has summarized the situation—

> The importance of the stars of the period 1912–1920 . . . transcends any single screen personality. The success of this early group proved an economic theory—that personalities can give a studio a kind of continuity of sales which could not be achieved by ideas, exploitation, or even art. With production and distribution apparatus already in place (and working well), with a technique of cinematic story-telling rapidly developing— thanks to Griffith, Ince, Sennett, and the director-stars, Chaplin and Hart —the perfection of the star system was the final touch needed to assure an infant industry that it would grow into healthy economic (if not aesthetic) adulthood. The production system that developed in the teens of this century is the system that prevailed, with very few changes, through all the years of Hollywood's greatness.[32]

SERIALS

The production system of filmmaking created another unique attraction: The Serial. Designed to appeal to a specific audience, this assembly line product, timed and patterned by fixed rules, was still another example of

30. DeWitt Bodeen, "Theda Bara," *Films in Review* 19, no. 5 (May 1968) : 266–87.

31. Gerald D. McDonald, "Origin of the Star System," *Films in Review* 4, no. 9 (November 1953) : 449–58; Douglas McVay, "The Goddesses: Part One," *Films and Filming* 11, no. 11 (August 1965) : 5–9; Douglas McVay, "The Goddesses: Part Two," *Films and Filming* 11, no. 12 (September 1965) : 13–18; Peter John Dyer, "The Face of the Goddess," *Films and Filming* 5, no. 9 (June 1959) : 13–15, 32–33; Eric Braun, "Where Have All the Stylists Gone?—Part One," *Films and Filming* 13, no. 8 (May 1967) : 50–55; Eric Braun, "Part Two," *Films and Filming* 13, no. 9 (June 1967) : 38–43; Eric Braun, "Part Three," *Films and Filming* 13, no. 10 (July 1967) : 12–16; Eric Braun, "Part IV," *Films and Filming* 13, no. 11 (August 1967) : 10–14; Eric Braun, "Part V," *Films and Filming* 13, no. 12 (September 1967) : 12–16.
For some helpful articles on film acting, see the following: Derek Prouse, "Notes on Film Acting," *Sight and Sound* 24, no. 4 (Spring 1955) : 174–80; Tony Richardson, "The Method and Why: An Account of the Actor's Studio," *Sight and Sound* 26, no. 3 (Winter 1956–57) : 132–36; Catherine de la Roche, "Stars," *Sight and Sound* 20, no. 4 (April–June 1953) : 172–74; Eric Rhode, "The Day of the Butterfly," *Sight and Sound* 33, no. 1 (Winter 1963–64) : 44–48; Bernard Miles, "The Acting Art," *Films in Review* 5, no. 6 (June–July 1954) : 267–82; Douglas McVay, "The Art of the Actor: Part One," *Films and Filming* 12, no. 10 (July 1966) : 19–25; Douglas McVay, ". . . Part Two," *Films and Filming* 12, no. 11 (August 1966) : 36–42; Douglas McVay, ". . . Part Three," *Films and Filming* 12, no. 12 (September 1966) : 44–50; Douglas McVay, ". . . Part Four," *Films and Filming* 13, no. 1 (October 1966) : 27–33; and Douglas McVay. ". . . Part Five," *Films and Filming* 13, no. 2 (November 1966) : 26–33.

32. Richard Schickel, *Movies: The History of an Art and An Institution* (New York: Basic Books, 1964) , pp. 172–73.

the early scenarios, which placed greater emphasis on a film personality than on art. Among the best of the "cliff hangers" were *The Perils of Pauline, The Hazards of Helen,* and *The Exploits of Elaine.* The serials were big business. Through them, the exhibitors and the newspapers began to develop a relationship that stimulated advertising and reviewing. Although a number of important productions in the serial field were released, most of them consisted of stock situations performed by a repertory group. These films became the forerunners of many radio and television programs.

Books[33]

* Barbour, Alan G. *Days of Thrills and Adventure.* Introduction by William K. Everson. New York: The Macmillan Company, 1970.

In addition to offering many nostalgic stills of old-time serials, Barbour presents a wealth of information about the styles of individual studios as they cleverly tried to outdo each other with weird and exciting situations and stunts. His major emphasis is on the sound period and those over thirty should enjoy rereading about such favorites as Buster Crabbe, Gene Autry, and Tom Mix. A useful appendix of the sound serials, arranged chronologically, is available. It includes the names of their stars.

* Barbour, Alan G. "Old Movies 2: The Serial," *A Screen Facts Reference Guide* (Screen Facts Press, Box 154, Kew Gardens, New York) .

This 1969 monograph has a host of annotated chapter-by-chapter accounts of serials from 1936 to 1954. Among the more famous ones are *Flash Gordon Conquers the Universe, Dick Tracy Returns, The Green Hornet* and *The Perils of Nyoka.* Marvelous memories are evoked if you saw the original films.

Fernett, Gene. *Next Time Drive Off the Cliff!* Cocoa, Florida: Cinememories Publishing Company, 1968.

A highly overpriced ($10.00) account of Nat Levine's Mascot Pictures Studio, filled with some excellent stills, but very light on critical and biographical content.

Lahue, Kalton C. *Bound and Gagged: The Story of the Silent Serials.* New York: A. S. Barnes and Company, 1968.

This time Lahue corrects many of his stylistic and critical flaws, presenting us with a well-illustrated and much more useful history of the silent cliffhangers. There is also a valuable appendix that contains Frank Leon

---

33. Some useful articles are William K. Everson, "Serials with Sound," *Films in Review* 4, no. 6 (June–July 1953) : 269–76; Edward Connor, "The Serial Lovers," *Films in Review* 6, no. 7 (August–September 1955) : 328–32; Frank Leon Smith, "The Man who made Serials," *Films in Review* 7, no. 8 (October 1956) : 375–83, 393; George Geltzer, "40 Years of Cliffhanging," *Films in Review* 8, no. 2 (February 1957) : 60–67; Edward Conner, "The 12 Tarzans," *Films in Review* 11, no. 8 (October 1960) : 452–63; William K. Everson, "The Silent Serial," *Screen Facts* 1, no. 1 (1963) : 1–14; Earl Michael, "The Serials of Republic," *idem.,* pp. 52–64; Edward Connor, "The First Eight Serials of Republic," *Screen Facts* 1, no. 1 (1964) : 52–63; Rudy Behlmer, "The Saga of Flash Gordon," *Screen Facts* 2, no. 4 (1965) : 53–63; Edward Connor, "The Golden Age of Republic Serials: Part I," *Screen Facts* 3, no. 5 (1968) : 48–61; Edward Connor, "Part Two," *Screen Facts* 3, no. 6 (1968) : 20–35; Wallace E. Davies, "Truth About Pearl White," *Films in Review* 10, no. 9 (November 1959) : 537–48; and George Geltzer, "Ruth Roland," *Films in Review* 11, no. 9 (November 1960) : 539–48.

Smith's original script for the first chapter of the 1920 Pathe serial, *Pirate Gold.*

Lahue, Kalton C. *Continued Next Week: A History of the Moving Picture Serials.* With a foreword by Kent D. Eastin. Norman: University of Oklahoma Press, 1964.

Lahue's first attempt is marred by shallow accounts of the serials, weak critical standards, and false information. Furthermore, the stills are not representative enough of the silent era. Some value exists, however, in the appendix—over 123 pages—which lists the majority of serials from 1912 to 1930. But here, too, there are a number of errors and omissions.

Stedman, Raymond William. *The Serials: Suspense and Drama by Installment.* Norman: The University of Oklahoma Press, 1971.

In this well-researched and authoritative guide to American film and TV serials, with a quick glance at radio's installment dramas, Stedman provides both an affectionate and useful 50 year history of the chapter plays. For those who are interested, he defines "serials" as "a narrative with continuing characters broken into a series of regularly appearing installments."

Weiss, Ken and Ed Goodgold. *To Be Continued . . .* New York: Crown, 1972.

Despite the forgetable introduction and the lack of any critical perspective, the authors do provide over 220 synopses and definitive production and cast credits to sound film serials beginning in 1929 and ending in 1956. Fans interested in reviving old memories from the profuse stills will be greatly annoyed by the poor production quality and an overabundance of incorrect captions.

Weltman, Manuel and Raymond Lee. *Pearl White, the Peerless Fearless Girl.* New York: A. S. Barnes and Company, 1969.

This is the only full-length biography of the greatest silent film serial queen and it is far from satisfactory. Written in superficial and fan magazine style, the authors opt for "cuteness" rather than seriousness. On the other hand, their selection of stills, together with good annotations, offers an invaluable collection of nostalgia and details.

Films[34]

The Story of the Serials (Walter Reade—16mm: 1968, 26 min., b/w, sound, R-WRS/S-WRS)

A very entertaining and useful teaching film that presents an edited version of the 1914 silent serial *The Perils of Pauline* plus other thrillers up to 1929.

The star system also gave rise to large advertising campaigns which tried, often successfully, to create images which were *continuously* reinforced by the publicity department. These stereotypes still exist and continue to have considerable influence on the audience, since our emotions cluster around

---

34. EM Gee Film library has a splendid rental collection of silent serials, available either by individual chapters or as a complete set. Titles include *The Perils of Pauline* and *The Hazards of Helen.* For an equally splendid rental collection of sound serials, send for a copy of Ivy Film/16's catalogue entitled "The Golden Age of Serials."

the figure of the star. The publicity campaigns were so blatant that they were subject to widespread attack. Criticism came from everywhere and almost anyone.

The excesses of publicity campaigns today stem from the original efforts of the film industry in 1913–19 to catch the public eye. The practice of deluging reviewers of new films with publicity material and readymade copy is now widespread. The material ranges from incidental facts to intimate and highly personal information. Hollywood avoids no expense in campaigns to publicize its product. Very rarely has there been any connection between a well-made film and a well-planned publicity campaign. A general rule of thumb is to avoid pictures that have large publicity programs.

So it was that the movie industry, confronted with the problems of supplying an ever-growing public demand for more films, tried to solve the problem in three significant ways: a star system, formula pictures, and advertising. The emphasis led to new forms of distribution, exhibition, and production.

Books

The Star System

Bull, Clarence Sinclair, with Raymond Lee. *The Faces of Hollywood.* New York: A. & S. Barnes and Company, 1969.

Conceived by a recognized photographer whose forty years in film began with Metro and followed through the great years of M-G-M, this volume presents his best portraits (almost 400) of the stars, accompanied with an assortment of chatty comments about such notables as Garbo, Norma Shearer, Jean Harlow, the Barrymores, Lon Chaney, and Elizabeth Taylor. It is a pleasant but not particularly important collection.

Carr, Larry. *Four Fabulous Faces.* New Rochelle: Arlington House, 1971.

By far the most deluxe production to date of collecting individual star's photographs, this book offers over 1000 beautiful pictures of Swanson, Garbo, Crawford, and Dietrich.

Griffith, Richard. *The Movie Stars.* New York: Doubleday and Company, 1970.

In this lavish and expensive book, Griffith surveys the rise and fall of many fabulous stars in a readable and useful historical chronology. It is a nostalgic journey and one well worth taking.

Lee, Raymond. *Not So Dumb: The Life and Times of the Animal Actors.* New York: A. S. Barnes and Company, 1970.

In this entertaining and informative book, Lee offers the first pictorial survey of the movies' most neglected stars, the animal actors who more than once saved the studios from bankruptcy. Among the favorites presented are Lassie, Rin Tin Tin, and the many Cheetahs.

* Levin, Martin (editor). *Hollywood and the Great Fan Magazines.* New York: Arbor House, 1970.

In this intelligently selected anthology of the best of *Photoplay, Motion*

Picture, Silver Screen, and a host of film fan magazines of the sound era, Levin offers his readers nostalgia, a sociological mirror, or a superb assortment of stills.

* Morin, Edgar. *The Stars.* Translated by Richard Howard. New York: Grove Press, 1961.

A very inventive and imaginary account of the invisible relationship between the screen gods and goddesses and their movie fans. Some interesting speculation about the psychological influence the players have on society is supplied.

* Ross, Lillian and Helen. *The Player: A Profile of an Art.* New York: Simon and Schuster, 1962.

A very helpful collection of interviews with 50 stars who discuss their professional lives and who emerge as clever, interesting, and very fallible human beings.

Schickel, Richard. *The Stars.* New York: The Dial Press, 1962.

A simplified picture of players who contribute to the social-cultural history of American film. Arranged in chronological order are two- to three-page descriptions and excellent stills of such stars as Chaplin, Valentino, Garbo, Cooper, Gable, and Taylor.

Shipman, David. *The Great Movie Stars: The Golden Years.* New York: Crown Publishers, 1970.

In the best of the reference works on the stars to date, Shipman presents an alphabetically arranged collection of biographies and critical comments on more than 450 performers from 1920 to 1945. Stills accompany each star's annotation.

Stuart, Ray (editor). *Immortals of the Screen.* New York: Bonanza Books, 1965.

Choosing from among his personal favorites, Stuart selected 100 stars from the silent days to the 1960s and provides over 650 stills of Hollywood's most famous players.

Trent, Paul and Richard Lawton. *The Image Makers: Sixty Years of Hollywood Glamour.* New York: McGraw-Hill Book Company, 1972.

In one of the most striking collections of studio portraits of major stars ever published, this book offers a fascinating experience for film buffs. Trent's narrative, coupled with Lawton's design, takes us decade by decade through pictures of the men and women who enchanted the world.

Twomey, Alfred E. and Arthur F. McClure. *The Versatiles: A Study of Supporting Actors and Actresses in the American Motion Picture, 1930–1955.* New York: A. S. Barnes and Company, 1969.

Written as a tribute to the supporting stars of yesteryear, this nostalgic collection of 400 familiar faces is accompanied by very brief biographical commentary. Unfortunately, the stills are often too poorly reproduced in size or clarity for effective use, and the majority of performers cited were less than versatile, considering the longevity of their type casting.

Walker, Alexander. *Stardom: The Hollywood Phenomenon.* New York: Stein and Day, 1970.

In this carefully documented and very readable study, Walker examines the origin, development, and effects of the star system. It is a valuable and accurate guide to famous personalities and periods.

Zierold, Norman J. *The Child Stars.* New York: Coward-McCann, Inc., 1965.
    Despite the absence of a much-needed index, this text offers a good but sympathetic review of the lives of Coogan, Temple, Rooney, Garland, Durbin, Bartholomew, Withers, and Baby Leroy.

Douglas Fairbanks

Cooke, Alistair. *Douglas Fairbanks: The Making of a Screen Character.* New York: Museum of Modern Art, 1940.
    Another useful MOMA monograph, which not only gives a valuable chronological account of a great star, but also outlines the formation of an image which captured the imagination of filmgoers all over the world for more than a decade. Fairbanks's pictures can be rented from the Museum of Modern Art and Audio Film Center or purchased from Blackhawk.

Hancock, Ralph, and Letita Fairbanks. *Douglas Fairbanks, The Fourth Musketeer.* New York: Henry Holt & Company, 1953.
    This lightweight and tender account by Fairbanks's niece traces his early stage career from 1902 until 1915 when he began making films at Triangle. We read about his love affairs, his motion picture successes, and his personal problems. But the book is most impressive when it records the lonely, forgotten, and aging star as the silent era ends and he lives beyond his time. Although the years are covered very quickly, and almost no documentation is presented, the book is a useful stopgap until a better one comes along.

Greta Garbo

Bainbridge, John. *Garbo.* New York: Holt, Rinehart and Winston, 1971.
    First written in 1955, this is a very entertaining and readable biography of a woman who starred in both the silent and sound eras, then retired at the peak of her career. Also helpful is his follow-up story, "Garbo is 65," *Look* 34, no. 18 (September 8, 1970) : 48–50, 52, 54, 56, 59.

Conway, Michael *et al. The Films of Greta Garbo.* Introduction by Parker Tyler. New York: Crown, 1963.
    A useful guide to Garbo's career, this book provides credits, synopses, and a variety of critical excerpts from reviewers. One of the best books of its kind.

Sjolander, Ture. *Garbo.* New York: Harper and Row, 1971.
    A marvelous addition to the growing number of Garbo books, this beautifully designed text offers a brief narrative together with more than 200 photographs of the famous star's personal and private lives.

* Zierold, Norman. *Garbo.* New York: Popular Library, 1969.
    This lightweight and breezy account of Garbo's career comes complete with filmography and bibliography. It is worth looking at for the collection of anecdotes.

William S. Hart

Hart, William S. *My Life East and West.* New York: Houghton Mifflin, 1929. Reissued by Benjamin Blom, 1968.

Although Hart rarely discusses the creative and technical aspects of his films, he gives us a valuable account of his concern with realistic western movies and the flavor of filmmaking from 1915 to 1925. A good companion to this book is George Mitchell, "William S. Hart," *Films in Review* 6, no. 4 (April 1955) : 145–54. Many of Hart's films can either be rented from the Museum of Modern Art or purchased from Blackhawk.

Buster Keaton[35]

* Blesh, Rudi. *Keaton*. New York: The Macmillan Company, 1966.
   One of the outstanding film biographies to date, this lovingly detailed and lucid book treats Keaton's career in a way that will interest both buffs and scholars. Don't miss reading this one.

Keaton, Buster, with Charles Samuels. *My Wonderful World of Slapstick*. New York: Doubleday and Company, 1960.
   Despite the undeveloped suggestions about his work and times, Keaton presents serious students with some clues to his problems at Metro, his respect for Fatty Arbuckle (who started him on his career), and his stint as gagman at M-G-M in the late 1930s and the 1940s. Many of Keaton's films can be rented from Audio Film Center and the Museum of Modern Art or purchased from Blackhawk.

* Lebel, J. P., translated by P. D. Stovin. *Buster Keaton*. New York: A. S. Barnes & Company, 1967.
   Another in Peter Cowie's *International Film Guide* series and a good account of Keaton's philosophy, characteristics, and methodology. It is very useful for studying *The General*.

* Robinson, David. *Buster Keaton*. Bloomington: Indiana University Press, 1969.
   Very helpful for adding to the background admirably supplied by the Blesh biography. The author, in a clear, chronological narrative, gives an overall introduction to Keaton's vaudeville career, emphasizing the main influences on the comedian's emerging grace and agility. Also helpful are Robinson's judicious comments on the shorts made during the actor's three years with Fatty Arbuckle, particularly Keaton's gags and camera techniques. Over and over, the writer points out how the great comedian avoided illogical and tricky shots to present one man's magnificent stand against the universe.

Mary Pickford

Lee, Raymond. *The Films of Mary Pickford*. New York: A. S. Barnes and Company, 1970.
   This is a useful pictorial survey of "America's Sweetheart," covering her

---

35. Some articles on Keaton are John Gillett and James Blue, "Keaton at Venice," *Sight and Sound* 35, no. 1 (Winter 1965–66) : 26–30; Penelope Houston, "The Great Blank Page," *Sight and Sound*, 37, no. 2 (Spring 1968) : 63–67; David Robinson, "Re-Discovery (4) : Buster," *Sight and Sound* 29, no. 1 (Winter 1959–60) : 41–43; Donald W. McCaffrey, *4 Great Comedians: Chaplin, Lloyd, Keaton, Langdon* (New York: A. S. Barnes & Company, 1968) : 83–137; Christopher Bishop, "The Great Stone Face," *Film Quarterly* 12, no. 1 (Fall 1958) : 10–15; Christopher Bishop, "An Interview with Buster Keaton," *idem.*, 15–22; and Arthur B. Friedman, "Buster Keaton: An Interview," *Film Quarterly* 19, no. 4 (Summer 1966) : 2–5.

23-year career with more than 200 stills and a complete filmography (credits included). Unfortunately, no index is provided, and it has shoddy work-manship.

Niver, Kemp. *Mary Pickford: Comedienne.* Edited by Bebe Bergsten. Los Angeles: Historical Films, 1970.
   Although this heavily illustrated edition is devoted to 37 Pickford films between 1909 and 1912, it contains some of the rarest shots of the star ever released. It also serves as a useful reminder of what can be done with the paper print collection at the Library of Congress. Pickford films can be purchased from Blackhawk.

Pickford, Mary. *Sunshine and Shadow.* Foreword by Cecil B. deMille. New York: Doubleday and Company, 1955.
   The most valuable part of this book is Miss Pickford's account of her family in the days leading up to and including the Biograph years. One gets a better understanding of how this clever, aggressive, and remarkable woman emerged from the hectic, early days of film not only a great actress but a highly successful business woman.

Gloria Swanson[36]

Hudson, Richard and Raymond Lee. *Gloria Swanson.* New York: A. S. Barnes and Company, 1970.
   Another pictorial survey of a great star, in which the authors present many rare stills plus a useful annotated filmography. The text is trite and slipshod.

DISTRIBUTION, EXHIBITION AND PRODUCTION

   With 1909 the American film industry was divided into two major camps. On one side were the well-known companies who had banded together in one giant organization—The Motion Picture Patents Company—to monopo-lize the movie world. Their avowed goal was to rule at home and abroad the making, leasing, and showing of all moving pictures. They had an exclu-sive agreement for raw film stock with Eastman Kodak, consented to theater owners' using their projectors for two dollars a week, and sold movies at a fixed rate, without making any allowances for artistic worth, through special film exchanges. Those who defied the Patents Company not only received court summonses but also were raided by gangs of thugs, hired to wreck their business.
   On the other side were the Independents, the outlaw firms who seriously challenged the legality of "The Trust." By 1912, led by their small film exchange operator Carl Laemmle and exhibitor William Fox, the opposition waged a brilliant, sarcastic campaign in the press and set into motion some expert legal machinery to destroy the Patents Company under the Sherman Anti-Trust Act of 1890. At the same time, these daring distributors and exhibitors began producing their own movies, mainly as insurance for their

36. DeWitt Bodeen, "Gloria Swanson," *Films in Review* 16, no. 4 (April 1965) : 193-217.

film theaters. In order to lure the important stars and directors away from the major companies, the aggressive Independents paid fabulous salaries and appealed to the performers' egos by promising to put their names in lights. Adolph Zukor, an Independent exhibitor, dealt another serious blow to the Trust in 1912 when he demonstrated with *Queen Elizabeth*[37] that feature films offered better entertainment than the Patent Company's standardized one- and two-reel films. And as 1913 got under way, it was all but over for the Motion Picture Patents Company.

The Trust War, however, was still active enough in 1913 to force many new production companies west to California. By the end of the year De-Mille had discovered Hollywood, Sennett had plans for a magnificent new studio, and Tom Ince was increasing his hold on a new method of studio-controlled productions.[38] Furthermore, the foundations for the would-be great companies were taking shape. The West Coast was now the center of production.

The structure of the film world also changed. Carl Laemmle, along with Pat Powers and several other Independents, had formed the Universal Pictures Corporation in 1912. That same year also saw the formation of Mutual by men like Harry E. Aitken and John R. Frueler. These two new firms modeled their distribution policies after the old General Film national exchange pattern of the Trust. That policy would soon change. In the meantime, Adam Kessel and Charles Baumann (the nominal heads of Sennett and Ince Productions) had planned to release their products through Universal, but sharp words and hot tempers soon forced them to choose Mutual. And so it was that Mutual obtained the likes of Griffith and Chaplin over the next three years.

Then in 1913, Lasky Feature Plays (originated by Jesse Lasky, Samuel Goldfish [later changed to Goldwyn], and Cecil B. DeMille), and Adolph Zukor's Famous Players in Famous Plays began operating. Because of their emphasis on the legitimate theater, a great exodus of stage stars and technicians started from New York to California, along with a new respectability for the movie industry.[39] Still in 1913, William W. Hodkinson sensed that the time was ready to rethink the patterns of distribution. He was one of the first to sense that the big money was in distribution and exhibition, not production. So Hodkinson started Paramount, a distributing agency that rented movies on a percentage basis instead of a flat fee for the old State's Rights method of booking. The new method was called "block-booking," and required an exhibitor to buy, sight unseen, almost *all* the motion pictures produced by a studio. If any theater owner objected, he soon found it difficult to get *any* picture from that studio.

---

37. Charles Ford (translated by Anne and Thornton K. Brown), "Sarah Bernhardt," *Films in Review* 5, no. 10 (December 1954) : 515–18.
38. George Mitchell, "Tom H. Ince," *Films in Review* 11, no. 8 (October 1960) : 464–84.
39. Gerald D. McDonald, "From Stage to Screen," *Films in Review* 6, no. 1 (January 1955) : 13–18.

In 1915 Aitken and Griffith began to find things uncomfortable at Mutual. They—along with Kessel, Baumann, Sennett and Ince—created the Triangle Film Corporation; and when that fizzled out, Zukor and Lasky picked up some of the remaining pieces, joined with Hodkinson, and created a new Paramount in 1916.[40] A couple of years later, Chaplin, Pickford, Griffith and Douglas Fairbanks (a refugee from Triangle) formed United Artists.[41] By 1919 William Fox had made his Fox Company a major force in the industry[42] and Samuel Goldfish,[43] who had changed his name in 1916 after joining with the Selwyn Brothers to form the Goldwyn Picture Corporation, left his fledgling firm to start a new production company.

Exhibitors had become quite alarmed at all these hectic and wild mergers as well as at the distributing policies over the years, and now they began to fight back. In 1917, many of the more successful theater owners decided to form their own production company, the First National Exhibitors Circuit. Marcus Loew, another prominent exhibitor, started his meteoric rise first by investing heavily in theaters and by 1919 taking the initial steps toward the eventual acquisition of the Metro and Goldwyn companies, which by 1924 would become the fabulous M-G-M operation.[44] Finally, the Warner brothers, owners of a minor chain of theaters, were beginning to test their business acumen and by 1929 would emerge with one of the major studios in motion picture history.

Almost every major studio began collecting large theater chains and operated on the following production-distribution-exhibition philosophy: (1) get important stars to appear in the picture; (2) make certain the story, taken from best-sellers, famous plays, or previously tried formulas, is familiar to the public; (3) keep the box-office in mind; and (4) build showcase theaters to display their prestige. The producers thus found it necessary to simplify stories, direction, acting, etc. This standardization of every aspect of motion pictures—studios, personalities, films, distrbution, exhibition—led to rising salaries, legal entanglements, new divisions of labor, and a host of other obstacles that the artist had to encounter in making a great film.

As the motion picture industry grew to embrace not only actors and directors but also cameramen, technicians, and editors, the general procedures of the past gave way to specialization. Hollywood saw the growth of a division of labor, which was characteristic of big business.

40. "Hollywood Sells Off The Splendor," *Life* 68, no. 7 (February 27, 1970) : 38–46.

41. Arthur L. Mayer, "The Origins of United Artists," *Films in Review* 10, no. 7 (August–September 1959) : 390–99; and Christopher North, "UA's 35th Birthday," *Films in Review* 5, no. 4 (April 1954) : 165–70.

42. George P. Erengis, "Twentieth-Century's Backlot," *Films in Review* 13, no. 4 (April 1962) : 193–205.

43. Herbert G. Luft, "Samuel Goldwyn," *Films in Review* 20, no. 10 (December 1969) : 585–604.

44. Albert Johnson, "Conversation with Roger Edens," *Sight and Sound* 27, no. 4 (Spring 1958) : 179–82; Penelope Houston, "Lion Rampant: The Record of M-G-M," *ibid.* 24, no. 1 (July–September 1954) : 21–30; Christopher North, "M-G-M's First 30 Years," *Films in Review* 5, no. 5 (May 1954) : 216–20; George P. Erengis, "M-G-M's Backlot," *Films in Review* 14, no. 1 (January 1963) : 5–22.

Books

General Introduction to the Film Moguls

French, Philip. *The Movie Moguls: An Informal History of the Hollywood Tycoons.* London: Weidenfeld and Nicolson, 1969.
   This is a well-written synthesis of the important books on the fabulous showmen like DeMille, Mayer, Schenck, Fox, Goldwyn, Laemmle, Lasky, and Zukor. French, in intriguing and clever prose, sketches the conduct of the film tycoons who restricted the showing of foreign movies in this country, exploited the performers and technicians who worked for them, and monopolized movies to further their personal vanity. It is also an excellent source for fictional accounts based upon the lives of Hollywood producers.

* Hampton, Benjamin B. *A History of the Movies.* New York: Covici, Friede, 1931. Reissued with minor corrections by Dover in 1970 under the new title *History of the American Film Industry: From Its Beginnings to 1931.* With an introduction by Richard Griffith.
   Hampton, writing from a first-hand acquaintance with the personalities and studios during the silent era, presents us with a remarkable account of the economics of the film world. It is must reading for naive students who never consider the overriding pressures of commerce in movie-making. Unfortunately, the book suffers from a heavy-handed American bias and a fuzzy knowledge of chronology, aesthetics, and experimentation.

Jobes, Gertrude. *Motion Picture Empire.* Hamden, Conn.: Archon Books, 1966.
   Although lacking Hampton's first-hand experience, Jobes does an outstanding job of combing files, records and newspaper accounts to produce a very readable and entertaining account of the American film industry up to 1965. This should be a basic source book for all serious students.

Rosenberg, Bernard and Harry Silverstein (editors). *The Real Tinsel.* New York: The Macmillan Company, 1970.
   The authors have collected a number of interesting and valuable essays by 24 of Hollywood's pioneers, including important information on Zukor, Roach Sr., Schary, Arthur Mayer, Mae Marsh, Lang, and Anita Loos.

Zierold, Norman. *The Moguls.* New York: Coward-McCann, Inc., 1969.
   Like the French book, this is a synthesis of old stories put into a new framework. For the uninitiated, it makes for pleasant and fast reading. Although nothing significant is revealed about the "moguls," it is worthwhile for its reminders of the kinds of men Laemmle, Goldwyn, Lasky, Zukor and Mayer were.

Producers

Harry Cohn

* Thomas, Bob. *King Cohn: The Life and Times of Harry Cohn.* New York: G. P. Putnam's Sons, 1967.
   This is a particularly well-documented record of an arrogant, crude, and lecherous individual who ran his film headquarters with an inflexible mind and an iron fist. Thomas does such an outstanding job of portraying the man's influence over Columbia Pictures that he presents us with many val-

uable insights into the buccaneering saga of the entire Hollywood film industry.

William Fox

Allvine, Glendon. *The Greatest Fox of Them All.* New York: Lyle Stuart, Inc., 1969.

Another one of those books which suggests an intimacy with the subject, but offers no documentation or evidence to support the dozens of direct quotations scattered throughout the text. Allvine has a pleasant and readable style, and this might make an entertaining evening with pseudo-history.

Sinclair, Upton. *Upton Sinclair Presents William Fox.* Los Angeles: Upton Sinclair, 1933.

Despite Sinclair's emotional and narrow commitment to Fox, the author does highlight the manner in which Fox began his fall from power in 1929 as well as the economics and politics of the financial wizards who took over the Fox Company.

Samuel Goldwyn

Goldwyn, Samuel. *Behind the Screen.* New York: Doran, 1923.

This is a highly unreliable and one-sided account of a man who personally dominated every aspect of production connected with his films. Nevertheless, it is worthwhile to examine how such a man thought in the first ten years of his film career.

* Griffith, Richard. *Samuel Goldwyn, The Producer and His Films.* New York: Museum of Modern Art, 1956.

Griffith presents the best reckoning so far of the individual who helped shape the careers of stars like Will Rogers, Ronald Coleman, and Eddie Cantor. This little monograph also comes with a valuable list of the producer's films, more than a dozen well-chosen stills, and a respectable bibliography.

Johnston, Alva. *The Great Goldwyn.* New York: Doubleday, 1937.

Johnston's book is a useful transition piece between Goldwyn's autobiographical sketch and Griffith's museum monograph. Some good comments are made on the ins and outs of production, distribution and exhibition.

Carl Laemmle

Drinkwater, John. *The Life and Adventures of Carl Laemmle.* New York: G. P. Putnam's Sons, 1931.

Legend has it that the author, commissioned in 1930 to write this biography, used it as a fantastic gamble to win himself a Nobel Peace Prize. Not only didn't he get the award, but this book may well be one of the most superficial records ever put together by a sympathetic author who had the opportunity to add a major contribution to film scholarship.

Jesse Lasky

Lasky, Jesse with Don Weldon. *I Blow My Own Horn.* London: Victor Gollancz, 1957.

Lasky prefers gossip and sentiment to an honest, informative history of his movie career from the early days in 1913 to the hectic years at Paramount. While he takes care to praise few people for his success and underscores the importance of a top-flight executive in film production, the author provides us with amusing and useful anecdotes about the beginning of the Hollywood era.

Louis B. Mayer

Crowther, Bosley. *Hollywood Rajah: The Life and Times of Louis B. Mayer.* New York: Holt, Rinehart and Winston, 1960.

The ex-New York Times film critic is not particularly fond of Mr. Mayer and goes to considerable pains to prove that his subject was a "psychopath" who hungered for power, an ignorant man who understood next to nothing about the contemporary world, and an unpredictable tyrant who considered himself a paternal leader. Nevertheless, Crowther fails to explain what made this Russian Jewish immigrant so successful. How was it that Mayer, leaving the junk business and going into film exhibition in 1907, was able to emerge out of the fantastic motion picture wars as one of the most important men in movie history? Incidentally, F. Scott Fitzgerald used Mayer as the prototype for Pat Brady, the mean and selfish producer in *The Last Tycoon.*

Crowther, Bosley. *The Lion's Share: The Story of an Entertainment Empire.* New York: E. P. Dutton & Company, Inc., 1957.

Crowther unfolds an uneven account of the controversial personalities and events that brought Loew's Incorporated to Culver City and helped produce one of the finest arrays of talent in film history during the 1930s and 1940s. The author provides useful commentary on Dore Schary, but downplays Irving Thalberg's value to M-G-M and says next to nothing about the studio's motion pictures.

David O. Selznick

Behlmer, Rudy (editor). *Memo from David O. Selznick.* With an Introduction by S. N. Behrman. New York: The Viking Press, 1972.

Based upon Selznick's copious memorandums, letters, telegrams, personal notes and autobiographical remarks, this fascinating book examines the late motion picture producer's career from 1926, when he joined M-G-M's story department, to his stay as a young producer at Paramount, and continues with his reign as executive producer at R-K-O, his triumphant return to M-G-M in the 1930s, and concludes with his fabulous years as head of his own major studio, Selznick International, where he produced such films as *Rebecca* and *Spellbound.*

Thomas, Bob. *Selznick.* New York: Doubleday and Company, 1970.

Another fine document on influential and significant figures in film production who helped shape the future of motion pictures. We are shown how Lewis J. Selznick during the silent era provided the skill and motivation for his sons, David and Myron. Thomas, a Hollywood columnist, enlivens the narrative with enjoyable and informative quotations, anecdotes, and facts. The book also has some good illustrations.

Albert E. Smith

Smith, Albert E. with P. A. Kowry. *Two Reels and a Crank*. New York: Doubleday and Company, 1952.

This is a rambling, anecdotal and unreliable account by one of the original partners of Vitagraph, which opened its doors in 1896. Nevertheless, Smith recreates the setting and flavor of the inventive years when a teenager who was an upstart technician and businessman could join in a partnership with J. Stuart Blackton and influence the direction of film history.

Irving Thalberg

Thomas, Bob. *Thalberg: Life and Legend*. New York: Doubleday and Company, 1969.

This is the weakest of Thomas's trilogy on the remarkable Hollywood executives. Thalberg was a man who at 20 took charge of Universal Studios, at 24 ruled the production of M-G-M films and at 37 was dead. Within that short span of time, he had directly or indirectly been responsible for such film classics as *The Merry Widow, Ben-Hur, Anna Christie, Grand Hotel, The Barretts of Wimpole Street, Mutiny on the Bounty,* and *A Night at the Opera*. Thalberg had also been the model for Monroe Stahr, the hero of Fitzgerald's *The Last Tycoon*. After reading Thomas's many entertaining anecdotes and details, we still come away with a very limited insight into Thalberg himself.

Jack L. Warner

Sennett, Ted. *Warner Brothers Presents: The Most Exciting Years from the Jazz Singer to White Head*. New Rochelle: Arlington House, 1971.

In a very interesting and readable fashion, Sennett surveys the major Warner Brothers output from 1927 to 1949. He provides a most extensive filmography of the studio, complete with cast, credits, and plot outlines. Profusely illustrated.

Warner, Jack L. with Dean Jennings. *My First Hundred Years in Hollywood*. New York: Random House, 1965.

The only survivor of the four brothers who helped revolutionize the motion picture industry argues that the best approach to life is a devil-may-care attitude. Consequently, the major tone of the book is cynical, tempered with frivolous comments. What emerges is his dislike of agents and specific personalities such as John Barrymore, Charles Chaplin, and Samuel Goldwyn. What does not emerge is a clear, much needed picture of the Warner Brothers Studio.

Darryl F. Zanuck

Dunne, John Gregory. *The Studio*. New York: Farrar, Straus and Giroux, 1968.

Here is a worthwhile examination of the complex world of Twentieth Century-Fox in 1967. Dunne, in a well-balanced tone of cynicism, amusement, and amazement, shows us life at a top studio during the production of movies like *Dr. Dolittle, Planet of the Apes, The Boston Strangler, Star!,* and *Hello, Dolly*. There are also some valuable statements on George Axelrod, Richard Zanuck, Pandro Berman, and Darryl Zanuck.

* Guild, Leo. *Zanuck: Hollywood's Last Tycoon.* Los Angeles: Hollywood House Publishing Company, 1970.
  A breezy and lightweight overview of Zanuck's fabulous career which should be read after the Gussow book below.

Gussow, Mel. *Don't Say Yes Until I Finish Talking: A Biography of Darryl F. Zanuck.* New York: Doubleday and Company, 1971.
  This highly entertaining and informative biography is the best source to date on the great showman's personal and public lives, but a more critical and scholarly book is still necessary to put Zanuck's contribution to motion picture history in better focus.

Adolph Zukor

Irwin, Will. *The House That Shadows Built.* New York: Doubleday, Doran and Company, Inc., 1928. Reissued by Arno Press in 1970.
  This unreliable but entertaining biography offers a number of personal anecdotes which should delight students and historians alike.

Zukor, Adolph with Dale Kramer. *The Public is Never Wrong: The Autobiography of Adolph Zukor.* New York: G. P. Putnam's Sons, 1953.
  This autobiography is almost as meaningless as Drinkwater's uncritical account of Laemmle. Zukor prefers to write pleasant accounts of his dealings with John Barrymore, Mary Pickford, W. S. Hart and Gloria Swanson. It would have been much more valuable to learn first hand how a Hungarian immigrant gave up the fur business and cleverly, with an iron will, dominated movie history for over thirty years. A better account of Zukor is given in Hampton's book.

Hollywood[45]

* Anger, Kenneth. *Hollywood Babylon.* Phoenix: Associated Professional Services, Inc., 1965.
  It's hard to find any book that beats this one for smut, scandal, and backstage stories of the movie industry. It is written by the director of *Scorpio Rising.*

Goodman, Ezra. *The Fifty-Year Decline and Fall of Hollywood.* New York: Simon and Schuster, 1961.
  Goodman, an outspoken and caustic writer, examines Hollywood in the 1950s and finds the town polluted. He presents many controversial views on major personalities, institutions and moving pictures. The book should be read by every serious student of film.

Higham, Charles. *Hollywood at Sunset.* New York: Saturday Review Press, 1972.
  This behind-the-scenes study of Hollywood since 1946 is must reading for anyone interested in learning about the intrigue and government interference that has helped destroy the fortunes of Nick Schenck, Louis B. Mayer, Spyros Skouras, Jack Warner, Harry Cohn, and the other movie moguls. Page after page of this fascinating narrative delves into the workings

---

45. For a good list of other contemporary books on Hollywood and its stars, see Margaret Tarratt, "Books," *Screen* 10, nos. 4, 5 (July–October 1969) : 174–78. Also useful are the following: Margaret Tarratt, "Reflections in a Golden Lens: Part One," *Films and Filming* 16, no. 3 (January 1970) : 4–8; and Margaret Tarratt, "Reflections in a Golden Lens: Part Two," *Films and Filming* 16, no. 4 (February 1970) : 14–18.

of the House Un-American Activities Committee, the effect of television on the industry, and the long battles to remove the old-timers and make way for a new brand of movie boss.

Knight, Arthur and Eliot Elisofon. *The Hollywood Style.* New York: The Macmillan Company, 1969.

Knight's easy flowing text and Elisofon's breathtaking photographs record the pretentious and glamorous homes of the wealthy stars from the 1920s to the present. Don't read this book when you're depressed.

MacCann, Richard Dyer. *Hollywood in Transition.* Boston: Houghton Mifflin, 1962.

Although I have reservations about some of MacCann's critical judgments of movies, he does have a good summary of Hollywood in the 1950s and raises some crucial questions about film censorship in general. It is quite an optimistic picture and a little disconcerting in comparison with Goodman's account.

Marlowe, Don. *The Hollywood that Was.* Fort Worth: Branch-Smith, Inc., 1969.

Some interesting anecdotes about Boris Karloff, Bela Lugosi and Stan Laurel are whipped off in this skimpy and sad little volume by a former member of "Our Gang" comedies.

* Mayersberg, Paul. *Hollywood, the Haunted House.* New York: Stein and Day, 1968.

Primarily a collection of interviews with Don Siegel, Richard Brooks, Blake Edwards, David Swift, Stanley Kramer, John Houseman, King Vidor, Nick Ray, Robert Aldrich, Joseph Losey, Dan Taradash, and Abby Mann. The main problem is that this dated material, most of which first appeared in *Cahiers du Cinema* and *Movie,* neglects to treat the end of the studio system and the new era of independent production.

* Powdermaker, Hortense. *Hollywood: The Dream Factory.* New York: Grosset and Dunlap, 1950.

This highly overrated book presents material that is generally known and often questioned. Powdermaker lacks first-hand knowledge of many aspects of production and direction, and the reader becomes aware of this in page after page of her discussion. Weakest of all is her attack on the production code. The anthropologist's contribution to film history is that she takes the first step and shows the errors and mistakes that future scholars should avoid.

Rivkin, Allen and Laura Kerr. *Hello Hollywood! The Story of the Movies by the People Who Make Them.* New York: Doubleday and Company, 1962.

This is a pseudo-documentary account of Hollywood which presents observations of the film town as seen by stars, producers, directors, writers and journalists. Very good for "legends."

Rosten, Leo C. *Hollywood: The Movie Colony, The Movie Makers.* New York: Harcourt, Brace and Company, 1941.

For three years, specialists in economics and sociology collected data on the studio system. They turned in the most complete and detailed study so far on what life was like on the Hollywood lot in the early days of sound.

Scott, Evelyn F. *Hollywood: When Silents Were Golden.* New York: Mc-Graw-Hill Book Company, 1972.

Written by a woman who grew up and went to school with many of the film capital's greats and near-greats, this book provides a chatty and nostalgic look back from the 1920s until now.

Spatz, Jonas. *Hollywood in Fiction: Some Versions of the American Myth.* Paris: Mouton, 1969.

In four interesting but uneven chapters, Spatz discusses the complex relationship between Hollywood's unique atmosphere and the concepts imbedded in the American dream: e.g., success, equality, and utopia. Most useful are his treatment of the success theme in Fitzgerald and Mailer's fiction in Chapter 2 and the analysis of the artist as a deceiver in mass media in Chapter 3.

Spears, Jack. *Hollywood: The Golden Era.* New York: A. S. Barnes and Company, 1971.

In a series of well-written essays (many of which first appeared in *Films in Review*), Jack Spears presents film buffs with a wealth of information and nostalgia concerning the history, growth, and personalities of the great Hollywood years. Among the more rewarding sections are those dealing with World War I, Max Linder, Chaplin's collaborators, and the American Indian. Also invaluable are two indices on names and films. Every library should get a copy of this book. It's fun reading.

Thorpe, Edward. *The Other Hollywood.* London: Michael Joseph, 1970.

This lightweight and breezy book is one Englishman's interesting observations on Hollywood today, its people, tourist traps, social and economical climates as well as the world of the high school kids.

Tyler, Parker. *The Hollywood Hallucination.* New York: Creative Art Press, 1944. Reissued by Simon and Schuster in 1970.

A perceptive and intriguing discussion on the effect that movies have on society that is filled with witty and sharp allusions to literature and the traditional arts. It should be read by serious students.

Wilk, Max (editor). *The Wit and Wisdom of Hollywood: From the Squaw Man to the Hatchet Man.* New York: Atheneum, 1971.

For those who love Hollywood anecdotes, Wilk offers a delightful collection of throw-away stories about the famous and near-famous personalities of the past sixty years. He divides the book up into unique and uneven sections such as "The Front Office," "Silent Days, Noisy Nights," "Life in Filmland," and "Hollywood Goes to War." A typical example from this potpourri is the DeMille story about Pharaoh and his daughter, who brought the infant Moses in for approval. Pharaoh looked at the baby and said, "My God, what an absolutely ugly kid! Where'd you get him?" "I can't understand it," his daughter sighed. "He looked so good in the rushes."

Film Theaters

Hall, Ben M. *The Best Remaining Seats: The Story of the Golden Age of the Movie.* New York: Branhall House, 1961.

Here is a book that is not totally accurate, suffers from an ineffectual organization, recounts its story in sentimental tones, and remains the major source for the history of motion picture theaters. Nowhere else has anyone taken the trouble to collect information about the exhibitors' lives, the magnificent organs, ushers' uniforms, architecture, and rare stills of the picture palaces themselves.

Sharp, Dennis. *The Picture Palace and Other Buildings for the Movies.* New York: Praeger, 1969.

Outside of Sharp's heavy reliance on Hall's record of American theaters, the author gives a new and fresh interpretation to the structure and growth of movie-houses in Britain and Europe. The book is beautifully produced and the comments are terse, sound and interesting. A good follow-up is Ernest Callenbach's "Temples of the Seventh Art," *Sight and Sound* 35, no. 1 (Winter 1965–66) : 12–17.

FILM CRITICISM

No one should get the impression that the big-business approach to moviemaking did not contribute to the art of the film. As the major companies grew, their concern with profits forced the industry, in spite of itself, to raise the standards of film production. Because the exhibitors demanded a steady flow of new films, the filmmakers worked regularly and had room for errors. Many of our most talented artists received their training while turning out quickly made films, and they had the chance to develop their skills, experiment with new ideas, and learn from their peers in the age when an undiscriminating audience flocked to see the newest movie, regardless of quality.

But not everyone accepted this point of view. By 1914, intellectuals, critics and reformers began arguing for standards in film production and for works of art. Movie critics appeared in most of the newspapers discussing, reviewing and complaining about tasteless films and spectacular breakthroughs. *Photoplay,* the archetype of a new trend in film periodicals, appeared in 1914 and today remains one of the most valuable records of the period. Over the next fifty years, a handful of talented and outstanding individuals would work against incompetent craftsmen, greedy producers, and an unconcerned public to condemn the motion picture industry for wasting its precious gift. These outspoken critics, ignored by most filmgoers, would have their greatest influence in helping to develop the principles separating good and bad films and in providing a source of encouragement to artists who felt themselves alienated in a crass, commercial system.

The period 1913–19, we can thus see, was an important one in the development of the film; and like formative periods in the traditional arts, it produced great works and developed magnificent talents. The major danger in teaching about such a valuable era is that the classwork will turn into a session on names, dates, and places. This is not my intention. I have tried to suggest that the primary concern should be with the experience of film and that the anecdotes, records, and biographical material should be used judiciously and only when they help to further an individual's interest, understanding, and enjoyment of movies.

Books

Early Commentators[46]

* Lindsay, Vachel. *The Art of the Moving Picture*. New York: The Macmillan Company, 1915. Reissued in 1970 by Liveright, with an introduction by Stanley Kauffmann.

The well-known American poet divides his thoughts on film into two sections: (1) a basis for "photoplay" criticism and (2) speculations. Although the prose suffers from a sentimental excess, Lindsay does provide a worthwhile commentary on the state of the motion picture between 1912 and 1915. It remains the major tribute by a literary mind to the then-new art.

* Münsterberg, Hugo. *The Film: A Psychological Study—The Silent Photoplay in 1916*. New York: D. Appleton and Company, 1916. Reissued in 1970 by Dover, with a new foreword by Richard Griffith.

This is the first major attempt by a distinguished psychologist to explain the relationship between film techniques and the movie audience. It is not dated. His treatment of depth, movement, attention, and emotions is thorough and his brilliant observations on the "phi phenomenon" are excellent in defining the limitations of the vision concept of film. The summarized lectures of Slavko Vorkapich, lovingly recorded by Barbara L. Kevles in *Film Culture* 38 (Fall 1965), are a good follow-up.

Since 1920

* Adler, Renata. *A Year in the Dark: Journal of a Film Critic 1968–1969*. New York: Random House, 1969.

An anthology highlighting the author's one disastrous year as film critic for the *New York Times*. This uneven volume suggests not only the problems of daily assignments, but also the value of not dismissing Adler offhand. Some discerning comments are made on black men in films, Bergman, Buñuel, *War and Peace, The Heart Is a Lonely Hunter*, and *Targets*.

* Agee, James. *Agee on Film, Volume One: Reviews and Comments*. New York: Grosset and Dunlap, 1967.

Agee was one of the foremost American critics during the 1940s and early 1950s. The importance of this collection is in reading an intelligent author's discussion of the issues and problems connected with film production and art.

Alpert, Hollis. *The Dreams and the Dreamer: Adventures of a Professional Movie Goer*. New York: The Macmillan Company, 1962.

This underrated movie critic who once shared the *Saturday Review* assignment with Arthur Knight demonstrates his style of popularizing movies and explaining the characteristics of well-made films. This volume includes ma-

---

46. See also E. R. Hagemann, "An Extraordinary Picture: The Film Criticism of Robert E. Sherwood," *The Journal of Popular Film* 1, no. 2 (Spring 1972) : 81–104.

terial from 1959 to 1962 and illustrates Alpert's values, prejudices, and strengths—particularly his wit in a delightful article on Hollywood clichés.

Cooke, Alistair (editor). *Garbo and the Night Watchman: A Selection Made in 1937 from the Writings of British and American Film Critics.* London: Jonathan Cape, 1937. Reissued by McGraw-Hill Book Company in 1971.
   The best available collection of movie criticism of the 1930s, with a particularly fine discussion by nine critics of Chaplin's *Modern Times.*

* Crist, Judith. *The Private Eye, the Cowboy and the Very Naked Girl: Movies From Cleo to Clyde.* New York: Holt, Rinehart, and Winston, 1968.
   Crist writes with a lively, honest point of view, and her judgments are both informed and reliable. Her audience for these reviews was mainly readers of the defunct *Herald Tribune, New York* magazine, *TV Guide,* and viewers of "The Today Show," and she is wonderful in criticizing the popular favorites of unselective audiences. Her trouble comes in the treatment of such artists as Bergman, Antonioni, and Fellini.

Farber, Manny. *Negative Space: Manny Farber on the Movies.* New York: Praeger Publishers, 1971.
   Farber, one of the most eccentric and highly praised critics of the last quarter century, has collected more than 25 diverse articles and published them in this worthwhile review. A major contribution to film criticism.

* Kael, Pauline. *Going Steady.* Boston: Little, Brown and Company, 1970.
   This collection contains Kael's best writing on the cinema to date and indicates the advantage of working for *The New Yorker.* Don't miss her reviews of Godard, the Beatles, and Bergman; or *If . . . , The Prime of Miss Jean Brodie,* or. . . .

* Kael, Pauline. *I Lost It at the Movies.* Boston: Little, Brown and Company, 1965.
   The first major book on film criticism in the 1960s. Kael magnificently attacks filmmakers and theorists who specialize in politics and social issues instead of the art of the film. She also lashes out at educators who might try to mummify movies the way some have successfully atrophied literature. In this compendium, American films receive better notices than foreign films.

* Kael, Pauline. *Kiss Kiss Bang Bang.* Boston: Little, Brown and Company, 1968.
   This volume contains Kael's reviews and articles written between 1965 and 1968, plus an excellent rendering of the production of *The Group* (which *Life* refused to print), and 280 short, useful and witty annotations on specific films over the past 40 years. Here is another knowledgeable, articulate and outspoken critic who balances her love for movies with a hatred for incompetence, qualities clearly evident in her treatments of Arthur Penn, Orson Welles, and Marlon Brando.

* Kauffmann, Stanley. *Figures of Light: Film Criticism and Comment.* New York: Harper and Row, 1971.
   Writing in a cold and dispassionate style, Kauffmann continues to attack the pretentious and erratic film elements so popular with modern-day audiences. His reviews are worth examining for their point of view and logic.

* Kauffman, Stanley. *A World on Film: Criticism and Comment.* New York: Harper & Row, 1966.

A collection of writings by this thoughtful and dedicated critic of *The New Republic* between 1958 and 1965. Kauffmann serves as a good contrast to Kael since he frowns on many American productions, dislikes the star system, and enjoys the art-house film crowd—particularly Antonioni. The book is arranged in an unusual and profitable manner; instead of reproducing his comments chronologically, Kauffmann organizes his material by subject or country of the film, allowing us to contrast and compare the work of artists of different nationalities.

* Macdonald, Dwight. *Dwight Macdonald on the Movies.* Englewood Cliffs, N.J.: Prentice-Hall, Inc., 1969.

An unusual collection of 40 years of observations by a critic thrilled to escape from film reviewing in 1966. Most of the writings center around his experiences as movie critic for *Esquire*—beginning in 1960—and reveal Macdonald's bitterness toward Hollywood, directors, and actors in general. Invaluable is his section on Eisenstein, taken from the remarkable appendices to his original, three-part study of the decline of Russian films, which first appeared (with 124 footnotes) in the *Partisan Review* (1939).

Pechter, William S. *Twenty-Four Times a Second: Films and Film-Makers.* New York: Harper and Row, 1971.

This free-lance film critic offers a stimulating collection of critical essays ranging from recent motion pictures to directors to film criticism itself. It is worth taking a couple of hours and reading through the book's four sections.

Reed, Rex. *Big Screen, Little Screen.* New York: The Macmillan Company, 1971.

In this collection of witty and fresh reviews taken from his writings in *Women's Wear Daily, Holiday,* and *The New York Times,* Reed takes on most of the major contemporary filmmakers.

* Sarris, Andrew. *Confessions of a Cultist: On the Cinema, 1955–1969.* New York: Simon and Schuster, 1970.

Here is a brief and spotty collection of film reviews and observations of movie personalities which first saw print in *Film Culture* and the *Village Voice.* In emphasizing the *auteur* theory, Sarris demonstrates his respect for men like Chaplin, Ford, Buñuel, and Renoir. Unfortunately, the essays are very uneven and do not reflect the depth of Sarris's very great talent.

Schickel, Richard. *Second Sight: Notes on Some Movies 1965–1970.* New York: Simon and Schuster, 1972.

The greatest value of this book is to make readers aware how dangerous initial film reviews are and how often, given more time and less concern for competitive cleverness among daily reviewers, the critics themselves have second thoughts about their first screenings. Schickel provides ample evidence of the problems and the reasons why.

Schickel, Richard and John Simon (editors). *Film 67/68.* New York: Simon and Schuster, 1968.

Founded in late 1966, The National Society of Film Critics sought four specific ends: (1) to give annual recognition to the outstanding film, director, and screen performances (male and female) of the previous year; (2) to promote worthwhile films; (3) to protest against possible dangers to movies or the film audience; and (4) to provide a common fraternal organization for filmmakers and critics. The idea for this annual anthology came in 1967, and we are the better for it. The book is divided into two main sections—The Year's Films and Reflections—which are each subdivided into such groupings as "Violence American Style," "Men and Arms," "Spoofs, and Adaptations." The volume will be published annually and is well worth reading on a yearly basis.

Sheed, Wilfrid. *The Morning After: Selected Essays and Reviews.* With a foreword by John Leonard. New York: Farrar, Straus and Giroux, 1971.

Taken from his reviews for *Esquire,* where he was film critic from 1967 to 1970, this book offers a good look at the ideas, detachment, and critical perceptions of a delightful critic who comments not only on movies, but also sports, theater, books, and politics. The emphasis is on original rather than on rehashed opinions.

Simon, John. *Acid Test.* Introduction by Dwight Macdonald. New York: Stein and Day, 1963.

Although this volume contains only four essays on film, Simon's razor-sharp criticism on Antonioni, Wilder, Bergman, and Dassin is provocative, unusual, and rewarding.

Simon, John. *Movies into Film: Film Criticism 1967–1970.* New York: Dial Press, 1971.

Insisting that there are differences between entertainment (movies) and art (film), Simon offers his reasons why so few good films are seen or appreciated. He is better at attacking rather than at praising, and one comes away from this third collection of his writings with the distinct feeling of having read it all before with only the names of the films changed.

* Simon, John. *Private Screenings: Views of the Cinema of the Sixties.* New York: The Macmillan Company, 1967.

No book on film criticism has a more splendid opening chapter on the principles of reviewing than does Simon's. He clearly and forcefully describes the values, the purposes, and the limitations of a dedicated and direct critic; and he does it with scholarship, wit, and excellent examples. Unfortunately, the remainder of the collection talks more about what is not good than what is art. Here is another side to Kael's and Sarris's views on Godard, another approach to Antonioni and Satyajit Ray.

Warshow, Robert. *The Immediate Experience: Movies, Comics, Theater and Other Aspects of Popular Culture.* New York: Doubleday and Company, 1962.

An outstanding film critic, in the fine tradition of Gilbert Seldes, Warshow prefers to condemn more often than praise, while at the same time demonstrating a great love for popular culture. No one should miss his articles on the gangster and on the cowboy.

Weinberg, Herman. *Saint Cinema: Selected Writings (1929–1970).* Preface by Fritz Lang. New York: Drama Book Specialists, 1970.

This is a rare book because it is written by one of the most knowledgeable film historians and critics, and covers the articles and comments made by a reviewer growing up with the great filmmakers themselves. Insightful comments on Chaplin, Dreyer, von Stroheim, Renoir, Welles, von Sternberg, and Disney.

Wilson, Robert (editor). *The Film Criticism of Otis Ferguson*. Foreword by Andrew Sarris. Philadelphia: Temple University Press, 1971.

    This significant collection of film criticism offers for the first time a bound edition of the writings of the *New Republic*'s influential and talented film critic of the 1930s and early 1940s. His tough-mindedness coupled with taste and humor helped elevate film as a serious art in the minds of intellectuals. Unfortunately, Ferguson was killed at the age of 36 in 1943 while he was serving with the merchant navy in World War II.

Nostalgia Books

* Gross, Martin A. *The Nostalgia Quiz Book*. New York: Signet, 1969.

    This book offers more than 1500 memory-teasers on mass media and what it was like growing up from the 1930s till now.

* Kennedy, Donald. *So You Think you Know the Movies?* New York: Ace Publishing Corporation, 1970.

    An easier quiz book for those who want to work their way up to the Gross text.

* Lamparski, Richard. *Whatever Became of . . . ?* New York: Ace Books, 1967.

    To date, there are three volumes of this useful little biographical series based on Lamparski's radio programs. More often than not, they provide information rarely found elsewhere.

7
Approaching the History
of Film

It is only very thoughtless and presumptuous people who can erect laws and an esthetic for cinema proceeding from premises of some incredible virgin-birth of this art! Let Dickens and the whole ancestral array, going back as far as the Greeks and Shakespeare, be superfluous reminders that both Griffith and our cinema prove our origins to be not solely as of Edison and his fellow inventors, but as based on an enormous cultured past; each part of this in its own moment of world history has moved forward the great art of cinematography. Let this past be a reproach to those thoughtless people who have displayed arrogance in reference to literature, which has contributed so much to this apparently unprecedented art and is, in the first and most important place, the art of viewing.

Sergei Eisenstein, Film Form

Films are a product of the age in which they are made, and nothing makes this clearer than the study of film in its historical context. This approach allows you to select, screen, and discuss movies in a chronological order, while learning about the historical and artistic conditions, trends, innovations, and major figures that bear on them. The arguments against it are that instructors deal more with facts than with film appreciation; the experience of film is ignored or destroyed; and often instructors struggle to escape from a rigid and dry schedule of historical progression. Nevertheless, creative teachers working with alert and responsive students can make the history of the cinema the most exciting experience in film study. If they come to it with interest, background, and purpose, students find this approach one of the best of all.

This chapter outlines the general history of film, while suggesting materials for implementing aspects of the method in individual classrooms.

Obviously, the best illustrative material for the history of film is the film itself. Usually 16mm prints are recommended. However, teachers should consider the advantages of 8mm versions: availability, accessibility, and cost. I have, therefore, suggested some 8mm. films within the course of this chapter.

Film history, although relatively short, includes a number of significant periods and trends. It is useful to present a brief overview of general film history and then investigate major film periods starting with the beginnings of motion pictures and then going on to American films (1914–1918), German films (1919–1925), Soviet films (1925–1928), Hollywood in the 1920s (1920–1928), the beginnings of sound films (1929–1941), French films (1933–1945), British and American documentary films (1933–1945), Italian and British films (1945–1952), Hollywood in the postwar years (1953–1963), film in the 1960s, and the contemporary cinema. Here are short introductory comments on the periods as well as an annotated list of books and films that help illustrate film developments.

General Books on the History of the Film[1]

Bardèche, Maurice and Robert Brasillach. *The History of Motion Pictures,* translated and edited by Iris Barry. New York: W. W. Norton, 1938. Reissued by Arno Press in 1970.

Written by two informed French authors, this fascinating book recounts the contributions of France and the United States, in particular, and England, Sweden, Italy, Germany, and Russia in general. Barry carefully notes the French text's errors, and also stresses the controversial nature of the original. The book's commentary ends with films in 1938.

Cowie, Peter. *Seventy Years of Cinema.* New York: A. S. Barnes and Company, 1969.

Considering the worthwhile articles the author has written, this is a particularly poor book filled with numerous errors and badly selected stills. The idea of a year-by-year chronology of important dates, names and films is an invaluable scheme, and if Cowie corrects his text and reissues it in a revised edition, this book might be one of the best sources in the field.

* Crowther, Bosley. *The Great Films: Fifty Golden Years of Motion Pictures.* New York: G. P. Putnam's Sons, 1967.

This well-illustrated and informative book represents Crowther's arbitrary selection of movies he has enjoyed, considers to have opened new ground and whose content has set the precedent for thousands of other films. Among the obvious are *The Birth of a Nation, Intolerance, The Cabinet of Dr. Caligari, Nanook of the North, Greed, Potemkin, The General, The Crowd, The Blue Angel, All Quiet on the Western Front, La Grande Illusion, The Bicycle Thief, Rashomon,* and *Blow-up.* The controversial ones include *The Public Enemy, King Kong* and *Camille.*

Durgnat, Raymond. *The Crazy Mirror: Hollywood Comedy and the American Image.* New York: Horizon Press, 1970.

---

1. An invaluable aid is the Fiftieth Anniversary issue of *American Cinematographer* 50, no. 1 (January 1969), which dealt with the history of the film industry.

Stressing that movies present an illuminating, although distorted, picture of the age in which they are made, Durgnat offers an unconventional and thought-provoking analysis of the great American comics. A useful index of comedy films is included.

Everson, William K. *The American Movie*. New York: Atheneum, 1963.

This short, well-written introduction to movies is a good beginning for young people who want a fast, knowledgeable overview. The printing is good, the illustrations intelligently chosen, and the text useful.

Griffith, Richard and Arthur Mayer. *The Movies: The Sixty-Year Story of the World of Hollywood and Its Effect on America from Pre-Nickelodeon Days to the Present*. New York: Bonanza Books, 1957. Reissued in 1970.

One of the best of the illustrated history film books. The authors almost always provide accurate information, rare stills, and delightful commentary. It is a pleasure to read.

Jobes, Gertrude. *Motion Picture Empire*. Hamden, Conn.: Archon Books, 1966.

Here is a good, penetrating overview of the film barons who built and controlled motion pictures for sixty years. Jobes describes their attitudes, accomplishments, and frustrated ambitions, as well as many interesting fights among exhibitors, distributors, and producers. Throughout, the text remains readable, informative, and often amusing.

* Knight, Arthur. *The Liveliest Art: A Panoramic History of the Movies*. New York: The Macmillan Company, 1957.

Written by one of the most informed and underrated film teachers today, this ambitious attempt to place film in the context of historical and artistic conditions is a fine text that covers events up to 1958. Its concern with key films and personalities naturally overlooks some masters and overemphasizes others. But you will find more to praise than condemn.

Lindgren, Ernest. *A Picture History of the Cinema*. London: Vista Books, 1960.

Despite the author's bias toward Russian films and his distaste for American movies, this useful book helps readers see stills from many significant motion pictures. For the most part, Lindgren's text is accurate, informative, and helpful.

* MacGowan, Kenneth. *Behind the Screen: The History and Techniques of the Motion Picture*. New York: Delacorte Press, 1965.

This general outline of film history really ends at the coming of sound, at which point MacGowan surveys the division of labor connected with film production. Very little serious commentary is given to European and Asian contributions. It makes for very enjoyable reading, mainly because of the author's delightful quoted materials and interesting statistics. In connection with this book, you might read Robert C. Dickson, "Kenneth Mac-Gowan," *Films in Review* 14, no. 8 (October, 1963) : 475–92.

Manvell, Roger, *et al. The International Encyclopedia of Film*. New York: Crown Publishers, Inc., 1972.

If I had to choose one book to own in my library, this text would come first. Not enough praise can be given to the editors, who have combined scholarship, production design, and information in order that the world of film could be so intelligently synthesized and yet maintain such depth and breadth. It is a classic work.

The Marshall Cavendish Learning System. *The Movies*. London: Marshall Cavendish Books, 1970.

Strictly for children. This beautifully illustrated volume gives a quick overview of movies, touching on production techniques, important personalities, and major trends. Particularly interesting is the last chapter and its treatment of *If . . .* from the film's inception till its completion.

* Mast, Gerald. *A Short History of the Movies*. New York: Bobbs-Merrill, Inc., 1971.

In one of the best one-volume studies of the art of the film, Mast emphasizes the techniques and the themes of major motion pictures which are available for 16mm rental. This book belongs on every film student's shelf.

* Robinson, David. *The Great Funnies: A History of Film Comedy*. New York: E. P. Dutton and Company, 1969.

This is a very brief pictorial history of the great movie comics, with a lovely selection of stills.

Rotha, Paul, in collaboration with Richard Griffith. *The Film Till Now: A Survey of World Cinema*. New York: Twayne Publishers, Inc., 1960.

This highly personal account of Rotha's opinions about the silent era is invaluable for its observations on artistic developments and appendices, while Griffith's commentary on sound films and their relationship to filmgoers is entertaining and stimulating reading. The book is one of the best and most accurate sources on film history in general.

Schickel, Richard. *Movies: The History of an Art and an Institution*. New York: Basic Books, 1964.

A short and underrated account of film history, written by *Life*'s film critic, with a heavy emphasis on American movies. Schickel's observations are perceptive, informative, and useful.

Smith, John M. and Tim Cawkwell (editors). *The World Encyclopedia of the Film*. New York: World Publishing, Inc.

A good and useful reference work for students interested in brief statistics on key directors, technicians, and players, plus the most extensive listing yet on films available to the general public.

Taylor, Deems, Bryant Hale, and Marcelene Peterson. *A Pictorial History of the Movies*. Revised and Enlarged. New York: Simon and Schuster, 1949.

Unfortunately this well-conceived book is poorly produced. Many valuable stills on films up to 1941 are badly reproduced, the chronology is muddled, and the commentary inaccurate.

Thomas, Bob. *The Heart of Hollywood: A 50-Year Pictorial History of the Film Capital and the Famed Motion Picture and Television Relief Fund*. Los Angeles: Price/Stern/Sloan, 1971.

Published for the express purpose of raising money for the Fund, this disappointing collection of "in-family" rather than standard production stills offers for film buffs some rare nostalgic moments. The idea was fine, but the research and editing were lacking.

* Tyler, Parker. *Classics of the Foreign Film: A Pictorial Treasury.* New York: Bonanza Books, 1962.

One of the best picture commentaries yet available on foreign films. The text is well-written, informative, and accurate. Tyler is particularly good on choosing excellent stills, and then putting down precise, useful annotations.

Wiseman, Thomas. *Cinema.* New York: A. S. Barnes and Company, 1965.

This useful, general history of movies makes up in a stimulating commentary what it lacks in illustrative excellence. Unfortunately, the text does not go deep enough for it to be serious history nor are there enough pictures to make it valuable as a pictorial guide. You wonder for whom it was intended.

Zinman, David. *50 Classic Motion Pictures: The Stuff that Dreams are Made of.* New York: Crown Publishers, Inc., 1970.

Although not so well-written as Crowther's book, this text is a respectable examination of Hollywood's fabulous period in the 1930s and 1940s. Zinman provides cast listings, production details, a fine selection of production stills and general comments on many standard film favorites, including *Casablanca, King Kong, Gone with the Wind,* and *Mutiny on the Bounty.*

Reference Books[2]

Bibliography: FIAF Members Publications. Edited annually by the Canadian Film Archives. Ottawa: Canadian Film Institute.

This is a useful annual bibliography of books, periodicals and other relevant printed material published by members of the International Federation of Film Archives.

Blum, Daniel. *Screen World.* New York: Crown Publishers, Inc., published annually.

Emphasizing mainly the credits for the yearly American releases, this handsomely illustrated review includes annual obituaries, box-office stars, and an invaluable index. Since 1969, the annual publication has been under the editorship of John Willis.

* Carey, Gary. *Lost Films.* New York: Museum of Modern Art, 1970.

Based mainly upon an exhibit Carey set up for the Museum, this nicely produced text presents an invaluable list of thirty presumably missing silent films, complete with plot synopses, cast and credit listings, and marvelous stills. Academicians will probably be most interested in the several Victor Seastrom movies (including Garbo's *The Divine Woman*) and a Lon Chaney film (one of two movies directed by Browning) . The major fault of the book is its limited printed commentary.

---

2. See Appendix V for a list of resources for scholarship. Some useful articles are collected in a special survey conducted by *Film Quarterly* and discussed in a special issue, "Our Resources for Film Scholarship," *Film Quarterly* 16, no. 2 (Winter 1962–63) : 29–50. Also helpful are Jerzy Toeplitz, "Film Scholarship: Past and Prospective," *Film Quarterly* 16, no. 3 (Spring 1963) : 27–37; George Mitchell, "The Library of Congress," *Films in Review* 4, no. 8 (October 1953) : 417–21; Jay Leyda, "A Note on Progress," *Film Quarterly* 21, no. 4 (Summer 1968) : 28–33; Iris Barry, "The Film Library and How it Grew," *Film Quarterly* 22, no. 4 (Summer 1969) : 19–27.

Copyright Entries (Cumulative Series): Motion Pictures 1960–69. Washington: Library of Congress (USGPO), 1971.

In what appears to be an exhaustive listing, this valuable catalog of the 1960s accounts for every movie (including TV films for TV series) produced in America. The preface explains the three-fold purpose of the volume: " (1) to provide correct index volumes to the legal profession, publishers, authors, and others interested in copyright, (2) to meet the administrative needs of the copyright office, and (3) to make available for other research uses, the information on record in the copyright office, much of which is not available elsewhere." Included in the catalog is information on more than 34,000 scripts (more than 11,000 deal with nonfiction films), date released (including copyright TV movie commercials) for each title, cast and director credits, running time, silent or sound, film mm, series title, and copyright date.

Council of the London Film Society. *The Film Society Programmes: 1925– 1939.* Introduction by George Amberg. New York: Arno Press, 1972.

This complete edition in one volume of the London Film Society's program notes represents an assortment of intellectual attempts to chronicle the rise of Soviet films, the demise of Germany's major film era, rare avant-garde experiments, the coming of sound, and the revolutionary use of color. The notes include brief biographical information, historical background material plus complete credits. It is an important contribution to film scholarship.

Cowie, Peter (editor). *International Film Guide.* New York: A. S. Barnes and Company, Inc., published annually.

Since 1963, this excellent guide to current films produced all over the world has been issued annually. It contains significant, valuable, and handy information.

Dimmitt, Richard B. *An Actor's Guide to the Talkies.* Two Volumes. Metuchen, New Jersey: The Scarecrow Press, Inc., 1967.

This alphabetically arranged list of more than 8,000 titles of feature-length movies covers the years from 1949 to 1964. It is a valuable source of information on production and cast credits.

Dimmitt, Richard B. *A Title Guide to the Talkies.* Two Volumes. Metuchen, N.J.: The Scarecrow Press, Inc., 1965.

The author provides a massive list of information on 6,000 feature-length film titles, copyright and release dates, producers, studios, screenwriters and original sources. It is a very useful research tool.

Everson, William K. *The Bad Guys: A Pictorial History of the Movie Villain.* New York: The Citadel Press, 1964.

In this finely illustrated text of film tough guys, Everson provides the best source for the villains in gangster films, monster movies, and suspense films. Not only are there 500 well-produced stills, but the author maintains a delightful and nostalgic tone throughout. After Everson, there is some value in consulting Ian and Elisabeth Cameron, *The Heavies* (New York: Praeger, 1967), and Ian and Elisabeth Cameron, *Dames* (New York: Praeger, 1969).

Fawcett, Marion. *An Index to Films in Review 1950–1959.* New York: The National Board of Review, 1961. *An Index to Films in Review 1960–1964.* New York: The National Board of Review, 1966.

These two handy references give a good cross-index to this invaluable magazine which belongs in every library interested in serious film study. Sandra Lester has brought the index up to 1969 in a just-announced publication, which I did not get a chance to review.

Film Daily Year Book of Motion Pictures. New York: Available on Microfilm, 18 reels from Arno Press.

The outstanding, comprehensive and definitive to date record of the history of motion pictures. The microfilm collection goes from 1918 to 1925. The first 4 years are available in two volumes from Arno Press as is the 1970 Yearbook.

* Gottesman, Ronald and Harry M. Geduld (editors). *Guidebook to Film: An Eleven-in-One Reference.* New York: Holt, Rinehart and Winston, Inc., 1972.

This useful but sketchy book contains brief descriptive comments about a number of areas in film study: Reference works (including foreign titles not covered here), film schools, and theses up to 1969.

* Graham, Peter (editor). *A Dictionary of the Cinema.* 2nd ed., rev. New York: A. S. Barnes & Company, 1968.

This useful volume contains 620 terse annotations plus a handy index to over 5000 movie titles. For quick, helpful, and usually accurate information, this is a good source book.

Halliwell, Leslie. *The Filmgoer's Companion: An International Encyclopedia.* Third Edition. New York: Hill and Wang, 1970.

One of the best available resources to date and getting better with each expanded and revised edition. There are more than 6000 entries on films, filmmakers, themes, and technical jargon. It should be on every student's shelf.

* Herrick, Margaret *et al.* (editors). *Academy Players Directory.* Published every four months.

This is a handy source of information about the members of the Academy of Motion Picture Arts and Sciences.

* Jordan, Thurston C. Jr. (editor). *Glossary of Motion Picture Terminology.* Menlo Park: Pacific Coast Publishers, 1968.

Written by a member of the personnel department of Twentieth-Century-Fox, this book, modeled after the employee's manual, presents a valuable definition of over 500 terms.

* Kone, Grace Ann (editor). *8mm Film Directory: A Comprehensive Descriptive Index.* New York: Comprehensive Service Corporation, 1969–70.

This handy guide to almost all 8mm films, regardless of length or subject matter, which are available today comes complete with dates, distributors, and pertinent information. Also listed and detailed are 8mm film equipment and distributors.

Lahue, Kalton C. *Collecting Film Classics.* New York: American Photographic Press, 1970.

Because there are so many missing entries, this first comprehensive guide to the hobby of collecting old films should be skimmed rather than owned.

Leonard, Harold (chief editor). *The Film Index—A Bibliography, Volume I, The Film as Art*. New York: The Museum of Modern Art, 1941. Reprinted in 1970 by Arno Press.
The best of its kind ever written, this valuable index to film writing—books, periodicals and newspapers—is an incredible example of compilation and annotation. It remains today an outstanding tribute not only to its editors but to the New York City Writers Program of three decades past. Every library should have a copy.

Library of Congress. *Motion Pictures 1912–1939*. Washington, D.C.: Library of Congress, Copyright Office, 1951.
Together with a valuable index, this publication offers information on films copyrighted during this period. In 1953, two further publications continued the work, covering the periods 1940–1949 and 1950–1959.

Limbacher, James L. (editor). *Feature Films on 8mm and 16mm. Third Edition. A Directory of Feature Films Available for Rental, Sale and Lease in the United States*. New York: R. R. Bowker Company, 1971.
By far the best and most comprehensive source of information about films in the United States, this book provides help on locating more than 15,000 movies. Limbacher adds new information at various intervals in *Sightlines*, published by the Educational Film Library Association.

McCarty, Clifford. *Published Screenplays: A Checklist*. Kent: The Kent State University Press, 1971.
In a valuable attempt to be inclusive rather than selective, McCarty includes not only complete screenplays but excerpts as well. All entries are arranged alphabetically by title, and also provide information on where the book or books are to be located, the film production company and date, the names of the director and screenwriters, and the source of the screenplay if not original.

* Meyers, Warren B. *Who is That? The Late Viewers Guide to the Old Old Movie Players*. New York: Personality Posters, Inc., 1967.
This invaluable, modest little paperback is a picture gallery of familiar faces arranged in eleven different categories such as "Tough Tomatoes," "Other Women," "Busybodies," "Losers," "Clean Old Men," and "Ethnic Types." Marvelous for trivia games with smart aleck colleagues.

Michael, Paul. General Editor. *The American Movies Reference Book: The Sound Era*. Englewood Cliffs: Prentice-Hall, Inc., 1969.
At present, everyone's favorite whipping boy for weak scholarship, omissions, and general presentation. Given time and encouragement, revision and expansion, this could become a valuable book. If you do decide to get a first edition, read Earl Anderson, "Sophomoric Scholarship," *Films in Review* 20, no. 8 (October 1969) : 496–501.

Munden, Kenneth W. (editor). *The American Film Institute Catalog: Feature Films 1921–30*. New York: R. R. Bowker Company, 1970. 2 Volumes.
One of the most valuable and scholarly works yet published, this comprehensive and almost perfect national filmography is just the beginning of a series on every motion picture filmed in the United States since 1893.

New York Motion Picture Critics' Reviews. New York: Critics' Theatre Reviews, Inc., 1944–46.

This is one of the most valuable sources for information about films shown in New York during the period. Reviews are from *New York Sun, Times, Post, Daily News, Newspaper PM, Herald Tribune, World Telegram,* and *Journal-American.*

New York Times Film Reviews, 1913–1968. 6 volumes. New York: Arno Press and The New York Times, 1970.

No matter how controversial the film revewers of the *Times* continue to be, this excellent reference source on the most powerful film force in motion picture history represents invaluable guidance to the cinematic taste, values, and opinions of Twentieth-Century America. Students will find it helpful for titles, credits, plots, and social revelations. A seventh volume was published in 1971, continuing the series into 1969–70.

Pate, Michael. *The Film Actor.* New York: A. S. Barnes and Company, 1970.

Based upon his professional acting career, Pate's fascinating and very helpful technical discussion of general film techniques is a first-rate handbook for novices. The book is divided into three main sections, with the greatest emphasis on screen terminology. For those who want specific help, the author provides twenty practical exercises and diagrams which should help in developing one's confidence prior to shooting actual scenes. Well worth getting for beginners.

Pickard, R. A. E. *Dictionary of 1000 Best Films.* New York: Association Press, 1971.

Arranged alphabetically, this interesting book gives a short, critical summary of each film, together with complete credits.

* Riggs, Ted (editor). *Film Collectors' Yearbook 1970.* Knoxville: Film Collectors' Registry, 1970.

If you're interested in special and private film collections, this is the book to use. Help is limited to American movies, particularly westerns, serials and comedies.

Salem, James M. *A Guide to Critical Reviews—Part IV: The Screenplay from "The Jazz Singer" to "Dr. Strangelove."* Two volumes. Metuchen, N.J.: The Scarecrow Press, Inc., 1971.

This is a superb research tool for anyone interested in locating popular reviews of over 12,000 American and foreign feature films released between October, 1927 and December, 1963. The films are listed alphabetically and cross references are frequently provided. The work's one serious flaw is its commitment to lay reviews instead of scholarly and critical evaluations.

* Sarris, Andrew. *The American Cinema: Directors and Directions, 1929–1968.* New York: E. P. Dutton and Company, 1968.

In a limited amount of space, Sarris manages to squeeze a lot of useful information about 200 directors. It is a very handy reference tool.

Schuster, Mel (editor). *Motion Picture Performers: A Bibliography of Magazine and Periodical Articles, 1900–1969.* Metuchen, New Jersey: The Scarecrow Press, 1969.

In this massive collection of entries that excludes the usual fan magazine tripe, Schuster arranges his information on the stars alphabetically and chronologically.

Steele, Robert. *The Cataloging and Classification of Cinema Literature.* Metuchen, New Jersey: The Scarecrow Press, Inc., 1967.
An interesting book which attempts to present more precise information about the flood of publications on the cinema. Steele extends the present classification system of the Library of Congress which should prove helpful to modern librarians.

Variety Film Reviews, 1913–1970. Nine Volumes. New York: Arno Press, 1972.
A major contribution to film scholarship, this publication provides one of the most complete records to date on commercial film making. Among the features of the revues are cast and production credits, running times, and synopses.

Weaver, John T. (editor). *Forty Years of Screen Credits 1929–1969.* Two Volumes. Metuchen, N.J.: The Scarecrow Press, Inc., 1970.
This extensive, alphabetically arranged coverage of performers' credits offers the most exhaustive listing to date. Unfortunately, it is not always accurate and too many omissions still exist.

Who Wrote the Movie and What Else Did He Write? An Index of Screen Writers and Their Film Works 1936–1939. Los Angeles: The Academy of Motion Picture Arts and Sciences and the Writers Guild of America, West. 1970.
Despite an overabundance of errors, this book provides a helpful start towards compiling writing and source credits for more than 13,000 American and some significant European screen writers. A revised edition should help considerably.

Young, William C. *Guide to Manuscripts and Special Collections in the American Theatre Arts in the United States and Canada.* New York: The American Library Association, 1971.
This listing and description of existing repositories and collections of film scripts and related documents will be updated annually in the *Journal of Theatre Documentation.*

Anthologies on Directors

Geduld, Harry M. (editor). *Film Makers on Film Making.* Bloomington: Indiana University Press, 1967.
A good collection of 30 directors' comments about their individual work. It is divided into two parts; section one includes Hepworth, Porter, Sennett, Griffith, Chaplin and Vertov. Section two, dealing with the sound period, has Hitchcock, Cocteau, Bergman, and Kurosawa.

* Gelmis, Joseph. *The Film Director as Superstar.* New York: Doubleday and Company, Inc., 1970.
This is the only collection to emphasize film independents as well as the more popular directors. Invaluable for insights into Robert Downey, Norman Mailer, Andy Warhol and John Cassavetes. It suffers, however, because

the filmographies are just titles without casts or credits and no index is available for cross-reference.

Kantor, Bernard R. *et al.* (editors). *Directors at Work: Interviews With American Film-Makers.* New York: Funk and Wagnalls, 1970.

This is a good collection of interviews with Richard Brooks, George Cukor, Norman Jewison, Elia Kazan, Stanley Kramer, Richard Lester, Jerry Lewis, Elliot Silverstein, and Robert Wise.

* Sarris, Andrew (editor). *Interviews with Film Directors.* New York: The Bobbs-Merrill Company, Inc., 1967.

The best directors' anthology yet available, it includes statements from 40 of the screen's most talented men, including Antonioni, Fellini, Buñuel, Chaplin, Dreyer, Eisenstein, Godard, Hawks, Losey, and von Sternberg. Sarris also has some excellent introductory material on most of the directors, plus a solid filmography following each interview.

Sherman, Eric and Martin Rubin. *The Director's Event: Interviews with Five American Film-Makers.* New York: Atheneum, 1970.

A worthwhile collection of ideas from and about Boetticher, Bogdanovich, Fuller, Penn and Polonsky. There are filmographies at the end of each interview, and incisive, clear introductions to each director.

Films[3]

History of the Motion Pictures Series

Originally designed for a half-hour television series entitled "Silents Please," this uneven and controversial collection traces the history of the movies from their infancy through the late 1920s.

Paul Killiam, the mastermind behind the series, has done a fine job of editing significant movies, adding new musical scores to enhance the viewing, and providing a nostalgic narration that points out the key facts about the individual film and its significant personalities.

Certain segments of the series are devoted, not to a single silent film, but to covering trends or careers. The running time for each segment is approximately 25 minutes, and all are in black and white.

Segments

FILM FIRSTS I. First examples of now familiar techniques, stories.

FILM FIRSTS II. Edwin S. Porter, Georges Méliès, Thomas Ince, Griffith.

AMERICA. Griffith's American Revolution shot on actual location with documentary realism.

FALL OF BABYLON. From *Intolerance,* using full-scale sets of old Babylon.

ORPHANS OF THE STORM I & II. The French Revolution with Lillian and Dorothy Gish.

---

3. For a thorough discussion of the series, see Richard Schickel, "The Silents Weren't Just Voiceless Talkies," *The New Times Magazine* Sunday, November 28, 1971, pp. 32–33, 54–64.

THE CROWN PRINCES. Chaplin, Harold Lloyd, Larry Semon, Charlie Chase, Laurel and Hardy, Ben Turpin and Billy West.

FUN FACTORY. Some of the best slapstick from Mack Sennett's studio.

SLAPSTICK. The era of visual comedy featuring death-defying stunts.

WILL ROGERS. His career from rodeo to radio.

DR. JEKYLL AND MR. HYDE. The first great American horror film, with John Barrymore.

DRACULA. The first screen version, directed by F. W. Murnau, 1922.

THE AMERICANO. Douglas Fairbanks quells a revolution.

GIRLS IN DANGER. Ladies in distress from Mae Marsh to Gloria Swanson.

THIEF OF BAGDAD. Douglas Fairbanks directed by Raoul Walsh.

SON OF THE SHEIK. Rudolf Valentino's last film.

YANKEE CLIPPER. William Boyd, typhoons and mutiny.

BLACK PIRATE. Douglas Fairbanks's duels, sea battles and acrobatics, including his famous slide-down-the-sail.

BLOOD AND SAND. Life of a matador, featuring Rudolf Valentino.

GARDEN OF EDEN. Glamorous adult fairytale from 1928.

THE GENERAL. The last and best classic silent comedy. directed by and starring Buster Keaton.

SAD CLOWNS. Charlie Chaplin, Buster Keaton, and Harry Langdon.

THE EAGLE. Rudolph Valentino as a Russian Robin Hood directed by Clarence Brown.

HUNCHBACK OF NOTRE DAME. Lon Chaney in the 1923 version.

ROAD TO YESTERDAY. Cecil B. DeMille's spectacular mix of feudal oppression and modern (1920s) hedonism.

TEMPEST. John Barrymore in one of the last, stylish silent classics.

WILLIAM S. HART. Film highlights climaxed by Hart's farewell to the screen.

VARIETY. The best film of its star, Emil Jannings, and its director, E. A. Dupont; technically innovative.

FILM BEGINNINGS

The nineteenth century provided the synthesis for all the inventions, patents, and claims to the birth of the motion picture. Henry V. Hopwood lists more than 160 related patents involved with film between 1851 and the end of 1898, while C. Francis Jenkins adds up close to 240 United States patents in a forty-seven-year period beginning in 1860.[4] But to this day the disagreement continues as to which were the most important patents and who were the founders.

There is, however, surprising agreement as to what the essential factors were: (1) the concept of persistence of vision, (2) a flexible and transparent material for photographing and projecting, (3) perforations on this photographic material, (4) a suitable camera and projector, (5) a shutter for this equipment, (6) storage for the photographic material before, during, and after its progression in the camera and projector, and (7) appropriate lens and lighting conditions for the use of the equipment.

From 1824 to 1896, screen history developed through the experiments of inventors concerned with vision, photographic processes,[5] animation, motion, sound, color,[6] and technical apparatus such as cameras and projectors.[7] Among the more famous of the early pioneers were Étienne-Jules Marey, Eadweard Muybridge,[8] Louis Aime Augustine Le Prince,[9] Emile Reynaud, Joseph Niepce, Louis-Jacques-Mande Daguerre, and Hannibal Goodwin. The major emphasis in the beginning was on reproducing realistic settings and providing entertainment rather than on developing an artistic medium. To a great degree, the early filmmakers emphasized the element of motion, a *tableaux vivant.* Late in 1888, W. K. L. Dickson started his film work for Thomas Edison, and by 1894 the two men had parted company. Within a year the seeds of the great patent wars had been planted as Edison sought recognition and control of the major film developments over men like Dickson, Herman Casler, the Latham Family, C. Francis Jenkins, Thomas Armat, the Lumière Brothers, R. W. Paul, William Friese-Greene,[10] and Charles Pathé.[11]

Georges Méliès was one director whose emphasis and techniques went beyond the problems of simply showing motion and explored "trick photography." His film work with theatrical tricks involving machines and double exposures laid the groundwork not only for animated films but also for many of the techniques connected with stop-motion photography.

As interest in developing narrative styles in film progressed, Edwin S.

---

4. Walter H. Stainton, "Movie Pre-History," *Film in Review* 16, no. 6 (June–July 1965) : 333.

5. John L. Fell, "Dissolves by Gaslight: Antecedents to the Motion Picture in Nineteenth-Century Melodrama," *Film Quarterly* 23, no. 3 (Spring 1970) : 22–34.

6. D. B. Thomas, *The First Colour Motion Pictures* (New York: B.I.S., 845 3rd Avenue, N.Y. 10022, 1969).

7. Helen Gibson as told to Mike Kornick, "In Very Early Days," *Films in Review* 19, no. 1 (January 1968) : 28–34.

8. Harlan Hamilton, "*Les Allures du Cheval,* Eadward James Muybridge's Contribution to the Motion Picture," *Film Comment* 5, no. 3 (Fall 1969) : 16–35.

9. Walter H. Stainton, "A Neglected Pioneer," *Films in Review* 14, no. 3 (March 1963) : 160–66.

10. Terry Ramsaye, "Friese-Greene Is a Legend," *Films in Review* 11, no. 7 (August–September 1951) : 15–18. For more information on the various competing patents, see Stainton, "Movies Pre-History," pp. 333–42.

11. Georges Sadoul, "Napoleon of the Cinema," *Sight and Sound* 27, no. 4 (Spring 1958) : 183.

Porter, in 1901, began his famous experiments. He emphasized cinematic rather than stage techniques to show movement. That is, he used parallel action (alternating two simultaneous actions) and cross-cutting (interweaving fragments of two separate scenes) instead of merely having the action take place in front of a fixed camera as on the stage.[12] Thus, we can see the growing tendency in the early part of the 1900s for filmmakers to move away from fantasy to the portrayal of reality.[13]

The next major milestone can be seen in the *Film d'art* movement, which began in France. Serious literary works were translated for the screen to try to bring a new social, economic, and artistic dignity to the neophyte medium which had, so far, been developed as mere entertainment. Some famous writers whose works were adapted for the screen were Shakespeare, Tolstoy, Balzac, and Maupassant. The stage's greatest actors and actresses were engaged to play in these films, the most famous probably being Sarah Bernhardt. The acting was not designed for films; the emphasis was theatrical and not cinematic. That is to say, the camera remained fixed while the actors and actresses performed in front of it rather than allowing the director to use techniques such as parallel editing and cross-cutting to tell the story. The average film during this period ran from five to twelve minutes. With the success of *Film d'art* motion pictures, the feasibility of longer films became evident.

As the film developed, techniques particularly suitable for the camera emerged. By 1908, such techniques as the pan shot, the close-up, cross-cutting, and parallel editing had been introduced. Although the French seem to have dominated the industry up to 1908, David Wark Griffith became the first great director. It was he alone who gave prestige, life, and art to the important but awkward experiments.

Books

Allister, Ray. *Friese-Greene: Close-up of an Inventor.* London: Marsland Publications, 1948. Reissued by Arno Press, 1972.

An English inventor's contributions to film development are discussed with biographical information providing an insight into one of the most tragic of the early pioneers. Here was a man, in terms of mechanical and scientific invention, who did more to further British motion pictures than any other pioneer, yet served three jail terms for debt and violation of bankruptcy laws. Unrecognized during his life, he has since become known as a great inventor. Unfortunately, few significant studies about his achievements have yet been done.

Balshofer, Fred J. and Arthur C. Miller. *One Reel a Week.* Berkeley: University of California Press, 1967.

Balshofer, one of the early film producers and founders of the New York

---

12. Jack Spears, "Edwin S. Porter," *Films in Review* 21, no. 6 (June–July 1970) : 327–54.
13. In this connection, see Raymond Fielding, "Hale's Tours: Ultrarealism in the Pre-1910 Motion Picture," *Cinema Journal* 10, no. 1 (Fall 1970) : 34–47.

Motion Picture Company, studied under Sigmund Lubin beginning in 1905. Within a few years, he was on his own and employing Miller as one of his cameramen. The fourteen-year-old Miller eventually went on to photograph *How Green Was My Valley, The Song of Bernadette, The Razor's Edge,* and *The Ox-Bow Incident.* Thus, their reflections on an emerging industry are not only interesting but first-hand recollections. They alternate chapters, commenting on personalities, techniques, and incidents. Their narrative plus well-chosen illustrations produces a valuable and delightful book.

Blum, Daniel C. *A Pictorial History of the Silent Screen.* New York: Grosset and Dunlap, 1953.
  This profusely illustrated text is fine for rare stills but weak on textual comments.

[British] National Film Archive. *Catalogue: Silent Films.* London: The British Film Institute, 1960. Three Volumes.
  Each of the three volumes provides a carefully indexed and comprehensive listing of films preserved in the British National Film Archives. Volume I lists silent news films 1895–1933; Volume II, silent nonfiction films 1895–1934; and Volume III, silent fiction films 1895–1930.

* Brownlow, Kevin. *The Parade's Gone By.* New York: Alfred A. Knopf, 1968.
  In this splendid re-creation of the atmosphere and successes of the silent era as remembered by the artists of the age, Brownlow gives us a fascinating record of the movies at the start. He interviewed silent film stars, supporting players, directors, cameramen, editors, and producers; and the results provide new insights for film historians. Although there are over 300 stills, the pictures are of less value than the text, since some are not identified. Serious students should also read Brownlow's letter to *Films in Review* 20, no. 4 (April 1969) : 257–8, where he lists corrections in the text.

Ceram, C. W. *Archaeology of the Cinema.* New York: Harcourt Brace & World, Inc., 1965.
  One of the most ambitious books on the pre-history of film, this account is balanced, usually accurate, and highly entertaining. The stills are plentiful and well-chosen, and you can spend several hours just enjoying 293 good reproductions.

Cook, Olive. *Movement in Two Dimensions: A Study of the Animated and Projected Pictures which Preceded the Invention of Cinematography.* London: Hutchinson & Co., 1963.
  The stress here is on the unusual rather than the relevant, and the narrative suffers from an overemphasis on the insignificant instead of the important figures in film history. Yet, you can enjoy some interesting discussions of the early mirror shows, panorama and peep performances, shadow plays, and magic lanterns.

* Cowie, Peter (editor). *A Concise History of the Cinema—Volume I: Before 1940.* New York: A. S. Barnes & Company, 1971.
  In a skeleton narrative, a number of well-known film historians list the key films and personalities in America, Britain, France, Italy, Germany, Austria, Scandinavia, and Eastern Europe; in addition they indicate trends in documentaries, animation, economics and technology.

Fielding, Raymond (editor). *A Technological History of Motion Pictures and Television. An Anthology From the Pages of the Journal of the Society of Motion Picture and Television Engineers.* Berkeley: University of California Press, 1967.

Here is an intelligent and useful anthology of articles selected from close to 475 issues of the Society's Journals. Fielding provides us with marvelous material from the recollections of Jenkins, Dickson, Armat, Paul, Louis Lumière, Gaumont, and Lauste. Unfortunately, no attempt is made to verify or correct conflicting claims, and the book suffers from the lack of an index.

Franklin, Joe. *Classics of the Silent Screen: A Pictorial Treasury.* New York: Bramhall House, 1959.

Written by a man in love with movies, this nostalgic and pleasant collection of film illustrations is a tender reminder of a marvelous era.

Grau, Robert. *The Theatre of Science.* New York: Broadway Publishing Company, 1944. Reissued by Benjamin Blom, 1969.

The most useful record of the early 1900s is this valuable study of the key figures of the American film industry.

* Hampton, Benjamin B. *A History of the Movies.* New York: Covici, Friede, 1931. Reissued with minor corrections by Dover in 1970 under the new title *History of the American Film Industry: From Its Beginning to 1931.* With a new introduction by Richard Griffith.

Written by a former newspaper editor, vice-president of the American Tobacco Company, and an associate of Adolph Zukor, this book presents a first-hand knowledge of the early days of the nickelodeons. Hampton, knowing the personalities of the day, is able to give important accounts of the behind-the-scenes activities of the tycoons—Zukor, Lewis J. Selznick, Harry Aitken, W. W. Hodkinson, and Marcus Loew—and describe the economic conditions that gave rise to the motion picture industry.

* Hendricks, Gordon. *The Edison Motion Picture Myth.* Berkeley: University of California Press, 1961.

Up to 1961, Edison was considered the father of the film, the Kinetoscope, the grandfather of all subsequent film projectors; and Dickson was a runaway son. No more. Hendricks, with a wealth of details gleaned from patents, notes, financial records, memoirs, diaries, and first-hand reports, presents a strong defense of the young Englishman. Although the text stops at 1892, Dickson emerges as one of the most important men in the history of motion pictures.

Hendricks, Gordon. *Beginnings of the Biograph: The Story of the Invention of the Mutoscope and the Biograph and their Supplying Camera.* New York: The Beginnings of the American Film, 1964.

On September 14, 1896, at the Alvin Theater in Pittsburgh, the finest cameras and projector yet known made their debut. The equipment heralded the start of the most important company of the first decade of motion pictures: Biograph. Hendricks, in clear and interesting prose, makes a very important contribution to film history by presenting an accurate and documented study of the company's key personalities: Harry Marvin, Elias Koopman, Herman Casler, and W. L. K. Dickson. This book is the major work on the subject, and corrects the errors of all history books to date.

Hendricks, Gordon. *The Kinetoscope. America's First Commercially Successful Motion Picture Exhibitor*. New York: The Beginnings of the American Film, 1966.

This is Hendricks's third book on reconstructing, rewriting, and reinterpreting the fuzzy historical records of the early, clumsy days of film experimentation. As a result of his wonderful and painstaking research, we learn more than ever before about the fantastic Kinetoscope, its films, and how it came to be. This invaluable document also comes with 60 important illustrations.

Hepworth, Cecil M. *Came the Dawn: Memories of a Film Pioneer*. London: Phoenix House, Ltd., 1951.

This useful and entertaining biography by a pioneer English film producer and inventor explains his work with arc lights and printing machines, the beginning of a British producing studio, and his love for movies about England. It also shows why he failed in commercial ventures. Although the "facts" are sometimes stretched, Hepworth is worth reading for his pleasant tales and recollections.

Hofmann, Charles. *Sounds for Silents*. New York: Drama Book Specialists Publications, Inc., 1970.

This lovely book on music offers valuable information on the method, use, and importance of background music in the silent era. It is thoughtfully written, technically correct, and well worth reading.

* Jacobs, Lewis. *The Rise of the American Film: A Critical History*. With an essay "Experimental Cinema in America 1921–1947." New York: Teachers College Press, 1968.

This reissue of the 1939 text is one of the best historical accounts of the period from 1890 to 1939. Jacobs presents a meaningful narrative about American films from the time they appeared as insignificant toys, to the emergence of artists and the advent of great sound movies. In clear, instructive and enjoyable prose, he provides helpful plot synopses, useful introductions and summaries of the trends, conditions, and attitudes of the significant periods, and remains one of the most important sources for the sociological study of motion pictures. For the new edition, Jacobs wrote a helpful commentary on the American experimental film from 1921–1947.

* Lennig, Arthur (editor). *Classics of the Film*. Madison: Wisconsin Film Society Press, 1965.

This collection, concerned with significant and enduring movies, is a provocative and entertaining book to read. Its first four sections, on American, German, French and Scandinavian films, leave something to be desired, but the essays on Buñuel movies and horror films are delightful.

* Lennig, Arthur (editor). *Film Notes*. Madison: Wisconsin Film Society Press, 1960.

This first Lennig edition presents some original, uneven, and controversial comments about the silent films of Germany, Russia, Scandinavia, and America. There is also a brief section on the great comedians of the 1920s. Not for film buffs the book will be valuable for serious students who might be interested in the discussion of relatively unknown movies like *The Ghost That Never Returns, Fragment of an Empire, Road to Heaven*, and *Warning Shadows*.

* Lennig, Arthur. *The Silent Voice—A Text, The Golden Age of the Cinema.* Troy: Lennig, 1969.

This enterprising book, written by the teacher for his students at the State University of New York, has some intriguing material on Lumière, Méliès, Porter, Griffith, The Fairbanks, Flaherty, and von Stroheim. Also enjoyable are Lennig's worthwhile comments on the early masterpieces.

Low, Rachael and Roger Manvell. *The History of the British Film: 1896–1906.* London: George Allen & Unwin, Ltd., 1948.

This invaluable book brings to light important information about the pioneer British producers—R. W. Paul, William Barker, Charles Urban, James Williamson, G. A. Smith, and Cecil Hepworth—and their early studios, their financial situations, and their ingenious exhibition procedures. Also valuable are the authors' insights into the trick photography of the "Brighton School," the efforts of J. Williamson and G. A. Smith. Unfortunately, for some strange reason, the book neglects the early inventors, particularly Friese-Greene.

Low, Rachel. *The History of the British Film: 1906–1914.* London: George Allen and Unwin, Ltd., 1949.

The second volume in this distinguished series is divided into two main sections. Part I examines the audience, the rise of theaters and circuits, early labor unions, censorship, the educational use of movies, special legislation, and other interesting sociological factors. Part II discusses the documentary, dramatic, and comic movies of the period.

Low, Rachel. *History of the British Film: 1914–1918.* London: Allen & Unwin, 1968.

In this third volume, the author again divides her study into two sections. Part I once more examines the audience size, distribution and exhibition, the growth of theaters, trade organizations, censorship and wartime restrictions. Part II discusses the subject matter of the movies made during the period, but this time there is a fascinating chapter on film technique plus a variety of excellent appendices—one lists the credits for more than 500 films made during those four years.

* McBride, Joseph (editor). *Persistence of Vision: A Collection of Film Criticism.* Madison: The Wisconsin Film Society Press, 1968.

Third in this active film society's publications, it is more valuable and better written than its predecessors. In particular, students should enjoy McBride's comments on Welles; Lennig's observations on Flaherty as well as his treatments of Lugosi and Karloff; Sarris on the 1940s; and the *Casablanca* dossiers. The first section, on the silent film, has some useful essays on Keaton, Gance, and Dreyer.

Manchel, Frank. *When Pictures Began to Move.* Englewood Cliffs, N.J.: Prentice-Hall Inc., 1969.

Strictly for children. This overview of the silent days of film traces the efforts of the early inventors up through the development of the motion picture industry and the rise of national cinemas. Readers are provided with helpful comments on personalities, periods, and film classics. Lovely illustrations.

Niver, Kemp R. *Biograph Bulletins 1896–1908.* Edited by Bebe Bergsten. Los Angeles: Historical Films, 1971.

In one of the most valuable publications in recent years, Niver offers a superb record of the first 12 years in the development of the pioneer film company eventually known as the Biograph. Throughout the 400 pages of the book are facsimile press opinions of the company's films, sales letters, film catalogs, and 200 handbills. The latter are great sources of information since they contain plot synopses and highlight the special features of the film described. In addition, each film has a still along with it, and the entire book is indexed with an alphabetical list of film titles, cameramen's names, date photographed, and copyright dates.

Niver, Kemp R. *The First Twenty Years: A Segment of Film History.* Edited by Bebe Bergsten. Los Angeles: Locale Research Group, 1968.

Like Hendricks, Niver is a dedicated and competent historian involved in correcting the errors of film texts. In this fine illustrated edition, the author presents important information about more than 100 of the films released between 1894–1913. The comments, stills, and statistics provide an intriguing account of these crucial years.

* Niver, Kemp R. *In the Beginning: Program Notes to Accompany One Hundred Early Motion Pictures.* New York: Brandon Books, 1967.

This invaluable monograph is a handy reference tool to the many programs Brandon Films has prepared for film courses. It is an abridged version of *The First Twenty Years.*

Niver, Kemp R. *Motion Pictures From the Library of Congress Paper Print Collection 1894–1912.* Edited by Bebe Bergsten. Berkeley: University of California Press, 1967.

This remarkable catalogue, confusingly indexed, is an indispensable guide to over 3000 motion pictures produced before the start of film copyrighting. Niver provides titles, copyright dates, producers' names, film lengths (on 16mm), their subject matter, and sometimes credits for the film, including cast and directors. Invaluable for its 300 Griffith films and three dozen Méliès listings.

Oakley, Charles. *Where We Came In: Seventy Years of the British Film Industry.* London: George Allen and Unwin, Ltd., 1964.

After first reading the Low histories, you might want to glance at this bumpy guide to British film development up to 1918. His two major weaknesses are lack of accuracy and a misguided emphasis.

* O'Leary, Liam. *The Silent Cinema.* New York: E. P. Dutton and Company, 1965.

A handy, quick runthrough of the history of the silent age with a generous and beautifully reproduced collection of 140 stills. The narrative reveals nothing new, but serves as a pleasant and useful guide to pictures of famous personalities and important national cinemas. This is one of the few good pictorial histories available in paperback.

* Pratt, George C. (editor). *Spellbound in Darkness: Readings in the History and Criticism of the Silent Film.* Rochester: The University of Rochester, 1966. Two Volumes.

Conceived and executed by one of our best living film historians, this valuable anthology has material collected from such diverse publications as *The New York Dramatic Mirror, The New York Times, Photoplay, The Moving Picture World,* and the *Motion Picture Almanac.* Volume One covers the early films up to Griffith's *Intolerance,* and Volume Two emphasizes individual directors—DeMille, Griffith, Chaplin, von Stroheim, Flaherty and Dreyer—as well as the influence of foreign cinemas on Hollywood. It is a fine assortment of essays, unique material, and shooting scripts.

Quigley, Martin Jr. *Magic Shadows: The Story of the Origin of Motion Pictures.* New York: Quigley Publishing House, 1960.
    In a seriously written style, Quigley presents a sketchy outline of the arguments against film having originated with the nineteenth century inventors. Although he makes very interesting if unconvincing statements about several periods in ancient history, his choice of illustrations makes it all worth reading. It was originally written in 1948.

* Ramsaye, Terry. *A Million and One Nights: A History of the Motion Pictures through 1925.* New York: Simon & Schuster, 1964.
    Here is a reissue of the 1926 edition of the most lively, the most enjoyable, and the least accurate history of the silent era. Ramsaye, a journalist with a fine imagination and a great love for movies, puts spice, gossip, and rumor into his charming version of the early days. Don't read it for facts, just for the pleasant and fascinating fiction that passes even today in many places for fact.

Reade, Eric. *Australian Silent Films: A Pictorial History, 1896–1929.* Melbourne: Lansdowne, 1970.
    This unique and concise volume covers the following significant periods: beginning films (1896–99), the Salvation Army successes (1900–03), the rise of feature films (1904–07), exciting showmen (1908–10), the golden age (1911–13 when two feature films were being made a month), the silent revolution (1914–19 when industrial problems arose), the tough years (1920–23), and the end of the silent era (1924–29). The book also has a valuable appendix on silent films and an index.

Rudisill, Richard. *Mirror Image: The Influence of the Daguerreotype on American Society.* Albuquerque: University of Mexico Press, 1971.
    In this handsomely produced and scholarly written book on the early days of pre-photography, Rudisill offers a superb look at the cultural, commercial and social aspects of the new science.

Wood, Leslie. *The Miracle of the Movies.* London: Burke Publishing Company, 1947.
    This talkative account of film history is a romantic story of the development of the motion picture industry, useful only in a marginal manner for learning about the problems, personalities, and products in those incredible early years.

Films

General

Animated Cartoons: The Toy That Grew Up (16mm: n.d., 17 min., b/w, sound, R-RAD/S-RAD)
    A wordy but worthwhile visual study of the early, primitive movie equip-

ment and the growth of the art and technique of animated drawings. Among the subjects presented are Plateau, Reynaud, and their machines: Phenakisti-cope and Praxinoscope.

Biography of the Motion Picture Camera (16mm: n.d., 21 min., b/w, sound, R-RAD/S-RAD)
    Another chatty but intriguing visual study of the early inventor, emphasizing Marey's investigations on recording motion, and the first films of the Lumières and Edison. Unfortunately, Dickson's work is omitted.

Daguerre: The Birth of Photography (16mm: n.d., 29 min., b/w, sound, R-RAD/S-RAD)
    This interesting film depicts the contributions of Daguerre, Niepce, and Talbot to the birth of photography. It illustrates how Niepce produced the Heliographic process, Daguerre the first permanent photograph, and Talbot the Calotype process.

In the Beginning. Unit I (16mm: 1893–1903, 22½ min., b/w, R-AUD) [14]
    These thirteen films produced and copyrighted by Thomas Alva Edison and photographed by Edwin S. Porter between 1898 and 1903 are superb for seeing the growth of film from its Kinetoscope days to the early days of matte shots and dissolves.

Origins of the Motion Picture (16mm: n.d., 21 min., b/w, sound, D-MMA)
    Based upon Quigley's book *Magic Shadows,* this worthwhile film provides some excellent visual material on Plateau, Stampfer, Marey, Edison, and the Lumières. The movie also includes some valuable footage on a prototype of Dickson's "Black Maria" and some insights into the films produced there.

George Méliès

The Films of Georges Méliès (16mm: n.d., 60 min., b/w, sound, kinescope, R-IND)
    This film shows the development of the famous French pioneer film maker with extracts from his films as well as useful comments by his grand-daughter.

Magic of Méliès (16mm: nof.,[15] R-AUD; 8mm: S-BLA)
    This film "anthology" of Méliès's early works includes "Jupiter's Thunderbolts" (1903), "The Magic Lantern" (1903), and "The Mermaid" (1904). All three show the techniques employed by Méliès in developing trick photography. The quality is poor.

Méliès Color Films (16mm: nof., R-AUD)
    A series of films which illustrate the early work by Méliès on color motion pictures, a technique involving the hand-painting of frames.

The Palace of the Arabian Nights (16mm: 1905, 17 min., b/w, R-MMA)
    Another example of trick photography and fantasy.

---

14. Kemp Niver has created 23 units, consisting of 99 films in all, to use in studying the history of film in the United States, Britain, France, and Denmark up to 1912. I recommend them very highly and suggest you get a copy of Audio's catalogue for a complete listing of all units.
15. No other information given.

The Doctor's Secret (16mm: 1908, 8 min., b/w, R-MMA)

While others were working away from fantasy, Méliès continued in the same direction begun at the turn of the century as evidenced by this film.

The Conquest of the Pole (16mm: 1912, 18 min., b/w, R-MMA)

By now Méliès had declined considerably in importance and production. This film is an example of the clumsy, but delightful pantomime of the stereotyped Old Father Pole who ate people who wandered in his domain.

A Trip to the Moon (16mm: 1902, 10 min., b/w, R-MMA)

Probably the best of Méliès's surviving works, this film is an example of how Méliès defied both the technical difficulties and fashions of filmmaking at the turn of the century. Despite all the obvious limitations of these pioneer films, they contain some of the richest examples we may ever see of an inventive, creative, and daring mind at work.

Edwin S. Porter

The Great Train Robbery (16mm: 1903, 11 min., b/w, R-AUD, MMA; 8mm: S-BLA)

Often called the first story film made in the United States, this movie was one of the most influential of the early attempts at screen narratives. It became the focal point for innovative filmmaking prior to the emergence of Griffith in 1908.

The Life of an American Fireman (16mm: 1903, 6 min., b/w, R-MMA)

Another film which may seem rather crude to today's audience, but was highly acclaimed in its day. Here was one of the first attempts at developing the last-minute rescue of a woman and her children from what seems an inevitable doom. It was this type of formula that Griffith was to develop in later years.

Film D'Art Movement

Queen Elizabeth (16mm: 1912, 65 min., b/w, R-MMA; 8mm: S-ENT)

Besides showing the great Sarah Bernhardt (illustrating how the acting of the period was theatrical not cinematic), this motion picture provided the filmmakers with a justification that films could be made that were longer in running time than the previous five- to twelve-minute films had been.

The Great Actresses of the Past Program (16mm: 90 min., b/w, R-MMA)

This anthology includes performances by theatrical stars such as Gabrielle Rejane, Sarah Bernhardt, Minnie Maddern Fiske, and Eleanora Duse.

David Wark Griffith

The Lonely Villa (16mm: 1909, 10 min., b/w, R-MMA)

While Griffith's films are discussed in Chapter 6, it might be important to point out a movie which can quickly illustrate the great director's talents in this early period of filmmaking. The story of an aborted robbery gives Griffith the chance to use cross-cutting and parallel editing to create the tension for a last-minute rescue, a technique which he was to use over and over again.

THE AMERICAN FILM (1914–1918)

The great names and films of this period are covered in Chapter 6. This was the era in which great improvements were made in camera techniques, acting ability, scenarios, and financial stability. This was the era in which movies grew into manhood.

THE GREAT GERMAN SILENTS (1919–1925)

By this time the film had developed considerably from the primitive techniques of Edison, the Lumières, and Méliès. The material of the film, the shot, and the editing technique, although primitive, had been carried forward by Griffith. The humor and sentiment of Sennett, Chaplin, and Griffith had developed the capacity of the film to convey a story. The Germans developed three aspects of cinema types: (1) costume and historical films; (2) expressionist films; and (3) melodramatic films. In this period Freidrich W. Murnau established the use of the moving camera as a subjective observer; G. W. Pabst used the camera for psychological commentaries; and a corps of directors was established, who soon would be imported by Hollywood.

Books[16]

General

Eisner, Lotte H. *The Haunted Screen: Expressionism in the German Cinema and the Influence of Max Reinhardt.* Berkeley: University of California, 1969.
     This work was first published as the French *L'Écran Démoniaque*, then as the expanded German *Dämonische Leinwand*, followed by the further revised and expanded French edition of 1965. Now this important study is available in English. Written with warmth and insight, it is an impressive analysis by a then young German journalist who saw the close connection between the State's policy toward film distribution, exhibition, and production and the artistic trends of the time. In addition, there are 300 well-chosen illustrations.

* Kracauer, Siegfried. *From Caligari to Hitler: A Psychological History of the German Film.* Princeton: Princeton University, 1969.

---

1. Some useful articles on the history of German films are the following: Louis Marcorelles, "Glimpses of the Nazi Cinema (1933–1945)," *Sight and Sound* 25, no. 2 (Autumn 1955) : 65–69; Enno Patalas, "The German Wasteland," *Sight and Sound* 26, no. 1 (Summer 1956) : 24–27; Robert Vas, "Fifteen Years After: Notes From West Germany," *Sight and Sound* 30, no. 4 (Autumn 1961) : 201–4; Herbert G. Luft, "Erich Pommer: Part I," *Films in Review* 10, no. 8 (October 1959) : 457–469; Herbert G. Luft, "Erich Pommer: Part II," *Films in Review* 10, no. 9 (November 1959) : 518–33; "Young German Film" *Film Comment* 6, no. 1 (Spring 1970) : 32–44; Ulrich Gregor, "The German Film in 1964: Stuck at Zero," *Film Quarterly* 18, no. 2 (Winter 1964) : 7–21; Robin Bean, "The Face of '63: Germany," *Films and Filming* 9, no. 9 (June 1963) : 41–48; and Robin Bean, "Hands Up, Hans!," *Films and Filming* 11, no. 1 (October 1964) : 53–57.

Originally published in 1947, this classic text suffers from a Freudian bias which sometimes forces Kracauer to label films arbitrarily. It also suffers from too heavy a sociological emphasis in trying to relate German film to the national state of mind. Nevertheless, the discussions, credits, and plot synopses make it the best available source on the silent period.

Manvell, Roger and Heinrich Fraenkel. *The German Cinema*. New York: Praeger Publishers, 1971.
In this invaluable and comprehensive study of the German film from the start to the present, the authors provide a much-needed discussion of the significant contributions of Reinhardt, Pabst, and Murnau. Throughout the book you sense the way in which the motion picture in Germany has been manipulated both for good and evil. Readers are also aided by a good bibliography and index, plus many useful illustrations.

Wollenberg, H. H. *Fifty Years of German Film*. London: The Falcon Press, 1948. Reissued by Arno Press, 1972.
A simpler account of the development of the German film industry. The emphasis is still sociological, but Wollenberg's comments add to Kracauer's thoughts. The book also contains some useful illustrations.

Fritz Lang[17]

* Bogdanovich, Peter. *Fritz Lang in America*. New York: Praeger, 1969.
Through the awkward use of the interview-article, Bogdanovich attempts to present a portrait of this unique artist. Unfortunately, we learn little about his films, and much of what passes for facts is more than questionable.

* Jensen, Paul M. *The Cinema of Fritz Lang*. New York: A. S. Barnes and Company, 1969.
This is a handy, brief, but detailed study of the great German director's work, told mainly through a thematic treatment of his movies. Very useful.

M by Fritz Lang. English translation and description of action by Nicholas Garnham. New York: Simon and Schuster, 1968. Screenplay.

Films

E. A. Dupont

Variety (16mm: 1925, 90 min., b/w, silent, R-AUD, CFS, EMG, MMA, RAD/S-MOV; 8mm: S-ENT, ESO, MOV)
E. A. Dupont's film is an example of Germany's melodramatic school and is the story of a pardoned criminal who is unable to escape from his crime. This film shows the growth in the art of the cinema by use of varied camera angles, multiple exposures, and fluid transitions, all in addition to creating a successful suspense story.

Fritz Lang

Destiny (16mm: 1921, 80 min., b/w, silent, R-EMG, MMA/S-ESS)

17. Some useful articles are John Russell Taylor, "The Nine Lives of Doctor Mabuse," *Sight and Sound* 31, no. 1 (Winter 1961–62) : 43–46; Axel Madsen, "Lang," *Sight and Sound* 36, no. 3 (Summer 1967) : 108–112; and Eric Rhode, "Fritz Lang (The German Period: 1919–33)," *Tower of Babel: Speculations on the Cinema* (Philadelphia: Chilton Books, 1967) , pp. 85–108.

While it is true that Griffith's *Birth of a Nation* (1915) and the earlier Méliès film *Civilization Through the Ages* (1906) are examples of historical films, nevertheless, no school of historical film comparable to that found in Germany during 1919–1925 developed earlier. Fritz Lang's film is part fairy tale and part legend. Two lovers are joined by a stranger, the Angel of Death, who eventually succeeds in bringing about their deaths but not in destroying their love. The film is preoccupied with fantasy, symbolism, and rhythm; it also shows the effect of the art movement of the times.

M (16mm: 1931, 90 min., b/w, English subtitles, sound, R-JAN)
Although this is Lang's first sound film, it was his last key German work and really ends the major period in Germany's film history. The story centers around a manhunt for a child murderer (Peter Lorre) and has some excellent examples of lighting, cutting, and camera angles.

Metropolis (16mm: 1926, 120 min., b/w, silent, R-AUD, COO, EMG, FNC, HPB, MMA, RAD, STA/S-HPB, MOV, NCS: 8mm: S-ENT, MOV)
Directed by Fritz Lang, this ambitious science-fiction spectacle represents one of the best examples of UFA's great studio work and the technical virtuosity of its highly skilled staff. The story of love overwhelming the divided forces of organized labor and big business still works for today's audiences.

Friedrich W. Murnau[18]

The Last Laugh (16mm: 1924, 81 min., b/w, silent, R-EMG, MMA, RAD; 8mm: COO/S-MOV)
Directed by F. W. Murnau and starring Emil Jannings, this brilliant film suggests the greatest achievements of Germany's Golden era. In addition, Carl Mayer's marvelous visual script enhances this superb story of an aging doorman's decline.

Nosferatu (16mm: 1922, 63 min., b/w, silent, R-MMA; 8mm: S-ENT, ESS)
Directed by Murnau just prior to his great *The Last Laugh*, this unauthorized adaptation of Bram Stoker's *Dracula* is fine so long as it stays in the streets and the countryside. Indoors, the awkward studio sets and limited budget glare out from the screen.[19]

Georg Wilhelm Pabst

The Joyless Street (16mm: 1925, 89 min., b/w, silent, R-AUD, MMA)
Directed by G. W. Pabst and featuring such stars as Asta Nielsen, Greta Garbo, and Werner Krauss, this realistic film points the way to most of Pabst's future work. Through the story of young lovers, trapped by economic and moral decay in postwar Vienna, the director develops the ability of the camera to depict psychological crises.[20]

Robert Wiene

The Cabinet of Dr. Caligari (16mm: 1919, 55 min., b/w, silent, R-JAN, RAD; 8mm: ENT)

18. Gilberto Perez Guillermo, "F. W. Murnau: An Introduction," *Film Comment* 7, no. 2 (Summer 1971) : 12–15.
19. Gilberto Perez Guillermo, "Shadow and Substance: Murnau's Nosferatu," *Sight and Sound* 36, no. 3 (Summer 1967) : 150–53, 159.
20. Herbert G. Luft, "G. W. Pabst," *Films in Review* 15, no. 2 (February 1964) : 93–116; and Herbert G. Luft, "G. W. Pabst," *Films and Filming* 13, no. 7 (April 1967) : 18–24.

This film shows the influence of the expressionist and the cubistic school of art, and is particularly useful for illustrating the Germans' subjective skill in handling lighting and background in film. This psychological tale is told by an inmate of a mental institution. By the use of camera angles integrated with horizontal and vertical sets, the idea of the narrator's distorted point of view is successfully communicated to the audience. This expressionist film by Robert Wiene is illustrative of the second group and is considered by many historians and critics to be one of the best movies ever made.

THE SOVIET FILMS (1925–1928)

The next major development in film history was away from formula pictures and a star system and toward a new form of cinematic technique, montage. In the early years following the 1917 revolution, the Russians revised every aspect of their society, including its artistic values. The new government, lacking film equipment, raw stock, technicians, and cinemas, decided to create new film aesthetics through socialist standards. Schools were started and people from all aspects of the culture drifted toward film production. From these ranks came such brilliant theorists and directors as Sergei Eisenstein, Vsevolod I. Pudovkin, Alexander Dovzhenko, Dziga Vertov,[21] and Lev Kuleshov.[22] But it was Eisenstein primarily, leaning heavily on his engineering and theatrical background, who developed montage, a method of editing that emphasized the importance of shots, selectively joined together, to create a new impression on the audience.[23] Intrigued with Pavlov's work, the young director saw in montage the means by which to provide a stimulus that would evoke a desired response from his audience. The work of all these men turned film into an object of intellectual pursuit.

Books

General[24]

Babitsky, Paul, and John Rimberg. *The Soviet Film Industry*. New York: Frederick A. Praeger, 1955.

21. David Bordwell, "Dziga Vertov: An Introduction," *Film Comment* 8, no. 1 (Spring 1972) : 38–45; "The Vertov Papers," Translated by Marco Carynnyk, *idem.*, pp. 46–51.
22. Ronald Levaco, "Kuleshov," *Sight and Sound* 40, no. 2 (Spring 1971) : 86–91, 109.
23. David Bordwell, "The Idea of Montage in Soviet Art and Film," *Cinema Journal* 11, no. 2 (Spring 1972) : 9–17.
24. Some useful articles on the history of Russian films are the following: Nina Hibbin, "Living on With Lenin," *Films and Filming* 16, no. 10 (July 1970) : 25–26; John Gillett, "Between the Acts," *Sight and Sound* 25, no. 4 (Spring 1956) : 201–4; Cynthia Grenier, "Soviet Cinema: The New Way," *Sight and Sound* 27, no. 5 (Summer 1958) : 236–37; Robert Vas, "Sunflowers and Commissars," *Sight and Sound* 31, no. 3 (Summer 1962) : 148–51; John Gillett, "Round About Moscow," *Sight and Sound* 32, no. 4 (Autumn 1963) : 187–89; David Robinson, "Russia Revisited," *Sight and Sound* 29, no. 2 (Spring 1960) : 70–75; Joseph L. Anderson, "Soviet Films Since 1945—Part One," *Films in Review* 4, no. 1 (January 1953) : 7–14; Joseph L. Anderson, "Soviet Films Since 1945," *Films in Review* 4, no. 2 (February 1953) : 64–73; Steven P. Hill, "Soviet Film Criticism," *Film Quarterly* 14, no. 1 (Fall 1960) : 31–40; Steven P. Hill, "The Soviet Film Today," *Film Quarterly* 20, no. 4 (Summer 1967) : 33–52; Nina Hibbin, "Ivan The Mag-

Written by a film writer (Babitsky) and a graduate student from Harvard, this useful book concentrates on the day-to-day production aspects of the Soviet cinema. Particularly useful is their discussion of politics, people, and pictures.

Dickinson, Thorold, and Catherine de la Roche. *Soviet Cinema.* London: The Falcon Press, 1948. Reissued by Arno Press, 1972.

Dickinson is helpful for his comments on the pre-sound days of Russian films and the techniques of many of the later moviemakers, while de la Roche's capsuled approach to the post-sound period suffers from the quality of the subject matter discussed.

Leyda, Jay. *Kino: History of the Russian and Soviet Film.* New York: The Macmillan Company, 1960.

In this, the best available book on the subject, Leyda describes the development of Russian cinema as an art form, relating Soviet films to their responsibility for implementing and maintaining the philosophy of the state. Beginning with the Czarist days, he explains the efforts of the revolutionary artists to glorify their political successes. Rarely in English does one even find mention of the significant filmmaker Leonid Andreyev; Leyda has excellent material on him and on other important figures of the first 40 years of Soviet film production. Good, detailed, and invaluable study. For updating purposes, read Jay Leyda, "Between Explosions," *Film Quarterly* 22, no. 4 (Summer 1970) : 33–38.

Sergei Eisenstein[25]

* Eisenstein, Sergei. *Film Essays and a Lecture.* Translated and edited by Jay Leyda. With an Introduction by Grigori Kozintsev. New York: Praeger Publications, 1970.

These almost verbatim notes suggest the master's classroom technique and offer important observations about the art of the film. Particularly interesting are his "The New Language of the Cinema," "The Dynamic Square," and "Lessons from Literature."

* Eisenstein, Sergei. *Film Form: Essays in Film Theory* and *Film Sense.*

---

nificent," *Films and Filming* 9, no. 5 (February 1963) : 56–61; Peter Baker, "The Other Side of the Curtain," *Films and Filming* 7, no. 6 (March 1961) : 8–9, 34; R. Yourenev, "A Short History of the Soviet Cinema," *Films and Filming* 7, no. 6 (March 1961) : 15–16, 39; John Peter Dyer, "Russian Youth in an Uproar," *Films and Filming* 5, no. 11 (August 1959) : 12–14, 32–33; Sergei Gerasimov, "Socialist Realism and the Soviet Cinema," *Films and Filming* 5, no. 3 (December 1958) : 11–12, 33; Nina Hibbin, "See No Evil," *Films and Filming* 12, no. 5 (February 1966) : 43–46; Y. Varshavsky, "From Generation to Generation," *Films and Filming* 13, no. 11 (August 1967) : 42–46; and Vladimir Baskakov, "After the Revolution," *Films and Filming* 16, no. 1 (October 1969) : 62–68.

25. Some useful articles are the following: Sergei Eisenstein, "One Path to Colour: An Autobiographical Fragment," *Sight and Sound* 30, no. 2 (Spring 1961) : 84–86, 102; Jay Leyda, "Eisenstein's Bezhin Meadow," *Sight and Sound* 28, no. 2 (Spring 1959) : 74–76, 105; Jay Leyda, "Eisenstein's Mexican Tragedy," *Sight and Sound* 27, no. 6 (Autumn 1958) : 305–8, 329; Marie Seton, "Eisenstein's Images and Mexican Art" *Sight and Sound* 23, no. 1 (July–September 1953) : 8–13; Evelyn Gerstein, "Ivan the Terrible: A Peak in Darien," *Film Comment* 5, no. 1 (Fall 1968) : 52–57; Eric Rhode, "Sergei Eisenstein," *Tower of Babel: Speculations on the Cinema* (New York: Chilton Books, 1967) , pp. 51–66; Dwight Macdonald, "Part Four: The Russian Cinema," *Dwight Macdonald on the Movies* (Englewood Cliffs, N.J.: Prentice-Hall, Inc., 1969) , pp. 181–190, 249–67; and Steven P. Hill, "A Quantitative View of Soviet Cinema," *Cinema Journal* 11, no. 2 (Spring 1972) : 18–25.

Translated and edited by Jay Leyda. New York: Meridian Books, 1957. Reissued separately by Harcourt, Brace in 1969.

Eisenstein's theories on film, presented in summary form, offer valuable insights into his films and his influence. Although difficult for beginners, they are a treasure-house for serious students of film.

Eisenstein, Sergei. *Notes of a Film Director*. Translated by X. Danko. London: Lawrence and Wishart, 1959.

Useful background information on the great director's methods and theories, plus an excellent collection of drawings he designed for *Alexander Nevsky* and *Ivan the Terrible*.

Geduld, Harry M. and Ronald Gottesman (editors). *Sergei Eisenstein and Upton Sinclair: The Making and Unmaking of Que Viva Mexico!* Bloomington: Indiana University Press, 1970.

Based mainly on the correspondence between Eisenstein and Sinclair, this book offers the most extensive information on the great Russian director's disastrous attempt to make a film in Mexico. An invaluable annotated bibliography is included.

* Montagu, Ivor. *With Eisenstein in Hollywood: A Chapter of Autobiography, Including the Scenarios of Sutter's Gold and An American Tragedy*. New York: International Publishers, 1967.

In 1930, Eisenstein, Alexandrov, and Tisse came to America, signed a contract with Paramount, wrote unsuccessful scenarios, worked on the abortive Mexican film project, and returned in disgrace to the Soviet Union. This excellent, entertaining book is a goldmine of information about the quartet (Montagu is included), and also reproduces the two scenarios.

* Moussinac, Leon. *Sergei Eisenstein: An Investigation into His Films and Philosophy*. Translated from the French by D. Sandy Petrey. New York: Crown Publishers, 1970.

Originally published in 1964 in the highly praised *Cinema d'Aujourd'hui* series of Editions Seghers in Paris, this first-rate study of Eisenstein, done by the pioneer French critic and close friend of the Russian director, is a must for all students of Russian cinema. It contains original essays, reviews, comments by critics and peers, letters, and an excellent bio-filmography.

Nizhny, Vladimir. *Lessons with Eisenstein*. Translated and edited by Ivor Montagu and Jay Leyda. New York: Hill and Wang, 1962.

This book provides valuable insights into scriptwriting and direction. Based upon selected records kept of Eisenstein's classes at the State Institute of Cinematography in 1928–29, Nizhny has written an outstanding source book for teaching about film direction.

Vsevolod I. Pudovkin[26]

Pudovkin, V. I. *Film Technique and Film Acting*, translated by Ivor Montagu. London: Vision, 1958.

Some good and useful theories about the relationship between the stage and the screen. No book comparable to this one has yet been written.

---

26. Herman G. Weinberg, "Vsevelod Pudovkin," *Films in Review* 4, no. 7 (August–September 1953) : 325–37.

In addition, there is a good article on Vertov's methods of filmmaking, which influenced Pudovkin: Dai Vaughan, "Great Films of the Century: The Man with the Movie Camera," *Films and Filming* 7, no. 2 (November 1960) : 18–20, 43.

Films

Sergei Eisenstein

Battleship Potemkin, or *Potemkin* (16mm: 1925, 70 min., b/w, music and sound effects only, R-AUD, L-CCM. Silent version is also available; R-AUD, FCE, MMA; 8mm: R-COO/S-ENT, MOV)

One approach to film montage came in the form of joining two unlike shots to create a new meaning. This film about the 1905 rebellion of the Battleship *Potemkin's* crew illustrates how, by montage, a work of art is created.

The teacher might find it helpful in explaining Eisenstein's techniques to show the famous "Odessa Steps" sequence from *Potemkin* (16mm: 1925, 20 min., b/w, R-MMA; 8mm: S-ENT) to illustrate how the great director manipulates time and space in film. That is to say, Eisenstein by the use of montage makes physical time and the actual event take longer and appear more dramatic and symbolic in the narrative film. The excerpt is also useful for showing the advantages of type casting (choosing individuals for their physical characteristics rather than for their acting ability) in creating a film metaphor.[27] A relationship between Griffith's and Eisenstein's work can be detected in the use of parallel editing and cross-cutting for creating tension.

Strike (16mm: 1925, 90 min., b/w, silent, R-AUD, MMA)

The story of a group of workers who are ruthlessly suppressed as a result of their demonstrations. This is Eisenstein's first film. A final portion of the film script is reproduced in *Film Sense* and there is an interesting examination of several possible endings that were considered.[28]

Ten Days That Shook the World, or *October* (16mm: 1928, 140 min., b/w, silent, R-AUD, EMG, MMA, STA/S-MOV: 8mm: R-COO/S-ENT, ESO, MOV).

The story of the Russian revolution of 1917 contains many famous episodes, an example of which is the raising of the bridge which is considered one of the most praised sequences in film history. Here, as in the other Eisenstein films, the director demonstrates that one can change the meaning of a film by changing the position of the shots.

Alexander Nevsky (Russia—16mm: 1938, 107 min., b/w, English subtitles, sound, R-AUD/L-AUD)

Helped by Sergei Prokofiev's brilliant musical score and Eduard Tisse's superb photography, Eisenstein presents one of the screen's outstanding historical recreations as he tells the heroic story of Prince Alexander Nevsky's

---

27. Two versions of the film script are available: David Mayer, *Eisenstein's Potemkin: A Shot-by-Shot Presentation.* New York: Grossman Publishers, 1972; and *Potemkin: A Film by Sergei Eisenstein.* Translated from the Russian by Gillon R. Aitken. New York: Simon and Schuster, 1968. See Norman Fruchter, "Film Critique No. 5: *Battleship Potemkin,*" *Screen Education* 30 (July–August 1965) : 37–52; and Sergei M. Eisenstein, "Organic Unity and Pathos in the Composition of *Potemkin,*" *Cahiers du Cinema in English* 3, CdC no. 82 (April 1958) : 36–43.

In this connection, it might be useful to read two articles on casting: Lola G. Yoaken, "Casting," *Film Quarterly* 12, no. 2 (Winter 1958) : 36–42; and Charles Winick, "The Face was Familiar," *Films and Filming* 11, no. 4 (January 1965) : 12–17.

28. Ivor Montagu, "Rediscovery: *Strike,*" *Sight and Sound* 26, no. 2 (Autumn 1956) : 105–8.

peasant army and their defeat of the 13th century invading German nobles. Nikolai Cherkasov plays the Russian prince who plans the great battle on the ice of Lake Peipus.

Ivan The Terrible (Part I) (Russia—16mm: 1944, 96 min., b/w, English subtitles, sound, R-AUD)
This film begins what Eisenstein wanted to be a trilogy on Russia's first Tsar (he died before a third part could be made). It is an outstanding example of cinematic and theatrical techniques interwoven to suggest how movies are a synthesis of traditional arts. Once more, Prokofiev and Tisse help create a film masterpiece.

Ivan The Terrible (Part II) (Russia—16mm: 1946, 90 min., b/w, English subtitles, sound, R-AUD)
Eisenstein's treatment here in showing how the Tsar squelched a Boyer's plot to overthrow him caused the film director great problems with Soviet censors. The film was not released until 1958, eight years after it was finished. Of particular interest is Eisenstein's experiment with color and his attempt to orchestrate it as he did images and sounds.

Sergei Eisenstein (16mm: 1958, 50 min., b/w, English narration, sound, R-AUD/L-CCM)
This is a film biography of the Russian director which not only treats his life but also shows extracts from his plays and major films.

Vsevolod I. Pudovkin

Mother (16mm: 1926, 100 min., b/w, silent, R-AUD, MMA)
This film concerns a plot from the Gorky novel about a working class mother and her relationship with individuals. One can readily see in the film Pudovkin's complex cutting methods combined with an emphasis on pictorial composition.

Storm over Asia (16mm: 1927, 98 min., b/w, silent, R-EMG, MMA. Music and sound effects version available from AUD)
The story of the exploitation of the Mongolians by foreigners. In this film set in Mongolia in 1918, we can see the effective use of naturalistic treatment; the camera often lingers over the faces of the people with their strange costumes, their mannerisms in the market place, as well as the sweeping scope of the landscape. Also evident is the director's experimentation which involves trying to show emotions in visual terms while at the same time telling the stereotyped story of the bad guys versus the good ones and using non-professional actors.

The End of St. Petersburg (16mm: 1927, 80 min., b/w, silent, R-AUD, MMA)
This story concerns the adventures of a country boy involved in the 1917 Russian Revolution. It covers the same historical period as that in *October* but uses the individual to represent the masses.

Pudovkin (16mm: 1960, 60 min., b/w, English narration, sound, R-AUD/L-CCM)
This film biography shows the great director at work and includes excerpts from his motion pictures.

Alexander Dovzhenko[29]

Arsenal (16mm: 1928, 80 min., b/w, silent, R-AUD, MMA)

While most of Dovzhenko's stories are concerned with a simple plot line (in this film, the revolt of the workers), he is one of the most poetic of silent directors. His major contributions to the film were in the form of a new realism coupled with a continuity of storytelling and lyrical beauty.

HOLLYWOOD IN THE TWENTIES (1920–1928)[30]

All the ferment in film began to change the style and industry of the motion picture capital of the world. Producers, distributors, and exhibitors sensed the need to merge forces and reap great profits. So in 1920 the rush for movie supremacy once more became paramount. Marcus Loew bought control of Metro Pictures to guarantee films for his vast chain operation; and the Cohns (Jack and Harry) and Joe Brandt established the C.B.C. Film Sales Company (the forerunner of Columbia Pictures, formed two years later).

But other trends also crept ominously onto the scene in the early 1920s. Reformers, politicians, and self-styled do-gooders began to attack the immorality and unconventional life style of Hollywood. By 1921, no less than thirty-six censorship bills were pending in state legislatures and the United States Congress. Faced by growing resentment and political interference, the movie tycoons hired William Harrison Hays in January 1922 to act as their official spokesman and bring dignity to the film industry. For the next six years, the ex-Postmaster General of the U.S. worked to create a self-censorship system within the industry. The result came in 1927 with the Motion Picture Production Code.[31]

These were the years that gave rise to the Film Booking Office of America (later to become Radio-Keith-Orpheum Corporation); to M-G-M; to the merger of Paramount, Balaban and Katz to establish Publix; to incredible revolutions with "talkies" through the efforts of Lee DeForest, Western Electric, William Fox, and Warner Brothers. This was the era in which Technicolor made dramatic advances in color processes. This too was the decade where Zukor's block-booking practices were declared illegal and the Academy of Motion Picture Arts and Sciences was formed.

But most important, this was the greatest age of silent films. These were the brilliant years of Erich von Stroheim, Joseph von Sternberg, Robert Flaherty, Charles Chaplin, Buster Keaton, Friedrich W. Murnau, Lon

---

29. Marco Carynnyk, "The Dovzhenko Papers," *Film Comment* 7, no. 3 (Fall 1971) : 34–41.

30. For most of the background information on this period, see Chapter 6. Two helpful articles for a brief overview are Christopher North, "Industry Highlights," *Films in Review* 19, no. 10 (December 1968) : 613–17; and Christopher North, "Film History for Exhibitors," *Films in Review* 21, no. 8 (October 1970) : 473–77.

31. See Appendices III and IV.

Chaney, Harold Lloyd, Rudolph Valentino, Douglas Fairbanks, Lillian Gish, Cecil B. DeMille, King Vidor, Gloria Swanson, Greta Garbo, and David Wark Griffith.

Books

General

Barry, Iris. *Let's Go to the Movies*. New York: Payson and Clark, 1926. Reissued by Arno Press, 1972.
   A clever and amusing commentary on the silent films. Barry is particularly good at presenting useful comments on the feature films of the period.

* McCaffrey, Donald W. *4 Great Comedians: Chaplin, Lloyd, Keaton, and Langdon*. New York: A. S. Barnes and Company, 1968.
   This is one of the most refreshing and original studies in the last decade. In his reevaluation of the great silent clowns, McCaffrey focuses his aim on the shorts and great features of the early days of comedy. A useful bibliography is included.

Manchel, Frank. *Yesterday's Clowns: The Rise of Film Comedy*. New York: Franklin Watts, Inc., 1973.
   Strictly for children. This book shows the relationship between the stars' childhood and their screen roles, while at the same time showing the history of film comedy from burlesque to the great features of the twenties.

Mayer, Arthur. *Merely Colossal: The Story of the Movies From the Long Chase to the Chaise Longue*. New York: Simon and Schuster, 1953.
   This marvelous man began his film career as a salesman for Samuel Goldwyn, produced copy for Mae West's publicity campaigns, wrote material to advertise Marlene Dietrich, operated a second-rate film theater on Broadway, and now has become one of the best film teachers around. This book, often unreliable on factual matters, is a delightful source of anecdotes on the greats of Hollywood and has some wonderful material on the 1920s.

Moley, Raymond. *The Hays Office*. New York: The Bobbs-Merrill Company, 1945. Reissued by Jerome S. Ozer, Publishers, Inc., 1971.
   This sympathetic but very useful portrait of the controversial Indiana film czar is an invaluable document on the origination of the Motion Picture Producers and Distributors of America in 1922 and the subsequent years up to 1944. All of the major resolutions are carefully appendixed at the end, and Moley's lucid prose and apt quotations suggest one side, an important one, of self-regulation.[32]

Marion, Frances. *Off With Their Heads: A Serio-Comic Tale of Hollywood*. With a Foreword by Gloria Swanson. New York: The Macmillan Company, 1972.
   Written by a very successful screenwriter of both the silent and sound

---

32. In this connection, the following articles suggest the problems Hays faced when he took office: DeWitt Bodeen, "Wallace Reid," *Films in Review* 18, no. 3 (April 1966) : 205–30; and Aydelott Ames, "Mary Miles Minter," *Films in Review* 20, no. 8 (October 1969) : 473–95, 501. Also useful are Herbert M. Levy, "The Case Against Film Censorship," *Films in Review* 1, no. 3 (April 1950) : 1–2, 38–42; and Frederick M. Wirt, "To See or Not to See: The Case Against Censorship," *Film Quarterly* 13, no. 1 (Fall 1959) : 26–31.

eras, this delightful anecdotal narrative about key personalities is very helpful in learning more about Hollywood life. It also contains some lovely illustrations.

* Robinson, David. *Hollywood in the Twenties.* New York: A. S. Barnes and Company, 1968.
   This tightly written and highly useful account of the 1920s is a good introduction to film production, distribution, and exhibition at the end of the silent era. In 9 fact-packed chapters, Robinson presents a provocative, entertaining and nostalgic overview of the important stars and the memorable films, lacing his narrative with perceptive and stimulating observations. My major objections are the poor quality of the stills and their almost negligible use.

Rosenberg, Bernard and Harry Silverstein (editors). *The Real Tinsel.* New York: The Macmillan Company, 1970.
   Two sociologists at the City College of New York have collected a wonderful series of 24 commentaries by film pioneers from all aspects of the movie industry: producers, directors, stars, publicist, stuntman, voice animator, music director, cameraman, sound director, writer, and critic. Among the notables are Adolph Zukor, Dore Schary, Arthur Mayer, Conrad Nagel, Mae Marsh, Fritz Lang, Max Steiner, and Arthur Knight.

* Seldes, Gilbert. *The Seven Lively Arts.* New York: A. S. Barnes and Company, 1957.
   This entertaining book was first published in 1924 and brought up to date in the 1957 edition. Its major chapters on film deal with Keystone, Chaplin and the film tycoons. Readers should also look at Seldes's related comments on comic strips, musical comedy, vaudeville, radio, popular music and the dance.

Lon Chaney

Anderson, Robert G. *Faces, Forms, Films: The Artistry of Lon Chaney.* New York: A. S. Barnes and Company, 1971.
   In a helpful narrative coupled with more than 150 stills, Anderson gives the best account of Chaney's contribution to the art of the film.

Allan Dwan

* Bogdanovich, Peter. *Allan Dwan: The Last Pioneer.* New York: Praeger Publishers, 1971.
   In a series of extensive interviews, Bogdanovich gives us a brief and useful overview of the veteran American director who ran the gamut of commercial filmmaking.

Cecil B. DeMille

DeMille, Cecil B. *The Autobiography of Cecil B. DeMille.* Edited by Donald Hayne. Englewood Cliffs, N.J.: Prentice-Hall, Inc., 1959.
   This posthumously published account is a nostalgic, honest, and discursive presentation of one of the most controversial men in film history. Although he sometimes takes credit for several firsts in film technique—e.g., "Rembrandt lighting," which Griffith and Bitzer had developed before him

—DeMille candidly presents an accurate description of his commercial commitment to box-office popularity. The book also presents some excellent stills. By way of introduction to DeMille, the student should first read Joseph and Harry Feldman, "Cecil B. DeMille's Virtues," *Films in Review* 1, no. 9 (December 1950) : 1–6; Cecil B. DeMille, "After 70 Pictures," *Films in Review* 7, no. 3 (March 1956) : 97–102; and Art Arthur, "C. B. DeMille's Human Side," *Films in Review* 23, no. 4 (April 1967) : 221–25.

DeMille, William C. *Hollywood Saga.* New York: E. P. Dutton, 1939.
Cecil's older brother gives a reflective and witty account of the film wars from the days of Triangle to the end of the 1930s. He also has some insightful comments on his kinsman's production methods and temperament.

Essoe, Gabe and Raymond Lee. *DeMille: The Man and his Pictures.* New York: A. S. Barnes and Company, 1970.
This pictorial survey combined with a brief biographical narrative is a good addition to the growing information of the most popular director of the 1920s.

* Ringgold, Gene and DeWitt Bodeen. *The Films of Cecil B. DeMille.* New York: The Citadel Press, 1969.
This is one of the outstanding picture collections about screen personalities and their movies. The pictures are well-chosen, many are new to publication, the comments and credits are accurate, and the narrative is more than suitable to make the necessary transition from work to work.

Robert Flaherty

Calder-Marshall, Arthur. *The Innocent Eye: The Life of Robert J. Flaherty.* New York: Harcourt, Brace and World, Inc., 1963.
This book is a descriptive approach to Flaherty's life, with summaries of his films and an inclusive index. The author's early chapters present a sober, detailed, and accurate account of Flaherty's experiences as an explorer in the Canadian arctic, and throughout other chapters we get a better understanding of the father of the documentary film's irregular work habits, his extravagance, and his marvelous talent. Much of the research in the biography was originally prepared by Paul Rotha and Basil Wright.

Flaherty, Frances Hubbard. *The Odyssey of a Film-Maker: Robert Flaherty's Story.* Urbana: Beta Phi Mu, 1960. Reissued by Arno Press in 1972.
This lovingly told biography by Flaherty's wife is a brief, very readable, and beautifully produced book. Although it is not very informative, the illustrations and the narrative are a tender reminder of a great artist.

Griffith, Richard. *The World of Robert Flaherty.* New York: Duell, Sloan and Pearce, 1953.
One of the best sources of material on the great pioneer documentary filmmaker. Many excerpts are taken from his letters, journals, and diaries. There are also some informative remarks by his wife and Pat Mullen.

Laurel and Hardy

* Barr, Charles. *Laurel and Hardy.* Berkeley: University of California Press, 1968.
In a well-thought-out interpretation, Barr analyzes the skill and art of the

great comedy team. The thesis is helped considerably by numerous illustrations.

* Everson, William K. *The Films of Laurel and Hardy*. New York: The Citadel Press, 1967.

Except for the scant biographical commentary, Everson presents a handy list of synopses and critical judgments together with many well-selected stills.

McCabe, John. *Mr. Laurel and Mr. Hardy*. With a Special Foreword by Dick van Dyke. New York: Grosset and Dunlap, 1961.

In the best study yet on the two marvelous comedians, McCabe gives a tender account of the sensitive Stan and the mirthful Oliver, their years together, and the importance of Laurel as the guiding genius.

Harold Lloyd[33]

Cahn, William. *Harold Lloyd's World of Comedy*. New York: Duell, Sloan and Pearce, 1964.

Unfortunately, there has not been a worthwhile study of this marvelous comic whose ingenious satirization of the healthy, All-American hero—the glass character—is once more getting its due recognition. Cahn's book tells us very little about Lloyd's production practices, his relationship with directors, fellow performers, or scriptwriters. Almost nothing is done with the films themselves or the similarities and dissimilarities between Lloyd and his competitors. And finally, a book like this should have included appendices and credit lists.

* Lloyd, Harold and Wesley W. Stout. *An American Comedy*. New York: Benjamin Blom, Inc., 1971.

Originally written in 1928, this autobiographical book is a chatty, rambling account of Lloyd's major years in film. Unfortunately, it offers little on technique, personalities or even a few good anecdotes.

Colleen Moore

Moore, Colleen. *Silent Star: Colleen Moore Talks about Her Hollywood*. New York: Doubleday and Company, Inc., 1968.

In this informal and chatty autobiography, we gain some insight into the famous Hollywood scandals involving Fatty Arbuckle and William Desmond Taylor.

Hal Roach[34]

* Everson, William K. *The Films of Hal Roach*. New York: The Museum of Modern Art, 1971.

In a brief but valuable overview, Everson comments on Roach's style, memorable pictures, and his great stars. There is also a recent interview with Roach plus a bibliography and several good stills.

---

33. Nelson E. Garringer, "Harold Lloyd," *Films in Review* 12, no. 7 (August–September 1962) : 407–22; and "Harold Lloyd Talks to Anthony Slide about His Early Career," *The Silent Picture* (Summer–Autumn 1971) , pp. 4–8.
34. Anthony Slide, "Hal Roach on Film Comedy," *The Silent Picture* 6 (Spring 1970) : 2–7.

Rudolph Valentino[35]

Arnold, Alan. *Valentino*. Foreword by John Paddy Carsairs. New York: Library Publishers, 1954.

In an attempt to debunk the usual myths surrounding Valentino's career, Arnold offers a good critical and interesting biography that reveals a sad and sensitive story of Hollywood in the 1920s.

Shulman, Irving. *Valentino*. New York: Trident Press, 1967.

This fascinating and entertaining biography examines many of the myths and foibles of Hollywood and provides more information and controversy than the Arnold text.

King Vidor

Vidor, King. *A Tree Is a Tree*. New York: Harcourt, Brace, 1952.

This exceptional director of *The Big Parade, The Crowd,* and *Hallelujah* presents us with a modest, well-written, and enjoyable account of film production and studio life. Although he fails to teach anything about his directing methods, Vidor relates some fascinating accounts of Hearst, John Gilbert, and the events that took place at Mabel Normand's funeral.

Vidor, King. *King Vidor on Film Making*. New York: David McKay Company, Inc., 1972.

This has to be one of the most fascinating books on filmmaking in the last decade. It weaves autobiography, history, and technique into an educational experience available nowhere else.

Josef von Sternberg

Sarris, Andrew. *The Films of Josef von Sternberg*. New York: Museum of Modern Art, 1966.

This short, handy, and informative survey of von Sternberg's 18 films beginning in 1925 provides good notes to particular movies and a valuable introduction to the great director's fascination with artificial settings, contrived lighting, and special effects. The book has many fine illustrations and important screen credits.

von Sternberg, Josef. *Fun in a Chinese Laundry*. New York: The Macmillan Company, 1965.

Von Sternberg's autobiography is a fascinating discussion of directing, personalities and a bygone age. The usual chatty and meandering anecdotal approach to a famous man's career is replaced by an intelligent, provocative, and meaningful discussion of theory and practice. This is a must for his students.

* Weinberg, Herman G. *Josef von Sternberg: A Critical Study of The Great Director* (New York: E. P. Dutton and Company, 1967) .

No book is more valuable for information on von Sternberg's style, subjects, and interests. Weinberg, in a loving tribute, presents chapters on the director's career, a personal interview with him, a collection of critical re-

---

35. Theodore Huff, "The Career of Rudolph Valentino," *Films in Review* 3, no. 4 (April 1952) : 145–63; and H. L. Mencken, "On Hollywood—and Valentino," *Cinema Journal* 9, no. 2 (Spring 1970) : 13–23.

views, extracts from the scenarios of *Shanghai Express*, and the entire narration of *Anatham*, the best available filmography and bibliography, and 50 important illustrations.

Erich von Stroheim[36]

Curtiss, Thomas Quinn. *Von Stroheim*. New York: Farrar, Straus and Giroux, Inc.

Except for some errors dealing with Griffith, Curtiss presents an in-depth study not only of a great director but also of a valuable era in film history. This is must reading for von Stroheim students.

* Finler, Joel W. *Stroheim*. Berkeley: University of California Press, 1968.

No figure in film history is more mysterious, more controversial, or more magnificent than the Viennese Jew who terrorized the studios and the stars of Hollywood; he was often labeled "the man you love to hate." The best part of this text is its lengthy and worthwhile discussion of *Greed*. Although von Stroheim's other films also are discussed in a useful fashion, an overall scholarly study of the man has not yet been written.

Noble, Peter. *Hollywood Scapegoat: The Biography of Erich von Stroheim*. London: The Fortune Press, 1950. Reissued by Arno Press, in 1972.

This first biography in English of von Stroheim is a general, loosely organized account of the great director's fascination with sex on the screen and his problems with the Hollywood censors and stars like the Gish sisters, Gloria Swanson, Douglas Fairbanks, and John Gilbert. For the most part, the facts are there along with many useful stills and a good list of cast credits and reference material.

Weinberg, Herman (editor). *The Complete "Greed" of Erich von Stroheim: A Reconstruction of the film in 348 still Photos Following the original Screenplay Plus 52 Production stills*. New York: Arno Press, 1971.

In providing us with a superb reconstruction of von Stroheim's brilliant film, Weinberg has performed a major contribution to film scholarship. The extraordinary stills, together with the foreword and epilogue in this handsome and expensive book, provide the reader with the story of one of the most horrendous filmmaking experiences ever in movie history.

Films

General

The Golden Age of Comedy (Youngson—16mm: 1957, 85 min., b/w, sound, R-AIM, AUD, CHA, CON, CWF, IDE, NAT, SWA, TWF, TWY, WHO/L-CAR)

This superb comedy anthology has scenes and sequences from some of the best of the Mack Sennett and Hal Roach comedies made between 1923 and 1928. Among the famous personalities shown are Will Rogers, Jean Harlow, Carol Lombard, Ben Turpin, Harry Langdon, The Keystone Cops, the Sennett Bathing Beauties, and Laurel and Hardy.

---

36. Herman Weinberg has an important filmography on von Stroheim in British Film Institute Index Series.

Directors and Personalities

Frank Borzage

Seventh Heaven (Fox—16mm: 1927, 120 min., b/w, music and sound effects only, R-MMA)

Director Frank Borzage deserves some of the credit for translating Austin Strong's play about two lovers in Paris whose lives become tragically affected by World War I into an immensely popular film. But the fame and the praise go mostly to the movie's stars: Janet Gaynor and Charles Farrell.

Charles Chaplin

The Gold Rush (United Artists—16mm: 1925, 81 min., b/w, silent, R-AUD, CFS, CON, CWF, EMG, HPB, NCS, RAD, SWA; 8mm: R-COO, S-ENT, ESS)

Chaplin wrote, produced, directed, and starred in this greatest of all the silent film comedies: the humorous and pathetic story of the sad little prospector who finds fortune and love in the Yukon.[37]

Cecil B. DeMille

Male and Female (Paramount—16mm: 1919, 97 min., b/w, silent, R-MMA)

Cecil B. DeMille, the most popular producer of the 1920s, was responsible for this visual guide to life among the wealthy in his stagey adaptation of James Barrie's *The Admirable Crichton*. The film featured Gloria Swanson, Thomas Meighan, and Bebe Daniels.[38]

Lon Chaney

The Hunchback of Notre Dame (Universal—16mm: 1923, 90 min., b/w, silent, R-AUD, CWF, HPB, MOG, RAD, SWA, TWF/S-HPB, NCS; 8mm: R-COO/S-BLA, FCE, MOG)

This classic Victor Hugo novel has been filmed three times, but no one ever topped Lon Chaney's incredible acting in this touching and memorable version of the tormented bellringer who is more pitied than feared. Wallace Worsley directed.[39]

The Phantom of the Opera (Universal—16mm: 1925, 75 min., b/w, silent, R-AUD, CHA, FNC, HPB, MOG, RAD, SWA/S-HPB, MOV, NCS; 8mm: S-BLA)

One of the best films of the 1920s, this marvelous story about a warped musician with a disfigured face who terrorizes the Paris Opera not only offers great moments of horror, but also superb production designs and photography. Rupert Julian directed.

---

37. Ernest Callenbach, "Classics Revisited: *The Gold Rush,*" *Film Quarterly* 13, no. 1 (Fall 1959) : 31–37; Bosley Crowther, "The Gold Rush," *The Great Films*, pp. 49–53; and Theodore Huff, "Chaplin as Composer," *Films in Review* 1, no. 6 (September 1950) : 1–5.

38. DeWitt Bodeen, "Bebe Daniels," *Films in Review* 15, no. 7 (August–September 1964: 413–40.

39. Richard E. Braff, "A New Lon Chaney Index," *Films in Review* 21, no. 4 (April 1970) :217–28.

James Cruze

The Covered Wagon (Paramount—16mm: 1923, 71 min., b/w, musical score only, R-AUD, MOG)
Directed by James Cruze, this film became recognized as the first successful western epic as the camera graphically portrayed the westward movement of the pioneers. It works best when the story is ignored and the camera records the Nevada locations.[40]

Robert Flaherty

Nanook of the North (Paramount—16mm: 1922, 60 min., b/w, sound version, R-CAL, CON, ILL, TF, UON/S-CON)
This Robert Flaherty masterpiece records the struggle of the Eskimos against the forces of nature and their short-lived victory over hunger. Originally, the director was hired by the Revillon Frères Fur Company to explore the Canadian arctic, but Flaherty's two gruelling years of research led him to make the first major documentary film.[41]

Greta Garbo

The Story of Gosta Berling (Sweden—16mm: 1924, 105 min., b/w, musical score only, R-MMA)
Although this film was made in Scandinavia, it brought director Mauritz Stiller and his great discovery, Greta Garbo, to Hollywood and gave the world one of its most enduring legends. The story of love is secondary to the extraordinary characterizations, photographic magnificence, and lyrical rhythm.[42]

David Wark Griffith

Way Down East (United Artists—16mm: 1920, 110 min., b/w, sound with musical score only, R-AUD, EMG, MIN, MMA, STA)
D. W. Griffith directed this unusual and highly successful story of a poor country girl, tricked into marriage by a city slicker, then deserted and finally ostracized by a puritanical community devoid of human understanding. It provided Lillian Gish with some of her finest moments.

William S. Hart

The Toll Gate (Paramount—16mm: 1920, 54 min., b/w, silent, R-MMA, RAD; 8mm: S-BLA)
Here is one of the best surviving films starring William S. Hart, the greatest cowboy star of the silent era, in his famous role as the "good-badman" who shuns his freedom to save a young child's life.[43]

---

40. George Geltzer, "James Cruze," *Films in Review* 5, no. 6 (June–July 1954) : 283–91; Alan Stanbrook, "Great Films of the Century: *The Covered Wagon*," *Films and Filming* 6, no. 8 (May 1960) :12–14, 35; and Bosley Crowther, "The Covered Wagon," *The Great Films*, pp. 26–30.
41. Helen von Dongen, "Robert J. Flaherty 1884–1951," *Film Quarterly* 18, no. 4 (Summer 1965) : 3–14; and Bosley Crowther, "Nanook of the North," *The Great Films*, pp. 24–26.
42. Bosley Crowther, "The Story of Gosta Berling," *The Great Films*, pp. 31–34.
43. See Chapter 2 for information about W. S. Hart and Westerns.

Buster Keaton

The General (Metro—16mm: 1927, 90 min., b/w, silent, R-AUD, CWF, MIN, RAD, STA, SWA/S-BLA, FIN; 8mm: R-COO/S-BLA, ENT)
Buster Keaton directed, wrote, and starred in this memorable film about a hero during the Civil War who decides to rescue a stolen train. Probably the best film Keaton ever made for showing his brilliant timing and superb visual gags.[44]

The Navigator (Metro—16mm: 1924, 70 min., b/w, silent, R-AUD)
This brilliant comedy deals with a rich playboy (Keaton) and his helpless girlfriend (Kathryn McGuire) who are stranded alone at sea aboard a mammoth ocean liner. Once more it was Keaton's timing and superb sight gags that made the film so successful.

Henry King

Tol'able David (First National—16mm: 1921, 85 min., b/w, sound, tinted version, R-RAD)
Henry King directed this highly acclaimed story of David (Richard Barthelmess), the youngest son of a simple mountain people, who becomes a man in the rugged outdoor world. Particularly outstanding are King's location shots and lucid continuity.[45]

Harold Lloyd[46]

The only 16mm Lloyd films, at this time, are 14 one- and two-reelers available on an individual rental basis from EM Gee Film Library. The supporting casts include Bebe Daniels and Snub Pollard.

Friedrich W. Murnau

Sunrise (Fox—16mm: 1927, 110 min., b/w, musical and sound effects only, R-FNC, MMA)
After *The Last Laugh* Murnau came to Hollywood and made this memorable parable about good and evil, starring Janet Gaynor and George O'Brien. Very evident in this love story of two country "greenhorns" who get confused in the big city are the masterly techniques first developed at UFA.[47]

---

44. Philip Strict, "Great Films of the Century: *The General*," *Films and Filming* 7, no. 12 (September 1961): 14–16, 40; and Bosley Crowther, "The General," *The Great Films*, pp. 60–65.
45. Jack Jacobs, "Richard Barthelmess," *Films in Review* 9, no. 1 (January 1958): 12–21; and Roy Pickard, "The Tough Race," *Films and Filming* 17, no. 12 (September 1971): 38–44.
46. The following material is worth reading in connection with the great screen clown: Harold Lloyd, "The Funny Side of Life," *Films and Filming* 10, no. 4 (January 1964): 19–21; Arthur B. Friedman, "Interview with Harold Lloyd," *Film Quarterly* 15, no. 4 (Summer 1962): 6–13; Bosley Crowther, "The Freshman," *The Great Films*, pp. 44–48; and Donald W. McCaffrey, *4 Great Comedians: Chaplin, Lloyd, Keaton, Langdon* (New York: A. S. Barnes and Co., 1968), pp. 60–83.
47. David Martin, "George O'Brien," *Films in Review* 13, no. 9 (November 1962): 541–60; Dorothy B. Jones, "*Sunrise*: A Murnau Masterpiece," *Introduction to the Art of the Film*, pp. 102–29; and Molly Haskell, "Sunrise," *Film Comment* 7, no. 2 (Summer 1971): 16–19.

Rudolph Valentino

Blood and Sand (Paramount—16mm: 1922, 75 min., b/w, silent, R-AUD, RAD; 8mm: S-BLA, ENT, ESO, MOG)
Fred Niblo directed this memorable screen version of Vincent Blasco Ibanez's romantic book about the tragic life of a Spanish bullfighter who is torn between his love for two women, and his love for the bull ring.

The Four Horsemen of the Apocalypse (MGM—16mm: 1921, 120 min., b/w, silent, R-FNC)
Director Rex Ingram brought Rudolph Valentino to stardom in this unusual screen adaptation of Ibanez's novel depicting the fortunes of war, love, and fate. Vincente Minnelli's 1962 remake, starring Glenn Ford, helped further no one's career.[48]

King Vidor

The Big Parade (MGM—16mm: 1925, 130 min., b/w, music and sound effects only, R-FNC)
In this great film, Vidor presented a classic image of war as seen through the experience of three men who fight in France during World War I. The picture not only made John Gilbert a famous leading man, but it also was the first major production of the newly formed M-G-M.[49]

The Crowd (MGM—16mm: 1927, 90 min., b/w, silent, R-FNC)
Director King Vidor also helped write the scenario for this socially conscious film about the dismal existence of an office worker in a large city. The picture gave James Murray's career a short boost of popularity and led to widespread recognition once more for Vidor's talent.[50]

Josef von Sternberg

Underworld (Paramount—16mm: 1927, 89 min., b/w, silent, R-MMA)
Josef von Sternberg directed this prototype of the gangster film and demonstrated his marvelous ability to use artificial reality in a creative and fascinating style. Some good performances by George Bancroft, Clive Brook, and Evelyn Brent.

Erich von Stroheim

Foolish Wives (Universal—16mm: 1922, 80 min., b/w, silent, R-EMG, MMA, RAD/S-MOV)
Despite von Stroheim's lavish production techniques, which resulted in the film's commercial flop, this is an intriguing story about a phony Russian nobleman (von Stroheim) who preys on the frailties of wealthy women visiting on the Riviera.

---

48. George Geltzer, "Hollywood's Handsomest Director," *Films in Review* 3, no. 5 (May 1952) : 213–19.
49. Roi A. Uselton, "Renee Adoree," *Films in Review* 19, no. 6 (June–July 1968) : 345–57; Joel Greenbert, "War, Wheat and Steel: King Vidor Interviewed." *Sight and Sound* 37, no. 4 (Autumn 1968) : 192–97; and Charles Higham, "King Vidor," *Film Heritage* 1, no. 4 (Summer 1966) : 14–25.
50. Vernon L. Schonert, "James Murray," *Films in Review* 19, no. 10 (December 1968) : 618–23; and Bosley Crowther, "The Crowd," *The Great Films*, pp. 66–70.

Greed (MGM—16mm: 1923, 156 min., b/w, silent, R-FNC)

Erich von Stroheim directed and wrote the screenplay of this memorable film adaptation of Frank Norris's novel *McTeague,* the story of a mismatched couple whose growing love for money eventually destroys them both. Outstanding performances by Zasu Pitts, Gibson Gowland, and Jean Hersholt.[51]

Raoul Walsh

The Thief of Bagdad (United Artists—16mm: 1924, 135 min., b/w, silent, R-AUD, EMG, MMA, STA)

Director Walsh took charge of this Douglas Fairbanks spectacular costume film which borrowed many of its special effects ideas from Lang's *Destiny.* Although unpopular among audiences, it stimulated Hollywood to begin once more with spectacular films.[52]

What Price Glory (Fox—16mm: 1926, 120 min., b/w, silent, R-EMG, MMA)

Director Walsh presented a memorable screen adaptation of the play about Flagg and Quirt, the officer and the soldier whose constant bickering underscored the stupidity and human waste that occurred in war. Fine acting turned in by Edmund Lowe, Victor McLaglen, and Dolores del Rio.[53]

SOUND COMES TO AMERICA (1929–1941)

In the silent days, the art of the film had achieved significant action and movement; the length of the motion pictures had increased sufficiently to tell an effective story. With the advent of sound, it was as if the film had begun all over again.[54]

Studio rivalries and mergers once more became rampant. The sound revolution and the Depression destroyed William Fox, forcing his company to merge with Twentieth Century; 2500 theaters folded, putting large companies like Paramount and RKO into receivership in 1933; the International Alliance of Theatrical Stage Employees struck the major studios, foreshadowing the tremendous struggle to come between the producers and the unions; and the Hays office stepped in to produce the strongest self-regulation code in the history of motion pictures.

51. Dennis Marion, "Erich von Stroheim: The Legend and the Fact," *Sight and Sound* 31, no. 1 (Winter 1961–62) : 22–23, 5; Jules V. Schwerin, "The Resurgence of von Stroheim," *Films in Review* 1, no. 3 (April 1950) : 3–6, 43–45; William K. Everson, "Erich von Stroheim 1895–1957," *Films in Review* 8, no. 7 (August–September 1957) : 305–14; and Bosley Crowther, "Greed," *The Great Films,* pp. 39–43.

52. Bosley Crowther, "The Thief of Bagdad," *The Great Films,* pp. 35–38.

53. DeWitt Bodeen, "Dolores del Rio," *Films in Review* 18, no. 5 (May 1967) : 266–83.

54. The following articles are useful: Leslie Halliwell, "Merely Stupendous: Part One," *Films and Filming* 13, no. 5 (February 1967) :4–12; ". . . Part Two," *Films and Filming* 13, no. 6 (March 1967) : 48–56; Leslie Halliwell, ". . . Part Three," *Films and Filming* 13, no. 7 (April 1967) : 44–52; Leslie Halliwell, ". . . Part Four," *Films and Filming* 14, no. 4 (January 1968) : 10–15; Leslie Halliwell, ". . . Part Five," *Films and Filming* 14, no. 5 (February 1968) : 38–44; Leslie Halliwell, ". . . Part Six," *Films and Filming* 14, no. 6 (March 1968) : 42–47; Leslie Halliwell, ". . . Part Seven," *Films and Filming* 14, no. 7 (April 1968: 49–53; Duncan Crow, "The First Golden Age," *Sight and Sound* 23, no. 3 (January–March 1954) : 148–51, 168; and William Thomaier, "Early Sound Comedy," *Films in Review* 9, no. 5 (May 1958) : 254–62.

Experimentation with sound also brought new attempts at revolutionizing screen sizes, acting methods, and screenwriting. But in the midst of this upheaval, certain directors came forward who effectively combined the revolutionary age with the art of the silent film and then furthered the development of the cinema: King Vidor, Lewis Milestone, Mervyn LeRoy, Walt Disney, Ernst Lubitsch, Fritz Lang, Josef von Sternberg, Howard Hawks, James Whale, and Rouben Mamoulian.

Books

General

Bandler, Bernard II *et al.* (editors). *Hound and Horn: Essays on Cinema.* New York: Arno Press, 1972.

From 1929 to 1933, the unique little periodical provided fascinating comments about the trends and developments in the cinema. Among the contributors were Allen Tate, Ezra Pound, Kenneth Burke, Francis Fergusson, and Herbert Read.

* Baxter, John. *Hollywood in the Thirties.* New York: A. S. Barnes and Company, 1968.

This is a useful, comprehensive, and fascinating account of the fabulous 1930s, with an emphasis on the major studios: Metro-Goldwyn-Mayer, Paramount, Warner Brothers, and Universal. Baxter is particularly good at recalling important personalities and pictures and should help in setting the scene for further study in the period. Unfortunately, the book has no bibliography, which is necessary for this type of study.

Bergman, Andrew. *We're in the Money: Depression America and Its Films.* New York: New York University Press, 1971.

Based upon his 1970 University of Wisconsin dissertation, Bergman's book is divided into twelve interesting and informative chapters on the films made in the depression years of 1930–1939. The emphasis is mainly on genres such as gangster movies, screwball comedies, and musicals.

* Blum, Daniel. *A New Pictorial History of the Talkies.* Revisions by John Kobal. New York: G. P. Putnam's Sons, 1968.

Originally issued in 1958, this visual survey of the sound era is hampered by its weak narrative and poor production design.

Davy, Charles (editor). *Footnotes to the Film.* London: Lovat Dickson, Ltd., 1938. Reissued by Arno Press in 1970.

Intended as a practical discussion of studio filmmaking, this book is a valuable guide to the techniques, artists, and movie-going public of the 1930s. The contributors are often key figures like Alfred Hitchcock, Robert Donat, Basil Wright, Graham Greene, Alberto Cavalcanti, John Grierson, Alexander Korda, Alistair Cooke, and Forsyth Hardy. Their brief essays are worthwhile, and the book contains more than 20 interesting illustrations.

* Fredrik, Nathalie. *Hollywood and the Academy Awards.* Foreword by Bob Hope. Beverly Hills: Hollywood Awards Publications, 1970.

A short and concise review of the Academy Awards since 1929, this is a handy reference tool.

Gregg, E. S. *The Shadow of Sound*. New York: Vantage Press, 1968.
Written by a man who was head of the export department of Electrical Research Products Inc.—the new company formed by Western Electric to handle their new sound inventions—this book deals with the turbulent years of the early talkies. Not only is this readable, brief narrative informative on Hollywood and its stars, but it is also very useful on the world scene and the business war that followed the exporting of sound devices to foreign countries.

Higham, Charles and Joel Greenberg. *The Celluloid Muse: Hollywood Directors Speak*. London: Angus and Robertson, Ltd., 1969.
This informative and interesting book provides some helpful information on Hitchcock, Lang, Cukor, Minnelli, Vidor, Wilder, and Milestone. The writing is clear, brief, and enjoyable.

Kiesling, Barrett C. *Talking Pictures: How They are Made, How to Appreciate Them*. Richmond: Johnson Publishing Co., 1937.
This is an interesting but outdated breakdown of the division of labor that went into making the sound motion picture in the early days of the Talkie revolution in films. Throughout the 28 short chapters, the author, a former publicity man with the old Famous Players-Lasky, presents the various roles of technicians, screenwriters, and directors.

Kirsten, Lincoln *et al.* (editors). *Films: A Quarterly of Discussion and Analysis*. Nos. I-IV. New York: Arno Press, 1972.
This unique magazine, with its international flavor, had some of the best contributors on the period 1938–1940—the time covered here—and the editors have taken extracts from the period to show the periodical's worth. Sample writers include Cavalcanti, R. Griffith, Grierson, and Arnheim. There is also some good information on film criticism, production and historical development.

MacPherson, Kenneth and Winifred Bryher (editors). *Close-Up, 1927–1933*. Foreword by Herman Weinberg. Ten Volumes. New York: Arno Press, 1972.
With the aid of a new cumulative index, consisting of three separate parts —author, film title, and subject—prepared especially for this reprint edition, this valuable magazine dealing primarily with aesthetics, theory and criticism provides a valuable addition to film scholarship. It also contains a rare collection of stills.

Maltin, Leonard. *The Great Movie Shorts: Those Wonderful One- and Two-Reelers of the Thirties and Forties*. New York: Crown, 1971.
This is the major source of information for those who want plot synopses and helpful commentaries about the important film personalities and significant shorts of the first two decades of the sound era.

* Maltin, Leonard. *Movie Comedy Teams*. With an Introduction by Billy Gilbert. New York: Signet, 1970.
A brief but handy reference tool, this book summarizes many of the familiar stories about the famous comic teams of American films.

Manchel, Frank. *When Movies Began to Speak*. Englewood Cliffs: Prentice-Hall, Inc., 1969.
Strictly for children. Written as a companion to *When Pictures Began*

to Move, the narrative covers the beginning of sound films originating in 1929 up to the revolutionary developments in film history that took place in the late sixties. In addition, there are many useful illustrations of key films and personalities.

Michael, Paul. *The Academy Awards: A Pictorial History.* New York: Crown, 1964.
This is a simple but attractive introduction to the history of the Awards. It contains a very helpful index.

Naumberg, Nancy (editor). *We Make the Movies.* New York: W. W. Norton and Company, Inc., 1937.
Designed to introduce readers to the fundamentals of film production, this book begins with Jesse Lasky's essay on what it means to be a film producer and follows with articles on story ideas, treatments, designing sets, casting, acting (written by Bette Davis and Paul Muni), sound recording, shooting, cutting, and a concluding chapter on exhibition by Walt Disney. All in all, an interesting and enjoyable reading assignment.

Parish, James Robert. *The Fox Girls.* New Rochelle: Arlington House, 1971.
In a well illustrated and nostalgic text, Parish reviews the careers of fifteen of Twentieth Century-Fox's most famous female stars, including Theda Bara, Loretta Young, Sonja Henie, Betty Grable, Anne Baxter, Jeanne Crain, Marilyn Monroe, and Raquel Welch. Each star's private and public careers are touched on, and a complete filmography is included.

Quigley, Martin Jr. and Richard Gertner. *Films in America, 1929–1969: A Panoramic View of Four Decades of Sound.* New York: Golden Press, 1970.
This book furnishes concise, comprehensive information about 400 significant movies, but fails to make any useful critical analyses. One still, at least, accompanies each film review.

Stern, Seymour and Lewis Jacobs (editors). *Experimental Cinema, 1930–1934.* With a New Cumulative Index. New York: Arno Press, 1972.
Aimed at a leftist audience, this controversial and militant magazine specialized in film aesthetics and Soviet techniques of montage. Among its many worthwhile contributors were Pudovkin, Eisenstein and Dovzhenko.

Scotland, John. *The Talkies.* With a Foreword by Cecil M. Hepworth. New York: The Industrial Book Company, 1931.
Useful for its discussion of the effects of sound development upon the production, distribution, and exhibition of motion pictures, this poorly written account by an unknown author (Scotland is a pseudonym) has over 30 valuable illustrations on equipment and studio conditions.

Seldes, Gilbert. *An Hour with the Movies and the Talkies.* Philadelphia: J. B. Lippincott, 1929.
Here is a provocative and insightful commentary on the significant changes that occurred as the result of sound movies. Seldes is primarily concerned with the industry's inability to produce another Chaplin and the film world's failure to reach its artistic destiny. The author offers some valuable suggestions for today's filmmakers as well.

Seldes, Gilbert. *The Movies Come from America.* With a Preface by Charles Chaplin. New York: Charles Scribner's Sons, 1937.

A general and informal history of the motion picture and the changes that took place in the industry when sound took over. Seldes, a wonderful commentator on a fascinating era, discusses with authority and ease the social, economic, and political forces that shaped the film world up to 1936.

Thrasher, Frederic (editor). *Okay for Sound: How the Screen Found Its Voice.* New York: Duell, Sloan and Pearce, 1946.

Written by a New York University professor of Education, this is a glossy and simplified approach to the development of sound and motion pictures. Most valuable, however, are Thrasher's more than 200 well-selected and reproduced stills of the films and studios of the day.

Film Personalities

Fred Astaire

Thompson, Howard. *Fred Astaire: A Pictorial Treasury of His Films.* New York: Falcon Enterprises, Inc., 1970.

Some rather unimpressive stills and a trite narrative mar what could have been a good study of a key figure in film musicals in the thirties and forties.

Mary Astor

Astor, Mary. *A Life on Film.* With an Introduction by Sumner Locke Elliott. New York: Delacorte Press, 1971.

In this nostalgic and sensitively written narrative, one of the screen's most underrated stars gives an insight into a stormy career which spanned almost 50 years of movie history.

John Barrymore

Alpert, Hollis. *The Barrymores.* New York: The Dial Press, 1964.

In a well-researched and entertaining book, Alpert studies the lives of Ethel, Lionel, and John Barrymore beginning with their theatrical parents in the nineteenth century and ending three generations later with the tragic death of Diana and the uneventful career of John Barrymore, Jr. Some good stills are used; an index is included.

Fowler, Gene. *Good Night, Sweet Prince: The Life and Times of John Barrymore.* Philadelphia: The Blakiston Company, 1944.

In this the best of Barrymore biographies Fowler offers a detailed, valuable, and fascinating inside story of the artist who, at his peak, was one of America's greatest talents. The tragedy of his four marriages and his alcoholic career are all fully treated as are his many triumphs. An index is provided but no stills.

Ingrid Bergman

Quirk, Lawrence J. *The Films of Ingrid Bergman.* New York: The Citadel Press, 1970.

This book offers a good introductory essay, plus the usual fine collection of stills, plot synopses, and cast credits.

Humphrey Bogart

* Gehman, Richard. *Bogart: An Intimate Biography*. Greenwich: Fawcett Publications, 1965.

This is an entertaining but lightweight biography of a very complex personality. Some very interesting stills are included.

Goodman, Ezra. *Bogey: The Good-Bad Guy*. New York: Lyle Stuart, Inc., 1965.

In typical Goodman fashion, this book offers a hard and critical side of Bogart found no where else in the lore that has risen about the great star. No study of the man is complete without the story written here.

* McCarty, Clifford. *Bogey: The Films of Humphrey Bogart*. New York: The Citadel Press, 1970.

This is a good source for information on Bogart's films, complete with synopses, cast credits, and many fine illustrations.

Michael, Paul. *Humphrey Bogart: The Man and His Films*. New York: Bobbs-Merrill, 1965.

Considering its fairly well developed essay and good collection of stills, this has to rate as the best book so far on Bogey.

Frank Capra[55]

* Capra, Frank. *The Name Above the Title: An Autobiography*. New York: The Macmillan Company, 1971.

In one of the best autobiographies to come out of Hollywood, Capra gives a nostalgic, entertaining and critical history not only of his great career, but also of the many famous personalities that crossed his path. Don't miss reading this one.

Gary Cooper

Carpozi, George Jr. *The Gary Cooper Story*. New Rochelle, Arlington House, 1970.

This breezy and fan magazine biography offers only a surface look at one of Hollywood's finest stars. More than 50 pictures, plus a complete filmography help to salvage the value of the text.

* Dickens, Homer. *The Films of Gary Cooper*. New York: The Citadel Press, 1970.

In a well-developed biographical text complete with a fine set of rare stills, Dickens provides the best source of information about the star whose career spanned more than 45 years.

Joan Crawford

* Quirk, Lawrence J. *The Films of Joan Crawford*. New York: The Citadel Press, 1970.

In a brief but valuable overview, Quirk offers a useful guide to one of Hollywood's most versatile and enduring stars. The book gives a good film-

---

55. An interesting monograph to glance at is James R. Silke, ed., *Frank Capra: One Man-One Film* (Washington, D.C.: The American Film Institute, 1971).

ography, including synopses, credits and superb stills from the star's 40 years of movie fame.

George Cukor

* Carey, Gary. *The Films of George Cukor and His Collaborators.* New York: The Museum of Modern Art, 1971.

This sketchy monograph offers a chance to compare the weak film plots of Cukor's films with his artistic nuances in such pictures as *Camille, A Star is Born, Little Women, The Philadelphia Story,* and *David Copperfield.* Carey also includes some of the director's preferences in personalities, places, and things as well as a complete filmography.

Lambert, Gavin. *On Cukor.* New York: G. P. Putnam's Sons, 1972.

In his first nonfiction attempt, screenwriter Lambert provides us with an important and revealing document on one of Hollywood's most enduring directors. The text is based upon extended interviews, sponsored by the American Film Institute's Louis B. Mayer Oral History Fund. There is also a good collection of stills from Cukor's 40 year career.

Bette Davis

Davis, Bette. *The Lonely Life: An Autobiography.* New York: G. P. Putnam's Sons, 1962.

Considered by some film historians to be one of the greatest actresses in the history of motion pictures, Davis gives us a rare and invaluable account of her fabulous career at Warner Brothers. This should be standard reading for those studying Hollywood.

* Ringgold, Gene. *The Films of Bette Davis.* New York: Bonanza Books, 1966.

This book is a useful supplement to the star's autobiography, providing a filmography which includes synopses, credits, and stills.

Marlene Dietrich[56]

* Dickens, Homer. *The Films of Marlene Dietrich.* New York: The Citadel Press, 1968.

This picture book of the great Prussian star is an adequate beginning to a study of her fabulous and long film career. The text, however, is less than adequate.

Frewin, Leslie. *Dietrich: The Story of a Star.* New York: Stein and Day, 1967.

Written by a man who takes extraordinary editorial license with the facts to create dramatic effects, this shoddy book would have been discarded except for 14 good pages of appendixed film credits.

* Kobal, John. *Marlene Dietrich.* New York: E. P. Dutton and Company, 1968.

Kobal combines the best available pictures with the most intelligent sketch

---

56. Three useful articles are Manfred George, "Marlene Dietrich's Beginnings," *Films in Review* 3, no. 2 (February 1952) : 77–80; Arthur Knight, "Marlene Dietrich," *Films in Review* 5, no. 10 (December 1954) : 497–514; and Ronald L. Bowers, "Marlene Dietrich: '54–'70," *Films in Review* 22, no. 1 (January 1971) : 17–22.

to date of the woman whom many historians consider one of the brightest and most talented screen stars in motion picture history.

Walt Disney[57]

* Schickel, Richard. *The Disney Version: The Life, Times, Art and Commerce of Walt Disney.* New York: Simon and Schuster, 1968.

In this unauthorized yet invaluable book, Schickel presents a controversial and fascinating account of Disney's youth, his rise to prominence, the make-up of his incredible empire during the past forty years, and the famous producer's personal problems. The definitive book is yet to be written, but this is a good stopgap in the meantime.

W. C. Fields[58]

* Anobile, Richard J. (editor). *Drat! Being the Encapsulated View of Life by W. C. Fields in his own Words.* Introduction by Ed McMahon. New York: Signet, 1969.

This is a pleasant and entertaining book to pass away an hour. It provides pictures and captions, plus some great throwaway lines like, "If at first you don't succeed, try, try again. Then quit. No use being a damn fool about it. . . ."

* Deschner, Donald. *The Films of W. C. Fields.* Introduction by Arthur Knight. New York: The Citadel Press, 1969.

This text gives a good filmography, including synopses, credits and critical extracts from reviewers. Contains the best stills of the great wit.

Everson, William K. *The Art of W. C. Fields.* New York: Bonanza Books, 1967.

Once more this unusual and first-rate film scholar goes about correcting the mistakes and the distortions of his predecessors in their descriptions of the one and only W. C. Fields. In addition to good descriptions of Fields's movies, Everson provides more than 100 useful illustrations.

Fields, W. C. *Fields for President.* Introduction and Commentary by Michael M. Taylor. New York: Dodd, Mead and Company, 1971.

Originally written in war-torn 1939, this book by one of the most fabulous anti-heroes of the twentieth century provides some amazing views. One of my favorites is his dividing the income tax problem into two divisions, ". . . whether you can add and subtract straight at your tax total; and whether you can pay the total once you arrive at it."

Monti, Carlotta with Cy Rice. *W. C. Fields and Me.* Englewood Cliffs, N.J.: Prentice-Hall, Inc., 1971.

Written by Fields's mistress for fourteen years, this entertaining and behind-the-scenes account of his personal and professional career is a delightful book with which to while away an evening.

---

57. Some worthwhile articles are Walt Disney, "How I Cartooned *Alice*," *Films in Review* 11, no. 5 (May 1951) : 7–12; and Leonard Maltin, "Walt Disney's Films," *Films in Review* 18, no. 7 (October 1967) : 457–69.

58. Two good articles are David Robinson, "Dukenfield Meets McGargle: Creation of a Character," *Sight and Sound* 36, no. 3 (Summer 1967) : 125–29; and Louise Brooks, "The Other Face of W. C. Fields," *Sight and Sound* 40, no. 2 (Spring 1971) : 92–96.

* Taylor, Robert Lewis. *W. C. Fields: His Follies and Fortunes.* New York: Doubleday and Company, 1949.
     This readable and pleasant biography suffers from too much editorial license in recounting the life story and style of the best natural comedian of motion pictures.

F. Scott Fitzgerald

Latham, Aaron. *Crazy Sundays: F. Scott Fitzgerald in Hollywood.* New York: The Viking Press, Inc., 1971.
     In a wonderful combination of biographical criticism and movie folklore, Latham offers a first-rate study of the tragic Fitzgeralds, the great writer's stay at M-G-M where he was bullied and mistreated beyond belief, and the final ordeals at the film colony which killed the man.

Errol Flynn[59]

* Flynn, Errol. *My Wicked, Wicked Ways.* New York: G. P. Putnam's Sons, 1959.
     One of the most candid and bold autobiographies ever to come out of Hollywood, this unusual book reveals the confused and hurt human being behind the public image of a brave and defiant hero. You get to see a different side of Bette Davis and Michael Curtiz by reading of Flynn's negative experiences.

* Thomas, Tony *et al. The Films of Errol Flynn.* Foreword by Greer Garson. New York: The Citadel Press, 1969.
     This is the best source for a filmography, including synopses, credits, and stills of the self-destructive star.

Henry Fonda

Springer, John. *The Fondas. The Films and Careers of Henry, Jane and Peter Fonda.* New York: The Citadel Press, 1970.
     It's fitting that the best part of this profusely illustrated text deals with Henry and not the children who have yet to demonstrate their durability as artists (although Jane is well on her way). The author presents biographies of the three, plus helpful plot synopses complete with cast and technical credits.

John Ford

* Baxter, John. *The Cinema of John Ford.* New York: A. S. Barnes and Company, 1972.
     This informative and serious study of Ford's filmic language and philosophy offers readers a valuable addition to the growing list of material of the great director. The book's major flaws are its lack of a comprehensive and detailed filmography as well as a much-needed index.

* Bogdanovich, Peter. *John Ford.* Berkeley: University of California Press, 1968.

---

     59. John Cutts, "Requiem for a Swashbuckler," *Films and Filming* 17, no. 1 (October 1970) : 14–18; and Gordon Gow, "Swashbuckling," *Films and Filming* 18, no. 4 (January 1972) : 34–40.

In this fascinating and invaluable examination of Ford, the author presents his own personal observations plus the director's own thoughts on his films, his collaborators, and his techniques. The book also contains an extended interview, many helpful stills, and a complete filmography.

Clark Gable

* Essoe, Gabe. *The Films of Clark Gable*. New York: The Citadel Press, 1970.

This is the best available biography of the great star's career, plus a complete filmography and many helpful stills.

Judy Garland

Deans, Mickey and Ann Pinchot. *Weep No More My Lady*. New York: Hawthorne Books, Inc., 1972.

Written by the tragic star's fifth and last husband, this sad and sensitive biography traces Garland's career from the days at M-G-M, where she was mercilessly exploited, to the closing days of her life when Judy Garland appeared to many as a pathetic victim of the star system.

* Steiger, Brad. *Judy Garland*. With a Special Introduction by Joe Cohen. New York: Ace Publishing Corporation, 1969.

This is a breezy and lightweight biography which does not do justice to its subject. Its one redeeming feature is its complete filmography with brief excerpts from the film reviews that appeared when the movies were released.

Tormé, Mel. *The Other Side of the Rainbow with Judy Garland on the Dawn Patrol*. New York: William Morrow and Company, Inc., 1970.

Although not the best book on the subject, this is the most moving because it deals in depth with the warm and wonderful star's television venture, which ended in frustration.

Jean Harlow

* Conway, Michael and Mark Ricci (editors). *The Films of Jean Harlow*. New York: Bonanza Books, 1965.

The best source for Harlow's filmography, including synopses, credits and stills.

Shulman, Irving. *Harlow: An Intimate Biography*. New York: Bernard Geis Associates, 1964.

Based upon the memoirs of Harlow's press agent and friend Arthur Landau, this sensational and behind-the-scenes biography only touches the surface of the lovely and tragic movie queen who died mysteriously at 26.

Howard Hawks[60]

* McBride, Joseph (editor). *Focus on Howard Hawks*. Englewood Cliffs: Prentice-Hall, Inc., 1972.

---

60. For some worthwhile articles, see the following: Peter John Dyer, "Sling the Lamps Low," *Sight and Sound* 31, no. 3 (Summer 1962) : 134–39, 155; Jacques Rivette and François Truffaut, "Howard Hawks," translated by Anne and Thornton K. Brown, *Films in Review* 7, no. 9 (November 1956) : 443–52; Andrew Sarris, "The World of

The editor has collected some unusual material for Hawks's students, including two new articles by Henri Langlois and Peter Bogdanovich, plus a superb essay by Andrew Sarris. In addition, there are a filmography and bibliography.

* Wood, Robin. *Howard Hawks*. New York: Doubleday and Company, 1968.
This well-written and intelligent study of Hawks is primarily a thematic analysis of the great director's work. The seven persuasive and controversial chapters offer good discussions of such films as *Only Angels Have Wings, To Have and Have Not, Rio Bravo, Scarface, The Thing from Another Planet, Red River* and *El Dorado*. Wood also provides a fine filmography and some excellent illustrations.

Katherine Hepburn

* Dickens, Homer. *The Films of Katherine Hepburn*. New York: The Citadel Press, 1970.
In one of the best introductions in this series, Dickens provides the star's many fans with a useful biography plus a lavish amount of stills, plot synopses, and credits.

Kanin, Garson. *Tracy and Hepburn: An Intimate Memoir*. New York: The Viking Press, 1971.
For more than 25 years two of Hollywood's greatest superstars maintained an open but unpublished secret life of their own, while they made nine good movies for M-G-M, Twentieth Century-Fox, and Stanley Kramer. Then following Tracy's death on June 10, 1967 reports filtered into the press about his private life with Miss Hepburn. So it became only a matter of time before one of their personal friends, in this case Kanin, decided to publish what were the behind-the-scenes events. What emerges in this book are two personalities neither personally attractive or likable. Hopefully, more will be done with the couple than the weak attempt so far.

Hedy Lamarr

* Lamarr, Hedy. *Ecstasy and Me: My Life as a Woman*. New York: Macfadden-Bartell, 1966.
This sensational autobiography is a very personal and inside account of the price some women pay to gain success.

Charles Laughton

Brown, William. *Charles Laughton: A Pictorial Treasury of his Films*. New York: Falcon Enterprises, Inc., 1970.
Although the narrative is trite and weak, the stills help salvage the book's value for Laughton fans.

Lanchester, Elsa. *Charles Laughton and I*. London: Faber and Faber, Ltd., 1968.
An entertaining and informative biography, this book describes Laughton as a husband and artist and is invaluable as a guide to his career.

Howard Hawks: Part One," *Films and Filming* 8, no. 10 (July 1962) : 21–23, 48–49; ". . . Part Two," *Films and Filming* 8, no. 11 (August 1962) : 44–48; and Joseph McBride and Michael Wilmington, "Do I Get to Play the Drunk This Time: An Encounter with Howard Hawks," *Sight and Sound* 40, no. 2 (Spring 1971) : 97–100.

Singer, Kurt. *The Laughton Story: An Intimate Story of Charles Laughton.* Philadelphia: The John C. Winston Company, 1954.

Filled with wonderful anecdotes, this biography reveals the actor's zest for life and the esteem in which Laughton was held.

Vivien Leigh

Robyns, Gwen. *Light of a Star.* New York: A. S. Barnes and Company, 1971.

This book, besides being the major source of information on the marvelous Vivien Leigh, is must reading for anyone who wants to seriously study such key films as *Gone with the Wind,* Olivier's *Hamlet* and *A Streetcar Named Desire.* There are also many worthwhile photographs of the British star's public and private life.

Mervyn LeRoy

LeRoy, Mervyn. *It Takes More Than Talent.* New York: Alfred A. Knopf, Inc., 1953.

One of the most enduring and entertaining of Hollywood's famous directors reveals the ins and outs of the movie business with some pleasant anecdotes peppered along the way.

Ernst Lubitsch[61]

* Weinberg, Herman G. *The Lubitsch Touch: A Critical Study of the Great Film Director.* New York: E. P. Dutton and Company, 1968.

Not only is this the first study on Lubitsch but it is also one that will be hard to better. Weinberg, as only he can, presents an in-depth, affectionate biography of the witty, brilliant, and creative king of satire. Also included are interviews, reminiscences, anecdotes, and tributes from Lubitsch's colleagues, excerpts from *Ninotchka* and *Trouble in Paradise,* an excellent filmography, and an invaluable bibliography.

Rouben Mamoulian[62]

* Milne, Tom. *Rouben Mamoulian.* Bloomington: Indiana University Press, 1969.

In this cautious, tender examination of an ignored filmmaker, Milne opens up a new area of study for those interested in an underrated craftsman. The films made by the former Armenian stage director were some of the best of the early sound period: *Applause* (1939), *Dr. Jekyll and Mr. Hyde* (1932), *Queen Christina* (1933), and *Becky Sharp* (1935). After those pictures, his reputation declined, unjustly. By reviewing Mamoulian's collaboration with Tyrone Power—the remakes of *The Mark of Zorro* (1940) and *Blood and Sand* (1941)—students should discover a valuable source of screen entertainment.

The Marx Brothers[63]

Anobile, Richard J. (editor). *Why a Duck? Visual and Verbal Gems from*

61. Andrew Sarris, "Lubitsch in the Thirties: Part One," *Film Comment* 7, no. 4 Winter 1971–72) : 54–57.

62. An interesting interview is available by James R. Silke (editor), *Rouben Mamoulian: Style Is the Man* (Washington, D.C.: The American Film Institute, 1971).

63. Robert Altman *et al.,* "Portrait of the Artist as an Old Man: Groucho Marx," *Take One* 3, no. 1 (September–October 1971) : 10–16; Joe Adamson, "Duck Soup for the Rest of Your Life," *ibid.,* pp. 18–21.

the Marx Brothers Movies. Introduction by Groucho Marx. Preface by Richard F. Shepard. New York: Darien House, Inc., 1971.

This book is a delightful re-creation of the Marx Brothers' films, with over 600 frame blow-ups and captions.

* Crichton, Kyle. *The Marx Brothers.* Abridged Edition. New York: Popular Library Edition, 1952.

Once five sons—Leonard (Chico), Adolph (Harpo), Julius (Groucho), Milton (Gummo), and Herbert (Zeppo)—lived in a house lorded over by their father, whom they nicknamed Frenchy, and wisely administered by their clever mother, Minnie. Unfortunately, this pleasant, easy-going chronology oversimplifies the art and development of Minnie's boys while totally ignoring the importance of such people as S. J. Perelman and Margaret Dumont in the Marx Brothers' films.

* Eyles, Allen. *The Marx Brothers: Their World of Comedy.* New York: A. S. Barnes and Company, 1966.

This invaluable book devotes most of its pages to a discussion of their films, providing fine synopses, good screen credits, some remarkable dialogue, and excellent filmographies. Begin your study with this book.

Marx, Arthur. *Life With Groucho.* New York: Simon and Schuster, 1954.

This affectionate and interesting biography is by Groucho's son. It unfortunately reveals very little about the great comic's techniques.

Marx, Groucho. *Groucho and Me.* New York: Bernard Geis Associates, 1959.

This is an entertaining but nontechnical account of Groucho's view of himself and his career.

Marx, Groucho. *The Groucho Letters: Letters from and to.* New York: Simon and Schuster, 1967.

Surely one of the most unusual collection of letters ever published by a show biz personality, this book offers a variety of laughs connected with men of letters, friends, family and strangers.

Marx, Harpo with Rowland Barber. *Harpo Speaks!* New York: Bernard Geis Associates, 1961.

In the most wonderful of books on the Marx Brothers, the ingenious Harpo tells of his personal and professional lives in critical and entertaining words.

Zimmerman, Paul D. and Burt Goldblatt. *The Marx Brothers and the Movies.* New York: G. P. Putnam's Sons, 1968.

This book covers the same ground as the Eyles text with the same emphasis and scholarship. It lacks the important bibliography, but surpasses its competitors with more than 200 well-chosen photographs and a much higher price.

Mickey Rooney

Rooney, Mickey. *I.E. An Autobiography.* New York: G. P. Putnam's Sons, 1965.

This is a disappointing book about a very talented man whose career started at 15 months of age and ran for the next 50 years on a stormy and exciting course. Readers may find some pleasure in the many candid anecdotes.

Spencer Tracy

Newquist, Roy. *A Special Kind of Magic*. New York: Rand McNally and Company, 1967.

For those who want to know more about *Guess Who's Coming to Dinner*, you will find some valuable and delightful comments about Tracy, Hepburn, Poitier, and Kramer in this unusually candid book.

* Swindell, Larry. *Spencer Tracy: A Biography*. New York: The World Publishing Company, 1969.

Except for the lack of critical commentary on the films made by Tracy, this rare biography presents most of the information available on the man, his lives, and loves.

Orson Welles[64]

* *The Citizen Kane Book, Including "Raising Kane" by Pauline Kael and the Shooting Script by Herman J. Mankiewicz and Orson Welles*. Boston: Little Brown and Company, 1971.

In one of the most widely discussed publications of the past decade, Kael in her original two-part *New Yorker* articles challenged Welles's contributions to the making of *Citizen Kane*. Now we have the material reprinted along with the actual script, more than eighty stills from the film, plus some helpful commentary by Gary Carey on RKO's cutting continuity of the film. Don't miss reading this one, but at the same time take a look at the reactions of people connected with the film itself, for example, George Coulouris and Bernard Herrmann with Ted Gilling, "The Citizen Kane Book," *Sight and Sound* 41, no. 2 (Spring 1972) : 71–73.

* Gottesman, Ronald (editor). *Focus on Citizen Kane*. Englewood Cliffs: Prentice-Hall, Inc., 1971.

This book should be a standard text on the film, not only because of the excellent articles on Welles, but also for the collection of original film revues, filmography, bibliography and index.

Mae West[65]

Weintraub, Joseph (editor). *The Wit and Wisdom of Mae West*. New York: G. P. Putnam's Sons, 1967.

In this collection of high-camp quotations, the fabulous Mae offers us her gawdy and riotous philosophy. A typical example is her classic remark on her films, "Why should I go good when I'm packing them in because I'm bad?"

* West, Mae. *Goodness Had Nothing to do with It*. 2nd ed. Enlarged and Revised. New York: Macfadden-Bartell, 1970.

---

64. Mike Prokosch, "Orson Welles: An Introduction," *Film Comment* 7, no. 2 (Summer 1971) :28–32; and David Bordwell, "Citizen Kane," *ibid.*, pp. 38–47.
65. Eric Braun, "Doing What Comes Naturally: Part I," *Films and Filming* 17, no. 1 (October 1970) : 27–28, 30–32; "Part II," *Films and Filming* 17, no. 2 (November 1970) : 38–42; and Steven V. Roberts, "76—And Still Diamond Lil," *The New York Times Magazine* Sunday, November 2, 1969, pp. 64–65, 67, 70–82.

Until someone else takes a more critical look at this lusty and delightful entertainer, Mae's autobiography should stand as the definitive work on her career.

Films

Musicals of the Thirties Anthology. (16mm: n.d., 78 min., b/w, sound, R-MMA)

Some useful excerpts are available from the following films: *Rio Rita* (1929), floorshow sequence; *42nd Street* (1933), "Shuffle off to Buffalo" and "Young and Healthy" sequences; *Gold Diggers of 1933,* Busby Berkeley[66] sequence; *Gold Diggers of 1935,* Busby Berkeley sequence; *Flying Down to Rio* (1933), "Carioca" sequence; *Music in the Air* (1934), excerpt with Gloria Swanson; and *In Caliente* (1935), "The Lady in Red" sequence.

Mervyn LeRoy[67]

I Am a Fugitive From a Chain Gang (Warners—16mm: 1932, 90 min., b/w, sound, R-ADF, CON, UAS)

Rarely in screen history has there been a more powerful attack on prison injustices than in this haunting and memorable story, based upon Robert Elliott Burn's semi-autobiographical novel, dealing with the misery and suffering of an ex-soldier (Paul Muni) unjustly placed on a Georgia chain gang.

Little Caesar (Warners—16mm: 1930, 80 min., b/w, sound. R-AUD, CON, TWF, UAS, WIL)

Another example of the artistic achievements of intelligent directors is Mervyn LeRoy's film about the petty gangster who rises to power in the rackets. The film illustrates how sound played a subordinate role to the picture and filmic technique. Its straightforward, economical cutting, with each sequence growing out of a particular detail, provided an organizational unity that only a first-rate craftsman could achieve. Excellent in its feeling for pace (dialogue was kept terse, images were cut to the essential) and sharp in characterization. The movie still remains as one of the classic examples of the gangster genre.[68]

Sound Film Anthology (16mm: n.d., 75 min., b/w, sound, R-MMA)

Some examples of camera technique, which once again became inflexible because of the limited knowledge of how to make the microphone mobile and how to use sound effectively in coordination with motion can be seen in this film "anthology." It includes excerpts from *The Jazz Singer* (1927), which was billed as a "talkie" but was essentially silent. One can see in the various scenes where sound is used how the actors had to stand close to a hidden microphone in order to be heard and filmed at the same time. A

---

66. William Murray, "The Return of Busby Berkeley," *The New York Times Magazine,* Sunday, March 2, 1969, pp. 26–27, 46, 48, 51, 53–54, 56, 58; Patrick Brion and René Gilson, "A Style of Spectacle: Interview with Busby Berkeley," *Cahiers du Cinema in English* 2, CdC no. 174 (January 1966): 26–37; Ralph Crandall, "Filmography," *ibid.,* pp. 38–41; and Jean-Louis Comolli, "Dancing Images: Busby Berkeley's Kaleidoscope," *idem.,* pp. 22–25.

67. Mervyn LeRoy, "The Making of Mervyn LeRoy," *Films in Review* 4, no. 5 (May 1953): 220–25.

68. Robert C. Roman, "Edward G. Robinson," *Films in Review* 17, no. 7 (August–September 1966): 419–34; and Allen Eyles, "Edward G. Robinson," *Films and Filming* 10, no. 4 (January 1964): 13–17.

second selection is *Lights of New York* (1927), the first all-talking picture, which reveals the early and naive preoccupations with sound. The players say anything as long as they keep talking, and the film demonstrates the artistic inferiority of the first sound motion pictures. In addition, this anthology includes *Shaw Talks for Movietone* (1927), a whimsical monologue by the eminent dramatist, which exemplifies the sound film's reaching out for new material, in this case getting famous people to speak for the movies; *The Sex Life of the Polyp* (1928), a funny monologue by Robert Benchley, which illustrates one of the first attempts at sustained dialogue; and *Steamboat Willie* (1928), not only the first Mickey Mouse cartoon to be shown publicly, but also an inventive approach to some of the mechanical problems involved in recording sound with motion.

Film Personalities

John Barrymore[69]

Svengali (Warners—16mm: 1931, 76 min., b/w, sound, R-STA, UAS)
    Archie Mayo directed this third version of George du Maurier's romantic novel about the evil genius Svengali (Barrymore) who hypnotized the beautiful Trilby (Marian Marsh). Don't miss Barrymore in this one.

Frank Capra

It Happened One Night (Columbia—16mm: 1934, 105 min., b/w, sound, R-COL)
    One of the great screwball comedies of the thirties, this excellent film presented Clark Gable as the tough, wisecracking newspaperman who catches up with Claudette Colbert, a runaway, spoiled brat. The movie remains today the most honored film by the Academy, receiving all four of the top Oscars (actor, actress, director, and film), plus an Oscar for screenwriting (Robert Riskin).

Lost Horizon (Columbia—16mm: 1937, 120 min., b/w, sound, R-AUD, CCC, CHA, CON, CWF, IDE, TWF, TWY/L-COL)
    Capra was at his best in adapting James Hilton's imaginative novel to the screen. Ronald Colman plays the kidnapped Englishman who finds his utopia in the mysterious Shangri-la, hidden away in the Tibetan mountains. Sam Jaffe is outstanding as the aged High Lama.

Merian C. Cooper and Ernest Schoedsack

King Kong (RKO—16mm: 1933, 100 min., b/w, sound, R-FNC, JAN)
    Directed and conceived by Merian C. Cooper and Ernest Schoedsack, this all-time fantasy classic recounts the story of a giant ape whose love for a beautiful woman (Fay Wray) destroys him. The film's special effects remain today as some of the best ever made.[70]

---

69. Spencer M. Berger, "The Film Career of John Barrymore," *Films in Review* 3, no. 10 (December 1952) : 481–99.
70. Bosley Crowther, "King Kong," *The Great Films*, pp. 92–97. See also Chapter 2 for further information of this horror film.

William Dieterle

The Story of Louis Pasteur (Warners—16mm: 1935, 87 min., b/w, sound, R-UAS)
   In this first of three outstanding biographies for Warner Brothers, Dieterle told of the struggle and prejudice that the great chemist (Paul Muni) had to overcome in his fight against disease and jealous colleagues.

W. C. Fields

Million Dollar Legs (Paramount—16mm: 1932, 65 min., b/w, sound, R-MMA, SWA, UNI)
   Director Edward F. Cline handled W. C. Fields in his first talking role as the President of Klopstokia. Picture is filled with knock-about comedy, wild chase scenes, and hilarious gags. Jack Oakie and Ben Turpin assist with the laughs.

John Ford[71]

The Informer (RKO—16mm: 1935, 91 min., b/w, sound, R-AUD, FNC, IDE, JAN)
   This sensitive and powerful film dealt with the pathetic Gypo Nolan (Victor McLaglen) who betrayed his friend for a handful of money. The music and the sets cannot be praised enough. Academy Awards went to Ford, McLaglen, screenwriter Dudley Nichols and musical director Max Steiner.

Stagecoach (United Artists—16mm: 1939, 96 min., b/w, sound, R-ROA, STA)
   John Wayne became a star in this memorable film about a stagecoach ride across the Arizona plains in the 1870s.

Greta Garbo

Camille (MGM—16mm: 1936, 108 min., b/w, sound, R-FNC)
   Director George Cukor did a masterful job in guiding Garbo to a New York Critics Award as the tragic, beautiful courtesan in 19th-century Paris who was capable of a great, unselfish love.

Grand Hotel (MGM—16mm: 1932, 115 min., b/w, sound, R-FNC)
   Producer Irving Thalberg deserves the credits for this remarkable film about the variety of people who populate a ritzy hotel. Among the stars were Greta Garbo, John Barrymore, Joan Crawford,[72] Wallace Beery, Lionel Barrymore,[73] Jean Hersholt, and Lewis Stone. The director was Edmund Goulding.

Ninotchka (MGM—16mm: 1939, 110 min., b/w, sound, R-FNC)

---

71. Lindsay Anderson, "John Ford," *Cinema* 6, no. 3 (Spring 1971) : 21–36; and Joseph McBride and Michael Wilmington, "Prisoner of the Desert," *Sight and Sound* 40, no. 4 (Autumn 1971) : 210–14.
   72. Lawrence J. Quirk, "Joan Crawford," *Films in Review* 7, no. 10 (December 1956) : 481–501; Ronald L. Bowers, "Joan Crawford's Latest Decade," *Films in Review* 17, no. 6 (June–July 1966) : 366–68; and Eric Braun, "Forty Years a Queen: The Joan Crawford Story," *Films and Filming* 11, no. 8 (May 1965) : 7–14.
   73. Bert Gray, "A Lionel Barrymore Index," *Films in Review* 13, no. 4 (April 1962) : 220–29.

Lubitsch directed this brilliant, cynical comedy about a priggish Russian trade official (Garbo) who finds herself in love with a devil-may-care capitalist (Melvyn Douglas).

Queen Christina (MGM—16mm: 1933, 100 min., b/w, sound, R-FNC)
Rouben Mamoulian directed Garbo and Gilbert in this romanticized story of a young girl, reared as a boy, who became a 17th-century queen of Sweden. A must for Garbo devotees.[74]

Howard Hawks

Bringing Up Baby (MGM—16mm: 1938, 102 min., b/w, sound, R-FNC)
Still one of the funniest films ever made, this madcap adventure involves an inhibited professor (Cary Grant) and a zany millionairess (Katherine Hepburn) who become involved with a runaway leopard and a hunt for a missing dinosaur bone.

Ernst Lubitsch

The Man I Killed (Paramount—16mm: 1931, 3 min., b/w, sound, R-MMA)
This short extract from Ernst Lubitsch's film deals with a sequence on Armistice Day in 1919 in France, suggesting the irony of the occasion. The original title of the film is *Broken Lullaby*.

Trouble in Paradise (Paramount—16mm: 1932, 86 min., b/w, sound, R-MMA, UNF, UNI)
Ernst Lubitsch directed this zany comedy of daring jewel thieves starring Herbert Marshall, Miriam Hopkins, and Kay Francis. Lubitsch considered it his best film.

The Marx Brothers

A Day at the Races (MGM—16mm: 1937, 105 min., b/w, sound, R-FNC)
Sam Wood directed this wild and zany story, in which the Marx Brothers are involved with running a sanatorium, which depends for its future on the good spirits of Margaret Dumont and a horse's fast reaction to a vicious man's picture.[75]

Duck Soup (Paramount—16mm: 1933, 70 min., b/w, sound, R-CON, MMA, SWA, UNI, WHO)
Director Leo McCarey teamed up with the zany Marx Brothers to wreak havoc on the sensible logic of the mythical kingdom of Fredonia. The tiny bankrupt nation is ordered by its wealthy benefactress (Margaret Dumont) to appoint as head of state Rufus T. Firefly (Groucho Marx) and no one has ever been the same since.[76]

A Night at the Opera (MGM—16mm: 1935, 90 min., b/w, sound, R-FNC)
Wood directed this greatest of the Marx Brothers films which involved the boys and Dumont in arranging a debut for friends at the New York Opera.

74. David Robinson, "Painting the Leaves Black: Rouben Mamoulian Interviewed," *Sight and Sound* 30, no. 3 (Summer 1961): 123–27.
75. Jerome S. Simon, "George Seaton," *Films in Review* 22, no. 9 (November 1971): 521–40.
76. Serge Davey and Jean-Louis Noames, "Taking Chances, Interview with Leo McCarey," *Cahiers du Cinema in English* 7, CdC no. 163 (February 1965): 42–54.

Lewis Milestone

All Quiet on the Western Front (Universal—16mm: 1930, 103 min., b/w, sound, R-CCC, CON, SWA, UNI/L-UNI)
Lewis Milestone's film version of the Erich Remarque novel about the First World War and the disillusioned German youth caused an uproar when it first appeared, mainly because of its sensational (for the times) camera mobility and cutting complexity. Also there was Lew Ayres's brilliant performance.

W. S. Van Dyke

San Francisco (MGM—16mm: 1936, 115 min., b/w, sound, R-FNC)
One of the best-loved films of the thirties, this far-fetched story, involving a saloon keeper (Clark Gable), an opera singer (Jeanette MacDonald), and a tough priest (Spencer Tracy), dealt with the fall of the Barbary Coast.

The Thin Man (MGM—16mm: 1934, 93 min., b/w, sound, R-FNC)
Myrna Loy and William Powell starred magnificently in this first screen presentation of Dashiel Hammett's funny and clever detective family who offer you both wit and suspense.

George Stevens

Gunga Din (RKO—16mm: 1939, 129 min., b/w, sound, R-FNC, JAN)
One of the most popular and entertaining films of the 1930s, this action-packed version of Rudyard Kipling's famous poem, starred Cary Grant, Douglas Fairbanks, Jr., and Victor McLaglen as the rugged British officers who save their regiment and learn the worth of an Indian watercarrier (Sam Jaffe).

King Vidor

Hallelujah (MGM—16mm: 1929, 107 min., b/w, sound, R-FNC)
King Vidor's film is an example of how the creative director effectively handled the problem of using sound with motion rather than relying on each as a separate entity. This motion picture is not only the first all-black sound film, but it is also one of the most important art films of the early thirties. Strangely enough, it's in the singing sequences that Vidor's cinematic skill is weakest.[77]

Josef von Sternberg

The Blue Angel (Germany—16mm: 1929, 94 min., b/w, sound, R-CFS, CON, EMG, JAN, STA/S-MOV)
Although made in Germany, this film about a staid schoolteacher (Emil Jannings) and his tragic love affair with a two-bit cabaret singer (Marlene Dietrich) brought Dietrich to Hollywood and started a memorable relationship in films between the star and her great director.

Morocco (Paramount—16mm: 1930, 92 min., b/w, sound, R-MMA, UNI)

---

77. Curtis Harrington, "The Later Years: King Vidor's Hollywood Progress," *Sight and Sound* 22, no. 4 (April–June 1953): 179–82, 203; and Herbert G. Luft, "King Vidor: A Career that Spans Half a Century," *The Film Journal* 1, no. 2 (Summer 1971): 26–46, 64–71.

Director Josef von Sternberg, after his great success the year before with Marlene Dietrich in *The Blue Angel,* now introduced his brilliant discovery to Hollywood and co-starred her with Gary Cooper and Adolph Menjou in a sexy love story of one woman's sacrifice for the French Foreign Legion. Even today one is amazed at von Sternberg's ability to retain the best of his silent techniques at a time when sound so dominated production techniques.

James Whale

Frankenstein (Universal—16mm: 1931, 71 min., b/w, sound, R-UNI)
James Whale directed this early sound masterpiece of Mary Shelley's novel about a monster who was more sinned against than sinner. Bela Lugosi always regretted that he had turned down the key role because the make-up would have disguised his suave appearance. But it made Boris Karloff a famous star.[78]

Orson Welles

Citizen Kane (RKO—16mm: 1941, 119 min., b/w, sound, R-AUD, CHA, FNC, IDE, JAN/L-FNC)
In this classic film about the meaning and values of a deceased tycoon, Welles set the standards by which great movies were to be measured.

Mae West

I'm No Angel (Paramount—16mm: 1933, 88 min., b/w, sound, R-UNI)
Wesley Ruggles directed Miss West as the honky-tonk dancer who has a flaming romance with a rich playboy (Cary Grant). In this film she issues the famous line, "Beulah, peel me a grape."

She Done Him Wrong (Paramount—16mm: 1933, 68 min., b/w, sound, R-MMA, UNI)
Lowell Sherman directed Mae West in her most famous role as the Bowery bombshell in the 1890s who captivated even the Salvation Army's legal eagle (Cary Grant). This is the film where she delivers the famous line, "Come up 'n' see me some time," and sings the suggestive songs, "Easy Rider," and "A Guy What Takes His Time."

THE FRENCH FEATURE FILM (1933–1945)[79]

Of all the European countries, France proved to be the most resilient when it came to revolution and art. While national cinemas like those of

---

78. William Thomaier, "James Whale," *Films in Review* 13, no. 5 (May 1962) : 278–90; Lillian Gerard, "Boris Karloff: The Man Behind the Myth," *Film Comment* 6, no. 1 (Spring 1970) : 46–48; Gordon Hitchens, "Historical Notes on Dr. Frankenstein and his Monster," *idem.,* pp. 49–51; and Paul Jensen, "James Whale," *Film Comment* 7, no. 1 (Spring 1971) : 52–57.
79. The following articles are useful: Louis Marcorelles, "French Cinema . . . The Old and the New," *Sight and Sound* 27, no. 4 (Spring 1958) : 190–95; Penelope Houston, "The Rewards of Quality," *Sight and Sound* 31, no. 2 (Spring 1964) : 71–72; Peter John Dyer, "Journey into the Night," *Films and Filming* 5, no. 10 (July 1959) : 12–14, 32–33; and Peter John Dyer, "Some Personal Visions,"*Films and Filming* 5, no. 2 (November 1958) : 13–15, 30–31; and Ronald H. Blumer, "The Camera as Snowball: France 1918–1927," *Cinema Journal* 9, no. 2 (Spring 1970) : 31–39.

Germany, Britain, and Russia depended heavily on government support, the French filmmaker prided himself on his independence and his individuality. Starting with the fiery Louis Delluc and his impressionistic school of filmmaking in the early twenties, a new group of artists began to emerge in the years just before the coming of sound: René Clair, Jacques Feyder, Jean Renoir, and Jean Vigo. France also became the haven for film refugees like Fritz Lang, Erich Pommer, Luis Buñuel, and Carl Dreyer. In spite of the staggering blow that the transition to sound dealt the French industry, these amazing artists continued their experimentations with new forms of story-telling, avant-garde projects, and psychological characterization.

Books

General

* Armes, Roy. *French Film.* New York: E. P. Dutton and Company, 1970.
This is a good and useful brief introduction to more than 40 major French directors. Many well chosen stills have been included.

* "The Art of the Cinema," *Yale French Studies* 17 (Summer 1956).
For those in search of critical material on pre-World War II French directors, this valuable monograph offers information on Ophuls, Cocteau, Clouzot, Renoir, plus some worthwhile commentary on *La Strada* and neorealism.

Sadoul, Georges. *French Film.* London: The Falcon Press, 1953. Reprinted by Arno Press in 1972.
This short and useful history of French films displays Monsieur Sadoul's great love for his country's work. Throughout his ten interesting chapters, this prolific writer presents many interesting insights into the cultural, economic, and artistic setting that produced so many outstanding artists. Don't miss his chapter on French cinema during the German occupation and its influence on Feyder, Renoir, Duvivier, and Carné.

Directors

Luis Buñuel[80]

Durgnat, Raymond. *Luis Buñuel.* Berkeley: University of California Press, 1967.
This very impressionistic and highly informative critic does a wonderful job in his early chapters on the great Spanish film exile, and no one has yet offered any analysis nearly so detailed as Durgnat's study of *Un Chien Andalou.* Even though Buñuel's other 26 films suffer by comparison, this should be a good source book for serious students. It comes with useful stills and a very helpful filmography and bibliography.

* *L'Age d'Or/Un Chien Andalou: Films by Luis Buñuel.* Translated from the French by Marianne Alexandre. New York: Simon and Schuster, 1968. Film Scripts.

---

80. Although Buñuel and Dreyer (listed below) are not French, they were working in France during this period.

Marcel Carné

* *Le Jour se Leve: A Film by Marcel Carné and Jacques Prévert*. Translated and described by Dinah Brooke and Nicola Hayden. New York: Simon and Schuster, 1970. Film script.

René Clair[81]

Clair, René. *Reflections on the Cinema*. London: William Kimber, 1953
   An outstanding French film director reminisces about the growth of the motion picture as an art form and provides the reader with insights into filmmaking. Clair, in particular, provides some additional insights on such artists as Griffith, Eisenstein, von Stroheim, Chaplin, and Douglas Fairbanks, Sr.

Clair, René. *Clair: Four Screenplays—Le Silence Est d'Or, La Beauté du Diable, Les Belles-de-Nuit, Les Grandes Manoeuvres*. Translated from the French by Piergiuseppe Bozzetti. New York: The Orion Press, 1970.

* *A Nous La Liberté/Entr'acte: Films by René Clair:* English Translation and Description of the Action by Richard Jacques and Nicola Hayden. New York: Simon and Schuster, 1970.

Carl Dreyer

* Milne, Tom. *The Cinema of Carl Dreyer*. New York: A. S. Barnes and Company, 1971.
   In a critical and valuable narrative, Milne examines how one of the screen's greatest directors was only able to make 14 films in 50 years. Some good stills plus a filmography are included.

* *Carl Theodor Dreyer: Four Screenplays—Passion of Joan of Arc/Vampyr/ Day of Wrath/Ordet*. Translated by Oliver Stallybrass. Introduction by Ole Storm. Bloomington: University of Indiana Press, 1970.

Jean Renoir

Braudy, Leo. *Jean Renoir: The World of His Films*. New York: Doubleday and Company, Inc., 1972.
   This excellent book on one of the cinema's greatest masters explores Renoir's cinematic genius in lucid, detailed and absorbing prose. Of particular interest is Braudy's treatment of the basic relationships in the filmmaker's art; the stage contrasted with realism, the magical versus the mechanical, the flexible versus the inflexible, and the social commitment contrasted with an aesthetic distance. Stills, a filmography, and an index are also provided.

* Leprohon, Pierre. *Jean Renoir*. Translated by Brigid Elson. New York: Crown Publishers, Inc., 1971.
   Originally published in 1967, this invaluable text serves as a perfect companion piece to the Braudy book, not only because of Leprohon's excellent biographical and critical essay, but also because it contains so much original, textual material on Renoir, including script excerpts, critical re-

views of his films, and first-hand observations by such artists as Cocteau and André-G. Brunelin. A filmography, bibliography and index are also included.

* *Grand Illusion: A Film by Jean Renoir*. Translated from the French by Marianne Alexandre and Andrew Sinclair. New York: Simon and Schuster, 1968. Film Script.

Jean Vigo

* Gomes, P. E. Salles. *Jean Vigo*. Translated by Allan Francovich. Berkeley: University of California Press, 1972.

In this useful and well-written biographical and critical study, Gomes offers an unusual portrait of a superb artist who made sharp and powerful social comments in his four important films before he died at 29.

* Smith, John M. *Jean Vigo*. New York: Praeger Publishers, Inc., 1972.

In this second-best account of Vigo's significant work, Smith presents some interesting and controversial comments about the relationship between the films and the critics over the years. Some good stills are provided along with a useful bibliography.

Films

Jean Benoit-Levy

La Maternelle (16mm: 1932, 86 min., b/w, English subtitles, sound, R-CON, MMA)

Jean Benoit-Levy and Marie Epstein's case study of an unwanted child is not only an example of the period's concern with psychological insight and concentrated characterization, but is also one of the early uses of the documentary approaches in a film.

Luis Buñuel[82]

Un Chien Andalou (16mm: 1928, 30 min., b/w, silent, R-AUD)

Luis Buñuel and Salvador Dali, two young Spaniards newly settled in Paris, combined their talents to make the most famous surrealistic film in movie history. It defies "logic," as the artists tried to present their insights and interpretation of Freudian psychology.

Alberto Cavalcanti

Rien que les Heures (16mm: 1926, 45 min., b/w, silent, R-MMA)

A dawn-to-dusk chronicle of the streets of Paris by the Brazilian ex-architect Alberto Cavalcanti, who, influenced by the French impressionist school of painting, avoids making any significant social commentary on the city.

82. Some useful articles are Tony Richardson, "The Films of Luis Buñuel," *Sight and Sound* 23, no. 3 (January–March 1954) : 125–30; Derek Prouse, "Interviewing Buñuel," *Sight and Sound* 29, no. 3 (Summer 1960) : 118–19; Robert M. Hammond, "Luis Alcoriza and the Films of Luis Buñuel," *Film Heritage* 1, no. 1 (Fall 1965) : 24–34; Peter Harcourt, "Luis Buñuel: Spanish and Surrealist," *Film Quarterly* 20, no. 3 (Spring 1967) : 2–19; J. F. Aranda, "Surrealist and Spanish Giant: First Part of An Analysis of Buñuel's Work for the Cinema," *Films and Filming* 8, no. 1 (October 1961) : 17–18; J. F. Aranda, ". . . Second Part," *Films and Filming* 8, no. 2 (November 1961) : 29–30, 45; and Alf MacLochlainn, "Pointed Horror: The Films of Luis Buñuel and Georges Franju," *The Film Journal* 1, no. 2 (Summer 1971) : 16–21.

Marcel Carné[83]

The Children of Paradise (16mm: 1946, 188 min., b/w, English subtitles, sound, R-CON)
   In one of the most moving and sensitive films in screen history, Carné and his screenwriter Jacques Prévert intertwined the lives of the Shakespearean actor Frédérick Lemaître (Pierre Braseur), the mime Debureau (Jean-Louis Barrault), the cynical villain Lacenaire (Marcel Herrand) and the woman who enchanted them all, Garance (Arletty).[83]

Le Jour se Leve (16mm: 1940, 85 min., b/w, English subtitles, sound, R-JAN)
   In this tragic story, Carné and Prévert demonstrated artistic greatness as they depicted the tale of a common man in love with a flower-girl who accidentally enters a world of crime and eventual death. Jean Gabin beautifully acted the part of a man unable to escape his destiny. Arletty, playing the role of a tramp, clearly foreshadowed her brilliant performance in *The Children of Paradise.*

René Clair

Entr'acte (16mm: 1924,   min., b/w, silent, R-MMA)
   Prepared especially as an intermission piece between the two acts of the ballet *Relache,* this impressionistic film is an avant-garde work showing a series of disconnected images.

The Italian Straw Hat (16mm: 1927, 76 min., b/w, English subtitles, sound, R-CON)
   This magnificent comedy deals with a befuddled bridegroom who finds himself obligated to save a lady's honor by replacing her unique straw hat. Albert Préjean had the lead role.

Le Million (16mm: 1930, 90 min., b/w, no English titles, sound, R-MMA)
   This is one of the only available examples of René Clair's experimental genius in treating motion with sound. It is the story of a penniless Bohemian whose fortune rests on a lottery ticket. There is a remarkable use by Clair of counterpoint and demonstrates the broad appeal of his screen technique.

A Nous la Liberté (16mm: 1931, 87 min., b/w, sound, English subtitles, R-CON)
   René Clair's memorable film is an example of the traditional technique in filmmaking and involves a satire on the industrial age, and man's eventual revolt against mass production.[84]

Sous les Toits de Paris (16mm: 1930, 80 min., b/w, sound, English subtitles, R-AUD)
   This was the early sound film about young love in the Paris garrets which set the great writer-director on his way to immortality.

Jean Cocteau

Blood of a Poet (16mm: 1932, 51 min., b/w, English subtitles, sound, R-AUD)

---

83. Nancy Warfield, "Notes on Les Enfants du Paradis," *The Little Film Gazette of N.D.W.* 2, no. 1 (March 1967).
84. Bosley Crowther, *"A Nous la liberté,"* *The Great Films,* pp. 88–91.

Cocteau began his first of many intriguing and puzzling film poems with this complex screenplay about a poet who has "to die" in order to be "reborn" as a true artist.

Carl Th. Dreyer

The Passion of Joan of Arc (16mm: 1928, 61 min., b/w, music and sound effects only, R-AUD, EMG, FCE/S-FCE)
Dreyer's masterpiece, done mainly in close-ups, re-creates the last days of the martyred peasant girl (Falconetti) and her execution. A great deal of credit also goes to the Polish cameraman Rudolph Maté, for his brilliant photography.

Germaine Dulac

The Sea Shell and the Clergyman (16mm: 1928, 38 min., b/w, silent, R-MMA)
This surrealistic film by Germaine Dulac about an impotent priest who in his dream-world pursues his ideal woman is an example of the filmmaker's attempt in the 1920s to create a unique French cinema. Not surprisingly, many censors failed to understand that the illogical images in the cryptic movie were mainly Freudian phallic and castration symbols.

Marcel Pagnol

The Baker's Wife (16mm: 1938, 120 min., b/w, English subtitles, sound, R-CON)
In one of the most remarkable reproductions of provincial life, Pagnol showed what happens when the baker (Raimu) has marital problems.

Jean Renoir

La Grande Illusion (16mm: 1937, 111 min., b/w, sound, R-JAN)
Another traditional approach, as opposed to an avant-garde method, is Jean Renoir's great anti-war film about a German prisoner-of-war camp for Allied soldiers. The Renoir–Charles Spaak script still remains one of the high marks in screen filmwriting.

La Règle de Jeu (16mm: 1939, 110 min., b/w, English subtitles, sound, R-JAN)
A wonderful illustration of counterpoint is Jean Renoir's satirical story of a man too sensitive for his pre-World War II society. This classic satire is a superb attack on the pre-World War II morality and mentality of the French nobility.[85]

Jean Vigo

L'Atalante (16mm: 1934, 82 min., b/w, English subtitles, sound, R-AUD)
This story is a lyrical expression of newlyweds and their problems aboard a barge. Vigo had a unique gift for mixing reality with lyricism, and some of that magic still comes through in this 16mm print.[86]

85. Jacques Joly, "Between Theater and Life: Jean Renoir and *Rules of the Games*," translated by Randall Conrad, *Film Quarterly* 21, no. 2 (Winter 1967–68) : 2–9; and Richard Whitehall, "Great Films of the Century: *La Règle du Jeu*," *Films and Filming* 9, no. 2 (November 1962) : 21–25. The script is available from Simon and Schuster.
86. Eric Rhode, "Jean Vigo," *Tower of Babel*, pp. 17–34.

Zéro de Conduite (16mm: 1933, 44 min., b/w, sound, English subtitles, R-AUD)

This is the first feature-length movie made by Jean Vigo and concerns life in a French boarding school. Its marvelous irony, satire, and great sensitivity to the oppressiveness of incompetent school teachers make the film a useful reminder to educators as to what teaching is all about.

THE DOCUMENTARY FILM IN GREAT BRITAIN AND AMERICA (1933–1945)[87]

The development of sound contributed to the growth of the documentary film. Although Flaherty had fathered the genre, it was John Grierson, a Scotsman, who provided the form with a label and a new direction. In Flaherty's movies, the emphasis was on showing man in relation to nature. In Grierson's work and that of his peers, the emphasis shifted to a realistic depiction of the problems of everyday people living in a complex, industrial environment. These filmmakers saw in the filmed documentary a unique opportunity to influence the ideas, emotions, and attitudes of a complacent public.[88]

Books

Baechlin, Peter and Maurice Muller-Strauss. *Newsreels Across the World.* New York: UNESCO, 1952.

A short but useful coverage of the history of newsreels and their production-distribution difficulties.

Balcon, Michael *et al.* (editors). *Twenty Years of British Films 1925–1945.* London: Falcon Press, 1947. Reissued by Arno Press in 1972.

A general introduction by periods to the history of British films, with comments by Forsyth Hardy on the documentary movement. There are many illustrations in this short book. Unfortunately it has no index, bibliography, or screen credits.

* Gifford, Denis. *British Cinema: An Illustrated Guide.* New York: A. S. Barnes and Company, 1968.

This is a wonderful, handy reference work to over 5000 films, dozens of leading artists and directors, and it has more than 100 photographs of important personalities.

Hardy, Forsyth (editor). *Grierson on Documentary.* New York: Harcourt, Brace and Company, 1947. Reissued in 1966.

This valuable collection of Grierson's writings shows the philosophy of

---

87. Some useful articles are David Robinson, "Looking for Documentary I: The Background to Production," *Sight and Sound* 27, no. 1 (Summer 1957): 6–11; and David Robinson, ". . . Part II," *Sight and Sound* 27, no. 2 (Autumn 1957): 70–75.

88. For additional information, see Raymond Fielding, "Mirror of Discontent: *The March of Time* and Its Politically Controversial Film Issues," *The Wisconsin Political Quarterly* 12, no. 1 (March 1959): 145–52; and Raymond Fielding, "Time Flickers Out: Notes on the Passing of the *March of Time*," *The Quarterly of Film, Radio, and Television* 11, no. 4 (Summer 1957): 354–60.

the documentary movement with its emphasis on subordinating form to content. A standard work for all film students.

Hopkinson, Peter. *Split Focus*. London: Hart-Davis, 1969.
Written by a British filmmaker who went through World War II, this excellent book provides invaluable information about the stock footage that is used in so many movies and television programs. Hopkinson recounts what it was like making the original films, but more important he writes about the political philosophy of the times, the people, and the filmmakers. It is one of the most worthwhile books to come out of the 1960s.

* Ivens, Joris. *The Camera and I*. New York: International Publishers, 1969.
In this revealing and fascinating autobiography of a documentary film-maker who's been around for more than 70 years we catch some valuable glimpses of the avant-garde movements of the 1920s, the great Russian directors and theorists, as well as the profound and dedicated thoughts of a committed human being.

* Jacobs, Lewis (editor). *The Documentary Tradition: From Nanook to Woodstock*. New York: Hopkinson and Blake, 1971.
In what amounts to the first real attempt to survey the documentary tradition, Jacobs tries valiantly to define the term by tracing its growth and its major exponents. The anthology, for the most part, relies heavily on modern source materials and the thoughts of filmmakers themselves.

* Levin, G. Roy. *Documentary Explorations: 15 Interviews with Filmmakers*. New York: Doubleday and Company, Inc., 1971.
This uneven anthology provides exhaustive filmographies and interesting interviews with Wright, Anderson, Franju, van Dyke, Leacock, Maysles Brothers, and Wiseman. In addition, there is a weak overview of the origins of the documentary tradition.

* Leyda, Jay. *Films Beget Films: Compilation Films From Propaganda to Drama*. New York: Hill and Wang, 1964.
This important, short account of the work done by film compilers is very helpful in showing how the philosophy begun by Grierson has been carried forward by other filmmakers. Leyda emphasizes the efforts of the Soviet artist Esther Schub and the German team of Andrew and Annelie Thorndike.

Rotha, Paul. *Documentary Film*. London: Faber and Faber, 1952.
This standard work on the documentary covers the genre's history and production techniques. Invaluable for relating motion picture theories and practices, it also has many worthwhile film credits, stills, and appendices.

Snyder, Robert L. *Pare Lorentz and the Documentary Film*. Norman: University of Oklahoma Press, 1968.
During the hard days of the Depression, the United States government decided to produce a series of motion pictures about the various crises facing the country. An unknown and untried filmmaker, working with dedicated artists and a meager budget of $6000, began to make film history with his first movie, *The Plow That Broke the Plains*. Before Congress and the war destroyed their organization, Lorentz had made two more memorable films —*The River* and *The Fight For Life*. Snyder puts it all into print in a useful, intelligent, and important document.

Wright, Basil. *The Use of the Film*. London: The Bodley Head, 1948. Reissued by Arno Press in 1972.

This valuable and concise book is a theoretical commentary of the documentary on filmmaking and its value to the public. It offers an interesting discussion of the film as a medium of information exchange, opinion-forming, and public service.

Films

Robert Flaherty

Man of Aran (16mm: 1934, 77 min., b/w, sound, R-CON/L-CON)
Robert Flaherty spent three years on the Aran Islands making this poignant and marvelous documentary of Irish fishermen living with and against their natural environment. Historians have cited it as one of the most influential films on the rising British documentary directors.

John Grierson[89]

The Granton Trawler (16mm: 1934, 11 min., b/w, sound, R-MMA)
A filmic essay on dragnet fishing, but more important for its lesson for filmmakers on the submission of form to content, combined with a masterful technique of counterpoint in movement and sound.

Night Mail (16mm: 1936, 24 min., b/w, sound, R-MMA)
An artistically exciting portrayal of a train trip on the postal special from London to Glasgow, with an excellent poem by W. H. Auden matched by superb cutting and visual images.

Song of Ceylon (16mm: 1934, 40 min., b/w, sound, R-MMA)
Praised as one of the masterpieces of documentary films, this motion picture tells the story of Singhalese people in the 1930s. Grierson produced the movie and Basil Wright directed.

Pare Lorentz

The Plow that Broke the Plains (16mm: 1936, 21 min., b/w, sound, R-MMA)
Lorentz wrote and directed this very important film about the social and economic situations in the Great Plains over a long period of time, suggesting at the same time the need for government intervention. The film was photographed beautifully by Paul Strand, Ralph Steiner, and Leo Hurwitz. Virgil Thomson contributed the marvelous music.

The River (16mm: 1937, 30 min., b/w, sound, R-MMA)
Again Lorentz wrote and directed, and helped by the brilliant photography of Willard Van Dyke and the superb musical anthology created by Virgil Thomson, this may well be one of the finest documentaries ever made. It shows the need for flood control on the Mississippi River and the creation of the Tennessee Valley Authority.

War Films

Desert Victory (16mm: 1943, 60 min., b/w, sound, R-MMA)

89. For an added dimension, see Jack G. Ellis, "John Grierson's First Years at the National Film Board," *Cinema Journal* 10, no. 1 (Fall 1970): 2–14.

David MacDonald's record of the rout of Rommel's Afrika Korps is a wartime example of the documentary film which tried to bring home to the English people the realistic element of combat. It is also indicative of filmmakers' attempts to raise the hopes and spirits of Englishmen during their days of crisis.

The Silent Village (16mm: 1943, 33 min., b/w, sound, R-MMA)
Humphrey Jennings's film about Nazi vengeance in a Czechoslovak village that was entirely destroyed is another example of the documentary film's use for propaganda purposes.[90]

World of Plenty (16mm: 1943, 45 min., b/w, sound, R-MMA)
Paul Rotha's documentary propaganda masterpiece about the end of the war and what was to come is an example of the way in which movies were used in time of war.

THE NEW REALISM IN ITALIAN AND ENGLISH FILMS (1945-1952)[91]

The influence of the documentary movement became evident in many countries following the end of the Second World War, particularly in Italy and England. Neo-realism was a new film movement that arose to depict the effects of the war upon the people. The stress was on presenting nonactors in a deliberately nonprofessionally photographed film that emphasized the difficult conditions existing for the underprivileged people. Audiences accepted this ragged style of pseudodocumentary filmmaking because they could identify with the characters and appreciate the film's sympathetic message. In fact, most of the movies that appeared after 1945 in Italy concerned Italian people. In England, the new films tried to relate the characters to the audience in three major types of motion pictures: literary or

90. *Film Quarterly* ran a special issue on Humphrey Jennings that should be consulted in all serious study of his work—*Film Quarterly* 15, no. 2 (Winter 1961–62).

91. Some useful articles on Italian Films are Cesare Zavattini, "Some Ideas on the Cinema," *Sight and Sound* 22, no. 3 (October–December 1953) : 64–69; Kevin Gough-Yates, "The Destruction of Neo-Realism," *Films and Filming* 16, no. 12 (September 1970) : 14–20, 22; Gavin Lambert, "The Signs of the Predicament: Italian Notes," *Sight and Sound* 24, no. 3 (January–March 1955) : 147–151, 166; Eric Rhode, "Why Neo-Realism Failed," *Sight and Sound* 30, no. 1 (Winter 1960–1961) : 26–32; Robert Kass, "50 Years of Italian Cinema," *Films in Review* 6, no. 7 (August–September 1955) : 313–17; Robert Kass, "The Italian Film Renaissance," *Films in Review* 4, no. 7 (August–September 1953) : 336–48; Vernon Young, "Italy: The Moral Cinema," *Film Quarterly* 15, no. 1 (Fall 1961) : 14–21; Vinicio Marinucci, "Fact, Fiction and History were in the Beginning: First Part of a History of Italian Cinema," *Films and Filming* 7, no. 4 (January 1961) : 15–16, 43; Vinicio Marinucci, ". . . Part Two," *Films and Filming* 7, no. 5 (February 1961) : 37–38, 40; Vinicio Marinucci, ". . . Part Three," *Films and Filming* 7, no. 7 (April 1961) : 33–35; Vinicio Marinucci, ". . . Part Four," *Films and Filming* 7, no. 8 (May 1961) : 33–34; Vinicio Marinucci, ". . . Part Five," *Films and Filming* 7, no. 9 (June 1961) : 31–32; Vinicio Marinucci, ". . . Part Six," *Films and Filming* 7, no. 10 (July 1961) : 33–34; Vinicio Marinucci, ". . . Final Part," *Films and Filming* 7, no. 11 (August 1961) : 41; Peter John Dyer, "The Realists—A Return to Life," *Films and Filming* 6, no. 2 (November 1959) : 12–14, 32; and John Francis Lane, "A Style is Born," *Films and Filming* 5, no. 7 (April 1959) : 13–15, 32.

dramatic translations, stories of personal problems, and comedies.[92]

Books

Italian Film Books

Armes, Roy. *Patterns of Realism.* New York: A. S. Barnes and Company and London: The Tantivy Press, 1972.

In the best book so far on Italian neo-realism, Armes examines the films themselves, the people who made them and the effect they have not only on the audience but also on other filmmakers and movements in the cinema. It is an invaluable document and should be read by anyone interested in the period.

Jarratt, Vernon. *The Italian Cinema.* London: Falcon Press, 1951. Reissued by Arno Press in 1972.

A very useful history of the early days of Italy's film development, and particularly good for showing the effects of Germany on film production during the occupation.

Malerba, Luigi. *Fifty Years of Italian Cinema.* Rome: Bestetti, 1954.

A standard work that covers the beginnings of Italy's film industry in 1904 to the middle 1950s.

Rondi, Gian Luigi. *Italian Cinema Today.* New York: Hill and Wang, 1966.

The most recent and best of the English writings about Italian cinema, containing comments about the major directors: Antonioni, Castellani, Fellini, Rossellini, and many others. Major difficulty is that it covers too many directors too quickly.

Zavattini, Cesare. *Zavattini: Sequences from a Cinematic Life.* Translated and with an Introduction by William Weaver. Englewood Cliffs, N.J.: Prentice-Hall, Inc., 1970.

Zavattini is regarded by many as one of the most important theorists in Italian film history. This is a valuable self-portrait that traces his career from the birth of neo-realism, while at the same time presenting interesting insights of many famous film personalities.

Roberto Rossellini

* Guarner, Jose Luis. *Roberto Rossellini.* Berkeley: University of California Press, 1970.

The only and most valuable full-length treatment of Rossellini's career from his early fascist films to his recent TV work, this book provides helpful critical and biographical observations plus many stills, a filmography and bibliography. Unfortunately, no index is provided.

General Films

Neo-Realism (Texture Films/RAI—16mm: 1971, 30 min., b/w, sound, R-TEX/S-TEX)

This is a helpful and interesting overview of Italian neo-realism because

---

92. For a helpful overview, see Alan Lovell, "The Unknown Cinema of Britain," *Cinema Journal* 11, no. 2 (Spring 1972) : 1–8.

it shows not only selected scenes from *Rome, Open City; Paisan;* and *Umberto D,* but also has recent comments from various filmmakers about the impact of the movement years ago. Among the people shown and interviewed are Roberto Rossellini, Vittorio de Sica, Cesare Zavattini, Pier Paolo Pasolini, Bernardo Bertolucci, and Michelangelo Antonioni.

Directors

Vittorio de Sica

The Bicycle Thief (16mm: 1949, 87 min., English subtitles, sound, R-BRA, BUR)
Vittorio de Sica's film deals with the effects of the war on the Italian people. Into this heartbreaking story about a man's search for the bicycle he needs to earn a living is interwoven a father-son relationship that concerns the moral collapse of a man because of economic deprivation.[93]

Miracle in Milan (16mm: 1951, 95 min., b/w, English subtitles, sound, R-AUD, BUR)
In a good attempt, de Sica shows how neo-realism can be used in a fantasy film about deadbeats who are rescued by a young, modern saint within their ranks.

Umberto D (16mm: 1951, 89 min., b/w, English subtitles, sound, R-AUD)
Vittorio de Sica's story of the pitiful conditions of old people and their loneliness is a brilliant illustration of the neo-realistic movement in Italian filmmaking.[94]

Roberto Rossellini[95]

Rome, Open City (16mm: 1945, 103 min., b/w, English subtitles, sound, R-CON)
Roberto Rossellini's film about Italy's days after German occupation is one of the most artistic films ever made. Anna Magnani is superb as the young widow shot down in the streets.[96]

English Film Books

General

Balcon, Michael. *Michael Balcon Presents . . . A Lifetime of Films.* London: Hutchinson and Company, 1969.
From this fascinating autobiography, we learn not only about the inner workings of Ealing Studio and its famous comedy series featuring Alec Guinness, but also about such outstanding films as *The Overlanders, Man of Aran,* and *The Cruel Sea.*

---

93. Peter Harcourt, "Film Critique No. 6: Bicycle Thief," *Screen Education* 30 (July–August 1965) : 53–61.
94. Douglas McVay, "Poet of Poverty: Part One—The Great Years," *Films and Filming* 11, no. 1 (October 1964) : 12–16; and Douglas McVay, ". . . Part Two," *Films and Filming* 11, no. 2 (November 1964) : 51–54.
95. Victoria Schultz, "Interview with Roberto Rossellini, February 22–25, 1971, in Houston, Texas," *Film Culture* (Spring 1971) : 1–43.
96. Richard Whitehall, "Gallery of Great Artists: Anna Magnani," *Films and Filming* 7, no. 10 (July 1961) : 15–16, 43; and Bosley Crowther, "Open City," *The Great Films,* pp. 193–97.

Durgnat, Raymond. *A Mirror for England: British Movies from Austerity to Affluence.* New York: Praeger Publishers, 1971.

In this very interesting history of British films since 1945, Durgnat points out the significant contributions the English have made to the world cinema, starting with Lean's *Great Expectations* and including the angry young men cycle (*Room at the Top, Look Back in Anger*) of the late 1950s up to the current Hammer movies.

* Manvell, Roger. *Film.* Baltimore: Penguin Books, 1950. Reissued in 1955 as *The Film and the Public.*

An outstanding film historian's comments about the film as an art form. His discussions of the influence of motion pictures on society, social realism in Hollywood films, documentaries, and British feature films from 1940–1945 are available to serious students of cinema.

* Manvell, Roger (editor). *The Cinema* (1950, 1951, 1952). London: Penguin Books, 1950, 1951, 1952.

Three paperback books that provide a series of philosophical essays on motion pictures as an art form. The collection includes writings by Robert Flaherty, Basil Wright, Karel Reisz, Herbert Read, Carol Reed, David Lean, Sergei Eisenstein, and John Gillett.

Alec Guinness

Tynan, Kenneth. *Alec Guinness.* New York: The Macmillan Company, 1954.

Written by one of England's finest film critics, this deceptively slim biography delves deeply and significantly into Britain's greatest character actor. Also very helpful are Tynan's observations on film acting and his exceptional stills.

Alexander Korda

Tabori, Paul. *Alexander Korda.* New York: Living Books, Inc., 1966.

Written by a fellow Hungarian and an ex-employee of Korda, this lightweight biography uses some dramatic license to tell the story of a farm bailiff's son who rose to become one of the most influential filmmakers on two continents. It is a good starting point for a study of the man who produced such spectaculars as *The Private Life of Henry VIII, The Shape of Things to Come, The Scarlet Pimpernel, Elephant Boy, The Four Feathers, The Thief of Baghdad, Jungle Book, The Tales of Hoffmann,* and *Richard III.*

J. Arthur Rank

Wood, Alan. *Mr. Rank: A Study of J. Arthur Rank and British Films.* London: Hodder and Stoughton, 1952.

This rather chatty and informal history of the Yorkshire flour-miller who entered the fabulous world of movies and high finance is the major source available on the Rank Organization. Wood also provides some useful discussion of American involvement in British production, government interference, and filmmaking problems in Britain up to 1951.

Alec Guinness

The Lavender Hill Mob (16mm: 1951, 80 min., b/w, sound, R-CCC, CON, ROA, SWA, TFC, TWY/L-TWY)
   This film is one of two examples given here of English comedies following the war which illustrate the effect of the realistic movement as well as the great talent of Alec Guinness. The story is about a gang's attempt to dispose of £100 million in gold bars. Charles Crichton directed.[97]

The Man in the White Suit (16mm: 1952, 85 min., b/w, sound, R-CCC, CON, ROA, TWF, TWY/L-TWY)
   Another Guinness film, this time about a chemist's discovery of an indestructible material that threatens the existence of the garment industry. Alexander Mackendrick directed.[98]

David Lean[99]

Breaking the Sound Barrier (16mm: 1952, 109 min., b/w, sound, R-AUD, IDE, WIL)
   This David Lean film explores the personal problems in people's lives. The subject of the film is the human conflicts of individuals interested in conquering the difficulties in flying faster than the speed of sound. Strong performances by Ralph Richardson[100] and Ann Todd.

Brief Encounter (16mm: 1946, 99 min., b/w, sound, R-WRS)
   Adapted from Noel Coward's stage play, this remarkably restrained romance between two middle-aged people who remain married to other spouses is still a sensitive film about life. Superbly acted by Trevor Howard[101] and Celia Johnson.

Laurence Olivier

Henry V (16mm: 1945, 137 min., color, sound, R-WRS)
   Laurence Olivier's version of Shakespeare's play is probably one of the greatest film adaptations ever made. It is an example of the influence of realism in theatrical films.[102]

Emeric Pressburger and Michael Powell

The Red Shoes (16mm: 1948, 139 min., color or b/w, sound, R-WRS)
   Emeric Pressburger and Michael Powell's adaptation of a Hans Christian Anderson tale is another example of the English interest at this time in

---

97. Douglas McVay, "Gallery of Great Stars: Alec Guinness," *Films and Filming* 7, no. 8 (May 1961) : 12–13, 36.
   98. J. B. Hoare, "The Man in the White Suit," *Screen Education Yearbook* (1960–1961), pp. 21–23.
   99. Douglas McVay, "Lean—Lover of Life," *Films and Filming* 5, no. 11 (August 1959) : 9–10, 34.
   100. Alan A. Coulson, "Ralph Richardson," *Films in Review* 20, no. 8 (October 1959) : 457–72.
   101. Richard Whitehall, "Gallery of Great Artists: Trevor Howard," *Films and Filming* 7, no. 5 (February 1961) : 12–13, 36; and A. R. Fulton, *Motion Pictures: The Development of an Art from Silent Films to the Age of Television* (Norman: University of Oklahoma Press, 1970), pp. 214–26.
   102. The film script is available in *Film Scripts One*, edited by George P. Garrett et al. (New York: Appleton-Century-Crofts, 1971).

literary or dramatic translations. It is one of the most beautifully photographed color films ever made, and the ballet scenes have yet to be surpassed.[103]

Carol Reed

The Fallen Idol (16mm: 1949, 92 min., b/w, sound, R-WRS)
This Reed motion picture is a drama about a boy's mistaken assumption that his friend has committed a murder. J. M. L. Peters has a good introduction to the film, plus many valuable illustrations.[104]

Odd Man Out (16mm: 1947, 117 min., b/w, sound, R-CON, JAN, WHO)
Carol Reed's treatment of a story dealing with a dying man's last hours and the manner in which it affects the lives of many others is an example of how English films tried to relate the characters on the screen to real-life situations. The film script has been published,[105] and there is also a film review of the movie, featuring comments by film critic Basil Wright, distributed by Contemporary Films.

The Third Man (Selznick—16mm: 1950, 93 min., b/w, sound, R-WRS)
Translated to the screen from a Graham Greene novel, this fascinating film focuses on finding a black-market leader (Orson Welles) in the postwar ruins of Vienna. In addition to the superb photography of Robert Krasker and the extremely popular theme music by Anton Karas, there are fine performances by Welles and Joseph Cotton.

HOLLYWOOD IN THE POSTWAR YEARS (1945–1955)[106]

The cultural, political, and economic forces shaping a new world dramatically and drastically revolutionized the Hollywood film. Beginning in 1947, the Federal Government began a concerted drive to destroy the old studio system. The Justice Department went after Technicolor and Eastman Kodak for price fixing and monopolizing the market for color raw stock and processing. The House Un-American Activities Committee started their deliberations on communists in the film industry.[107] One year later the United States Supreme Court ruled that theaters must not be owned by

103. Marian Eames, "Gray Thoughts on *Red Shoes,*" *Films in Review* 1, no. 9 (December 1950) : 20–24.
104. J. M. L. Peters, *Teaching About Film* (New York: UNESCO, 1961), pp. 22–30.
105. Roger Manvell (ed.), *Three Screen Plays: Brief Encounter, Odd Man Out, Scott of the Antarctic* (London: Methuen, 1950).
106. A useful article on Hollywood in the Forties is John Russell Taylor, "The High 40's," *Sight and Sound* 30, no. 4 (Autumn 1961) : 188–91. Some useful articles on Hollywood in the 1950s are the following: Penelope Houston, "Hollywood in the Age of Television," *Sight and Sound* 26, no. 4 (Spring 1957) : 175–79; John Gillett, "The Survivors," *Sight and Sound* 28, nos. 3–4 (Summer–Autumn 1959) : 150–55; Theodore Huff, "Hollywood on Hollywood," *Films in Review* 4, no. 4 (April 1953) : 171–83; Colin Young, "The Hollywood War of Independence," *Film Quarterly* 12, no. 3 (Spring 1959) : 4–15; and Colin Young, "The Old Dependables," *Film Quarterly* 13, no. 1 (Fall 1959) : 2–17.
107. For important information on blacklisting, see the following: John Cutts and Penelope Houston, "Blacklisted," *Sight and Sound* 27, no. 1 (Summer 1957) :15–19, 53; Alvah Bessie, "Jail, Freedom and the Screenwriting Profession," *Film Comment* 3, no. 4 (Fall 1965) : 57–64; Roger Tailleur, "Elia Kazan and the House Un-American Activities Committee," translated by Alvah Bessie, *Film Comment* 4, no. 1 (Fall 1966) : 43–48, 50–58; and a special double issue on "Blacklisting" published by *Film Culture* 50–51 (Fall–Winter 1970).

the producers. In 1949, Paramount Pictures, Inc., separated into two companies: one for production, one for distribution. And in 1950, the United States Supreme Court reaffirmed that the once vertical system of filmmaking could no longer exist.

The Hays office also was undergoing change. Hays resigned in 1945 and was succeeded by Eric Johnston, who renamed the office the Motion Picture Association of America. The code began to undergo revisions, and the United States Supreme Court's decision on the exhibition of *The Miracle* in 1952 set in motion the sweeping reforms that appear in today's code.

The old guard was fast disappearing. By 1958, RKO, United Artists, M-G-M, Loews' Inc., Twentieth Century-Fox, and Columbia had undergone major changes in management. And there was more to come.

But the greatest threat of the decade came from television. In 1945, a jurisdictional strike had halted Hollywood film production for eight months, and six years later the city of dreams still faced tremendous economic problems. So the producers searched for a novelty to get back its customers. The new attraction was wide screens.[108] In 1952, Cinerama and 3-D movies appeared. One year later Twentieth Century-Fox brought out Cinemascope. Paramount came out with Vista-Vision in 1954, the same year that exhibitors began to organize once more against a common enemy: television. In 1954, the new craze of drive-in theaters reached its peak. But by 1955, film studios began falling over themselves to unload their old movies on television and buy into the new medium.

For the first time in decades, the independent artist in America began to assert himself. Not only did individuals make personal films, but the New York "underground" searched for new areas of technique and subject matter. The fresh approaches to filmmaking soon appeared in the commercial cinema, and people like Jonas Mekas, Marlon Brando, Billy Wilder, Burt Lancaster, Otto Preminger, Frank Sinatra, Elia Kazan, and James Dean offered new challenges to the older, more recognized Hollywood names.

Books

General

Deming, Barbara. *Running Away From Myself: A Dream Portrait of Amer-*

---

108. Some useful articles on wide-screens and spectaculars are the following: Editors, "The Big Screens," *Sight and Sound* 24, no. 4 (Spring 1955) : 209–12; Derek Prouse, "Dynamic Frame," *Sight and Sound* 25, no. 3 (Winter 1955–56) : 159–60; Gavin Lambert, "Report on New Dimensions," *Sight and Sound* 20, no. 4 (April–June 1953) : 157–60; Richard Kohler and Walter Lassally, "The Big Screens," *Sight and Sound* 24, no. 3 (January–March 1955) : 120–26; Penelope Houston and John Gillett, "The Theory and Practice of Blockbusters," *Sight and Sound* 32, no. 2 (Spring 1963) : 68–74; Barry Day, "Beyond the Frame," *Sight and Sound* 37, no. 2 (Spring 1968) : 80–85; Henry Hart, "Cinerama," *Films in Review* 3, no. 9 (November 1952) : 433–35; Edward Connor, "3-D on the Screen," *Films in Review* 17, no. 3 (March 1966) : 159–74; Charles Barr, "Cinemascope," *Film Quarterly* 16, no. 4 (Summer 1963) :4–24; David Robinson, "Spectacle," *Sight and Sound* 25, no. 1 (Summer 1955) : 22–27, 55–56; William K. Everson, "Film Spectacles," *Films in Review* 5, no. 9 (November 1954) : 459–71; Stephen Farber, "The Spectacle Film: 1967," *Film Quarterly* 20, no. 4 (Summer 1967) : 11–22; and Raymond Durgnat, "Epic," *Films and Filming* 10, no. 3 (December 1963) : 9–12.

ica Drawn from the Films of the 40's. New York: Grossman Publishers, Inc., 1969.

This uneven and controversial study is based upon the thesis that the audience in the 1940s used their screen stars as a means of escaping from the problems of the decade. Miss Deming analyzes in detail many movies in attempting to illustrate what she means by "escape," but she refuses to interpret what she uncovers. I'm never certain, for example, if the author believes that the more important films—dealing with archetypical heroes—were unique to America. If so, then they would not be archetypes. As you can see, it's a stimulating book.

* Deren, Maya. "An Anagram of Ideas on Art, Form and Film," *Film Culture* 39 (Winter 1965) .

This book, originally published in 1946, is republished along with other comments about and by Maya Deren, one of the most unusual filmmakers in the last twenty years. It is an interesting and valuable commentary for those interested in the avant-garde movement.

* Gow, Gordon. *Hollywood in the Fifties.* New York: A. S. Barnes and Company, 1971.

One of the best of the narrative histories presented in this series, Gow offers more than the usual critical commentaries on important personalities, pictures, and studios. The stills, on the other hand, are below par.

* Higham, Charles and Joel Greenberg. *Hollywood in the Forties.* New York: A. S. Barnes and Company, 1968.

In this compendium of brief critical comments neatly tied together by a nostalgic narrative, the authors present a useful, accurate, and informative guide to hundreds of personalities, pictures, and trends.

MacCann, Richard Dyer. *Hollywood in Transition.* Boston: Houghton Mifflin Co., 1962.

Here is a perceptive study of the effects of television on the movie industry, although his comments on film leave something to be desired. MacCann, formerly a Hollywood correspondent for *The Christian Science Monitor,* uses many of his former articles to diagnose Hollywood's problems in the 1950s.[109]

* Manvell, Roger. *New Cinema in the USA: The Feature Film Since 1946.* New York: E. P. Dutton and Company, 1968.

This beautifully illustrated paperback guide to American feature films since 1946 is a useful introduction to beginners who want a quick survey on Kazan, Sturges, Wyler, Stevens, Donen, Huston, Welles, and Wilder.

* Mayer, Michael F. *Foreign Films on American Screens.* Introduction by Arthur Knight. New York: Arco Publishing Company, 1965.

One of the most useful collections of film stills, listing of awards, and general comments on foreign film distribution available.

---

109. For some useful information on the relationship between television and film see the following: Duncan Crow, "From Screen to Screen: Cinema Films on Television," *Sight and Sound* 27, no. 2 (Autumn 1957) : 61–64, 106; André Bazin, "Cinema and Television: Jean Renoir and Roberto Rossellini," *Sight and Sound* 28, no. 1 (Winter 1958–59) : 26–30; and Jean R. Debrix, "TV's Effect on Film Esthetics," translated by David A. Mage, *Films in Review* 3, no. 10 (December 1952) : 504–6.

Film Personalities

Alfred Hitchcock

* LaValley, Albert J. (editor) . *Focus on Hitchcock.* Englewood Cliffs, N.J.: Prentice-Hall, Inc., 1972.

One of the best collections in this series, LaValley divides his essays into three parts: Part I treats the director's own observations; Part II, controversies surrounding his ability, and Part III, comments on his films. A filmography and bibliography are included.

* Perry, George *The Films of Alfred Hitchcock.* New York: E. P. Dutton and Company, 1965.

A helpful beginning to the study of Hitchcock's works, with some good illustrations. Perry's style is straightforward; his text short and useful; and the information accurate.

* Truffaut, François, with the collaboration of Helen G. Scott. *Hitchcock.* New York: Simon and Schuster, 1967.

This book should be read first because of its mnay important observations, its useful chronology and well-balanced comments, the rare photographs, and the insights it offers into both directors.

* Wood, Robin. *Hitchcock's Films.* 2nd enlarged ed. New York: A. S. Barnes and Company, 1969.

An analysis of Hitchcock's *Strangers on a Train, Rear Window, Vertigo, North by Northwest, Psycho, The Birds, Marnie,* and *Torn Curtain.* This book has the weakest production of photographs.

* *North by Northwest.* Edited by Ernest Lehman. New York: The Viking Press, 1972. Film Screenplay.

Marilyn Monroe

* Conway, Michael and Mark Ricci (editors) . *The Films of Marilyn Monroe.* With a Tribute by Lee Strasberg and an Introductory Essay by Mark Harris. New York: The Citadel Press, 1964.

Although Marilyn Monroe was one of the most talked about stars in the history of motion pictures, there is no really worthwhile information available about her. This is as good a book as any to find out about her films, plot synopses, credits, critical reactions and stills.

Guiles, Fred Lawrence. *Norma Jean: The Life of Marilyn Monroe.* New York: McGraw-Hill Book Company, 1969.

The greatest value of this book is the author's considerable research dealing with Monroe's life prior to her becoming a star. After that, the narrative and the critical comments dwindle to fan-magazine level and next to nothing is revealed about the confusion and unbearable strain that forced the beautiful star to commit suicide.

Robert Rossen

* Casty, Alan. *The Films of Robert Rossen.* New York: The Museum of Modern Art, 1969.

In spite of the book's brevity, Casty offers the best source of critical and biographical help on the socially conscious director who gave us such good films as *Body and Soul, All the King's Men,* and *The Hustler.*

Billy Wilder[110]

* Madsen, Axel. *Billy Wilder,* Bloomington: Indiana University Press, 1969.
    In this hurried examination of an important Hollywood director, Madsen gives us some stimulating thoughts on films like *The Lost Weekend, Sunset Boulevard, Witness for the Prosecution, Some Like It Hot,* and *The Apartment.*

Wood, Tom. *The Bright Side of Billy Wilder, Primarily.* New York: Doubleday and Company, Inc., 1970.
    This refreshing and entertaining book treats the behind-the-scenes events of Wilder's productions and relations with famous film personalities. It is well worth the reading.

Blacklisting[111]

Cogley, John. *Report on Blacklisting I: Movies.* New York: The Fund for the Republic, Inc., 1956.
    This invaluable document describes the 1947 HUAC hearings, communism in Hollywood, the labor problems connected with blacklisting, and contains the best appendices anywhere on the subject. In particular, Cogley has lists of the movies made by the Hollywood Ten: Alvah Bessie, Herbert Biberman, Lester Cole, Edward Dmytryk, Ring Lardner, Jr., John Howard Lawson, Albert Maltz, Samuel Ornitz, Adrian Scott, and Dalton Trumbo.

Trumbo, Dalton. *Additional Dialogue: Letters of Dalton Trumbo 1942–1962.* Edited by Helen Manfull. New York: J. B. Lippincott Company, 1970.
    From these artistically written letters, we get some marvelous insights into the 64-year-old screenwriter of *Kitty Foyle, Thirty Seconds Over Tokyo,* and *Our Vines Have Tender Grapes.* He made no secret that his Communist Party membership began in 1943 but argued strenuously that HUAC had no right to question his political beliefs. The conviction for contempt of Congress, the ten-month prison sentence, and the terrible years after are all handled honestly and forcefully.

Experimentation

* Battcock, Gregory (editor). *The New American Cinema: A Critical Anthology.* New York: E. P. Dutton and Company, 1967.
    In this compendium of 29 essays mainly concerned with the New York underground, the editor tries, not always successfully, to shed some light on the techniques and theories of the avant-garde filmmakers. Among the contributors are Jonas Mekas, Andrew Sarris, Rudolf Arnheim, Parker Tyler, Amos Vogel, Stan Vanderbeek, Carl Linder, Gregory Markopoulous, Dwight Macdonald, Susan Sontag, and Stan Brakhage.

---

110. Joseph McBride and Michael Wilmington, "The Private Life of Billy Wilder," *Film Quarterly* 23, no. 4 (Summer 1970) : 2–9; and Stephen Farber, "The Films of Billy Wilder," *Film Comment* 7, no. 4 (Winter 1971–72) : 8–22.
    111. For more information on blacklisting, read the section in Chapter 3 entitled "Censorship."

Curtis, David. *Experimental Cinema.* New York: Universe Books, 1971.

Working from the thesis that the experimental film is vital to the art and development of motion picture history, Curtis presents a short but critical and absorbing history of the crucial stages and personalities who discovered and expanded film technique. In addition, there is an excellent collection of stills.

Manvell, Roger (editor). *Experiment in the Film.* London: Grey Walls, 1949. Reissued by Arno Press in 1972.

A collection of essays by 8 important critics who have difficulty in agreeing on an interpretation of "experimentation." Manvell has a useful introductory article suggesting the range that the experiments take and commenting on the influences of early pioneers like Griffith, Porter, Méliès, Eisenstein, Pudovkin, and Dreyer. Also useful are essays by Hans Richter, Jacques Brunius, and Lewis Jacobs.

* Mekas, Jonas. *Movie Journal: The Rise of the New American Cinema, 1959–1971.* New York: The Macmillan Company, 1971.

Taken from much of his writings in the *Village Voice,* this book gives an excellent example of Mekas' attacks on traditional films and intellectual critics. It is difficult to read if you're used to rational, objective prose, but for those who prefer impressionistic and emotional outbursts, this text is not to be missed.

* Renan, Sheldon. *An Introduction to the American Underground Film.* New York: E. P. Dutton and Company, 1967.

Six biased and brief chapters serve as a useful guide to the low-budget, mainly non-profit world of the unique *auteurs* of the American cinema. Most useful is the good appendix on where to rent these movies.

* Sitney, P. Adams (editor). *Film Culture Reader.* New York: Praeger Publishers, 1970.

This is by far the best available introductory text on American avant-garde films. In 5 valuable sections, we have some of the best material published from *Film Culture*'s indispensable and unique press. Among the contributors are Hans Richter, Jonas Mekas, Carl Dreyer, Andrew Sarris, Parker Tyler, Rudolf Arnheim, Herman G. Weinberg, Erich von Stroheim, Maya Deren, and Stan Brakhage.

Stauffacher, Frank (editor). *Art in Cinema.* San Francisco: Museum of Modern Art, 1947.

Written as a companion piece to accompany the experimental film program at the Museum, this handy, brief guide is an informative, entertaining, and useful publication.

Tyler, Parker. *The Three Faces of the Film: Art, Dream, Cult.* New York: Thomas Yoseloff, 1960.

If you can get over your initial response to dismiss Tyler as a windbag, you will find this book a worthwhile experience. Tyler, avoiding any serious discussion of the quality of the films he reviews, makes bold and provocative statements about the problems connected with experimental moviemaking and the relationship between film and myth. Well worth reading!

Tyler, Parker. *Sex Psyche Etcetera in the Film.* New York: Horizon Press, 1969.

In his sixth film book, Tyler probes the delicate relationship of ritual and aesthetics, and offers some very controversial opinions about major experimentators like Eisenstein, Chaplin, Warhol, and the film *I Am Curious.*

* Tyler, Parker. *Underground Film: A Critical History.* New York: Grove Press, Inc., 1969.

In an attempt to distinguish between experimental and commercial films, Tyler offers a positive and invaluable guide through the avant-garde history of film. In addition, a selected filmography is included.

Films

Avant-Garde

Stan Brakhage[112]

The Way to Shadow Garden (16mm: 1955, 10 min., b/w, sound, R-C16, FMC)

Brakhage is an independent filmmaker who works extensively in 8mm. This film is an example of his use of experimental sound. The content of the film concerns the experiences of a disturbed youth. Other films by this artist can be obtained from Cinema 16 or the Film-Makers' Cooperative.

Jame Broughton

Four in the Afternoon (16mm: 1951, 15 min., b/w, sound, R-C16, RAD)

This poetical film presents four different interpretations of love.

Loony Tom (16mm: 1953, 11 min., b/w, sound, R-C16, RAD)

Here, the San Francisco filmmaker produces a satirical takeoff on the early Charlie Chaplin comedies.

James Davis

Thru the Looking Glass (16mm: 1954, 10 min., color, sound, R-RAD)

Davis seems to be the only filmmaker from the East Coast who has gained recognition for intriguing abstract films. Here the former painter shows some of his skill with illuminated plastics, lights, and colors.

Maya Deren

Meditation on Violence (16mm: 1948, 12 min., b/w, sound, R-C16)

This poetic dance film by one of the early avant-garde filmmakers is an exciting example of the work produced by independent artists. The action of the film involves visual rhythms and movements corresponding to Chinese boxing.

Meshes of the Afternoon (16mm: 1943, 14 min., b/w, sound, R-C16)

A classic of the experimental cinema, this film explores the shades of difference between reality and fantasy.

---

112. For some helpful insights, see Stanley Brakhage, "The Art of Vision," *Film Culture* 30 (Fall 1963); Jerome Hill, "Brakhage's Eyes," *Film Culture* 52 (Spring 1971): 43–47; and Stan Brakhage, "Some Remarks," *Take One* 3, no. 1 (September–October 1971): 6–9.

Norman McLaren

Blinkety Blank (Canada—16mm: 1955, 6 min., color, sound, R-NFB)
McLaren represents a new force in animation, going away from the style of Walt Disney and more towards the techniques developed by UPA. This film is an experiment in intermittent animation and spasmodic imagery.

Neighbors (Canada—16mm: 1953, 9 min., color, sound, R-NFB)
An animated film about two individuals who symbolize a breakdown of communications between people.

Hollywood

Howard Hawks

The Big Sleep (Warners—16mm: 1946, 114 min., b/w, sound, R-AUD, CON, IDE, UAS, WIL)
In this very involved but entertaining Raymond Chandler detective story, Philip Marlowe (Bogart) becomes involved with eight murders plus two incredible sisters (Lauren Bacall and Martha Vickers), and one of the greatest two-bit thugs in film history (Elisha Cook, Jr.). Faulkner wrote the screenplay.[113]

John Huston

The Treasure of Sierra Madre (Warners—16mm: 1948, 126 min., b/w, sound, R-CHA, SWA, UAS)
In his first film after leaving the service, Huston did such an outstanding job of examining the power that greed has over three men (Bogart, Tim Holt, and Walter Huston), that he won two Oscars (writing and directing), while his father won one for his supporting role.

Elia Kazan

Boomerang (Fox—16mm: 1947, 88 min., b/w, sound, R-FNC)
Dana Andrews gave one of his finest performances as the honest and relentless district attorney who is unable to prosecute an innocent man for the unsolved murder of a New England priest.

On the Waterfront (Columbia—16mm: 1954, 108 min., b/w, sound, R-AUD, CCC, CON, CWF, ICS, IDE, NAT, ROA, SWA, TWF, TWY, WHO/L-COL)
This was one of those rare films about corruption and brutality on the New York waterfronts where the outstanding techniques of Leonard Bernstein, Boris Kaufman, and Budd Schulberg were combined with superb performances by the cast, which included Marlon Brando, Karl Malden, and Rod Steiger.[114] The film won eight Academy Awards, including best movie, direction, actor (Brando), screenplay and photography.

---

113. Paxton Davis, "Bogart, Hawks and *The Big Sleep* Revisited—Frequently," *The Film Journal* 1, no. 2 (Summer 1971): 2–9. In addition, the script is available in *Film Scripts One.*
114. John Dennis Hall, "Method Master: Rod Steiger's Career—Part I," *Films and Filming* 17, no. 3 (December 1970): 28–32; and "Part II," *Films and Filming* 17, no. 4 (January 1970): 28–33.

Gene Kelly[115] *and Stanley Donen*

Singin' in the Rain (MGM—16mm: 1952, 103 min., color, sound, R-FNC)
    Gene Kelly and Stanley Donen teamed up to direct this superb musical spoof of what happened to Hollywood during the early days of sound. It may well be one of the finest musicals ever made.

Joseph Mankiewicz[116]

All About Eve (Fox—16mm: 1950, 130 min., b/w, sound, R-FNC)
    Joseph Mankiewicz directed this all-star cast in a cynical interpretation of what unbridled ambition does to a human being. Some outstanding performances by Bette Davis,[117] Anne Baxter, Celeste Holm, and George Sanders. The latter won an Oscar for his superb supporting role as the vicious theater columnist. Two other Academy Awards went to Mankiewicz for his direction and writing, and the film was selected the best film of 1950.

Delbert Mann

Marty (United Artists—16mm: 1955, 91 min., b/w, sound, R-UAS)
    This low-budget film momentarily revolutionized the film industry when producers realized that a sensitive and poignant story about a lonely, unappealing New York butcher (Ernest Borgnine) and his search for love with a bashful school teacher could draw millions to the box-office. Borgnine received an Oscar for his starring role, while the film, director and screenwriter (Paddy Chayefsky) were also honored.

Vincente Minnelli

An American in Paris (MGM—16mm: 1951, 113 min., color, sound, R-FNC)
    Vincente Minnelli directed his choreographer and star Gene Kelly in a marvelous musical about an ex-GI who decides to stay in Paris and become an artist. The film contains one of the best ballet sequences ever photographed. It was honored with six Oscars, including best picture, story and screenplay, color photography, art direction, costume design, and musical scoring.

Billy Wilder

Sunset Boulevard (Paramount—16mm: 1950, 108 min., b/w, sound, R-FNC)
    Billy Wilder co-wrote and directed this memorable story of a forgotten

    115. Rudy Behlmer, "Gene Kelly," *Films in Review* 15, no. 1 (January 1964) : 6–22; John Cutts, "Kelly: Part One . . . dancer, . . . actor . . . director," *Films and Filming* 10, no. 11 (August 1964) : 38–42; and John Cutts,". . . Part Two," *Films and Filming* 10, no. 12 (September 1964) : 34–37.
    116. Gordon Gow, "Cooking a Snook," *Films and Filming* 17, no. 2 (November 1970) : 18–22, 84; and John Springer, "The Films of Joseph L. Mankiewicz," *Films in Review* 22, no. 3 (March 1971) : 153–57.
    117. For some information on Bette Davis see the following: Lawrence J. Quirk, "Bette Davis," *Films in Review* 6, no. 10 (December 1955) : 481–99; Gary Carey, "The Lady and the Director: Bette Davis and William Wyler," *Film Comment* 6, no. 3 (Fall 1970) : 18–24; David Shipman, "Whatever Happened to Bette Davis," *Films and Filming* 9, no. 7 (April 1963) : 8–9; Bette Davis, "What is a Star," *Films and Filming* 11, no. 12 (September 1965) : 5–7; and Ann Guerin, "Bette Davis: Part One," *Show* 2, no. 2 (April 1971) : 28–30; and "'Part Two," *Show* 2, no. 3 (May 1972) :28–29.

silent film actress who decides to make a comeback. Gloria Swanson and Erich von Stroheim give brilliant performances.[118]

Robert Wise[119]

The Day the Earth Stood Still (Fox—16mm: 1951, 92 min., b/w, sound, R-FNC)
    Edmund A. North's well-conceived screenplay helped make this science-fiction film about a stranger from outer space (Michael Rennie) who comes to warn the world about the dangers of a nuclear competition. One of the best movies of its kind.

William Wyler

Roman Holiday (Paramount—16mm: 1953, 118 min., b/w, sound, R-FNC)
    This romantic fantasy about 24 hours in the life of a princess (Audrey Hepburn) and an American journalist earned Miss Hepburn an Oscar.[120]

Fred Zinnemann

High Noon (United Artists—16mm: 1952, 85 min., b/w, sound, R-AIM, AUD, CCC, CHA, CON, CWF, NAT, ROA, SPF, SWA, TWF, TWY, WHO, WIL)
    For those who remember Gary Cooper in *The Virginian*, this film, in which he plays a retiring marshall who on his wedding day learns that four killers are after him, sounded the end of an era. Academy Awards went to Cooper and to Dimitri Tiomkin for his musical score and for the film's theme song.

THE CONTEMPORARY CINEMA

The changes continue to come in what is now a world cinema. First, a polarization exists between the mass film (e.g., *Oliver, Funny Girl,* and *Patton*) and the personal film (e.g., Godard's *Weekend,* Bergman's *Shame,* and Satyajit Ray's *Charulata*) ; in other words, the spectacle theater versus the art house.[121] Second filmmakers, educators, and critics are working together to help develop a more discriminating audience. This has given rise to the third important trend, that of a specialized audience interest in retrospective screenings and the revival of key films. A fourth development con-

118. Charles Higham, "Cast a Cold Eye: The Films of Billy Wilder," *Sight and Sound* 32, no. 2 (Spring 1963) : 83–87, 103; and Charles Higham, "Meet Whiplash Wilder," *Sight and Sound* 37, no. 1 (Winter 1967–68) : 21–23.
    119. Roy Pickard, "The Future . . . A Slight Return," *Films and Filming* 17, no. 10 (July 1971) : 26–31.
    120. Gene Ringgold, "Audrey Hepburn," *Films in Review* 22, no. 10 (December 1971) : 585–605.
    121. For useful information on the *auteur* theory, see the following: Pauline Kael, "Circles and Squares," *Film Quarterly* 16, no. 3 (Spring 1963) : 12–26; Andrew Sarris, "The *Auteur* Theory and the Perils of Pauline," *Film Quarterly* 16, no. 4 (Summer 1963) : 26–33; and Andrew Sarris, "Notes on the *Auteur* Theory in 1970," *Film Comment* 6, no. 3 (Fall 1970) : 6–9.

cerns the growing activity of filmmakers outside the commercial cinema, particularly film students and avant-garde groups throughout the world.[122]

The films themselves represent the revolutions in taste, conventions, and political institutions. Censorship has been sharply curtailed, more and more production involves getting together a "package deal" where artists join together to make a specific film, and soon it may well be that films will be transferred to tape to be sold in stores for people to take home much as they do a book.[123] This development promises to be dramatic. And it's only the beginning.

General Books

Guback, Thomas H. *The International Film Industry: Western Europe and America Since 1945.* Bloomington: Indiana University Press, 1969.

Very rarely has this subject been so intensely and capably approached. Guback, in a finely documented text, explores American and European film-markets, exports and imports, coproductions, financial arrangements and procedures, and policy making practices. Beginners might avoid this one; serious students should not.[124]

Limbacher, James L. *Four Aspects of the Film.* New York: Brussel and Brussel, 1969.

One of the best researched, documented and discussed accounts of the growth of film color, sound, 3-D and widescreen techniques now available. Besides a helpful commentary, Limbacher provides over a hundred pages of appendices which deal with marvelous chronologies of the specific areas covered.

---

122. For unique developments in film, consult the following: "Bruce Connor," *Film Comment* 5, no. 4 (Winter 1969) : 16–25; Albert Johnson, "The Dynamic Gesture: New American Independents," *Film Quarterly* 19, no. 4 (Summer 1966) : 6–11; Stan Vander-beek, "The Cinema Delimina: Films from the Underground," *Film Quarterly* 14, no. 4 (Summer 1961) : 5–16; James Lithgow and Colin Heard, "Underground U.S.A. and the Sexploitation Market," *Films and Filming* 15, no. 11 (August 1969) : 18–29; Gordon Gow, "The Underground River: Agnes Varda," *Films and Filming* 16, no. 5 (March 1970) : 6–10; David MacDougall, "Prospects of the Ethnographic Film," *Film Quarterly* 23, no. 2 (Winter 1969–70) :16–30; Robert Siegler, "Masquage: The Multi-Image Film," *Film Quarterly* 21, no. 3 (Spring 1968) : 15–21; Judith Shatnoff, "Expo '67—A Multiple Vision," *Film Quarterly* 21, no. 1 (Fall 1967) : 2–13; Edgar F. Daniels, "Plain Words on Underground Film Programs," *The Journal of Popular Film* 1, no. 2 (Spring 1972) : 112–21; and Gordon Gow, "Up From the Underground, I: Curtis Harrington," *Films and Filming* 17, no. 11 (August 1971) : 16–22; and "II: Conrad Rooks," *ibid.,* pp. 24–28.

123. Peter Guber, "The New Ballgame: The Cartridge Revolution," *Cinema* 6, no. 1 (1970) : 21–31; Richard Kahlenberg and Aaron Chloe, "The Cartridges are Coming," *Cinema Journal* 9, no. 2 (Spring 1970) : 2–12; and Henry Hart "Cassettes," *Films in Review* 21, no. 9 (November 1970) : 521–24.

124. In connection with postwar production, the following three articles are useful: David Paletz and Michael Noorau, "The Exhibitors," *Film Quarterly* 19, no. 2 (Winter 1965–66) : 14–40; Arthur Mayer, "Hollywood's Favorite Fable," *Film Quarterly* 12, no. 2 (Winter 1958) : 13–20; and Richard Dyer MacCann, "Film and Foreign Policy: The USIA, 1962–67," *Cinema Journal* 9, no. 1 (Fall 1969) : 23–42.

A COUNTRY-BY-COUNTRY ANALYSIS OF SOURCE MATERIALS[125]

CZECHOSLOVAKIA[126]

Books

* Hibbin, Nina. *Eastern Europe: An Illustrated Guide*. New York: A. S. Barnes and Company, 1970.

This is the best available guide to postwar movies because it is accurate on leading personalities, films, and technicians, and the index and photographs help fill in the gaps.

Films

Milos Forman[127]

The Loves of A Blonde (Czechoslovakia—16mm: 1965, 88 min., b/w, sound, English subtitles, R-AUD)

Writer-director Milos Forman created this comic tale of two young people in love. Good performances by Vladimir Pucholt and Hana Brejchova.[128]

---

125. Although no films are listed here for the following countries, you might wish to read about their work. Argentina: Domingo Di Nubila, "Argentina Way—Part One," *Films and Filming* 7, no. 3 (December 1961) : 16, 39; Domingo Di Nubila, ". . . Part Two," *Films and Filming* 7, no. 4 (January 1961) : 41–42; and Peter Baker, "Argentine Way," *Films and Filming* 6, no. 8 (May 1960) : 8–9, 33. The People's Republic of China: Mark J. Scher, "Film in China," *Film Comment* 5, no. 2 (Spring 1969) : 8–21; Leonard Rubenstein, "Report From China," *Film Society Review* 7, no. 1 (September 1971) : 36–39; Leonard Rubenstein, "Red China," *Film Society Review* 7, no. 2 (October 1971) : 40–43; Leonard Rubenstein, "Revolution in China," *Film Society Review* 7, no. 3 (November 1971) : 37–42; and Leonard Rubenstein, "China: The Red Sons," *Film Society Review* 7, no. 4 (December 1971) : 41–44. Cuba: Andi Engel, "Solidarity and Violence," *Sight and Sound* 38, no. 4 (Autumn 1969) : 196–200; William Johnson, "Report from Cuba," *Film Quarterly* 15, no. 2 (Winter 1961–62) : 42–49. Holland: Peter Cowie, "Dutch Films," *Film Quarterly* 19, no. 2 (Winter 1965–66) : 41–46. Hungary: Louis Marcorelles, "Hungarian Cinema: The Fight for Freedom," *Sight and Sound* 26, no. 3 (Winter 1956–57) : 124–30; Robert Vas, "Yesterday and Tomorrow: New Hungarian Films," *Sight and Sound* 29, no. 1 (Winter 1959–60) : 31–34; and David Robinson, "Quite Apart from Miklos Jansso . . . Some Notes on the New Hungarian Cinema," *Sight and Sound* 39, no. 2 (Spring 1970) : 84–89. Mexico: Manuel Michel, "Mexican Cinema: A Panoramic View," translated by Neal Oxenhandler, *Film Quarterly* 18, no. 4 (Summer 1965) : 46–55. Yugoslavia: Ronald Holloway, "Social Documentary in Yugoslavia," *Film Society Review* 6, no. 7 (March 1971) : 42–48.

126. Some useful articles are John Peter Dyer, "Star-Crossed in Prague," *Sight and Sound* 35, no. 1 (Winter 1965–66) : 34–35; Antonin Liehm, "A Reckoning of the Miracle: An Analysis of Czechoslovak Cinematography," *Film Comment* 5, no. 1 (Fall 1968) : 64–69; Kirk Bond, "The New Czech Film," *ibid.*, pp. 70–78; Jan Zalman, "Question Marks on the New Czechoslovak Cinema," *Film Quarterly* 21, no. 2 (Winter 1967–68) : 18–27; and Jaroslav Broz, "Here Come the Czechs: Grass Roots," *Film and Filming* 11, no. 9 (June 1965) : 39–42.

127. James Conaway, "Milos Forman's America is Like Kafka's—Basically Comic," *The New York Times Magazine* Sunday, July 11, 1971, pp. 8–12; and Gordon Gow, "A Czech in New York: An Interview with Milos Forman," *Films and Filming* 17, no. 12 (September 1971) : 20–24.

128. Claire Clouzot, "Loves of A Blonde," *Film Quarterly* 21, no. 1 (Fall 1967) : 47–48.

Jan Kadar

The Shop on Main Street (Czechoslavakia—16mm: 1964, 128 min., b/w, English subtitles, sound, R-AUD, MMM)

Jan Kadar and Elmer Klos co-directed this screen masterpiece on the moral dilemma that simple people face in war. Memorable performances by Ida Kaminska and Josef Kroner.

ENGLAND[129]

Books

Kelly, Terence, with Graham Norton and George Perry. *A Competitive Cinema*. London: The Institute of Economic Affairs, 1967.

The two major distributors in England, Rank and Associated British Cinemas (ABC), exert a monopoly that may prove fatal to a national growth. In one way or another, Kelley explains how and why and points out how American interests are involved: Columbia, Disney, Twentieth Century-Fox, and United Artists go to Rank; Warners, Seven Arts, M-G-M and Paramount go to ABC. It is an interesting book and one worth reading, particularly for its discussion about a proposed film school.[130]

* Manvell, Roger. *New Cinema in Britain*. New York: E. P. Dutton and Company, 1968.

This concise, readable, and well-illustrated guide to English film covers the period from 1946 to the present. Manvell emphasizes the work of serious directors like Tony Richardson, Lindsay Anderson, and Karel Reisz.

The Monopolies Commission. *Films: A Report on the Supply of Films for Exhibition in Cinemas*. London: Her Majesty's Stationary Office, 1967.

A good companion volume to the Kelley book and useful for examining the government's relationship to Rank, ABC, and British Lion.

Lindsay Anderson

* Sussex, Elizabeth. *Lindsay Anderson*. New York: Praeger Publishers, 1969.

129. The following articles are helpful: Penelope Houston, "The Undiscovered Country," *Sight and Sound* 25, no. 1 (Summer 1955) : 10–14; Richard Roud, "Britain in America," *Sight and Sound* 26, no. 3 (Winter 1956–57) : 119–23; John Berger, "Look at Britain," *Sight and Sound* 27, no. 1 (Summer 1957) : 12–14; Penelope Houston, "Time of Crisis," *Sight and Sound* 27, no. 4 (Spring 1958) : 166–75; Penelope Houston, "Whose Crisis," *Sight and Sound* 33, no. 1 (Winter 1963–64) : 26–28, 50; John Gillett, "State of the Studios," *Sight and Sound* 33, no. 2 (Spring 1964) : 54–61; Kenneth Cavander et al., "British Feature Directors: An Index to Their Work," *Sight and Sound* 27, no. 6 (Autumn 1958) : 289–304; Penelope Houston and Duncan Crow, "Into the Sixties," *Sight and Sound* 29, no. 1 (Winter 1959–60) : 4–8; Derek Hill, "A Writer's Wave," *Sight and Sound* 29, no. 2 (Spring 1960) : 56–60; John Russell Taylor, "Backing Britain," *Sight and Sound* 38, no. 3 (Summer 1969) :112–15; Penelope Houston, "Seventy," *Sight and Sound* 39, no. 1 (Winter 1969–70) :2–5; Jan Dawson and Clair Johnston, "More British Sounds," *Sight and Sound* 39, no. 3 (Summer 1970) : 144–47; Ian Jarvie, "Media and Manners: Film and Society in Some Current British Films," *Film Quarterly* 22, no. 3 (Spring 1969) : 11–17; and Ian Johnson, "The Decade—Britain: We're All Right Jack," *Films and Filming* 8, no. 12 (September 1962) : 44–48.

130. For more information on the economic situation, read Bernard Husra, "Patterns of Power," *Films and Filming* 10, no. 7 (April 1964) : 49–56; Raymond Durgnat, "TV's Young Turks: Part One," *Films and Filming* 15, no. 6 (March 1969) : 4–8, 10; and Raymond Durgnat, ". . . Part Two," *Films and Filming* 15, no. 7 (April 1969) : 26–30.

This rather shallow text fails to present a serious critical study and background material about the enterprising Anderson. The quotations, narrative, general information, and photographs tease you with thoughts of what might have been had more time and effort gone into the text.

Joseph Losey[131]

* Leahy, James. *The Cinema of Joseph Losey*. New York: A. S. Barnes & Company, 1967.
This is a good study to introduce Joseph Losey to his fans. Filled with quotations, arranged in chronological fashion, and complete with an important bibliography and screen credits, Leahy's text highlights the themes of Losey's works and suggests the reasons why the American expatriate prefers to work in England.

* Milne, Tom (editor). *Losey on Losey*. New York: Doubeday and Company, 1968.
Written by a writer who has done better work, this hodgepodge of quotations, uneven critical comments, and rambling organization should be tasted, rather than digested.

Films

Lindsay Anderson

If . . . (Paramount—16mm: 1969, 111 min., b/w and color, sound, R-FNC)
In this somewhat updated version of Vigo's *Zèro de Conduite,* Anderson examines the outmoded and nonsensical aspects of English public schools. Malcolm McDowell is first-rate as the rebellious student leader.[132]

This Sporting Life (16mm: 1963, 129 min., b/w, sound, R-WRS)
This is a realistic story of an ambitious rugby player who refuses to let anything interfere with his ambitions. Strong performances by Richard Harris and Rachel Roberts.[133]

Donald Cammell and Nicolas Roeg

Performance (16mm: 1970, 110 min., color, sound, R-WSA)
In the pop star film genre, this film centers on a rock singer (Mick Jagger) who retires to an obscure house and takes for a tenant a gangster (James Fox) hiding out from members of his own gang and the police. Eventually, the men's personalities exert reciprocal influences on them and the character studies are interestingly handled.[134] Jagger sings on the sound track as well.

---

131. Gordon Gow, "Weapons: An Interview with Joseph Losey," *Films and Filming* 18, no. 1 (October 1971) : 36–41.
132. Albert Johnson, "If . . .," *Film Quarterly* 22, no. 4 (Summer 1969) : 48–52.
133. Robert Vas, "Arrival and Departure," *Sight and Sound* 32, no. 2 (Spring 1963) : 56–59; Tom Milne, "This Sporting Life," *Sight and Sound* 31, no. 3 (Summer 1962) : 113–15; and Ernest Callenbach, "This Sporting Life," *Film Quarterly* 17, no. 4 (Summer 1964) : 45–48.
134. Philip French, "Performance," *Sight and Sound* 40, no. 2 (Spring 1971) : 67–69; Foster Hirsch, "Underground Chic: Performance," *Film Heritage* 6, no. 3 (Spring 1971) : 1–6, 36; and Gordon Gow, "Identity: An Interview with Nicolas Roeg," *Films and Filming* 18, no. 4 (January 1972) : 18–24.

Lewis Gilbert

Alfie (16mm: 1966, 114 min., cinemascope, color, sound, R-FNC)
   Lewis Gilbert directed this exceptional film about Alfie, the cad, who suddenly loses his touch with women and sinks into despair. Michael Caine does a fine job as the stud.[135]

Richard Lester[136]

Help! (16mm: 1965, 90 min., color, sound, R-CHA, UAS)
   This mad and delightful film tries every type of cutting and camera technique that comes to mind so that the Beatles can sing and romp through the world in entertaining fashion.[137]

The Knack (United Artists—16mm: 1965, 84 min., b/w, sound, R-CHA, UAS)
   Another whacky and merrymaking film, this time about an inexperienced school teacher who wishes to learn his roommate's "knack" with women. He does, and more. A fine performance by Rita Tushingham.

Joseph Losey[138]

Accident (16mm: 1967, 105 min., color, sound, R-COL)
   Losey directs Harold Pinter's fascinating screenplay about a neurotic teacher and father who tries extramarital relations and nearly destroys himself. Good acting jobs turned in by Dirk Bogarde and Stanley Baker.[139]

The Servant (16mm: 1963, 115 min., b/w, sound, R-AUD)
   The same team of Losey, Pinter, and Bogarde presents an extraordinary tale of depravity as a weak aristocrat becomes the pawn of a degenerate servant. Fine performances by James Fox, Sarah Miles, and Bogarde.[140]

Karel Reisz

Morgan! (16mm: 1966, 97 min., b/w, sound, R-COL)
   Reisz turns David Mercer's screenplay into a marvelous comedy about a nonconformist painter loose in London. Both Vanessa Redgrave and David Warner are outstanding.

---

   135. David Austen, "Playing Dirty: Michael Caine—Part One," *Films and Filming* 15, no. 7 (April 1969) : 4–8, 10; David Austen, ". . . Part Two," *Films and Filming* 15, no. 8 (May 1969) : 15–18; and Stephen Farber, "Alfie," *Film Quarterly* 20, no. 3 (Spring 1967) : 42–46.
   136. George Bluestone, "Lunch with Lester," *Film Quarterly* 19, no. 4 (Summer 1966) : 12–16.
   137. Robin Bean, "Keeping Up with The Beatles," *Films and Filming* 10, no. 5 (February 1964) : 9–12.
   138. Penelope Houston and John Gillett, "Conversation with Nicholas Ray and Joseph Losey," *Sight and Sound* 30, no. 4 (Autumn 1961) , 182–87; Gilles Jacob, "Joseph Losey or the Camera Calls," *Sight and Sound* 35, no. 2 (Spring 1966) : 62–67; Raymond Durgnat, "Losey: Modesty and Eve—Part One," *Films and Filming* 12, no. 7 (April 1966) : 26–33; and Raymond Durgnat, ". . . Part Two," *Films and Filming* 12, no. 8 (May 1966) : 28–33.
   139. John Russell Taylor, "Accident," *Sight and Sound* 35, no. 4 (Autumn 1966) : 179–84; Tom Milne, "Accident," *Sight and Sound* 36, no. 2 (Spring 1967) : 56–59; and Margaret Tarratt and Kevin Gough-Yates, "Playing the Game: Stanley Baker," *Films and Filming* 16, no. 11 (August 1970) : 30–34.
   140. Richard Whitehall, "Dirk Bogarde," *Films and Filming* 10, no. 2 (November 1963) : 13–16.

Saturday Night and Sunday Morning (16mm: 1961, 90 min., b/w, sound, R-WRS)

This exceptional film details the life and loves of a blue-collar cad from the English industrial world. Albert Finney is perfect for the role.

Tony Richardson

The Entertainer (16mm: 1960, 97 min., b/w, sound, R-WRS)

Richardson did a good job with John Osborne's screenplay about an egocentric, second-rate song-and-dance man whose sick ambitions destroy him in the end. Laurence Olivier is superb.

FRANCE[141]

Books

* Armes, Roy. *French Cinema Since 1946: Volume One—The Great Tradition.* 2nd enlarged ed. New York: A. S. Barnes and Company, 1970.

This is a valuable general introduction to important filmmakers like Clair, Cocteau, Bresson, Tati, and Ophuls. There is a useful filmography on each director with some handy biographical information.

* Armes, Roy. *French Cinema Since 1946: Volume Two—The Personal Style.* 2nd enlarged. New York: A. S. Barnes and Company, 1970.

As good as the first, this volume, using auteurism as a measuring rod, introduces Astruc, Chabrol, Demy, Franju, Godard, Marker, Resnais, Truffaut, Vadim, and Varda.

* Cameron, Ian (editor). *Second Wave.* New York: Praeger Publishers, 1970.

In an attempt to assess the impact of the *nouvelle vague* on present-day films, the editors examine the styles of eight unusual contemporary directors who admittedly are reacting to French influences: Dusan Makavejev, Jerzy Skolimowski, Nagisa Ohima, Ruy Guerra, Glauber Rocha, Gilles Groulx, Jean-Pierre Lefebvre, and Jean-Marie Stroub. Filmographies and stills are included.

* Graham, Peter (editor). *The New Wave: Critical Landmarks.* New York: Doubleday and Company, 1968.

This breezy, lightweight treatment suffers from lack of detail, depth, and style. Most serious are its missing filmographies and poorly reproduced illustrations.

---

141. Some useful articles are the following: Jacques Siclier, "New Wave and French Cinema," *Sight and Sound* 30, no. 3 (Summer 1961) : 116–20; Gabriel Pearson and Eric Rhode, "Cinema of Appearance," *Sight and Sound* 30, no. 4 (Autumn 1961) : 160–68; Gilles Jacob, "Nouvelle Vague or Jeune Cinema," *Sight and Sound* 34, no. 1 (Winter 1964–65) : 4–8; Georges Sadoul, "Notes on a New Generation," *Sight and Sound* 28, nos. 3, 4 (Summer–Autumn 1959) : 111–16; François Truffaut, "A Certain Tendency of the French Cinema," *Cahiers du Cinema in English* 1 (January 1966) : 30–41; Stephen Taylor, "After the Nouvelle Vague," *Film Quarterly* 18, no. 3 (Spring 1965) : 5–9; Colin Young, and Gideon Bachmann, "New Wave or Gestures," *Film Quarterly* 14, no. 3 (Spring 1961) : 6–14; Eugen Weber, "An Escapist Realism," *Film Quarterly* 13, no. 2 (Winter 1959) : 9–16; Noel Burch, "Qu'est-ce que la Nouvelle Vague," *ibid.,* pp. 16–30; Peter Graham, "The Face of '63—France," *Films and Filming* 9, no. 8 (May 1963) : 13–22; Raymond Durgnat, "The Decade: France—A Mirror for Marianne," *Films and Filming* 9, no. 2 (November 1962) : 48–55; and David Austen, "All Guns and Gangsters," *Films and Filming* 16, no. 9 (June 1970) : 52–56, 58–60.

Schrader, Paul. *Transcendental Style in Film: Ozu, Bresson, Dreyer*. Berkeley: University of California Press, 1972.

Working on the theory that a common universal style links divergent artists in various cultures, Schrader presents a stimulating and thoughtful analysis of film transcendentalists whose concern is with spiritual art, non-psychological interpretations, and lean techniques. A useful bibliography is included.

Film Personalities

Robert Bresson

* Cameron, Ian (editor). *The Films of Robert Bresson*. New York: Praeger Publishers, 1969.

In this uneven and disappointing collection, seven critics discuss Bresson's major films. An interview and filmography are also included.

Claude Chabrol

* Wood, Robin and Michael Walker. *Claude Chabrol*. New York: Praeger Publishers, 1970.

Stressing the influence of Hitchcock on the ex-film critic, the authors discuss in hurried terms the major movies of Chabrol. A filmography is included plus a small number of stills.

Jean Cocteau

Cocteau, Jean. *Cocteau on the Film,* recorded by André Fraigneau and translated by Vera Traill. London: Dennis Dobson Limited, 1954.

A discussion by one of France's greatest directors on the relationship between the film and the audience. The book is in the form of an extempore conversation and thus may offer some difficulty to the reader. Serious students may appreciate the artist's ability to be objective about his art and his work.

Cocteau, Jean. *The Journals of Jean Cocteau*. Translated by Wallace Fowlie. Bloomington: Indiana University Press, 1964.

This is an invaluable collection of the great filmmaker's thoughts about a host of topics and should be in every collection on French film.

* Cocteau, Jean. *Screenplays and Other Writings of the Cinema: The Blood of A Poet. The Testament of Orpheus*. Translated from the French by Carol Martinsperry. New York: Grossman, 1968.

The scripts of two of Cocteau's most famous films, *The Blood of a Poet* (1930–1932) and *The Testament of Orpheus* (1959) are supplemented by over 50 stills from the productions. The comments, scenarios, and illustrations add considerably to our understanding of the filmmaker's art.

* Gilson, René. *Jean Cocteau*. New York: Crown Publishers, Inc., 1969.

Originally published in the *Cinema d'Aujourd'hui* series in 1964, this invaluable translation sheds enormous light on one of the most important Renaissance filmmakers in motion picture history. It should be read by every serious student of French films particularly for Cocteau's marvelous thoughts.

Hammond, Robert M. (editor). *Beauty and The Beast.* Bilingual Script Annotated. New York: New York University Press, 1970.

A helpful introduction by this resourceful scholar provides us with the only accurate and complete text of this rare film.

Phelps, Robert (editor). *Professional Secrets: An Autobiography of Jean Cocteau—Drawn from his Lifetime Writings.* Translated from the French by Richard Howard. New York: Farrar, Straus and Giroux, Inc., 1970.

Drawing from more than 30 books and memoirs on the great French artist, Phelps has put together a stimulating and valuable record of the man and his thoughts.

Steegmuller, Francis. *Cocteau: A Biography.* Boston: Atlantic-Little, Brown, 1970.

Winner of the National Book Award, this outstanding biography separates the fact from the fiction of the 50 year history of Cocteau's fights, failures and triumphs. The author, in lively, interesting, and scholarly writing presents a revealing history of Paris as well as an indepth study of Cocteau's homosexual world.

Georges Franju[142]

* Durgnat, Raymond, *Franju.* Berkeley: University of California Press, 1968.

Although this book, like most written by Durgnat, suffers from a heavy literary emphasis, it also provides the usual provocative and entertaining observations by a very perceptive student of film. The emphasis here is on a relatively unknown and unpopular commercial artist who specialized in slow, dismal, pessimistic films which were preoccupied with pain, torture, and death. Yet, Franju was a master of *mise-en-scène*, and Durgnat, in considerable detail, discusses how, why, and where.

Jean-Luc Godard

* Collet, Jean. *Jean-Luc Godard.* Translated by Ciba Vaughan. New York: Crown Publishers, Inc., 1968.

Originally published in the Cinema d'Aujourd-hui series in 1963, this is another splendid introduction to a unique and brilliant filmmaker. It comes with an excellent filmography and bibliography for each film.

* Mussman, Tony (editor). *Jean-Luc Godard: A Critical Anthology.* New York: E. P. Dutton and Company, 1968.

This is a fine compendium of articles, interviews and critical commentaries. Among the many worthwhile contributors are Sarris, Sontag, Kael, and Godard (very often).

* Narboni, Jean and Tom Milne (editors and translators). *Godard on Godard: Critical Writings by Jean-Luc Godard.* With an Introduction by Richard Roud. New York: The Viking Press, 1972.

Here is an invaluable collection of the famous filmmaker's critical writings from his early attempts for *La Gazette au Cinéma* starting in 1950, to his

---

142. Cynthia Grenier, "Franju," *Sight and Sound* 26, no. 4 (Spring 1957) : 186–90; and Alf MacLochlainn, "Pointed Horror: The Films of Luis Buñuel and Georges Franju," *The Film Journal* 1, no. 2 (Summer 1971) : 16–21.

later works in *Cahiers du Cinéma*. Anyone who intends to seriously view Godard's films will discover many important keys to his visual syntax in these provocative essays.

* Roud, Richard. *Jean-Luc Godard*. New York: Doubleday and Company, 1968.

  This is the weakest of the three popular books on Godard, primarily because Roud lacks enthusiasm and ability to handle this elusive filmmaker. Once more Doubleday has reproduction problems.

* *Le Petit Soldat: A Film by Jean-Luc Godard*. English translation and description of action by Nicholas Garnham. New York: Simon and Schuster, 1971.

Alain Resnais

* Armes, Roy. *The Cinema of Alain Resnais*. New York: A. S. Barnes and Company, 1968.

  This highly intelligent introduction presents an important study of Resnais's formative film years as a documentary filmmaker. Armes also is very helpful in giving us some perspective about Resnais's relationship to his peers, his preoccupations in movies, and his mental outlook. Very good filmography and bibliography are available.

* Ward, John. *Alain Resnais, or the Theme of Time*. New York: Doubleday and Company, 1968.

  This is one of the best of the Cinema One Series, mainly because its author takes pains to limit his subject and then present some intelligent, informative, and coherent comments. Even the photographs seem better printed. But still the editor refuses to ask his writers to include bibliographies.

François Truffaut

* Petrie, Graham. *The Cinema of François Truffaut*. New York: A. S. Barnes and Company, 1971.

  What is best about his book is Petrie's emphasis on aspects of Truffaut's talent and a chronological examination of his films. The writing is lucid and informative if not always stimulating. Regretfully no index is included and the binding is poor. Still, this is the only full length study of an important director and belongs in every library.

Truffaut, François. *The Adventures of Antoine Doinel: Four Screenplays— The 400 Blows, Love at Twenty, Stolen Kisses, Bed and Board.* Translated by Helen G. Scott. New York: Simon and Schuster, 1972.

  This is a superb anthology not only of Truffaut's fine films about adolescence, love, and maturity, but also of his work notes in making these movies and the various relationships existing among them. This is a must for Truffaut fans.

* *Jules and Jim: A Film by François Truffaut*. Translated from the French by Nicholas Fry. New York: Simon and Schuster, 1968.

Film

Robert Bresson

Le Journal d'Un Curé de Campagne (16mm: 1951, 95 min., b/w, English subtitles, sound, R-AUD)
    In this moving story of a country priest's conflict between his abilities and his ambitions, Bresson magnificently captures the isolation and loneliness of an individual.[143]

Claude Chabrol[144]

Les Biches (16mm: 1968, 97 min., color, English subtitles, sound, R-AUD)
    In this strange but simplistic film, Chabrol centers on the involved relationship among three unusual people: a rich lesbian photographer (Stephane Andran), her female lover (Jacqueline Sassard), and the disrupting architect (Jean-Louis Trintignant) who eventually seduces both women.

Costa-Gavras

The Confession (16mm: 1970, 138 min., color, English subtitles, sound, R-GEN)
    In an attempt to introduce topics of political concern to mass audiences, director Costa-Gavras relates the story of a former Stalinist who is arrested by the Czechoslovakian Communist party and accused of crimes against the state. In showing the cruelty and brutality of the protagonist's interrogation, Costa-Gavras displays his distaste for violence and oppression, regardless of the political affiliation. Yves Montand and Simone Signoret give fine performances as the family undergoing great moral stress.[145]

Z (16mm: 1969, 131 min., color, English subtitles, sound, R-CIV)
    Based upon Vassili Vassilikos's novel, this masterful political thriller focuses on the moral dilemma of a conscientious government investigator who discovers that the state has murdered an important pacifist leader of the

143. Some useful articles on Bresson are the following: Roland Monod, "Working with Bresson," *Sight and Sound* 28, no. 1 (Summer 1957) : 30–32; Gavin Lambert, "Notes on Robert Bresson," *Sight and Sound* 33, no. 1 (July/September 1953) : 35–39; Tom Milne, "The Two Chambermaids," *Sight and Sound* 33, no. 4 (Autumn 1964) : 174–79; Charles Ford, "Robert Bresson," translated by Anne and Thornton K. Brown," *Films in Review* 10, no. 2 (February 1959) : 65–67, 79; Jean-Luc Godard and Michel Delahaye, "The Question: Interview with Robert Bresson," *Cahiers du Cinema in English* 7 (CdC #178, May 1966) : 5–27; Colin Young, "Conventional-Unconventional," *Film Quarterly* 13, no. 3 (Spring 1960) : 4–10; Richard Roud, "French Outsider with the Inside Look: A Monograph of Robert Bresson's Early Work," *Films and Filming* 6, no. 7 (April 1960) : 9–10, 35; Raymond Durgnat, "Diary of a Country Priest," *Films and Filming* 13, no. 3 (December 1966) : 28–32; Donald S. Skoller, "*Praxis* as a Cinematic Principle in Films by Robert Bresson," *Cinema Journal* 9, no. 1 (Fall 1969) : 13–22; Marvin Zemon, "The Suicide of Robert Bresson," *Cinema* 6, no. 3 (Spring 1971) : 37–42; and Mike Prokosch, "Bresson's Stylistics Revisited," *Film Quarterly* 25, no. 2 (Winter 1971–72) : 30–32.
    144. Rui Noqueria and Nicoletta Zalaffi, "Chabrol," *Sight and Sound* 40, no. 1 (Winter 1970–71) : 2–6.
    145. Len Rubenstein, "The Confession," *Film Society Review* 6, no. 5 (January 1971) :25–27; Michael Sragnow, "The Confession: Pro," *idem.*, pp. 27–35; and Patrick MacFadden, "The Confession: Con," *idem.*, pp. 35–40.

opposition party. Yves Montand and Jean-Louis Trintignant are superb as the pacifist and government official respectively.[146]

Jean Cocteau

Beauty and the Beast (16mm: 1946, 90 min., b/w, English subtitles, sound, R-JAN)
In his first feature film, the gifted and unusual Cocteau adapted the classic fable to the screen. He gave it a unique interpretation in terms of man's feelings about love, isolation, greed and self-sacrifice. A fine performance by Jean Marais.

Orphée (16mm: 1949, 94 min., b/w, English subtitles, sound, R-JAN)
Cocteau wrote and directed this strange, haunting film loosely based upon a modern-day version of the myth of Orpheus and Eurydice. Georges Auric's memorable music and Nicolas Hayer's bewitching photography contributed to the weird effect.[147]

The Testament of Orpheus (16mm: 1960, 79 min., b/w, English subtitles, sound, R-CON)
This was Cocteau's sequel, with even more mysterious goings on.[148]

Jean-Luc Godard[149]

Alphaville (16mm: 1965, 100 min., b/w, English subtitles, sound, R-CON)
Here is Godard at his best, mixing literary allusions, science fiction, gangsters, and social satire. Eddie Constantine and Anna Karina star.[150]

Breathless (16mm: 1959, 89 min., b/w, English subtitles, sound, R-CON)

---

146. Joan Mellen, "Fascism in the Contemporary Cinema," *Film Quarterly* 24, no. 4 (Summer 1971) : 2–19.
147. Jean R. Debrix, "Cocteau's *Orpheus* Analyzed," translated by Edith Morgan King, *Films in Review* 11, no. 6 (June–July 1951) : 18–23; Raymond Durgnat, "Orphée," *Films and Filming* 10, no. 1 (October 1963) : 45–48; and Robert M. Hammond, "The Mysteries of Cocteau's *Orpheus*," *Cinema Journal* 11, no. 2 (Spring 1972) : 26–33.
148. George Amberg, "The Testament of Jean Cocteau," *Film Comment* 7, no. 4 (Winter 1971–72) : 23–27.
149. The following articles are useful on Godard: Norman Silverstein, "Godard and Revolution," *Films and Filming* 16, no. 9 (June 1970) : 96–98, 100, 102–105; Raoul Coutard, "Light of Day," *Sight and Sound* 35, no. 1 (Winter 1965–66) : 9–11; Jean-Luc Godard, "One or Two Things," *Sight and Sound* 36, no. 1 (Winter 1966–67) : 2–6; Jean-Luc Godard, "'Three Thousand Hours of Cinema," *Cahiers du Cinema in English* 10, CdC no. 184 (November 1966) : 10–15; Michel Delahaye, "Jean-Luc Godard and the Childhood of Art," *idem.*, CdC no. 179 (June 1966) : 18–29; Luc Moullet, "Jean-Luc Godard," 12 CdC no. 106 (April 1960) : 22–33; Jean-Luc Godard, "A Woman is a Woman," *idem.*, CdC no. 98 (August 1959) : 34–37; Jean-Andre Fieschi, "The Difficulty of Being Jean-Luc Godard," *idem.*, CdC no. 137 (November 1962) :38–43; Jean-Luc Godard, *et al.*, "Two Arts in One," *Cahiers du Cinema in English* 6, CdC no. 177 (April 1966) : 24–33; Claire Clouzot, "Godard and the US," *Sight and Sound* 37, no. 3 (Summer 1968) : 110–14; Raymond Federman, "Jean-Luc Godard and Americanism," *Film Heritage* 3, no. 3 (Spring 1968) : 1–10; Joel E. Siegel, "Between Art and Life," *idem.*, pp. 11–22, 47–48; Molly Haskell, "Omegaville," *idem.*, pp. 23–26; John Simon, "Bull in the China Shop: Godard's *La Chinoise*," *idem.*, pp. 35–47; Paul J. Sharits, "Red, Blue Godard," *Film Quarterly* 19, no. 4 (Summer 1966) : 24–29; James Roy MacBean, "Politics, Painting and the Language of Signs in Godard's *Made In USA*," *Film Quarterly* 22, no. 3 (Spring 1969) :18–25; David Cast, "Godard's Truths," *Film Heritage* 6, no. 4 (Summer 1971) :19–24; Brian Henderson, "Toward a Non-Bourgeois Camera Style," *Film Quarterly* 24, no. 2 (Winter 1970–71) : 2–14; and James Roy MacBean, "See You at Mao," *idem.*, pp. 15–23.
150. Richard Roud, "Anguish: Alphaville," *Sight and Sound* 34, no. 4 (Autumn 1965) : 164–66; and Jack Edmund Nolan, "Eddie Constantine," *Films in Review* 19, no. 7 (August–September 1968) : 431–44.

Most interesting about this adaptation of the American gangster genre is the director's experimentation and improvisation with editing. Jean-Paul Belmondo starred.[151]

Le Petit Soldat (16mm: 1960, 95 min., b/w, English sub-titles, sound, R-NYF)
Godard's second film was banned for two years because its hero, a member of a fascist terror organization, was considered subversive. It is really a cops-and-robbers film and very enjoyable.

Max Ophuls[152]

Lola Montes (16mm: 1955, 110 min., cinemascope, color, English subtitles, sound, R-AUD)
Max Ophuls's last movie depicts the amorous affairs of a famous circus courtesan, told mostly in flashback. The film stars Martine Carol, Anton Walbrook, and Peter Ustinov.[153]

Alain Resnais[154]

Hiroshima Mon Amour[155] (16mm: 1959, 88 min., b/w, English subtitles, sound, R-CON)
An exciting experience in filmic editing by one of the best of the New Wave French directors. The story involves a love affair between a French actress and a Japanese architect, and suggests the effects of the atomic bomb on our civilization.

Last Year at Marienbad[156] (16mm: 1961, 93 min., b/w, English subtitles, sound, R-AUD)
Resnais experimented in this film with time and its relationship to characters, to plot, and to the audience's confused reactions and interpretations.

---

151. David Shipman, "Belmondo," *Films and Filming* 10, no. 11 (August 1964) : 7–11.
152. Max Ophuls, "My Experience," *Cahiers du Cinema in English* 1, CdC no. 81 (January 1966) : 63–68; Forrest Williams, "The Mastery of Movement: An Appreciation of Max Ophuls," *Film Comment* 5, no. 4 (Winter 1969) : 70–74; Eric Rhode, "Max Ophuls," 159–70; Howard Koch, "Script to Screen with Max Ophuls," *Film Comment* 6, no. 4 (Winter 1970–71) : 40–43; Andrew Sarris, "Max Ophuls: An Introduction," *Film Comment* 7, no. 2 (Summer 1971) : 56–59; Michael Kerbel, "Letter From an Unknown Woman," *idem.*, pp. 60–61; Gary Carey, "Caught," *idem.*, pp. 62–64; William Paul, "The Reckless Moment," *idem.*, pp. 65–66; and Foster Hirsch, "Madame De," *idem.*, pp. 67–68.
153. Robin Bean, "Art and Artlessness: Peter Ustinov," *Films and Filming* 15, no. 1 (October 1968) : 4–8.
154. The following articles are helpful: Roy Armes, "Resnais and Reality," *Films and Filming* 16, no. 8 (May 1970) : 12–14; Richard Roud, "The Left Bank: Marker, Varda, Resnais," *Sight and Sound* 32, no. 1 (Winter 1962–63) : 24–27; Richard Roud, "Memories of Resnais," *Sight and Sound* 38, no. 3 (Summer 1969) :124–29, 162; and Noel Burch, "A Conversation with Resnais." *Film Quarterly* 13, no. 3 (Spring 1960) : 27–29.
155. Louis Marcorelles, "Alain Resnais and *Hiroshima Mon Amour:* Rebel With A Camera," *Sight and Sound* 39, no. 1 (Winter 1959–60) : 12–14; Henri Colpi, "Editing Hiroshima Mon Amour," *Sight and Sound* 39, no. 1 (Winter 1959–60) : 14–16; Richard Roud, "Conversation with Marguerite Duras," 39, no. 1 Winter 1959–60) : 16–17.
156. Alain Robbe-Grillet, "'L'Année Dernière à Marienbad," *Sight and Sound* 30, no. 4 (Autumn 1961) : 176–79; Jacques Brunius, "Every Year in Marienbad or the Discipline of Uncertainty," *Sight and Sound* 31, no. 3 (Summer 1962) : 122–27, 153; Alain Resnais, "Trying to Understand My Own Film," *Films and Filming* 8, no. 5 (February 1962) : 9–10, 41; Penelope Houston, "Resnais: *L'Année Dernière à Marienbad*," *Sight and Sound* 31, no. 1 (Winter 1961–62) : 26–28.

It is one of the most controversial films ever made, either considered a masterpiece or a complete bore.

François Truffaut[157]

The 400 Blows (16mm: 1959, 98 min., b/w, English subtitles, sound, R-JAN)
   This is Truffaut's first major film, semi-autobiographical, in which he recounts the terrifying events in a lonely boy's world.

Jules and Jim (16mm: 1962, 104 min., b/w, English sub-titles, sound, R-JAN)
   The story takes place in 1914 and involves a curious triangular love affair of three cosmopolitan young people. There is an outstanding performance given by Jeanne Moreau.[158] The film may well be Truffaut's masterpiece.[159]

INDIA[160]

Books

Barnouw, Erik and Subrahmanyam Krishnaswamy. *Indian Film*. New York: Columbia University Press, 1963.
   India, one of the largest filmmaking countries in the world, has her filmmakers treated sympathetically and perceptively in this standard book. For many who have never been to India, this text offers some interesting observations as well as some significant information on the start of Indian filmmaking, the influence that mythology has on her artists, and a very helpful chapter on Ray.

Satyajit Ray[161]

Seton, Marie. *Portrait of a Director: Satyajit Ray*. Bloomington: Indiana University Press, 1971.
   In this superbly written and exhaustive study of the famed Indian director, Seton, as always in her work, offers a critical and biographical examination of the man, his films, and his unique cinematic contributions, particu-

---

157. The following articles are useful: Michael Klein, "The Literary Sophistication of François Truffaut," *Film Comment* 3, no. 3 (Summer 1965) : 24–29; Paul Ronder, "François Truffaut: An Interview," translated and abridged from *Cahiers du Cinema,* no. 138 (December 1962) , *Film Quarterly* 18, no. 1 (Fall 1963) : 3–13; Judith Shatnoff, "François Truffaut: Anarchist Imagination," *Film Quarterly* 16, no. 3 (Spring 1963) : 3–11; and David Bordwell, "François Truffaut: A Man can Serve Two Masters," *Film Comment* 7, no. 1 (Spring 1971) : 18–23.
158. Alan Stanbrook, "The Stars They Couldn't Photograph," *Films and Filming* 9, no. 5 (February 1963) : 10–14.
159. Louis Marcorelles, "Interview with Truffaut," *Sight and Sound* 31, no. 1 (Winter 1961–62) : 35–37, 48; and Roger Greenspun, "Elective Affinities: Aspects of Jules and Jim," *Sight and Sound* 32, no. 2 (Spring 1963) : 78–82.
160. The following articles offer some help: Marie Seton, "Journey Through India," *Sight and Sound* 26, no. 4 (Spring 1957) : 198–202; and Chidananda Das Gupta, "Indian Cinema Today," *Film Quarterly* 22, no. 4 (Summer 1969) : 27–35.
161. The following articles are useful: Eric Rhode, "Satyajit Ray: A Study," *Sight and Sound* 30, no. 3 (Summer 1961) : 132–36; Marie Seton, "Kanchenjunga: Satyajit Ray at Work on His Film," *Sight and Sound* 31, no. 2 (Spring 1962) : 73–75; Folke Isaksson, "Conversation with Satyajit Ray," *Sight and Sound* 39, no. 3 (Summer 1970) : 114–20; Satyajit Ray, "From Film to Film," *Cahiers du Cinema in English* 3, CdC no. 175 (February 1966) : 12–19, 62–63; and James Blue, "Satyajit Ray: An Interview," *Film Comment* 4, no. 4 (Summer 1968) : 4–17.

larly his debts to the documentary and the neo-realistic traditions. Many useful stills and a helpful index are included.

"Special Issue on Satyajit Ray," *Montage* 5–6 (July 1966).

Up to the Seton book, this was the best available source on the man who put Indian films on a world circuit. There are useful articles by Ray on his work as well as essays by his collaborators.

* Wood, Robin. *The Apu Trilogy.* New York: Praeger Publishers, Inc., 1971.

This book provides a good study of the three films that catapulted Ray to international fame. Wood's comments are stimulating, perceptive, and entertaining. Stills and a helpful bibliography are included.

Films

Satyajit Ray

Pather Panchali (16mm: 1956, 112 min., b/w, English subtitles, sound, R-AUD)

This cinematic poem of the life of a poor but dedicated Indian scholar and his family struggling to survive in a tiny Bengali hamlet was the first film to bring Ray justly deserved fame. It was awarded a significant prize at the 1956 Cannes Film Festival.

The World of Apu (16mm: 1960, 103 min., b/w, English subtitles, sound, R-AUD)

In this final part of the film trilogy, Ray reaches his greatest heights as he poignantly and magnificently follows the difficult life of Apu, the now grown-up son of the poor scholar's family, whose meager living and happy marriage are tragically disrupted by his wife's death in childbirth. The movie ends on an optimistic note as the bereaved husband finally becomes reconciled to the child.

ITALY[162]

Books

Michelangelo Antonioni[163]

* Antonioni, Michelangelo. *Screenplays: L'Avventura/Il Grido/La Notte/*

---

162. The following articles on Italian Cinema are useful: Giulio Cesare Castello, "Cinema Italiano 1962," translated by Isabel Quigley, *Sight and Sound* 32, no. 1 (Winter 1962–63) : 28–33; John Francis Lane, "A Case of Artistic Inflation," *Sight and Sound* 32, no. 3 (Summer 1963) : 130–35; John Francis Lane, "The Face of '63—Italy," *Films and Filming* 9, no. 7 (April 1963) : 11–21; John Francis Lane, "Italy's Angry Young Directors," *Films and Filming* 15, no. 1 (October 1968) : 74–80; John Francis Lane, "A Style is Born," *Films and Filming* 5, no. 7 (April 1959) : 13–15, 32; Geoffrey Nowell-Smith, "Italy Sotto Voce," *Sight and Sound* 37, no. 3 (Summer 1968) : 145–47; and Merando Morandini, "The Year of *La Dolce Vita*," *Sight and Sound* 29, no. 3 (Summer 1960) : 123–27.

163. The following articles are helpful: Michele Manceaux, "An Interview with Antonioni," *Sight and Sound* 30, no. 1 (Winter 1960–61) : 4–8; Richard Roud, "Five Films," *idem.*, pp. 8–11; Geoffrey Nowell-Smith, "The Event and the Image: Michelangelo Antonioni," *Sight and Sound* 33, no. 1 (Winter 1964–65) : 14–20; Penelope Houston, "Keeping Up with the Antonionis," *Sight and Sound* 33, no. 4 (Autumn 1964) : 163–68; Marsha Kinder, "Antonioni in Transit," *Sight and Sound* 36, no. 3 (Summer 1967) : 132–37; Jean-Luc Godard, "Night, Eclipse, Dawn: An Interview with Michelangelo Antonioni," *Cahiers du Cinema in English* 1 CdC, no. 160 (January 1966) : 19–29; and Gordon Gow, "Antonioni Men," *Films and Filming* 16, no. 9 (June 1970) : 40–44, 46.

L'Eclisse. With an Introduction by the Author. New York: Orion Press, 1963.

* Cameron, Ian and Robin Wood. *Antonioni.* Revised Edition. New York: Praeger Publishers, 1970.
     Basically, Cameron's useful monograph listed below, with additional comments by Wood on *Blow-Up, The Red Desert* and *Zabriskie Point.*

* Cameron, Ian. "Special Issue: Antonioni," *Film Quarterly* 16, no. 1 (Fall 1962) .
     A carefully written and perceptive analysis of Antonioni's basic camera work.

* Huss, Roy (editor) . *Focus on Blow-Up.* Englewood Cliffs, N.J.: Prentice-Hall, Inc., 1971.
     This valuable anthology of the film, in addition to a variety of critical reviews, includes an outline of the film, three sequences and shot analysis, and a filmography.

* Leprohon, Pierre. *Michelangelo Antonioni.* New York: Simon and Schuster, 1963.
     A translation from the *Cinema D'Aujourd'hui* series, the book is valuable mainly for its many Antonioni quotations and its appendix.

* Strick, Philip. "Antonioni: A Monograph," *Motion* 5 (March 1963) .
     A brief sketch of the author's life with an uneven discussion of his major films. Strick concludes with a series of critical quotations on Antonioni's films by reviewers.

Federico Fellini[164]

Boyer, Deena. *The Two Hundred Days of 8½.* Translated by Charles Lam Markmann. With an Afterword by Dwight Macdonald. New York: The Macmillan Company, 1964.
     This diary of the day-by-day shooting of the film is a film buff's bargain, filled with cutesy stories and behind-the-scenes stills. Considering the movie, the book is lacking in depth and serious insights.

* Budgen, Suzanne. *Fellini.* London: The British Film Institute, 1966.
     This is a short, useful, and readable reference work on Fellini's works up to *La Dolce Vita.* It contains extracts from a Belgian television interview with the director and *La Strada.*

Hughes, Eileen Lanouette. *On the Set of Fellini's Satyricon: A Behind-the-Scenes Diary.* New York: William Morrow and Company, 1972.
     One of the best books of its kind, this fast-reading and entertaining account of the movie is a superb bedside companion and a useful source for behind-the-camera comments and details.

---

164. The following articles are useful: Gideon Bachmann, "An Interview with Federico Fellini," *Sight and Sound* 30, no. 2 (Spring 1963) : 82–87; Eric Rhode, "Federico Fellini," *Tower of Babel,* pp. 121–36; Pierre Kast, "Giulietta and Federico: Visits with Fellini," *Cahiers du Cinema in English* 5, CdC no. 164 (March 1965) : 24–33; Irving R. Levine, "I Was Born for the Cinema," *Film Comment* 4, no. 1 (Fall 1966) : 77–84; Peter Harcourt, "The Secret Life of Federico Fellini," *Film Quarterly* 19, no. 3 (Spring 1966) : 4–19; Forrest Williams, "Fellini's Voices," *Film Quarterly* 21, no. 3 (Spring 1968) : 21–25; Enzo Peri, "Fellini: An Interview," *Film Quarterly* 15, no. 1 (Fall 1961) : 30–33; Eugene Walter, "The Wizardry of Fellini," *Films and Filming* 12, no. 9 (June 1966) : 18–26; and James R. Silke (editor) , *Federico Fellini* (Washington, D.C.: The American Film Institute, 1970) .

* Salachas, Gilbert. *Federico Fellini.* Translated by Rosalie Siegel. New York: Crown Publishers, Inc., 1969.

Originally published in the *Cinema d'Aujourd'hui* Series in 1963, this is the weakest in the French studies but more important than the Budgen book. Salachas provides some entertaining anecdotes, critical reviews, excerpts from seven screenplays, and a badly constructed biographical essay. There are also a good filmography and bibliography.

Solmi, Angelo. *Fellini.* Translated by Elizabeth Greenwood. New York: Humanities Press, Inc., 1968.

Divided into two major sections, the book first charts the familiar themes in Fellini's movies by discussing their relationship to his life and secondly shows in detail how the director's life is incorporated into the films. Solmi is particularly good when it comes to presenting the economic and artistic difficulties Fellini has encountered.

* Taylor, John Russell. *Cinema Eye Cinema Ear: Some Key Film-Makers of the Sixties.* New York: Hill and Wang, 1964.

Here is a basic and valuable introduction to some of the best filmmakers: Antonioni, Buñuel, Bergman, Bresson, Hitchcock, Truffaut, and Godard. But the best essay is on Fellini. It is original, insightful, and essential.

* Fellini, Federico. *La Dolce Vita.* New York: Ballantine Books, 1963.

* Fellini, Federico. *Juliet of the Spirits.* New York: Ballantine Books, 1965.

* Fellini, Federico. *Three Screenplays: I Vitelloni/Il Bidone/The Temptations of Doctor Antonio.* Translated from the Italian by Judith Green. New York: The Orion Press, 1970.

Pier Paola Pasolini[165]

* Stack, Oswald. *Pasolini on Pasolini: Interviews.* Bloomington: Indiana University Press, 1969.

During two weeks in Rome in 1968, Stack interviewed the talented director and the results are the best and most valuable information available on his career, theories and filmography.

Luchino Visconti[166]

* Nowell-Smith, Geoffrey. *Luchino Visconti.* New York: Doubleday and Company, 1968.

Another Renaissance filmmaker who also has deep roots in the Italian opera and theater, Visconti has had a long cinema career but made few movies. Nowell-Smith does his best to help illuminate the man, his work, and his virtues. Since this is the only book in English on Visconti, it is important. Best use of illustrations in the Cinema One series.

* Visconti, Luchino. *Three Screenplays: White Nights, Rocco and His*

---

165. Roy Armes, "Pasolini," *Films and Filming* 17, no. 9 (June 1971) : 55–58.
166. Some useful articles are Giulio Cesare Castello, "Luchino Visconti," *Sight and Sound* 25, no. 4 (Spring 1956) : 184–90, 220; Luchino Visconti, "Drama of Non-Existence," *Cahiers du Cinema in English* 2, CdC no. 174 (January 1966) : 12–18; Jean Collet, "The Absences of Sandra," *idem.*, pp. 18–21; Gianfranco Poggi, "Luchino Visconti and the Italian Cinema," *Film Quarterly* 13, no. 3 (Spring 1960) : 11–22; and Walter F. Korte, Jr., "Marxism and Formalism in the Films of Luchino Visconti," *Cinema Journal* 11, no. 1 (Fall 1971) : 2–12.

Brothers, The Job. Translated from the Italian by Judith Green. New York: The Orion Press, 1970.

* Visconti, Luchino. *Two Screenplays: La Terra Trema/Senso.* Translated from the Italian by Judith Green. New York: The Orion Press, 1970.

Films

Michelangelo Antonioni

L'Avventura (16mm: 1960, 145 min., b/w, English subtitles, sound, R-JAN)
   This unusual story of an unsuccessful search for a lost friend illustrates the director's view of man's helplessness. Antonioni makes it a point here, and also elsewhere, to concern himself with the paradoxes inherent in many human beings.[167]

Blow-Up (MGM—16mm: 1967, 108 min., color, sound, R-FNC)
   In his first English film, Antonioni explored different kinds of visual reality by focusing attention on a peculiar weekend in the life of a fashionable London photographer. Outstanding performances by David Hemmings and Vanessa Redgrave.[168]

Red Desert (16mm: 1964, 116 min., color, English subtitles, sound, R-AUD)
   Another clinical study, starring Monica Vitti, of a woman confused, trapped, and neurotic in an industrial society.[169]

Mario Bellocchio

China is Near (16mm: 1968, 108 min., b/w, English subtitles, sound, R-COL)
   Here is a good example of one of Italy's new directors in a screenplay of an egocentric woman, her two brothers, and a dangerous romance. Elda Tattloli doubled as scriptwriter and actress. This revolutionary film about left wing politics was temporarily banned in Italy.[170]

Bernardo Bertolucci

The Conformist (16mm: 1970, 115 min., color, English subtitles, sound, R-GEN)
   In a tightly constructed film, Bertolucci magnificently manipulates time to show a fascist secret agent (Jean-Louis Trintignant) involved in three

---

167. John Francis Lane, "Oh! Oh! Antonioni," *Films and Filming* 9, no. 3 (December 1962) : 58–66.
168. Carey Harrison, "Blow-Up," *Sight and Sound* 36, no. 2 (Spring 1967) : 60–62; Arthur Knight, "Blow-Up," *Film Heritage* 2, no. 3 (Spring 1967) : 3–6; Hubert Meeker, "Blow-Up," *idem.*, pp. 7–15; Bosley Crowther, "Blow-Up," *The Great Films*, pp. 242–46; and Max Kozloff, "The Blow-Up," *Film Quarterly* 20, no. 3 (Spring 1967) : 28–31.
169. Michele Manceaux, "In the Red Desert," *Sight and Sound* 33, no. 3 (Summer 1964) : 118–19; Richard Roud and Penelope Houston, "The Red Desert," *Sight and Sound* 34, no. 2 (Spring 1965) : 76–81, 103; and Colin Young, "Red Desert," *Film Quarterly* 19, no. 1 (Fall 1965) : 51–54.
170. Claire Clouzot, "China is Near," *Film Quarterly* 22, no. 1 (Fall 1968) : 70–72; and William Starr *et al.*, "Mario Bellocchio: An Interview," *Film Society Review* 7, no. 5 (January 1972) : 33–40. The script is available from Grossman Publishers in New York.

murders and his eventual reactions years later as he watches the end of the fascist party in Italy.[171]

Vittorio de Sica

The Garden of the Finzi-Continis (Italian-German—16mm: 1970, 103 min., color, English subtitles, sound, R-CIV)

Adapted from Giorgio Bassani's novel, de Sica's thoughtful and depressing film follows the adolescent love in the late 1930s of a middle-class Jewish boy (Lino Capolichio) for the aristocratic and beautiful Jewess Micol (Dominique Sanda). Neither the boy's parents nor the wealthy Finzi-Continis family can avoid at the end their eventual arrest by Mussolini's fascist government. In between we are shown a remarkable recreation of a frightening era which might yet occur again.

Two Women (16mm: 1961, 105 min., b/w, English sub-titles, sound, R-AUD)

The story of a mother and daughter who try desperately to stay alive in Italy toward the end of World War II. There is an excellent performance given by Sophia Loren, for which she won an Oscar.

Federico Fellini[172]

La Dolce Vita (16mm: 1961, 180 min., b/w, English sub-titles, sound, R-AUD)

In its initial release, this was a sensational and significant exposé of Roman high society, which centered around the newsgathering activities of a scandal magazine reporter searching for smut. Outstanding performances by Marcello Mastroianni, Anouk Aimée, and Anita Ekberg.

8½ (16mm: 1963, 135 min., b/w, plus color, English subtitles, sound, R-AUD)

This extraordinary autobiographical film explores the psychological and actual world of a famous Italian film director who seeks rest at a spa as he is preparing for a new movie. Another fine job turned in by Mastroianni and Aimée.

La Strada (16mm: 1954, 107 min., b/w, English subtitles, sound, R-AUD, MMM)

The story of three people whose loneliness on the roads of Italy communicates such emotional appeals to the audience that the film is one of the most acclaimed pictures in film history. Magnificent performances by Anthony Quinn, Giulietta Masina, and Richard Basehart.

Satyricon (16mm: 1969, 136 min., color, English subtitles, sound, R-UAS)

In this stunning commentary on man's struggle to survive, Fellini follows the adventures of a young and serious Roman (Martin Potter) who faces death-defying challenges successfully because he understands his own strengths and weaknesses.[173]

---

171. Richard Roud, "Fathers and Sons," *Sight and Sound* 40, no. 2 (Spring 1971) : 60–64; Marilyn Goldin, "Bertolucci on *The Conformist*," *idem.*, pp. 64–66; and Amos Vogel, "Bernardo Bertolucci: An Interview," *Film Comment* 7, no. 3 (Fall 1971) : 24–29.

172. Joseph McBride, "The Director as Superstar," *Sight and Sound* 41, no. 2 (Spring 1972) : 78–81.

173. Joseph O'Mealy, "Fellini Satyricon: A Structural Analysis," *Film Heritage* 6, no. 4

Pier Paolo Pasolini

The Gospel According to St. Matthew (16mm: 1964, 136 min., b/w, English subtitles, sound, R-CCM)

Told in the *cinema verité* style, this Biblical film is one of the most artistic motion pictures of our time. Jesus, depicted as a magnificent revolutionary figure, has neven been presented more forcefully on the screen.[174]

Gillo Pontecarvo

The Battle of Algiers (16mm: 1967, 120 min., b/w, English subtitles, sound, R-ADF, AUD, MMM)

This extremely powerful film of the Algerian uprising against the French between 1954 and 1957 is a model for mixing documentary technique with a fictional narrative.[175]

Burn (United Artists—16mm: 1970, 115 min., color, sound, R-UAS)

In this fascinating attempt to make a contemporary statement on black Caribbean heritage and the modern struggle for freedom, Pontecorvo tells a mid-19th-century story of a Caribbean Bolivar (Evaristo Marquez) who is first used and then destroyed by a British secret agent (Marlon Brando).[176]

Francesco Rosi

Moment of Truth (16mm: 1965, 110 min., color, English subtitles, sound, R-AUD)

Rosi co-directed and wrote the screenplay for this incredible semi-documentary film about a poor boy who grows up to be a bullfighter. The fight scenes are some of the best ever filmed.[177]

JAPAN[178]

General Books

Anderson, Joseph and Donald Richie. *The Japanese Film: Art and Industry*. With a Foreword by Akira Kurosawa. Rutland: Charles E. Tuttle Company, 1959.

The best book of its kind on the subject and invaluable for studying the films of Kon Ichikawa and Akira Kurosawa. The authors present important

(Summer 1971) : 25–29; and Marsha Kinder and Beverle Houston, "Satyricon," *Close-Up: A Critical Perspective on Film* (New York: Harcourt Brace Jovanovich, Inc., 1972), pp. 313–19.

174. Pier Paolo Pasolini, "The Cinema of Poetry," *Cahiers du Cinema in English* CdC no. 171 (October 1965) : 34–43; "Pier Paolo Pasolini: An Epical-Religious View of the World," *Film Quarterly* 18, no. 4 (Summer 1965) : 31–45; and James Blue, "Pier Paolo Pasolini: An Interview," *Film Comment* 3, no. 4 (Fall 1965) : 24–32.

175. Marsha Kinder and Beverle Houston, "The Battle of Algiers," *Close-Up: A Critical Perspective on Film*, pp. 332, 334–37.

176. David Wilson, "Politics and Pontecorvo," *Sight and Sound* 40, no. 3 (Summer 1971) : 160–61.

177. John Francis Lane, "Moments of Truth: Francesco Rosi Interviewed," *Films and Filming* 16, no. 12 (September 1970) : 6–10.

178. The following articles are helpful: Masayoshi Iwabutchi, "1954 in Japan," *Sight and Sound* 24, no. 4 (Spring 1955) : 202–5; J. L. Anderson, "Seven From the Past: Aspects of the Pre-War Japanese Cinema," *Sight and Sound* 27, no. 2 (Autumn 1957) : 82–87; Lindsay Anderson, "Two Inches off the Ground," *Sight and Sound* 27, no. 3 (Winter

insights into the Japanese directors' attempts to revere or revolt against tradition.

Richie, Donald. *Japanese Movies*. Tokyo: Japanese Travel Bureau, 1961.
A more condensed version of *The Japanese Film*.

* Richie, Donald. *Japanese Cinema: Film Style and National Character*. New York: Doubleday and Company, Inc., 1971.
This text is an extensively revised, expanded, and updated version of *Japanese Movies* offering readers capsule views on the history of Japan's film industry from 1896 to 1971. Richie also provides an appendix on Japanese films now available in the United States in 16mm with addresses of the distributors.

* Svensson, Arne. *Japan*. New York: A. S. Barnes and Company, 1971.
This valuable "dictionary" provides us with the only available English guide to career filmographies of the major Japanese directors, players and technicians. together with accurate credits and useful plot synopses to the most significant films of Japan. In addition, there is a welcome index and over 100 well-produced illustrations.

Akira Kurosawa

* Richie, Donald. *The Films of Akira Kurosawa*. Berkeley: University of California Press, 1964.
Probably one of the best studies to date done on any director. Richie analyzes Kurosawa's moral emphasis and his great concern with illusion and reality.

* *Ikiru: A Film by Akira Kurosawa*. English Translation and Introduction by Donald Richie. New York: Simon and Schuster, 1969.

* *Rashomon: A Film by Akira Kurosawa*. English Translation by Donald Richie. New York: Grove Press, 1969.

* *The Seven Samurai: A Film by Akira Kurosawa*. English Translation and Introduction by Donald Richie. New York: Simon and Schuster, 1970.

Films

Kon Ichikawa

Fires on the Plain (16mm: 1959, 105 min., b/w, English subtitles, sound, R-AUD, JAN)

1957–58) : 131–32, 160; Donald Richie, "Japan: The Younger Talents," *Sight and Sound* 29, no. 2 (Spring 1960) : 78–81; Donald Richie, "Yasujiro Ozu: The Syntax of His Films," *Film Quarterly* 17, no. 2 (Winter 1963–64) : 11–16; Donald Richie, "The Later Films of Yasujiro Ozu," *Film Quarterly* 13, no. 1 (Fall 1959) : 18–25; Donald Richie, "The Face of '63: Japan," *Films and Filming* 9, no. 10 (July 1963) : 15–18, 35–36; Donald Richie, "A Personal Record," *Film Quarterly* 14, no. 1 (Fall 1960) : 20–30; Clifford V. Harrington, "Japanese Film-Making Today," *Films in Review* 8, no. 3 (March 1957) : 102–7; James Blue, "Susumu Hani," *Film Comment* 5, no. 2 (Spring 1969) : 24–36; Alan Stanbrook, "Break with the Past: Part One," *Films and Filming* 6, no. 6 (March 1960) : 9–11, 30; and Alan Stanbrook, ". . . Part Two," *Films and Filming* 6, no. 7 (April 1960) : 13–14, 30; and Larry N. Landrum, "Popular Asian Film: A Checklist of Sources, Part I," *Journal of Popular Film* 1, no. 3 (Summer 1972) : 249–52. Part II was not ready when this book went to press.

This example of Japanese personal style in filmmaking concerns the story of a Japanese survivor's attempt to exist on Leyte toward the end of the Second World War.[179]

Akira Kurosawa[180]

Rashomon (16mm: 1951, 87 min., b/w, English subtitles, sound, R-AUD)
   A film dealing with the relativity of truth and one of the best films ever made.

Ikiru (16mm: 1952, 140 min., b/w, English subtitles, sound, R-AUD)
   This movie is another example of Kurosawa's philosophical bent. The story involves a dying man's search for the meaning of life.

The Seven Samurai (16mm: 1954, 141 min., b/w, English subtitles, sound, R-AUD)
   This epic story of seven Samurai warriors who defend a village against bandits is considered by many to be Japan's masterpiece.[181]

Hiroshi Teshigahara

Woman in the Dunes (16mm: 1964, 130 min., b/w, English subtitles, sound, R-CON)
   Based upon Kobo Abe's allegorical novel, this haunting film explores one man's values of life, freedom, and love as he is held prisoner with a woman at the bottom of a sandpit in a remote desert area. It is one of the most memorable films of the last decade.[182]

POLAND[183]

Books

Banaszkiewicz, Wladyslaw *et al. Contemporary Polish Cinematography.* Warsaw: Polona Publishing House, 1962.
   Interest for most Americans in Polish cinema began with men like Roman Polanski and Andrezej Wajda, with the excellent Polish animated films,

179. Donald Richie, "The Several Sides of Kon Ichikawa," *Sight and Sound* 35, no. 2 (Spring 1966) : 84–86; and Tom Milne, "The Skull Beneath the Skin," *Sight and Sound* 35, no. 4 (Autumn 1966) : 185–89.

180. Jay Leyda, "The Films of Kurosawa," *Sight and Sound* 24, no. 2 (October–December 1954) : 74–78, 112; Donald Richie, "Kurosawa on Kurosawa: Part One," *Sight and Sound* 33, no. 3 (Summer 1964) : 108–13; Donald Richie, ". . . Part Two," *Sight and Sound* 33, no. 4 (Autumn 1964) : 200–203; Douglas McVay, "The Rebel in Kimono: First Part of an Analysis of Kurosawa's Work for the Cinema," *Films and Filming* 7, no. 10 (July 1961) : 9–10, 34; and Douglas McVay, ". . . Part Two," *Films and Filming* 7, no. 11 (August 1961) : 15–16.

181. S. G. P. Alexander, "The Magnificent Seven," *Screen Education Yearbook* (1964) : 66–68.

182. Judith Shatnoff, "Woman in the Dunes," *Film Quarterly* 18, no. 2 (Winter 1964) : 43–46.

183. The following articles are helpful: Gene Moskowitz, "The Uneasy East: Aleksander Ford and the Polish Cinema," *Sight and Sound* 27, no. 3 (Winter 1957–58) : 136–40; David Robinson, "Better Late than Never," *Sight and Sound* 31, no. 2 (Spring 1962) : 67–70, 103; Boleslaw Michalek, "The Polish Drama," *Sight and Sound* 29, no. 4 (Autumn 1960) : 198–200; David Stewart Hull, "New Films from Poland," *Film Quarterly* 14, no. 3 (Spring 1961) : 24–29; and Mira Coopman, "Report from Poland," *Films and Filming* 10, no. 4 (January 1964) : 47–51.

and certain key documentaries. The collective authors (seven in all) decided that the foreign audience should know more about Poland's film history and present operating procedures. This book helps learn about those areas and gives some useful information about important filmmakers.

Roman Polanski

* Butler, Ivan. *The Cinema of Roman Polanski.* New York: A. S. Barnes and Company, 1970.
   This informative and lucid book is the only full-length study available on the director of *Knife in the Water, Repulsion,* and *Rosemary's Baby.*

Films

Roman Polanski[184]

Knife in the Water (16mm: 1962, 95 min., b/w, English subtitles, sound, R-JAN)
   A couple having marital problems pick up a hitchhiker and take him for a weekend on their yacht. Polanski develops this simple relationship into a significant experience for everyone, all in his first film.[185]

Repulsion (Columbia—16mm: 1965, 105 min., b/w, sound, R-COL)
   Polanski made his second film in England and used Catherine Deneuve in this macabre story of a mentally ill woman whose tormented lusts and disgust for men turn her into a murderess.[186]

Rosemary's Baby (Paramount—16mm: 1968, 136 min., color, sound, R-FNC)
   In a fascinating and striking screen version of Ira Levin's novel, Polanski centers on a young married couple's involvement with the followers of witch-craft and Satan. Ruth Gordon won an Oscar for her supporting role as the wife of the evil coven leader. Fine performances are also turned in by Mia Farrow and John Cassavetes as the naive couple.[187]

Andrzej Wajda[188]

Ashes and Diamonds (16mm: 1959, 105 min., b/w, English subtitles, sound, R-JAN)
   Rarely has anyone captured the disillusionment and horror that follow a town's revenge on its former Quislings. Wajda is splendid in showing how it destroys a young idealist in war-torn Poland.

Kanal (16mm: 1957, 96 min., b/w, English subtitles, sound, R-JAN)
   This grim film traces the parallels between discouraged soldiers existing

---

184. See the following: Michel Delahaye and Jean-Andre Fieschi, "Landscape of a Mind: Interview with Roman Polanski," *Cahiers du Cinema in English* 3, CdC no. 175 (February 1966) : 28–35; Harrison Engle, "Roman Polanski in New York," *Film Comment* 5, no. 1 (Fall 1968) : 4–11; and Gordon Gow, "Satisfaction—A Most Unpopular Feeling," *Films and Filming* 15, no. 7 (April 1969) : 15–18.
   185. Krzysztof-Teodor Toeplitz, "Jerzy Skolimowski: Portrait of a Debutant Director," *Film Quarterly* 26, no. 1 (Fall 1967) : 25–31.
   186. T. J. Ross, "Roman Polanski, Repulsion and the New Mythology," *Film Heritage* 4, no. 4 (Winter 1968–69) : 1–10.
   187. Robert Chappetta, "Rosemary's Baby," *Film Quarterly* 22, no. 3 (Spring 1969) : 35–38.
   188. Eric Rhode, "Andrzej Wajda," *Tower of Babel,* pp. 171–90.

in Poland's sewers with the nation's personal dejection. There is also a tragic romance that shows Wajda's wonderful ability to mix sentiment with tension.

SPAIN[189]

Books

* Kyrou, Ado. *Luis Buñuel*. New York: Simon and Schuster, 1963.

A translation from the *Cinema d'Aujourd'hui* collection, this book is valuable for its script extracts, footnotes, letters, and interviews.

* Buñuel, Luis. *Three Screenplays: Viridiana/The Exterminating Angel/ Simon of the Desert*. New York: The Orion Press, 1969.

Films

Luis Buñuel

Viridiana (16mm: 1961, 90 min., b/w, English subtitles, sound, R-AUD)

A cynical account of a young novitiate whose personal tragedy is told with emotional and forceful cinematic action.[190]

Belle de Jour (France—16mm: 100 min., color, English subtitles, sound, R-CIN)

Buñuel is brilliant as he creates a fantistic story about a woman's sexual desires, her relationships with men, and her marriage. Catherine Deneuve gives an outstanding performance.[191]

SWEDEN[192]

Books

* Cowie, Peter. *Swedish Cinema*. New York: A. S. Barnes and Company, 1966.

This handy, comprehensive guide to the history of Swedish films offers some very useful information about directors, movies, and personalities and helps us to place it all in a specific context.

---

189. Juan Cobos, "The Decade: Spain," *Films and Filming* 9, no. 4 (January 1963) : 67–71; and Juan Cobos, "The Face of '63: The Spanish Influence," *Films and Filming* 10, no. 1 (October 1963) : 39–43.

190. David Robinson, "Thank God—I Am Still an Atheist: Luis Buñuel and *Viridiana*," *Sight and Sound* 31, no. 3 (Summer 1962) : 116–18, 155.

191. Elliott Stein, "Buñuel's Golden Bowl," *Sight and Sound* 36, no. 4 (Autumn 1967) : 172–75; and Margot S. Kernan, "Belle de Jour," *Film Quarterly* 23, no. 1 (Fall 1969) : 38–41.

192. Vernon Young, "After Bergman," *Sight and Sound* 32, no. 2 (Spring 1963) : 96–99; Peter Cowie, "Swedish Films at Sorrento," *Film Comment* 6, no. 2 (Summer 1970) : 22–25; Frederic Fleischer, "Export or Die," *idem.*, pp. 36–37, Rune Waldekranz, "Young Swedish Cinema: In Relation to Swedish Film Tradition," *idem.*, pp. 38–43; Ann Morrissett, "The Swedish Paradox," *Sight and Sound* 30. no. 4 (Autumn 1961) : 192–94, 207; and Ann Morrissett, "Sweden: Paradise or Paradox," *Film Quarterly* 15, no. 1 (Fall 1961) : 22–29.

* Cowie, Peter, in collaboration with Arne Svensson. *Sweden I/II.* Two Volumes. New York: A. S. Barnes and Company, 1970.

These illustrated dictionaries of key figures, credits, and plot outlines are worthwhile reference books and very nicely produced. Book II is an updated version of *Swedish Cinema.*

Ingmar Bergman[193]

* Cowie, Peter. "Ingmar Bergman: A Monograph," *Motion* 4 (March 1962) .

A brief sketch of Bergman's life, with a commentary that shows the regard that many people have for the great Swedish director.

Donner, Jorn. *The Personal Vision of Ingmar Bergman.* Translated by Holger Lundbergh. Bloomington: Indiana University Press, 1964.

A more critical analysis by a Swedish critic on Bergman's existential tendencies in filmmaking; its major drawback is the eclectic organization of its very useful information.

Gibson, Arthur. *The Silence of God: Creative Response to the Films of Ingmar Bergman.* New York: Harper and Row, 1969.

Throughout seven of Bergman's major films—*The Seventh Seal, Wild Strawberries, The Magician, Through a Glass Darkly, Winter Light, The Silence, Persona*—the question of God's silence remains uppermost in this critic's mind. By providing us with a detailed analysis of each film, Gibson offers some fascinating and significant opinions.

* Gill, Jerry H. *Ingmar Bergman and the Search for Meaning.* Grand Rapids: William B. Eerdmans Publishing Company, 1969.

This ambitious Assistant Professor of Philosophy tries to analyze Bergman's attitudes toward an ideal community implied in *The Seventh Seal, Wild Strawberries, Through a Glass Darkly, Winter Light,* and *The Silence.* A good idea, but not in 44 pages!

* Isaksson, Ulla. *The Virgin Spring.* New York: Ballantine Books, 1960.

A copy of the script for the film of the same name. Scripts used by Bergman are extremely useful for studying his films since he writes most of his material himself.

Simon, John. *Ingmar Bergman Directs.* New York: Harcourt Brace Jovanovich, Inc., 1972.

Without question this study of four key Bergman films—*The Clown's*

---

193. The following articles are helpful: Erik Ulrichsen, "Ingmar Bergman and the Devil," *Sight and Sound* 27, no. 5 (Summer 1958) : 224–30; Jerry Vermilye, "An Ingmar Bergman Film Index," *Films in Review* 12, no. 5 (May 1961) : 280–92; Jean-Luc Godard, "Bergmanorama," *Cahiers du Cinema in English* 1, CdC no. 85 (January 1966) : 56–62; Ingmar Bergman, "My Three Powerfully Effective Commandments," translated by P. E. Burke and Lennart Swahn, *Film Comment* 6, no. 2 (Summer 1970) : 8–20; Ingmar Bergman, "The Serpent's Skin," *Cahiers du Cinema in English* 11, CdC no. 188 (March 1967) : 24–29; Jean-Louis Comolli, "The Phantom of Personality," *idem.,* pp. 30–33; David Madden, "The Virgin Spring: Anatomy of a Mythic Image," *Film Heritage* 2, no. 2 (Winter 1966–67) : 2–20; Birgitta Steene, "The Isolated Hero of Ingmar Bergman," *Film Comment* 3, no. 2 (Spring 1965) : 68–78; Robert Rosen, "The Relationship of Ingmar Bergman to E. T. A. Hoffmann," *Film Comment* 6, no. 1 (Spring 1970) : 26–31; Eugene Archer, "The Rock of Life," *Films in Review* 12, no. 4 (Summer 1959) : 3–16; Birgitta Steene, "Images and Words in Ingmar Bergman's Films," *Cinema Journal* 10, no. 1 (Fall 1970) : 23–33; and Art Carduner, "Nobody Has Any Fun in Bergman's Movies," *Film Society Review* 7, no. 5 (January 1972) : 27–32.

312   FILM STUDY: A Resource Guide

Evening (Naked Night/Sawdust and Tinsel), Smiles of a Summer Night, Winter Light, and *Persona*—is a superb illustration of Simon's great critical powers and standards. It is also an excellent model for analyzing films. Don't miss this one.

* Steene, Birgitta (editor). *Focus on the Seventh Seal.* Englewood Cliffs: Prentice-Hall, Inc., 1972.
   This excellent anthology contains serious essays, critical reviews, commentaries, an outline, a script extract and *Wood Painting: A Morality Play,* plus a filmography and bibliography.

Steene, Birgitta. *Ingmar Bergman.* New York: Twayne Publishers, Inc., 1968.
   This comprehensive and insightful book is an expansion of Steene's *Film Comment* article and is one of the best sources of information on Bergman's early theater training, where he directed and studied. Very fine footnotes and bibliography.

* Wood, Robin. *Ingmar Bergman.* New York: Praeger Publishers, 1969.
   Probably the best book in the Praeger Film Library series to date. Unabashedly a Bergman devotee, Wood synthesizes a number of critical issues on the Swedish director's films and then offers valuable, intelligent, and lucid suggestions on their meanings. He also provides a comprehensive bibliography and biography.

* *Four Screenplays of Ingmar Bergman: Smiles of a Summer Night/The Seventh Seal/Wild Strawberries/The Magician.* Translated by Lars Malstrom and David Kushner. New York: Secker and Warburg, 1960.

Films

Ingmar Bergman

The Seventh Seal (16mm: 1957, 96 min., b/w, English subtitles, sound, R-JAN)
   This allegorical story of a knight's search for the meaning of life presents marvelous images of suffering, fear, and optimism.[194]

Wild Strawberries (16mm: 1957, 90 min., b/w, English subtitles, sound, R-JAN)
   Bergman offers a memorable story of a septuagenarian doctor who recalls his past experiences on the day he is to receive an honorary degree from his university.[195]

Carl Th. Dreyer[196]

Gertrud (16mm: 1964, 115 min., b/w, English subtitles, sound, R-CON)
   Dreyer's last film is a controversial screenplay about one woman's deter-

194. Roger Manvell, "The Seventh Seal," *Screen Education Yearbook* (1966), 95–99; and Peter Cowie, "Great Films of the Century: The Seventh Seal," *Films and Filming* 9, no. 4 (January 1963): 44–46.
   195. Eleanor McCann, "The Rhetoric of Wild Strawberries," *Sight and Sound* 30, no. 1 (Winter 1960–61): 44–46.
   196. Tom Milne, "Darkness and Light: Carl Dreyer," *Sight and Sound* 34, no. 4 (Autumn 1965): 167–72; Carl Dreyer, "Film Style," *Films in Review* 3, no. 1 (January 1952): 15–21; Carl Dreyer, "Thoughts on My Craft," *Sight and Sound* 25, no. 1 (Winter

mination, in middle age, to live her life according to her desires. I think it to be one of the finest films ever made.[197]

Ordet (16mm: 1954, 126 min., b/w, English subtitles, sound, R-CON)
This is an amazing story of young love, religious controversy, and the power of faith. The end is something to behold.[198]

UNITED STATES[199]

Books

* Billings, Pat and Allen Eyles. *Hollywood Today.* New York: A. S. Barnes and Company, 1971.
This handy dictionary provides a biography and filmography of more than 370 film personalities, plus a small collection of illustrative stills.

* Higham, Charles. *Hollywood Cameramen: Sources of Light.* New York: Doubleday and Company, 1970.
This valuable compendium is a worthwhile introduction to such famous cameramen as James Wong Howe, Lee Garnes, Stanley Cortez, and William Daniels. The interviews make for interesting reading.

Rosenthal, Alan. *The New Documentary in Action: A Casebook in Film-Making.* Berkeley: University of California Press, 1971.
In an attempt to provide some behind-the-scenes information on documentary production, Rosenthal interviewed a number of important people connected with key filmmakers and producers, writers, cameramen, and editors. The result is an excellent text on creative perspectives as seen by Fred Wiseman, Al Maysles, Mort Silverstein, Peter Watkins, and Don Pennebaker.

* Wanger, Walter and Joe Hyams. *My Life with Cleopatra.* New York: Bantam Books, 1963.
This producer's view of one of the most widely covered and exploited films of the 1960s supplies a good reason why the Hollywood empire is in trouble today.

1955–56) : 128–29; Dale D. Drum, "Carl Dreyer's Shorts," *Films in Review* 20, no. 1 (January 1969) : 34–41; and Michel Delahaye, "Between Heaven and Hell: Interview with Carl Dreyer," *Cahiers du Cinema in English* 4, CdC no. 170 (September 1965) : 7–17.
197. Elliott Stein, "Gertrud," *Sight and Sound* 34, no. 2 (Spring 1965) : 56–58; Carl Lerner, "My Way of Working is in Relation to the Future: A Conversation with Carl Dreyer," *Film Comment* 4, no. 1 (Fall 1966) : 62–67; Kirk Bond, "The Basic Demand of Life for Love," *idem.,* pp. 67–69; Don Skoller, "To Rescue *Gertrud." idem.,* pp. 70–76; and Elsa Gress Wright, "Gertrud," *Film Quarterly* 19, no. 3 (Spring 1966) : 36–40.
198. Jorn Donner's book is the best source of information for this film.
199. Some useful articles are the following: Penelope Houston, "After the Strike," *Sight and Sound* 29, no. 3 (Summer 1960) : 108–12; Axel Madsen, "The Changing of the Guard," *Sight and Sound* 39, no. 2 (Spring 1970) : 63–65, 11; Harriet R. Polt, "Notes on the New Stylization," *Film Quarterly* 19, no. 3 (Spring 1966) : 25–29; Stephen Farber, "End of the Road," *Film Quarterly* 23, no. 2 (Winter 1969–70) : 3–16; William Johnson, "Hollywood 1965," *Film Quarterly* 19, no. 1 (Fall 1965) : 39–51; Richard Dyer MacCann, "From Technology to Adultery," *Films and Filming* 9, no. 4 (January 1963) : 73–77; Richard Dyer MacCann, "Independence with a Vengeance," *Film Quarterly* 15, no. 4 (Summer 1962) : 14–21; "Discussion: Personal Creation in Hollywood—Is it Possible? Fred Zinnemann, John Houseman, Irvin Kershner, Kent MacKenzie, Pauline Kael, Colin Young," *Film Quarterly* 15, no. 3 (Spring 1962) : 16–34; and George Fenin, "The Face of '63: United States," *Films and Filming* 9, no. 6 (March 1963) : 55–63.

Film Personalities

John Cassavetes

* Cassavetes, John. *Faces.* Book compiled by Al Ruban. New York: Signet Books, 1970.

Peter Fonda

* Hardin, Nancy and Marilyn Schlossberg (editors). *Easy Rider: Original Screenplay by Peter Fonda, Dennis Hopper, Terry Southern. Plus Stills, Interviews and Articles.* New York: Signet Books, 1969.

John Frankenheimer

* Pratley, Gerald. *The Cinema of John Frankenheimer.* New York: A. S. Barnes and Company, 1970.

Here is a readable, competent, and helpful study of the ex-television director whose fascination with technique has resulted in such unusual films as *The Birdman of Alcatraz, The Manchurian Candidate, Seven Days in May,* and *The Fixer.*

Samuel Fuller

* Hardy, Phil. *Samuel Fuller.* New York: Praeger Publishers, Inc., 1970.

This study of one of the most neglected but visually exciting American directors is the only available full-length treatment of his work. Hopefully more will be done with the brief narrative and filmography started here.

Stanley Kubrick

Kagan, Norman. *The Cinema of Stanley Kubrick.* New York: Holt, Rinehart and Winston, 1972.

Since this is the only in-depth study of Kubrick to date, it is a must for serious students. Kagan offers much important information by establishing the great director's working principles, collecting Kubrick's comments on each of the films, and synthesizing critical reactions to the movies themselves. He also includes a good bibliography and filmography.

Walker, Alexander. *Stanley Kubrick Directs.* New York: Harcourt, Brace, Jovanovich, Inc. 1971.

Based upon extended interviews, the book offers a superb visual and printed discussion of the brilliant director's feelings about *Paths of Glory, Dr. Strangelove, 2001: A Space Odyssey,* and *A Clockwork Orange.*

Arthur Penn

* Wood, Robin. *Arthur Penn.* New York: Praeger Publishers, 1969.

In one of the better books in this uneven series, Wood presents a sensitive and useful study of the director's films, including *The Left-Handed Gun, The Miracle Worker, Mickey One, Bonnie and Clyde,* and *Little Big Man.*

Otto Preminger

* Pratley, Gerald. *The Cinema of Otto Preminger.* New York: A. S. Barnes and Company, 1971.

In lucid and entertaining prose, Pratley gives a good analysis of the controversial director and his views on such works as *Laura, Anatomy of a Murder, Exodus, Advise and Consent,* and *Tell Me You Love Me, Junie Moon.*

Alan Schneider

* Beckett, Samuel. *Film.* With an Essay on Directing *Film* by Alan Schneider. New York: Grove Press, Inc., 1969.

Orson Welles

* Bessy, Maurice. *Orson Welles.* New York: Crown Publishers, Inc., 1971.
In this invaluable and well-researched book, Bessy offers a good evaluation of the director and his works, plus useful quotations from Welles himself. In addition, a host of French and American critics review specific films and a good filmography is included.

* Cowie, Peter. *The Cinema of Orson Welles.* New York: A. S. Barnes and Company, 1965.
A good introduction to the great director, with a full listing of other sources on the subject.

* Higham, Charles. *Films of Orson Welles.* Berkeley: University of California Press, 1970.
A well-intentioned book, but with poorly researched materials and a lightweight perspective.[200]

Noble, Peter. *The Fabulous Orson Welles.* London: Hutchinson, 1956.
This early journalistic account on Welles provides some useful information on his fights with the American Federal Theater, *The War of the Worlds* fiasco, and the butchering of *The Magnificent Ambersons.*

* *The Trial: A Film by Orson Welles.* English translations from the French by Nicholas Fry. New York: Simon and Schuster, 1970.

American Films

Robert Aldrich[201]

The Dirty Dozen (MGM—16mm: 1967, 140 min., color, sound, R-FNC)
This raw and fantasized glorification of twelve condemned men who are given a chance for freedom if they destroy a German military resort during the invasion of Normandy is a good example of the brutality and cynicism evident in American films during the late 1960s. Strong performances by Lee Marvin, John Cassavetes, and Charles Bronson.

Kenneth Anger

Scorpio Rising (16mm: 1962–63, 31 min., color, sound, R-FUC)
This underground Brooklyn film is one example of how the low-budget

---

200. In connection with the book, see Richard Wilson, "It's Not Quite All True," *Sight and Sound* 39, no. 4 (Autumn 1970) : 188–93.
201. Paul Schrader, "Notes on Film Noir," *Film Comment* 8, no. 1 (Spring 1972) : 8–13; Alain Silver, "Mr. Film Noir Stays at the Table: An Interview with Robert Aldrich," *idem.,* pp. 14–23.

movie breaks with the conventions of Hollywood film and uses the old themes for new, dramatic effects.

John Boorman

Point Blank (MGM—16mm:. 1967, 92 min., color, sound, R-FNC)
   In one of the most unusual and well-made underworld films ever, Boorman centers on a revengeful hood (Lee Marvin) and his decision to pay back key members of the Organization who have double-crossed him.[202]

John Cassavetes[203]

Faces (Continental—16mm: 1968, 130 min., b/w, sound, R-WRS)
   Cassavetes, always concerned with human relations, presents the problems of a middle-class marriage in an original, engrossing, and thought-provoking manner.[204]

Shadows (Lion International—16mm: 1960, 81 min., b/w, sound, R-AUD, ROA)
   In this highly unusual movie, Cassavetes experiments with improvisation. The question of prejudice is treated in a simple but startling fashion.

John Ford[205]

The Man Who Shot Liberty Valance (Paramount—16mm: 1962, 122 min., b/w, sound, R-FNC)
   This marvelous story about the relationship between an Eastern lawyer (James Stewart), a rough frontier cowboy (John Wayne), and a vicious killer (Lee Marvin) is Ford's last great tale about the end of the Western frontier.

John Frankenheimer[206]

The Fixer (MGM—16mm: 1968, 132 min., color, sound, R-FNC)
   Based upon Bernard Malamud's story, this amazing and absorbing film centers on a simple Jew who becomes a scapegoat in Czarist Russia and how he emerges as an international figure. Dalton Trumbo's fine script is powerfully performed by Alan Bates.[207]

The Manchurian Candidate (United Artists—16mm: 1962, 126 min., b/w, sound, R-CHA, UAS)

---

   202. Gordon Gow, "Playboy in a Monastery: An Interview with John Boorman," *Films and Filming* 18, no. 5 (February 1972) : 18–22.
   203. John Cassavetes, ". . . And the Pursuit of Happiness," *Films and Filming* 7, no. 5 (February 1961) : 7–8, 36; and David Austen, "Masks and Faces: An Interview with John Cassavetes," *Films and Filming* 14, no. 2 (September 1968) : 4–6, 8.
   204. "Playboy Interview: John Cassavetes," *Playboy* 18, no. 7 (July 1971) : 55–70, 210–12; and Claire Clouzot, "Faces," *Film Quarterly* 22, no. 3 (Spring 1969) : 31–35. The script is available from Signet Books in New York.
   205. Robin Wood, "Shall We Gather at the River: The Late Films of John Ford," *Film Comment* 7, no. 3 (Fall 1971) : 8–17; and David Bordwell, "The Man Who Shot Liberty Valance," *idem.*, pp. 18–20.
   206. Charles Higham, "Frankenheimer," *Sight and Sound* 37, no. 2 (Spring 1968) : 91–93; and Alan Casty, "Realism and Beyond: The Films of John Frankenheimer," *Film Heritage* 2, no. 2 (Winter 1966–67) : 21–33.
   207. Gordon Gow, "Reflections: An Interview with Alan Bates," *Films and Filming* 17, no. 9 (June 1971) : 22–28.

A superb examination of macabre politics which offers some marvelous moments of suspense, entertainment, and editing. Best thing about the film is George Axelrod's screenplay.[208]

Stuart Hagmann

The Strawberry Statement (MGM—16mm: 1970, 107 min., color, sound, R-FNC)

Based upon James Simon Kunen, this controversial film centers loosely on the student uprisings of 1968 and is set at a mythical San Francisco college.[209]

George Roy Hill

Butch Cassidy and the Sundance Kid (Fox—16mm: 1969, 112 min., color, cinemascope, sound, R-FNC)

In this disturbing but well-made film about two of the West's most vicious gunmen, Hill presents Butch (Paul Newman) and Sundance (Robert Redford) as two fun-loving outlaws who flee to Bolivia with their girl friend (Katharine Ross).[210]

The Making of Butch Cassidy and the Sundance Kid (EYR—16mm: 1969, 52 min., color, sound, R-EYR)

This is a first-rate behind-the-scenes account of a major film production and is a very useful teaching aid.

Alfred Hitchcock[211]

North by Northwest (MGM—16mm: 1959, 136 min., color, sound, R-FNC)

In one of his best films, Hitchcock offers us a fast, action-packed adven-

---

208. John Thomas, "John Frankenheimer: The Smile on the Face of the Tiger," *Film Quarterly* 19, no. 2 (Winter 1965–66) : 2–13; John Hanhardt, "George Axelrod and *The Manchurian Candidate*," *Film Comment* 6, no. 4 (Winter 1970–71) : 8–13; and Gordon Gow, "I Was a Young Woman of Parts: An Interview with Angela Lansbury," *Films and Filming* 18, no. 3 (December 1971) : 18–22.

209. Stephen Farber, "Movies from Behind the Barricades," *Film Quarterly* 24, no. 2 (Winter 1970–71) : 24–33.

210. Michael Shedlin, "Conrad Hall: An Interview," *Film Quarterly* 24, no. 3 (Spring 1971) : 2–11.

211. The following articles are helpful: John Peter Dyer, "Young and Innocent," *Sight and Sound* 30, no. 2 (Spring 1961) : 80–83; Penelope Houston, "The Figure in the Red Carpet," *Sight and Sound* 32, no. 4 (Autumn 1963) : 158–64; Gerald Pratley, "Alfred Hitchcock's Working Credo," *Films in Review* 3, no. 10 (December 1952) : 500–503; André Bazin, "Hitchcock versus Hitchcock," *Cahiers du Cinema in English* 2, CdC no. 39 (October 1954) : 51–59; François Truffaut, "Skeleton Keys," *idem.*, pp. 60–66; Claude Chabrol, "Hitchcock Confronts Evil," *idem.*, pp. 67–71; John Pett, "A Master of Suspense: An Analysis of Hitchcock's work for the Cinema," *Films and Filming* 6, no. 2 (November 1959) : 9–10, 33; John Pett, ". . . Part Two," *Films and Filming* 6, no. 3 (December 1959) : 9–10, 32; Raymond Durgnat, "The Strange Case of Alfred Hitchcock— Part One," *Films and Filming* 16, no. 5 (February 1970) : 58–62; Raymond Durgnat, ". . . Part Two," *Films and Filming* 16, no. 6 (March 1970) : 58–62; Raymond Durgnat, ". . . Part Three," *Films and Filming* 16, no. 7 (April 1970) : 58–60; Raymond Durgnat, ". . . Part Four," *Films and Filming* 16, no. 8 (May 1970) : 58–61; Raymond Durgnat, ". . . Part Five," *Films and Filming* 16, no. 9 (June 1970) : 114–18; Raymond Durgnat, ". . . Part Six," *Films and Filming* 16, no. 10 (July 1970) : 52–58; Raymond Durgnat, ". . . Part Seven," *Films and Filming* 16, no. 11 (August 1970) : 57–61; Raymond Durgnat, ". . . Part Eight," *Films and Filming* 16, no. 12 (September 1970) : 84–88; Raymond Durgnat, ". . . Part Nine," *Films and Filming* 17, no. 1 (October 1970) : 60–64; and Raymond Durgnat, ". . . Part Ten," *Films and Filming* 17, no. 2 (November 1970) : 35–37.

ture story about a case of mistaken identity when an unsuspecting advertising man (Cary Grant) becomes involved with international spies.[212]

Psycho (Paramount—16mm: 1960, 109 min., b/w, sound, R-CCC, CWF, ROA, UNI)
Considered by many to be Hitchcock's greatest film, this bizarre story centers on a mentally disturbed young man (Anthony Perkins) who sees the world as his enemy. Fine performances by Perkins, Janet Leigh[213] and Martin Balsam.

Norman Jewison[214]

The Russians Are Coming, The Russians Are Coming (United Artists—16mm: 1966, 126 min., color, sound, R-CHA, UAS)
This is a delightful farce that depicts what happens to a sleepy New England town when an incompetent Russian captain accidentally gets his submarine stuck on the beach. Alan Arkin gives a magnificent performance as a befuddled sailor. The skipper was Theodore Bickel.[215]

Ben Maddow

The Savage Eye (Trans-Lux—16mm: 1959, 67 min., b/w, sound, R-AUD)
This story of a self-pitying divorcée is told in a semi-documentary and semi-fantasy style. One unusual aspect of the movie is the absence of dialogue.

The Maysles Brothers[216]

Gimme Shelter (Cinema V—16mm: 1970, 91 min., color, b/w, R-CIV)
This is a strange and disturbing film that recounts the Rolling Stones' American tour, their bizarre free concert at Altamont, California, and the singers' reaction to the murder that took place there.[217]

Salesman (The Maysles Brothers—16mm: 1969, 90 min., b/w, sound, R-NTS)
Shot in *cinema vérité* style, this unusual and exceptional film captures the frustrations and life of a traveling Bible salesman.[218]

---

212. A. W. Richardson, "North by Northwest," *Screen Education Yearbook* (1963), pp. 45–47.

213. Rui Nogueira, "Psycho, Rosie and a Touch of Orson: Janet Leigh Talks," *Sight and Sound* 39, no. 2 (Spring 1970) : 66–70; and Kevin Gough-Yates, "Private Madness and Public Lunacy," *Films and Filming* 18, no. 5 (February 1972) : 26–30.

214. Gordon Gow, "Confrontations: Norman Jewison Interviewed," *Films and Filming* 17, no. 4 (January 1971) : 20–24.

215. Gordon Gow, "Vibrations: An Interview with John Phillip Law," *Films and Filming* 18, no. 7 (April 1972) : 18–22.

216. Maxine Haleff, "The Maysles Brothers and 'Direct Cinema,'" *Film Comment* 2, no. 2 (1964) : 19–23; James Blue, "Thoughts on *Cinema Vérité* and a Discussion with the Maysles Brothers," *Film Comment* 3, no. 4 (Fall 1965) : 22–30; Colin Young, "Cinema of Common Sense," *Film Quarterly* 17, no. 4 (Summer 1964) : 26–29, 40; Peter Graham, "*Cinema-Vérité* in France," *idem.*, pp. 30–36; Henry Breitrose, "On the Search for the Real Nitty-Gritty: Problems and Possibilities in *Cinema Vérité*," *idem.*, pp. 36–40.

217. Patrick MacFadden, "Gimme Shelter," *Film Society Review* 6, no. 3 (November 1970) : 39–42; Robert Phillip Kolker, "Circumstantial Evidence: An Interview with David and Albert Maysles," *Sight and Sound* 40, no. 4 (Autumn 1971) : 183–86; and Peter Buckley, "Why Are We Fighting: A Closer Look at Gimme Shelter," *Films and Filming* 17, no. 11 (August 1971) : 32–37.

218. Patrick MacFadden, "Salesman," *Film Society Review* 4, no. 6 (February 1969) : 11–17.

Alan Pakula

Klute (Warners—16mm: 1971, 114 min., color, sound, R-WSA)
In this rather average film, Jane Fonda gives a great performance as the cynical but sensitive call-girl who provides a detective's only link with a psychopathic killer.[219]

Sam Peckinpah[220]

Ride the High Country (MGM—16mm: 1962, 94 min., cinemascope or regular, color, sound, R-FNC)
This Peckinpah classic sums up thirty years of "B" westerns as Joel McCrea and Randolph Scott plays two aging, ex-marshals who escort a gold shipment from the mines and reflect over the value of honesty, dedication, and rewards.[221]

The Wild Bunch (Warners—16mm: 1969, 135 min., color, sound, R-WSA)
In his best film so far, Peckinpah presents a violent Western drama about an outlaw gang's final days along the Texas border. Outstanding performances turned in by William Holden as the bandit leader and Emilio Fernandez as the grinning Mexican outlaw.[222]

Arthur Penn

Bonnie and Clyde (Warners—16mm: 1967, 111 min., color, sound, R-WSA)
In one of the all-time great gangster films, Penn superbly mixes comedy and violence as he re-creates the Depression-era milieu of Bonnie Parker (Faye Dunaway) and Clyde Barrow (Warren Beatty).

Frank and Eleanor Perry[223]

Last Summer (Allied Artists—16mm: 1969, 97 min., color, sound, R-CIN)
Loosely based upon Evan Hunter's novel, this sensitive and moving film centers on Sandy (Barbara Hershey), Peter (Richard Thomas), Dan (Bruce Davidson), and their senseless and violent treatment of their lonely friend (Cathy Burns).

Sydney Pollack

They Shoot Horses Don't They (ABC—16mm: 1969, 129 min., color, sound, R-FNC)

---

219. Tom Milne, "Not a Garbo or a Gilbert in the Bunch: Alan Pakula Talks," *Sight and Sound* 41, no. 2 (Spring 1972) : 88–93; Robin Wood, "Klute," *Film Comment* 8, no. 1 (Spring 1972) : 32–37; and Ann Guerin, "Jane Fonda Takes on the World," *Show* 2, no. 2 (March 1971) : 44–48.

220. The following articles are helpful: Richard Whitehall, "Talking with Peckinpah," *Sight and Sound* 38, no. 4 (Autumn 1969) : 172–75; and Ernest Callenbach, "A Conversation with Sam Peckinpah," *Film Quarterly* 17, no. 2 (Winter 1963–64) : 3–10.

221. Colin McArthur, "Sam Peckinpah's West," *Sight and Sound* 36, no. 4 (Autumn 1967) : 180–83.

222. John McCarty, "Sam Peckinpah and *The Wild Bunch*," *Film Heritage* 5, no. 2 (Winter 1969–70) : 1–10; Stephen Farber, "Peckinpah's Return," *Film Quarterly* 23, no. 1 (Fall 1969) : 2–11; John Cutts, "Shoot!—Sam Peckinpah," *Films and Filming* 16, no. 1 (October 1969) : 4–6, 8; and William Blum, "Toward a Cinema of Cruelty," *Cinema Journal* 10, no. 2 (Spring 1972) : 19–33.

223. Kay Loveland and Estelle Changas, "Eleanor Perry: One Woman in Films," *Film Comment* 7, no. 1 (Spring 1971) : 64–69.

Following closely Horace McCoy's significant Depression novel, Pollack offers a disturbing and haunting story of American life in the 1930s as reflected in a shabby ballroom marathon dance contest. Outstanding performances by Jane Fonda and Gig Young (who won an Oscar for his supporting role as the contest emcee).[224]

Stan Vanderbeek

À la Mode (16mm: 1958, 5 min., b/w, sound, R-FMC, C16)
  A filmmaker who works primarily in animation, Vanderbeek describes his film as "A montage of women and appearances, a fantasy about beauty and the female, a formage, a mirage."[225]

Science Friction (16mm: 1959, 9 min., color, sound, R-FMC, C16)
  Vanderbeek describes this movie as "A social satire aimed at the rockets, scientists, and competitive mania of our times."[226]

Breathdeath (16mm: 1964, 15 min., b/w, sound, R-FMC)
  One of his best films. Vanderbeek explains the movie as

  . . . a film experiment that deals with the photo reality and the surrealism of life. It is a collage-animation that cuts up photos and newsreel film and reassembles them; producing an image that is a mixture of unexplainable fact (Why is Harpo Marx playing a harp in the middle of a battlefield?) with the inexplicable act (Why is there a battlefield?). It is black comedy that mocks at death . . . a parabolic parable.[227]

Andy Warhol[228]

Kiss (16mm: 1963–4, 50 min., b/w, silent, R-FMC)
  Warhol brings a new look to the cinema as evidenced by this film that involves many routines and styles of kissing.

Orson Welles

The Trial (France—16mm: 1962, 118 min., b/w, sound, R-AUD)
  This adaptation of the Franz Kafka novel is an excellent rendition of a terrifying story about a man who wakes up one morning to find himself accused of an unknown crime which he didn't commit and can't avoid being punished for.

Cornel Wilde[229]

The Naked Prey (Paramount—16mm: 1966, 94 min., cinemascope and regular, color, sound, R-FNC)

224. Michael Buckley, "Gig Young," Films in Review 22, no. 2 (February 1971) : 66—84.
225. Film-Maker's Cooperative Catalogue, p. 61.
226. Ibid.
227. Ibid., p. 62.
228. Gretchen Berg, "Nothing to Love: Interview with Andy Warhol," Cahiers du Cinema in English 10 (May 1967) : 38–43; Andrew Sarris, "The Sub-New York Sensibility," idem., pp. 43–45; Serge Gavronsky, "Warhol's Underground," idem., pp. 46–49; and James Stoller, "Beyond Cinema: Notes on some Films by Andy Warhol," Film Quarterly 20, no. 1 (Fall 1966) : 35–38.
229. John Coen, "Cornel Wilde: Producer/Director," Film Comment 6, no. 1 (Spring 1970) : 52–61; and Gordon Gow, "Survival!" Films and Filming 17, no. 1 (October 1970) : 4–8, 10.

This outstanding and neglected film deals with a white hunter's agonizing race against death and the desperate measures he takes to avoid his pursuing hunters. Wilde directs and stars in this true cinematic achievement.

Frederick Wiseman[230]

The Titicut Follies (Evergreen—16mm: 1967, 85 min., b/w, sound, R-GRO/L-GRO)
One of the most haunting and overpowering documentaries of its kind, this revealing and pathetic look at Bridgewater State Prison Hospital in Massachusetts is a shocking condemnation of society's inhumane treatment of the mentally ill.

230. Donald E. McWilliams, "Frederick Wiseman," *Film Quarterly* 24, no. 1 (Fall 1970) : 17–26; and John Graham, "There Are No Simple Solutions—Frederick Wiseman on Viewing Film," *The Film Journal* 1, no. 1 (Spring 1971) : 44–47.

8
Film Study

We are all amateurs and we never live long enough to be anything else.

Charles Chaplin, Limelight

SUMMARY

In this last chapter we shall try to synthesize the thousands of bits of information now available for film study, to indicate the areas that need developing, and to draw attention to future needs. To help do this, let's take a look backwards before we move forward.[1] The history of film scarcely encompasses the expected life span of the average American. However, the technological age has intensified the artistic pace, as well as created new types. The advancements of radio and television show how quickly such new media develop. Movies have made even more dramatic achievements. Because of the hundreds of thousands of film theatres and television programs regularly showing motion pictures, it would take centuries of readers to equal the number of people who have seen films in their seventy-odd years of existence.

The film has its own language, composition, and literature. Years ago, most screen adaptations of novels and plays showed no awareness of the demands of cinematic treatment. Today that has changed; and as a result, any adaptations have to be concerned with translating the original into cinematic terms. The situation is somewhat similar for artists using traditional literary language. The poet must write in terms of poetry; the dramatist in terms of drama; and the novelist in terms of narrative fiction. So, the filmmaker must work in terms of film. But it would be a mistake to disassociate that new form completely from traditional literature and its best purposes.

---

1. The writer wishes to express a debt of gratitude to the strategy suggested by Milton Allen Kaplan in his conclusions on the relationship between poetry and radio. See Milton Allen Kaplan, *Radio and Poetry* (New York: Columbia University Press, 1949), pp. 231–60.

As our emphases and our world change, schools constantly reexamine their curriculums. For example, in their efforts to keep up with an expanding literature, more and more teachers are replacing the traditional hard-covered anthologies with selected paperbacks. These same teachers realize, too, that television, radio, and motion pictures are legitimate fields for classroom study. This shift in the curriculum led me to examine the way films are taught in our schools and colleges. This examination has been based on the knowledge that film is a major art form that has its own language, composition, and literature; that the value of film goes beyond entertainment; and that we have a responsibility to help others understand more about motion pictures.

Recognizing the diversity that exists within the film world, I began by examining an approach to teaching film in Chapter 2: the study of genres. By surveying the various types of movies, students see how the social and political forces of an age influence not only the production process but the treatment of conventions itself. Knowing how, why, where, and when film changes its approaches helps in discriminating between art and mere propaganda.

Sometimes it becomes necessary to emphasize that film history is also a branch of social history. The cinema is worthy of that emphasis in at least two major ways. First, the filmmaker is a member of his society as well as a product of his times. His work therefore reflects his environment. Second, and too often overlooked, a generation sometimes may be studied more rationally and calmly through film than through printed material. When we see, for example, the kinds of screen myths and stereotypes perpetuated over the years, we sense the social changes developing before our eyes.

A second approach to film study, described in Chapter 3, examines movie stereotypes. It should help in selecting materials for student-centered programs. The treatment of Afro-Americans, for instance, suggests the dramatic difference between the attitudes of today's young people and those of their grandparents.

Movies also reflect our tastes and our customs, primarily because filmmakers try to appeal to an audience's desires. As a result, there is a constant and perennial recurrence of themes, plots, and stock figures. This continual exposure affects the values of our society, for good and for bad. Franklin Fearling, more than twenty years ago, summarized the two valid generalizations that can be made regarding the relations between film content and our behavior and attitudes:

(1) In the first place, on the basis of evidence from several lines of research, it is possible to demonstrate that any film, regardless of its character—documentary, musical, western or realistic—has some measurable effects on specific attitudes of those exposed to it, provided a measuring instrument (e.g., attitude scale) is devised for it, and provided the audience is sufficiently interested to give it sustained attention.

(2) In the second place, motion pictures afford an opportunity for the expression of the basic meanings inherent in the relationships of human beings to each other, to their environment, and to the society of which they are a part. This is not limited to a passive reflection of these meanings, but may be a dynamic and creative interpretation.[2]

Realizing that teachers more and more are discussing films through themes of general and universal significance—e.g., courage, survival and rebellion— I suggested, in Chapter 4, certain movie groupings that appeal to students. The purpose in such a thematic arrangement is to emphasize the experience of film, to help the student reflect about what he sees, how it affects him and why. My feeling is that the thematic approach offers the viewer the best chance to examine his personal attitudes and values at the same time he is learning about the art of the cinema.

One of the most popular methods of introducing the discussion of film art is to compare movies with traditional literature. I tried, in Chapter 5, to present materials that point to the film's unique conventions, restrictions and techniques. I also tried to show that the relationship between movies and literature is a strong, healthy and historical fact.

From the start, it became obvious that students needed a sense of historical perspective in order to better understand, appreciate, and enjoy movies. One way of giving them that perspective is by examining a particular period. In Chapter 6, I tried to show how the film industry in 1913–1919 pointed the way to the movies we see today. This formative film period produced many significant works, artists, and trends. It initiated the film industry as one of the most influential forms of media in the world. And much of today's films had their start in those seven crucial years. By studying that part of motion picture history, students should gain a better perspective on the art of the cinema.

Based on the view that better understanding of film requires an acquaintance with its development as an art form, the last approach suggested in this book, in Chapter 7, outlines the times and trends that led to today's movies. The world cinema we now have had its roots more than a hundred years ago when people were concerned mainly with preserving motion—the physical movement of bodies and objects. But through the creative efforts of men like Méliès, Porter, Griffith, Sennett, and Chaplin, the grammar and art of the film became in a relatively short period of time an important form of communication. By the end of the 1920s, the movies, because of outstanding American, Russian, French, and German film artists, caused a notable shift in emphasis in communication from the written word to the visual.

Then, in 1927, there was a dramatic setback in the development of motion pictures. With the advent of sound, it was as if the film had begun all over

2. Franklin Fearing, "Influence of the Movies on Attitudes and Behavior," *The Annals of the American Academy of Political and Social Science* 154 (September 1947) : 78–79.

again. But the film industry met the challenge through the creative efforts of international artists, and today we see the results of dedicated and ingenious people like Vidor, Milestone, Cocteau, Renoir, Welles, Lean, Reed, Antonioni, Fellini, Bergman, Truffaut, Resnais, Kurosawa, Ray, and many others. To ignore their work, to neglect the value of films in our lives, is to remain a semieducated man.

My great fear, however, is that the study of film's historical process will degenerate into "units" on biography and the memorization of dates, *auteurs*, and works. This common survey course often bores students and makes them disillusioned about film. It is my hope that if we provide them with a historical perspective, young people will learn to understand, appreciate, and enjoy the great art we have.

CONCLUSIONS

Each of these approaches is related in one way or another to four major factors in the study of the film: materials, methods, scholarship, and teacher training.

First, we should recognize that in the past it has been extremely difficult to obtain worthwhile books and articles that have seriously examined film aesthetics. The present paperback revolution has, in combination with the rising number of film courses, changed the minds of publishers, librarians, and educators. Many books that were out of print or accessible only at great expense are now being reprinted in relatively inexpensive editions. For example, such important publications as Terry Ramsaye's *A Million and One Nights,* Sergei Eisenstein's *Film Form and Film Sense,* Siegfried Kracauer's *From Caligari to Hitler,* Theodore Huff's *Charlie Chaplin,* and Rudolf Arnheim's *Film as Art* are now available in soft cover. Schools, teachers, and students may now study these works without great expense to themselves.

Film study has also been helped considerably by the availability of scripts. No less than five years ago I had a heated discussion with the president of an important publishing house. I tried to convince him that teachers wanted screenplays. He said there was no market for these books. Today, however, houses like Simon and Schuster and Grossman are providing invaluable material with their film scripts.

The increased availability of 16mm and 8mm films is yet another boon to motion picture study. With this growth has come a much needed improvement in the quality of film distributors' catalogues. In the past, it had been difficult to find important information about films for use in the classroom. Now, to cite an example, Janus Films includes in its catalogue production dates, running times, plot summaries, and critical comments about the pictures. Another distributor, Continental 16, gives, in addition to the aforementioned, a list of related materials—available recordings, books, and articles. Other film catalogues—such as those provided by Twyman and Films, Incorporated—categorize films according to themes, directors, awards, and genres. Interested teachers should get on the mailing lists of these distributors since prices, films, and addresses constantly change.[3] One word of warning about film rentals: films sometimes come damaged, and there is no reason to pay for a bad print; if you complain to the distributor, he usually will not charge you.

This brings us to a discussion of buying films, projectors, and cameras. The cry of the neophyte is that film study is too expensive; his school cannot afford the equipment. The old-timers refuse to purchase new equipment because, years ago, the school paid "a lot of money" for those sturdy old machines. And the critic complains that all this talk about new hardware is just the businessman's smooth way of making money for himself. A good answer to those arguments was given almost a decade ago:

> . . . we in education must learn, and must learn to budget accordingly, that the procedures and devices of a technological society are *always obsolescent*. The school administrator who is forced to spend money for equipment on the assumption that it must forever withstand the assaults of technical advances is asked to do the impossible. We who are schoolmen, we who are citizens, must learn the lesson of industry that obsolescence in plant and equipment is assumed; yes, is built into the industrial tax structure.[4]

The point is that good education requires modern methods, excellent equipment, and the best educational environment we can create.

Film teaching methods, like those of the humanities, depend on oral interpretation (with or without films in the classroom), student discussions, and analysis. Our students expect us to know something about film art, worthwhile materials, and accessible resources. This book has tried to fill that gap. And we need to remind others that enthusiasm is no substitute for good teaching.

We come, next, to the situation of film scholarship. To study film seriously, students need printed material and a film library. *Film Quarterly* once performed a major service to cinema scholars when it surveyed the major film archives in the United States as well as the book collections containing valuable film materials[5]

While it is more common to talk about teaching before discussing scholarship, it seems evident that there can be no valid teaching unless there is scholarship. Scholarship and research, however, cannot exist in a vacuum. As Ernest Callenbach pointed out in 1962:

---

3. See Appendix II for a current list of film distributors.
4. Louis and Joan Rosengren Forsdale, "The New 8mm Format," *Audio-Visual Instruction* 11 (January 1966) : 33.
5. See Appendix V.

It is time for serious film students to begin holding themselves to the same standards of documentation and evidence which prevail in other scholarly endeavors. . . .

It is time for our museums to make a concerted effort to solve their perennial problems of financing; for upon their success in saving films, and making them accessible, all serious study depends.

It is time for private collectors to lay plans whereby their films may become, by bequest or earlier, part of the public wealth in museums or other responsible institutions.

It is time for scholars in sociology, anthropology, psychology, economics, law, literature, to realize that the social and aesthetic problems raised by the motion picture are central to an understanding of modern man, and that rich resources exist wherein studies of these may be conducted.

It is time for the foundations to support the work of those scholars who are attempting to outgrow the academic handicaps of the field.

It is time for the universities to regard films as more than a convenient fund-raising device for the support of less popular arts, and to organize film research and teaching programs with the same kind of devotion they bring to nuclear physics, plant-breeding or even the study of Middle English.

It is a time for the Congress to augment the shamefully tiny budget for the Library of Congress film collection, so that it can be maintained, augmented, and serviced in a manner befitting an important national archive.[6]

These are only some of the problems. The one major addition is the unfortunate state of the American Film Institute's educational program. It is time for that department to receive a larger share of the total budget, get support from splinter groups around the country, and coordinate the various film programs in our public schools and universities.

This leads into the area of teacher training. In May 1964, a six-month survey of the place of film in higher education was conducted by the American Council on Education. At a national meeting on film study held at Lincoln Center for the Performing Arts in New York in October 1964, the results of that survey were discussed. The assumptions of the report were that

(1) motion pictures are a major, contemporary, artistic expression; (2) their cultural value lies far beyond pure entertainment; and (3) higher education, as part of its continuing responsibility in the broad field of the arts, should contribute to the development of a more informed and discerning film audience.[7]

The report itself centered on identifying, recording, and disseminating information about present higher education courses in film history, criticism, and appreciation. It also surveyed informal campus activities that had a

---

6. Ernest Callenbach, "Editor's Notebook," *Film Quarterly* 16, no. 2 (Winter 1962–63) : 2.

7. David Stewart (editor), *Film Study in Higher Education* (Washington, D.C.: American Council on Education, 1966), pp. 2–3.

direct bearing on the creation of formal courses. David Stewart, reporting the committee's findings, stated,

> As this report indicates, higher education has only just begun to respond to motion pictures as a contemporary art. The traditionalists' insistence upon custom as a guide to subjects which merit serious inquiry is ever-present. And in the academic field in which film is most often studied, there will always be those who maintain that human experience can be effectively recorded only in print. But against all the odds, film study will advance. The print-versus-film argument is irresistible and inevitable. And the general differences between traditionalists and those who would radically revise the curriculum will persist. But there is a basic understanding: films are not made by cameras any more than books are made by typewriters.[8]

The conference recommended that a second meeting be held to study the role of film courses in higher education. That meeting, held at Dartmouth College in October 1965, addressed itself to the examination of various ways of teaching film, as well as to the major problems and requirements of film study. The major speeches of that conference have been published in a paperback volume.[9]

As the colleges have manifested an increased interest in the art of the film, there has been a change in the college curriculum. In May of 1964, Professor Jack C. Ellis reexamined the film-study courses (originally done in 1952–53) in 100 of the largest colleges and universities in the United States. His report divided the courses into four broad categories:

audio-visual (concentrating on the use of the film as an aid to instruction); *production* (emphasizing film writing, directing, acting, etc.); *history, criticism, and appreciation;* and *communication* (primarily concerned with film as one of the mass media reflecting and affecting society). The surveys showed that these categories were divided in the following manner:

Category	1952–53 %	1952–53 No.	1964–65 %	1964–65 No.
Audio-visual	39	236	34	284
Production	28	161	32	265
History, criticism, and appreciation	17	98	18	148
Communication	16	80	16	128
Total	100	575	100	825[10]

Recent findings are even more encouraging. According to a questionnaire

8. David Stewart, "The Study of Motion Pictures," p. 37.
9. *Ibid.*
10. Jack C. Ellis. Reported in David Stewart, "The Study of Motion Pictures," p. 49.

completed by colleges and universities listed in the American Film Institute's *Guide to College Film Courses* 1971–72:

A total of 2,392 film courses are being offered during the 1971–72 academic year.
There are 47 schools which offer degrees in film, from AA to Ph.D. (This includes the degree in cinema, in motion pictures, and in radio-TV-film.)
Of the schools listed, 96 offer a major in film. These include schools where the major is in related fields (e.g., radio-TV-film), with an emphasis, specialization or concentration in film.
4,619 students are majoring in films on the undergraduate level and 1,508 on the graduate level in the schools surveyed.
Of the schools offering a major in film, there are 294 full-time faculty members, 333 part-time, including lecturers and assistants.
In these same 96 schools, film production is felt to be the most important aspect, with film history and criticism coming second, followed by an interest in television filmmaking. Documentary and experimental filmmaking are primarily emphasized, then dramatic fiction and animation in that order.
Of the 427 schools listed 104 offer *further* training for teachers of film, just over double the amount listed for last year.[11]

Compared with the courses offered in the other arts, film study, although increasing, is sadly neglected. There is no question that this situation will change, but the point needs to be made that the change will come more quickly if informed educators take a more active role in their respective colleges and universities.

The implications of this study for teachers, schools, and students have been discussed in the previous pages. There are two other areas for which this work also has implications: the film industry and the film audience.

IMPLICATIONS FOR THE FILM INDUSTRY

Many educators realize that there are moviemakers who continue to exploit the schools and the students for profit. And it is becoming clearer to teachers at large that film is not a panacea for incompetence, boredom, and lack of ability. No matter how many inferior film texts are put into book rooms, no matter how much foolish administrators pander to federal programs just to get money to buy technological tools that they don't use properly, the motion picture industry is going to suffer financial hardships until it raises the quality of its product. Producers claim that their function is to give the public what it wants. If the audience is undiscriminating, it is not the producer's responsibility. The fact is that many people enjoy poor films, that often the senseless values come from the spectator as well as the movie, and that there is no conclusive evidence to support many of the

11. American Film Institute Report (December 1971), p. 14.

charges of harmful effects leveled against the film industry.

But there is a need for a more responsible film industry concerned with worthwhile motion pictures. And I'm not talking about esoteric, art house movies alone. I like good entertainment as much as anyone. What we need are adults who don't do only what is easiest, simplest, and quickest. Pauline Kael said it beautifully:

> The movies that are popularly considered the best movies at any given time may or may not be good movies—they may be important bad movies —but they touch a nerve, express a mood that is just coming to popular consciousness, or present heroes who connect in new ways. They not only reflect what is going on in the country but, sometimes by expressing it and sometimes by distorting it, affect it, too—such movies as "The Wild One," "Rebel Without a Cause," "Blackboard Jungle," "On the Waterfront," "Morgan!," "Bonnie and Clyde," "The Graduate," "Midnight Cowboy," "Easy Rider," the new "Joe," and probably the new "Five Easy Pieces." Movies like these enter the national bloodstream. . . .[12]

While it is true that the film industry cannot change or improve the present situation by itself, filmmakers should try to help.

IMPLICATIONS FOR THE FILM AUDIENCE

Since 1946, one of the best years in motion picture box-office history, the movie industry has had great problems with its film audiences. Recently, *Variety* published a chart showing the seriousness of the situation. (See Figure 1.)

The newspaper explained that in 1946, the chart's beginning, although there was a lot of spending money around, few luxury and recreation items were available, and television did not yet offer any serious commercial challenge to films.

The chart's upper trace (the dashed line) represents the U.S. theatrical box-office totals in annual dollars as reported by the U.S. Department of Commerce. The one change—and a significant one at that—from the 1946 peak to the 1962–63 bottom is the reversal in 1954–56. *Variety* attributes this departure to technical innovations, which are generally labeled "the Cinemascope rebound." Following this change, however, the decline resumed at an even greater pace. Then in 1962–63, the curve begins to rise to the present levels, which in real money is 30 percent down from the 1946 starting point. *Variety* is quick to point out that owing to current inflation and increased ticket prices this level is misleading.

To show a more realistic picture, the chart traces the same period "in

---

12. Pauline Kael, "The Current Cinema," *The New Yorker* 46, no. 3 (October 3, 1970) : 80.

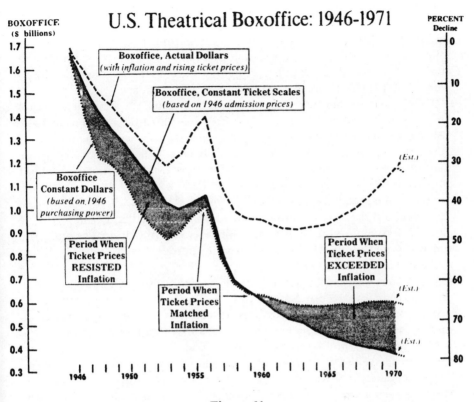

BOXOFFICE
($ billions)

U.S. Theatrical Boxoffice: 1946-1971

PERCENT
Decline

Boxoffice, Actual Dollars
(with inflation and rising ticket prices)

Boxoffice, Constant Ticket Scales
(based on 1946 admission prices)

**Boxoffice
Constant Dollars**
*(based on 1946
purchasing power)*

**Period When
Ticket Prices
RESISTED
Inflation**

**Period When
Ticket Prices
Matched
Inflation**

**Period When
Ticket Prices
EXCEEDED
Inflation**

Figure 1[1]

terms of receipts adjusted for the steady debasement of currency, in combination with the change in admission prices."

The dotted line represents the adjusted box-office receipts and follows the financial crisis in terms of 1946 purchasing power. Except for 1954–56 reversal again, the decline is now shown to place the box-office receipts at a level some 65 percent below the 1946 standard. The one qualifying comment is that admission prices have varied considerably from overall inflation and do not accurately represent the total picture.

The most meaningful representation then is the solid line, which represents the annual U.S. box-office total adjusted to 1946 admission prices. Between 1946 and 1956, the solid line is above the dotted line of 1946 adjusted receipts, which shows that ticket prices were not affected by inflation for at least a decade after 1946.

Then, starting in the 1957–59 period, ticket prices began to rise exactly as inflation increased, so both lines are locked tightly together.

---

1. *Variety* (May 10, 1972), p. 6. Reprinted by permission.

Following 1959, however, and continuing to the present, ticket prices have outstripped inflation, and the annual U.S. box-office total adjusted receipts (represented by the solid line) has continued to decline. It is this solid line that tells the true story, because it alone represents the actual film audience, independent of inflation figures since 1946. In other words, 80 percent of 1946 audience is missing in the 1972 audience.

These data are another way of showing that today's estimated weekly film audience of 20 million is a far cry from the 100 million patrons of 1946. *Variety* concludes with the reminder that since they are weekly figures which fluctuate severely from season to season, "It is far safer simply to conclude that, whatever the attendance was at 1946 theatre prices, it is now only about 20 percent of that peak amount."

To get film audiences and the movie industry back to where they were in the "good old days" is an important and difficult job. But I believe that if patrons were more visually literate, more concerned with quality and taste when it came to films, that business would improve. Better audiences result in better films. Better films increase box-office receipts. And for all the jargon about this being a multi-media society, visual illiteracy is more rampant than ever before. Schools can help by developing and maintaining strong and meaningful film programs. In addition, serious students need to read the works of reputable film critics, see a lot of movies, and *think*.

The future for film study is excellent. The danger is our complacency. Some of us have become arrogant, smug, and irresponsible toward tradition. Others, because of the academicians' past ignorance of film, are neglecting standards, scholarship, and cooperation with other disciplines. This must not continue. The future of the film is at stake.

Glossary

ABERRATION: Any distortion of the image by optical elements, e.g., lens, prism, mirror.

ABRASIONS: Unwanted marks or scratches on the surface of film caused by improper threading or projection.

ACADEMY MASK: A camera mask used to fix the rectangularity of the camera image on the screen to approximately a 3:4 ratio. Since the Academy of Motion Picture Arts and Sciences set the standards the enclosed area is known as an Academy aperture.

ACETATE: A slow-burning base for movie film composed mainly of Cellulose triacetate. Often referred to as a safety base.

ACHROMATIC: A lens designed for handling chromatic aberrations and achieving a common focus.

ACTION: The movement that takes place in front of the lens.

ACTION!: The director's signal to begin filming.

ANGLE: The point of view from which the action is filmed.

APERTURE: In the camera, it determines how each frame is exposed. The lens aperture controls the amount of entering light, the printer aperture regulates the light needed to expose film being reproduced, and the projector aperture limits the section of each projected frame.

ASPECT RATIO: The ratio by height and width of a single movie frame.

ATMOSPHERE: The mood, setting, or background effect of a shot. What the French call *mise en scene*.

AUTEUR: A director who leaves his individual mark on a film.

B-PICTURE: Movies run as second features or Saturday morning television flicks.

BACK-LIGHTING: In order to contrast lighting effects, the lights are set up behind or facing the lens (without distorting the lens's control of light).

BASE (film): The transparent, flexible material mixed with chemicals to create film.

BOOM: Camera booms are mobile cameras that allow shots to be taken from almost any angle. Microphone booms provide the same flexibilities.

BREAKAWAY: The fragile, specially constructed props designed for action sequences.

CALL: The schedule sheet which tells everyone connected with the production when to report.

CAMERA STYLO: Alexandre Astruc's term for creating with a camera the way a writer works with a pen.

CINÉASTE: Someone who loves films.

CINÉMA VÉRITÉ: The on-the-scene, "natural" documentary effect that suggests reality is being recorded just as it happened.

CLAPPER BOARD: The wooden chalk board used to signal the start of a take and to provide visual and oral cues to the editor.

COMPOSITION: The artistic arrangement of the visual aspects in a frame before shooting.

CONTRAST: The manipulation of light and shadows with a shot.

CRANE SHOT: A camera shooting from a boom.

CUE: An action, sound or gesture that indicates the start of something new.

CUT: A visual transition from one shot to another.

CUT!: The director's signal to call a halt to the shooting.

CUT AWAY: A fast shift away from the main action. A cut back returns you quickly back.

DEFINITION: The sharpness of the visual image.

DEPTH OF FIELD: The visual range between the foreground and the background.

DIAPHRAGM: The instrument that monitors the light going through the lens.

DISSOLVE: A visual effect that causes a transition between one shot and another by first dimming and then brightening.

DOLLY: A mobile truck used to move the cameraman around the set.

DUBBING: Substitution of a soundtrack in the national language for the foreign speech.

ESTABLISHING SHOT: Placement of the scene in a specific context: time, place, setting.

FADE IN/OUT: Motion from darkness to light or from light to darkness in visual terms.

FAST MOTION: Slowing of the camera's recording speed so that the projected action on the screen moves unnaturally fast.

FRAME: In one sense, the individual picture on a strip of celluloid. In another sense, the actual composition of the shot. The traditional projection method used for silent films was 16 frames per second; sound has 24 frames.

FREEZE FRAME: The use of a single picture printed repeatedly to convey the impression of a photographic still.

INTERMITTENT MOVEMENT: The process of moving the film through the camera and the projector in a stop-go fashion, thus making it possible for individual frames to be exposed, projected, and then replaced by the following frame.

IRIS: The gradual opening or closing of the lens, designed for dramatic effect.

JUMP CUT: Abrupt cutting from shot to shot, scene to scene.

LENS: Any optical system that organizes light rays to create an image.

MASK: A device designed to control light transmission.

MATTE: A masking technique used to block out a particular part of the frame.

MATTE SHOT: Mixing actual shots with artificial scenes to create a new setting.

MOVIOLA: A machine used to examine film foot by foot and to coordinate the visual and the audio.

OUT-TAKES: Shots and scenes that have been deleted from the final print of the film.

PAN: A horizontal camera movement.

PRINT: A positive copy made from a negative film (one that has its primary tone inverted).

RAW STOCK: Unprocessed or unused film.

RETAKE: New shots of bad rushes.

ROUGH CUT: A crudely put together version of an evolving film.

RUSHES: Also called "dailies." The immediate screening of recently developed shooting, unedited.

SCENE: A specific section of the film shot in one set-up.

SET-UP: The fixing of equipment and blocking of performers prior to shooting.

SHOT: The single running of the camera without stopping.

SLOW MOTION: The technique by which the camera is run more quickly than usual so that the projected film moves more slowly than normal.

SOFT FOCUS: The hazy photographic effect that glamorizes fading stars.

TAKE: The total scene shot, numbered and ready for processing.

TRACKING: Parallel movement of the camera with the subject being shot. It can also be used to photograph a continuous, but motionless, scene— à la *Marienbad, Weekend.*

WIPE: Visually, the technique in which one image pushes another image off the screen.

ZOOM: Quick movement by the camera toward or away from the center of attention.

Appendix I

A SELECTED LIST OF FILM CRITICS AND PERIODICALS

Films are regularly reviewed in the following publications: *Commonweal,* Philip Hartung; *Esquire,* Jacob Brackman; *Life,* Richard Schickel and Brad Darrach; *The New Leader,* John Simon; *The New Republic,* Stanley Kauffmann; *New York Magazine,* Judith Crist; *New York Times,* Vincent Canby and Roger Greenspun; *The New Yorker,* Penelope Gilliatt, Pauline Kael, and Brendan Gill; *Newsweek,* Paul D. Zimmerman; *Saturday Review,* Arthur Knight; *Time,* Jay Cocks and Stefan Kanfer; *Village Voice,* Jonas Mekas and Andrew Sarris; *Women's Wear Daily,* Rex Reed.

Films are also reviewed and discussed regularly in the following periodicals:
Action. 7950 Sunset Boulevard, Hollywood, California 90046. $4.00.
American Cinematographer. 1728 North Orange Drive, Hollywood, California 90028. $6.00.
A-V Communication Review. Department of Audio-Visual Instruction, NEA, 1201 16th Street, N.W., Washington, D.C. 20036. $8.00.
Cineaste. 144 Bleecker Street, New York, New York 10012. $3.00.
Cinema. 9667 Wilshire Boulevard, Beverly Hills, California 90212. $4.00.
Cinema Journal. 217 Flint Hall, University of Kansas, Lawrence, Kansas. 66044. $2.00 per issue.
Cinema Studies. 1 Dane Street, High Holborn, London, WC1, England. $2.40.
Classic Film Collector. 734 Philadelphia Street. Indiana, Pennsylvania 15701. $1.25 per issue.
CTVD: Cinema TV Digest. Hampton Books, Box 738, Newberry, South Carolina 29108. $3.00.
Film Comment. 100 Walnut Place, Brookline, Massachusetts 02146. $9.00.
Film Critic. 144 Bleecker Street, New York, New York 10012. $5.00.
Film Culture. GPO Box 1499, New York, New York 10001. $4.00.
Film Facts. P. O. Box 213, Village Station, New York, New York 10014. $25.00.
The Film Journal. Box 9602, Hollins College, Virginia 24020. $3.50.
Film Heritage. Box 42, University of Dayton, Dayton, Ohio 45409. $2.00.
Film Library Quarterly. 17 West 60th Street, New York, New York 10023. $8.00.
Film Quarterly. University of California Press, Fulton Street, Berkeley, California 94720. $5.00.
Film Review Digest. 22 West Madison Street, Chicago, Illinois 60602. $1.00 per issue.

Films and Filming. Hansom Books, Artillery Mansions, 75 Victoria Street, London, SW1, England. $11.50.

Films in Review. 210 East 68th Street, New York, New York 10021. $7.50.

Filmmakers' Newsletter. 80 Wooster Street, New York, New York 10012. $4.00.

Focus! Doc Films, 5811 South Ellis Avenue, Chicago, Illinois 60637. $1.00 per issue.

Focus on Film. 108 New Bond Street, London, W1Y OQX, England. $5.00.

Hollywood Reporter. 6715 Sunset Boulevard, Hollywood, California 90028. $30.00.

Journal of Popular Film. University Hall 101, Bowling Green State University, Bowling Green, Ohio 43403. $4.00.

Journal of the University Film Association. 156 West 19th Avenue, Ohio State University, Columbus, Ohio 43210. $4.00.

Media and Methods: Exploration in Education. 134 North 13th Street, Philadelphia, Pennsylvania 19107. $5.00.

Monthly Film Bulletin. The British Film Institute, 81 Dean Street, London, WIV6AA, England. $6.80 for two years.

Motion Picture Daily. 1270 Sixth Avenue, New York, New York 10020. $15.00.

Motion Picture Herald. 1270 Sixth Avenue, New York, New York 10020. $5.00.

Movie. 21 Ivor Place, London, NW1, England. $4.00.

Movie Digest. Star Guidance Inc., 315 Park Avenue South, New York, New York 10010. $3.00.

Photon. 801 Avenue C., Brooklyn, New York 11218. $6.00.

Screen Actor. 7750 Sunset Boulevard, Hollywood, California 90046. $4.00.

Screen Facts. P. O. Box 154, Kew Gardens, New York 11415. $7.00.

Show. H&R Publications, Inc., 866 United Nations Plaza, New York, New York 10017. $8.00.

Sight and Sound. The British Film Institute, 81 Dean Street, London, WIV6AA, England. $5.00.

Sightlines. Educational Film Library Association, 17 West 60th Street, New York, New York 10023. $8.00.

The Silent Picture. 613 Harrow Road, London, W10, England. $3.00.

Take One. Unicorn Publishers, P. O. Box 1788, Station B, Montreal 2, P.W., Canada. $4.00.

Variety. 154 West 46th Street, New York, New York 10036. $20.00.

The Velvet Light Trap. The 602 Club, 602 University Avenue, Madison, Wisconsin 53703. $2.00.

Women and Film. 2802 Arizona Avenue, Santa Monica, California 90404. $2.00.

Appendix II

SELECTED LOT OF 16mm FILM DISTRIBUTORS[1]

American Documentary Films (ADF)
336 W. 84th Street
New York, New York 10024
(212) 799-7440

Audio Film Center (AUD)
866 Third Avenue
New York, New York 10022
(212) 935-7854

Avco Embassy Pictures Corp. (AVC)
1301 Avenue of the Americas
New York, New York 10019
(212) 956-5500

Bailey/Film Associates (BAI)
11559 Santa Monica Blvd.
Los Angeles, California 90025
(213) 464-7491

Blackhawk Films (BLA)
Eastin-Phelan Corporation
Davenport, Iowa 52808
(319) 323-9736

Buchan Pictures (BUC)
122 W. Chippewa Street
Buffalo, New York 14202

Cine-Craft Company (CCC)
709 SW Ankeney
Portland, Oregon 97205
(503) 228-7487

Cinema 5 Ltd. (CI V)
595 Madison Avenue
New York, New York 10022
(212) 421-5555

Crowell Collier Macmillan Inc.
(CCM)
866 Third Avenue

New York, New York 10022
(212) 935-7854

Charard Motion Pictures (CHA)
2110 E. 24th Street
Brooklyn, New York 11229
(212) 891-4339

Ciem Williams Films (CWF)
2240 Noblestown Road
Pittsburgh, Pennsylvania 15205
(412) 921-5810

Columbia Cinemateque (COL)
711 Fifth Avenue
New York, New York 10022
(212) 751-4400

Contemporary Films (CON)
McGraw-Hill Book Company
Princeton Road
Hightstown, New Jersey 08520
(609) 448-1700

Em Gee Film Library (EMG)
4931 Gloria Avenue
Encino, California 91316
(213) 981-5506

Film Classic Exchange (FCE)
1926 S. Vermont Avenue
Los Angeles, California 90007
(213) 731-3854

Films Incorporated (FNC)
4420 Oaktown Street
Skokie, Illinois 60076
(312) 676-1088

Genesis Films, Ltd. (GEN)
40 West 55th Street
New York, New York 10019
(212) 765-3750

1. For a more extensive list consult *Feature Films on 8mm and 16mm*, 3rd ed. Compiled and Edited by James L. Limacher (New York: R. R. Bowker Co., 1971).

338

Ideal Pictures (IDE)
34 MacQuesten Parkway, S.
Mount Vernon, New York 10550
(914) 664-5051

Indiana University (IND)
Audio-Visual Center
Bloomington, Indiana 47401
(812) 337-2103

Institutional Cinema Service (ICS)
915 Broadway
New York, New York 10010
(212) 673-3990

Ivy Film 16 (IVY)
120 East 56th Street
New York, New York 10022
(212) 758-5305

Mass Media Ministries (MMM)
2116 North Charles St.
Baltimore, Maryland 21218
(301) 727-3270

Museum of Modern Art (MMA)
Department of Film
11 W. 53rd St.
New York, New York 10019
(212) 245-8900

National Film Service (NAT)
14 Glenwood Avenue
Raleigh, North Carolina 27602
(919) 832-3901

Newman Film Library (NEW)
2021 Eastern Ave. S.E.
Grand Rapids, Michigan 49507
(616) 245-2277

Pyramid Films (PYR)
Box 1048
Santa Monica, California 90406
(213) 395-5200

Radim Films/Film Images (RAD)
17 W. 60th Street
New York, New York 10023
(212) 279-6653

Roa's Films (ROA)
1696 N. Astor Street
Milwaukee, Wisconsin 53202
(414) 271-0861

Samuel Goldwyn/16mm (SGS)
1041 N. Formosa Avenue
Los Angeles, California 90046
(213) 815-1234

Swank Motion Pictures (SWA)
201 S. Jefferson Avenue
St. Louis, Missouri 63166
(314) 531-5100

Teaching Film Custodians, Inc.
(TMC)
25 West 43rd Street
New York, New York 10036
(212) 695-1640

Texture Films, Inc. (TEX)
1600 Broadway
New York, New York 10019
(212) 586-5960

"The" Film Center (TFC)
915 Twelfth Street, N.W.
Washington, D.C. 20005
(202) 393-1205

Time-Life Films (TIM)
43 W. 16th Street
New York, New York 10011

Trans-World Films (TWF)
322 S. Michigan Avenue
Chicago, Illinois 60604
(312) 922-1530

Twyman Films (TWY)
329 Salem Avenue
Dayton, Ohio 45401
(513) 222-4014

United Artists 16 (UAS)
279 Seventh Avenue
New York, New York 10019
(212) 245-6000

United Entertainment, Inc. (UEI)
1124 S. Cheyenne
Tulsa, Oklahoma 74119

United Films (UNF)
1425 S. Main St.
Tulsa, Oklahoma 74119
(918) 584-6491

Universal 16 (UNI)
221 Park Avenue S
New York, New York 10003
(212) 777-6600

University of California (CAL)
Extension Media Center
2223 Fulton Street
Berkeley, California 94720
(415) 845-6000

Walter Reade 16 (WRS)
241 E. 34th Street
New York, New York 10016
(212) 683-6300

Warner Brothers (WSA)
Non-Theatrical Division
4000 Warner Boulevard
Burbank, California 91503
(213) 843-6000

Wholesome Film Center (WHO)
20 Melrose Street

Boston, Massachusetts 02116
(617) 426-0155

Willoughby-Peerless (WIL)
110 W. 32nd St.
New York, New York 10001
(212) 564-1600
and
415 Lexington Avenue
New York, New York 10017
(212) 687-1000

SELECTED LIST OF 8mm FILM DISTRIBUTORS[2]

Blackhawk Films (BLA)
29 Eastin-Phelan Building
Davenport, Iowa 52808

Castle Films (CAS)
221 Park Avenue South
New York, New York 10003

Cooper's Classic Film Rental Service
(COO)
Northedge Shopping Center
Eaton, Ohio 45320

Enrique J. Bouchard (EJB)
Charcas 2762
Buenos Aires, Argentina

Entertainment Films Co., Inc.
(ENT)
850 Seventh Avenue
New York, New York 10019

Film Classic Exchange (FCE)
1926 South Vermont Avenue
Los Angeles, California 90007

I. K. Meginnis (IKM)
Box 5803, Bethesda P.O.
Washington, D.C. 20014

John Griggs' Moviedrome (JGM)
139 Maple Street
Englewood, New Jersey 07631

Movie Classics (MC)
P. O. Box 1463
Philadelphia, Pennsylvania 19105

Parkchester Films (PAR)
1775 Mansion Street
Bronx, New York 10560

United Artists EIGHT (UA8)
555 Madison Avenue
New York, New York 10022

2. For a more complete list, see *8mm Film Directory: A Comprehensive and Descrip tive Index*. Compiled and Edited by Grace Ann Kone (New York: Comprehensive Service Corporation, 1969–70) .

Appendix III

"THE DON'TS AND BE CAREFULS"

I. Crimes Against the Law;
There shall never be presented in such a way as to throw sympathy with the crime against law and justice or to inspire others with a desire for imitating.
A. *Murder*
1. The technique of murder must be presented in such a way that will not inspire imitation.
2. Brutal killings are not to be presented in detail.
3. Revenge in modern times shall not be justified.
B. *Methods of Crime* should not be explicitly presented.
1. Theft, robbery, safe-cracking and dynamiting of trains, mines, buildings, etc., should not be detailed in methods.
2. Arson must be subject to the same safeguards.
3. The use of firearms should be restricted to essentials.
4. Methods of smuggling should not be presented.
C. *The Illegal Drug Traffic* must not be portrayed in such a way as to stimulate curiosity concerning the use of, or traffic in, such drugs; nor shall scenes be approved which show the use of illegal drugs or their effects in detail (as amended Sept. 11, 1946.)
D. *The use of liquor* in American life, when not required by the plot or for characterization, will not be shown.
II. *Sex*
The sanctity of the institution of marriage and the home shall be upheld. Pictures shall not imply that low forms of sex relationships are the accepted or common thing.
A. *Adultery and illicit sex,* sometimes necessary plot material, must not be explicitly treated or justified or presented attractively.
B. *Scenes of passion*
1. These should not be introduced except where they are definitely essential to the plot.
2. Excessive and lustful kissing, lustful embraces, suggestive postures and gestures are not to be shown.
3. In general, passion should be treated in such a manner as not to stimulate the lower or baser emotions.
C. *Seduction or Rape*
1. These should never be more than suggested, and then only when essential for the plot. They must never be shown by explicit method.
2. They are never the proper subject for comedy.
D. *Sex perversion* or any inference to it is forbidden.

341

E. *White Slavery* shall not be treated.
F. Miscegenation (sex relationship between black and white races) is forbidden.
G. *Sex hygiene* and venereal diseases are not proper subjects for theatrical motion pictures.
H. Scenes of *actual childbirth,* in fact or silhouette, are never to be presented.
I. Children's sex organs are never to be exposed.

III. *Vulgarity*

The treatment of low, disgusting, unpleasant, though not necessarily evil subjects should be guided always by the dictates of good taste and a proper regard for the sensibilities of the audience.

IV. *Obscenity* in word, gesture, reference, song, joke, or by suggestion (even when likely to be understood only by part of the audience) is forbidden.

V. *Profanity*

Pointed profanity and every other profane or vulgar expression, however used, is forbidden. No approval by the Production Code Administration shall be given to the use of words and phrases in motion pictures including, but not limited to, the following:

Alley cat (applied to a woman); bat (applied to a woman); broad (applied to a woman; Bronx cheer (the sound); chippie, cocotte; God; Lord, Jesus, Christ (unless used reverently); cripes; fanny; fairy (in a vulgar sense); finger (the); fire, cries of; Gawd, goose (in a vulgar sense); "hold your hat"; louse; lousy; hot (applied to a woman); "in your hat," nance; nerts; nuts (except when meaning crazy); pansy; razzberry (the sound); slut (applied to a woman); S.O.B.; son-of-a-tart; toilet gags; tom cat (applied to a man); traveling salesman and farmer's daughter jokes; whore; damn; hell; (excepting when the use of said last two words shall be essential and required for portrayal, in historical fact or folklore, or for the presentation in proper literary context of a Biblical, or other religious quotation, or a quotation from a literary work provided that no such use shall be permitted which is intrinsically objectionable or offends good taste.)

In the administration of Section V of the Production Code, the Production Code Administration may take cognizance of the fact that the following words are offensive to the patrons of motion pictures in the United States and more particularly to the patrons of motion pictures in foreign countries: Chink, Dago, Frog, Greaser, Hunkie, Kike, Nigger, Spic, Wop, Yid.

VI. *Costume*

A. *Complete Nudity* is never permitted. This includes nudity to the fact or in silhouette, or any licentious notice thereof by other characters in the pictures.
B. *Undressing Scenes* should be avoided, and never used save where essential to the plot.
C. *Indecent or undue exposure* is forbidden.
D. *Dancing Costumes* intending to permit undue exposure or indecent movements in the dance are forbidden.

VII. *Dances*

A. Dances suggesting or representing sexual actions or indecent passion are forbidden.

B. Dances which emphasize indecent movements are to be regarded as obscene.

VIII. *Religion*
   A. No film or episode may throw *ridicule* on any religious faith.
   B. *Ministers of religion* in their characters as ministers of religion should not be used as comic characters or villains.
   C. Ceremonies of any definite religion should be carefully avoided and respectfully handled.

IX. *Locations*
   The treatment of bedrooms must be governed by good taste and delicacy.

X. *National Feelings*
   A. The use of the flag shall be consistently respectful.
   B. The history, institutions, prominent people and citizenry of all nations shall be represented fairly.

XI. *Titles*
   Salacious, indecent or obscene titles shall not be used.

XII. *Repellent Subjects*
   The following subjects must be treated within careful limits of good taste:
   A. Actual hangings or electrocutions as legal punishment for crime.
   B. Third-degree methods.
   C. Brutality and possible gruesomeness.
   D. Branding of people or animals.
   E. Apparent cruelty to children or animals.
   F. The sale of women or a woman selling her virtue.
   G. Surgical operations.

Appendix IV

THE MOTION PICTURE CODE AND RATING PROGRAM
A SYSTEM OF SELF-REGULATION[1]

The Code of Self-Regulation of the Motion Picture Association of America shall apply to production, to advertising, and to titles of motion pictures.

The Code shall be administered by the Code and Rating Administration, headed by an Administrator.

There shall also be a Director of the Code for Advertising, and a Director of the Code for Titles.

Non-members are invited to submit pictures to the Code and Rating Administration on the same basis as members of the Association.

DECLARATION OF PRINCIPLES OF THE CODE OF SELF-REGULATION OF THE MOTION PICTURE ASSOCIATION

This Code is designed to keep in close harmony with the mores, culture, the moral sense and change in our society.

The objectives of the Code are:
1. To encourage artistic expression by expanding creative freedom;
2. To assure that the freedom which encourages the artist remains responsible and sensitive to the standards of the larger society.

Censorship is an odious enterprise. We oppose censorship and classification by governments because they are alien to the American tradition of freedom.

Much of this nation's strength and purpose is drawn from the premise that the humblest of citizens has the freedom of his own choice. Censorship destroys this freedom of choice.

It is within this framework that the Motion Picture Association continues to recognize its obligations to the society of which it is an integral part.

In our society parents are the arbiters of family conduct. Parents have the primary responsibility to guide their children in the kind of lives they lead, the character they build, the books they read, and the movies and other entertainment to which they are exposed.

The creators of motion pictures undertake a responsibility to make avail-

---

1. For further information write to: Motion Picture Association of America, 522 Fifth Avenue, New York, New York 10036.

344

able pertinent information about their pictures which will assist parents to fulfill their responsibilities.

But this alone is not enough. In further recognition of our obligation to the public, and most especially to parents, we have extended the Code operation to include a nationwide voluntary film rating program which has as its prime objective a sensitive concern for children. Motion pictures will be reviewed by a Code and Rating Administration which, when it reviews a motion picture as to its conformity with the standards of the Code, will issue ratings. It is our intent that all motion pictures exhibited in the United States will carry a rating. These ratings are:

G SUGGESTED FOR GENERAL AUDIENCES
This category includes motion pictures that in the opinion of the Code and Rating Administration would be acceptable for all audiences, without consideration of age.

M² SUGGESTED FOR MATURE AUDIENCES—ADULTS & MATURE YOUNG PEOPLE
This category includes motion pictures that in the opinion of the Code and Rating Administration, because of their theme, content and treatment, might require more mature judgment by viewers, and about which parents should exercise their discretion.

R RESTRICTED—Persons under 16 not admitted, unless accompanied by parent or guardian
This category includes motion pictures that in the opinion of the Code and Rating Administration, because of their theme, content or treatment, should not be presented to persons under 16 unless accompanied by a parent or adult guardian.

X PERSONS UNDER 16 NOT ADMITTED
This category includes motion pictures submitted to the Code and Rating Administration which in the opinion of the Code and Rating Administration are rated X because of the treatment of sex, violence, crime or profanity. Pictures rated X do not qualify for a Code Seal. Pictures rated X should not be presented to persons under 16.
The program contemplates that any distributors outside the membership of the Association who choose not to submit their motion pictures to the Code and Rating Administration will self-apply the X rating.

The ratings and their meanings will be conveyed by advertising; by displays at the theaters; and in other ways. Thus, audiences, especially parents, will be alerted to the theme, content, and treatment of movies. Therefore, parents can determine whether a particular picture is one which children should see at the discretion of the parent; or only when accompanied by a parent; or should not see.

We believe self-restraint, self-regulation, to be in the American tradition. The results of self-discipline are always imperfect because that is the nature of all things mortal. But this Code, and its administration, will make clear that freedom of expression does not mean toleration of license.

---

2. Later this was changed to GP, then PG (parental guidance suggested).

The test of self-restraint—the rule of reason . . . lies in the treatment of a subject matter for the screen.

All members of the Motion Picture Association, as well as the National Association of Theatre Owners, the International Film Importers and Distributors of America, and other independent producer-distributors are co-operating in this endeavor. Most motion pictures exhibited in the United States will be submitted for Code approval and rating, or for rating only, to the Code and Rating Administration. The presence of the Seal indicates to the public that a picture has received Code approval.

We believe in and pledge our support to these deep and fundamental values in a democratic society:

Freedom of choice . . .

The right of creative man to achieve artistic excellence . . .

The importance of the role of the parent as the guide of the family's conduct . . .

Standards for Production

In furtherance of the objectives of the Code to accord with the mores, the culture, and the moral sense of our society, the principles stated above and the following standards shall govern the Administrator in his consideration of motion pictures submitted for Code approval:

The basic dignity and value of human life shall be respected and upheld. Restraint shall be exercised in portraying the taking of life.

Evil, sin, crime, and wrong-doing shall not be justified.

Special restraint shall be exercised in portraying criminal or anti-social activities in which minors participate or are involved.

Detailed and protracted acts of brutality, cruelty, physical violence, torture and abuse shall not be presented.

Indecent or undue exposure of the human body shall not be presented.

Illicit sex relationships shall not be justified. Intimate sex scenes violating common standards of decency shall not be portrayed.

Restraint and care shall be exercised in presentations dealing with sex aberrations.

Obscene speech, gestures or movements shall not be presented. Undue profanity shall not be permitted.

Religion shall not be demeaned.

Words or symbols contemptuous of racial, religious, or national groups, shall not be used so as to incite bigotry or hatred.

Excessive cruelty to animals shall not be portrayed and animals shall not be treated inhumanely.

Standards for Advertising

The principles of the Code cover advertising and publicity as well as production. There are times when their specific application to advertising may be different. A motion picture is viewed as a whole and may be judged that way. It is the nature of advertising, however, that it must select and emphasize only isolated portions and aspects of a film. It thus follows that what may be appropriate in a motion picture may not be equally appropriate in advertising. Furthermore, in application to advertising, the principles and standards of the Code are supplemented by the following standards for advertising:

Illustrations and text shall not misrepresent the character of a motion picture.

Illustrations shall not depict any indecent or undue exposure of the human body.

Advertising demeaning religion, race, or national origin shall not be used.

Cumulative overemphasis on sex, crime, violence, and brutality shall not be permitted.

Salacious postures and embraces shall not be shown.

Censorship disputes shall not be exploited or capitalized upon.

Standards for Titles

A salacious, obscene, or profane title shall not be used on motion pictures.

REGULATIONS GOVERNING THE OPERATION OF THE MOTION PICTURE CODE AND RATING ADMINISTRATION

The Motion Picture Code and Rating Administration (hereinafter referred to as the Administration) is established to be composed of an Administrator and staff members, one of whom shall be experienced in the exhibition of motion pictures to the public.

(a) All motion pictures produced or distributed by members of the Association and their subsidiaries will be submitted to the Administration for Code and rating.

(b) Non-members of the Association may submit their motion pictures to the Administration for Code approval and rating in the same manner and under the same conditions as members of the Association or may submit their motion pictures to the Administration for rating only.

Members and non-members who submit their motion pictures to the Administration for approval and rating should, prior to the commencement of the production of the motion picture, submit a script or other treatment.

The Administration will inform the producer in confidence whether a motion picture based upon the submitted script appears to conform to the Standards of the Code and indicate its probable rating. The final judgment of the Administration shall be made only upon reviewing of the completed picture.

(a) When a completed motion picture is submitted to the Administration and is approved as conforming to the Standards of the Code, it will be rated by the Administration either as G [suggested for general audiences], M [suggested for mature audiences—adults and mature young people], or R [restricted], according to the categories described in the DECLARATION OF PRINCIPLES.

(b) Completed motion pictures submitted by non-members for rating only will be rated according to the categories described in the DECLARATION OF PRINCIPLES as G, M, R, or X.

Motion pictures of member companies or their subsidiaries which are approved under the Code and rated G, M, or R shall upon public release bear upon an introductory frame of every print distributed in the United States the official seal of the Association with the word "Approved" and the words "Certificate Number," followed by the number of the Certificate of Approval and the symbol of the rating assigned to it by the Administration. So far as possible the Seal of the Association and the rating shall be displayed in uniform type, size and prominence. All prints of an approved motion picture bearing the Code Seal shall be identical.

Motion pictures of non-member companies submitted for Code approval and rating or for rating only which receive a G, M, or R rating shall bear such ratings upon an introductory frame of every print distributed in the United States, in uniform shape, type, size and prominence. Prints of such pictures may also display the official Seal of the Association if application is made to the Association for the issuance of a Code Certificate number.

If the Administration determines that a motion picture submitted for approval and rating or rating only should be rated X in accordance with the description of that category in the DECLARATION OF PRINCIPLES, the symbol X must appear on all prints of the motion picture distributed in the United States in uniform type, size and prominence and in all advertising for the picture.

The Administration in issuing a Certificate of Approval and Rating or a Rating Certificate shall condition such issuance upon the agreement by the producer or distributor that all advertising and publicity to be used for the picture shall be submitted to and approved by the Director of the Code for Advertising.

The producer or distributor upon applying for a Certificate of Approval for a picture or a Rating Certificate for those pictures receiving a rating only shall advance to the Administration at the time of application a fee in accordance with the uniform schedule of fees approved by the Board of Directors of the Association.

The standards for titles for motion pictures shall be applied by the Administration in consultation with the Director of the Code for Titles to all motion pictures submitted for approval and rating only and no motion picture for which a Certificate of Approval or Rating Certificate has been issued shall change its title without the prior approval of the Administration.

ADVERTISING CODE REGULATIONS

These regulations are applicable to all members of the Motion Picture Association of America, to all producers and distributors of motion pictures with respect to each picture for which the Association has granted its Certificate of Approval or Rating Certificate; and to all other producers and distributors who apply the X rating to their motion pictures and voluntarily submit their advertising.

The term "advertising" as used herein shall be deemed to mean all forms of motion picture advertising and exploitation and ideas thereof, including the following: pressbooks; still photographs; newspaper, magazine and trade paper advertising; publicity copy and art intended for use in pressbooks or otherwise intended for general distribution in printed form or for theater use; trailers; posters, lobby displays and other outdoor displays; advertising accessories, including heralds and throwaways; novelties; copy for exploitation tieups; and all radio and television copy and spots.

All advertising for motion pictures which have been submitted to the Code and Rating Administration for approval and Rating, or for rating only, shall be submitted to the Director of the Code for Advertising for approval before use, and shall not be used in any way until so submitted and approved. All advertising shall be submitted in duplicate with the exception of pressbooks, which shall be submitted in triplicate.

The director of the Code for Advertising shall proceed as promptly as feasible to approve or disapprove the advertising submitted.

The Director of the Code for Advertising shall stamp "Approved" on one copy of all advertising approved by him and return the stamped copy to the Company which submitted it. If the Director of the Code for Advertising disapproves of any advertising, the Director shall stamp the word "Disapproved" on one copy and return it to the Company which submitted it, together with the reasons for such disapproval; or, if the Director so desires, he may return the copy with suggestions for such changes or corrections as will cause it to be approved.

The Director of the Code for Advertising shall require all approved advertising for pictures submitted to the Code and Rating Administration by members of the Motion Picture Association of America and their subsidiaries to carry the official Code seal and a designation of the rating assigned to the picture by the Code and Rating Administration. Uniform standards as to type, size and prominence of the display of the seal and rating will be set forth by the Advertising Code Administrator.

Approved advertising for pictures submitted to the Code and Rating Administration by companies other than members of the Motion Picture Association of America, and their subsidiaries, for Code approval and rating, or for rating only, may bear the official seal at the distributor's option, but all such advertising shall bear the assigned rating.

Approved advertising for pictures rated X by the Code and Rating Administration shall bear the X rating but may not bear the official seal.

All pressbooks approved by the Director of the Code for Advertising shall bear in a prominent place the official seal of the Motion Picture Association of America and a designation of the rating assigned to the picture by the Code and Rating Administration. The word "Approved" shall be printed under the seal. Pressbooks shall also carry the following notice:

All advertising in this pressbook, as well as all other advertising and publicity materials referred to herein, has been approved under the Standards for Advertising of the Code of Self-Regulation of the Motion Picture Association of America. All inquiries on this procedure may be addressed to:

Director of Code for Advertising
Motion Picture Association of America
522 Fifth Avenue
New York, New York 10036

Appeals. Any Company whose advertising has been disapproved may appeal from the decision of the Director of the Code for Advertising, as follows:

It shall serve notice of such appeal on the Director of the Code for Advertising and on the President of the Association. The President, or in his absence a Vice President designated by him, shall thereupon promptly and within a week hold a hearing to pass upon the appeal. Oral and written evidence may be introduced by the Company and by the Director of the Code for Advertising, or their representatives. The appeal shall be decided as expeditiously as possible and the decision shall be final.

On appeals by companies, other than members of the Motion Picture Association of America and their subsidiaries, the President shall, if requested, decide the appeal in consultation with a representative of International Film Importers and Distributors of America, as designated by its Governing Board.

Any company which has been granted a Certificate of Approval and which uses advertising without securing the prior approval of the Director of the Code for Advertising or if such advertising does not include the assigned rating may be brought up on charges before the Board of Directors by the President of the Association. Within a reasonable time, the Board may hold a hearing, at which time the company and the Director of the Code for Advertising or their representatives, may present oral or written statements. The Board, by a majority vote by those present, shall decide the matter as expeditiously as possible.

If the Board of Directors finds that the company has used advertising for a Code approved and rated picture without securing approval of the Director of the Code for Advertising, or without including the assigned rating, the Board may direct the Code and Rating Administration to void and revoke the Certificate of Approval granted for the picture and require the removal of the Association's seal from all prints of the picture.

Each company shall be responsible for compliance by its employees and agents with these regulations.

CODE AND RATING APPEALS BOARD

1. A Code and Rating Appeals Board is established, to be composed as follows:

(a) The President of the Motion Picture Association of America and 12 members designated by the President from the Board of Directors of the Association and executive officers of its member companies;

(b) Eight exhibitors designated by the National Association of Theatre Owners from its Board of Directors;

(c) Two producers designated by the Producers Guild of America;

(d) Two distributors designated by the International Film Importers and Distributors of America.

2. A pro tempore member for any particular hearing to act as a substitute for a member unable to attend may be designated in the same manner as the absent member.

3. The President of the Motion Picture Association shall be Chairman of the Appeals Board, and the Association shall provide its secretariat.

4. The presence of 13 members is necessary to constitute a quorum of the Appeals Board for a hearing of any appeal.

5. The Board will hear and determine appeals from:

(a) A Decision of the Code and Rating Administration withholding Code approval from a picture submitted for approval and rating and which consequently received an X rating.

(b) A decision by the Code and Rating Administration applying an X rating to a picture submitted for rating only.

On such appeals a vote of two-thirds of the members present shall be required to sustain the decision of the Administration. If the decision of the Administration is not sustained, the Board shall proceed to rate the picture appropriately by majority vote.

6. The Board will also hear and determine appeals from the decision of the Code and Rating Administration applying any rating other than X to a motion picture.

Such appeals shall be decided by majority vote. If the decision of the Administration is not sustained the Board shall proceed to rate the picture appropriately.

7. (a) An appeal from a decision of the Administration shall be instituted by the filing of a notice of appeal addressed to the Chairman of the Appeals Board by the party which submitted the picture to the Administration.

(b) Provision shall be made for the screening by the members of the Appeals Board at the hearing or prior thereto of a print of the motion picture identical to the one reviewed and passed upon by the administration.

(c) The party taking the appeal and the Administration may present oral or written statements to the Board at the hearing.

(d) No member of the Appeals Board shall participate on an appeal involving a picture in which the member or any company with which he is associated has a financial interest.

(e) The appeal shall be heard and decided as expeditiously as possible and the decision shall be final.

8. The Board will also act as an advisory body on Code matters and, upon the call of the Chairman, will discuss the progress of the operation

of the Code and rating program and review the manner of adherence to the Advertising Code.

INFORMATION FOR PARENTS

With the adoption of the voluntary film rating system described in this booklet the creators, distributors and exhibitors of motion pictures fulfill an important responsibility to the parents of this country. Through this system guidance is now provided as to the suitability of certain films for young audiences.

The ratings are applied by the experienced staff of the Code and Rating Administration. Those few film companies that do not choose to submit a film for rating will self-apply the strictest rating to that film, an X. The symbols which indicate audience suitability can be found easily . . . in movie advertising, in theater boxoffice windows, in lobby displays, and in numerous newspapers and magazines.

This new system goes into effect on November 1, 1968, but there will be a period from 3 to 6 months during which time movies in release prior to that date will continue to be shown without ratings. Their number will diminish rapidly, however, after the new system begins to operate.

The film industry is doing all in its power to make these ratings easily accessible, but we must rely on the public to become familiar with the symbols and their meanings, and to respect and follow the guidance offered. Parents especially must teach their own children to understand and observe the symbols. Theater managers will enforce all those which restrict children's admission.

ADDENDUM[3]

RESOLVED, that the resolution adopted September 18, 1968, creating and establishing a Code and Rating Appeals Board under the Motion Picture Code and Rating Program, as revised by resolution dated October 5, 1970, be and is hereby amended so that the resolution reads as follows:

Code and Rating Appeals Board

1. A Code and Rating Appeals Board is established, to be composed as follows:

(a) The President of the Motion Picture Association of America and 12 members designated by the President from the Board of Directors of the Association and executive officers of its member companies;

(b) Eight exhibitors designated by the National Association of Theatre Owners;

(c) Four distributors designated by the International Film Importers and Distributors of America.

2. A pro tempore member for any particular hearing to act as a substitute for a member unable to attend may be designated in the same manner as the absent member.

---

3. (Revised September 16, 1971; effective September 22, 1971.)

3. The President of the Motion Picture Association shall be Chairman of the Appeals Board, and the Association shall provide its secretariat.

4. The presence of eleven members is necessary to constitute a quorum of the Appeals Board for the hearing of any appeal, provided that at least four members each, designated by MPAA and NATO, respectively, and one member designated by IFIDA are present.

5. The Board will hear and determine appeals from decisions by the Code and Rating Administration withholding Code approval from a picture submitted for approval and rating and decisions applying any rating to a motion picture.
No decision of the Code and Rating Administration shall be reversed upon appeal unless two-thirds of those present and voting shall vote to reverse. Upon reversal of any decision, the Code and Rating Administration shall rate the picture involved in conformity with the decision of the Appeals Board.

6. (a) An appeal from a decision of the Administration shall be instituted by the filing of a notice of appeal addressed to the Chairman of the Appeals Board by the party which submitted the picture to the Administration.
(b) Provision shall be made for the screening by the members of the Appeals Board at the hearing or prior thereto of a print of the motion picture identical to the one reviewed and passed upon by the Administration.
(c) The party taking the appeal and the Administration may present oral or written statements to the Board at the hearing.
(d) No member of the Appeals Board shall participate on an appeal involving a picture in which the member or any company with which he is associated has a financial interest.
(e) The appeal shall be heard and decided as expeditiously as possible and the decision shall be final.

7. (a) The Appeals Board may adopt supplemental regulations governing its procedures but not inconsistent with those set forth above, including provision for payment of a uniform filing fee by a party taking an appeal, to be used toward the costs involved in the hearing of appeals.
(b) The Board will also act as an advisory body on Code matters and, upon the call of the Chairman, will discuss the progress of the operation of the Code and Rating Program and review the manner of adherence to the Advertising Code.
FURTHER RESOLVED, that this resolution shall be effective immediately.

Appendix V

SELECTED LIST OF SOURCES FOR FURTHER FILM STUDY[1]

Archives

George Eastman House of Photography, 900 East Avenue, Rochester, New York 14607.

Hollywood Museum, 7046 Hollywood Boulevard, Los Angeles, California 90028.

Los Angeles County Museum, History Division, Exposition Park, Los Angeles, California 90007.

Museum of Modern Art, 11 West 53rd Street, New York, New York 10019.

Library Resources

Academy of Motion Picture Arts and Sciences, 9038 Melrose Avenue, Hollywood, California 90069.

Baker Library, Dartmouth College, Hanover, New Hampshire 03755.

Columbia University Library, Columbia University, New York, New York 10027.

De Forest Research Service, 780 North Gower Street, Los Angeles, California 90038.

The Free Library of Philadelphia, Logan Square, Philadelphia, Pennsylvania 19144.

The Library of Congress, First Street Between E. Capital Street and Independence Avenue, S.E., Washington, D.C. 20540.

New York Public Library, Fifth Avenue and 42nd Street, New York, New York 10036.

New York Museum of the Performing Arts, Lincoln Center at 111 Amsterdam Avenue, New York, New York 10023.

Sterling Memorial Library, Yale University, New Haven, Connecticut 06520.

Twentieth Century Fox Film Corporation Research Library, 10201 W. Pico Boulevard, Los Angeles, California 90064.

UCLA Library, Department of Special Collection, Powell Library, UCLA, Los Angeles, California 90024.

Biographical and Reference Tools

Library of Congress Catalogue Books

---

1. This appendix is indebted to Jay Leyda, *et al.*, "Special Features on Film Scholarship," *Film Quarterly* 16, no. 2 (Winter 1962–63) : 29–50.

National Union Catalogue
Union List of Serials
Readers' Guide to Periodicals
Subject Index to Periodicals
Film as Art
Filmfacts
New York Times Index
How and Where to Look It Up
American Library Resources: a bibliographical guide, Supplement 1950–61
Who's Who in the Theatre

Bookstores

Booklord's, P. O. Box 177, Peter Stuyvesant Station, New York, New York
   10009.
Cinemabilia, 10 West 13th Street, New York, New York 10011.
Gotham Book Mart, 41 West 47th Street, New York, New York 10036.
Hampton Books, Box 738, Newberry, South Carolina 29108.
Larry Edmunds Bookshop, 6658 Hollywood Boulevard, Hollywood, Cali-
   fornia 90028.

Stills

The Bettmann Archive, Incorporated, 136 East 57th Street, New York, New
   York 10022. (212) 758-0362.
Brandon Memorabilia, 13 East 53rd Street, New York, New York 10022.
   (212) 752-9864.
British Film Institute, 81 Dean Street, London WIV6AA, England.
Culver Pictures, 660 First Avenue, New York, New York 10016. (212)
   684-5054.
Memory Shop, 100 Fourth Avenue, New York, New York 10003. (212)
   473-2404.
Museum of Modern Art, 11 West 53rd Street, New York, New York 10019.
   (212) 245-8900.

Appendix VI

A SELECTIVE LIST OF DISSERTATIONS ON FILMS

1955

Parker, David Wilson. A descriptive analysis of the Lone Ranger as a form of popular art. Northwestern University, 1955. Deals broadly with the popular arts but specifically with the Lone Ranger radio scripts.
(D.A.[1] vol. 15, 1955, p. 2600)

1957

Chenoweth, Stuart Curran. A study of the adaptation of acting technique from stage to film, radio, and television media in the United States, 1900–1951. Northwestern University, 1957.

1958

Fell, John L. A comparison between sponsored and educational motion pictures. New York University 1958–59.
(Under American Doctoral Dissertations 1958–59, p. 161)
Rider, Richard Lee. A comparative analysis of directing television and film drama. University of Illinois, 1958.
(D.A. vol. 18, 1958, p. 1900)

1960

Kuiper, John Bennett. An analysis of the four silent films of Sergei Mikailovich Eisenstein. State University of Iowa, 1960.
(D.A. vol. 20, 1959–60, p. 4755)
Thayer, David Lewis. A study of the influence of conventional film lighting on audience response. State University of Iowa, 1960.
(D.A. vol. 20, 1959–60, p. 4758)

1961

Gregory, John Robert. Some psychological aspects of motion picture montage. University of Illinois, 1961.
(D.A. vol. 22, 1961–62, p. 317)

---

1. D.A. stands for *Dissertation Abstracts*.

Sanderson, Richard Arlo. A historical study of the development of American motion picture content and technique prior to 1964. University of Southern California, 1961.

(D.A. vol. 22, 1961–62, p. 235)

Tyo, John Henry. A comparative analysis of motion picture production courses offered in selected colleges and universities in the United States. Indiana University, 1961.

(D.A. vol. 22, 1961–62, p. 819)

1962

Byrne, Richard Burdick. German cinematic expressionism: 1919–1924. State University of Iowa, 1962.

(D.A. vol. 23, 1962–63, p. 3021)

Nasir, Sari Jamil. The image of the Arab in American popular culture. University of Illinois, 1962.

(D.A. vol. 23, 1962–63, p. 4003)

McCaffrey, Donald William. An investigation of three feature length silent film comedies starring Harold Lloyd. State University of Iowa, 1962.

(D.A. vol. 23, 1962–63, p. 3550)

Warden, James William. The portrayal of the Protestant minister in American pictures, 1951–1960, and its implications for the Church today. Boston University, 1962.

(D.A. vol. 23, 1962–63, p. 1440)

1963

Huaco, George Arthur. The sociology of film styles. University of California at Berkeley, 1963.

(D.A. vol. 24, 1963–64, p. 5594)

Sargent, John Alan. Self-regulation: The Motion Picture Production Code, 1930–1961. University of Michigan, 1963.

(D.A. vol. 24, 1963–64, p. 897)

Schwartz, Jack. The portrayal of education in American motion pictures, 1931–1961. University of Illinois, 1963.

(D.A. vol. 24, 1963–64, p. 5377)

Schweitzer, Harold Clayton, Jr. Comparison of color and black and white films in the modification of attitudes. Fordham University, 1963.

(D.A. vol. 24, 1963–64, p. 874)

See, Carolyn Penelope. The Hollywood novel: An historical and critical study. University of California at Los Angeles, 1963.

(D.A. vol. 24, 1963–64, p. 5418)

Selby, Stuart Alan. The study of film as an art form in American secondary schools. Columbia University, 1963.

(D.A. vol. 24, 1963–64, p. 5098)

1964

Carmen, Ira Harris. State and local motion picture censorship and constitutional liberties with special emphasis on the communal acceptance of Supreme Court decision-making. University of Michigan, 1964.

(D.A. vol. 25, 1964–65, p. 6038)

Dart, Peter Arnold. Pudovkin's film legacy. University of Iowa.
(American Doctoral Dissertations, vol. 25, 1964–65, p. 220)
(Also D.A. vol. 26, 1965–66, p. 2918)

Giglio, Ernest David. The decade of *The Miracle,* 1952–1962: A study of the censorship of the American motion picture. Syracuse University, 1964.
(D.A. vol. 25, 1964–65, p. 5889)

Guback, Thomas Henry. The film industry in post-war Western Europe; the role of the Euro-American interaction in the shaping of economic structure and operations. University of Illinois, 1964.
(D.A. vol. 25, 1964–65, p. 4681)

Rawlins, Mary Jane. A Q-Methodological Study of Some Effects of a Fictional and Documentary Treatment of a Controversial Issue. University of Missouri, 1964.

(D.A. vol. 25, 1964–65, p. 1184)
(Uses commercial film: *A Raisin in the Sun*)

Seymour, Victor. State director's workshop; a descriptive study of The Actors Studio Directors Unit, 1960–64. University of Wisconsin.
(American Doctoral Dissertations vol. 25, 1964–65, p. 221)

1966

Burke, William Lee. The presentation of the American Negro in Hollywood films 1946–61; analysis of a selected sample of feature films. Northwestern University.
(American Doctoral Dissertations 1965–1966, p. 208)

Gollub, Judith Podselver. *Noveau roman et nouveau cinema* (French text). University of California at Los Angeles, 1966.
(D.A. vol. 26, 1966, p. 712)

Lounsbury, Myron Osborn. The origins of American film criticism, 1909–1939. University of Pennsylvania, 1966.
(D.A. vol. 27, 1966, p. 1373-A)

Manchel, Frank. Film literature: A resource study for secondary school English teachers. Columbia University, 1966.
(D.A. vol. 27, 1967, p. 3875-A)

McGuire, Jerry Carter. Value philosophy and contemporary cinema. University of Southern California, 1966.
(D.A. vol. 26, 1966, p. 6712)

Perry, Donald LeRoy. An analysis of the financial plans of the motion picture industry for the period 1929 to 1962. University of Illinois, 1966.
(D.A. vol. 27, 1967, p. 4019-A)

Snyder, Robert Louis. A history of the early productions of Pare Lorentz and the United States film service, 1935–1940. University of Iowa.
(American Doctoral Dissertations 1965–1966, p. 208)

Whitaker, Rodney William. The content analysis of film: A survey of the field, an exhaustive study of *Quai des Brumes* and a functional description of the elements of the film language. Northwestern University, 1966.
(D.A. vol. 27, 1967, p. 3543-A)

Wolfe, Glenn Joseph. Vachel Lindsay: The poet as film theorist. State University of Iowa, 1964.
(D.A. vol. 26, 1966, p. 1222)

1967

Lawder, Standish Dyer. Structuralism and movement in experimental film and modern art, 1896–1925. Yale University, 1967.
(D.A. vol. 28, 1968, p. 4555-A)

Miller, William Charles III. An experimental study of the relationship of film movement and emotional involvement response, and its effect on learning and attitude formation. University of Southern California, 1967.
(D.A. vol. 29, 1968, p. 716-A)

Penn, Roger. An experimental study of meaning of cutting-rate variables in motion pictures. University of Iowa, 1907.
(D.A. vol. 28, 1967, p. 788-A)

Randall, Richard Stuart. Control of motion pictures in the United States. University of Wisconsin, 1967.
(D.A. vol. 28, 1967, p. 2751-A)

Ritze, Frederick Henry. Responses of Pakistani college students to a selected American film. Columbia University, 1967.
(D.A. vol. 25, 1967, p. 1455-A)

Staples, Donald Edward. A statistical study of award-winning American films and their makers, 1930–1964. Northwestern University.
(D.A. vol. 28, 1967, p. 2371-A)

Wood, James Allen. An application of rhetorical theory to filmic persuasion. Cornell University, 1967.
(D.A. vol. 28, 1967, p. 2808-A)

1968

Lamson, Robert Doane. Motion picture exhibition: An economic analysis of quality, output and production. University of Washington, 1968.
(D.A. vol. 29, 1968, p. 716-A)

Phelan, Rev. John Martin, S.J. The National Catholic Office for Motion Pictures: An investigation of the policy of film classification. New York University, 1968.
(D.A. vol. 29, 1969, p. 3087-A)

Reynolds, James Conrad. The effect of viewer distance on film induced anxiety. Indiana University, 1968.
(D.A. vol. 29, 1969, p. 3341-A)

Suber, Howard. The anti-Communist blacklist in the Hollywood motion picture industry. University of California at Los Angeles, 1968.
(D.A. vol. 29, 1969, p. 4131-A)

1969

Basti, Abdul Zaher. Impact of the American motion picture industry on the United States balance of payments. University of Colorado, 1969.
(D.A. vol. 30, p. 881-A)

Blumenberg, Richard Mitchell. The manipulation of time and space in the novels of Alain Robbe-Grillet and in the narrative films of Alain Resnais, with particular reference to Last Year at Marienbad. Ohio University, 1969.
(D.A. vol. 30, p. 4051-A)

Karpf, Stephen Louis. The gangster film: emergence, variation and decay of a genre, 1930–1940. Northwestern University, 1969.

(D.A. vol. 30, p. 4587-A)

Kosower, Herbert. A study of an independent feature film you don't have time. University of Southern California, 1969.

(D.A. vol. 30, p. 4599-A)

Margolies, Alan. The impact of theatre and film on F. Scott Fitzgerald. New York University, 1969.

(D.A. vol. 30, p. 3467-A)

Musun, Chris. The marketing of motion pictures. University of Southern California, 1969.

(D.A. vol. 30, p. 4075-A)

Nulf, Jr., Frank Allen. Luigi Pirandello and the cinema: a study of his relationship to motion pictures and the significance of that relationship to selected examples of his prose and drama. Ohio University, 1969.

(D.A. vol. 30, p. 4055-A)

Reynolds, Lessie Mallard. An analysis of the non-verbal symbolism in Frederico Fellini's film trilogy: La Dolce Vita, 8½, and Juliet of the Spirits. University of Michigan, 1969.

(D.A. vol. 31, p. 2536-A)

Snyder, John J. James Agee: A study of his film criticism. St. John's University, 1969.

(D.A. vol. 30, p. 3477-A)

1970

Beaver, Frank Eugene. Bosley Crowther: Social critic of the film, 1940–1947. University of Michigan, 1970.

(D.A. vol. 31, p. 2413-A)

Dimas, Chris. The effect of motion pictures portraying black models on the self-concept of black elementary school children. Syracuse University, 1970.

(D.A. vol. 31, p. 2609-A)

Gardner, Martin Allan. The Marx Brothers: An investigation of their films as satirical social criticism. New York University, 1970.

(D.A. vol. 31, p. 3695-A)

Hoover, William Franklin. Replicating photographic lighting effects to elicit certain conditioned responses in motion picture audiences. Wayne State University, 1970.

(D.A. vol. 32, p. 470-A)

Karimi, Amir Massoud. Toward a definition of the American film noir (1941–1949). University of Southern California, 1970.

(D.A. vol. 31, p. 4807)

Koch, Christian Herbert. Understanding film as process of change: A metalanguage for the school of film developed and applied to Ingmar Bergman's Persona and Alan J. Pakula's The Sterile Cuckoo. University of Iowa, 1970.

(D.A. vol. 31, p. 3936-A)

Korte, Jr., Walter Francis. Marxism and the scenographic baroque in the films of Luchino Visconti. Northwestern University, 1970.

(D.A. vol. 31, p. 5562-A)

Latham, John Aaron. The motion pictures of F. Scott Fitzgerald. Princeton University, 1970.
(D.A. vol. 31, p. 6617-A)

Laurence, Frank Michael. The film adaptations of Hemingway: Hollywood and the Hemingway myth. University of Pennsylvania, 1970.
(D.A. vol. 31, p. 5411-A)

Mapp, Edward Charles. The portrayal of the Negro in American motion pictures 1962–1968. New York University, 1970.
(D.A. vol. 31, p. 2415-A)

Meyer, Timothy P. The effects of viewing justified and unjustified fictional versus real film violence on aggressive behavior. Ohio University, 1970.
(D.A. vol. 31, p. 4264-A)

Schlosser, Anatol I. Paul Robeson: His career in the theatre, in motion pictures, and on the concert stage. New York University, 1970.
(D.A. vol. 31, p. 2538-A)

Schwartz, Stanley. Film music and attitude change: A study to determine the effect of manipulating a musical sound-track upon changes in attitude toward militarism-pacifism held by tenth grade social studies students. Syracuse University, 1970.
(D.A. vol. 31, p. 5677-A)

Von Hanwehr, Wolfram. A critical analysis of the structure of the East German film Berlin Wall. University of Southern California, 1970.
(D.A. vol. 31, p. 6088-A)

Wight, Warland Davis. The relevance of selected theories for developing systematic research on film communications. University of Washington, 1970.
(D.A. vol. 31, p. 5050-A)

1971

Callahan, S.J., Michael Anthony. A critical study of the image of marriage in the contemporary American cinema. University of Southern California, 1971.
(D.A. vol. 32, p. 4644-A)

Embler, Jeffrey Brown. A historical study of the use of film to provide additional content to theatrical productions on the legitimate stage. University of Pittsburgh, 1971.
(D.A. vol. 32, p. 3473-A)

Garrison, Jr., Lee Cedric. Decision processes in motion picture production: A study of uncertainty. Stanford University, 1971.
(D.A. vol. 32, p. 1124-A)

Hecht, Chandra Mukerji. Flashes and pans: The careers of student filmmakers. Northwestern University, 1971.
(D.A. vol. 32, p. 3442-A)

Holman, Loyd Bruce. The history and technique of puppet animation in cinema. Syracuse University, 1971.
(D.A. vol. 32, p. 5817-A)

Koolik, Murry Wolf. A content analysis of educational films about Israel. New York University, 1971.
(D.A. vol. 32, p. 2403-A)

May, Thomas Stephen. An analysis of twelve films by Arne Sucksdorff. University of Wisconsin, 1971.

(D.A. vol. 32, p. 1111-A)

McGregor, Edgar Russell. A design for a mediated first course in film production. University of Southern California, 1971.

(D.A. vol. 32, p. 3342-A)

Moore, Douglas Cameron. A study in the influence of the film, The Birth of a Nation, on the attitudes of selected high school white students towards Negroes. University of Colorado, 1971.

(D.A. vol. 32, p. 5617-A)

Poteet, George Howard. A computer-assisted content analysis of film criticism in popular American periodicals from 1933 through 1967. Columbia University, 1971.

(D.A. vol. 32, p. 2920-A)

Rosene, James Melvin. The effects of violent and sexually arousing film content: An experimental study. Ohio University, 1971.

(D.A. vol. 32, p. 6469-A)

Indexes

1

ARTICLE TITLES INDEX

AUTHORS–ARTICLES INDEX

AUTHORS–BOOKS INDEX

BOOK TITLES INDEX

FILM PERSONALITIES INDEX

FILM TITLES INDEX